SECOND EDITION

International Financial Reporting and Analysis

A Contextual Emphasis

SECOND EDITION

International Financial Reporting and Analysis

A Contextual Emphasis

Mark E. Haskins
Darden Graduate School of Business, The University of Virginia

Kenneth R. Ferris
The American Graduate School of International Management

Thomas I. Selling
The American Graduate School of International Management

Irwin
McGraw-Hill

Boston • Burr Ridge, IL • Dubuque, IA • Madison, WI • New York • San Francisco • St. Louis
Bangkok • Bogotá • Caracas • Lisbon • London • Madrid
Mexico City • Milan • New Delhi • Seoul • Singapore • Sydney • Taipei • Toronto

McGraw-Hill Higher Education

A Division of **The McGraw-Hill** *Companies*

INTERNATIONAL FINANCIAL REPORTING AND ANALYSIS:
A CONTEXTUAL EMPHASIS

This book printed on acid-free paper.

1 2 3 4 5 6 7 8 9 0 KGP/KGP 9 0 9 8 7 6 5 4 3 2 1 0 9

ISBN 0-07-228762-4

Vice president/Editor-in-chief: *Michael W. Junior*
Publisher: *Jeffrey J. Shelstad*
Sponsoring editor: *Stewart Mattson*
Editorial coordinator: *Jennifer Jackson*
Senior marketing manager: *Melissa Caughlin*
Project manager: *Christine Parker*
Production supervisor: *Kari Geltemeyer*
Coordinator freelance design: *Mary L. Christianson*
Freelance cover designer: *Kay Fulton*
Cover image: © *PhotoDisc*
Supplement coordinator: *Craig S. Leonard*
Compositor: *Black Dot*
Typeface: *10/12 Times Roman*
Printer: *Quebecor Printing Book Group/Kingsport*

Library of Congress Cataloging-in-Publication Data

Haskins, Mark E.
    International financial reporting and analysis: a contextual
emphasis / Mark E. Haskins, Kenneth R. Ferris,
Thomas I. Selling.
  — 5th ed
     p. cm.
    Includes index.
    ISBN 0-07-228762-4
    1. Accounting. 2. Financial statements. 3. Comparative
accounting. I. Ferris, Kenneth R. II. Selling, Thomas I. III.
Title.
HF5635 .H35 2000
657 — dc21

99-34881
CIP

http://www.mhhe.com

Preface

The globalization of financial markets has increased the value of knowledge about how business is conducted in other countries. One important aspect of that understanding is an awareness of the way in which international financial results are reported. Indeed, understanding the measurement and reporting process has a special urgency when considered as part of the capital formation and allocation process. Thus, one of the principal objectives of this book is to explore and understand the financial reporting practices used by companies from various countries around the world.

The book is intended for graduate students and upper-level undergraduates. In an undergraduate setting, the book assumes an intermediate-level accounting background. In an MBA setting, the book assumes student proficiency in a strong introductory financial accounting course prerequisite. In either instance, the book (1) provides an opportunity for students to learn about diverse financial reporting practices from around the world, (2) provides students with sufficient understanding of contextual factors so that they may begin to understand the reasons for diverse financial reporting practices across countries, and (3) in achieving (1) and (2), a meaningful decision context, namely the review and analysis of firm performance by analysts, investors, and managers, is offered.

In the pursuit of these objectives, this book adopts a threefold emphasis. First, like some other international financial reporting books, it chronicles and discusses some of the more significant similarities and differences in generally accepted accounting practices found in a selected number of countries. *Unlike other books,* however, this book posits the importance of understanding country context as a necessary prerequisite to comprehending the story being told by the specific accounting practices used by a particular company domiciled in a particular country. Indeed, the importance of and insights into the cultural, governmental, and business contexts of the book's focal countries is a constant theme throughout. Last, and *in contrast to other books* on international financial reporting, this book emphasizes a user's perspective, explicitly devoting three chapters to financial analysis issues and highlighting such pertinent issues within each of the country-specific chapters. These three chapters are set apart with a bold border on each page, thus highlighting their distinctiveness and allowing instructors to incorporate them into varied course sequences and to varying extents.

The book is divided into three parts:

I. International Financial Reporting and Standard Setting
II. Financial Statement Analysis
III. Financial Reporting Practices and Contexts in Selected Countries

The first chapter presents Geert Hofstede's framework for analyzing the significant cultural contexts present in a country. This framework is referred to throughout the country-specific chapters. Chapter 1 also highlights the pertinent legal/political and business environment factors likely to influence the practice and developments of financial reporting. Chapters 2 and 3 provide background on the major international alliances working toward large-scale geographic harmonization of financial reporting: the International Accounting Standards Committee and the European Economic Union.

Part II of the book is devoted to the fundamentals of financial statement analysis as well as some of the special challenges presented by a desire to analyze annual reports of non-U.S. companies. In the latter section of this part of the book, the special challenges in financial reporting for multinational companies is considered.

The third part of the book takes the reader on a macro-level journey to the financial reporting contexts of seven countries: Great Britain, Germany, Japan, Sweden, Mexico, South Korea, and Italy. The emphasis in these chapters is on country context and the major similarities/differences in financial reporting practices across these seven countries and the United States. Included in these chapters are numerous annual report excerpts, highlighting particular financial reporting practices prevalent in a country's corporate annual reports. These seven countries were chosen because of the comparative differences and similarities they exhibit between each other and the United States.

As an additional avenue for learning about the evolving, dynamic, fascinating world of international financial reporting, the end-of-chapter materials provide varied and provocative forums for further exploration. Each chapter presents some study opportunities drawn from the business press and/or recent academic business literature, as well as assignments that focus on a specific international financial reporting practice. The accompanying instructor's manual is intended to assist instructors in identifying the key and/or provocative insights imbedded in each student assignment.

We would like to draw your attention to two other subtle, but valuable, features of the text. Throughout the text, the first appearance of a key word, name, or phrase is highlighted by bold type. These bolded words or phrases then appear in the glossary that can be found at the end of the text. Also, at the end of the text is an extensive set of tables summarizing comparative accounting and reporting practices for 10 additional countries (in addition to the text's 7 focal countries). Together, these end-of-text materials are intended to be a resource for students of international financial reporting.

It is important to note that the book is about generalized tendencies and attributes. Generalizations make comparisons possible, and the comparisons we make are intended to be purely informative, not verdicts of better versus worse. It is in that spirit that we undertake this investigation of international financial reporting.

This book has benefitted from numerous students and colleagues, in large and small ways. We thank them all, especially Chris Wenger and Lynna Martinez. We would like to acknowledge the tireless manuscript processing of Lee Pierce, Dot Govoruhk, Bessie Truzy, and Kathleen Collier; and our colleagues Bob Sack, Brandt Allen, and E. Richard Brownlee II who continuously bring their insights in international financial reporting to the classroom.

We would also like to thank the survey respondents who provided us with feedback for the second edition: Carol Adams, University of Glasgow; Mark Finn, Northwestern University; Gerhard Gniewosz, University of Wollongong; Elizabeth A. Gordon, University of Chicago; Jeannie Harrington, Middle Tennessee State University; Gilbert W. Joseph, The University of Tampa; Chan-Jane Lin, National Taiwan University; Thomas McGhee, Savannah State University; Lynn Rees, Texas A & M University; Mike Robinson, Saint Mary's College; Kurt S. Schulzke, Kennesaw State University; Frederic M. Stiner, Jr., University of Delaware; and Fergus WT Wong, City University of Hong Kong—Visiting Fellow.

A special thanks goes to Ignacio Navarro, Tax Partner, Ernst & Young, LLP—Guadalajara, Mexico, and Jose Garcia-Figueroa Narro, ITESM—Campus Guadalajara, for their insightful comments and valuable feedback on the Mexico chapter.

Finally, we would like to thank the editorial staff at Irwin/McGraw-Hill for their assistance and guidance— Jeffery Shelstad, Stewart Mattson, Jennifer Jackson, Melissa Caughlin, Christine Parker, Mary Christianson, and Craig Leonard.

Mark E. Haskins
Kenneth R. Ferris
Thomas I. Selling

Contents in Brief

Contents

SECOND
EDITION

International Financial Reporting and Analysis

A Contextual Emphasis

PART I

International Financial Reporting and Standard Setting

International financial reporting is a dynamic, evolving field of inquiry. Powerful new technologies and communications devices have opened the world for an explosion in cross-border commerce and capital creation. Never before has there been so much pressure on, and opportunity for, leaders of financial reporting thought to help shape the most useful "language" by which suppliers of capital and seekers of capital communicate across companies, industries, countries, and cultures.

The first three chapters of this text set the stage for our inquiries into country-specific financial reporting practices and the fine art of financial analysis. Students of international financial reporting need to be aware of the forces that shape financial reporting as well as the progress to date on the harmonization of contemporary accounting practices. Toward that end, Chapters 1 through 3 provide the backdrop for all subsequent chapters and discussions.

Accounting and Its Global Contexts

Accounting reporting and disclosure standards and practices do not develop in a vacuum but reflect the particular environment in which they are developed.[1]

Accounting cannot be culture free.[2]

Introduction

The importance of putting data in a context is no secret. Educators and psychologists have long known that people learn and retain information more easily if they integrate it with what they already know. This process of contextualizing data contributes to the creation of meaning from data. Indeed, managers, investors, and analysts constantly strive to contextualize the financial data with which their desks are strewn daily. Consequently, one of the main goals of this book is to highlight and elaborate on a set of analytical considerations that readers of international financial statements should be aware of as they seek to interpret the data contained therein for the purpose of making informed decisions.

Accounting is often called the *language of business.* Although not every financial information user must be able to create the "language," all users must be able to "read" it fluently and appreciate the assumptions and complexities that condition its production. As the intricacy of financial reporting increases, those who can use financial information adroitly will find themselves in possession of an increasingly valuable skill. Those who are deficient run greater risk of being victimized by their ignorance.

With the advent of a global economy, characterized by electronically accessible stock exchanges and multinational enterprises operating in scores of countries, the production, dissemination, and use of financial information are no longer restricted by national borders. Understanding the context within which information from other nations is generated often imposes special demands on both managers and investors. More specifically, the premises on which financial data are constituted in other parts of the world are now a matter of crucial importance. For financial reporting, a new imperative for interpretation has begun.

The knowledge that one needs to interpret and understand financial statements from other countries goes beyond merely acquainting oneself with what financial reporting methods and practices were used in preparing the documents (although this is, of course,

---

[1]A. Adhikari and R. H. Tondkar. "Environmental Factors Influencing Accounting Disclosure Requirements of Global Stock Exchanges," *Journal of International Financial Management and Accounting,* Summer 1992, p. 76.

[2]M. H. B. Perera, "Toward a Framework to Analyze the Impact of Culture in Accounting," *The International Journal of Accounting* 24, no. 1 (1989), p. 43.

important). Even if complete harmonization of international financial reporting standards were achieved—which is not likely to happen for some time to come—one would still need important contextual information to assess the significance of the financial data.

Accordingly, the chapters that follow are designed to familiarize the reader with some of the contextual and analytical issues surrounding financial reporting in a variety of countries. They discuss how cultural, legal, political, and economic contexts shape financial information. Because each chapter presents a number of issues, they are necessarily broad in their approach. The aim is not to make readers expert analysts or masters of technical detail; rather, the objective is to enlighten readers as to the various key questions germane to just about any set of foreign financial statements that come under review: What is the relationship of financial reporting to tax law in this country? What role, if any, does a country's accounting profession play in the creation of local reporting and disclosure standards? Who are the primary users of the financial statements—investors, unions, legal authorities? The concern for and understanding of these and other sociocultural issues will make the reader a more intelligent consumer of international financial information.

The content of this book is organized as follows. Chapters 1 through 3 provide the reader with a background of some of the larger, more important institutional issues: Along what dimensions and to what extent do country contexts differ and potentially influence the development of financial reporting practices? Who is responsible for international accounting principles, and how are they set? What is the European Union and how has it assisted in the harmonization of accepted accounting practice across a diverse set of nations? From these broad, macrolevel considerations, the text then moves to a review of microlevel issues in Chapters 4 through 6. For example, how do analysts, investors, and managers make economic decisions, and how are those decisions impacted by diverse and inconsistent international accounting practices? How do the decisions of these individuals change when dealing with international, as opposed to domestic, companies? Finally, Chapters 7 through 13 focus on seven countries selected because they represent a varied set of economic, political, and social dimensions.

Although only seven countries are specifically considered, the potential benefits of this book are more extensive than such a small sample would immediately suggest. As readers become more familiar with financial reporting around the world, they will find a considerable amount of similarity among particular nations, for reasons both cultural and historical. These transnational similarities make it possible to develop classifications of key international financial reporting characteristics. For example, a basic understanding of British financial reporting will help one understand financial reporting in numerous other Commonwealth countries such as Australia, Hong Kong, and New Zealand. Becoming familiar with the Mexican system of monetary correction should yield general insights about financial reporting in other inflationary economies (especially South American ones). The presence of common themes helps not only to situate whole systems in relation to each other but also to gauge the importance of particular variations. The goal is to highlight and discuss some of the key contextual factors pertinent to understanding a variety of international financial reporting practices.

As the more or less common structure of the country-specific chapters implies, the framework used here makes rough distinctions among cultural, legal, political, and business influences. These categories are not meant to be definitive by any means; other approaches might have been used as well. The important point about the framework adopted here is that it implicitly proposes a set of long-term factors—national culture, statutory and tax law, labor, capital markets, role of the accounting profession—that affect the structure and use of financial accounting information. Any such list, of course, is hardly likely to be either exhaustive or universal; hence, the reader will notice that the structure of the country-specific chapters will vary somewhat, but the basic sections remain the same throughout. The following is a description of the general approach used in the country-specific chapters of this book.

Cultural Environment

Information is more than words; it is words that fit into a cultural framework.[3] Familiarization with a language is, by itself, necessary but not sufficient. Language is but a "means of communication within a particular culture."[4] Indeed, the "language" of financial reporting is conditioned by a nation's cultural influences.

Accounting, the language of business, is the handling of symbols that have meaning to those initiated in business.[5] Universally speaking, however, the same symbols may mean different things to financial information users of different cultures. What should we conclude, for example, if we find that the shareholders' equity of a Japanese steelmaking firm is 10 percent of its total capitalization and its current ratio is .75 as compared to 40 percent and 1.2, respectively, for a U.S. steelmaker? Is this cause for alarm or applause?

The cultural analysis in the country-specific chapters begins by drawing on the work of Geert Hofstede, director of the Institute for Research on Intercultural Cooperation, at the University of Limburg, Maastricht, The Netherlands. Defining *culture* as a kind of "collective mental programming" that affects the way people perceive and act in the world, Hofstede discusses five important cultural "dimensions": power distance, individualism, long-term orientation, uncertainty avoidance, and masculinity.[6] These cultural dimensions serve to identify the core values that explain the general similarities and differences in cultures around the world. These dimensions reflect the different ways in which societies answer basic questions about the organization and the conduct of their institutions. The distinctive cultural dimensions that Hofstede discusses, although subject to criticisms of simplification, have been time tested[7] and found to be associated with nations' economic growth, management accounting systems in use, support for global financial accounting harmonization, business failures, and cross-border corporate acquisitions.[8]

---

[3]G. Hofstede, *Cultures and Organizations: Software of the Mind* (Berkshire, England: McGraw-Hill, 1991), p. 217.

[4]V. Terpstra and K. David, *The Cultural Environment of International Business* (Cincinnati: South-Western, 1985), p. 18.

[5]Hofstede, *Cultures and Organizations*, p. 155.

[6]The cultural dimension of masculinity (MAS) is a construct that describes the extent to which social gender roles tend to be distinct in a given society. Although interesting and important for understanding some aspects of societal attitudes, we believe that it does not bear on financial reporting attitudes and it is therefore not a part of subsequent discussions.

[7]G. Hofstede and M. Bond, "Hofstede's Culture Dimensions: An Independent Validation Using Rokeach's Value Survey," *Journal of Cross-Cultural Psychology,* December 1984, pp. 417–33. See also R. Hodgetts, "A Conversation with Geert Hofstede," *Organizational Dynamics,* Spring 1993, pp. 53–61, and The Chinese Culture Connection, "Chinese Values and the Search for Culture-Free Dimensions of Culture," *Journal of Cross-Cultural Psychology,* June 1987, pp. 143–64. Interested readers may also want to read J. Scarborough, *The Origins of Cultural Differences and Their Impact on Management* (Westport, Conn.: Quorum Books, 1998).

[8]See S. Ueno and U. Sekaran, "The Influence of Culture on Budget and Control Practices in the USA and Japan: An Empirical Study," *Journal of International Business Studies,* 4th Quarter 1992, pp. 659–74; and G. L. Harrison, "The Cross-Cultural Generalizability of the Relation between Participation, Budget Emphasis, and Job-Related Attitudes," *Accounting, Organizations, and Society* 17, no. 1 (1992), pp. 1–15. See also R. H. Franke, G. Hofstede, and M. H. Bond, "Cultural Roots of Economic Performance: A Research Note," *Strategic Management Journal* 12 (1991), pp 165–73; and A. Smith, D. R. Deis, Jr., and R. Holland, "Cultural Mapping of Attitudes toward International Harmonization Efforts: A Cross-National Study," paper presented at annual meeting of the American Accounting Association, San Francisco, 1993; J. Li and S. Guisinger, "How Well Do Foreign Firms Compete in the United States?" *Business Horizons,* November–December 1991, pp. 49–53; P. C. Brewer, "National Culture and Activity-Based Costing Systems: A Note," *Management Accounting Research* 9, no. 2 (1998), pp. 241–260; and P. Morosini, S. Shane, and H. Singh, "National Cultural Distance and Cross-Border Acquisition Performance," *Journal of International Business Studies* 29, no. 1 (1998), pp. 137–158.

*Large Power
Distance versus
Small Power
Distance*

The concept of **power distance** (PD) refers to the degree to which people are willing to live with unequally distributed power within and across their institutions and organizations. A high score on the PD index indicates that a national culture has a high tolerance for inequality. In such a society, people accept a hierarchy that is justified by those in power and by the historical tradition of those positions. In contrast, people from societies scoring low on the PD index are more egalitarian and require justification for power inequalities.

The basic issue addressed by this cultural dimension is how a society handles inequalities among people. In large PD societies, the

> political spectrum . . . is characterized by strong right and left wings with a weak center. Incomes in these countries are very unequally distributed, with a few very rich and many very poor people. Moreover, taxation protects the wealthy, so that incomes after taxes can even be more unequal than before. Labor unions tend to be government controlled; where they are not, they are ideologically based and involved in politics. . . . The political spectrum in [small PD] countries usually shows a powerful center and weaker right and left wings. Incomes are less unequally distributed than in large power distance countries. Taxation serves to redistribute income, making income after taxes less unequal than before. Labor unions are independent and less oriented to ideology and politics than to pragmatic issues on behalf of their members.[9]

The relevance of a PD notion to financial reporting is twofold.[10] First, large PD countries are likely to tend toward greater statutory control over financial reporting practices to achieve and maintain a uniformity in reporting that is not likely to be achieved if financial reporting practices predominantly emanate from the deliberative processes of a professional organization that airs ideas for debate and seeks consensus from a diverse constituency. Indeed, the national statutes pertaining to financial reporting that exist in Korea and Japan exert a much greater influence over external financial reporting than those in the United States, Great Britain, or Germany (all of which have substantially lower PD scores than Korea or Japan), where professional organizations more actively shape practice.[11] Second, the PD concept suggests important implications for understanding a society's attitude toward access to and availability of information. It seems likely that high PD societies may be characterized by the restriction of information to preserve secrecy, power, and/or role inequalities. Thus, in terms of financial reporting providing a more or less full and open view of a business entity, high PD societies are likely to provide fewer financial disclosures than small PD societies. Results from at least one broad-based study that ranked countries according to the extensiveness of the financial disclosures made by their companies identify Mexico, Korea, and Italy (relatively high PD countries) as providing less extensive disclosures than Sweden, Great Britain, and Germany (relatively low PD countries).[12]

Some examples of the key differences between small and large PD societies are presented in Table 1–1. The PD scores of the countries discussed in the following chapters are shown here.

---

[9]Hofstede, *Cultures and Organizations,* pp. 38–39.

[10]See S. J. Gray, "Towards a Theory of Cultural Influence in the Development of Accounting Systems Internationally," *Abacus* 24, no. 1 (1988), pp. 9–11.

[11]See F. D. S. Choi, *Handbook of International Accounting* (New York: John Wiley, 1991).

[12]Center for International Financial Analysis and Research, *International Accounting and Auditing Trends* (Princeton, N.J.: CIFAR, 1995), esp. pp. 366–430.

Hofstede's Power Distance (PD) Scores*
(higher scores = larger PD)

Country	PD Score
Mexico	81
South Korea	60
Japan	54
Italy	50
Great Britain	35
Germany	35
Sweden	31
United States	40

*Of primary importance is the relative position of the countries, not the absolute values of the scores.

Source: G. Hofstede. *Cultures and Organizations* (Berkshire, England: McGraw-Hill, 1991). Reproduced with permission.

TABLE 1–1   Key Differences between Large and Small Power Distance Societies

Small Power Distance	Large Power Distance
• Inequalities among people should be minimized.	• Inequalities among people are both expected and desired.
• There should be, and there is to some extent, interdependence between less and more powerful people.	• Less powerful people should be dependent on the more powerful; in practice, less powerful people are polarized between dependence and counterdependence.
• Hierarchy in organizations means an inequality of roles, established for convenience.	• Hierarchy in organizations reflects the existential inequality between higher-ups and lower-downs.
• Decentralization is popular.	• Centralization is popular.
• There is a narrow salary range between top and bottom of organization.	• Salary range between top and bottom of organization is wide.
• Subordinates expect to be consulted.	• Subordinates expect to be told what to do.
• The ideal boss is a resourceful democrat.	• The ideal boss is a benevolent autocrat or good father.
• Privileges and status symbols are frowned upon.	• Privileges and status symbols for managers are both expected and popular.
• All should have equal rights.	• The powerful have privileges.
• Powerful people try to look less powerful than they are.	• Powerful people try to look as impressive as possible.
• Power is based on formal position, expertise, and ability to give rewards.	• Power is based on family or friends, charisma, and ability to use force.
• The way to change a political system is by changing the rules (evolution).	• The way to change a political system is by changing the people at the top (revolution).
• The use of violence in domestic politics is rare.	• Domestic political conflicts frequently lead to violence.
• Pluralist governments based on outcome of majority votes.	• Autocratic or oligarchic governments are based on cooptation.
• Political spectrum shows strong center and weak right and left wings.	• Political spectrum, if allowed to be manifested, shows weak center and strong wings.
• Small income differentials in society are further reduced by the tax system.	• Large income differentials in society are further increased by the tax system.
• Prevailing religions and philosophical systems stress equality.	• Prevailing religions and philosophical systems stress hierarchy and stratification.
• Prevailing political ideologies stress and practice power sharing.	• Prevailing political ideologies stress and practice power struggle.
• Native management theories focus on role of employees.	• Native management theories focus on role of managers.

Source: G. Hofstede, *Cultures and Organizations* (Berkshire, England: McGraw-Hill, 1991). Reproduced with permission.

Individualism versus Collectivism

Societies that exemplify the **individualism** (IDV) construct tend to be those in which the ties between individuals are loosely coupled (i.e., people are expected to look after themselves and their immediate family). In contrast, a low score on the IDV index corresponds to a collectivist society. **Collectivism** pertains to societies in which people are integrated into strong, cohesive in-groups, which throughout people's lifetimes continue to protect them in exchange for their loyalty. The fundamental issue addressed by the IDV cultural dimension is the degree of interdependence that a society maintains among individuals. For example, according to Hofstede, employees of organizations in individualistic societies tend to place great value on the freedom to adopt their own approach to their work assignments. In contrast, employees of collectivist societies place less value on freedom to do their work their way; instead, they place a higher value on training and opportunities to improve their work skills so they become full-fledged members of the team, making their expected contribution. Other examples of some key differences between individualist and collectivist societies can be examined in Table 1–2. The IDV scores of the countries discussed in the following chapters are shown here.

Hofstede's Individualism Scores* (higher scores = greater IDV)	
Country	*IDV Score*
Great Britain	89
Italy	76
Sweden	71
Germany	67
Japan	46
Mexico	30
South Korea	18
United States	91

*Of primary importance is the relative position of the countries, not the absolute values of the scores.

Source: G. Hofstede, *Cultures and Organizations* (Berkshire, England: McGraw-Hill, 1991). Reproduced with permission.

It has been hypothesized that societies with less IDV exhibit tendencies toward greater statutory control over financial reporting, leading to less flexibility accorded companies in the application of specific financial reporting practices than in societies with greater IDV.[13] Furthermore, such a tendency also suggests the likelihood of financial information being more closely held by the companies domiciled in societies with less IDV. Together, such tendencies lead one to expect more conservative financial reporting from companies in societies with less IDV.

The merits of such hypothesized relationships warrant continued testing and refinement. Results from two recent studies, however, provide evidence of a profile of conservative financial reporting that ranks Japan as more conservative than Germany, which is more conservative than Italy, which is more conservative than Great Britain.[14] As the reader will note, these four countries are more or less IDV in the same order.

---

[13]Gray, "Towards a Theory of Cultural Development of Accounting Systems."

[14]See S. J. Gray and L. H. Radebaugh, *International Accounting and Multinational Enterprises* (New York: John Wiley, 1993), esp. pp. 386–90. It should be noted that the United States was included in these studies and was found to be more conservative than Great Britain but less conservative than Germany or Japan.

TABLE 1–2   Key Differences between Individualist and Collectivist Societies

Individualist	*Collectivist*
• Everyone grows up to look after him- or herself and his or her immediate family only.	• People are born into extended families or other in-groups that continue to protect them in exchange for loyalty.
• Identity is based in the individual.	• Identity is based on the social network to which one belongs.
• Children learn to think in terms of "I."	• Children learn to think in terms of "we."
• Speaking one's mind is a characteristic of an honest person.	• Harmony should always be maintained and direct confrontations avoided.
• Purpose of education is learning how to learn.	• Purpose of education is learning how to do.
• Employer-employee relationship is a contract supposed to be based on mutual advantage.	• Employer-employee relationship is perceived in moral terms, like a family link.
• Hiring and promotion decisions are supposed to be based on skills and rules only.	• Hiring and promotion decisions take employees' in-group into account.
• Management is management of groups.	• Management is management of individuals.
• Task prevails over relationship.	• Relationship prevails over task.
• Individual interests prevail over collective interests.	• Collective interests prevail over individual interests.
• Everyone has a right to privacy.	• Private life is invaded by group(s).
• Everyone is expected to have a private opinion.	• Opinions are predetermined by group membership.
• Laws and rights are supposed to be the same for all.	• Laws and rights differ by group.
• Restrained role of the state in the economic system.	• Dominant role of the state in economic system.
• Economy is based on individual interests.	• Economy is based on collective interests.
• Political power is exercised by voters.	• Political power is exercised by interest groups.
• Native economic theories are based on pursuit of individual self-interests.	• Imported economic theories are largely irrelevant because unable to deal with collective and particularist interests.
• Ideologies of individual freedom prevail over ideologies of equality.	• Ideologies of equality prevail over ideologies of individual freedom.
• Self-actualization by every individual is an ultimate goal.	• Harmony and consensus in society are ultimate goals.

Source: G. Hofstede, *Cultures and Organizations* (Berkshire, England: McGraw-Hill, 1991). Reproduced with permission.

Uncertainty Avoidance versus Uncertainty Acceptance

The concept of **uncertainty avoidance** (UAV) can be thought of as the extent to which the members of a society feel threatened by uncertain or unknown situations. This feeling is usually expressed through a need for predictability expressed in written and unwritten rules. Uncertainty-avoiding cultures generate, nurture, and uphold explicit codes of belief and behavior and tend to be unaccepting of behaviors, attitudes, and ideas opposite to the group norms. The need for laws and rules in a strong UAV culture often leads to the establishment of rules or rule-oriented behavior that sometimes is puzzling to others from a low UAV environment. Consider, for example, Japan (UAV score = 92), which has a law stating that before a merchant can open a business in a given locale, existing merchants—including competitors—must first approve the merchant's entrance.[15] Another characteristic of a strong UAV culture is that its citizens tend to be pessimistic about their possibilities to influence authorities. Few citizens are ready to protest decisions made by authorities; they depend on the government's expertise and believe that this is how things should be. The authorities and the citizens share the same norms about their mutual roles.[16] In contrast, low UAV cultures tend to be flexible, prefer fewer rules, and are willing to, and often do, participate in politics to influence official rule-making activities.

[15]Interview with Brian Rawson in summer 1992. Mr. Rawson lived and worked in Japan as a business consultant for seven years.

[16]Hofstede, *Cultures and Organizations: Software of the Mind.*

Another example of the differences between high and low UAV cultures is that low UAV countries tend to be innovative and high UAV cultures tend to focus on full-scale implementation of innovations, requiring a considerable sense of detail and punctuality. Hofstede cites as an example Great Britain (UAV score = 35), which has produced more Nobel Prize winners than Japan (UAV score = 92), which has put more new products on the world market.[17] One other aspect of low UAV cultures is that they are not as focused on trying to craft the future and extend greater tolerance to those members of society who hold different ideas and attitudes.

From a financial reporting perspective, it has been posited that relatively higher UAV societies exhibit greater tendencies toward conservatism than do lower UAV societies, due to the caution with which the former approach the uncertainty of future events.[18] Moreover, to avoid conflict and preserve security—both attributes of higher UAV societies—secrecy (i.e., more limited disclosures) is likely to be an attitude underlying financial reporting practices in high UAV countries. As one might expect, therefore, uniformity rather than flexibility in reporting practices is the preference imposed on the companies residing in relatively higher UAV societies. In a recent study of preferences for the international harmonization of accounting principles, preliminary evidence suggests that higher UAV societies do exhibit stronger preferences in support of current international harmonization efforts than do low UAV societies.[19]

Table 1–3 provides additional examples of some of the general differences between uncertainty-avoiding cultures and uncertainty-accepting cultures. The following are UAV scores for the countries discussed at length later in this book:

Hofstede's Uncertainty Avoidance Scores*
(higher scores = greater UAV)

Country	UAV Score
Japan	92
South Korea	85
Mexico	82
Italy	75
Germany	65
Great Britain	35
Sweden	29
United States	46

*Of primary importance is the relative position of the countries, not the absolute values of the scores.

Source: G. Hofstede, *Cultures and Organizations* (Berkshire, England: McGraw-Hill, 1991). Reproduced with permission.

Long-Term Orientation versus Short-Term Orientation

In practical terms, a society with a **long-term orientation** (LTO) values persistence, ordering of relationships by status and observing this order, thrift, and having a sense of shame, whereas a society with a **short-term orientation** (STO) values personal stability, protecting face, and respect for tradition.[20] Hofstede notes that the attributes akin to an

---

[17]Ibid.

[18]Gray, "Towards a Theory of Cultural Development of Accounting Systems."

[19]Smith, Deis, and Holland, "Cultural Mapping of Attitudes."

[20]G. Hofstede and M. Bond, "The Confucius Connection: From Cultural Roots to Economic Growth," *Organizational Dynamics,* 1988; and Hofstede, *Cultures and Organizations: Software of the Mind.*

TABLE 1–3   Key Differences between Uncertainty-Avoiding Cultures and Uncertainty-Accepting Cultures

Uncertainty Avoiding	Uncertainty Accepting
• The uncertainty inherent in life is felt as a continuous threat that must be fought.	• Uncertainty is a normal feature of life, and each day is accepted as it comes.
• High stress and a subjective feeling of anxiety are prevalent.	• Low stress and a subjective feeling of well-being are prevalent.
• There is an acceptance of familiar risks and fear of ambiguous situations and of unfamiliar risks.	• Society is comfortable in ambiguous situations and with unfamiliar risks.
• What is different is dangerous.	• What is different is curious.
• Students are comfortable in structured learning situations and concerned with the right answers.	• Students are comfortable with open-ended learning situations and concerned with good discussions.
• Emotional need for rules, even if these will never work, is characteristic.	• There should not be more rules than are strictly necessary.
• Time is money.	• Time is a framework for orientation.
• Society feels an emotional need to be busy and an inner urge to work hard.	• Society feels comfortable when lazy and hardworking only when needed.
• Precision and punctuality come naturally.	• Precision and punctuality have to be learned.
• Deviant ideas and behavior resistance to innovation are suppressed.	• Tolerance of deviant and innovative ideas and behavior exists.
• Society is motivated by security and esteem or belongingness.	• Society is motivated by achievement and esteem or belongingness.
• Many and precise laws and rules exist; if rules cannot be respected, members are sinners and should repent.	• Few and general laws and rules exist; if rules cannot be respected, they should be changed.
• Citizens are negative toward institutions.	• Citizens are positive toward institutions.
• Conservatism, extremism, and law and order prevail.	• Tolerance and moderation prevail.
• Nationalism, xenophobia, and repression of minorities prevail.	• Regionalism, internationalism, and attempts at integration of minorities are common.
• There is a belief in experts and specialization.	• There is belief in generalists and common sense.
• There is only one Truth, ours.	• One group's truth should not be imposed on others.
• Religious, political, and ideological fundamentalism and intolerance characterize society.	• Human rights—nobody should be persecuted for beliefs—are respected.
• In philosophy and science, the tendency is toward grand theories.	• In philosophy and science, the tendency is toward relativism and empiricism.

Source: G. Hofstede, *Cultures and Organizations:* (Berkshire, England: McGraw-Hill, 1991). Reproduced with permission.

LTO are more oriented toward the future (especially perseverance and thrift); they are more dynamic and support entrepreneurial activity. For example, perseverance or tenacity in the pursuit of goals is an important attribute for both intrapreneurs and entrepreneurs. Similarly, thrift leads to savings and the accumulation of capital for reinvestment. Moreover, having a sense of shame contributes to a sensitivity to social contacts and keeping one's commitments (a Japanese example of this, *dantai ishiki,* or group consciousness, is discussed in more detail in Chapter 9).

The societal attributes more closely aligned with a STO tend to focus on the past and present, and they tend to be more static. At the STO end of the spectrum, personal stability and saving face, if overemphasized, tend to dampen initiative and risk taking. Also, too much respect for tradition impedes innovation. Part of the reason for the post–World War II economic success of the Five Dragons (i.e., Japan, Taiwan, Singapore, South Korea, and Hong Kong) is the apparent ease with which these countries have accepted Western technological innovations.[21] Table 1–4 summarizes key differences between countries with long-term orientation versus short-term orientation.

---

[21]Hofstede, *Cultures and Organizations: Software of the Mind,* p. 169.

Hofstede's Long-Term Orientation Scores*
(higher scores = greater LTO)

Country	LTO Score
Japan	80
South Korea	75
Sweden	33
Germany	31
Great Britain	25
Italy & Mexico	Not available
United States	29

*Of primary importance is the relative position of the
countries, not the absolute values of the scores.

Source: G. Hofstede, *Cultures and Organizations* (Berkshire,
England: McGraw-Hill, 1991). Reproduced with permission.

Because an LTO orientation emphasizes thrift, perseverance toward steady results, and the willingness to subordinate oneself to a purpose, a positive linkage to financial reporting tendencies of conservatism and uniformity is likely. In general, Japan and South Korea tend to exhibit strong LTO orientations and, indeed, their financial reporting tends to manifest these traits.

To briefly summarize, then, Hofstede's cultural dimensions have been introduced as a way to think about the possible cultural root causes of differences in financial reporting practices across countries. The Hofstede scores are useful not in the sense that they are absolute measures of anything but because they indicate the relative extent to which certain attributes typify various countries' "collective programming." A limited number of countries are discussed in this text. The seven countries discussed share some cultural similarities and exhibit certain cultural differences as previously conveyed in the Hofstede scores.

Legal and Political Environment

One of the fundamental aspects of any financial reporting system is its relationship to tax law. In the United States and Great Britain, the influence of tax provisions on the calculation of accounting income is minimal: Companies may report one set of figures in their financial statements and a substantially different set on their tax returns. In many other

TABLE 1–4   Key Differences between Long-Term Orientation and Short-Term Orientation

Long-Term Orientation	Short-Term Orientation
• Adaptation of traditions to a modern context.	• Respect for traditions.
• Respect for social and status obligations within limits.	• Respect for social and status obligations regardless of cost.
• Thrift, sparing resources.	• Social pressure to "keep up with the Joneses" even if it means overspending.
• Large savings, funds available for investment.	• Small savings, little money for investment.
• Perseverance toward slow results.	• Quick results expected.
• Willingness to subordinate oneself for a purpose.	• Concern with "face."
• Concern with respecting the demands of Virtue.	• Concern with possessing the Truth.

Source: G. Hofstede, *Cultures and Organizations:* (Berkshire, England: McGraw-Hill, 1991). Reproduced with permission.

countries, however, taxable income is more closely related to accounting income. In Japan and Germany, for example, expenses must be recorded on the books of accounts—hence, included in financial statements—to qualify for deduction on a company's tax return. The requirement that accounting and taxable income be substantially the same naturally prompts companies to measure income as conservatively as legally possible. Certain expenses, most notably depreciation, are calculated according to legislative requirements and incentives instead of sound business experience. As a consequence, accountants and auditors become less concerned with fair presentation than with legal compliance. And because tax law is formulated by national legislative bodies in response to varying political and economic agendas, its influence on financial reporting is one of the most obvious and immediate hindrances to establishing a common set of international reporting standards.

Although corporate tax law and its relationship to financial reporting have a more direct effect on financial reporting standards, individual tax law also plays a role. Tax incentives for individuals are some of the tools that governments use to encourage or discourage share ownership among small investors, which in turn has an impact on the nature and orientation of corporate financial reporting. Nations eager to develop stronger stock exchanges—Italy is a good example—are not only adjusting government regulation in an attempt to ensure fair and free markets but also are implementing tax incentives to encourage their citizens to buy and hold stocks. If this trend persists, it is likely to move financial reporting standards in the direction of the market-driven practices of Anglo-American countries.

Tax law is a factor in the development and practice of specific countries' financial reporting norms as is the general nature of a country's legal system. For example, a hierarchical classification scheme of the world's legal systems has been found to be useful in identifying clusters of countries employing similar accounting practices.[22] Other legal and political factors impinge on financial reporting systems as well: the role of government in formulating principles and standards, the volatility of the political system (which may affect the frequency of reform), as well as the existence of external pressures (such as European Union membership) on governments to revamp systems. Such matters are considered in subsequent chapters.

Business Environment

Because modern financial reporting springs from the development of the publicly held corporation (with its separation of ownership and management and its limitation on liability exposure), the dominant form of business in an economy can have a material effect on the sophistication of financial reporting standards in a country. In Italy, for example, the continuing prominence of small, family-owned companies (and large ones as well) has undoubtedly contributed to the slow development of public-minded financial reporting standards in that country. Every developed nation recognizes some version of the publicly owned corporation as a primary business entity, but the reporting requirements imposed on such companies can vary widely. Company law in most countries distinguishes between publicly and closely held corporations and between "large" and "small" companies (however they may be defined) and adjusts financial reporting requirements accordingly. Moreover, the prevalence of, or the desire to build, world-class multinational corporations may also influence a country's willingness to accommodate financial reporting practices

---

[22]S. B. Salter and T. S. Doupnick, "The Relationship between Legal Systems and Accounting Practices: A Classification Exercise," *Advances in International Accounting* 5 (1992), pp. 3–22.

amenable to interested parties in other countries. In terms of the number of major multinational companies propagated by the economies of this text's focal countries, Table 1–5 depicts quite a variation. We might at times find it insightful to posit a company's, if not a country's, adoption of internationally accepted accounting standards to be consistent with that company's expressed desire to elevate its overall international image and awareness (e.g., Fiat and Bayer). These ma`tters are considered in the Form of Business section of each chapter dealing with a focus country.

Closely related to the forms of business in a country is the state of its capital markets (i.e., stock and bond markets). The nature of financial reporting standards and the fundamental purpose of the entire financial reporting system depend on customary sources of capital. In such countries as Germany and Japan, where banks have long played a very powerful role in stoking economic growth, disclosure tends to be deemphasized because lenders (who are usually major investors as well) generally have ready access to internal corporate information. In addition to the banking system, the development of stock exchanges—the distribution of share ownership, the mix of domestic and international listings, the effectiveness of regulation, the stringency of listing requirements—has a powerful effect on financial reporting standards and the quality of disclosure. Table 1–6 provides some recent data exhibiting the disparity among nations in some of these areas.

TABLE 1–5
Number of Companies in *Fortune* Global 500 from Focal Countries

	1997	1993
United States	175	159
Japan	112	135
Great Britain	37	41
Germany	42	32
Korea	12	12
Sweden	4	12
Italy	13	7
Mexico	1	3

Source: "Guide to the Global 500," *Fortune*, July 25, 1994, pp. 137–96; "The FORTUNE Global 500," *Fortune*, August 3, 1998, pp. F-1 to F-10.

A sophisticated and modern system of financial disclosure requires an accounting profession that is well educated and numerous enough to ensure its proper functioning. One certainly sees this in countries such as Great Britain and the United States, where the accounting profession shares responsibility for creating financial reporting standards. But even in nations where financial reporting standards are largely a matter of central legislation, the sophistication and training of the accounting profession (usually because it serves as an adviser to the legislature and is itself charged with developing auditing standards) noticeably affect the quality of financial reporting. For example, Swedish multinationals under the guidance of a professional elite able and willing to debate reporting practices consistently publish some of the most comprehensive annual reports throughout the world even though Swedish accounting standards are dictated by commercial law.

The final major element discussed in the business environment section of the country chapters is the influence of organized labor on financial reporting practices. This influence has rarely been a matter of labor unions changing the way income is measured or assets

TABLE 1–6

Various International Securities Exchange Information

Panel A: Number of Companies Listed and P/E ratio

Country	No. of Companies	P/E Ratio
Mexico	193	13.4
Italy	244	21.7
Great Britain	2,433	16.2
Japan	2,334	54.4
South Korea	760	21.8
Sweden	229	18.8
Germany	681	23.5
United States	8,479	19.5

Source: "By the Numbers," *The Wall Street Journal* (June 26, 1997), pp. R16–R17. All data as of 12/31/96 except share price in P/E ratios, which was as of 4/17/97.

Panel B: Number of Domestic and Foreign Companies with Shares listed on Major Stock Exchanges (1997)

Exchange	Total Listings	Domestic Companies	Foreign Companies
Mexico	198	194	4
U.S. (NYSE)	2,626	2,271	355
Germany	2,696	700	1,996
Italy	239	235	4
London	2,513	2,046	467
Stockholm	261	245	16
Korea	776	776	0
Tokyo	1,865	1,805	60

Source: Web site of the International Accounting Standards Committee (www.iasc.org.uk).

Panel C: New Listings of non-U.S. Issuers on NYSE, 1986–1996 (common shares only)

1986	8	1992	16
1987	16	1993	37
1988	12	1994	52
1989	13	1995	35
1990	10	1996	59
1991	12		

Source: J. Fanto and R. Karmel, "A Report on the Attitudes of Foreign Companies Regarding a U.S. Listing," *NYSE Working Paper 97-01,* (March 6, 1997).

Panel D: Foreign Companies Listed on the NYSE: 1998

Country of Origin	No. of Companies
Germany	8
Italy	11
Japan	12
Korea	3
Mexico	27
Sweden	3
UK	48

Source: Web site of the NYSE (www.nyse.com).

are valued; rather, it generally has taken the form of ancillary disclosures—compensation of directors and top management, employment figures by region and business sector, and so on—and an increase in social reporting. European firms are much more apt to use their annual reports as a platform for responding to public concerns on a variety of social issues, employment being one of the most prominent. Most of these companies respond to labor-related and other social concerns by including a statement of policies and programs or some other form of narrative presentation. Some, however, go beyond this to include a value-added set of financial statements designed to measure a company's creation of wealth and show its distribution among major stakeholders: employers, investors, and government. The growth of the labor movement, with its demands for more socially responsible corporate behavior, has undoubtedly helped to create a social climate that requires such disclosure from companies.

Selected Financial Reporting Practices and Illustrations

Each chapter includes a number of illustrations taken from the annual reports (English-language versions) of companies headquartered in the country under consideration. The illustrations are offered in the belief that whatever explanations are provided here will be inadequate without the experience of actually confronting foreign financial statements, with all the bafflement that may attend such a confrontation. Accordingly, readers should take sufficient time to peruse additional complete sets of financial statements from various countries to discover points of differences as well as common themes and practices within the various reports. The Selected Financial Reporting Practices section of each country-specific chapter (i.e., in Chapters 7–13) includes a list of significant practices that extend the narrative part of the chapter. Readers should not consider these practices as carved in stone because financial reporting practices are changing rapidly in many parts of the world to accommodate the emerging global economy. Nevertheless, this section should supplement a discussion that may at times seem theoretical and speculative with useful detail, and it should give the reader some idea of practices around the world with regard to such items as, say, research and development expenditures.

Summary

Context is critical for interpreting and understanding financial data. This chapter and, indeed, this book posit that financial reporting practices are a consequence of various contextual factors that include a country's (1) dominant culture, (2) system of taxation, (3) role of capital markets, and (4) business-government relations. The financial reporting differences that are exhibited around the world are rooted in nationalistic preferences, attitudes, and systems. The following chapters attempt to highlight the international and country-specific forces influencing the financial reporting practices employed by publicly held companies around the world. Generally accepted accounting practices do differ across countries to varying degrees. Reasons for their similarity and their differences can be explained and understood, to a large extent, by understanding the context within which the practices exist.

Suggested Readings

Choi, F. D. S., and R. M. Levich. "Behavioral Effects of International Accounting Diversity." *Accounting Horizons,* June 1991, pp. 1–13.

Doupnik, T. S. and S. B. Salter, "External Environment, Culture, and Accounting Practice: A Preliminary Test of a General Model of International Accounting Development," *International Journal of Accounting* 30 (1995), pp. 189–207.

Franke, R.; G. Hofstede; and M. Bond. "Cultural Roots of Economic Performance: A Research Note." *Strategic Management Journal* 12 (1991), pp. 165–73.

Gernon, H. and R. S. O. Wallace, "International Accounting Research: A Review of Its Ecology, Contending Theories and Methodologies," *Journal of Accounting Literature,* (1995), pp. 54–106.

Gray, S. "Cultural Influences and the International Classification of Accounting Systems." Presented at EIASM Workshop on Accounting and Culture. Amsterdam, 1985.

——. "Towards a Theory of Cultural Influence on the Development of Accounting Systems Internationally." *ABACUS* 24, no. 1 (1988).

Hofstede, G. *Culture's Consequences: International Differences in Work-Related Values.* Sage Publications, 1980.

——. *Cultures and Organizations: Software of the Mind.* Berkshire, England: McGraw-Hill, 1991.

——, and M. Bond. "Hofstede's Culture Dimensions: An Independent Validation Using Rokeach's Survey." *Journal of Cross-Cultural Psychology* 15, no. 4 (December 1984), pp. 417–33.

——. "The Confucius Connection from Cultural Roots to Economic Growth." *Organizational Dynamics,* Spring 1988, pp. 4–21.

Meek, G. K., and S. Sandagaran. "A Survey of Research on Financial Reporting in a Transnational Context." *The Journal of Accounting Literature* (1990), pp. 145–82.

Nobes, C., and R. Parker. *Comparative International Accounting.* Englewood Cliffs, NJ: Prentice-Hall, 1991.

Raimond, P.; M. Hinard; and J. Weitkamp. "Comparing European Companies." *European Management Journal* 6, no. 4 (1988), pp. 367–74.

The Chinese Culture Connection. "Chinese Values and the Search for Culture-Free Dimensions of Culture." *Journal of Cross-Cultural Psychology* 18, no. 2 (1987). The Chinese Culture Connection is the name given to an international network of 23 colleagues orchestrated by Michael Bond.

Zarzeski, M. T., "Spontaneous Harmonization Effects of Culture and Market Forces on Accounting Disclosure Practice," *Accounting Horizons* (March, 1996), pp. 18–37.

Exercises

1.1 American Depositary Receipts

In an October 6, 1993, *Financial Times* article (p. 28), "Kaufhof Holding Plans Sponsored ADR Scheme," writer David Waller notes that there are "three ways that shares in non-U.S. companies can be traded in North America." At one end of the spectrum, a company can list on a U.S. stock exchange just as any U.S. company might. At the other end of the spectrum is the unsponsored American depositary receipt (ADR) mechanism. Between these two is the third option utilizing sponsored ADRs.

Required:

Investigate and report on the two types of ADR programs, making sure to note how they work, their pros and cons, and their financial reporting requirements. Why might a non-U.S. company choose a sponsored ADR plan versus a full listing?

1.2   Audit Reports

In a December 15, 1994, *Financial Times* article (p. 20), "Accountancy: Cookbook May Be Put on the Back Burner," author Jim Kelly asserts that "the role of auditors, the scope of their duties and responsibilities, are issues too long left to the almost glacial pace of change in the accountancy profession."

Required:

Choose any two of the seven focal countries in this text and obtain a copy of an annual report of a company from each of those countries. Compare and contrast the audit report noting such things as to whom the report is addressed, the date of the report relative to the company's fiscal year-end, the scope of work noted, the conclusion rendered, and any other interesting features. As a potential investor in those companies, what is your conclusion about the auditors' reports?

1.3   Culture-Based Business Propositions

In a 1993 *Journal of Business Ethics* (vol. 12, pp. 753–60) article, "The Effects of Culture on Ethical Decision-Making: An Application of Hofstede's Typology," S. J. Vitell, S. L. Nwachukwu, and J. Barnes present a number of propositions related to Hofstede's cultural dimensions of uncertainty avoidance, individualism, and power distance. Those propositions are as follows:

a. *Proposition:* Business practitioners in countries that are high on individualism (i.e., the United States) will be less likely to consider professional, industry, and organizational norms (formal and informal) when forming their own [moral] norms than business practitioners in countries that are high on collectivism (i.e., Japan).

b. *Proposition:* Business practitioners in countries with a small power distance (i.e., the United States) are likely to consider informal professional, industry, and organizational norms as more important than formal codes of ethics when forming their own [moral] norms.

c. *Proposition:* Business practitioners in countries that are high in uncertainty avoidance (i.e., Japan) will be more likely to consider formal professional, industry, and organizational codes of ethics when forming their own [moral] norms than business practitioners in countries that are low in uncertainty avoidance (i.e., the United States).

d. *Proposition:* Business practitioners in countries that are high on individualism (i.e., the United States or Canada) will be likely to consider themselves as more important stakeholders than owners/stockholders and other employees while business practitioners in countries that are high on collectivism (i.e., Japan) will be likely to consider the owner/stockholders and other employees as more important stakeholders than themselves.

e. *Proposition:* Business practitioners in countries with high uncertainty avoidance (i.e., Japan) will be likely to consider the owners/stockholders and other employees as more important stakeholders than themselves while business practitioners in countries with low uncertainty avoidance (i.e., the United States or Canada) will be likely to consider themselves as more important stakeholders than the owners/stockholders and other employees.

f. *Proposition:* Business practitioners in countries that are high in uncertainty avoidance (i.e., Japan) will be less likely to perceive ethical problems than business practitioners in countries that are low in uncertainty avoidance (i.e., the United States).

Required:

Prepare a brief summary of the financial reporting issues/concerns/considerations that spring from each proposition. Are the conclusions contained in your summary important to you as a potential user of financial statements from around the world? Why or why not?

1.4   Culture-Based Business Research

Professor Scott Shane of MIT University is one of the leading authors in the field of culture-based business research. Among his many articles are "Uncertainty Avoidance and the Preference for Innovation Championing Roles," *Journal of International Business Studies* (First Qtr., 1995), pp. 47–68 and "National Cultural Distance and Cross-Border Acquisition Performance," with P. Morosini and H. Singh, *Journal of International Business Studies* (First Qtr., 1998), pp. 137–58.

Required:

Obtain copies of these two articles and prepare a brief overview of the key business issue(s) raised, the hypotheses offered, and the conclusions reached. Opine as to how these results might be suggestive of some cultural implications related to financial reporting across countries.

Harmonization of International Accounting and Reporting Standards

The objective of harmonization is the comparability of accounts.[1]

Internationally accepted accounting standards are good for business, good for investors, good, in short, for the world economy.[2]

In the 21st century, the IASC, with the support of national standard-setting bodies, will be the paramount force in the setting of financial reporting standards.[3]

Introduction

Even a brief survey of the financial press from the last 10 years reveals that articles on the **harmonization** of world accounting standards have appeared with ever-increasing frequency. Everyone, it seems, is talking about it—academics, standards setters, securities regulators, analysts, columnists, and practitioners alike. Its ramifications—economic, political, cultural, technical—are routinely examined and debated. Once deemed by many to be little more than a utopian fantasy, financial-reporting harmonization has become a major theme in almost any discussion of international business.

More important, the talk is increasingly being followed with action. With the promulgation of standards by the **International Accounting Standards Committee** (IASC), since 1973 harmonization has moved from the realm of theoretical debate to the arena of practical reality. In the 1990s, as **European Union** (EU) member countries implemented the Fourth and the Seventh Directives—the EU policies regarding the presentation of annual accounts and consolidated accounts of companies (discussed at length in Chapter 3)—and as more firms voluntarily adopted IASC standards, the possibilities and limitations of harmonization came into sharp focus. But what exactly does harmonization mean, and why has it become such an important issue?

On the simplest level, *harmonization* is the process of bringing international accounting standards into some sort of agreement so that the financial statements from different coun-

---

[1]K. Van Hulle, "Harmonization of Accounting Standards in the EC," *European Accounting Review,* November 2, 1993, p. 387.

[2]P. N. Roy, "International Accounting Standards—Why Bother?" *Financial Executive,* November/December 1995, p. 1.

[3]A quote attributed to Michael Sharpe, who stepped down as chair of IASC on December 31, 1997. The quote was in A. Carey, "Towards Some Truly Global Standards," *Accountancy,* December 1995, p. 64.

tries are prepared according to a common set of principles of measurement and disclosure. To the uninitiated, this might seem to be a rather straightforward matter, requiring perhaps four to five years (or less) for study and a few more for implementation. In fact, harmonization is an amazingly complex process fraught with political and technical pitfalls.

As is true of any transnational effort, harmonization must address the issue of national sovereignty and its changing role in a world community that is continually becoming more economically and technologically interdependent. National governments have a vested interest in the financial information produced by private companies, frequently using these data as the basis for tax collection, statistics gathering, and implementation of macroeconomic policy. Governments are understandably reluctant to allow international agencies to influence the shape of financial information in ways that could disrupt the basic legal and fiscal structures of their countries. Because international financial reporting agencies (such as the IASC) generally have no means to force national governments to accept their recommendations, they must rely on the delicate arts of negotiation and persuasion. Success requires the achievement of a widespread consensus, which takes considerable time and patience.

Moreover, would-be harmonizers must weigh these national sovereignty political problems against technical and conceptual issues. For example, what degree of uniformity in financial reporting practices is most useful and desirable? Many scholars and practitioners believe that complete uniformity would not necessarily yield the best results; it might actually distort financial statements by stressing form over substance. In fact, many differences in financial reporting methods are far from arbitrary, reflecting divergences in economic "infrastructures" as well as cultural habits. To understand these differences, one must appreciate something of the diversity of business practices around the world.

International accounting standards must therefore maintain a delicate balance between counterproductive rigidity and confusing and needless diversity. For such standards to be viewed as worthwhile, they must be comprehensive and detailed enough to provide positive guidance for the well-educated provider of the financial data, yet simple enough to be comprehensible to the consumer with relatively little training who relies on the financial data for important insights. International standards must be useful in many different cultural and economic contexts. These and other problems ensure that harmonization will be a long and difficult process, requiring careful consideration at every step.

Market Forces

The process of harmonization continues, propelled by the profound economic forces of international trade and capital movements. In spite of all the obstacles created by widely divergent financial reporting methods, the adoption of global financing strategies by multinational corporations and of global investment strategies by institutional and individual investors is causing the flow of financial information to increase among nations and continents. The search for less costly capital on the one hand, and higher returns on the other, has transformed securities markets into international marketplaces with listings and buyers from all corners of the globe. As of early 1999, almost 400 non-U.S. companies, from nearly 50 countries, were listed on just the New York Stock Exchange. Likewise, over 2,100 non-German companies, from over 60 countries, were listed on the various German exchanges. Such listings are in many cases quite important in meeting the capital needs of companies, as well as in raising their visibility in strategically significant markets. From the viewpoint of investors, the listing of foreign companies on domestic exchanges provides the opportunity to buy shares in enterprises that they may have previously admired only from afar. Table 2–1, for example, provides

TABLE 2–1

Partial Listing of Non-U.S. Equity Securities Traded on the New York Stock Exchange*

Country	Company	New York Stock Exchange Symbol
Australia	Broken Hill Proprietary Ltd.	BHP
Bermuda	ADT Ltd.	ADT
British West Indies	Club Med, Inc.	CMI
Canada	Placer Dome, Inc.	PDG
Chile	Compania de Teléfonos de Chile	TCH
Denmark	Novo-Nordisk A/S	NVO
France	Rhone-Poulenc S.A.	RPV
Great Britain	British Petroleum Plc	BP
Hong Kong	Hong Kong Telecommunications Ltd.	HKT
Ireland	Allied Irish Banks Plc	AIB
Israel	Elscint Ltd.	ELT
Italy	Benetton Group S.p.A.	BNG
Japan	Hitachi Ltd.	HIT
Mexico	Teléfonos de Mexico S.A.	TMX
Netherlands	Phillips N.V.	PHG
Netherlands Antilles	Schlumberger Ltd.	SLB
New Zealand	Telecom Corp. of New Zealand Ltd.	NZT
Norway	Norsk Hydro a.s.	NHY
Philippines	Benguet Corporation	BE
South Africa	ASA Ltd.	ASA
Spain	Repsol S.A.	REP

*Foreign securities traded on the NYSE represent either actual equity securities or ADRs (American depositary receipts).

a partial listing of the non-U.S. companies whose equity securities trade on the New York Stock Exchange.

The trend toward globalization in the world's securities markets has created formidable challenges in the areas of communications and investor relations, however, especially for those firms listing their securities on exchanges in several countries. Multinationals must determine how to communicate with current and prospective foreign investors in terms that they can readily understand. Prudent investors quite naturally expect a premium from companies that seem "risky," a perception that is more likely to haunt firms with less than totally understood financial reporting practices. As a result, many companies listed on major securities exchanges voluntarily exceed minimum disclosure requirements. For a company seeking capital in two or three countries with different financial reporting standards and practices, the necessity of keeping investors informed is burdensome; for one pursuing it in six or eight, it can be a serious and costly matter indeed. Timely, informative, comprehensive financial reporting becomes a major effort requiring considerable planning and coordination.

With no universally accepted set of international financial reporting and disclosure guidelines, multinationals have responded with a variety of strategies: (1) translating the text of home-country annual reports into the reader's language (**convenience translations**); (2) translating the text of home-country annual reports into the reader's language and into the reader's currency (**convenience statement**); (3) preparing several sets of statements that report results in different languages and currencies according to different countries' accounting principles (**multiple reporting**); (4) providing reconciliations in annual reports and filing forms with a foreign country's equivalent of the Securities and Exchange Commission to meet its minimum financial reporting requirements based on local GAAP (**reconciliation report**); and (5) preparing financial reports in accordance with IASC accounting standards (**world standards report**).[4]

Tables 2–2 through 2–6 present examples of these five strategies. Obviously, reporting strategies that ignore differences in local accounting principles present problems for local analysts and investors; on the other hand, those reports that consider them require considerably more time and expense on the part of the preparer. Either way, someone absorbs the costs of divergent principles and standards of financial reporting; generally, the multinational preparers do so. It is not surprising, then, that multinationals are supporting harmonization, in part, because it promises to reduce differences in reporting requirements and that analysts and investors are supporting it because it promises to provide a more comparable basis from which well-informed investing decisions can be made.

Unquestionably, market forces are providing a much-needed impetus for harmonization of financial reporting standards. However, the influence of the market on international financial reporting standards should not obscure the importance of political and professional initiatives in this area. This point sometimes escapes the financial press, which has an unfortunate tendency to ascribe progress to the demands of the financial industry and to blame inevitable difficulties on the governments and professional groups

TABLE 2–2
Convenience Translation: Income Statement—Swedish Match AB

Language: Reader's   **Currency:** Home Country's   **GAAP:** Home Country's

SEK million	*1997*	*1996*
Sales inclusive tobacco tax	15,231	15,007
Less, tobacco tax	−7,766	−7,591
Sales	**7,465**	**7,416**
Cost of goods sold	−3,615	−3,653
Gross margin	**3,850**	**3,763**
Selling expenses	−1,572	−1,352
Administrative expenses	−759	−729
Other operating income	84	30
Other operating expenses	−34	−5
Share of earnings in associated companies	17	16
Items affecting comparability	−	−123
Operating profit	**1,586**	**1,600**
Interest income	48	97
Interest expenses	−65	−178
Exchange rate differences and other financial items	−11	11
Profit after financial items	**1,558**	**1,530**
Taxes	−512	−439
Minority interest	−1	18
PROFIT FOR THE YEAR	**1,045**	**1,109**

The annual report follows the recommendations of the Swedish Financial Accounting Standards Council.

---

[4]G. Meek, "Competition Spurs Worldwide Harmonization," *Management Accounting,* August 1984, pp. 47–49.

TABLE 2–3
Convenience Statement: Income Statement—Toyota Motor Corp.

Language: Reader's   **Currency:** Reader's and Home Country's   **GAAP:** Home Country's

	Millions of yen			Thousands of U.S. Dollars
	1997	*1996*	*1995 (9 months)*	*1997*
Net Sales	¥12,243,835	¥10,718,740	¥8,120,975	$98,740,603
Cost of Sales	9,925,775	9,015,040	6,876,796	80,046,571
Gross profit	2,318,060	1,703,700	1,244,179	18,694,032
Selling, General and Administrative				
Expenses	1,652,946	1,355,631	988,459	13,330,207
Operating income	665,114	348,069	255,720	5,363,825
Other Income (Expenses):				
Interest and dividend income	78,464	88,598	82,513	632,771
Interest expense	(45,489)	(44,255)	(39,311)	(366,842)
Other, net	10,210	28,389	(24,109)	82,337
Income before income taxes	708,299	420,801	274,813	5,712,091
Income Taxes:				
Current	370,788	187,121	149,007	2,990,222
Tax effect of timing differences	(16,674)	(3,590)	9,782	(134,467)
Minority Interests in Income of				
Consolidated Subsidiaries	5,893	5,239	4,210	47,527
Amortization of Consolidation Difference	(230)	59	21	(1,859)
Equity in Earnings of Affiliates	37,854	24,887	20,118	305,275
Net income	¥ 385,916	¥ 256,977	¥ 131,953	$ 3,112,225

	Yen			U.S. Dollars
Amounts per Share:				
Net income	¥100.21	¥66.55	¥34.40	$0.808
Dividends	22.00	19.00	14.50	0.177

Note:

The accompanying consolidated financial statements have been prepared in accordance with the accounting principles generally accepted in Japan from accounts and records maintained by Toyota Motor Corporation (the "Parent") and its subsidiaries.

The financial statements presented here are expressed in yen. Solely for the convenience of the reader, they have been translated into U.S. dollars at the rate of ¥124=US$1, the approximate exchange rate on the Tokyo Foreign Exchange Market on March 31, 1997. These translations should not be construed as representations that the yen amounts have been or could be converted into U.S. dollars at the rate used here or at any other rate.

In 1995, the Parent changed its fiscal year-end to March 31, from June 30, which resulted in a nine-month fiscal period ended March 31, 1995.

that first began pushing for harmonization. For example, a headline in the May 8, 1985, edition of *The Wall Street Journal* boldly proclaimed: "Where Boards and Governments Have Failed, the Market Could Internationalize Accounting." Likewise, *Forbes* reported that the internationalizing of capital markets was producing results when public and professional groups such as the IASC and the EU supposedly had failed.[5] Perhaps such descriptions simply indicate the ideological predilections of journal editors, showing the

---

[5]"Take the Cash and Let the Standards Go," *Forbes,* July 2, 1984.

forces of free enterprise succeeding when the efforts of everyone else (most notably "boards and governments") have failed. However, this is simply no longer a fair characterization. The fact of the matter is that market forces are speeding up a process that has been under way for some time—one that has been created, nurtured, and guided by the farsightedness of several political and professional organizations. Harmonization efforts not only currently depend on the groundwork laid by these groups over the last 25 years but also will continue to look to them for guidance and coordination in years to come. The vigorous growth of the IASC, which claimed members from nine nations in 1973 as compared with more than 100 twenty-five years later, indicates that its efforts are gaining recognition and credibility as capital markets become more international. Following are brief descriptions of the international organizations that to a greater or lesser extent have been promoting the cause of harmonization. (A more extensive discussion of the impact of the EU is included in Chapter 3.) Indeed, as *The Wall Street Journal* more recently noted in an August 29, 1995, headline, "All Accountants Soon May Speak the Same Language."

TABLE 2–4

Multiple Reporting: Income Statement—Hitachi Ltd.

Language: Reader's   **Currency:** Reader's and Home Country's   **GAAP:** Reader's

	Millions of Yen			Thousands of U.S. Dollars
	1997	*1996*	*1995*	*1997*
Net sales	¥8,523,100	¥8,123,810	¥7,592,266	$68,734,677
Cost of sales	6,250,895	5,828,887	5,393,757	50,410,443
Gross profit	2,272,205	2,294,923	2,198,509	18,324,234
Selling, general and administrative expenses	1,975,039	1,962,341	1,893,919	15,927,734
Operating income	297,166	332,582	304,590	2,396,500
Other income				
Interest	37,632	51,126	74,550	303,484
Dividends	8,638	8,010	8,003	69,661
Other	41,561	51,827	13,319	335,170
	87,831	110,963	95,872	708,315
Other deductions:				
Interest and discount charges	60,669	63,375	74,998	489,266
Other	61,004	31,543	41,821	491,968
	121,673	94,918	116,819	981,234
Income before income taxes and minority interests	263,324	348,627	283,643	2,123,581
Income Taxes	138,495	165,764	153,443	1,116,895
Income before minority interests	124,829	182,863	130,200	1,006,686
Minority interests	36,498	41,093	16,288	294,339
Net income	¥ 88,331	¥ 141,770	¥ 113,912	$ 712,347
	Yen			**U.S. dollars**
Net income per share of common stock	¥25.55	¥40.09	¥33.02	$0.21

The consolidated financial statements presented herein have been prepared in a manner and reflect the adjustments which are necessary to conform them with United States generally accepted accounting principles. Management of the Company has made a number of estimates and assumptions relating to the reporting of assets and liabilities and the disclosure of contingent assets and liabilities to prepare these financial statements. Actual results could differ from those estimates.

TABLE 2–5

Reconciliation Report: Income Statement—Volvo Group

Language: Reader's **Currency:** Reader's **GAAP:** Reconciled

SEKM	*1995*	*1996*	*1997*
Net sales	171,511	156,060	**183,625**
Cost of sales	(128,529)	(121,249)	**(138,990)**
Gross income	42,982	34,811	**44,635**
Research and development expenses	(7,343)	(8,271)	**(8,659)**
Selling expenses	(17,418)	(14,895)	**(17,160)**
Administrative expenses	(7,399)	(6,685)	**(7,018)**
Other operating income	4,168	5,086	**3,187**
Other operating expenses	(5,966)	(6,336)	**(6,567)**
Operating income before nonrecurring items	9,024	3,710	**8,418**
Nonrecurring items	1,215	—	**—**
Operating Income	10,239	3,710	**8,418**
Income from investments in associated companies	2,119	314	**2,929**
Income from other investments	788	9,007	**1,168**
Interest income and similar credits	3,996	4,817	**3,486**
Interest expenses and similar charges	(3,757)	(3,271)	**(2,748)**
Other financial income and expenses	(337)	(374)	**(77)**
Income after financial items	13,048	14,203	**13,176**
Taxes	(3,741)	(1,825)	**(2,705)**
Minority interests	(45)	99	**(112)**
Net income	9,262	12,477	**10,359**

The consolidated accounts of AB Volvo and its subsidiaries are prepared in accordance with Swedish accounting principles. These principles differ in certain significant respects from American accounting principles.

A summary of the Volvo Group's approximate net income and shareholders' equity determined in accordance with U.S. GAAP, is presented in the accompanying tables

Net Income	*1995*	*1996*	*1997*
Net income in accordance with Swedish accounting principles	9,262	12,477	10,359
Items increasing (decreasing) reported net income:			
Foreign currency translation 5,457	(89)	(4,994)	
Income taxes	(523)	494	122
Tooling costs	(633)	(312)	—
Business combinations	355	(529)	(529)
Shares and participations	(116)	176	—
Interest costs	2	15	28
Leasing	49	49	46
Debt and equity securities	368	(147)	123
Other	111	(95)	65
Minority interests	2	—	—
Tax effect of above U.S. GAAP adjustments	(1,399)	178	1,336
Net increase (decrease) in net income	3,673	(260)	(3,803)
Approximate net income in accordance with U.S. GAAP	**12,935**	**12,217**	**6,556**
Approximate net income per share, SEK in accordance with U.S. GAAP	**28.20**	**26.40**	**14.50**
Weighted average number of shares outstanding (in thousands)	457,984	463,558	452,540

TABLE 2–6

World Standards Report: Income Statement—Hoechst AG

Language: Reader's   **Currency:** Home Country's   **GAAP:** IASC

		1997 DM Million	1996 DM Million
Net sales		**52100**	**50927**
Cost of sales	−	31533	30902
Gross profit	=	20567	20025
Distribution and selling costs	−	10206	10112
Research and development costs	−	3990	3880
General and administrative costs	−	2808	2522
Other operating income	+	1834	2377
Other operating expense	−	1744	1875
Operating profit	=	**3653**	**4013**
Result on sale and transfer of businesses	+	304	1792
Investment income, net	+	309	212
Interest expense, net	−	1019	780
Other financial expense, net	−	90	91
Non-operating expenses	=	**−800**	**−659**
Profit before taxes on income	=	**3157**	**5146**
Taxes on income	−	1383	2372
Income before minority interests	=	**1774**	**2774**
Minority interests	−	431	660
Net income	=	**1343**	**2114**
		DM	DM
Earnings per share		**2.28**	**3.60**

The 1997 consolidated financial statements are based on the International Accounting Standards ("IAS") of the International Accounting Standards Committee ("IASC") in the version valid on the respective balance sheet dates. Additionally, the promulgated standards IAS 12 (revised 1996) "Income Taxes," IAS 14 (revised 1997) "Segment Reporting," and IAS 33 "Earnings per Share" have been adopted prior to their effective dates, as encouraged by the IASC. In order to comply with the provisions of the German Commercial Code and Generally Accepted Accounting Principles in Germany ("German GAAP"), appropriate use is made of the existing options under the German Commercial Code and IAS, thereby permitting conformance with both sets of accounting standards. Insofar as classification rules are stipulated by the German Commercial Code for the consolidated financial statements, this is taken into consideration in the balance sheet or in the form of additional information and explanations in the notes. Classification is based on the principles of clarity, understandability, and materiality.

Political Organizations

United Nations   The interest of the United Nations (U.N.) in financial disclosure is primarily motivated by its desire to control the impact of **multinational enterprises** (MNEs)—including **multinational corporations** (MNCs)—on the economies and quality of life in newly industrialized countries. Accordingly, since 1972 the U.N. has formed a variety of councils and study groups, such as the Centre on Transnational Corporations, that have examined the international activities of MNEs and developed a code of conduct to encourage socially responsible behavior. In 1977, the Group of Experts on International Standards of Accounting and Reporting, an ad hoc study group formed by the U.N. Centre, created a list of minimum financial and nonfinancial disclosures that should be included in the annual reports of

MNEs.[6] Recommended financial reporting disclosures on the list include financial statements for individual firms within consolidated groups, segment information by line of business, research and development expenditures, employment information, and transfer pricing policies. In addition, the U.N. group pointed out that useful disclosure would be facilitated by the preparation of comparable reports regardless of national origin. Because the U.N. has no jurisdiction over MNEs, it cannot enforce these disclosure recommendations, and its attempts to influence governments to enact them as law have met with little success.

Obviously, the approach to standard setting taken by the U.N. is highly politicized and more concerned with curbing exploitation than with ensuring the efficient allocation of capital. The primary user groups envisioned by the U.N. initiatives are national governments. As a result, the main beneficiaries of the U.N.'s efforts have been those governments that have used its guidelines as an unofficial framework for regulating MNEs. Thus, the needs of investors and multinationals have generally been subordinated.

OECD

The **Organization for Economic Cooperation and Development** (OECD), formed in 1960, is an association of 29 governments of industrialized nations from the noncommunist world. Its purpose, as its title suggests, is to promote cooperation among industrialized nations by serving as a forum in which member countries can consult each other with regard to important policy matters such as exchange rates or the balance of trade. It also facilitates the circulation of economic information by compiling statistics and preparing forecasts.

In 1976, the OECD issued a code of conduct for MNEs that included guidelines for disclosures in annual reports.[7] Historically the OECD has taken a relatively moderate line on multinationals, stressing voluntary restraint instead of national regulation. Although the OECD has been promoting harmonization and hosted a major conference in 1985 that examined the issue from a variety of perspectives, it does not actually propose specific accounting standards and does not intend to do so. The organization did, however, in October of 1998 issue a report titled "Report of the Working Group on Strengthening Financial Systems."[8] This report, in large measure, was prompted by the financial crises that occurred in East Asia during the 1997–98 time period. Among its recommendations, the report stressed the need to "enhance transparency and accountability" of the international financial system. In particular, the report highlighted the need to enhance "the relevance, reliability, comparability and understandability of information disclosed by the private sector [with priority] given to compliance with and enforcement of high-quality accounting standards" (p. ii). Toward such an end, the report made a special point to "underscore the importance of the IASC completing its set of core accounting standards" (p. viii).

Professional Organizations

International Accounting Standards Committee

The **International Accounting Standards Committee** (IASC), founded in 1973 by a group of professional accounting organizations from nine countries, has since grown to 143 professional accounting bodies (e.g., the American Institute of Certified Public Accountants) from over 103 nations (as of November 1998). Headquartered in London, the IASC is the most widely recognized professional group in charge of developing and issuing interna-

---

[6]United Nations Centre on Transnational Corporations, "International Standards of Accounting and Reporting" (New York: U.N. Publications, 1984), E/C.10/1982/8/Rev.1.

[7]"Declaration on International Investment and Multinational Enterprises," *The OECD Guidelines for Multinational Enterprises* (Paris: OECD, 1986).

[8]The report can be found at the OECD Web site—www.oecd.org.

tional accounting and reporting standards. The committee is governed by a board of 16 members representing 13 countries (as of 1998 these were: United States, United Kingdom, South Africa, the Nordic Federation of Public Accountants, India, Netherlands, Mexico, Malaysia, Japan, Germany, France, Canada, and Australia) and the International Association of Financial Executives Institute, the Federation of Swiss Industrial Holding Companies, and the International Coordinating Committee of Financial Analysts' Associations. It takes a 3/4 vote of the board to issue a reporting standard. The IASC's stated objectives are:

(a) To formulate and publish accounting standards to be used in the presentation of financial statements and to promote their worldwide acceptance;
(b) To work for the improvement and harmonization of regulations, accounting standards, and procedures relating to the presentation of financial statements.

Lacking some of the political and technical barriers that must inevitably slow the harmonization process, the IASC has made considerable headway, at least on paper, issuing 38 **international accounting standards** (each known as an IAS) since its founding. Appendix 2A provides a list of the IASs as of November 1998, as well as the IASC's other active projects.

Lacking the authority to enforce observance of its standards, the IASC has had to exercise a great deal of diplomacy and discretion both in formulating standards and in urging their adoption by national standard-setting bodies. The IASC must continually weigh the benefits of greater uniformity (i.e., less diversity) in financial reporting practices against the social and economic costs of retooling accounting systems, and it must remember that many financial reporting practices arise from legitimate local needs. Consequently, the typical IAS attempts to build in a certain amount of flexibility. It may mix levels of conformity, prescribing a particular accounting method in one instance while allowing alternative treatments in another so long as the one selected is adequately disclosed and its effects noted.

This approach by the IASC has won some important endorsements for IASC pronouncements. Today over 500 prominent companies prepare their statements in conformity with international accounting standards (e.g., ABB, Bayer, Fiat, and Nestlé). Moreover, the International Stock Exchange in London allows foreign firms seeking a listing to do so if they follow IASC guidelines and new laws in Belgium, France, Germany, and Italy permit publicly traded companies, foreign or domestic, to use IASs in consolidated financial statements.

The IASC has, until now, focused on obvious targets—financial reporting practices that are clearly arbitrary or unsound—in the belief that filtering out such practices is an important first step toward harmonization. In countries that have not yet issued financial reporting standards or that allow more than one accounting treatment of a given transaction, the IASC has urged local officials to adopt uniform practices consistent with existing IASs. In short, rather than immediately pushing toward complete uniformity, it has instead sought to reduce or prevent excessive diversity. This pluralistic approach has won a hearing for IASC standards in the private as well as the public sector, from multinational corporations as well as developing countries.

In early 1987, the IASC began a significant move toward a new level of international harmonization. At that time, a steering committee on comparability of financial statements was appointed to review existing international accounting standards with the objective of reducing the number of alternative treatments permissible—a movement spearheaded by the International Organization of Securities Commissions and Similar Organizations (IOSCO) (discussed later in this chapter).

In January 1989, the IASC released Exposure Draft 32, *Comparability of Financial Statements* (E32). It dealt with 29 accounting issues for which the choice of alternative accounting treatments permitted by IASs may have a material effect on the definition, recognition, measurement and display of income, expenses, assets, liabilities, or shareholders' equity in the financial statements of an enterprise. The objectives of the E32 proposals were to:

1. Eliminate all but one accounting method for which the alternative methods represent an unrestricted choice for like transactions and events.
2. Ensure that the appropriate method is used where the alternatives represent different methods that should be used in different circumstances.

In deciding which alternative treatments should be required, preferred, or eliminated, the IASC invoked a multifaceted set of criteria:

1. Current worldwide practice and trends in national accounting standards, law, and generally accepted accounting principles.
2. Conformity with the Framework for the Preparation and Presentation of Financial Statements (which was in exposure draft form at the time E32 was issued).
3. The views of regulators and their representative organizations, such as IOSCO.
4. Consistency within an international accounting standard and with other international accounting standards.

In these circumstances, E32 identified a preferred treatment and an allowed alternative. E32 proposed that an enterprise that presents financial statements using allowed alternative treatments and that purport to conform with IASs should reconcile its reported net income and shareholders' interests to those amounts determined using the preferred treatments. The original E32 proposals are listed in Appendix 2B.

The IASC received more than 160 comment letters on the proposals in E32. The letters were virtually unanimous in supporting the objective of greater comparability of financial statements and the exposure draft as a whole. Inevitably, however, many respondents disagreed with one or more of the detailed proposals in E32.

In some instances, the consequence of adopting the E32 revisions would have a significant impact on the financial reporting results of corporations in certain countries. For example, if the United States chose to follow the IASC's recommendations as outlined in E32, the net income reported by U.S. companies would be significantly affected by at least two of these revisions: IAS 22, *Accounting for Business Combinations,* and IAS 2, *Valuation and Presentation of Inventories in the Context of the Historical Cost System.*

IAS 22, Accounting for Business Combinations

This pronouncement deals with goodwill (among other things). Prior to E32, IAS 22 allowed positive goodwill to be recognized as an asset and amortized to income *or* to be adjusted immediately (i.e., written off) to shareholders' equity (it was silent on the issue of the length of the amortization period). The proposed treatment of positive goodwill eliminated one acceptable approach—the immediate adjustment (write off) to shareholders' equity—a method widely used by corporations in Great Britain until just recently and some other countries still (e.g., the Netherlands). The E32 treatment proposed that positive goodwill be recognized as an asset and that it usually be amortized over a 5- (but not to exceed a 20) year period. This change would have had a profound effect on the reported net income of U.S. companies since U.S. GAAP recognizes positive goodwill as an asset and amortizes it to income over as long as a 40-year period. The proposed shorter amortization period would significantly increase reported expenses and dampen net income. Should countries decide to adopt the proposed IAS 22 as a worldwide norm, the effects on financial reporting results could have other repercussions throughout the international business community:

> The implication of the revised IAS 22 for potential corporate buy-outs cannot be overlooked. The higher annual goodwill charges implied by IAS 22's five-year amortization period in countries permitting a longer period could drive down the amount in excess of fair value of net assets which purchasers would be willing to pay. In order to keep goodwill amortization charges to income as low as possible, buyers are likely to pay less for purchased goodwill. Thus prices are likely to decline.[9]

In finalizing its Comparability Project in November 1993, the IASC passed the E32 suggested revision to IAS 22. Thus, the IASC narrowed the acceptable alternative treatments for positive goodwill. More recently, in E61, the IASC recommended removal of the arbitrary maximum length of time for amortizing goodwill (20 years) as long as companies could justify the longer life and were in accordance with IAS 36 guidelines (Impairment of Assets).

IAS 2, Valuation and Presentation of Inventories in the Context of the Historical Cost System

This pronouncement deals with the type of cost-flow assumption used in valuing inventories. Prior to the revisions to E32 proposed in the *Statement of Intent,* IAS 2 recommended using FIFO or a weighted-average cost formula but also allowed LIFO, specific identification, and the base stock formula. The proposed amended treatment would eliminate LIFO as an alternative. Under the LIFO cost-flow method, costs are assigned to units sold on the basis that inventories represent the earliest purchases or production. As a result, the use of this method usually results in a material difference in both the carrying value of inventories and the cost of sales when compared with that obtained using the FIFO or weighed-average cost formulas. Since the LIFO cost-flow approach does not assign the most current costs to ending inventories, the IASC argued that its use may distort the balance sheet. Be that as it may, there was so much public sentiment to keep LIFO as an allowed alternative that the IASC reversed its E32 position and has continued to pose LIFO as an allowed alternative in IAS 2.[10]

In November 1993, after six years of debate and reconsideration, the final versions of the IAS revisions springing from the Comparability of Financial Statements Project were approved by the IASC board. In the end, of 24 accounting alternatives available in the original versions of the IASs, 16 were eliminated.[11] Thus ended one of the most ambitious IASC undertakings. The relative speed with which it was accomplished and the broad-based debate it sparked portended a new era of IASC importance. While acknowledging the progress achieved by the IASC in this regard, *The Economist* magazine also reminded the financial community that "To provide investors with good information, accounting standards must accomplish two things: they must increase firms' disclosure and limit their choices."[12]

A second major initiative in recent years by the IASC was the creation of a Standing Interpretations Committee (SIC) in January 1997. This committee's objective is to "enhance the rigorous application and worldwide comparability of financial statements that are

---

[9]R. Brunovs and R. Kirsch, "Goodwill Accounting in Selected Countries and the Harmonization of International Standards," *ABACUS* 27, no. 2 (1991), pp. 135–61.

[10]V. Pereira, "Fewer Alternatives Permitted," *Accountancy,* July 1994, pp. 121–22.

[11]Ibid.

[12]"Global Accounting's Roadblock," *The Economist,* April 27, 1996, p. 79.

prepared using International Accounting Standards by interpreting contentious accounting issues."[13] Moreover, SIC interpretations approved by the IASC board become a part of the IASC's authoritative literature. As of October 1998, the committee had issued 16 interpretations, 10 of which have been approved by the IASC board. These 10 dealt with interpretations of such IASs as IAS 2 (Inventories), IAS 23 (Borrowing Costs), IAS 32 (Financial Instruments), and IAS 22 (Business Combinations). There is little doubt that as more and more companies, from more and more countries, choose to implement the IASC's pronouncements, there will be an increasing need for interpretations to bridge cross-national paradigms and to clarify implementation issues arising from an extremely diverse corporate constituency.

As with anything that attempts to change or coordinate products of culture, albeit in an effort to benefit all parties concerned, the IASC has drawn considerable criticism from various quarters. It has been accused of allowing industrialized nations to dominate the standard-setting process, of legislating from on high with little regard for the needs of practitioners and financial analysts, and of serving multinationals and ignoring smaller domestic enterprises. At a conference on harmonization held by the OECD in 1985, John L. Kirkpatrick, then IASC chairman, addressed some of these criticisms. The IASC, he pointed out, owes no allegiance to any nation and makes a point of including developing nations on its governing board. It consults analysts, executives, managerial accountants, and industry groups as standards are developed, and it recognizes that the acceptance of each IAS depends on its usefulness to users and preparers of statements. Small domestic companies as well as giant multinationals are included in its jurisdiction, a fact that the IASC implicitly recognizes by trying to make its standards concise, clear, and simple enough to be useful around the world. Echoing a similar sentiment 13 years later, Stig Enevoldsen, the 1998 IASC chairman, observed that "the whole world in actual fact has an influence on the standards issued based on the hearing responses reaching the IASC [and] I think that the IASC is the natural solution in an ever smaller world."[14]

Two other complaints, somewhat broader in scope than those mentioned, are sometimes leveled against the IASC. The first and most common is that the IASC is ineffectual. The truth of this charge depends largely on how one chooses to measure effectiveness. The lack of an enforcement mechanism has undoubtedly slowed progress toward harmonization, but one can hardly blame the IASC itself for the limitations imposed on it by the politics of national sovereignty. In the endeavor in which the IASC may properly be held accountable—winning acceptance of its standards by dint of negotiation and consultation—studies indicate that the committee is making significant progress. A study conducted in 1996 by the IASC found that 56 of the 67 nations studied either adopted IAS standards as their national standards or developed national standards based primarily on IAS.[15] Perhaps the most important contribution of the IASC in this respect is that it has provided a focus for debate and has created what has been referred to as an *international subculture* for accounting standards that is beginning to have a visible impact on the formation of accounting policy around the world.[16]

The second charge, less frequently made but more serious, is that the IASC is too concerned with technical conformity and is not sensitive enough to the cultural and eco-

---

[13]IASC, *Interpretations of International Accounting Standards,* "Preface to Section 3," 1997, p. 1.

[14]IASC, "A Look Back and a Look Forward," *Insight,* June 1998, p. 16.

[15]IASC, "Current Status of IAS in 67 Countries," *Insight,* October 1997, p. 15.

[16]J. Gaertner and N. Rueschhoff, "Cultural Barriers to International Accounting Standards," *CA Magazine,* May 1980, pp. 36–39.

nomic issues underlying national accounting systems. This is a troubling charge, one that ultimately calls into question the feasibility of harmonization. It implicitly asks us to consider what level of engagement and reform is necessary for the creation of meaningful international standards. Is it enough to change an accounting system alone, or must legal systems, economic habits, and basic cultural attitudes be altered as well to achieve financial reporting harmonization? This is a difficult question to answer because the interaction between cultural contexts and accounting norms is not understood fully. In this regard, the IASC, like the European Union, can be regarded as a large-scale experiment that will, as time goes on, yield valuable information about harmonization. Likewise, the IASC's recent creation of a Joint Working Group (JWG) to develop an "integrated and harmonised standard on financial instruments" represents a small-scale experiment to see if such good intentions can be forthcoming with a specifically narrowed, critically important topical focus. The group comprises 17 accounting standard setters from nine countries plus the IASC. The countries represented are Australia, Canada, France, Germany, Japan, New Zealand, a Nordic country representative, the U.K., and the United States (two FASB members). The JWG's work is to be completed by the end of 2000.

International Organization of Securities Commissions and Similar Organizations	In February 1985, the U.S. Securities and Exchange Commission (SEC) published a document calling for comments on eased requirements for multinational securities offerings and the use of a common prospectus by companies in the United States, Great Britain, and Canada. Two distinct approaches for multinational securities offerings were considered: (1) *reciprocal*—the prospectus used by an issuer in its own country would be accepted for offerings in each of the other countries and (2) *common prospectus*—all three countries would agree on disclosure standards for an offering document (prospectus) that would then be usable in more than one country. More than 70 responses were received from issuers, securities exchanges, and industry representatives: 50 favored the reciprocal approach and 21 (including the IASC) favored the common prospectus approach.[17] At the time, however, the SEC could not decide how to proceed, partly due to the desire to extend the arrangement to other countries, especially Japan.[18] The desire to include countries outside the Americas and Europe in multinational securities offerings led, in part, to the transformation of the Interamerican Conference of Securities Agencies and Similar Organizations from a regional group to a global body in 1987 with a new name—the **International Organization of Securities Commissions and Similar Organizations** (IOSCO).[19] This new and influential organization has almost 150 securities regulatory agencies (or securities exchanges if a country has no government regulatory agency) from around the world as members,

---

[17]C. Sampson, "Facilitation of Multinational Securities Offerings," in *Research in Accounting Regulation,* ed. Gary J. Previts (Greenwich, CT: JAI Press, 1988), p. 216.

[18]In June 1991, the United States and Canada agreed on a multijurisdictional disclosure system (MJDS), which allows companies in one jurisdiction to file home-country documents in the other's jurisdiction. The British were not included. As of July 1992 there were 21 filings, 19 issuers, and $3 billion in debt capital moved from Canada to the United States as a result of a reciprocity agreement between the U.S. SEC and the Ontario SEC; fewer have gone from the United States to Canada. Information based on a phone interview in July 1992 with an attorney at the International Affairs Dept., SEC.

[19]R. S. O. Wallace, "Survival Strategies of a Global Organization: The Case of the International Accounting Standards Committee," *Accounting Horizons,* June 1990, pp. 1–22.

representing coverage of a substantial percent of the world's capital markets.[20] IOSCO members have resolved to

    a. cooperate together to ensure a better regulation of the markets, on the domestic as well as on the international level in order to maintain just and efficient securities markets;

    b. exchange information on their respective experiences in order to promote the development of domestic markets;

    c. unite their efforts to establish standards and an effective surveillance of international securities transactions; and

    d. provide mutual assistance to ensure the integrity of the markets by a rigorous application of the standards and by effective enforcement against offenses.[21]

IOSCO has a number of working committees to review and propose solutions to regulatory problems related to international securities transactions. One committee works with the IASC to identify accounting standards that securities regulators might be ready to accept in the case of multinational offerings. In 1987, IOSCO accepted an invitation to join the IASC consultative group. IOSCO's membership has meant that it can influence the work of the IASC, and IOSCO is credited with having spearheaded the movement to reduce options in IASs (i.e., IOSCO informed IASC that it would enforce the IASC's standards if the IASC would reduce the number of acceptable treatments in its existing standards and if it would buttress the existing set of IASs to meet the needs of capital markets and the international business community). With an eye toward harmonization, two noted authorities have stated that "the acceptability of the IASC's accounting rules eventually will be determined by IOSCO as well as the individual securities exchanges making up IOSCO."[22] Indeed, to this end, in October 1993, IOSCO endorsed the IASC's standard on cash flow statements stating:

> the President's Committee recommends that the members of IOSCO take all steps necessary and appropriate in their respective home jurisdictions to accept cash flow statements prepared in accordance with IAS 7, as amended, as one alternative to statements prepared in accordance with the regulator's domestic accounting standards relating to cash flow statements in connection with cross-border offerings and continuous reporting by foreign issuers.[23]

At about the same time that IOSCO endorsed IAS 7, it also promulgated a list of 40 core accounting issues (see Table 2–7) that it asserted must be included in IASC pronouncements for IOSCO to endorse those pronouncements for use by issuers in connection with cross-border securities offerings and multiple listings. The IASC was very optimistic about an imminent, comprehensive, significant endorsement of the IASC's pronouncements by IOSCO since IAS 7 had just been endorsed and because all of IOSCO's core issues, except one (interim reporting), were addressed in existing IASs or were being addressed in its active projects. In 1994, such optimism was soon dashed when the IASC received written communication from IOSCO concerning the acceptability of other existing IASs. To the dismay of the IASC, it was made clear that "IOSCO will not endorse further Standards [beyond the endorsement of IAS 7], . . . until IASC has completed all the core standards to IOSCO's satisfaction."[24] According

---

[20]*IOSCO Annual Report 1997* (Montreal: IOSCO, undated).

[21]*IOSCO Annual Report 1991* (Montreal: IOSCO, undated).

[22]A. R. Wyatt and J. F. Yospe, "Wake-up Call to American Business: International Accounting Standards Are on the Way," *Journal of Accountancy,* July 1993, p. 82.

[23]IASC, "Agreement on Cash Flow Statements and Core Standards," *IASC Insight,* December 1993, p. 4.

[24]E. Shiratori, "Time for a Different Approach from IOSCO," *IASC Insight,* December 1994, p. 10.

TABLE 2–7
IOSCO List of Desired Core International Accounting Standards and the IASC's Progress Toward Completion (as of 1998)

Core Standards as Set Forth in IOSCO's 1993 List	Current Status of IASC Work			*Core Standards as Set Forth in IOSCO's 1993 List*	Current Status of IASC Work		
	Current IAS (Last Revision)	*IASC Work Completed*	*Project Under Way*		*Current IAS (Last Revision)*	*IASC Work Completed*	*Project Under Way*
General				22. Investments	IAS 25 (1985)		E62
1. Disclosure of accounting policies	IAS 1 (1997)	X		23. Financial instruments/ off balance sheet items	IAS 32 (1995)		E62
2. Changes in accounting policies	IAS 8 (1993)	X		24. Joint ventures	IAS 31 (1990)	X	
3. Information disclosed in financial statements	IAS 1 (1997)	X		25. Contingencies	IAS 37 (1998)	X	
				26. Events occurring after the balance sheet date	IAS 10 (1974)	X	
Income Statement				27. Current assets and current liabilities	IAS 1 (1997)	X	
4. Revenue recognition	IAS 18 (1993)	X		28. Business combinations (including goodwill)	IAS 22 (1998)	X	
5. Construction contracts	IAS 11 (1993)	X		29. Intangibles other than R&D and goodwill	IAS 38 (1998)	X	
6. Production and purchase costs	IAS 2 (1993)	X					
7. Depreciation	IAS 4 (1974) and IAS 16 (1998)	X		**Cash Flow Statement**			
8. Impairment	IAS 36 (1998)	X		30. Cash flow statements	IAS 7 (1992)	X	
9. Taxes	IAS 12 (1996)	X					
10. Extraordinary items	IAS 8 (1993)	X		**Other Standards**			
11. Government grants	IAS 20 (1982)	X		31. Consolidated financial statements	IAS 27 (1988)	X	
12. Retirement benefits	IAS 19 (1998)	X		32. Subsidiaries in hyper inflationary economies	IAS 21 (1993) and IAS 29 (1989)	X	
13. Other employee benefits	IAS 19 (1998)	X		33. Associates and equity accounting	IAS 28 (1988)	X	
14. Research and development	IAS 38 (1998)	X		34. Segment reporting	IAS 14 (1997)	X	
15. Interest	IAS 23 (1993)	X		35. Interim reporting	IAS 34 (1998)	X	
16. Hedging	None		E62	36. Earnings per share	IAS 33 (1997)	X	
				37. Related party disclosures	IAS 24 (1984)	X	
Balance Sheet				38. Discontinuing operations	IAS 35 (1998)	X	
17. Property, plant and equipment	IAS 16 (1998)	X		39. Fundamental errors	IAS 8 (1993)	X	
18. Leases	IAS 17 (1997)	X					
19. Inventories	IAS 2 (1993)	X					
20. Deferred taxes	IAS 12 (1996)	X					
21. Foreign currency	IAS 21 (1993)	X					

Source: *IASC Insight,* October 1998, p. 14. Reproduced with permission. (See note at end of Chapter 2.)

to the IASC chairman at the time, IOSCO's position raised two fundamental questions: Should IOSCO endorse the process of setting international accounting standards in the same way that its members endorse the process of setting national standards? Or should it review, in detail, each international accounting standard? IOSCO is currently following the second approach, something that most of its members do not do in their own jurisdiction.[25] Moveover, the IASC chairman described the approach that he believed

---

[25]Ibid.

would be most appropriate for IOSCO to adopt in the pursuit of the shared objective of multinational companies being able to use one set of financial statements for listing shares and raising capital on any stock exchange. His recommendation was for IOSCO to

- Accept international accounting standards as a comprehensive set of standards.
- Acknowledge that international accounting standards may require different treatments from those preferred by individual IOSCO members.
- Endorse the process of setting international accounting standards rather than review each standard in detail.
- As an interim step, pending endorsement of the process, endorse those international accounting standards that it accepts and those that have recently been revised through an extensive due process in which IOSCO played an important part—this will drastically reduce the need for restatement or reconciliation by foreign issuers.[26]

As can be seen from Table 2–7, the IASC's concerted effort to address IOSCO's core standards imperative is complete as of late 1998 except for issues pertaining to financial instruments. Although IAS 32 (Financial Instruments: Disclosure and Presentation) was issued about the time that IOSCO and IASC were agreeing on a core standards work program, the standard was determined to not satisfy IOSCO's required minimums. Shortly thereafter, in order to meet a 1999 targeted deadline for all 40 core standards being addressed and IOSCO minimum requirements met, the IASC developed a two-pronged approach with regard to financial instruments. First, as an interim measure, revisions to IAS 32 would be pursued. That endeavor produced Exposure Draft (ED) 62, whose comment period ended September 30, 1998. Based on the comments received, the IASC is hopeful of a revised IAS 32 that will allow the IOSCO core standards requirements to be met by mid-1999. The second aspect of the financial instruments project is that giving rise to the Joint Work Group mentioned earlier. This group is to review the topic more comprehensively, with an eye to international integration and harmonization. The JWG's work is not scheduled for completion until 2000.

International Federation of Accountants

An important ally of the IASC in the harmonization process is the **International Federation of Accountants** (IFAC), an association of over 140 professional accounting organizations from more than 100 nations. Headquartered in New York, IFAC was formed in 1977 to encourage a consistently high standard of professionalism among accountants around the world. IFAC has largely devoted itself to providing international guidelines for the accounting profession in the areas of auditing, ethics, management accounting, and professional education. It has become the primary source of statements on international auditing standards, having issued over 45 international auditing guidelines that attempt to codify a body of acceptable auditing practices for all independent examinations of financial statements.

In 1982, the IFAC and the IASC entered into an agreement under which the IFAC recognized the IASC as the sole official source of international accounting standards, affirmed the autonomy of the IASC in their development, and promised to promote the use of international standards in all the IFAC member countries. In return, the IASC recognized the IFAC as the authorized representative of the accounting profession worldwide, accepted all members of the IFAC as members of the IASC, and gave the IFAC

---

[26]Ibid., p. 11.

authority to nominate candidates for membership on the governing board of the IASC. The cooperation of the two organizations effectively enlists the accounting profession in the promotion of international accounting standards issued by the IASC and should help to win favor for them among the international business community as a whole.

Summary

Undoubtedly, today's world markets and cross-border economies are anything but static. Certainly, the domino effect of the Asian financial crisis, the increased numbers of nondomestic companies listing on the world's major stock exchanges, the European single currency, and recent mergers such as Daimler-Chrysler are but a few examples that change, when desired and needed, can come quickly. Moreover, such changes are testimony to diverse interests working toward shared objectives and finding ways mutually satisfying to all. Never before have there been such promising precedents against which the possibility for generally accepted international financial reporting practices has been sought and anticipated. It seems clear that the desire, willingness, and need for such principles exist; the issues now involve priorities, time, and enforcement. A recent chairman of the U.S.-based Financial Accounting Standards Board has gone on record stating that the "FASB would support an objective that seeks to create superior international standards that would gradually supplant national standards as the superior standards become universally accepted."[27]

Suggested Readings

Beresford, D. R. "Internationalization of Accounting Standards." *Accounting Horizons,* March 1990, pp. 99–107.

Bloomer, C., *The IASC-U.S. Comparison Project.* Norwalk, Conn.: FASB, 1996.

Choi, F. D. "Economic Effects of Multinational Accounting Diversity." *The Journal of International Financial Management and Accounting,* Summer 1989, pp. 105–29.

——, and R. Levich. *The Capital Market Effects of International Accounting Diversity.* Homewood, IL: Dow Jones–Irwin, 1990.

Gray, S. J. "The Impact of International Accounting Differences from a Security Analysis Perspective." *The Journal of Accounting Research,* Spring 1980, pp. 64–76.

Harris, T. S., *International Accounting Standards versus US-GAAP Reporting: Empirical Evidence Based on Case Studies.* Cincinnati, OH: South-Western College Publishing, 1995.

International Accounting Standards Committee. *International Accounting Standards 1998.* London, England: IASC, 1998.

Pacter, P., "International Accounting Standards," *The CPA Journal,* July 1998, pp. 14–21.

Park, J., and K. Park. *Global Equity Markets.* Chicago: Probus Publishing, 1991.

Roll, R. "Industrial Structure and the Comparative Behavior of International Stock Market Indices." *The Journal of Finance,* March 1992, pp. 3–41.

Street, D. L. and K. A. Shaughnessy, "The Quest for International Accounting Harmonization: A Review of the Standard Setting Agendas of the IASC, US, UK, Canada, and Australia, 1973–1997." *The International Journal of Accounting* 33, no. 2 (1998), pp. 179–209.

---

[27]D. R. Beresford, "Internationalization of Accounting Standards: The Role of the Financial Accounting Standards Board," *Financial Accounting Standards Board Status Report,* series 065, no. 195, June 1988, p. 4.

Tay, J., and R. Parker. "Measuring International Harmonization and Standardization." *ABACUS.* January 1990, pp. 71–88.

Wallace, R. S. O. "Survival Strategies of a Global Organization: The Case of the International Accounting Standards Committee." *Accounting Horizons,* June 1990, pp. 1–22.

Wyatt, A. R., and J. F. Yospe. "Wake-Up Call to American Business: International Accounting Standards Are on the Way." *Journal of Accountancy,* July 1993, pp. 80–85.

APPENDIX 2A
INTERNATIONAL ACCOUNTING STANDARDS IN FORCE
as of November 1998

		Issuance Date
IAS 1	Disclosure of Accounting Policies	January 1975 (revised 8/97)
IAS 2	Valuation and Presentation of Inventories in the Context of the Historical Cost System	October 1975 (revised 11/93)
IAS 4	Depreciation Accounting	October 1976
IAS 7	Statement of Changes in Financial Position, as amended to become Cash Flow Statements	October 1977, December 1992
IAS 8	Unusual and Prior Period Items and Changes in Accounting Policies	February 1978 (revised 11/93)
IAS 10	Contingencies and Events Occurring After the Balance Sheet Date	October 1978
IAS 11	Accounting for Construction Contracts	March 1979 (revised 11/93)
IAS 12	Accounting for Taxes on Income	July 1979 (revised 10/96)
IAS 14	Reporting Financial Information by Segment	August 1981 (revised 8/97)
IAS 15	Information Reflecting the Effects of Changing Prices	November 1981
IAS 16	Accounting for Property, Plant and Equipment	March 1982 (revised 11/93 and 9/98)
IAS 17	Accounting for Leases	September 1982 (revised 12/97)
IAS 18	Revenue Recognition	December 1982 (revised 11/93)
IAS 19	Accounting for Retirement Benefits in the Financial Statements of Employers	January 1983 (revised 11/93 and 2/98)
IAS 20	Accounting for Government Grants and Disclosure of Government Assistance	April 1983
IAS 21	Accounting for the Effects of Changes in Foreign Exchange Rates	July 1983 (revised 11/93)
IAS 22	Accounting for Business Combinations	November 1983 (revised 11/93 and 9/98)
IAS 23	Capitalization of Borrowing Costs	March 1984 (revised 11/93)
IAS 24	Related Party Disclosures	July 1984
IAS 25	Accounting for Investments	March 1986
IAS 26	Accounting and Reporting by Retirement Benefit Plans	January 1987
IAS 27	Consolidated Financial Statements and Accounting for Investments in Subsidiaries	April 1989
IAS 28	Accounting for Investments in Associates	April 1989 (revised 9/98)
IAS 29	Financial Reporting in Hyperinflationary Economies	July 1989
IAS 30	Disclosures in the Financial Statements of Banks and Similar Institutions	August 1990
IAS 31	Financial Reporting of Interests in Joint Ventures	December 1990 (revised 9/98)
IAS 32	Financial Instruments: Disclosure and Presentation	June 1995
IAS 33	Earnings per Share	February 1997
IAS 34	Interim Financial Reporting	February 1998
IAS 35	Discontinuing Operations	June 1998
IAS 36	Impairment of Assets	June 1998
IAS 37	Provisions, Contingent Liabilities, and Contingent Assets	September 1998
IAS 38	Intangible Assets	September 1998

Note: Missing IAS #s are those IASs that have been superceded by subsequent IASs.

IASC ACTIVE PROJECTS
as of November 1998

> Agriculture
> Business Combinations
> Developing Countries and Economies in Transition
> Discounting
> Events After the Balance Sheet Date
> Extractive Industries
> Financial Instruments
> Insurance
> Investment Properties

APPENDIX 2B
PROPOSALS IN EXPOSURE DRAFT 32, COMPARABILITY OF FINANCIAL STATEMENTS

Issues	*Required or Benchmark Treatment*	*Allowed Alternative Treatment*	*Treatment Eliminated*
1. Correction of fundamental errors and omissions; adjustments resulting from accounting policy changes	Adjust opening retained earnings (subject to certain exceptions)	Include in income of the current period	
	Amend comparative information	Present amended pro forma comparative information	
2. Recognition of revenue and net income on construction contracts	Percentage of completion method		Completed contract method
	When the conditions for profit recognition are not met, recognize revenue to the extent of related costs		
3. Measurement of property, plant, and equipment	Measure at cost	Measure at revalued amounts	
4. Measurement of property, plant, and equipment acquired in exchange for another asset	Fair value for dissimilar assets acquired		Net carrying amount of asset given up for dissimilar assets acquired
	Net carrying amount of asset given up for similar assets acquired		Fair value for similar assets acquired
5. Recognition of a revaluation increase relating to a revaluation decrease previously charged to income	Recognize in income of the current period		Recognize in shareholders' interests
6. Recognition of revenue on transactions involving the rendering of services	Percentage of completion method		Completed contract method
7. Determining the cost of retirement benefits	Accrued benefit valuation methods	Projected benefit valuation methods	

APPENDIX 2B   (continued)

Issues	Required or Benchmark Treatment	Allowed Alternative Treatment	Treatment Eliminated
8. Use of projected salaries in determining the cost of retirement benefits	Incorporate an assumption about projected salaries		Do not incorporate an assumption about projected salaries
9. Recognition of past service costs, experience adjustments, and the effects of changes in actuarial assumptions	Recognize systematically over a period approximating the average of the expected remaining working lives of participating employees		Recognize in income of the current period as they arise
10. Recognition of foreign exchange gains and losses on long-term monetary items	Recognize in income of the current period unless hedged		Defer and recognize in income of current and future periods
11. Recognition of foreign exchange losses on the acquisition of an asset that result from a severe devaluation against which there is no practical means of hedging	Recognize in income of the current period	Recognize as part of the cost of the asset	
12. Exchange rate for use in translating income statement items of foreign entities	Exchange rates at the dates of the transactions (or average rate)		Closing exchange rates
13. Treatment of differences on income statement items translated at other than the closing rate	Recognize in shareholders' interests		Recognize in income of the current period
14. Subsidiaries operating in hyperinflationary economies	Restate financial statements in accordance with IAS 29, *Financial Reporting in Hyperinflationary Economies,* before translation		Translate financial statements without prior restatement
15. Exchange differences on foreign operations integral to those of the parent	Recognize in income of the period unless hedged	Recognize as part of the cost of an asset when they result from a severe devaluation against which there is no practical means of hedging	Defer and recognize in income of current and future periods
16. Accounting for business combinations	Purchase method for acquisitions Pooling of interests method for uniting of interests		 Purchase method for uniting interests
17. Positive goodwill	Recognize as an asset and amortize to income on a systematic basis over its useful life. The amortization period should not exceed 5 years unless a longer period can be justified which should not, in any case, exceed 20 years		Adjust immediately to shareholders' interests

APPENDIX 2B   (concluded)

Issues	Required or Benchmark Treatment	Allowed Alternative Treatment	Treatment Eliminated
18. Negative goodwill	Allocate over individual nonmonetary assets. After such an allocation, if negative goodwill remains, treat as deferred income and recognize in income on a systematic basis as for positive goodwill	Treat as deferred income and recognize in income on a systematic basis as for positive goodwill	Adjust immediately to shareholders' interests
19. Measurement of minority interest arising on a business combination	Measure at preacquisition carrying amounts	Measure at postacquisition fair values	
20. Measurement of investment properties	Measure at cost with depreciation	Measure at revalued amounts	Measure at cost without depreciation
21. Recognition of a realized gain previously recognized in revaluation surplus	Transfer to retained earnings		Recognize in income of the current period
22. Assignment of cost to inventories	FIFO and weighted average cost formulas	LIFO formula	Base stock inventories
23. Recognition of development costs	Recognize immediately as expenses	Recognize as assets when they meet specified criteria	
24. Recognition of borrowing costs	Recognize immediately as expenses	Recognize as part of the cost of an asset if it takes a substantial period of time to get it ready for its intended use or sale	
25. Measurement of long-term investments	Measure at cost	Measure at revalued amounts	
26. Measurement of marketable equity securities held as long-term investments	Measure at cost recognizing declines in value that are other than temporary on an individual investment basis	Measure at revalued amounts	Measure at the lower-of-cost-or-market value on a portfolio basis
27. Measurement of current investments	Measure at market value	Measure at the lower-of-cost-or-market value on an individual investment basis	Measure at the lower-of-cost-or-market value on a portfolio basis
28. Recognition of increases and decreases in market values of current investments	Recognize in income of the current period		Recognize in revaluation surplus
29. Recognition of finance income on finance leases by a lessor	Net investment method for finance leases other than leveraged leases Net cash investment method for leveraged leases		Net cash investment method for finance leases other than leveraged leases Net investment leases method for leveraged leases

Source: International Accounting Standards Committee, "Statement of Intent, Comparability of Financial Standards (E32)" (London: IASC, July 1990). Reproduced with permission. (See note at end of Chapter 2.)

Exercises

2.1 Harmonization

a. In a November 2, 1993, *European Accounting Review* (pp. 387–96) article, K. Van Hulle asserted that harmonization of financial reporting can probably be achieved in one of three ways:

1. Development of uniform rules (similar to U.S. practice).

2. Compromises allowing different financial reporting options that are viewed as equivalent as long as appropriate disclosures are made in the notes (this is the current EU approach).

3. Allowance of options but clearly labeling them as *preferred, not preferable but allowed,* and *not allowed;* use of a method other than that labeled *preferred* requires a reconciliation of the method used to the preferred one (this is the IASC approach).

Required:

Assuming that harmonization is a worthy goal, write an essay discussing the pros and cons of each of these approaches. Begin your essay with a statement as to which approach you endorse.

b. In the same article, Van Hulle reported the views on financial reporting harmonization expressed by the CFOs of two major international companies:

Hugh Collum of Smith Kline Beecham: There are only two major stock exchanges in the world: London and New York. The accounting standard setting bodies of the UK and the US should therefore get together and develop the accounting standards. The rest of the world should merely follow their lead.

Gerhard Liener of Daimler-Benz: During the last few decades the English language has become the world language without a resolution of the UN or any other institution. It just happened. Well, something very similar is happening in international accounting. The Anglo-Saxon principles are gaining more ground and thus getting nearer and nearer to becoming the world's accounting language.

The expression "Anglo Saxon" . . . as used by Mr. Liener . . . does not include the UK . . . [it] is clearly an option for US GAAP.

Required:

Write an essay discussing your agreement or disagreement with these statements. Do not devote space in your essay summarizing or paraphrasing these comments. Your thoughts and rationale are important.

c. Van Hulle ended the same article with a series of questions posited to encourage thinking on the need for/role of the international harmonization of financial reporting practices.

Question 1: Do capital markets "need" harmonization of accounting standards?

Question 2: What does comparability mean? Is absolute comparability possible or desirable?

Question 3: Does reconciliation of different accounting methods serve to provide useful information or is it likely to confuse the user?

Required:

Write an essay presenting your well-reasoned thinking for each of these questions.

2.2 Standard-Setting Roles

Write a one- to two-page brief, spelling out what you believe _____ role should be in the international standard-setting process. The blank is to be filled in according to the following:

Letter Beginning Your Last Name	Fill in Blank with
A to D	the Financial Accounting Standards Board's
E to K	the Security and Exchange Commission's
L to N	the New York Stock Exchange's
O to Z	multinationals'

2.3 Comparative Assumptions

What underlying assumptions make it possible to compare/contrast the financial statements of two U.S. companies such as Ford and General Motors? Do such assumptions hold for similar cross-border comparisons? Why or why not?

2.4 Disclosure Harmonization?

In a March 1996, *Accountancy* article, Marilyn Zarzeski reports quite a disparity in the disclosure levels of 256 companies, domiciled across seven countries. From a list of 58 possible disclosures, she found the sample of companies in France reporting only 11, Germany 17, Hong Kong 17, Japan 15, Netherlands 19, U.K. 19, and the United States 32. Moreover, she found only five disclosures required in all seven countries.

Required:

What conclusions do you draw from these summary results and why? What is your best thought as to what the five shared disclosures might be? Why?

2.5 MNCs: What Nationality?

One of the consequences of the globalization of corporate entities has been the creation of what is commonly called the *multinational corporation* (MNC). For example, Exxon Corp., founded in the United States, generates more sales and holds more assets outside the United States than it does within it. This phenomenon is happening all over the world as companies expand beyond their original national borders.

The development of domestic companies into MNCs raises important accounting, economic, legal, and political issues. For example, how does an MNC determine which accounting principles to follow, those of the country of its incorporation or those of the country in which it generates the most income or sales? In what country should it pay taxes? To what country does it owe its allegiance?

Required:

How should an MNC determine which country's accepted accounting practices it should follow for financial reporting purposes? Be prepared to justify your position.

2.6 U.S. versus Non-U.S. GAAP

In a comparison of reported earnings and shareholders' equity using U.S. and home-country GAAP, the following 1997 results were obtained:

	U.S. GAAP		Home-Country GAAP	
	Net Income	*Shareholders' Equity*	*Net Income*	*Shareholders' Equity*
Repsol Group (Spain) (pesetas, millions)	142,919	859,621	126,028	924,622
Volvo (Sweden) (kronor, millions)	6,556	66,612	10,359	60,431

Required:

What generalizations would you draw from these data with respect to (1) U.S. versus Spanish GAAP and (2) U.S. versus Swedish GAAP?

2.7 U.S. GAAP Waivers

According to a news report in the May 1998 *Journal of Accountancy,* the U.S. Securities and Exchange Commission allows foreign corporate registrants several deviations from pure U.S. GAAP reporting required of U.S. corporate registrants. Those reporting allowances are:

- statements of cash flow in accordance with IAS 7;
- use of any currency deemed best for U.S. readers;
- use of IAS 21 for operations in a hyperinflationary environment;
- use of purchase method for consolidation according to IAS 22 even if the circumstances of the business combination meet U.S. GAAP's for the pooling-of-interests method; and
- dropped the requirement of foreign issuers having to reconcile the differences in net income and shareholders' equity arising from a difference in amortization periods (generally 5 years under IASC and up to 40 years under U.S. GAAP).

Required:

Do these five exceptions represent a major breakthrough on the part of those who have been staunch proponents that the United States needs to be more in line with the rest of the world in its financial reporting requirements? Explain. If you were the chief financial officer of a U.S. multinational corporation, would you petition the SEC to be allowed to utilize one or more of these exceptions afforded foreign registrants? Why? Which one(s)? Why?

2.8 Economic Consequences of Harmonization

In May 1994, Swiss pharmaceutical company Roche Holdings Ltd. acquired Syntex Corporation (a U.S. company) for $5.3 billion. One month later, Sandoz Ltd., another Swiss pharmaceutical company, offered $3.7 billion for Gerber Products Co.

According to analysts familiar with the two transactions, the purchases were motivated by two factors. The first is a strong Swiss franc relative to the U.S. dollar, which made the acquisition of Syntex and Gerber appear relatively inexpensive despite the high U.S. dollar price tag. The second is a dramatic change in IASC accounting standards with respect to the accounting for goodwill that would become effective year-end 1994. Goodwill refers to the amount paid for a company in excess of its fair market value. For example, Roche's offer price exceeded Syntex's fair market value by approximately $3.0 billion, and Sandoz's offer for Gerber exceeded that company's fair market value by about $2.0 billion.

Prior to 1995, most European companies had a choice as to how they accounted for goodwill: They could either capitalize goodwill to the balance sheet and then amortize it against earnings, or they could write it off in total against existing shareholders' equity. Most European firms, including Roche and Sandoz, chose the latter method. Beginning in 1995, the charge-to-equity method is no longer available for many European companies as part of the IASC's harmonization efforts.

Required:

(a) What is the advantage of the charge-off method of accounting for goodwill to companies such as Roche and Sandoz? Why would they prefer it to the alternative of capitalizing and amortizing goodwill?

(b) How do U.S. companies account for goodwill?

(c) Which method do you prefer, and why?

2.9 Harmonizing International Accounting Standards

To facilitate the orderly flow of capital among and between international capital markets, the International Accounting Standards Committee (IASC) is attempting to harmonize the reporting practices followed in different countries. To understand why harmonization is important, it is first necessary to understand the financial effects produced by differing disclosure and reporting practices. This exercise focuses on two controversial areas: the accounting for goodwill, and research and development costs.

The following are two different scenarios. Analyze each scenario independently and identify the financial statement effect of each alternative accounting or reporting practice.

(a) **Goodwill**   Throughout the world, it is commonly accepted that *goodwill* results when an acquiring company (the acquiror) purchases another company (the acquiree) and pays more than the fair market value for the acquiree's identifiable net assets. How this excess purchase price—or goodwill—is accounted for varies considerably from country to country. In the United States, for example, goodwill is capitalized to the acquiror's balance sheet and then is amortized against earnings over the goodwill's expected useful life (but not in excess of 40 years). In the Netherlands, however, goodwill may be capitalized and amortized or charged, in total, directly to owners' equity at date of acquisition. The IASC states that when goodwill arises as a consequence of a merger or acquisition, it should be capitalized to the acquiror's balance sheet and then amortized against earnings over a period not to exceed 20 years, preferably over only 5 years.

Scenario:

During 1991, American Telephone and Telegraph Company (AT&T) made a successful acquisition bid for the NCR Corporation. The initial bid of $6.12 billion (U.S.) came at a time when NCR's net assets were reportedly worth $1.77 billion (U.S.).

Required:

Calculate the effect on AT&T's annual earnings of accounting for the NCR goodwill under each of the three approaches (i.e., those of the United States, the Netherlands, and the IASC). Does the accounting treatment for goodwill affect the price that an acquiror would (or should) be willing to pay for an acquiree in a merger or acquisition?

(b) **Research and Development Costs**   The accounting for research and development (R&D) costs around the world is quite diverse. In some countries, such as the United States, all R&D costs must be expensed against earnings in the year in which they are incurred. In other countries, however, R&D costs may be capitalized to the balance sheet and then amortized against earnings over the expected period of benefit. Currently, the IASC permits the capitalization of development costs if a company can prove that a market does (or will) exist for its proposed product. The IASC does not permit the capitalization of research costs.

Scenario:

The 1997 financial statements of General Electric Company reveal that R&D costs deducted against earnings totaled $1,891 million, $1,886 million, and $1,892 million in 1997, 1996, and 1995, respectively.

Required:

Assume that the IASC standard is implemented and that GE is able to demonstrate that a market will exist for its proposed products. Furthermore, assume one-third of GE's R&D costs pertained to development. Calculate the after-tax dollar effect on GE's 1996 and 1997 earnings, assuming the capitalization of developments costs and a 40 percent tax rate.

2.10   IASC vs U.S. GAAP

In late November 1996, the U.S.'s Financial Accounting Standards Board published a book titled *The IASC-U.S. Comparison Project: A Report on the Similarities and Differences Between IASC Standards and U.S. GAAP.* That report identifies 255 differences between IASC standards and U.S. GAAP as classified below:

Similar (but not identical) approach and guidance	56
Similar approach but different in guidance	79
Different approach	56
Alternative approaches permitted	27
Covered by either IASC or U.S. GAAP but not the other	37
	255

There was also a sixth category that identified all the specialized topics that U.S. GAAP dealt with but IASC did not (e.g. certain industry pronouncements).

Required:

If you were the chair of the U.S. Securities and Exchange Commission and you had just read this summary table, and nothing more, what resultant questions would arise in your mind as you tried to assess whether there was ever any chance of the SEC ultimately accepting the IASC's standards as the internationally acceptable mode for cross-border listings of corporate securities? How would you proceed in getting answers to those questions?

Special note regarding the reproduction of IASC materials contained in Table 2–7 and Appendix 2B:

International Accounting Standards, Exposure Drafts, and other IASC documents are copyright of the International Accounting Standards Committee, 167 Fleet Street, London EC4A 2ES, United Kingdom. Telephone: +44 (171) 353-0565, Fax: +44 (171) 353-0562. All rights reserved. No part of these publications may be translated, reprinted or reproduced or utilised in any form either in whole or in part, without permission in writing from IASC. The extracts from IASC's "Statement of Intent, Comparability of Financial Statements" (published July 1990), and IASC's *Insight* newsletter (October 1998) have been reproduced and published by the authors, and publisher (McGraw-Hill/Irwin Inc.), of *International Financial Reporting and Analysis: A Contextual Emphasis,* with the permission of IASC. Copies of the full English text of the "Statement of Intent," and IASC *Insight* can be obtained directly from IASC.

Financial Reporting and the European Union

It is a fundamental objective of the European Union (EU) that a common economic market be achieved which allows for free mobility of capital, labour and enterprise, as well as trade, across the borders between member countries. This requires that the infrastructure of markets be harmonized, and financial accounting is a part of that infrastructure.[1]

The quality of financial reporting in the EU has considerably improved with the implementation of the accounting directives.[2]

Introduction

Founded in 1957 when six nations—France, West Germany, Italy, Belgium, the Netherlands, and Luxembourg—signed a series of international treaties, the **European Union** (EU) as we know it today, sprang from the merger of three cooperative alliances intended to improve the efficiency and competitive ability of its members: the European Coal and Steel Community, the European Atomic Energy Commission, and the European Economic Community (EEC). From its tentative and experimental beginnings, the European Union has grown in size and ambition, attracting nine new members—the United Kingdom, Ireland, and Denmark in 1973; Greece in 1981; Portugal and Spain in 1986; and Sweden, Austria, and Finland in 1995—eager to avail themselves of the benefits of belonging to a large trading bloc. These 15 member[3] nations have a combined population of almost 400 million (the United States is almost 300 million), a gross domestic product similar to the U.S.'s and an employed workforce of nearly 150 million people (the United States is about 130 million). At the same time, these 15 nations' combined

---

[1] P. Thorell and Whittington, G., "The Harmonization of Accounting within the EU," *The European Accounting Review* 3, no. 2 (1994), p. 216.

[2] K. Van Hulle, "Harmonization of Accounting Standards in the EU," *The European Accounting Review* 2, no. 2 (1993), p. 390.

[3] In November 1994, Norway voted not to join the European Union. Moreover, negotiations began in November 1998 with representatives of the Czech Republic, Estonia, Hungary, Poland, Slovenia, and Cyprus, setting the stage for their possible membership in 2002 or 2003. Bulgaria, Latvia, Lithuania, Romania, and Slovakia have also applied to be considered but currently comprise a "second wave" of later possibilities.

consumer spending is less than that of the United States, their publicly traded companies number about 6,500 compared to the U.S.'s roughly 9,000, the equity market capitalization is half that of the United States, and their unemployment rate is double the U.S.'s.[4]

The goal of the EU is to create the world's largest free market economy by removing all physical, technical, and fiscal barriers that hinder the free movement of capital, goods, and people within the EU. The economic union of these nations, however, has proven to be a gargantuan and multifaceted task involving debate and compromise on a staggering array of issues: trade policy, company and tax law, product regulation, labor relations, monetary policy, financial markets, and legal and financial reporting requirements. Inevitably, the arduous process of negotiating these issues has forced member nations not only to confront the laws and traditions separating their respective economies but also to consider in a new light the economic structures—their history and purpose, their implicit cultural values—that have been responsible for these barriers. In the broadest terms, the existence of the European Union is prompting a reevaluation of the place of national sovereignty and cultural diversity in an increasingly supranational and transcultural economic order.

Several cases in point typify this basic need for reconsidering long-standing national positions in attempting to comply with specific EU rules. For example, Luxembourg has had to reevaluate its role as a haven for holding companies as it seeks to adhere to EU rules regarding consolidated financial statements. In hammering out an agreement on insider trading laws, the Italians have had to examine the prominence of close-knit groups (i.e., families) in their economy and to revise their notions of acceptable business behavior. Similarly, the British have had to defend their rigid notion of fair play rather than simply assume its universal applicability. Even many apparently "objective" guidelines, such as technical standards concerning product quality, may express essentially cultural preferences. A German law requiring a minimum alcohol content in alcoholic beverages, for example, was struck down by EU officials in 1979 because it prevented the import of French alcoholic beverages. It was ruled that a product legally produced and marketed in one member country has the right to be sold in other member countries, barring genuine public health or safety concerns. (This principle, incidentally, undergirds the London International Stock Exchange's granting of listings to European continent–based companies that might not otherwise qualify for exchange membership. For further information, see the following section on Securities Exchanges.) In effect, the ruling implied that the German "technical" standard was an arbitrary cultural preference, expressing a German idea of "purity" and "quality" among alcoholic beverages that could not be used to restrict the import of goods meeting different but legitimate standards.

Despite the fact that financial statements prepared in one member state must be accepted in all other member states for purposes of cross-listing shares on stock exchanges, the EU continues to be a major force in (and a major forum for) the international movement to harmonize financial reporting practices. The efficient movement of capital within the European Union depends to a great extent upon an acceptable level of comparability among financial statements assembled in different member nations. While the goal of comparability does not require absolute uniformity in the reporting systems of all member nations, it does call for a considerable degree of coordination and the elimination of needlessly diverse reporting practices. Even this more limited goal presents a formidable challenge.

---

[4]These data were obtained from charts presented on p. IV of a special survey section titled, "Welcome to Euroland," that appeared in the April 30, 1998, *Financial Times.*

The European Union includes countries with extremely diverse economies, ranging from the highly concentrated industrial base of the Netherlands to the prevalent agrarian economy of Portugal. Even the highly industrialized members, such as the United Kingdom and Germany, provide sharp contrasts in the style and orientation of their financial reporting practices, the surface variations often indicating deeply rooted divergences in philosophy and purpose. Indeed,

> In most Continental countries, the accountant's goal is to comply with strict rules and to hold down tax liabilities—and not to impress investors. In Britain, the Netherlands, the U.S. and other countries with more of an Anglo-Saxon business tradition, reports to shareholders are distinct from tax calculations and accounting rules are much more flexible; accountants use lots of judgment and don't let rigid rules get in the way of presenting a "true and fair view" of the company . . . [Continental] and Anglo-Saxon accountants don't even share the same basic aims.[5]

Whatever the difficulties facing the EU harmonization efforts, the consequences of its success or failure reach far beyond its borders. Users and preparers of financial statements around the world are watching intently for a number of reasons. First, the ultimate success of global financial-reporting harmonization requires that everyone in the movement be aware of what everyone else is doing. Otherwise, harmonization will merely create new layers of reporting requirements on top of existing national practices, exacerbating the problem that it is intended to solve. Second, while proponents and skeptics have long debated the possibility of harmonization, the European Union is actually putting the question to a major test. Its efforts, uniting the political assent of 15 national governments with the international economic forces drawing Europe and the world together, constitute a large-scale example of harmonization's challenges and feasibility. Third, the financial reporting requirements developed and approved by the European Union directly affect a large number of foreign multinationals who operate in member countries. Fourth, the European Union is becoming such a formidable member of the world economy that foreign managers and regulators will feel increasingly obliged to conform to its standards. In a very real sense, then, much of the world has a stake in what is decided in the EU's headquarters in Brussels. To appreciate its true significance, one must see European harmonization in a global context.

The European Commission (responsible for the implementation of the various EU treaties and the rules issued by the EU's Council of Ministers) demonstrated its awareness of the global implications of the European experiment when it announced in January 1990 that it would join the International Accounting Standards Committee's Consultative Group. In addition, in 1991 the European Union created an Accounting Advisory Forum of financial statement regulators, preparers, and users. (This forum merely discusses standards, not sets them.) By taking these steps, the European Commission hoped to accomplish two important objectives. First, by actively coordinating its efforts with the IASC, it would avoid duplication of effort and the needless proliferation of reporting requirements. Second, it hoped to take advantage of the IASC's more detailed treatment of accounting issues not currently addressed by EU directives, thereby improving the comparability of financial statements within the European Union without itself having to formulate further standards. In November 1995, the European Commission in effect opted not to pursue any sort of European Accounting Standards Board by announcing that it would "ally itself with the efforts undertaken by the IASC and IOSCO towards international harmonization of accounting standards."[6] A 1996 commission task force reported no major conflicts

---

[5]B. Haggerty, "Differing Accounting Rules Snarl Europe," *The Wall Street Journal,* September 4, 1992, pp. A3C.
[6]From remarks of IASC chair Stig Enevoldsen titled "IASC Current Trends and Future Perspectives," presented at the 50th Anniversary of the Japanese Institute of CPAs, Tokyo, October 23, 1998.

between the EU's two primary accounting directives and IASC standards, and for the minor conflicts that do exist, the commission has gone on record as saying it will propose amending its directives to eliminate the conflict.[7] To preempt criticism that it has given up on accounting harmonization, "the commission stresses . . . on the contrary, it is strengthening its commitment and contribution to the international standard-setting process."[8] From the viewpoint of users, the linkage between the EU and the IASC holds the promise that the two most active and influential players in the harmonization movement will create widely acceptable standards.

A uniquely important element of European harmonization resides in the Union's ability, unlike that of the Organization for Economic Cooperation and Development, the United Nations, and even the IASC, to enforce its pronouncements on financial reporting. Under the terms set out by the Treaty of Rome (1957) that formed the European Union, the European Union's ruling bodies may issue regulations, which are specific and immediately binding on members of the Union, or directives, which are broad and must be incorporated by members into national law by a given deadline. (It should be noted that these deadlines may be, and often are, pushed back or missed.) Members that fail to incorporate directives in a timely fashion may be brought before the European Court of Justice and ordered to comply. To date, the EU Council of Ministers has issued two major directives that bear directly on accounting matters. The Fourth Directive, adopted by the European Union in 1978, establishes acceptable formats for financial statements as well as basic reporting requirements for companies operating in EU territory, and the Seventh Directive, adopted in 1983, promulgates standards governing the preparation of consolidated statements for business groups. As a matter of political necessity, some latitude has been granted to member nations as to the precise mode of implementation and enforcement of these two directives. Hence, their objective has been mutual recognition based on minimum rules rather than uniformity. Indeed, a representative from the German Ministry of Justice was paraphrased along these lines:

> Mutual recognition of financial statements is not dependent on harmonization. . . . Mutual recognition is guaranteed in EU Member States for general purposes and listings at stock exchanges for all financial statements drawn up under the requirements of the Fourth [and] Seventh Directives.[9]

More specific discussion of each of these directives follows.

The Fourth Directive

Purpose

The Fourth Directive (a summary of its contents is presented in Appendix 3A) was adopted by the European Union on July 25, 1978, after 15 years of gestation, debate, and revision. The text of the directive calls for member states to incorporate its requirements into their respective legal systems.

The Fourth Directive has two strategic objectives. First, by coordinating company law in member nations, it seeks to eliminate needless legal and bureaucratic obstacles to

---

[7]See IASC, "EU Directives and IAS," *Insight,* December 1996, p. 22. The two minor conflicts noted by the task force were: (1) treatment of negative goodwill, and (2) the IASC requirement to consolidate all subsidiaries (the EU allows distinctly different subsidiaries to remain unconsolidated).

[8]IASC, "EU Puts Weight Behind IASC," *Insight,* March 1996, p. 3.

[9]IASC, "Mutual Recognition of Financial Statements in International Capital Markets," *Insight,* December 1993, p. 11.

economic activity within the Union. Second, by establishing basic reporting requirements and acceptable financial statement formats, it attempts to create a minimum level of comparability among financial statements throughout the European Union. In pursuit of these objectives, the directive not only sets out minimum auditing and disclosure requirements but also enjoins particular auditing and accounting principles on examiners and preparers of financial statements. The directive applies to all public and private limited liability companies, with the exception of banks and insurance companies. In addition, it allows some concessions such as abridged statement formats and more lenient audit requirements to small and medium-sized companies. Small and medium-sized companies are defined as those that do not exceed two of the following three limits[10]:

	Small	*Medium*
1. Balance sheet total assets	2 million ECU[11]	8 million ECU
2. Net sales	4 million ECU	16 million ECU
3. Average employees during year	50	250

Audit and Public Filing Requirements

Under EU law, each member state must establish and maintain a public registry of companies operating in that nation. Each company must submit to this registry an annual report that includes a balance sheet, a profit-and-loss statement, explanatory footnotes, and a report of an independent and professionally qualified auditor. (A statement of cash flows is *not* required under the Fourth Directive. Acceptable qualifications for auditors are set forth in the Eighth Directive.) The auditor must not only examine the financial statements themselves but also verify their consistency with the annual report in which they appear. Small companies (as defined previously) may be exempted from the audit requirement at the discretion of the member state.

True and Fair View

An important and much-discussed feature of the Fourth Directive is its adoption of the **true and fair view** as the ultimate criterion for financial reporting in the European Union. According to Article 2 of the directive, preparers should ignore any provision therein if compliance with that provision would conflict with presentation of a true and fair view of a company's financial position and income. (Any such departure and the reason for it must be disclosed in the notes.) To understand the full significance of this choice of policy, one must appreciate something of the implicit cultural values lurking behind it, as well as its relation to accounting practices of various countries in the Union, especially Great Britain and Germany.

The phrase *true and fair view* has long been included in British audit reports; it represents a concept analogous to *fair presentation* in U.S. auditing. Fraught with philosophical implications, it signifies a particular approach to financial reporting in which financial statements are valued not so much for their compliance with particular rules as their ability to create an overall picture of a company's financial affairs. At least in theory, the true and fair view criterion ensures that statements are not only correct but also are useful indicators of a company's financial health. The fulfillment of this criterion requires a concern for *substance over form* and the application of professional judgment. The indepen-

---

[10]In an effort to simplify obligations of small and medium companies, the original limits set in 1978 were doubled by an amendment to the Fourth and Seventh Directives in November 1990. The limits shown above reflect those set out in the 1990 amendment. Limits 1 and 2 were the only ones raised in 1990; the limits regarding the number of employees remain unchanged since 1978.

[11]At the end of November 1998, one ECU (European currency unit, a basket currency that serves as the monetary unit of the European Union) was worth approximately $1.16 US.

dent auditor, according to this view, serves as a referee as well as a reporter/preparer. Ultimately, the true and fair view suggests a culturally conditioned distrust of rules—a skepticism of their efficacy unless they are subordinated to human judgment—and a belief in an abstract fairness that can never be completely codified.

German audit reports (see Table 3–1), on the other hand, have traditionally emphasized technical conformity of financial statements, with the auditor expressing an opinion that they fulfilled all legal requirements set out by existing company and tax law. (It is worth noting that in Great Britain, as in the United States, financial reporting is separated from tax compliance, while in Germany the two are linked.) Until the adoption of the

TABLE 3–1

Comparison of an Audit Report from British and German Annual Reports

A British Audit Report	*A German Audit Report*
Report of the auditors	**Auditors' Certificate**
To the Members of The British Petroleum Company p.l.c. We have audited the accounts on pages 28 to 50, which have been prepared under the historical cost convention and on the basis of the accounting policies set out on pages 28 and 29. We have also audited the information specified for audit by the London Stock Exchange which is set out on pages 59 to 61 in the Report of the Remuneration Committee.	**Bayerische Motoren Werke** Aktiengesellschaft The Board of Management The Consolidated Financial Statements, which we have audited in accordance with professional standards, comply with the German legal provisions. The Consolidated Financial Statements present, in compliance with required accounting principles, a true and fair view of the Group's assets, liabilities, financial position and net income. The Group's Economic Review is consistent with the Consolidated Financial Statements.
Respective responsibilities of directors and auditors As described above, the company's directors are responsible for the preparation of the accounts. It is our responsibility to form an independent opinion, based on our audit, on those accounts and to report our opinion to you.	
	Munich, March 5, 1998
Basis of opinion We conducted our audit in accordance with Auditing Standards issued by the Auditing Practices Board. An audit includes examination, on a test basis, of evidence relevant to the amounts and disclosures in the accounts. It also includes an assessment of the significant estimates and judgements made by the directors in the preparation of the accounts, and of whether the accounting policies are appropriate to the group's circumstances, consistently applied and adequately disclosed. We planned and performed our audit so as to obtain all the information and explanations which we considered necessary in order to provide us with sufficient evidence to give reasonable assurance that the accounts are free from material misstatement, whether caused by fraud or other irregularity or error. In forming our opinion we also evaluated the overall adequacy of the presentation of information in the accounts.	**KPMG Deutsche Treuhand-Gesellschaft** Aktiengesellschaft Wirtschaftsprüfungsgesellschaft Dr. Hoyos Kilgert Wirtschaftsprüfer Wirtschaftsprüfer (independent auditors)
Opinion In our opinion the accounts give a true and fair view of the state of affairs of the company and of the group as at 31 December 1997 and of the profit of the group for the year then ended and have been properly prepared in accordance with the Companies Act 1985.	
Ernst & Young Chartered Accountants Registered Auditor London *10 February 1998*	

Fourth Directive, such concepts as true and fair view or fair presentation held relatively little importance in German auditing. Now, however, German audit reports must express an opinion not only on the correctness of company accounts and their compliance with appropriate laws but also on whether they render a true and fair view. Unfortunately, the mere presence of a phrase in the audit report does not guarantee that the concept will (or can) be similarly applied in various countries. Time will tell whether the gap between the German and British approaches has actually been narrowed.

Valuation Principles

The Fourth Directive adopts several general principles of valuation that must be adhered to in the preparation of financial statements. Among the key ones are the following:

- The company must be assumed to be a *going concern.*
- Methods of valuation must be *consistent* from year to year.
- Profit calculations must be based on the concept of *prudence* (including only profits earned as of the balance sheet date while also including all foreseeable losses).
- Income and expenses must conform to the *matching* principle and be calculated on the *accrual* basis.

As in the case of the true and fair view, one should remember that these concepts are broadly stated and may be applied rather differently in different countries.

Other Reporting Practices

The Fourth Directive also sets out a number of other minimum standards for reporting covering a variety of areas. The following are some of the highlights:

- Companies generally must use *historic cost* as the basis for asset valuation, but member states may allow *replacement value accounting* for certain fixed assets so long as there is full disclosure of the impact on the financial statements.
- Companies need not disclose the effects of *inflation* on financial statements unless required by the member state. Any revaluation reserve created by the application of methods of accounting for inflation may not be distributed as dividends unless realized.
- If a member nation allows the *capitalization* of research and development expenses, any capitalized amount should be written off in five years or less. Longer periods may be allowed under exceptional circumstances if appropriate disclosure is made in the notes.
- Taxes on ordinary profit and extraordinary items should be disclosed separately, though the two may be combined on the face of the profit and loss statement. When income tax expense differs materially from income tax payable, the difference must be disclosed. *Deferred income tax* accounting is not required.
- Pension costs charged against income must be disclosed. However, the directive contains no detailed guidance for determining *pension expenses or liabilities.*
- Subscribed capital, paid-in capital, revaluation reserve (if applicable), other reserves, and retained earnings must be disclosed on the balance sheet. The number and par value of shares issued during the year, the number and par value of each class of stock outstanding, and a description of convertible debentures, stock rights, or other such instruments must be disclosed in the notes.
- The Fourth Directive makes no specific requirements with regard to accounting for leases, related-party transactions, or foreign currency translation. The only segment reporting requirements are net sales broken down by line of business and geographical market, and average number of employees by category.

As these examples suggest, the Fourth Directive concerns itself with broad issues rather than detailed guidance, an approach that has the advantage of making the document politically palatable but one that also has the drawbacks of leaving many important accounting issues unresolved and perhaps allowing too much flexibility in accounting method selection.

Statement Formats

The Fourth Directive allows two formats for balance sheets, horizontal and vertical, and four formats for profit and loss statements, two that present results by type of expenditure (e.g., all salaries and wages shown as personnel expense) and two that present them by type of operation (e.g., all salaries and wages distributed across cost of goods sold, marketing expense, and administration expense). Member nations may require any one of these formats or allow companies to choose among them. Some of the formats look similar to U.S. statements; others differ markedly. Tables 3–2 and 3–3 present the income statements and balance sheets of BMW, a German automotive company, and British Petroleum, a British oil concern. Note that BMW's balance sheet employs a horizontal format similar to U.S. balance sheets but presents assets and liabilities by increasing liquidity instead of decreasing liquidity, as is the U.S. custom. Unlike U.S. practice, BMW's income statement is organized by type of expenditure. On the other hand, BP's balance sheet employs a vertical format, one that balances net assets with shareholders' equity. Note that BP's income statement employs a format similar to that used by U.S. companies.

Amendments

In November 1990, the EU council amended the Fourth and Seventh directives. With the intent to simplify financial reporting obligations of small and medium-sized companies, the council increased the minimum requirements used to define small and medium-sized companies. Another purpose of this amendment was to promote the use of ECUs as the primary currency in the annual reports of those companies required to file annual reports.[12]

Status

Although more than 20 years have passed since the adoption of the Fourth Directive, its effects are still being debated. The directive unquestionably has had a major impact on reporting standards around Europe, even in countries outside the European Union, and it has reduced the diversity of national reporting practices. For example, a survey conducted by the Fédération, des Experts–comptables Européens (FEE)—an organization representing European accounting bodies—compares various forms of accounting and reporting practices between three groups of countries: (1) those in the European Union that must comply with the Fourth Directive, (2) those for which this was not compulsory (in 1989), and (3) non-EU countries comprising the European Free Trade Association (EFTA). In aggregate, the survey found that more similarities than differences exist between EU and non-EU countries' accounting in Europe and that listed companies disclose more detailed information than do unlisted ones. It also notes that, strikingly enough, Italy, Spain, and the EFTA countries surveyed disclose more information in certain instances than companies from the other countries.[13] In summary, the results of the survey indicate that a high

---

[12]"Council Directive of 8 November 1990 Amending: Directive 78/660/EEC on Annual Accounts, and Directive 83/349/EEC on Consolidated Accounts, as Concerns the Exemption for Small and Medium-sized Companies and the Publication of Accounts in ECUs," *Official Journal of the European Communities,* No. L 317/57, 16. 11. 90.

[13]"FEE European Survey of Published Accounts 1991," press release; copy provided by Fédération des Experts Comptables European. See also the FEE's 1994 publication titled *Discussion Paper on the Application of Prudence and Matching in Selected European Countries.*

TABLE 3–2

BMW CONSOLIDATED STATEMENTS (000s DM)

Balance Sheets

	31.12.1997 DM million	31.12.1996 DM million
Assets		
Intangible assets	325	464
Tangible assets	14,204	12,376
Financial assets	705	589
Fixed assets	**15,234**	**13,429**
Inventories	5,900	5,340
Leased products	11,962	8,921
Receivables from sales financing	9,283	7,877
Assets from sales financing	21,245	16,798
Trade receivables	4,091	3,245
Other receivables and miscellaneous assets	2,151	1,812
Marketable securities and notes	1,244	1,335
Liquid funds	2,458	2,698
Current assets	**37,089**	**31,228**
Prepaid expenses and deferred taxes	**957**	**685**
	53,280	**45,342**
Shareholders' equity and liabilities		
Subscribed capital	990	989
Capital reserve	1,635	1,614
Revenue reserves	7,097	6,043
Unappropriated profit available for distribution	397	297
Minority interest	129	124
Shareholders' equity	**10,248**	**9,067**
Registered profit-sharing certificates	**76**	**77**
Pension provisions	2,415	2,279
Other provisions and accruals	10,321	8,593
Provisions and accruals	**12,736**	**10,872**
Bonds	1,959	1,633
Liabilities to banks	756	1,745
Trade payables	3,573	3,014
Other liabilities	4,627	3,872
Liabilities	**10,915**	**10,264**
Liabilities from sales financing	18,148	12,977
Deferred income from lease financing	968	1,894
Liabilities from sales financing	**19,116**	**14,871**
Deferred income	**189**	**191**
	53,280	**45,342**

Income Statement

Net sales	**60,137**	**52,265**
Increase in product inventories and own work capitalised	1,905	· 696
Total value of production	**62,042**	**52,961**
Other operating income	2,215	2,078
Material costs	35,595	31,057
Personnel costs	10,825	9,844
Depreciation on intangible and tangible fixed assets	3,543	3,002
Other operating expenses	11,457	9,248
Net income from investments	61	69
Net interest income	237	204
Interest expense from lease financing	607	501
Result from ordinary business activities	2,528	1,660
Taxes on income	1,153	714
Other taxes	129	126
Net income	**1,246**	**820**

TABLE 3–3

BRITISH PETROLEUM GROUP

	£ Million	
Balance Sheet	*1997*	*1996*
Fixed assets		
Intangible assets	1,130	959
Tangible assets	19,639	18,805
Investments	2,414	2,056
	23,183	21,820
Current assets		
Stocks	2,581	3,009
Debtors—amounts falling due:		
Within one year	5,460	6,276
After more than one year	1,487	1,314
Investments	53	58
Cash at bank and in hand	113	95
	9,694	10,752
Creditors—amounts falling due within one year		
Finance debt	1,137	1,058
Other creditors	8,980	9,559
Net current (liabilities) assets	(423)	135
Total assets less current liabilities	22,760	21,955
Creditors—amounts falling due after more than one year		
Finance debt	3,211	3,474
Other creditors	1,362	1,530
Provisions for liabilities and charges		
Deferred taxation	390	405
Other provisions	3,629	3,642
Net assets	14,168	12,904
Minority shareholders' interest	56	109
BP shareholders' interest	14,112	12,795
Represented by Capital and reserves		
Called up share capital	1,453	1,425
Share premium account	2,078	2,012
Capital redemption reserve	197	197
Reserves	10,384	9,161
	14,112	12,795

Income Statement		
Turnover	43,460	44,731
Replacement cost of sales	35,177	36,325
Production taxes	617	823
Gross profit	7,666	7,583
Distribution and administration expenses	3,652	3,704
Exploration expense	199	203
	3,815	3,676
Other income	506	516
Replacement cost operating profit	4,321	4,192

TABLE 3–3   (concluded)

BRITISH PETROLEUM GROUP

	£ Million	
	1997	*1996*
Loss on sale or termination of operations	**(105)**	(175)
Refinery network rationalisation	**43**	—
European refining and marketing joint venture implementation	**—**	(341)
Replacement cost profit before interest and tax	**4,259**	3,676
Stock holding gains (losses)	**(317)**	402
Historical cost profit before interest and tax	**3,942**	4,078
Interest expense	**296**	411
Profit before taxation	**3,646**	3,667
Taxation	**1,168**	1,107
Profit after taxation	**2,478**	2,560
Minority shareholders' interest	**8**	8
Profit for the year	**2,470**	2,552
Distribution to shareholders	**1,262**	1,102
Retained profit for the year	**1,208**	1,450
Earnings per ordinary share	**43.3p**	45.5p
Replacement cost results		
Historical cost profit for the year	**2,470**	2,552
Stock holding (gains) losses	**317**	(402)
Replacement cost profit for the year	**2,787**	2,150
Exceptional items, net of tax and minority shareholders' interest	**35**	470
Replacement cost profit before exceptional items	**2,822**	2,620
Earnings per ordinary share		
On replacement cost profit before exceptional items	**49.5p**	46.7p

level of basic harmonization has been achieved. Yet critics argue that the directive allows too much latitude on important issues such as leases, pensions, taxation, and currency transactions, and they are calling for further reform. EU officials are undoubtedly hoping that the Union's affiliation with the IASC will enable them to effectively address any remaining accounting issues without having to endure the arduous negotiations and lengthy delays that issuing a new directive would entail.

The Seventh Directive

Purpose

The **Seventh Directive** (a summary of its contents is presented in Appendix 3B), adopted by the European Commission and Council of Ministers in 1983 after eight years of sometimes heated debate, establishes basic rules for preparing consolidated statements in EU nations. To comply with the directive, member states are required to enact legislation to incorporate it. Until the formulation of the Seventh Directive, many EU countries had few if any regulations requiring consolidated accounts or governing their preparation; others had devised sophisticated guidelines. Because of this wide variation, the process of negotiation and compromise leading up to the directive's adoption involved a number of difficult issues, such as which forms of business should be covered by its provisions, whether entities should be defined by legal control or economic integration, and how the technical process of consolidation should be handled. In the end, the directive's mandatory provisions, which were intended to provide a minimum level of disclosure and comparability, generally followed the Anglo-American approach with its emphasis on legal control.

Who Must Consolidate?

As a matter of political necessity, the Seventh Directive allows member states considerable latitude in deciding who must prepare consolidated statements. Each state decides whether the directive should apply to all groups that include a limited liability company as a member or only to groups whose parent firm is a limited liability company. In addition, member states may exempt financial holding companies from consolidation requirements if the company to be exempted can show that it has not influenced the management decisions of its subsidiaries for the past year and has not influenced the appointment of any directors or management personnel for the past five years. Finally, member states may also exempt firms that meet the criteria for a medium-sized company stated in the Fourth Directive, unless any of the companies to be consolidated is listed on a securities exchange in an EU nation. A transitional clause, effective only for 10 years pursuant to 1990, expands the size limits for a medium-sized firm (for this purpose only) to a maximum amount of up to 2.5 times the criteria expressed in ECUs (see section covering Fourth Directive), thus, a maximum amount of 20 million ECU ($24 million) for the balance sheet total asset amount, maximum sales of 40 million ECU ($48 million), and an average of 500 employees.

Intermediate-size parent companies (i.e., heads of a subgroup) that are at least 90 percent owned by another EU company need not prepare consolidated financial statements if minority shareholders do not request them and their parent company prepares consolidated statements. Member nations may also grant exemptions to subgroups owned by non-EU enterprises if these non-EU parents provide consolidated statements prepared and audited in a manner consistent with the provisions of the Seventh Directive. This last exemption avoids placing an undue burden (i.e., two different sets of consolidated statements) on groups headquartered in such countries as the United States or Canada.

Scope of Consolidation

In general, parent companies must consolidate all domestic and foreign subsidiaries. (This represents a significant departure for German groups, which had previously been required to consolidate only domestic subsidiaries.) Certain exceptions may apply, as in the case of subsidiaries held for resale, those whose activities are so different from other members that their inclusion would not give a true and fair view of the group, or those whose results are immaterial relative to the consolidated group.

Definition of Control

A parent is deemed to have *control* if one of the following applies:

- It owns or controls the majority of the voting rights in another undertaking (including those voting rights held by a subsidiary or a nominee).
- It is a shareholder or member in another undertaking and has the right to appoint or remove a majority of the members of its administrative, management, or supervisory body.
- It is a member or shareholder in another undertaking and exercises control over it by virtue of a contract.
- It is a member or shareholder in another undertaking and exercises control by virtue of an agreement with other shareholders (this provision being at the discretion of each member state).

In addition, member states may require consolidation if a parent holds a "participating interest" in another firm and either exercises a dominant influence over the affiliate or shares a common management with it. A "participating interest" is a long-term shareholding exceeding a statutory percentage set by each nation: 10 percent in France and Belgium and 20 percent in Denmark, the Netherlands, and Great Britain. This option is a concession to those countries—primarily Germany and France—that have tended to emphasize de facto rather than de jure control in their consolidation requirements.

Member states may also require horizontal groups to consolidate if they share a common management or a majority of directors even if they are not linked by share ownership. One example of this arrangement is Unilever, which is an association of a British company with a Dutch company, both of which have the same board of directors.

Methods of Consolidation

Consolidated statements, like those prepared for individual companies, must include a balance sheet, an income statement, and explanatory footnotes, and they must present a true and fair view of the group's activities and financial position. As in the case of the Fourth Directive, if any provision of the Seventh Directive conflicts with a true and fair view, preparers should depart from it, disclosing the divergence and the reason for it in a note. The format of group statements must be chosen from those described in the Fourth Directive and must remain consistent from year to year. Likewise, the method of consolidation must remain consistent from year to year.

If group members have been using different valuation methods in their own statements, the differences must be adjusted so that all assets and liabilities are valued consistently in the group statements. This requirement covers not only those cases in which a subsidiary has employed replacement cost or some other method of restating fixed assets, but also methods of inventory costing. Thus, *all* inventory in the group must be restated according to the same method, be it LIFO, FIFO, weighted average, or some other method.

Accounts must be consolidated line by line, with all intercompany balances and transactions eliminated. *Goodwill,* defined as the excess of acquisition price over the fair market value of the assets purchased, must be identified separately in the consolidated accounts and amortized. Member states are allowed to choose the precise manner of the amortization: they may require companies to amortize goodwill over a period of five years or less (a procedure recommended, but not required, by the directive), they may allow companies to write it off over some longer period not to exceed its useful economic life, or they may allow companies to write it off immediately against reserves without charging it against income. Negative goodwill, or a bargain purchase, is not discussed in detail in the directive and remains open to a variety of treatments. (A primer on consolidated accounting practices is presented in Appendix 5A).

Equity Method

Under Article 33 of the Seventh Directive, companies must use the equity method to account for the profits and losses of unconsolidated affiliates in which they hold a participating interest (defined by national statute previously noted) and over which they exercise significant influence.[14] The parent company must calculate goodwill arising from the purchase of its share of the affiliate (i.e., the excess of the cost of the investment over the fair market value of the investor's share of the affiliate's net assets) and amortize it according to the guidelines mentioned. The parent company also records its share of the affiliate's income or loss in the investment account, as well as any dividends received.

---

[14]A company is considered to exercise a "significant influence" over another company when it has 20 percent or more of the shareholders' voting rights in that company.

Proportionate Consolidation Method

The Seventh Directive provides jointly owned entities the option of using the proportionate consolidation method in lieu of the equity method. Under proportionate consolidation, an investor consolidates with its financial statements its proportionate share of each asset, liability, revenue, and expense item of an investee.

Audit Requirements

Until the adoption of the Seventh Directive, consolidated financial statements, if and when they were prepared, were not always audited in many European countries. The directive, however, requires all consolidated statements to be examined by an auditor, authorized by the applicable national laws. (The Eighth Directive requires auditors to be professionally competent and independent.) The auditor of the parent company's consolidated accounts need not audit each subsidiary (which in many cases will be located in another country); instead, they may rely on the opinion of the subsidiary's auditor as to the information passed on to the parent corporation. As is the case with auditors of single-company financial statements, the auditors of group statements must ascertain that the annual report and the analyses contained therein are consistent with the consolidated financial statements.

Status

The provisions of the Seventh Directive provide a radical departure for many EU member states, some of whom (e.g., Greece, Luxembourg, Italy, Portugal) have had few or no requirements for companies to publish consolidated statements. Others that do require consolidated statements (e.g., Belgium, France, Germany) have had to include many more companies under the new laws and to change significantly the methods by which consolidation is carried out. The FEE survey (referred to earlier in this chapter) found that companies in some countries tend to use internationally harmonized accounting policies in consolidated accounts rather than in the single accounts. This relates to those countries where the application of Article 29 of the Seventh Directive makes possible the use of different accounting policies in the consolidated accounts than those used in the single accounts. This plays an important role in those countries, such as Germany and France, where the single accounts are used for tax purposes, and, thus, the accounting methods and valuation methods are strongly influenced by legal and taxation requirements. Progress toward the improvement of the comparability of financial information may therefore lie with the consolidated accounts rather than the single accounts. Although it is too early to tell precisely what the outcome of these reforms will be, the large disparity between the consolidation requirements and practices that existed before the adoption of the Seventh Directive ensures that it will represent a major improvement in reporting standards.

As even this brief review of the Fourth and Seventh Directives should indicate, the guidance they offer tends to be broad, leaving some issues untouched and others open to a variety of interpretations and practices. While the two directives represent a major step forward in the effort to harmonize accounting methods and reporting practices within the EU, comparability remains something of an unreached ideal. Union members have begun to wonder whether directives, which involve years of negotiation, are too cumbersome to achieve the desired ends. Thus, as the EU enters the next phase of integration, it may have to face the broader question of an appropriate regulatory mechanism.

Securities Exchanges

In their quest to facilitate the free movement of capital among member nations, EU leaders have spent considerable time thinking about the form and regulation of securities exchanges. The Union contains 35 stock exchanges, in contrast to 8 in the United States, with those in London, Frankfurt, Paris, Amsterdam, and Milan having the largest market capitalizations, respectively.[15] Each exchange is locally regulated, with its own legal and cultural peculiarities. In the face of this diversity, the challenge facing EU officials is twofold. The first and most immediate is to harmonize local regulations so that companies may cross-list their shares and investors can expect reasonable protection of their interests on any exchange in any member nation. This in itself will be a major task requiring the achievement of consensus on such issues as listing requirements and insider trading.[16] The second and more strategic concern is to consider what system of securities exchanges will ultimately best serve European interests: a group of regional markets with similar regulations but still basically competing with each other for listings and investors, or a fully integrated electronic network that would list all major European securities and provide investors with the greatest possible variety and liquidity.

Listing Requirements

To accomplish the first job—harmonization of exchange regulations—the EU has issued a series of directives covering listing requirements. The first directive, issued in 1980, established minimum standards for a local exchange to qualify as an EU stock exchange. Although exchanges in member countries could not offer more lenient listing rules, they were free to exceed the basic requirements. This arrangement made compliance for more developed and sophisticated exchanges, notably the **International Stock Exchange** (ISE) in London, a fairly simple matter involving only minor adjustments.

The next logical step is for an EU plan in which a company meeting the listing requirements of one EU-approved local exchange will be entitled to a listing on all of them. This so-called Eurolist plan makes it possible for an Italian company listed in Milan to gain a listing on the ISE in London.[17] In effect, the higher standards of the ISE are being struck down as impediments to trade. As noted earlier, goods (in this case, securities) that meet the minimum standards of the EU cannot be prevented from entering particular countries because of higher national standards.

Insider Trading

Another EU directive, whose deadline for implementation was mid-1992, requires member nations to enact laws banning insider trading on securities exchanges. Few issues have so effectively illustrated the cultural obstacles to EU integration as this one, highlighting as it does not only differences in practice but also divergences in values. Specifically, the debate surrounding insider trading has exposed widely varying attitudes toward secrecy (i.e., the ownership of information), commercial fairness, and insider status.

At one extreme is Great Britain, with its toughly worded insider trading laws and its cultural ideals of fair play and sportsmanship. (This is not to assert that the cultural ideals are scrupulously observed but that they exist.) In Great Britain, perhaps because so many corporations are owned by thousands of shareholders, the general public (investors and potential investors) is deemed to have certain informational rights that insider trading laws are intended to safeguard. At the other extreme is Italy, where the family is the more dominant social unit, economically as well as culturally. Large financial empires are still controlled by families. This fact and the belief that group membership (i.e., insider status) should confer advantages have led Italians, until very recently, to accept insider trading as

---

[15]"Too Many Trading Places," *The Economist,* June 19, 1993, pp. 21–23. The three newest members of the EU have one securities exchange each. See also B. Riley, "Aim for Bourse without Borders," *Financial Times,* May 18, 1998, p. 15.

[16]As previously noted, member states must accept financial statements prepared in accordance with the standards of other member states. Thus, the listing requirement issues pertain to such things as number of shareholders, discussed later in this chapter.

[17]*The Economist,* June 19, 1993.

a legitimate activity. Between these two extremes fall most of the other EU nations, including Germany, which until now has depended on voluntary agreements rather than legal sanctions to prevent insider trading.

As a consequence of these disparate attitudes and widely varying business practices, the EU directive has rather vaguely defined *insider information* as any knowledge that would have a significant effect on share prices if it were to become publicly known. Thus, trading on inside information will be a crime not only for those who work for or advise the company in question but also for those who learn it secondhand, such as journalists. The main questions at this point concern whether the law will be enforceable, given its broad definition of insiders and inside information, and whether in any case it will be vigorously enforced by national authorities. The effect of a law, like the effect of other norms, depends to a large extent on how it is handled within its sociocultural setting.

A European Equity Market?

History is likely to record 1999 as the beginning of a major change in the nature of, and conduct of business in, the European equity markets. With the advent of the euro's phased introduction in 1999 (more on the euro is presented later), a pan-European attitude, ability, and affinity toward corporate equities will be greatly facilitated and fostered. Historically, European capital has been invested in home-country assets, with equities generally comprising a significant, but not majority, share of portfolio allocations. Of the large European countries

> only the U.K. invested more than 15 percent of its financial assets abroad in 1996 . . . in Germany, France, and Italy [it is] around 5 percent. [Moreover, in the U.K. just] over half of private sector financial assets were in equities in 1996 [and it] is the glaring exception among the big countries. The figures in Germany, France, and Italy were all around 20 percent.[18]

It is generally believed that removing the currency risk associated with cross-European investments will spur such investments by individuals; according to one report, only 22 percent of the U.K. population, 13 percent of France's population, and about 7 percent of Germany's directly or indirectly owned shares—in contrast to 33 percent of Americans.[19] Likewise, pan-European investments by insurance companies and pension funds are likely to be spurred, as they have been heretofore restricted by national laws from investing in foreign-currency-based securities.

From the perspective of corporate management, attitudes are also changing in ways that add to a pan-European equity market reality. "Shareholder value" is no longer purely an American mantra—it is gaining acceptance in many European corporations. This is, however,

> still a controversial subject in several European countries where banks and trade unions have been much more important *shareholders.*[20]

Be that as it may, Europe is already seeing a slight rise in share buybacks, the linking of executive compensation to share price performance, and stock options, and it is speculated that hostile takeovers may materialize.[21] Once the single-currency euro is in full play and European companies become predominantly Eurocentric as opposed to country-centric, shareholders and analysts alike will be inclined to be more concerned with companies from an industry-sector, rather than country-sector, perspective. Such a notion

---

[18]H. Dixon, "Emu's Capital Consequences," *Financial Times,* April 30, 1998, p. 13.
[19]V. Boland, "Continent of Shareholders?" *Financial Times,* October 15, 1997, p. 15.
[20]Riley, "Aim for Bourse without Borders."
[21]Dixon, "Emu's Capital Consequences."

would clearly parallel that within the United States. Indeed, some have referred to Europe's economic future as alien to a "United States of Europe."

From the perspective of Europe's fragmented, country-oriented stock exchanges, life is also changing, and it is likely to do so in profound ways. First, with a single European currency looming on the horizon, Europe will not need the more than 30 stock exchanges it now has—consolidation and linkages will abound.[22] In July 1998, the London and Frankfurt exchanges announced a strategic link wherein they will

> harmonize their listing rules [including accounting standards] and market conventions, offer reciprocal access to each other's members, and eventually build a single electronic trading platform for the 300 largest European companies.[23]

Moreover, the Paris exchange has raised the specter of linking with those in Milan, Madrid, and the Benelux countries. The Stockholm exchange is already partnering with the Copenhagen exchange and is discussing the prospects of a pan-Nordic exchange. There is even the possibility of one or more European exchanges seeking linkages with the U.S.'s NASDAQ or NYSE.

A second development with a bit more longevity actually foreshadows more of what is likely to happen as noted above. The European Association of Securities Dealers (EASD) was created in 1995 and at the beginning of 1999 consisted of 140 member organizations from 16 European countries as well as the United States. The EASD created a pan-European stock market, the European Association of Securities Dealers Automated Quotation (EASDAQ), for high-growth, internationally-oriented companies. This market is modeled on the U.S.'s NASDAQ market.

> EASDAQ offers seamless trading and settlement across Europe within a highly regulated, liquid market. EASDAQ was born of a unique collaboration between venture capitalists, investment bankers, securities dealers, and investment institutions to provide a mechanism for economic development and innovation in Europe. EASDAQ considers applications from companies that are duly incorporated with total assets of at least ECU 3.5 million and capital and reserves of at least ECU 2.0 million. EASDAQ expects 20% of the company's capital to be publicly held and recommends a minimum number of 100 shareholders. A company must report its financial results in accordance with either (i) International Accounting Standards (IAS), (ii) U.S. GAAP or (iii) the standards of its home state with a reconciliation to IAS or U.S. GAAP.[24]

In just three short years, the EASD's membership has increased over fivefold. The calculation and publication of the EASDAQ All Share Index (EASI) began on July 1, 1998, covering all listed companies. As of mid-1998, the EASDAQ's total market capitalization was almost $14 billion (38 listed companies, 8 of which are U.S.) with a per company average of about $370 million.

As existing European exchanges merge and link and as the EASDAQ grows, one thing is for certain—Europe's equity markets are likely to be transformed. With the EU embracing IASC standards and with the EASDAQ sanctioning both IASC and U.S. accounting standards, there is a clear move toward an implementable, useful set of common accounting standards and guidelines that are not solely rooted in the history and context of a particular European country. It is likely that an economic version of a unified, borderless Europe will occur well before a political or cultural version.

---

[22]See S. Davies and G. Graham, "Europe's Big Bang," *Financial Times,* July 8, 1998, p. 15; see also "What About the Others?" *The Economist,* July 25, 1998, pp. 69–70.

[23]G. Graham, "Tyrannosaurus Lex?" *Financial Times,* July 11, 1998, p. 6. See also G. Graham and S. Davies, "London–Frankfurt Link Paves Way for Pan-Europe Exchange," *Financial Times,* July 8, 1998, p. 1.

[24]Information taken from the EASD Web site at http://www.easd.com/ as of December 12, 1998.

Corporate Taxation

One of the thorniest issues still facing the European Union is that of corporate taxation. Proposals for tax harmonization, as is true of every EU measure, must balance respect for national sovereignty with the need for economic rationalization. For more than 20 years, EU negotiators have struggled to achieve a satisfactory compromise, but only recently has real progress begun to be evident.

The divergences in tax law facing EU negotiators fall into three categories: tax rates, tax bases, and tax systems. Tax rates are not all that similar, with basic corporate tax rates between about 25 and 45 percent. The equation becomes more complex, however, because nations charge this rate against different tax bases, which they manipulate by granting such allowances as accelerated depreciation and investment credits. Finally, countries may employ a classical tax system, in which corporate profits are taxed in the hands of shareholders as well as in the hands of the corporation (e.g., the Netherlands and Luxembourg); an imputation system, in which profits are taxed once at the same rate regardless of whether they are retained in the business or distributed to shareholders (e.g., Great Britain); or a split-rate system, in which distributed profits are subject to a lower corporate tax rate than those retained in the business (e.g., Germany).

The case for tax law harmonization is usually cast in terms drawn from classical economics, stressing the efficiency of the markets and the need for investment decisions based on economic, not legal, criteria. Analysts have pointed out, for example, that variations in tax codes distort the competitive ability of corporations (specifically, their ability to achieve a given after-tax rate of return) and their decisions concerning the location of new investments. But it should also be remembered that variations in tax law are often responsible for major differences in financial reporting practices as well. Particularly in those nations in which financial reporting is linked to macroeconomic and tax policies—that is, most EU nations except Great Britain and the Netherlands—calculation of financial net income and the valuation of assets may be materially affected by tax considerations. Thus, harmonization of tax law has the potential to facilitate the harmonization of financial accounting standards. But whether this proves to be the case with EU deliberations remains to be seen.

The Euro

On January 1, 1999, Germany, France, Spain, Italy, Ireland, the Netherlands, Austria, Belgium, Finland, Portugal, and Luxembourg began conducting selected business affairs, and the trading of equities and most governmental debt in a single, shared currency—the euro. The exchange rates between these countries' national currencies and the euro were irrevocably fixed on midnight December 31, 1998. Corporate financial statements may be reported in euros after January 1, 1999, and they *must* use the euro for fiscal years ending after January 1, 2002. On this latter date, the euro currency physically replaces national currencies, bringing about complete monetary union for these 11 countries.[25] Among other things, these countries have given up their sovereign ability to devalue their currencies, increase deficit spending beyond a certain level, and set interest rates (the latter under the control of the newly created Frankfurt-based European Central Bank as of January 1, 1999).

---

[25]As of the beginning of 1999, Greece failed to qualify for joining these 11 countries, and the U.K., Sweden, and Denmark have opted not to join this move for fear that phasing out their currencies will undermine their independence.

These 11 countries have worked for years to meet the five economic criteria for monetary union spelled out in the Maastricht Treaty:[26]

1. Price stability (average rate of inflation less than or equal to that of the three best national rates plus 1.5 percent).
2. Exchange-rate stability (at least two years of "normal" fluctuations without any devaluations).
3. Interest-rate stability (long-term rates less than or equal to that of the three best national rates plus 2 percent).
4. Sustainability of public finances (public deficit should be less than or close to 3 percent of GDP).
5. Public debt should not exceed 60 percent of GDP unless the trend in debt is satisfactorily close to and approaching 60 percent.

Between each of these 11 nations there will be transparency of wages and prices as arbitrage reduces the wage and price differentials that have historically existed across these borders. The euro will lead to a European-based pool of liquid capital that should lower companies' cost of capital and transactions costs, thus improving the efficient allocation and deployment of capital. Moreover, consumer prices should come down, corporations and financial institutions will consolidate, and there is likely to be an increase in entrepeneurialism. The euro is also likely to accelerate privatization of companies in these countries. In sum, these 11 nations' combined population is slightly more than the U.S.'s and many observers think that the euro can potentially displace the U.S. dollar as the preeminent currency in global business.

The move to the euro is not without some significant downside possibilities. Among those noted by interested parties are the possibility of declining wages, increased unemployment, the failure of one monetary policy "fitting" the needs of 11 different nations, pressure on high-tax countries to lower taxes, and a widening of the gap between rich and poor.[27] Perhaps the most uncertain and most potentially damaging issue for the euro's success pertains to the labor force. Historically, the European labor pool is higher paid, works fewer hours, has more lucrative and extensive unemployment benefits, and has higher unemployment rates than their counterparts in the United States or Japan.[28] With much of the euro's predicted effects likely to make European companies more competitive, European workers are likely to lose some of these excesses while also having, at least under intermediate-term pressures, greater unemployment. Historically, few European workers have moved across borders to look for work. "While business is freer than ever to cross borders, workers remain divided by culture, language, and benefit systems."[29] It remains to be seen whether workers' attitudes, tendencies, and proclivities will change in concert with the other economic changes these 11 countries will experience.

From a financial reporting perspective, the euro can only accelerate the harmonization of standards. This is likely to manifest in three distinct ways. First, the ease and

---

[26]L. Barber, "Safe Landing Expected for 11 Countries," *Financial Times,* March 23, 1998, p. I.

[27]Many of the possibilities, positive and negative, presented here are put forth in "The Euro: A Special Report," *Business Week,* April 27, 1998, pp. 90–108; "The Merits of One Money," *The Economist,* October 24, 1998, pp. 85–86; J. B. Quinn, "Here Comes the Euro," *Newsweek,* October 26, 1998, p. 63; D. Aalund, "What's the Euro?" *The Wall Street Journal,* September 28, 1998, p. R6; and J. Kelly, "Big Changes Ahead for Accountants," *Financial Times,* October 8, 1998, p. 23.

[28]See E. Tucker, "Workers Pay for Europe's Rigidities," *Financial Times,* February 13, 1998, p. 2; and D. Lavin, "The Achilles' Heel?" *The Wall Street Journal,* September 28, 1998, p. R17.

[29]"Workplace Earthquake?" *Business Week,* April 27, 1998, p. 106.

comfort of reading financial statements with a common currency are bound to create a demand for a similarly comfortable common base of principles employed in creating the financial statements. Second, as the corporate cost of capital declines due to the euro, companies will seek means to lower it even further, and the use of harmonized standards harbors that potential. Third, and perhaps most significantly, the euro is seen by many as a powerful catalyst for accelerating Europe's development of an equity culture. One estimate predicts $1.3 trillion of new money will flow into Europe's equity markets in the next decade.[30] The providers of such a 50 percent increase in these 11 nations' market capitalization will demand transparent accounting, and companies will have to respond.

Summary

A number of regional economic blocs exist around the world. For example, there is Mercosur (Uruguay, Argentina, Brazil, and Paraguay), NAFTA (United States, Mexico, and Canada), the Association of Southeast Asian Nations (ASEAN) (Singapore, Brunei, Indonesia, Laos, Malaysia, Myanmar, the Phillipines, Thailand, and Vietnam), as well as the 21-nation Asia Pacific Economic Corporation (APEC) group (Australia, Chile, Indonesia, Malaysia, Papua New Guinea, Chinese Taipei, Brunei, the People's Republic of China, Japan, Mexico, the Phillipines, Thailand, Canada, Hong Kong, the Republic of Korea, New Zealand, Singapore, the United States, Vietnam, Peru, and Russia). These affiliations are fairly recent and appear to not have the depth and breadth of agreed on purposes, principles, and practices that the EU has achieved. Whatever difficulties and disagreements remain for the EU to overcome, one message emerges consistently from EU member states: We've come too far to turn back now. Too much is at stake. An EU-sponsored study, The European Challenge 1992 (usually referred to as the *Cecchini Report*),[31] attempted to gauge the economic benefits of achieving a single market. Its authors estimated that, in the medium term, the aggregate gross domestic product of EU nations would grow approximately 4.5 percent per year (representing about $200 to $300 billion of economic benefits annually), that an additional 1.8 million jobs would be created in the European Union (representing a 1.5 percent reduction in unemployment), and that the consumer price index would fall 4.5 percent. Over the long term, the report estimates, aggregate gross domestic product could rise 7 percent, 5.7 million new jobs could be created, and prices could fall 6 percent. All of this is expected to result from the increased efficiencies of a single market.

Economic incentives of this magnitude simply cannot be ignored—either by the EU officials who are working to make them real or by outsiders watching the process happen. Everyone will be affected; there will be no casual bystanders. Regulators in nonmember countries—especially in Europe, but in other parts of the world as well—are already feeling the pressure to coordinate their requirements with those of the European Union. U.S. banks, it has been suggested, will be hard-pressed to compete with larger European counterparts globally unless the patchwork of state and federal regulations that govern their domestic operations is reformed and brought into line with

---

[30]J. Martinson, "Why Eggs Will Move to Many Baskets," *Financial Times,* September 3, 1998, p. 21.

[31]Paolo Cecchini, *The European Challenge, 1992: The Benefits of a Single Market* (Aldershot, England: Wildwood House Limited, 1988), summary of the *Cecchini Report*. The *Cecchini Report* (Brussels, Belgium: The Commission of the European Communities, 1988).

EU regulations. Governments and businesses that fail to respond to the challenges and opportunities presented by European unification may find themselves shouldered to the margins of the global marketplace.

Inevitably, the prospect of dealing with this new economic colossus has inspired some nervousness among nonmember states and multinational businesses headquartered in other countries. The most persistent fear is that the European Union will turn out to be a new trading bloc, an economic fortress that will close its markets to imports and use its power to subordinate old trading partners. Essentially, this thinking fuels fears that a unified Europe will damage the all-important transatlantic alliance that has provided an anchor for the Free World since 1945. European business leaders have discounted this scenario, pointing out that many EU members depend heavily on exports to overseas markets, especially the United States. (The United States and the European Union are each other's largest trading partner.) To ensure continued access to these markets, they will keep the European market open to imports. Although European nations will undoubtedly gain leverage in trade negotiations by presenting a united front, the door to Europe will by no means be nailed shut. The more likely scenario, then, is continued—probably increasing—international trade, with the benefits of the single market being diffused around the globe.

Most U.S. multinationals currently operating in Europe seem to be adopting an attitude of optimism toward the European Union, regarding the fundamental changes under way as an opportunity not a threat. While new EU regulations may create unprecedented problems by redefining trade restrictions with regard to the rest of the world, many companies will use the emergence of a unified European market as the opportunity (or justification) to enter new markets and consolidate their European operations. Since Europe will primarily operate with one currency and will no longer be a patchwork of conflicting regulations and trade barriers, U.S. companies will be freer to move plants and people to more efficient and profitable locations without losing access to established markets. In addition, previously restricted markets, especially in such areas as financial services, will be more open. U.S. multinationals, like their European and Japanese counterparts, are increasing their investment in Europe to take advantage of these new possibilities.

Far from resulting in intercontinental isolation, then, continued European unity is likely to result in even stronger ties with the rest of the world, including Europe's old ally and trading partner, the United States. It is true that the United States will be less able to take the lead than formerly, a change that will require some adjustment in attitudes, and, as is ever the case in cross-cultural communication, forbearance. Likewise, in the development of workable international financial reporting standards, the United States will have to share more of the limelight with European concerns and spokespeople. But the opportunities for reciprocal and mutually beneficial influence between the European Union and the United States will be—already are—unprecedented. What is made of these opportunities will, in large part, depend on a willingness to learn to speak a common financial language. There is no question that the EU's affiliation with the IASC's activities raises the specter of a heightened importance for IASC standards that the U.S. cannot, should not, ignore. If one word signifies Europe's next decade, it is "change" . . . change in many fundamental facets of its business. The United States can choose to partner in that change or to stand alone, insisting on change to American models. Indeed,

> The Continent's old way of running an economy, dominated by big companies, big banks, big labor unions, and big government, just isn't up to the relentless new demands of globalized markets.[32]

---

[32]J. Fox, "Europe is Heading for a Wild Ride," *Fortune,* August 17, 1998, p. 145.

Suggested Readings

Alexander, D. "A European True and Fair View?" *European Accounting Review* 1 (1993), pp. 59–80.

Batt, M., "European Accounting Harmonisation," *Accountancy,* April 1998, p. 70–71.

Cecchini, P. *The European Challenge, 1992: The Benefits of a Single Market.* Aldershot, England: Wildwood House Limited, 1988.

Diggle, G., and C. Nobes. "European Rule-Making in Accounting: The Seventh Directive as a Case Study." *Accounting and Business Research* 24, no. 96 (1994), pp. 319–33.

"The Economics of European Disintegration." *The Economist,* May 22, 1993, p. 56.

"The European Single Market." *Financial Times,* January 19, 1993, survey section.

Gumbel, P. "Customs of the Countries." *The Wall Street Journal,* September 30, 1994, p. R10.

Hegarty, J. "Accounting Integration in Europe—Still on Track." *Journal of Accountancy,* May 1993, pp. 92–95.

Hoarau, C., "American Hegemony or Mutual Recognition," *European Accounting Review* 4, no. 2 (1995), pp. 217–33.

Hopwood, A. G. "The Future of Accounting Harmonization in the Community." *European Accounting* (1991), pp. 12–21.

Nobes, C. "EC Group Accounting: Two Zillion Ways to Do It." *Accountancy,* December 1990, pp. 84–85.

"A Survey of the European Community." *The Economist,* July 11, 1992, pp. 1–30.

"A Survey of the European Union," *The Economist,* May 31, 1997, pp. 1–18.

"Too Many Trading Places." *The Economist,* June 19, 1993, pp. 21–23.

Wilson, A. "Harmonisation: Is It Now or Never for Europe?" *Accountancy,* November 1994, p. 98.

APPENDIX 3A
A BRIEF SUMMARY OF THE EU'S FOURTH DIRECTIVE

- Article 1 states that the directive relates to public and private companies throughout the European Union, except that member states need not apply the provisions to banks, insurance companies, and other financial institutions.
- Article 2 defines the annual accounts to which it refers as the balance sheet, profit and loss account, and notes.
- Articles 3–7 contain general provisions about the consistency and detail of the formats for financial statements; there is a specified order of items, some items cannot be omitted, and corresponding figures for the previous year must be shown.
- Articles 8–10 detail two formats for balance sheets: horizontal or vertical; one or both may be allowed by member states.
- Articles 11 and 12 allow member states to permit small companies to publish considerably abridged balance sheets.
- Articles 13 and 14 concern details of disclosure, particularly contingent liabilities, which were shown in the United Kingdom but not in some other countries.
- Articles 15–21 concern the definition and disclosure of assets and liabilities.
- Articles 22–26 specify four formats for profit and loss accounts that member states may choose.

- Article 27 allows member states' medium-sized companies to avoid disclosure of the items making up gross profit.
- Articles 28–30 contain definitions relating to the profit and loss accounts.
- Articles 31 and 32 provide general rules of valuation.
- Article 33 is a lengthy explanation of the directive's stance toward accounting for inflation or for specific price changes.
- Articles 34–42 relate to detailed valuation and disclosure requirements for various balance sheet items.
- Articles 43–46 concern the disclosures that are obligatory in the annual report, including the notes to the accounts. Small companies may be partially exempted.
- Articles 47–51 relate to the audit and publication of accounts. Member states may exempt "small companies" from publishing profit and loss statements; "medium-sized companies" can abridge their balance sheets and notes.
- Articles 52–62 deal with the implementation of the directive and with transitional problems, particularly those relating to consolidation, which await the seventh directive.

Source: Student report.

APPENDIX 3B
A Brief Summary of the EU's Seventh Directive

- Articles 1–4 require undertakings (which member states may restrict to mean limited companies) to draw up consolidated accounts that include subsidiaries and subsubsidiaries, and so on, irrespective of their location.
- Article 5 allows member states to exempt financial holding companies that neither manage their subsidiaries nor take part in board appointments.
- Article 6 allows member states to exempt medium-sized and small groups, using the criteria of the Fourth Directive and assuming that no listed company is included.
- Articles 7–11 exempt a company from the requirement to consolidate its own subsidiaries if it is itself a wholly owned subsidiary of an EU company.
- Article 12 allows member states to require consolidation when companies are managed by the same persons.
- Articles 13–15 allow various subsidiaries to be excluded from the consolidation if they are immaterial.
- Article 16 requires that consolidated accounts shall be clear and shall give a true and fair view.
- Article 17 requires the Fourth Directive's formats to be used, suitably amended.
- Article 18 requires consolidation to be 100 percent.
- Article 19 requires there to be a once-and-for-all calculation of goodwill based on fair values at the date of first consolidation or at the date of purchase.
- Article 20 allows merger accounting when any cash payment represents less than 10 percent of the nominal value of shares issued.
- Articles 21–23 require minority interest to be shown separately, and 100 percent of income of consolidated companies to be included.
- Articles 24–28 require consistency, elimination of intragroup items, use of the parent's year-end as the group's year-end, and disclosure of information to enable meaningful temporal comparisons when the composition of the group has changed.
- Article 29 requires the valuation rules of the Fourth Directive to be used and uniform rules to be used for the consolidation of all subsidiaries.

- Articles 30 and 31 require positive goodwill on consolidation to be depreciated or to be immediately written off against reserves and that negative goodwill only to be taken to profit if it is realized or when it was due to the expectation of future costs or losses.
- Article 32 allows member states to require or permit proportional consolidation for joint ventures.
- Article 33 requires associated companies to be recorded as a single item, initially valued at cost or at the proportion of net assets.
- Articles 34–36 specify the number of disclosures relating to group companies and consolidation methods.
- Articles 37 and 38 deal with publication and audit.
- Articles 39–51 deal with transitional and enabling provisions.

Source: Student report.

Exercises

3.1 Institutional Plumbing

In a *Financial Times* article titled "Stock Markets Slow Down on Road to Convergence" (January 4, 1993, p. 29), author Peter Martin asserts that "the institutional plumbing necessary for an integrated European stock market was lacking [due in part to the belief that] substantial national differences in accounting and tax practice remained." Given such a situation, he reports that European securities markets cope by "using valuation measures that minimize the differences between national accounting and tax policies."

Required:

Through inquiries to investment banking houses and/or library research, report on some of the valuation measures used to "minimize the differences."

3.2 Mutual Recognition

K. Van Hulle, a member of the EU Commission, recently posed the following question:

> What are the prerequisites (i.e., shared objectives, not political concerns) necessary for a mutual recognition of accounting practices between the EU and the US?[1]

Required:

Prepare a short essay presenting your answer to this question.

3.3 Consolidated Reporting: The Seventh Directive

In November 1993, Akzo NV of the Netherlands agreed to acquire Sweden's struggling Nobel Industrier AB. The merger would create one of Europe's largest specialty chemical concerns. Akzo agreed to pay 16.7 billion Swedish kronor (or approximately $2.06 billion) in cash and stock and to assume an estimated 8 billion kronor in debt for Nobel's core chemical operations. To help finance the purchase, Akzo also disclosed a proposed 1.3 billion Dutch guilder (about $684.1 million) stock offering.

---

[1]K. Van Hulle, "Harmonization of Accounting Standards in the EU: Is It the Beginning or Is It the End?" *European Accounting Review* 2 (1993), p. 396.

In response to the news release, the price of Akzo shares tumbled 6 percent, from 197.2 to 185.1 guilders, and Nobel's share price rose 23 percent. Akzo's bid price of 29.6 kronor was 35 percent above Nobel's most recent closing share price.

Required:

(a) Under the Seventh Directive, how should Akzo account for its pending merger with Nobel Industrier? Prepare the entry for Akzo's investment in Nobel.

(b) Summarize the financial statement effects on Akzo of a merger with Nobel; be sure to consider the related equity offering.

(c) What inferences would you draw from the market price movements in the shares of Akzo and Nobel? Why did Akzo offer a 35 percent premium above Nobel's recent share price?

3.4   Mergers, Acquisitions, and State-Controlled Companies

In mid-1993, AB Volvo of Sweden and Renault of France announced plans to merge and create the world's sixth largest automobile manufacturer. The merger was hailed as a milestone for consolidation of Europe's fragmented auto industry, as well as an important display of the kind of economic cooperation that was expected to emerge in the wake of the formation of the European Union. By early December 1993, however, AB Volvo announced that the merger had been canceled. According to a Volvo spokesperson, Volvo's big institutional shareholders challenged the merger agreement because of "suspicion about Renault as a state-owned French company." The large investor groups felt that any kind of control by a state or local government was simply incompatible with the need to make business decisions based on economic or industrial logic.

Following the merger cancellation announcement, Volvo's benchmark Class B shares surged to 458 kronor, up more than 3 percent. Shortly thereafter, Volvo's president and chairman of 22 years, Pehr Gyllenhammar, resigned.

Required:

(a) Unlike those in the United States, many EU companies are controlled and supported, in whole or in part, by national, state, or local governments. What risks does this control and support pose for foreign investors?

(b) How might the risks identified in question 1 be reflected in a company's financial statements?

3.5   EU Accounting Practices

An article in *The Financial Times* ("Report Calls for Accounting Harmonization," February 16, 1993) expressed concern over the lack of conformity in accepted accounting practices among EU member-nations. Specifically, the writers expressed concern about the following divergent practices:

- Upward revaluation of assets on the balance sheet (e.g., in Italy and the United Kingdom).

- Excess or special depreciation on the income statement to reduce taxable earnings (e.g., in Germany and Switzerland).
- Capitalization of certain intangible assets, such as interest costs and R&D costs, on the balance sheet (e.g., in France and Italy).
- Goodwill written off to reserves and negative goodwill credited to retained earnings (e.g., Italy and Netherlands).
- Creation of discretionary provisions and reserves to help smooth reported earnings (e.g., Germany).

Required:

Consider the preceding list of accounting policies and try to identify parallel practices under U.S. GAAP. Consider also how you might overcome such differences in accounting practice to generate comparative financial data in companies from different countries.

3.6 Harmonization of EU Equity Markets

As the European Union matures, an expectation held by many is that the securities markets of EU-member nations will converge to form, in essence, a pan-EU marketplace. Preliminary evidence indicates that this is already happening.

Required:

Prepare a list of the factors that you believe are important in establishing a common EU equity market. Be prepared to discuss how those factors affect equity markets.

3.7 Comparing Auditors' Reports

One element of published financial data that financial statement users have come to take for granted is the independent auditors' report. Although an audit examination by a licensed independent professional is not required in every country nor of all companies (i.e., the requirement is often linked to the issuance of publicly held securities or to firm size—small companies that can least afford the cost of an audit examination are often permitted to waive the requirement), sophisticated financial statement users have come to expect the issuance of an unqualified or "clean" auditors' opinion.

The presence of an independent audit report provides assurances to the statement user that the reasonableness and reliability of the financial information, as well as the integrity of the system that generated the information, have been evaluated. Standards of integrity and reasonableness, however, are very much culturally dependent, and, thus, it is quite likely to find the presence of cultural diversity reflected in both the form and content of the auditors' report.

Required:

Following are the auditors' report of three international companies. Compare and contrast their form and content, and when possible, identify the presence of cultural diversity.

1. PSA Peugeot Citroën

Peugeot Citroën, a leading manufacturer of cars and light commercial vehicles, is head-quartered in Paris, France. The company's 1997 auditors' report contained the following:

**Auditors' Report on the Consolidated
Financial Statements for the Years Ended
December 31, 1997 and 1996**

To the Shareholders of Peugeot S.A.

We have audited the consolidated balance sheets of Peugeot S.A. as of December 31, 1997 and 1996, and the consolidated statements of income, cash flows and retained earnings for the years then ended, as attached to this report. These financial statements have been pre-pared by the Managing Board. Our responsibility is to express an opinion on these financial statements based on our audits.

We conducted our audits in accordance with generally accepted international accounting standards. These standards require that we plan and perform the audit to obtain reasonable assurance about whether the financial statements are free of material misstatement. An audit includes examining, on a test basis, evidence supporting the amounts and disclosures in the financial statements. An audit also includes assessing the accounting principles used and sig-nificant estimates made by management, as well as evaluating the overall financial statement presentation. We believe that our audits provide a reasonable basis for our opinion.

In our opinion, the consolidated financial statements prepared in accordance with the accounting principles described in note 1 to the consolidated financial statements give a true and fair view of the assets and liabilities, financial position and results of operations of the companies consolidated as of December 31, 1997 and 1996.

We have also verified the information given in the Management Review. We are satisfied that this information is fairly stated and agrees with the consolidated financial statements.

Neuilly-sur-Seine and Paris, March 10, 1998

The Statutory Auditors

Barbier Frinault & Autres   Coopers & Lybrand Audit

Gilles Puissochet   Aldo Cardoso   Yves Nicolas   Pierre Anglade

---

2. Electrolux

Electrolux is a Swedish company with significant operations in household appliances, floor-care products, compressors, professional laundry equipment, and forestry equipment. The company's 1997 auditors' report contained the following:

Auditors' report

To the Annual General Meeting of the shareholders of AB Electrolux (Reg. no. 556009-4187)

We have audited the parent company and the consolidated financial statements, the accounts and the administration of the Board of Directors and the President of AB Electrolux for the 12-month period ending December, 1997. These accounts and the administration of the Company are the responsibility of the Board of Directors and the President. Our responsibility is to express an opinion on the financial statements and the administration based on our audit.

We conducted our audit in accordance with Generally Accepted Auditing Standards in Sweden. Those Standards require that we plan and perform the audit to obtain reasonable assurance that the financial statements are free of material misstatement. An audit includes examining, on a test basis, evidence supporting the amounts and disclosures in the financial statements. An audit also includes assessing the accounting principles used and their application by the Board of Directors and the President, as well as evaluating the overall presentation of information in the financial statements. We examined significant decisions, actions taken and circumstances of the Company in order to be able to determine the possible liability to the Company of any Board member or the President or whether they have in some other way acted in contravention of the Companies Act, the Annual Accounts Act or the Articles of Association. We believe that our audit provides a reasonable basis for our opinion set out below.

In our opinion, the parent company and the consolidated financial statements have been prepared in accordance with the Annual Accounts Act, and, consequently we recommend

that the income statements and the balance sheets of the Parent Company and the Group
be adopted, and

that the profit of the Parent Company be dealt with in accordance with the proposal in the
Administration Report.

In our opinion, the Board members and the President have not committed any act or been guilty of any omission which could give rise to any liability to the Company. We therefore recommend

that the members of the Board of Directors and the President be discharged from liability
for the financial year.

Stockholm, March 10, 1998

Ernst & Young AB
GUNNAR WIDHAGEN
Authorized Public Accountant

---

3. *Nestlé S.A.*

Nestlé is a Swiss company principally involved in the manufacture and sale of beverages, confectionary, and pharmaceutical products. The company's 1997 auditors' report contained the following:

Report of the Group auditors to the General Meeting of Nestlé S.A.

As Group auditors we have audited the Group accounts (balance sheet, income statement, cash flow statement and annex) of the Nestlé Group on pages 50 to 74 for the year ended 31st December 1997.

These Group accounts are the responsibility of the Board of Directors. Our responsibility is to express an opinion on these Group accounts based on our audit. We confirm that we meet the legal requirements concerning professional qualification and independence.

Our audit was conducted in accordance with auditing standards promulgated by the profession, and with International Standards on Auditing issued by the International Federation of Accountants (IFAC), which require that an audit be planned and performed to obtain reasonable assurance about whether the Group accounts are free from material misstatement. We have examined on a test basis evidence supporting the amounts and disclosures in the Group accounts. We have also assessed the accounting principles used, significant estimates made and the overall Group accounts presentation. We believe that our audit provides a reasonable basis for our opinion.

In our opinion, the Group accounts give a true and fair view of the financial position, the net profit and cash flows and comply in all respects with International Accounting Standards (IAS), the Listing Rules of the Swiss Exchange and the law.

We recommend that the Group accounts submitted to you be approved.

KPMG Klynveld Peat Marwick Goerdeler SA

| W.M. Tannett | S.R. Cormack | B.A. Mathers |
| Chartered accountant | Chartered accountant | Chartered accountant |

Auditors in charge
London and Zurich, 26th March 1998

3.8 A Comparison of Three EU Corporate Income Statements to U.S. GAAP

Many non-U.S. companies prepare annual reports based on their national GAAP and then provide a reconciliation to U.S. GAAP. (If a company's shares are traded on an American stock exchange, they must do this or prepare their annual report based on U.S. GAAP.) Presented below are three such reconciliations.

PetroFina
(a Belgian Oil Company Listed on the NYSE in 1997):

Restating the 1996 income statement to comply with U.S. GAAP has generated a BEF 100 million reduction in net income.

This BEF 100 million change can be attributed to the following:	*(in BEF million)*
• Bonuses granted to managing directors, officers and senior management which under the Belgian accounting rules are accounted for directly in retained earnings (without passing through the income statement)	(223)
• Following U.S. GAAP, general and administrative/overheads and training expenses are not capitalized	(380)
• The change in functional currency (from dollars to pounds) of the U.K. upstream affiliates. The functional currency is defined as the currency in which the affiliate carries out most of its activities (sells goods, pays taxes and pays suppliers)	637
• Other changes	(134)
TOTAL	**(100)**

At December 31, 1996, Shareholder's Equity had increased by BEF 1.9 billion subsequent to the restatement of the Group accounts to comply with the US GAAP.

An overview of the components of the increase follows:		*(in BEF billion)*
• Subsidies were accounted for as an offset to tangible assets		(0.5)
• The U.S. GAAP balance sheet was established before allocation to dividends payable. Consequently, shareholder's equity increased while debts (dividends payable) decreased.		9.5
• Fina Life, which manages pension funds for Belgian affiliates, was excluded from the scope of consolidation. This variation in scope generated the following balance sheet changes:		
Long-term receivables	(6.0)	
Cash/Marketable securities	(0.5)	
Other receivables	(0.2)	
Provisions for pensions	(6.3)	
Other debts	0.3	
Shareholder's equity	(0.7)	(0.7)
• The adoption of accounting standard SFAS 87 dealing with pensions has resulted in an increase in shareholder's equity (the counterpart being booked in other long-term assets)		1.2
• According to US accounting standards general and administrative, overhead and training expenses must not be capitalized in the context of a reorganization or the implementation of a new software. Shareholder's equity has therefore been reduced by the amounts capitalized under the Belgian accounting rules. (the counterpart was recorded to intangible assets)		(1.6)
• The adoption of FAS 109 (accounting for deferred taxes) has resulted in a decrease in shareholder's equity, with the counterpart being a provision for deferred taxes of 6.5 billion and a receivable of 2.2 billion resulting from recognizing tax loss carry-forwards. The increase in the provision for deferred taxes is substantially related to capital gains which have generated temporary differences. Those capital gains should be taxed in case of distribution.		(4.3)
• Because U.S. accounting standards dealing with site restoration are more strict than those existing under Belgian accounting rules, the existing provision for site restoration was increased by 2.1 billion.		(2.1)
• The change in functional currency of the U.K. upstream affiliates has resulted in an increase in shareholder's equity which has as its counterpart an increase in tangible assets of 0.5 billion and an increase in provisions for deferred taxes of 0.1 billion.		0.4
TOTAL		**1.9**

Repsol (a Spanish Energy and Petrochemicals Company Whose ADRs Trade on the NYSE)

Following is a summary of the adjustments to consolidated net income and shareholders' equity that would have been required had U.S. GAAP been applied instead of Spanish GAAP.

	Net Income				Shareholders' Equity		
	For the Years Ended December 31,				At December 31,		
	Pesetas			U.S. Dollars	Pesetas		U.S. Dollars
	1995	*1996*	*1997*	*1997*	*1996*	*1997*	*1997*
Amounts per accompanying consolidated financial statements	117,715	119,222	126,028	861	847,848	924,622	6,314
Increase (decrease) due to:							
1. Elimination of legal restatements of fixed assets	1,372	1,372	1,202	8	(1,826)	(624)	(4)
2. Elimination of legal restatements of fixed assets as of December 31, 1996	—	—	19,310	132	(119,981)	(100,671)	(687)
3. Effect of changes in accounting for reflagging expenses (see Note 1–c)	(2,555)	(2,026)	(1,157)	(8)	1,157	—	—
4. Labor force reduction plan	—	(4,826)	4,826	33	(4,826)	—	—
5. Deferred taxation under SFAS 109	(5,446)	33,707	(5,585)	(38)	41,759	36,174	247
6. Tax effect of the above adjustments*	493	1,918	(1,705)	(12)	1,825	120	1
Approximative amounts under U.S. GAAP	111,579	149,367	142,919	976	765,956	859,621	5,871
Net income per share in accordance with U.S. GAAP	372	498	476	3,3			

(Amounts in Millions)

*Includes the tax effect of the above numbers 1, 3 and 4 adjustments.

	Millions of Pesetas	
	1996	*1997*
U.S. GAAP shareholders' equity at December 31	665,984	765,956
Net income for the year	149,367	142,919
Translation adjustment	3,705	5,865
Other	—	2,181
Interim dividend	(23,700)	(30,600)
Supplementary dividend	(29,400)	(26,700)
U.S. GAAP shareholders' equity at December 31	765,956	859,621

Legal restatements of property, plant and equipment As described in Note 2-b, the cost and accumulated depreciation of property, plant and equipment have been restated, including the 1996 legal restatement. Under U.S. GAAP, such restatements are not acceptable. The adjustments shown in the reconciliation at the end of this Note include a reduction of consolidated shareholders' equity due to elimination of these restatements, and an increase in consolidated net income for each year, resulting from the recalculation of the annual depreciation expense on an historical basis. The effect of the tax credit arising from deductibility of future depreciation of the restated assets in 1996 was recorded as an income for the year, net of the 3% tax, in according to SFAS N° 109 (Note 4).

Reflagging expenses Through December 31, 1990, the estimated cost of reflagging service stations owned by third parties was expensed by Repsol when the contracts with the respective owners were signed. In line with the industry's new commercial environment and the standard practice in the industry, from January 1, 1991, the costs relating to service station reflagging contracts were recorded as "Deferred Expenses" and amortized by the straight-line method over 5 years. In 1992 the Company changed the amortization period (prospectively) for these costs from 5 years to 8 years based on experience gained in 1991 and on the terms of contracts entered into in 1992.

For U.S. GAAP purposes the 1991 change in accounting for the reflagging expenses was treated as a change in accounting principles and the cumulative effect as of January 1, 1991, was included in the reconciliation to U.S. GAAP.

The adjustments shown in the reconciliation include a decrease in consolidated net income for 1995 and 1996 of Ptas. 1,582 million and 1,247 million and of Ptas. 695 million for 1997 (net of taxes and minority interests) as a result of the annual depreciation of the 1991 recalculation.

Income taxes For U.S. financial reporting purposes, the Group elected to adopt as of January 1, 1993, the tax accounting requirements contained in SFAS N°. 109. The accounting rules that are applicable under Spanish GAAP in relation to the recording of income taxes differ from those under U.S. GAAP with respect to when deferred tax assets and liabilities are recognized and, secondly, in the disclosures required.

The principal differences between the Company's accounting policy for deferred tax accounting and U.S. GAAP (SFAS N° 109) are:
- under Spanish GAAP, deferred tax assets arising from tax loss carryforwards are recognized only when their future realization is assured "beyond any reasonable doubt", as opposed to when they are "more likely than not" under U.S. GAAP.
- under Spanish GAAP, deductible temporary differences that are expected to reverse in more than ten years from the balance sheet date are not recorded as deferred tax assets.

Unilever
(a Dutch/British Consumer Products Company Whose ADRs are Traded on the NYSE).

The following is a summary of the more important differences between Unilever's accounting principles and US GAAP.

Profit on Sale of Chemicals Businesses
Unilever calculates profit on sale of businesses after writing back any goodwill previously charged directly to reserves but without adjusting for currency retranslation differences recognised through the statement of total recognised gains and losses. Under U.S. GAAP the profit on disposal of the discontinued speciality chemicals businesses is adjusted to reflect the write-back of cumulative currency retranslation and the difference between the total goodwill written back and the unamortised balance charged under U.S. GAAP.

Dividends
The proposed final ordinary dividends and related United Kingdom Advance Corporation Tax are provided for in the Unilever accounts in the financial year in respect of which they are subsequently recommended by the Boards of Directors for approval by the shareholders. Under US GAAP such dividends are not provided for until they become irrevocable.

Goodwill and Other Intangibles
Unilever writes off goodwill and all other intangible assets arising on the acquisition of new interests in group companies and associated companies directly to profit retained in the year of acquisition. Under U.S. GAAP, goodwill and identifiable intangibles, principally trademarks, are capitalised and amortised against income over their estimated useful lives, not exceeding 40 years.

Restructuring Costs
Unilever charges all restructuring costs to the profit and loss account in the period in which the decision has been made to restructure a part of the Group's activities. Under U.S. GAAP, certain types of restructuring costs are only recognised when further specific criteria are also met.

Interest
Unilever treats all interest costs as a charge to the profit and loss account in the current period. Under U.S. GAAP interest incurred during the construction periods of tangible fixed assets is capitalised and depreciated over the life of the assets.

Pensions
Under Unilever's accounting policy the expected costs of providing retirement pensions are charged to the profit and loss account over the periods benefiting from the employees' services. Variations from expected cost are similarly spread. Under US GAAP, pension costs are also spread, but based on prescribed actuarial assumptions.

The following is a summary of the approximate effect on the Unilever Group's net profit, combined earnings per share and capital and reserves of the application of US GAAP.

	US $ million	
	1997	*1996*
Net profit as reported in the consolidated profit and loss account	**5,568**	2,504
U.S. GAAP adjustments:		
Profit on sale of speciality chemicals businesses	**123**	—
Goodwill	**(167)**	(211)
Identifiable intangibles	**(110)**	(132)
Restructuring costs	**46**	(118)
Interest	**(11)**	9
Pensions	**(99)**	(3)
Taxation effect of above adjustments	**40**	78
Net decrease	**(178)**	(377)
Approximate net income under U.S. GAAP	**5,390**	2,127
Approximate combined net income per share under U.S. GAAP		
Per Fl. 1 of ordinary capital	**$4.80**	$1.89
Per 5p of ordinary capital	**$2.88**	$1.14
Capital and reserves as reported in the consolidated balance sheet	**12,200**	8,802
U.S. GAAP adjustments:		
Goodwill	**4,931**	4,988
Identifiable intangibles	**3,273**	3,344
Restructuring costs	**266**	238
Interest	**604**	748
Pensions	**222**	290
Dividends	**768**	790
Taxation effect of above adjustments	**(1,332)**	(1,201)
Net increase	**8,732**	9,197
Approximate capital and reserves under U.S. GAAP	**20,932**	17,999
Net gearing under U.S. GAAP (%)	—	13

Required:

Compare and contrast the three net income and owners' equity reconciliations. What tentative conclusions can be made regarding the national GAAPs represented by these three companies versus U.S. GAAP?

3.9 The Seventh Directive*

Equity Method versus Proportional Consolidation.   The Seventh Directive, adopted in 1983, established the basic principles and standards for EU companies to follow in preparing consolidated financial statements. The key aspects of the directive are

- A parent company must consolidate all subsidiaries unless the subsidiary is held for resale, the subsidiary's results are immaterial relative to the group, or the subsidiary's principal line of business is sufficiently different from that of the group that consolidation would result in misleading data.

- Consolidation is to be effected by purchase accounting unless certain circumstances exist (e.g., a 90 percent or more shareholding is achieved by means of an exchange of shares), in which case pooling of interests accounting may be used *if* permitted by the EU-member nation.

- Associated companies are to be accounted for using the equity method, and joint ventures may be accounted for using either the equity method or proportional consolidation.

This case concerns the later issue.

Background.   On January 1, 1999, Global Enterprises Ltd. (GE) formed a joint venture with European Investments SpA. Each of the venture partners was to hold a 50 percent shareholding in the new company, which was to be called Global J.V., Inc., and consequently each contributed the equivalent of 500,000 British pounds (about $780,000 U.S.) in exchange for its one-half ownership interest.

Immediately *prior* to the formation of the joint venture, Global Enterprises' balance sheet appeared as follows:

	£000's
Assets	9,000
Liabilities	1,500
Shareholders' equity	7,500
	9,000

GE financed its investment in Global J.V. by a EuroBond offering of £500,000.

During the joint venture's first year of operations, business was not very robust, as expected, and costs exceeded revenues for a net loss of £100,000. At year-end 1999, Global J.V.'s auditors approved the balance sheet as "true and fair."

GLOBAL J.V., INC.
BALANCE SHEET
As of 31 December, 1999
[£000s]

Assets	1,300
Liabilities	400
Shareholders' equity	
Share capital	1,000
Profit and loss	(100)
	1,300

As usual, 1999 was a very successful year for GE, producing a net profit (excluding the joint venture's results) of £600,000.

Required:

   (a) Prepare GE's year-end earnings statement and balance sheet, including the results of Global J.V. assuming the use of (a) the equity method and (b) proportionate consolidation. (Ignore tax considerations.)
   (b) Which method do you prefer, and why?

3.10 The World's Largest Companies

The September 28, 1998, *Wall Street Journal* provided several rankings of the world's largest companies. In particular, of the world's 100 largest publicly held companies (as measured by June 30, 1998, market value), the United States was home base for 59, the U.K. for 12, Germany for 9, Sweden for 1, Italy for 3, and Japan for 3. Of the world's 100 largest banks (as measured by 1997 fiscal year-end assets), the United States was home for 12, the U.K. for 8, Germany for 16, Sweden for 2, Italy for 7, and Japan for 22. Of the world's 25 largest securities firms (as measured by 1997 fiscal year-end capital), the United States was home for 15, the U.K. for 2, and Japan for 6.

Required:

Opine as to how the absolute and relative positions of these countries' institutions might influence the future of accounting harmonization.

PART II

Financial Statement Analysis

The objective of any financial statement analysis is ultimately to make an informed decision—to invest or divest, to lend or call a loan, to expand a business or to contract it. The information necessary to make an informed decision may be self-generated or obtained from second- or third-party sources. In either case, much, if not most, of the needed information will be provided by a process known as **financial statement analysis.**

In this section, the fundamentals of financial statement analysis are introduced. The limitations and constraints of this process are considered, as well as the considerable problem of translating the results of foreign operations into a domestic currency. The objective of this section is to provide the reader with a foundation in financial statement analysis *before* considering the eccentricities of financial data found in the financial disclosures of companies operating in specific foreign countries.

Financial Statement Analysis: An Overview

[T]here is much to learn from the financial ratios of a business enterprise.[1]

Financial statement analysis is the process of reviewing and interpreting financial information for the purpose of appraising the financial health and operating performance of a company. Many individuals associate financial statement analysis exclusively with an activity commonly known as **ratio analysis,** or the process of analyzing ratios formed from two or more financial statement numbers (e.g., the return on sales is the ratio of net income to net sales). This book adopts a broader perspective, however, in which financial statement analysis is seen to include not only the development and interpretation of ratios using historical accounting data but also the preparation of pro forma financial data and the critical evaluation of the accounting measurement rules used in the presentation of the financial data being analyzed. This broader perspective on financial statement analysis is necessary for two reasons.

First, it is widely recognized that almost all financial decisions—to merge or acquire, to expand operations, to invest, or to lend—are based largely on *expectations* about the future. Thus, when buying shares of stock in a company, it is frequently said that "an investor pays for future, not past earnings." Hence, the price that an informed investor should be willing to pay for an interest in a company will depend substantially on his or her projections of the future state of the firm: its earnings, cash flow, liquidity, and so on. One important source of information to aid in the development of such expectations is the recent *historical* performance of a company, particularly when combined with informed assessments about industry-specific and general economic trends. Thus, the value of historical financial statements can be seen to derive from their contribution in helping analysts and managers predict the future on the basis of the recent past.

Second, one of the principal conclusions reached in the first section of this book was that harmonization of accounting and reporting practices throughout the world is unlikely to occur in the near future. As a consequence, financial statement users will continue to face the difficult analytical problem of interpreting financial data from different countries prepared using accounting concepts and measurement approaches reflective of those unique

---

[1]J. E. Kristy, "Striking the Right Balance and Proportion," *Business Credit,* February 1993, p. 20.

business, cultural, and legal environments. Even if international harmonization of accounting principles were attainable in the foreseeable future, there would undoubtedly still exist a diversity of practice in applying generally accepted accounting principles and, thus, the need to be able to analyze, interpret, and perhaps restate the diverse set of practices to a common benchmark. Thus, before an informed analysis of financial data—either domestic or international—can occur, the analyst or manager must first understand the specific accounting concepts and measurement rules in use. A second thing the analyst or manager must understand is the country context in which the financial data are grounded. For example, is the cultural context such that secretive approaches to accounting disclosure and conservative judgment are the norm? Do local tax laws, as in the case of Germany and Japan, drive the principal financial reporting practices? An understanding of these unique country-specific considerations will facilitate the user's interpretation of reported financial data.

To summarize, in this book *financial statement analysis* is seen to include the following:

- Preparation and interpretation of ratios and other summary measures of financial performance using data from accounting reports and other sources.
- Development of financial forecasts, primarily in the form of pro forma financial statements.
- Understanding the country-specific context in which the financial data are prepared.
- Critical evaluation of accounting methods used in the presentation of the financial data being analyzed. The objective of this aspect of financial statement analysis is to make the fullest use of accounting data in a given set of circumstances.

Uses of Financial Statement Analysis

The uses of financial statements are many and varied. Senior corporate executives and boards of directors analyze internal financial statements to assess the performance of operating divisions and their managers. Money lenders such as banks, insurance companies, pension funds, and others analyze statements to assess the ability of potential borrowers to repay principal and interest. Merger and acquisition specialists analyze financial statements to determine the desirability of acquiring a takeover target and the purchase price that should be paid. Brokerage house analysts review financial statements to arrive at buy, sell, or hold recommendations for their clients. For these analysts, and others, the contents of a company's financial statements are often the key input in arriving at their financial decisions.

Not all elements of a company's financial statements, however, are relevant to the decisions of the varied financial statement users. Thus, the credit review manager whose job it is to review the creditworthiness of applicants for working capital loans is likely to pay particular attention to an applicant's recent and projected cash-generating ability, whereas a long-term credit assessment is likely to focus on a company's potential for profitability and its capital structure. Just which elements of the financial statements will be most informative depends on the goals and objectives of the financial statement user.

The common link between virtually all reasons for financial statement analysis, however, is that analysts form assessments of (1) the expected future returns from courses of action (e.g., to invest, divest, or do nothing) and (2) the possibility that some return other than the expected one will occur. A business decision, at its most basic level, often reduces to the question of whether expected returns are worth the attendant risks, and financial statement analysis is one important way to assess these dimensions of a business decision.

Financial Health and the Basic Financial Statements

The Content of a
Financial Report

Although the format, style of presentation, and terminology may differ dramatically from one country to the next, almost all countries require companies with publicly traded securities to issue two basic financial statements: the **balance sheet** and the **income statement.** Many countries also require that additional statements be presented, principally a **statement of cash flows.**

The analysis of foreign-based companies is often impeded by a diverse set of factors, one of which has historically been the lack of disclosure of a statement of cash flows. Other differences include those related to language, financial disclosure standards for information to supplement the basic financial statements, and accounting methods. Frequently, however, these differences are mitigated when a foreign-based company desires access to the capital markets of another country. Foreign issuers are usually required to prepare and submit various accounting and legal documents that comply with the securities laws of that country, and this is the case in the United States.

Since the United States is one of the three largest capital markets in the world (Japan and the U.K. are the others), it is an obvious candidate for companies needing or desiring foreign investment. The U.S. capital markets, however, are the most strictly regulated markets in the world; and consequently, foreign companies seeking access to U.S. investors often find compliance with U.S. disclosure regulations a considerable burden, as well as quite costly.[2]

Public offerings by foreign companies in the United States are regulated by the U.S. Securities and Exchange Commission (SEC), and the reporting requirements for foreign issuers are essentially the same for domestic companies. In reality, however, the SEC frequently grants accommodations to foreign issuers, for example by waiving requirements such as the disclosure of salaries and shareholdings of individual officers and major shareholders. Initial public offerings in the U.S. by non-U.S. companies are registered with the SEC on Form F-1, whereas subsequent public offerings are registered via Forms F-2, F-3 or F-4. Non-U.S. companies whose securities are publicly held must file periodic financial reports with the SEC, although these statements need not be prepared according to U.S. GAAP so long as they contain a reconciliation of significant variations in net income and shareholders' equity from U.S. GAAP. U.S. domestic companies are required to make an annual filing via Form 10-K; non-U.S. companies make such filings via Form 20-F. When non-U.S. companies sell their securities in the United States through means of a **private placement,** the disclosure requirements of the SEC do not apply; thus, no reconciliation with U.S. GAAP is required.

The Balance
Sheet

A major determinant of financial health is financial position—the nature and extent of a company's resources, as well as the claims by nonowners on those resources—and, this information can be found principally in a company's balance sheet. The balance sheet is similar to a photograph of the financial health of a company in that the statement describes the assets and equities of a company *as of* a particular point in time. By comparing a sequence of consecutive balance sheets, it is possible to assess the growth (or decline) in a company's financial position.

---

[2]Foreign stock traded publicly in the United States is usually done through trades of **American depositary receipts** (ADRs) or **stock depositary receipts** (SDRs). ADRs and SDRs do not represent actual shareholdings in a foreign company but are securities *backed* by actual shareholdings wherein the actual shares are held in trust for the investor by a bank or other recognized trustee. These beneficial ownership shares are issued to avoid such problems as the collection of dividends denominated in a foreign currency and to facilitate rapid ownership transfer.

Exhibit 4–1 contains consecutive (and thus, comparative) financial statements for Cray Electronics Holding Plc.[3] Cray Electronics is a British company engaged in the manufacture of communications software and the provision of information systems consulting services. One way to begin an analysis of the balance sheet of such a company is the same as we might approach a picture in a museum. Standing at a distance we see the broadest features: total assets, total liabilities and shareholders' equity.

EXHIBIT 4–1

CRAY ELECTRONICS HOLDINGS PLC
Panel A—Comparative Balance Sheets as of April 30
(in thousands)

	19x9	19x8	19x7
Assets			
Cash and short-term investments	£ 2,637	£ 324	£ 600
Accounts receivable	29,583	24,823	31,258
Inventories	18,092	18,059	21,175
Prepaid expense and accrued income	1,625	1,271	1,725
Current assets—sundry	1,737	6,597	2,145
Total current assets	£53,674	£51,074	£56,903
Fixed assets	24,507	23,093	45,478
Depreciation and amortization	(13,532)	(10,712)	(15,160)
Fixed assets—net	£10,975	£12,381	£30,318
Investments and advances	82	1,472	2,457
Total assets	**£64,731**	**£64,927**	**£89,678**
Liabilities			
Short-term borrowings	£ 8,134	£18,772	£32,973
Accounts payable/creditors—trade	10,824	6,974	12,047
Current liabilities—other	15,634	10,685	15,005
Total current liabilities	£34,592	£36,431	£60,025
Long-term debt	9,360	9,146	11,482
Total liabilities	**£43,952**	**£45,577**	**£71,507**
Shareholders' equity			
Common/ordinary capital	13,451	10,492	9,411
Share capital—other	400	400	400
Capital surplus/share premium reserve	3,234	2,113	2,113
Revaluation reserve	1,252	4,656	4,498
Retained earnings	2,442	568	(1,075)
Equity reserves—other	–0–	1,121	2,824
Total shareholders' equity	**£20,779**	**£19,350**	**£18,171**
Total liabilities and shareholders' equity	**£64,731**	**£64,927**	**£89,678**

---

[3]The financial statements of Cray Electronics in Exhibit 4–1 have been placed in a standard format. Beginning in Chapter 7, we will begin analyzing company data in its original country-specific format; however, at this stage, to control the level of data complexity encountered, we will focus on the process of financial analysis using the more familiar U.S. format for financial data.

EXHIBIT 4–1   (concluded)

Panel B—Comparative Income Statements for Years Ended April 30
(in thousands)

	19x9	*19x8*
Sales/Turnover (net)	**£84,786**	**£107,286**
Operating expense		
Cost of goods sold	51,233	68,255
Selling, general and administrative	24,039	27,004
Operating expense—total	75,272	95,259
Depreciation of fixed assets	2,117	2,621
Operating Income	**£ 7,397**	**£ 9,406**
Interest and related expense	2,745	6,076
Nonoperating income (expense)—total	135	179
Net income before income taxes	£ 4,787	£ 3,509
Income taxes		
Current	978	1,027
Deferred	331	146
Other	24	(94)
Income taxes—total	1,333	1,079
Net income before extraordinary items	3,454	2,430
Extraordinary items net of tax effects	(542)	(769)
Net income	£ 2,912	£ 1,661

Panel C—Comparative Statements of Cash Flows
For Years Ended April 30
(in thousands)

	19x9	*19x8*
Operating activities		
Net income before extraordinary items	£3,454	£ 2,430
Depreciation and amortization	2,117	2,621
Deferred income taxes	331	146
Accounts receivable	(4,760)	6,435
Inventories	(33)	3,116
Prepaid expenses and accrued income	(354)	454
Sundry current assets	4,860	(4,452)
Accounts payable	3,850	(5,073)
Cash flows from operations	9,465	5,677
Investing activities		
Investments	1,390	985
Fixed assets (net)	(4,657)	14,705
Cash flows from (for) investing	(3,267)	15,690
Financial activities		
Ordinary capital	4,080	1,081
Short-term borrowings	(10,638)	(14,201)
Current liabilities—other	4,949	(4,320)
Long-term debt	(117)	(2,482)
Dividends	(2,159)	(1,721)
Cash flows from (for) financing	(3,885)	(21,643)
Change in cash and cash equivalents	£ 2,313	£ (276)

- Cray's total assets of £64.7 million in 19x9 declined slightly from its 19x8 total of £64.9 million. The company's total liabilities also declined, although shareholders' equity was up from £19.4 million to £20.8 million.

A closer look at Cray's assets reveals that a substantial amount are classified as current. Is it significant that fewer than 18 percent of the company's total assets are classified as noncurrent? Definitely; information as to the relative mix of a company's assets reveals the nature of the company's business. In this instance, we can see that Cray is not a capital-intensive company, and instead maintains a substantial investment in such working capital assets as inventories and receivables.

As you can see, an analysis of the balance sheet at this broad level may raise more questions than are answerable without knowledge of the other basic financial statements, the notes accompanying the financial statements, and other data. That is not to say that our overview to this point would be valueless: an analyst would get some idea as to where to focus a search for more information and what types of accounts contain material balances.

The Income Statement

The income statement, or statement of earnings, summarizes the events and transactions that produce revenues for a company as a consequence of selling a product or providing a service, as well as the events and transactions that result in expenses for the company. Unlike the balance sheet, which reflects the financial health of a company as of a particular point in time, the income statement summarizes the recent *operating performance* of a company *for* a given period of time, usually a quarter or a year.

When analyzing the income statement, one of the key analytical activities involves the identification of (1) recurring and nonrecurring income or loss and (2) nonoperating items. As noted earlier, financial decisions should be predicated largely on expectations about the future: the ability to pay *future* dividends, the ability to deliver *future* innovative products, and the ability to repay *future* incremental interest and principal. Nonrecurring and nonoperating items usually provide few insights about a company's future operations and, thus usually have little information value for financial analysts.

An analysis of Cray's income statements could also begin by viewing them from a distance and then moving closer to see some of the detail:

- Net income increased substantially in 19x9 despite a material decline in sales (or turnover).
- Cost of goods sold is by far the largest expense item. As a consequence, an important consideration is how, and in what proportion, the cost of goods sold varies with sales activities. Although Cray's sales declined by 21 percent, its costs of sales declined by 25 percent—a factor clearly responsible for some of the improvement in net income despite the drop in sales.
- Interest and related expense declined by nearly 55 percent while long-term debt actually increased. What financing decisions were undertaken during 19x9 to enable Cray to achieve this dramatic reduction in interest costs?

The Statement of Cash Flows

The statement of cash flows reveals how a company has obtained and utilized its most liquid assets: cash and cash equivalents.[4] The statement summarizes and categorizes the inflows and outflows of cash from various sources for a given period of time. Under both

---

[4]**Cash equivalents** refer to short-term government securities that are readily converted to cash or have a very short maturity period, and are essentially risk-free.

U.S. and IASC GAAP, the cash inflows and outflows are usually categorized into three areas of activity: cash flows from *operations,* cash flows for *investing activities,* and cash flows from *financing activities.* In some countries, the presentation of a statement of cash flows is not a required financial statement disclosure. Nonetheless, a financial analysis of any company would be seriously deficient without a consideration of where cash came from and where it has gone.

The analysis of a company's cash flows usually involves the identification of several key measures. At the broadest definitional level are the *net cash flows* for the period. This figure represents the increase (or decrease) in a company's overall cash position; it is a summation of the cash inflows and outflows from all sources.

- Cray's cash and cash equivalents increased £2.3 million in 19x9. Where did this cash come from, and how did Cray utilize it?

Although each of the subcomponents of cash flow is important, greatest emphasis is usually placed on the **cash flows from operations** (CFFO). The CFFO is considered to be a highly significant indicator of a company's short-term financial health; it is essentially equivalent to a company's net income measured on a cash basis instead of an accrual basis.

- Cray's CFFO in 19x9 was £9.5 million, up from £5.7 million in 19x8. Most of the company's 19x9 CFFO was provided by net income adjusted for the noncash depreciation and amortization expenses, and an increase in accounts payable.

Ideally, a company generates substantially all of its cash needs from operating activities, but this is seldom, if ever, the case. Usually, a company must borrow, generate new equity capital, and sometimes even liquidate revenue-producing assets to support its cash-consuming operations. An analyst needs to answer the following questions: When are these other cash-generating activities appropriate? Do they create excess risk under the circumstances? Are they the result of poor management decisions in past periods?

- Although Cray issued new ordinary shares valued at over £4.0 million in 19x9, much of this new cash inflow was utilized to reduce the company's short-term borrowings. The company also had net new capital investment totaling £4.7 million and increased its dividends to shareholders to £2.2 million.

When the CFFO is negative, a company is likely to be forced to borrow, generate new equity capital, or sell its revenue-producing assets to support its cash-consuming operations. Obviously, a prolonged period of negative CFFO can be disastrous for a company, often leading to bankruptcy. However, the CFFO must be analyzed carefully. A financially sound company undertaking a significant growth or expansion effort is very likely to experience a negative CFFO largely as a consequence of the significant cash investment in receivables and inventory that is necessary to support such expansionary efforts. Thus, of primary concern to analysts are those companies experiencing a negative CFFO in a nongrowth period or in ways that indicate that growth is not being managed properly.

A final key measure of cash flows is **discretionary cash flow.** Although not specifically defined in official accounting literature or expressly reported in financial statements, discretionary cash flow is generally viewed as that portion of a company's CFFO available to finance discretionary corporate activities (e.g., the acquisition of another company, the early retirement of debt or equity, or some form of capital asset expansion). Thus, a company's discretionary cash flow is usually measured as its CFFO less any nondiscretionary cash disbursements or payments in the subsequent period (e.g., "regular" dividends, currently maturing debt payments, replacement of productive capacity, and the like). Discretionary cash flow is important to analysts because it represents a source of cash for growth, and to lenders because it is a source of cash for principal and interest repayment relating to any new (incremental) debt agreements. Clearly, the greater a company's discretionary cash flows, the greater the company's ability to undertake new opportunities when they arise.

It should be noted that the concept of discretionary cash flows is forward looking (i.e., the current period CFFO less any required disbursements in the following period). As a consequence, analysts frequently treat a company's discretionary cash flows as if they were a *permanent* stream, particularly if the time frame of analysis is relatively short-term (e.g., the next three to five years). Thus, as with the income statement, an important aspect of the analysis of cash flows involves the identification of the permanent and transitory cash flows. As always, permanent cash (or income) flows are valued more highly than transitory (nonrecurring) cash (or income) flows.

A Model of Financial Statement Analysis

Format Standardization

Anyone who has read even a few annual reports knows that apart from major categories, financial statements are not presented in a standard format. Differences in presentation occur across companies within a given country, across years for a given company, as well as across countries (as we will see beginning in Chapter 7).

The financial statements of Cray in Exhibit 4–1 were placed in a standard format by a data services company and were presented in this book with minor modifications to aid in their readability. Beginning with Chapter 7, we will begin analyzing company data in its original country-specific format; however, at this stage, to control the level of data complexity encountered, as well as to illustrate how foreign financial data can be and are reformatted, we will focus on the *process* of financial analysis using the more familiar U.S. format for financial data. If we had wanted to present Cray's original financial statements and did not have a database service available, clear presentation would have required a compilation of as many as four different annual reports, all of which may have been prepared in a different format. An additional advantage of financial databases is that all other industrial companies in the database are presented in the same format, facilitating comparisons across companies as well as across time.

The principal disadvantage of standardized formatting is that some information may be lost through overaggregation of account balances or it may lose its meaning through the use of standardized categories. For example, a more detailed presentation of the Current Assets—sundry category on Cray's balance sheets would be useful. The label "sundry" can mean many different things to different companies in different countries. An analyst may need at least to scan the original financial reports to verify that the standardized format of the database service is not too highly aggregated for the purpose of his or her analysis.

Trend and Cross-Sectional Analysis

One way to cut through the complexity of financial statements, related disclosures, and other available information is to think of the starting point as seeking answers to the following two broad questions:

1. What significant patterns and relationships exist in the financial statements?
2. What is observed that explains any patterns and relationships or that may cause the observed patterns or relations to change in the future?

Trend analysis and **cross-sectional analysis** are methods by which to answer the first question. Trend analysis involves the identification of patterns within financial statements across time; cross-sectional analysis involves identification of relationships within the same time period. Informative cross-sectional relationships are usually sought across financial statements from firms within the same industry or by comparing one or more sets of financial statements with industry averages.

The level of analysis that is most comprehensive is that of the *consolidated entity.* This is because disclosures and financial statements tend to be most detailed at this level for public companies from all around the world. Depending upon the disclosure standards of a given country, however, an informative financial analysis could occur at any one of the following levels as well:

Business segment.

Geographic sales region.

Product line.

Interim reporting dates (e.g., by quarter) during the fiscal year.

Two popular analysis methods for investigating trend and cross-sectional relationships are common-size financial statements and financial statement ratios.

Common-Size Financial Statements.   In **common-size financial statements,** all amounts are expressed as a percentage of some base financial statement item. For example, a **common-size balance sheet** might express all asset (equity) account balances as a percentage of total assets (equities); a **common-size income statement** might express all revenue and expense account balances as a percentage of net revenues, gross revenues, or total assets. Trend analysis of common-size balance sheets permits the analyst to determine, for example, how the relative composition (or mix) of total assets or total equities is changing over time, whereas a trend analysis of common-size income statements reveals the changing relation of various expense accounts to the reported revenues of a company.

Exhibit 4–2 presents common-size financial statements for Cray Electronics for 19x7 through 19x9, and reveals that a significant shift in the composition of the company's assets took place: The level of fixed assets decreased from 33.8 percent to just 17 percent. Exactly why Cray appears to be reducing its investment in its long-term revenue-producing assets is unclear; perhaps it represents a shift in emphasis from the more capital-intensive segment of its business (software manufacturing) to the less capital-intensive service side (information system consulting). Whatever the reason, the change in asset mix is sufficiently material as to signal a major corporate redirection that should be investigated.

Exhibit 4–2 also reveals a significant shift in Cray's financial structure. In 19x7, shareholders' equity represented only 20.3 percent of total equities, while in 19x9, it totaled 32.1 percent. This increase in equity financing was achieved largely by the sale of ordinary shares in 19x8 and again in 19x9, and may represent an attempt by management to reduce the company's dependency on interest-bearing financing. The common-size income statements in Exhibit 4–2 reveal that interest expense as a percent of net sales did decline from 5.6 percent in 19x9 to 3.1 percent in 19x9. This reduction accounted for almost all of Cray's increase in net income over the same period. It appears that, without the financial restructuring, Cray would have just broken even or possibly lost money in 19x9.

Common-size financial statements can help the analyst form impressions about the direction of a company's financial health or operating performance over time and the relative importance of any given account within a given period. The other principal

EXHIBIT 4–2

CRAY ELECTRONICS HOLDINGS PLC
Common-size Comparative Balance Sheets and Income Statements
For Years Ended April 30

	19x9	19x8	19x7
Assets			
Cash and short-term investments	4.1%	0.5%	0.7%
Accounts receivable	45.7	38.2	34.9
Inventories	28.0	27.8	23.6
Prepaid expenses and accrued income	2.5	2.0	1.9
Current assets—sundry	2.7	10.2	2.4
Total current assets	83.0	78.7	63.5
Fixed assets	37.9	35.6	50.7
Depreciation and amortization	(20.9)	(16.5)	(16.9)
Fixed assets (net)	17.0	19.1	33.8
Investments and advances	.1	2.3	2.7
Total noncurrent assets	17.1	21.4	36.5
Total assets	**100.0%**	**100.0%**	**100.0%**
Liabilities			
Short-term borrowings	12.6%	28.9%	36.8%
Accounts payable/creditors—trade	16.7	10.7	13.4
Current liabilities—other	24.2	16.5	16.7
Total current liabilities	53.5	56.1	66.9
Long-term debt	14.5	14.1	12.8
Total liabilities	68.0	70.2	79.7
Shareholders' Equity			
Common/ordinary capital	20.8	16.2	10.5
Share capital—other	0.6	0.6	0.5
Capital surplus/share premium reserve	5.0	3.3	2.4
Revaluation reserve	1.9	7.1	5.0
Retained earnings	3.8	0.9	(1.2)
Equity reserves—other	0.0	1.7	3.1
Total shareholders' equity	32.1	29.8	20.3
Total Equities	**100.0%**	**100.0%**	**100.0%**

Common-size Comparative Income Statements

	19x9	19x8
Sales/Turnover (net)	100.0%	100.0%
Cost of goods sold	(60.4)	(63.6)
Selling, general and administrative	(28.4)	(25.2)
Depreciation of fixed assets	(2.5)	(2.4)
Operating income	**8.7**	**8.8**
Interest and related expense	(3.1)	(5.6)
Nonoperating income (expense)	(0.1)	(0.1)
Net income before income taxes	5.5	3.1
Income taxes	(1.5)	(1.0)
Net income before extraordinary items	4.0	2.2
Extraordinary items (net of tax effects)	(0.6)	(0.6)
Net Income	3.4%	1.6%

use is to aid in predicting the future financial performance of a company. Most companies prepare projections or **pro forma financial statements** based on assumptions about the future for their own *internal* planning purposes, but very few companies issue those projected financial statements publicly.[5] Analysts, however, may prepare pro forma financial statements based on published history and carefully constructed assumptions about a company's future. For example, based on expected product demand, an analyst can formulate an estimate of a company's future sales under various selling price scenarios. From this estimate of revenues, a pro forma income statement can be prepared after identifying those expenses that vary as a function of sales level (e.g., cost of goods sold) and those that are relatively fixed (e.g., depreciation and certain overhead costs). Thus, with a reasonable estimate of revenues and knowledge of the relationship between the various expense categories and revenues that can be gained from common-size statements, a pro forma income statement can be prepared.

For example, based on Cray's financial statements in Exhibit 4–1 and the common-size statements in Exhibit 4–2, an analyst might feel safe in predicting that overall net income will remain a relatively constant percentage of net revenues if net revenues fluctuate in the same range as it has over the previous two years; however, such an analysis would be too superficial to warrant such a definitive statement. Given the importance of estimated revenues to pro forma income statements (i.e., almost all other numbers are derived from it), a more in-depth analysis is warranted. A consideration of expected inflation rates, population growth, and market demand for Cray's products would, at a minimum, also be necessary. The topic of pro forma statements will be revisited in greater detail shortly.

Ratio Analysis   While common-size financial statements facilitate comparisons of financial statement categories, it fails to capture informative aggregations of categories. Ratio analysis effectively summarizes multiple financial statement categories into one or a few relative indices of performance and financial position.

The numerator of a financial ratio can usually be interpreted as the financial statement element being measured and the denominator as the scale, or units of measure. For example, consider a firm with $100 of cash and $1,000 of total assets. The ratio of cash to total assets is 0.1; consequently, it can be said that, as of one point in time, the amount of cash per dollar of total assets was 10 cents. If this ratio decreased over time, even while the total cash balance was increasing, one might investigate whether the firm's actual cash needs were changing disproportionately to the change in the size of the firm, or whether there was some other reason for the change in the value of the ratio of cash to total assets.

The **return on equity** (ROE) is an example of a ratio that summarizes a large amount of information in one number as well as controlling for scale. ROE is often expressed as net income available to common shareholders for a given period divided by average total shareholders' equity for the same period. It is the amount of net income of a period per average dollar of total shareholders' equity invested during the period. A richer description of this ratio is that it is a summary indicator of the degree to which a company achieved the goal of maximization of common (or ordinary) shareholder wealth.

---

[5]The one exception to this general rule in the United States involves the distribution of a prospectus in conjunction with a merger or an initial public offering. The acquiring (or offering) company often issues pro forma statements to reflect the current (or pending) period results as if the merger (public offering) had already transpired.

The preceding calculation of ROE also illustrates the dilemma of how to combine numbers that represent "flows" over an interval of time (e.g., net income, revenues, expenses) with numbers that represent "stocks" at a particular point in time (e.g., assets, liabilities, owners' equity). When flows and stocks are combined to form a single ratio, the following conventions are adopted throughout this book:

- When flows and stocks are combined to form a single ratio, the *average* level of stocks for the relevant time period is used. This averaging process can usually be adequately approximated by the arithmetic mean of the beginning and ending value of stocks for the period. The principal benefit of this approach is to lessen any distortions in a ratio caused by a significant contraction or expansion of stocks during a given period.
- When data availability restricts calculation of arithmetic means, the level of stock as of the end of the relevant time period is used.

Numerous ratios have been developed to assist in the analysis of financial statements, and they typically fall into five principal categories:

Financial Health

1. Liquidity
2. Solvency

Operating Performance

3. Asset management
4. Profitability
5. Return to investors

Professional analysts have always faced the problem of deciding how to organize a financial review of a company. It is commonly acknowledged that the key areas of interest are firm profitability, asset management, liquidity, solvency, and shareholder returns. But a coherent framework that linked the five key areas of analysis was elusive.

One framework that has been successfully utilized is the **DuPont Model,** so named for the company in which it was developed. This model successfully integrates the areas of profitability and asset management, emphasizing a company's return on assets (ROA). The advantage of the DuPont framework (see Figure 4–1) is that it highlights the important interplay between effective asset management and firm profitability, namely that a company's ROA can be increased by:

- Increasing the net profit margin on each individual sale transaction;
- Increasing the volume of sales transactions per dollar of assets employed; or,
- Some combination of the above.

Unfortunately, the DuPont Model ignores the important issue of how a company finances its investment in assets—with debt or equity, and if debt, whether it is short-term or long-term debt.

To overcome this limitation, many analysts turned to an extension of the DuPont Model known as the **ROE Model.** The strength of the ROE Model is that not only does it integrate all five areas of analysis, but it is also premised on the widely held notion that the *principal goal of management is to maximize shareholder wealth.*

The cornerstone of the ROE Model is a single overall index of firm performance called the **return on equity,** or ROE:

FIGURE 4–1

The DuPont Model

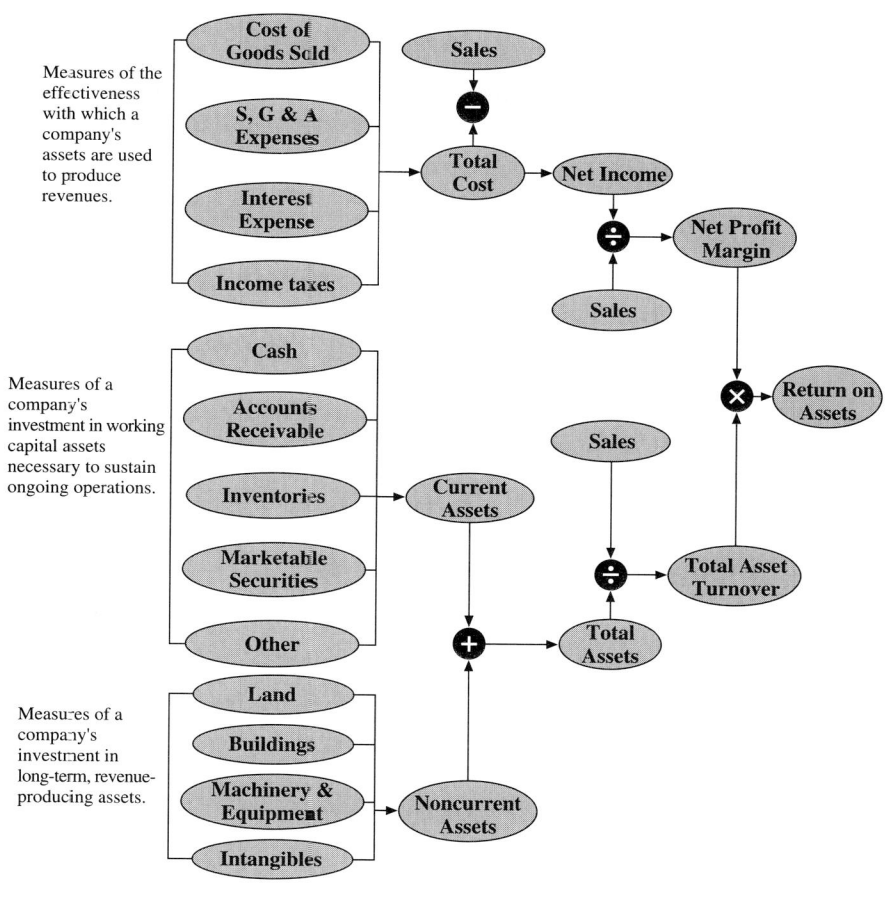

Measures of the effectiveness with which a company's assets are used to produce revenues.

Measures of a company's investment in working capital assets necessary to sustain ongoing operations.

Measures of a company's investment in long-term, revenue-producing assets.

$$\text{ROE} = \frac{\text{Net income after taxes} - \text{Preferred stock dividends}}{\text{Average common shareholders' equity}} \quad (1)$$

ROE measures the rate of return generated by a company for its owners—the voting shareholders.[6] This return is largely determined by two factors: (1) How profitably a company is able to utilize the assets that it has at its disposal; and, (2) The relative size of the owners' investment in the firm. Clearly, the more profitably a company employs its assets, the greater the returns to the owners. A second way that the owners' returns can be maximized, however, is through the use of **financial leverage,** or borrowing. If a company can generate a return on its assets that exceeds its cost of borrowing, then the company can enhance its ROE by leveraging the owners' investment. Thus, the ROE model highlights the fact that corporate management can impact shareholder wealth both through its operating decisions *and* its financing decisions.

---

[6]Preferred stock dividend distributions are not tax deductible in most countries. In those countries (e.g., Germany) where preferred stock dividends (PD) are tax deductible, a tax adjustment of 1 minus the incremental tax rate (tx) must be incorporated into the calculation of ROE as follows:

$$\text{ROE} = \frac{\text{NIAT} - \text{PD}\,(1 - \text{tx})}{\text{Average common shareholders' equity}}$$

These relationships become apparent by deconstructing ROE into its two principal components—profitability and financial leverage:[7]

$$\textbf{ROE = Profitability} \times \textbf{Financial Leverage} \qquad (2)$$

$$= \frac{\text{Net income after taxes}}{\text{Average total assets}} \times \frac{\text{Average total assets}}{\text{Average common shareholders' equity}}$$

Notice that the first component of ROE is nothing more than a company's return on assets (ROA), the cornerstone of the DuPont Model. **ROA** tells us about a firm's profitability, whereas the second component, financial leverage, tells us how successfully the company has been able to lever the owners' investment. It is important to observe that leverage, or the extent to which a company is able to borrow, is a double-edged sword: Leverage will enhance a company's ROE only so long as the cost of borrowing is *less* than the returns generated on the borrowed assets; thereafter, leverage will reduce a firm's ROE and destroy shareholder value.

ROE can be further deconstructed by examining the factors that contribute to a company's profitability. A firm's profitability, as measured by ROA, can be seen to be dependent on two factors: (1) the relative profitability of each sale that a company generates—that is, its net profit margin; and (2) the number of sales, or turnover, that a company is able to generate given its existing asset base. These relationships are observable by deconstructing ROA into its component elements—net profit margin and asset turnover:[8]

$$\textbf{Profitability = Net profit margin} \times \textbf{Asset turnover} \qquad (3)$$

$$= \frac{\text{Net income after tax}}{\text{Net sales}} \times \frac{\text{Net sales}}{\text{Average total assets}}$$

Deconstructing ROA into its components highlights the two principal ways that management can enhance shareholder returns through its operating decisions. Equation (3) reveals, for example, that shareholder returns can be increased by either increasing a company's net profit margin or by increasing the number (or volume) of its sales transactions. That is, the higher a company's net profit margin, the greater will be the share-

---

[7]For convenience, we assume from this point forward that our sample firm has only common stock outstanding, and hence preferred stock dividends are ignored.

[8]Some analysts question the internal consistency of ROA as a measure of profitability. Their concern stems from the fact that the traditional accounting income statement deducts an opportunity cost for debt capital (i.e., "interest expense"), but makes no similar deduction for the opportunity cost of equity capital. These analysts believe that a more consistent measure of firm profitability is given by **unlevered ROA,** or UROA:

$$\text{UROA} = \frac{\text{NIAT} + \text{Interest expense}(1 - \text{tx})}{\text{Average total assets}}$$

where tx = incremental tax rate.

UROA is a measure of firm profitability *before* interest charges and its role in the ROE Model is discussed further in Appendix 4A. The adjustment for taxes is designed to recognize the tax benefit resulting from the interest expense deduction. Another refinement utilized by some analysts is to replace average total assets with the sum of shareholders' equity and interest-bearing debt—that is, to eliminate those assets obtained through non-interest-bearing debt. This refinement creates a measure called **return on net assets** (RONA):

$$\text{RONA} = \frac{\text{NIAT} + \text{Interest expense}(1 - \text{tx})}{\text{Shareholders' equity} + \text{Debt}}$$

holder returns on any given sale; and, the higher the number of sales that are generated for a given investment in assets, the higher the overall profitability.

Returning to our cornerstone ratio and incorporating these latest concepts yields the following equation:

$$\text{ROE} = [\text{Net profit margin} \times \text{Asset turnover}] \times \text{Financial leverage} \qquad (4)$$

Equation (4) reveals that the three principal drivers of shareholder returns are (1) the relative profitability of each sale transaction, (2) the number of sale transactions generated given a company's investment in operating assets, and, (3) the extent to which a company has been able to successfully lever the shareholders' investment. Figure 4–2 presents a graphical illustration of how the ROE model both builds upon, as well as extends, the DuPont Model.

To illustrate the relationship of these performance drivers, consider the financial data for Cray Electronics. In 19x9, Cray's ROE was 14.5 percent, up from 8.9 percent in 19x8 (see shaded area in Exhibit 4–3). To understand the causal factors of this growth, Cray's ROE for 19x9 can be deconstructed as follows:

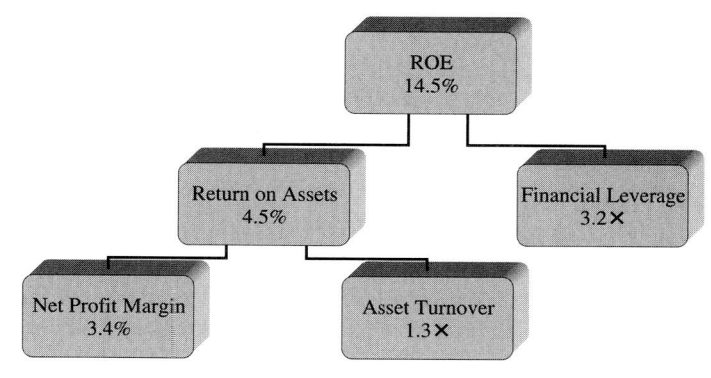

FIGURE 4–2

The Return on Shareholders' Equity Model

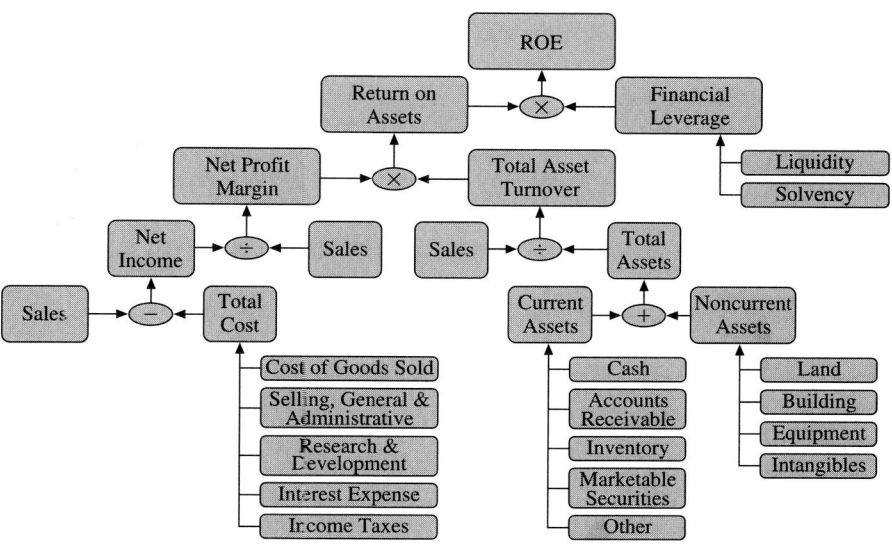

EXHIBIT 4–3

Cray Electronics Holdings Plc
Return on Equity Decomposition Analysis

Ratio	19x9	19x8
ROE	14.5%	8.9%
ROA	4.5%	2.2%
Financial leverage	3.2×	4.1×
Net profit margin	3.4%	1.6%
Asset turnover	1.3×	1.4×

Considering the company's trend data in Exhibit 4–3, we see that the growth in Cray's ROE has largely come from its increasing net profit margin, up from 1.6 percent in 19x8 to 3.4 percent in 19x9. Cray's asset turnover, decreased from 1.4 times in 19x8 to 1.3 times in 19x9; and its financial leverage decreased from 4.1 times to 3.2 times in 19x9.

Deconstruction Analysis

Just as it is possible to deconstruct ROE into the three key drivers of profit margin, asset turnover, and financial leverage, so is it possible to decompose each of these three key drivers into their subcomponents. **Decomposition analysis** is the process of segmenting a component of ROE into its principal sub-elements, and in so doing, enabling the analyst to identify the *specific* causes of change in each of the key ROE drivers.

Deconstructing Profit Margin. A company's net profit margin reveals the relative profitability of its basic operating activity. To help the analyst identify just which components of operations were responsible for generating an increase (or decrease) in profitability, it is instructive to decompose the net profit margin ratio into the various sub-ratios that, collectively, comprise the net profit margin ratio.

The most effective way to decompose a company's net profit margin into its subcomponents is by means of common-size income statements. Trend analysis of common-size income statements permits an analyst to assess how a company's income statement accounts are changing over time relative to sales, and thus how the various income statement items contribute to the net profit margin. Exhibit 4–2, for example, presents the common-size income statement data for Cray for 19x8 and 19x9. This data reveals the following:

- Cray's net income as a percentage of net sales grew from 1.6 percent in 19x8 to 3.4 percent in 19x9.
- Cray's cost-of-goods sold declined from 63.6 percent to 60.4 percent over the two-year period.
- Selling, administrative and general expenses (S, G & A) increased from 25.2 percent in 19x8 to 28.4 percent in 19x9.
- Interest expense declined over the two-year period from 5.6 percent of sales to 3.1 percent, whereas income taxes increased from 1.0 to 1.5 percent.

As the above analysis of Cray's common-size income statement data reveals, deconstructing the net profit margin enables the analyst to address the following types of questions:

- Is the company's net profit margin changing over time? If so, what factors are causing the changes: cost-of-goods sold, research and development outlays, selling and administrative costs, interest costs, income taxes, or what?

- How well is company management managing its cost of doing business? Has the company reached sufficient volume levels to gain any economies-of-scale? In what areas, if any, does the company seem to be overspending?

Deconstructing Asset Turnover.   Asset turnover, or what is sometimes called "asset management," refers to the degree of productivity that a company is able to achieve with respect to its operating assets. It is a measure of the effectiveness with which a company's management is able to employ the valuable resources provided by creditors and owners alike. Not surprisingly, there is a strong link between the effective utilization of a company's assets and the degree of profitability that a company is able to achieve. While the net profit margin focuses on the *rate* at which profit is generated from each unit of sales, the asset turnover ratio focuses on the *volume* of sales generated from a given investment in operating assets. Thus, in Exhibit 4–3, we see that in 19x9, Cray generated .034 British pounds in net profit from each pound of sales revenue, while generating 1.3 pounds in sales revenue from each pound invested in operating assets. It can be readily seen from this data that Cray can increase its return to shareholders *either* by increasing the rate of profit per pound of sales or by increasing the number of sales [pounds] generated from its existing investment in operating assets.

The deconstruction of asset turnover traditionally focuses on two groups of assets that are closely linked to the operations of a company—the working capital assets, which include cash, trade receivables, and inventory, and the noncurrent revenue-producing assets such as property, plant, and equipment. For most companies, the following ratios are calculated by analysts when analyzing how effectively corporate management has utilized a company's operating assets:

Working capital ratios:

Current asset turnover $\quad = \quad \dfrac{\text{Net sales}}{\text{Average current assets}}$

A measure of the value of net sales generated from a given investment in current assets.

Accounts receivable turnover $\quad = \quad \dfrac{\text{Net sales}}{\text{Average accounts receivables}}$

A measure of the number of collection cycles (i.e., credit sale → account receivable → cash collection) occurring in a given period of time (usually one quarter or one year).

Receivable collection period $\quad = \quad \dfrac{365 \text{ days}}{\text{Receivable turnover}}$

A measure of the number of days, on average, required to collect an outstanding account receivable.

Inventory turnover $\quad = \quad \dfrac{\text{Cost of goods sold}}{\text{Average ending inventory}}$

A measure of the number of production cycles (i.e., inventory production → sale) occurring in a given period of time.

$$\text{Days' inventory on hand} = \frac{365 \text{ days}}{\text{Inventory turnover}}$$

A measure of the quantity of inventory on hand, expressed in terms of the number of days needed to sell the existing inventory

$$\text{Accounts payable turnover} = \frac{\text{Cost of goods sold}}{\text{Average accounts payable}}$$

A measure of the number of account payment cycles (i.e., buy inventory on credit → sell inventory → payment on account) occurring in a given period of time.

$$\text{Days' payable period} = \frac{365 \text{ days}}{\text{Payable turnover}}$$

A measure of the number of days, on average, required to pay an outstanding account payable.

Noncurrent asset ratios:

$$\text{Noncurrent asset turnover} = \frac{\text{Net sales}}{\text{Average noncurrent assets}}$$

A measure of the value of net sales generated for a given investment in noncurrent assets.

$$\text{Property, plant, and equipment turnover} = \frac{\text{Net sales}}{\text{Average property, plant, and equipment}}$$

A measure of the value of net sales generated for a given investment in property, plant, and equipment.

Several observations about the above ratios are noteworthy. First, in most cases, the denominator of each ratio is an average. The purpose of averaging a beginning-of-period and an end-of-period balance is to try to eliminate the effects of any significant increases or decreases in a given account. For example, it would be distortive to the inventory turnover ratio to divide a company's cost of goods sold by its ending inventory if the firm had experienced either a dramatic increase or decrease in inventory at year-end; in either case, the inventory turnover ratio would be biased by the end-of-period contraction/expansion in inventory. Second, not all of the above ratios are relevant for all companies. For example, a company like The McDonald's Company, a worldwide chain of fast-food restaurants, maintains an insignificant balance in accounts receivables. Few, if any, of the company's customer sales are undertaken on a credit basis. Thus, the analysis of receivable turnover for a company like McDonald's is unnecessary. Third, some of the ratios are merely transformations of other ratios. For example, the days' inventory-on-hand ratio is merely a transformation of the inventory turnover ratio. It is often unnecessary to calculate both ratios, although many analysts do. Fourth, it is probably obvious that, in almost all cases, a high rate of turnover is to be preferred to a lower rate. This generality will hold except in those cases in which management is liquidating its revenue-producing assets—a dangerous situation for any company in the long term. Finally, the above set of ratios should not be considered to be exhaustive—analysts frequently add to, and subtract from, the above list.

To illustrate the use of these ratios, consider Exhibit 4–4, which contains the asset turnover ratios for Cray. The data in Exhibit 4–4 reveal the following:

- In 19x9, Cray generated 1.62 pounds in net sales for each pound invested in current assets, down 19 percent from 1.99 pounds in 19x8.
- Cray's receivable turnover cycle slowed from 3.83 times in 19x8 to 3.12 times in 19x9. This decline is reflected in Cray's increasing receivable collection period, which is up over 21 days from 19x8 to 19x9.
- Cray's inventory turnover cycle count also declined, from 3.48 to 2.83. The lower rate of inventory turns is reflected in Cray's higher days' inventory on hand—103.5 days in 19x8 versus 127.2 days in 19x9.
- Cray's PP&E turnover, on the other hand, increased over the same period from 5.03 pounds to 7.26 pounds per invested pound. This indicates that Cray has increased the efficiency of its investment in PP&E: The company is able to generate a 44 percent higher volume of sales for an equivalent investment in PP&E.
- Cray's accounts payable turnover declined from 7.18 times in 19x8 to 5.76 times in 19x9. This decline is reflected in an increase in Cray's average accounts payable period, from 50.1 days to 62.5 days. When contrasted with Cray's receivable collection period, it suggests that Cray may not be efficiently managing these working capital assets.

The deconstruction analysis of Cray's asset turnover suggests that the decrease in the company's asset turnover almost certainly resulted from a diminished effectiveness in the management of Cray's key working capital components: accounts receivable, inventory, and accounts payable.

Deconstructing Financial Leverage.   Financial leverage refers to the ability of a company to increase its asset base through borrowing. Financial leverage can be a powerful tool for enhancing shareholder returns, but the effectiveness of leverage in maximizing shareholder returns is directly linked to the spread between a company's cost of borrowing and the returns on those borrowed funds. As this spread declines, the ability of financial leverage to enhance shareholder returns also declines.

The ability of financial leverage to enhance shareholder returns can thus be seen to be a function of a firm's cost of borrowing and its return on borrowed assets (which we ignore for the moment). Further, a firm's cost of borrowing is directly linked to its ability to repay debt—what is commonly called **default risk.** A company with low default risk (i.e., a high

---

Exhibit 4–4

Cray Electronics Holdings Plc
Asset Turnover Decomposition Analysis

Ratio	19x9	19x8
Asset Turnover	1.31×	1.39×
Current asset turnover	1.62×	1.99×
Accounts receivable turnover	3.12×	3.83×
Receivable collection period (days)	115.4	94.0
Inventory turnover	2.83×	3.48×
Days' inventory on hand (days)	127.2	103.5
Property, plant, and equipment turnover	7.26×	5.03×
Accounts payable turnover	5.76×	7.18×
Days' payable period (days)	62.5	50.1

ability to repay debt and debt service charges) will be able to borrow at a lower cost than a company with a higher default risk. Hence, one way that analysts evaluate the extent and effectiveness of financial leverage is by evaluating a company's default risk.

The analysis of financial leverage usually focuses on two types of default risk—short-term risk, or liquidity, and long-term risk, or solvency. For most companies, the following ratios are calculated when analyzing this risk:

Short-term risk:

$$\text{Quick ratio}[9] = \frac{\text{Cash + Marketable securities + Trade receivables}}{\text{Current liabilities}}$$

A measure of the highly liquid current assets available to repay short-term liabilities.

$$\text{Operating cash flow ratio} = \frac{\text{Cash flow from operations}}{\text{Current liabilities}}$$

A measure of the cash flow from operations available to repay short-term liabilities.

Long-term risk:

$$\text{Total liabilities-to-equity ratio} = \frac{\text{Total liabilities}}{\text{Common shareholders' equity}}$$

A measure of the relative investment of creditors versus common shareholders in a company.

$$\text{Long-term debt-to-equity ratio} = \frac{\text{Long-term debt}}{\text{Common shareholders' equity}}$$

A measure of the relative investment of long-term creditors versus common shareholders in a company.

$$\text{Interest coverage ratio} = \frac{\text{Income before taxes + Interest expense}}{\text{Interest expense}}$$

A measure of the extent to which operations can pay debt service charges

Several observations about the above ratios are important. First, a company's short-term obligations can be repaid using cash generated from a variety of sources: operations, existing liquid assets (as reflected by the current asset section of the balance sheet), the sale of assets, the sale of stock, or new borrowings. The short-term liquidity ratios focus on the two sources of liquid resources that are immediately available to managers—cash from operations and cash (or other highly liquid current assets) on hand. Second, the long-term solvency ratios themselves focus on two separate aspects of risk: (1) the ability of a company to cover the cost of debt from the income generated by existing operations; and (2) the existing level of financial leverage that currently characterizes a company. If a company is already highly leveraged (i.e., already has a high proportion of assets from creditors), then further financial leverage will not be as effective

---

[9]A close variant of the quick ratio is the **current ratio,** measured as current assets divided by current liabilities. The quick ratio is generally preferred to the current ratio because the current ratio includes *all* current assets, some of which (e.g., inventory and prepaid expenses) are not always liquid.

in enhancing shareholder returns. As previously stated, as the degree of leverage increases, so too does a firm's riskiness, and lenders will charge commensurately higher interest costs.

To illustrate the use of these ratios, consider Exhibit 4–5 which contains a deconstruction analysis of Cray's financial leverage ratios. The data in Exhibit 4–5 reveal:

- Cray's use of financial leverage declined from 4.1 times in 19x8 to 3.23 times in 19x9. This decline in use of leverage is reflected in significant increases in Cray's liquidity and solvency over the same time period.
- With respect to liquidity, the quick ratio increased from 69 percent in 19x8 to 93 percent in 19x9. Similarly, the operating cash flow ratio increased from 16 percent to 27 percent over the same period. Both ratios indicate improved levels of liquidity, and hence a reduced utilization of short-term leverage.
- With respect to solvency, the total debt-to-equity ratio declined from 2.36 times in 19x8 to 2.12 times in 19x9, and the long-term debt-to-equity ratio declined marginally from 47 percent to 45 percent over the same period. The interest coverage ratio showed marked improvement, from 1.58 times in 19x8 to 2.74 times in 19x9.

Overall, the deconstruction analysis of Cray's financial leverage indicates a dramatic reduction (over 21 percent) in the use of leverage.

Analytical Framework: Putting It All Together

Figure 4–3 presents a composite framework for the ratio analysis of a company. The framework is premised on the notion that the principal goal of corporate management is to maximize shareholder wealth. As such, the cornerstone of the model is the return on common shareholders' equity, or ROE. As discussed above, ROE can be deconstructed into the three key drivers of profitability, asset turnover, and financial leverage. And, each of the three key drivers can themselves be deconstructed into various subcomponents, as depicted in Figure 4–3.

Cash Flow Analysis

With the exception of the operating cash flow ratio, all of the ratios discussed thus far are derived from income statement and balance sheet data. Given that cash is the one asset that a company cannot operate without, the analysis of cash flows is an important component of any financial review. Since the use of cash flow data in financial analysis has become widespread, most countries now require the presentation of a statement of cash flows (SCF).

EXHIBIT 4–5

Cray Electronics Holdings Plc
Financial Leverage Decomposition Analysis

Ratio	19x9	19x8
Financial Leverage	3.23×	4.10×
Short-term liquidity:		
Quick ratio	93%	69%
Operating cash flow ratio	27%	16%
Long-term solvency:		
Total liabilities-to-equity ratio	2.12×	2.36×
Long-term debt-to-equity ratio	45%	47%
Interest coverage ratio	2.74×	1.58×

FIGURE 4–3

ROE Model for Financial Review

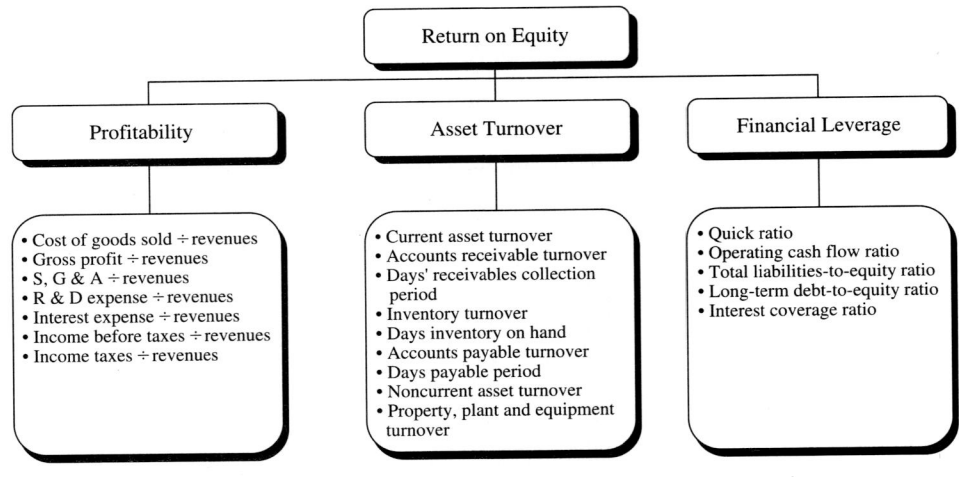

The structure of the SCF worldwide has evolved into a fairly consistent presentation, composed of three categories:

- Cash flows from operating activities (CFFO)
- Cash flows from investing activities (CFFI)
- Cash flows from financing activities (CFFF)

The CFFO represents the cash generated from the sale of goods or the provision of services, less the cash paid for operations. The CFFI represents the cash paid for intercorporate investments (both short and long term), the cash paid for new capital investments, and the cash received from the sale or disposal of noncurrent assets. The CFFF represents the cash generated from the sale of stock and from long- and short-term borrowings, less the cash paid to retire outstanding debt, repurchase treasury stock, or pay dividends.

Cash flow analysis enables the analyst to address a variety of key questions, such as:

- Is the company generating a positive CFFO, and if so, is it also generating a positive discretionary cash flow?
- What types of strategic investments has the company been making?
- How has the company been financing its operations and its strategic investments?
- How has the company financed its dividend payments?

To illustrate this type of analysis, consider the data in Panel C of Exhibit 4–1. This exhibit contains the SCF for Cray for 19x8 and 19x9; this data reveals the following:

- Cray generated a positive CFFO of 9.5 million pounds in 19x9, an increase of about 67 percent over 19x8. The company also generated a positive discretionary cash flow of 2.532 million pounds:

CFFO	9.465 million
Less: Dividend payments	(2.159)
Debt retirements	(0.117)
Capital expenditures	(4.657)
Discretionary cash flow	2.532

- Cray's 19x9 CFFI was a negative 3.267 million pounds. The company made significant investments in new PP&E (4.657 million), although these investment outlays were partially offset by the proceeds generated from disposing of select investments (1.390 million).
- Cray's 19x9 CFFF was a negative 3.885 million pounds, largely due to the company's program of debt reduction and continuing dividend payments.

Pro Forma Financial Statements: Projecting Financial Results

The purpose of projected or **pro forma financial statements**[10] is to aid analysts and managers in the formation of explicit, detailed forecasts of future profitability, financial health, and cash flow. As noted earlier, the historical financial statements prepared under the GAAP of any country in the world are not intended to be forecasts of the future. For the most part, the reported accounting data reflect only past cash flows and reasonably certain future cash flows that are the result of past events. For example, costs of inventory and equipment measure past cash flows, whereas principal amounts of receivables and debt measure highly probable future cash flows resulting from past transactions.

Pro forma analysis can enhance the analysis of historical financial statements by incorporating forecasts of future events into the traditional accounting framework. At one extreme, a set of pro forma financial statements can be prepared by projecting one determinant of a company's financial results and holding all other historical results constant, or at the other extreme, by forecasting changes in all determinants of financial results. The fundamental accounting equation is used as an organizing framework in preparing projected financial statements for the same reason that it is used for presentation of historical financial statements: to reduce the possibilities for reflecting the economic impact of transactions to those that conform to the simple and familiar logic of the fundamental accounting equation. A second reason is that if projections are prepared on the same basis as historical financial statements, it is easier to compare the projections to historical results. Projections are frequently extrapolations of patterns exhibited in the financial statements of past periods because historical patterns frequently can reasonably be presumed to recur in future periods.

Projected financial statements have many uses. Company management generates projected financial statements as part of the budgeting process: to set goals for profitability, anticipate future cash needs, evaluate opportunities for expansion, control the rate of growth, or perform sensitivity analyses on key determinants of financial results. Outside financial analysts may generate forecasts for many of the same reasons, and they may use projected financial statements to evaluate the feasibility of business acquisition opportunities, opportunities to provide debt or equity financing, or, in general, to value a business. The final section of this chapter (see pp. 113–122) illustrates the use for pro forma financial statements in valuation decisions.

---

[10]For the purposes of this book, the terms *projected* and *pro forma* financial statements are used interchangeably. However, the reader should be aware that the term *pro forma financial statements* has a more general meaning in practice, referring to either projected financial statements *or* restatements of historical financial statements to reflect hypothetical events. For an example of the latter, SEC regulations state in regard to acquisitions of significant subsidiaries that took place during the most recent fiscal year: "Pro forma financial information should provide investors with information about the continuing impact of a particular transaction by showing how it might have affected historical financial statements if the transaction had been consummated at an *earlier* [emphasis supplied] time." See SEC Regulation S-X, Rule 11–02.

*Developing
Projected
Financial
Statements*

Even the simplest set of projected financial statements requires numerous forecasts, assumptions, and simplifications. After all, historical financial statements for a period are a summarization of thousands of events, prices, quantities, and so on. Usually with the aid of commonly available and popular electronic spreadsheet software, an analyst or manager can make judgments as to how to express these many details as a manageable number of determinants of projected financial results. Major determinants usually include such items as sales forecasts, cost structure, interest rates, tax rates, and capital expenditures. The care with which an analyst or manager expresses these determinants depends on their significance, available information, and the desired level of complexity and detail in the pro forma financial statements. For example, forecasted sales may reflect not only historical sales patterns but also industry and economywide trends, stage of products in their life cycles, and known product R&D projects.

The analyst must also be aware of assumptions that are inherent in the preparation of projected financial statements that are both subtle and unnecessary in the preparation of historical financial statements. For example, in forecasting interest expense, the analyst must consider the timing of financing events within a period and the timing of operating events that will either generate or use cash. In forecasting changes in fixed assets, the analyst must be aware of the interactions between depreciation expense, purchases of new fixed assets, and dispositions of existing fixed assets.

The simple example to follow examines the types of forecasting and modeling choices that can be made and, with the aid of personal computer spreadsheet software, illustrates procedures by which these forecasts can be reflected in projected financial statements. We begin in Exhibit 4–6 with the condensed historical income statements and balance sheets of Kaufmann & Hess, GmbH (K&H) in the first numerical column. K&H is a hypothetical German manufacturing firm with sales totaling 1,000,000 DM for the most recently completed fiscal year (1999) and a historical growth rate in sales of 10 percent per year. The task at hand is to generate projected financial statements for the upcoming fiscal year (2000). In practice, an analyst would ordinarily prepare financial statements for more than one period into the future (perhaps as much as three to five years) and base those projections on financial statements going back more than one year, but the simple circumstances portrayed in Exhibit 4–6 should be sufficient for our purposes at this point. (We will consider projections for additional future periods later in Exhibit 4–10.)

Exhibit 4–6 also includes a partial forecast for 2000 for K&H. The following steps were undertaken to create this partial forecast. Shaded areas of the projected income statement and balance sheet will be completed in later steps.

Step 1. *Forecast sales growth.* This is frequently the most crucial assumption since, as we will soon see, many other elements of both the pro forma income statement and balance sheet will be based on this number. For simplicity, we assume a sales growth equal to the historical average of 10 percent.

Step 2. *Forecast operating expenses (excluding interest).* We assume that operating expenses are a constant percentage of sales, but this assumption is almost certainly unrealistic. Expense behavior is usually modeled by fixed and variable components. Fixed expenses remain at the same level over relatively wide fluctuations in sales; variable expenses move in proportion to changes in sales.

Step 3. *Forecast the change and composition of total assets.* We assume that total assets vary in direct proportion to sales. This is roughly equivalent to assuming a constant total asset turnover ratio. In addition, the composition of projected total assets is assumed to follow the most recent common-size balance sheet. (A more refined analysis could focus on individual asset categories. For example, it is quite reasonable to expect that fixed asset turnover would decrease with small increases in sales and that current asset

EXHIBIT 4–6

KAUFMANN & HESS, GmbH
Historical and Projected Financial Statements
Projection of Operating Results, Asset Mix and Long-term Financing Policy

	Historical Amounts (1999)		Projected (2000)
Income Statement			
Sales	DM1,000.0		DM1,100.0
Cost of goods sold	550.0	55%	605.0
Other operating expenses	200.0	20%	220.0
Operating income	**DM 250.0**		**DM 275.0**
Interest	26.0		
Net income before taxes	**DM 224.0**		
Taxes	89.6		
Net income	**DM 134.4**		
Less: dividends	10.0		
Change in retained earnings	**DM 124.4**		
Balance Sheet			
Cash	DM 10.0	2%	DM 11.0
Accounts receivable	100.0	20	110.0
Inventory	50.0	10	55.0
Fixed assets, net	340.0	68	374.0
Total assets	**DM 500.0**	**100%**	**DM 550.0**
Accounts payable—trade	DM 45.0		
Short-term debt	210.0		
Long-term debt	50.0		
Total liabilities	**DM 305.0**		
Paid-in capital	30.0		
Beginning retained earnings	40.6		165.0
Add: Net income	134.4		
Less: Dividends	10.0		
Ending retained earnings	**DM 165.0**		
Total equities	**DM 500.0**		**DM 550.0**

turnover would remain relatively constant. Moreover, the analyst would certainly want to review the most recent annual report to see if management has made any explicit statements about planned capital acquisitions or divestitures that would assist in forecasting the composition of total assets.)

Step 4. *Set total equities equal to total assets, and beginning retained earnings equal to ending retained earnings of the previous period.*

The shaded areas of the balance sheet of Exhibit 4–6 can be thought of as projections of financing decisions to be made by management, and the shaded areas on the income statement can be thought of as the consequences on net income of these financing decisions. These management actions can be partitioned into those that are part of long-term plans and those that are in response to short-term cash surpluses and deficits. Exhibit 4–7 reflects the following steps to project long-term financing policies:

Step 5. *Forecast net proceeds from the issuance and purchase of capital stock.* We assume that no new issuances or repurchases will occur during the period; hence, paid-in capital is unchanged.

EXHIBIT 4–7

KAUFMANN & HESS, GmbH
Historical and Projected Financial Statements
Projection of Operating Results, Asset Mix, and Long-Term Financing Policy

	Historical Amounts (1999)		Projected (2000)
Income Statement			
Sales	DM1,000.0		DM1,100.0
Costs of goods sold	550.0	55%	605.0
Other operating expenses	200.0	20%	220.0
Operating income	DM 250.0		DM 275.0
Interest	26.0		
Net income before taxes	DM 224.0		
Taxes	89.6		
Net income	DM 134.4		
Less: dividends	10.0		10.0
Change in retained earnings	DM 124.4		
Balance Sheet			
Cash	DM 10.0	2%	DM 11.0
Accounts receivable	100.0	20	110.0
Inventory	50.0	10	55.0
Fixed assets, net	340.0	68	374.0
Total assets	DM 500.0	100%	DM 550.0
Accounts payable—trade	DM 45.0	9%	49.5
Short-term debt	210.0		
Long-term debt	50.0		50.0
Total liabilities	DM 305.0		
Paid-in capital	30.0		30.0
Beginning retained earnings	40.6		165.0
Add: Net income	134.4		
Less: Dividends	10.0		10.0
Ending retained earnings	DM 165.0		
Total equities	DM 500.0		DM 550.0

Step 6. *Forecast issuances and retirement of long-term debt.* We assume that no new issuances or retirements will occur during the period; hence, total long-term debt is unchanged.

Step 7. *Forecast dividends for the period.* We assume that management policy is to maintain a constant dividend.

For each of steps 4–7, it would be wise to review a firm's most recent annual report to see whether management has made any explicit statements about anticipated stock sales or repurchases, new debt issuances or retirements, or dividend payment policy. These explicit statements can be used to verify or modify the analyst's assumptions.

Step 8. *Forecast changes in non-interest-bearing liabilities.* We will assume, for simplicity, that management's policy is to maintain accounts payable at 9 percent of total assets, as reflected by the common-size balance sheet. A more refined analysis might focus on forecasting the future accounts payable turnover ratio.

The projected income statement and balance sheet can be completed by considering the effect of short-term cash surpluses and deficits. This is necessary because we have fixed the amount of cash on the projected balance sheet to be 11.0 million DM, without any idea as to how much cash will actually be generated by the next period's operating, investing and, financing activities. A simple way to handle the problem of cash surpluses (deficits) relative to the projected ending cash balance of 11 million DM is to assume purchases (issuances) of capital stock during the period sufficient to affect the surplus (deficit); however, in reality, capital stock is rarely manipulated in this manner by management. A more complex but realistic method that can be used is to adjust the amounts of short-term interest-bearing debt for cash deficits and surpluses. This method is more complex because the level of debt on the balance sheet reflects the level of interest expense on the income statement and, hence, the amount of cash used to pay interest. However, it is more realistic because many companies maintain bank lines of credit or similar types of revolving short-term debt arrangements to handle exactly these circumstances.

The following steps describe the completion of the projected income statement and balance sheet as shown in Exhibit 4–8:

Step 9. *Project an average tax rate.* We assume a flat rate of 40 percent.

Step 10. *Create an equation for the calculation of interest expense.* We assume that cash receipts and disbursements will occur evenly over the period. Hence, interest expense will be a function of both the beginning and ending amounts of debt. We also assume that the interest rates on short- and long-term debt are 10 percent and 12 percent, respectively. Thus, our algebraic expression for interest expense is

$$\text{Interest expense} = .1 \frac{STD_1 + STD_2}{2} + .12 \frac{LTD_1 + LTD_2}{2} \tag{5}$$

where the subscripts 1 and 2 denote the beginning and end of the period, respectively, and *STD* and *LTD* are short- and long-term debt, respectively.

Step 11. *Create an equation for the calculation of end-of-period short-term debt.*

$$STD_2 = \text{Total equities} - \text{Retained earnings} - \text{Paid-in capital} \tag{6}$$
$$- \text{Long-term debt} - \text{Accounts payable}$$

where all amounts in Equation (6) are as of the end of the period to be forecast.

Calculation of short-term debt using Equation (6) is not as straightforward as it may first appear. The problem is one of circular logic in the equations caused by double-entry accounting. Although not shown explicitly, STD_2 is in both sides of the equation: retained earnings is a function of net income for the period, which is in turn a function of interest expense for the period, which is in turn a function of STD_2, which is what we are trying to solve for! Circular logic creates a calculational problem that is best handled by iterative calculations on a spreadsheet program.

The amounts added by steps 9 through 11 remain shaded in Exhibit 4–8.

The final step in the process of preparing projected financial statements for K&H is to prepare a statement of cash flows. This is a fairly mechanistic process that does not differ from the preparation of historical cash flows once the income statement and balance sheet have been prepared. In essence, the pro forma statement of cash flows is not independently prepared but is derived from the pro forma income statement and balance sheet just prepared. The statement of cash flows in Exhibit 4–9 has only one "twist": operating and investing cash flows are combined into one category.

EXHIBIT 4–8

KAUFMANN & HESS, GmbH
Historical and Projected Financial Statements Completed with Amounts
Added by Steps 9–11 Shaded

	Historical Amounts (1999)		Projected (2000)
Income Statement			
Sales	DM1,000.0		DM1,100.0
Cost of goods sold	550.0	55%	605.0
Other operating expenses	200.0	20%	220.0
Operating income	**DM 250.0**		**DM 275.0**
Interest	26.0		21.2
Net income before taxes	**DM 224.0**		**DM 253.8**
Taxes	89.6		101.5
Net income	**DM 134.4**		**DM 152.3**
Less: dividends	10.0		10.0
Change in retained earnings	**DM 124.4**		**DM 142.3**
Balance Sheet			
Cash	DM 10.0	2%	DM 11.0
Accounts receivable	100.0	20	110.0
Inventory	50.0	10	55.0
Fixed assets, net	340.0	68	374.0
Total assets	**DM 500.0**	**100%**	**DM 550.0**
Accounts payable—trade	**DM 45.0**	9%	**DM 49.5**
Short-term debt	210.0		113.2
Long-term debt	50.0		50.0
Total liabilities	**DM 305.0**		**DM 212.7**
Paid-in capital	30.0		30.0
Beginning retained earnings	40.6		165.0
Add: Net income	134.4		152.3
Less: Dividends	10.0		10.0
Ending retained earnings	**DM 165.0**		**DM 307.3**
Total equities	**DM 500.0**		**DM 550.0**

See Appendix 4B for a printout of the formulas used to calculate the figures in this exhibit using Microsoft *Excel.*

There are two reasons for not distinguishing between operating and investing cash flows. First, there may not be enough information to make the distinction accurately in a projected statement of cash flows. In analyzing the change in fixed assets, it is necessary to know the amount of depreciation expense for the period, an operating item, versus net fixed asset acquisitions/dispositions, an investing item. In historical financial statements, depreciation expense is often aggregated with cost of sales. Second, the distinction between operating and investing cash flows is not always informative. For example, fixed asset acquisitions to maintain existing productive capacity are arguably operating cash flows, even though no accounting standard requires preparers to distinguish in the statement of cash flows between fixed asset expenditures for expansion versus maintenance of productive capacity. For purposes of preparing projected financial statements, we believe that capital expenditures made to maintain existing product capacity should be classified as operating cash flows (as in the calculation of free or discretionary cash flows). An investing category is informative when a major asset

EXHIBIT 4–9

KAUFMANN & HESS, GmbH
Projected Statement of Cash Flows
For the Year 2000

Operations

Net income		DM 152.3
Adjustments		
Change in accounts receivable	(10.0)	
Change in inventory	(5.0)	
Change in fixed assets	(34.0)	
Change in accounts payable	4.5	(44.5)
Cash provided by operations		**DM 107.8**
Financing		
Additions (reductions) in short-term debt	(96.8)	
Additions (reductions) in long-term debt	0.0	
Additions (reductions) in paid-in capital	0.0	
Dividends	(10.0)	
Net cash from financing		**(106.8)**
Change in cash		**DM 1.0**

expenditure or divestiture is planned that significantly changes the firm's productive capacity.

In summary, although the use of K&H as an illustration emphasizes an organizing framework for preparing projected financial statements, analysts should not lose sight of the applicability of various financial analysis techniques discussed thus far as aids in projecting financial results. Ratio analysis and common-size financial statements are used to analyze trends in relationships among numbers on the financial statements. In making projections, the analyst must forecast how certain trends and relationships will change (or not change, as the case may be) with time. In the next section, we illustrate how to use financial statement projections to value a firm (or other investment opportunity) for sale or acquisition, which is just one way in which pro forma statements can be used by professional analysts and managers.

Valuing Ownership Interests

Financial analysis does not always involve business valuation, but it frequently does. The two most common reasons that business valuation is an important aspect of financial analysis are due to (1) the existence of illiquid markets for trading the stock of a company to be bought or sold and (2) the identification of mispriced securities. Before discussing the common approaches to business valuation, these two reasons are explored.

Illiquid Markets   Many companies, even large ones, are not publicly traded. For example, in the United States, Hughes Aircraft was a privately held corporation until purchased by General Motors over 10 years ago. Mars, Inc. (the U.S. candy company) is still privately owned, and E. Merck, Germany's largest pharmaceuticals company, made its initial public offering of shares as recently as 1995.

The market for corporate control is also illiquid, and prices may differ from the market for noncontrolling interests in a company's stock (e.g., quoted prices on stock exchanges).

For example, it is well known that successful tender offers almost always require that the purchaser pay a substantial premium over the trading price per share of a target firm, whereas no premium is required to purchase, say, 100 shares. Financial projections and valuation methods help to determine how a change in control would affect a corporation's financial results and how much of a premium over the current share price is justified.

Market Mispricing

Although many financial theorists argue that securities markets are efficient in the sense that all publicly available information is reflected in an unbiased manner in stock prices, legions of analysts persist in applying the tools of financial analysis for the purpose of identifying over- and under-priced stocks. Analysts seek opportunities to create insights into financial information that they believe are not noticed by others, or to incorporate information in their analysis that they believe other market participants have not discovered or have improperly valued. In addition, some markets may be less informationally efficient than others: smaller companies may not be followed as closely as larger companies by the market, and in some countries (e.g., Germany), actual "information asymmetries" exist. For example, larger shareholders may have access to information that small shareholders do not have, and in some countries, trading on inside information is much less restrictive than in the United States.

Valuation Methods

Theoretically, the valuation of an ownership interest in a business entails the calculation of the present value of expected future cash flows to owners for all future periods. The details and variants of the discounted cash flow (DCF) method are described in many finance textbooks. The problem is that direct application of financial theory to valuation often yields results that appear unreasonable. This is usually due to the lack of accuracy of assumptions that generate projected future cash flows into the too distant future. Therefore, the best method of determining value depends on the circumstances: Every business has its own unique characteristics, and available information relevant to its valuation can vary considerably. In addition to the DCF approach to valuation, other methods to be discussed in this section are based on direct comparison with the market price of similar businesses, or adjustments to balance sheet and income statement numbers for the relationship between observed market prices of "comparable" businesses and their accounting numbers.

Discounted Cash Flow Methods.   Under the DCF method, a potential buyer (or seller) analyzes a company's operations and on the basis of that analysis, which usually includes the preparation of pro forma financial statements, estimates of the amount and timing of the future cash flows that are expected to accrue to the potential buyer. The degree of **nondiversifiable risk** is assessed,[11] and is usually incorporated into the analysis via the selection of a discount rate. The process of discounting future cash flows is captured by the following equation:

$$V = \sum_{t=1}^{n} \frac{D_t}{(1 + r)^t}$$

where

V = The net present value of the future cash flows to the owners   (7)
D_t = The dividend payment (or any cash distribution) at time t
r = The risk-adjusted required rate of return

---

[11]*Nondiversifiable risk* refers to the unique, nonsystematic risk associated with an investment. Most risk can be hedged by investing in a diverse set of assets (e.g., a portfolio of securities), whereas nondiversifiable risk usually cannot be effectively, or completely, hedged.

As mentioned earlier, the most critical issue in applying this equation is the forecast horizon or, more specifically, the number of periods (months, quarters, or years) for which pro forma financial statements are prepared. There is no widely accepted answer, although most analysts agree that forecasts beyond five to seven years are highly suspect because of the uncertainties that may arise. One way to mitigate these uncertainties is to substitute so-called discretionary or free cash flows for dividend flows. By definition, discretionary cash flows are greater than dividends, since dividends are themselves a discretionary cash outflow. This substitution has the effect of increasing V, implicitly by the present value of cash flows used to sustain the business for a longer period of time than explicitly considered in the DCF calculation. Other variants include substituting a company's cash flow from operations (*CFFO*) for *D*. However, neither method may be an adequate substitute for an estimate of the "terminal value" of the business (i.e., the value at the end of the time period over which expected dividend or cash flows have been forecast).

A related issue is whether future dividend streams adequately describe the benefits of ownership in a company. The following equation portrays the additional benefits to be derived through ownership of a target company by another business:

$$V_{sub} = \sum_{t=1}^{n} \frac{(D_s + P_{is} + MSC_s)}{(1 + r)^t} \tag{8}$$

where for simplicity, time subscripts are excluded and

V_{sub} = The parent's net present value of subsidiary cash flows
D_s = The dividend payment from subsidiary
P_{is} = The profit on intracompany sales
MSC_s = The miscellaneous payments from the subsidiary (fees, royalties, interest and principal repayments, income tax credits)

Market Comparables. This method of valuing a firm assesses value through a process of comparison with similar, recently sold (or purchased) businesses. This process is quite common in the real estate industry, particularly in real estate transactions involving a single asset, but it is somewhat difficult to apply to businesses involving a bundle of diverse assets, largely because of the difficulty of finding recently sold businesses with comparable bundles of assets. Nonetheless, for asset-dependent businesses, this approach may provide an approximate basis for assessing firm value. For example, companies involved in the oil and gas industry are often valued relative to the market value of their oil and gas reserves. This rough approximation of value may be useful in those situations where only the reserves (or assets) of the company are being purchased, not the liabilities, and where the costs of extraction are nominal. When differences in cost structure or asset composition are material, comparables enhanced by accounting values may be an alternative approach for valuation. This is the rationale for the balance sheet and income statement-based valuation methods to be described next.

Balance Sheet Valuation Methods. Balance sheet-based valuation methods are essentially grounded in the notion that a buyer (seller) purchases (sells) the net assets of a company, and the economic value of the net assets bears some relationship to their book values. Before the U.S. savings and loan debacle of the 1980s, the purchase price of an S&L was typically quoted as a multiple of the institution's net book value (e.g., 1.5 times net book value). This valuation approach was followed for many years because of the relative stability of interest rates and the stability of the markets in which S&Ls provided financing. Investors who paid a price in the range of 1.5 times net book value generally earned an adequate return for the risks taken.

A significant limitation of the balance sheet valuation approach arises, however, when interest rates shift or other changes in business conditions cause the market value of assets (and liabilities) to differ from their recorded balance sheet values. One way to deal with this limitation is to "adjust" individual balance sheet values for an estimate of the amounts by which accounting valuations misstate fair values. This approach is often used today to evaluate the reasonableness of selling prices for banks, insurance companies, securities firms, and other financial institutions, whose principal assets are primarily driven by interest rates. For example, industry analysts suggest that insurance companies in the United States usually sell for 1.4 times adjusted book value and securities firms for 1.5 times adjusted book value. Although these adjustments are appealing because of their simplicity, they also have limitations. First, multiples of book values are usually not transferable across borders because of differences in governmental regulations and risk profiles. Second, adjustment to net asset book values is not ordinarily undertaken as a valuation method when large portions of a company's assets are nonfinancial: it is much more difficult for an external analyst to accurately estimate the fair values of assets other than financial assets.

It is also possible to combine balance sheet valuation methods with the DCF method. For example, projected dividend cash flows for five to seven years are estimated, and the terminal value of the business is estimated as a multiple of net worth from the projected balance sheet as of the terminal date. This procedure is reflected in the following valuation equation:

$$V = \sum_{t=1}^{n} \frac{D_t}{(1 + r)^t} + \frac{(NW_n)(X)}{(1 + r)^n} \qquad (9)$$

where

NW_n = Book value of net worth at the terminal date, n
X = A multiple of book value based on market prices of comparable companies

Earnings-Based Methods.   Under this approach, the value of a company is assumed to be a multiple of its operating earnings or operating cash flow. For example, the value of a newspaper company might be quoted as 14 times operating cash flow. The advantage of this approach is its simplicity and the use of widely available data. Price/earnings ratios are also widely quoted in the financial press, and it is a simple matter to calculate an average P/E ratio for companies in the same industry that are otherwise comparable. The particular limitations of this approach involve the possibility that a single earnings number may not represent a company's worth; it may be distorted by uncharacteristically good (or poor) recent company performance. Also, earnings for a period are particularly sensitive to a company's accounting policies and may not be comparable with earnings numbers for companies that have available market prices. Finally, as was noted in Chapter 1 and as will be seen in Chapters 7–13, P/E ratios vary dramatically across borders as a consequence of cultural, business, and legal factors.

Evaluating International Investment Opportunities

The use of DCF analysis in conjunction with pro forma financial statements is a powerful tool for evaluating the value of almost any firm or investment opportunity. In this section, we illustrate this approach in the context of an international investment opportunity.

The process of evaluating *international* investment opportunities involves greater complexity than evaluating purely domestic ones.[12] Although the fundamental approach

---

[12]We are indebted to T. H. Woodland for her input on this topic.

is similar for both domestic and international opportunities, the number of factors to be considered increases substantially when projects cross national borders. In this section, we explore the process of multinational capital budgeting and show how the DCF framework discussed above can be implemented in the face of such additional concerns as foreign currency risk, country (or political) risk, foreign taxes, and repatriation laws, among others.

Multinational Capital Budgeting: Project versus Parent Cash Flows. A primary difference between evaluating domestic versus foreign investments involves the risks associated with a project's cash flows. For domestic investments, the parent's and the project's cash flows are equivalent, whereas for a foreign investment, the parent's cash flow stream rarely equals that of the project. The cash flows between a parent and its foreign subsidiary are exposed to the additional considerations of foreign income (or withholding) taxes, exchange rate fluctuations, and restrictions on the movement of capital (e.g., the repatriation of profits from the subsidiary's domicile to that of the parent).

Thus, multinational capital budgeting usually involves the added complexity of generating *two* sets of pro forma statements, one for the parent and one for the project (or subsidiary). *Project cash flows* are usually computed in the **functional currency** of the subsidiary: the inflows are the after-tax funds received from the parent and the outflows are the after-tax profits generated by the project.[13] Project cash flows, however, must be considered in light of two special risks: the risk of expropriation and the risk of blocked funds. **Expropriation risk** refers to the probability that a project's assets and operations will be taken over by a foreign government, with or without compensation to the parent.[14] **Blocked funds risk,** on the other hand, refers to existing or pending foreign laws that restrict the flow of funds out of a given locale. Although blocked funds cannot be repatriated, they can usually be reinvested in the foreign country and at some point in the future may be transferable.

Parent cash flows are usually computed twice, once in the functional currency of the subsidiary and then translated into the functional currency of the parent. This latter computation requires an assumption with respect to the movement of exchange rates and thus requires an explicit consideration of exchange rate exposure.[15] For the parent, the outflows are represented by the pretax dollars sent to (or paid for) the subsidiary, whereas its inflows are represented by the subsidiary's after-tax profits, adjusted to reflect profit repatriation limitations and exchange rate fluctuations. The parent's inflows usually take the

---

[13]The "functional currency" of a company is the currency in which it primarily conducts its business operations. For example, a British company, headquartered in London and with shares traded on both the London Stock Exchange and the New York Stock Exchange, but whose principal operations involve trading in Hong Kong (in transactions denominated in Hong Kong dollars), would have a functional currency of Hong Kong dollars, not British pounds or U.S. dollars.

[14]When expropriation is uncompensated, the parent company can usually seek some form of recompensation (i.e., a tax loss deduction or insurance recovery) in its own domicile. Alternatively, the parent may seek recovery from the Overseas Private Investment Corporation (OPIC), which provides insurance coverage against currency inconvertibility by law, expropriation, civil war or revolution, and wrongful or improper calling of a guarantee. These payments, of course, must be considered when evaluating an international investment opportunity.

[15]The topics of foreign exchange exposure and accounting for exchange rate fluctuations are addressed in detail in Chapter 6.

form of dividends, although some multinational companies also use interest and principal repayments, transfer pricing, management fees, rents, and royalties to shift income across national boundaries (or from a subsidiary to a parent). Sophisticated international tax law writers, however, have adopted the position that virtually *all* forms of repayment to a parent company constitute dividends and thus are subject to local income tax laws.

A measure of the net present value of cash flows received by a parent from a foreign subsidiary can be modeled by the following equation:

$$V_{sub} = \sum_{t=1}^{n} \frac{(D_s + P_{is} + MSC_s)FX - (D_s + P_{is} + MCS_s)(FX)(T_d)}{(1 + r)^t} + \frac{(NW_n)(X)}{(1 + r)^n} \qquad (10)$$

where

$$FX = \text{The foreign exchange rate}$$
$$T_d = \text{The domestic tax rate}$$

Reinvestment versus Repatriation.   The desirability of embarking on a foreign investment may, in large measure, be linked to local repatriation laws. Consider, for example, the decision by McDonald's in the early 1990s to invest $40 million in a restaurant in Moscow. This multimillion dollar investment in the former Soviet Union was made with the full realization that existing (and current) Soviet laws prevented the repatriation of any of the restaurant's profits. Obviously, McDonald's Moscow investment was predicated on market growth objectives, not on cash flow repatriation.[16]

In the absence of repatriation constraints, an issue often arises as to where (i.e., in what country) a parent should invest its scarce resources. This decision is usually resolved using the following investment maxim: invest in that locale with the highest rate of return, adjusted for foreign exchange risk and political risk.

Blocked funds—either partially or fully—may have considerable value to a parent company, depending on its cash needs. Blocked funds, particularly those that can be reinvested at rates of return that equal or exceed those experienced by the parent company, can have considerable value if the objectives of the parent are market share oriented, as in the case of McDonald's. Blocked funds, however, also can be quite costly when the local rates of return are low and prospects for future repatriation of the blocked funds are negligible. When these conditions exist, alternative payment schemes from the subsidiary to the parent (i.e., intracompany loans, management fees, transfer prices) should be considered to reduce the magnitude of blocked funds.

Multinational Capital Budgeting: A Process Approach.   The analysis of international investment opportunities presents a challenge to most analysts. The complexity of this challenge can be managed, however, by sequentially addressing the problem in a stepwise fashion, as follows:

Step 1. *Develop rational assumptions.* The backbone of any DCF analysis is the forecasted cash flow data and, hence, pro forma financial statements. The key to meaningful pro forma data is the use of rational, well-reasoned assumptions regarding the subsidiary's future performance, local political risk, and the general economic conditions. Examining the local and regional business and political environment (i.e., country risk

---

[16]Since McDonald's original investment of $40 million, the exchange rate of the ruble relative to the U.S. dollar has fallen by more than 1,000 percent, causing a parallel decline in the value of this foreign investment as reflected on the parent's financial statements. This type of foreign exchange exposure can be hedged against in a variety of ways—a topic for consideration in Chapter 6.

analysis), as well as the structure of a subsidiary's industry, provide a useful starting point.[17] Assumptions as to market growth, inflation, changes in market share, and changes in costs must be incorporated in a project's pro forma analysis. The parent must also provide a rough business plan that identifies and quantifies the value and effects that can be obtained by putting the project under new, foreign ownership, as well as the effects of any restructuring activities, technology upgrades, and synergy exploitation. These plans should represent an important input to the project pro formas.

Step 2. *Develop project forecasts.* The parent should always first develop a set of profitability projections for the venture assuming status quo. This enables the investor to estimate the value of the project in its current state to the parent. A second set of projections should then be prepared incorporating the effects of any proposed reorganization or restructuring, infusion of capital, expertise, or technology, and the exploitation of any economies of scale or other synergies. This allows the parent to carefully consider the value of changes to the existing project.

As part of this phase, scenarios regarding changes in exchange rates and governmental regulations should be drafted. Also, at this stage, these scenarios, as well as all assumptions previously developed, should be subjected to **sensitivity analysis,** which refers to evaluating how changes in a given assumption or scenario will affect a project's operating performance or cash flows. This type of analysis is useful for two reasons. First, it highlights those assumptions or scenarios that create the greatest risk for project success; these assumptions and scenarios must be reevaluated for their reasonableness (i.e., if it is unlikely that a purchaser for an asset exists, assuming that an asset will be sold is an unrealistic scenario). Second, it identifies for parent management those assumptions that need to be most closely tracked after a project begins. Tracking the most influential factors will enable management to control, as much as humanly possible, the success of a foreign project.

Step 3. *Determine the appropriate discount rate.* Determining the appropriate discount rate (r) for any capital budgeting analysis is, at best, a tenuous science. In the typical domestic DCF analysis, the discount rate is usually set equal to the firm's weighted-average cost of capital (WACC) or some desired (or required) rate of return (in essence, a hurdle rate of return). For international investment opportunities, however, additional considerations are necessary.

---

[17]The use of country risk analysis has increased in recent years in both its importance and its sophistication. Interested readers should consider the related readings in the Suggested References at the end of this chapter. On a regular basis, *Euromoney* provides a country risk ranking. Its rankings for this text's focal countries are

Country Risk Ratings (1 = least risky)

	1995	*1998*
Japan	2	23
United States	5	2
Germany	7	3
United Kingdom	10	9
Sweden	21	13
Italy	22	17
S. Korea	26	34
Mexico	58	47
*No. of countries ranked	187	187

Source: *Euromoney,* March 1995, pp. 376–81, and October 1998, pp. 91–93.

In theory, the discount rate should be the *risk-adjusted* required rate of return on invested funds for a given company.[18] Thus, if the net cash flows for a given investment opportunity are less certain than would normally be the case for a firm (i.e., the probable distribution of returns is more dispersed than usual), the discount rate must be adjusted to reflect this uncertainty. Thus, increasing the discount rate is a fairly straightforward mechanism to capture the additional risk exposure that tends to characterize international investment projects. One disadvantage to the approach of adding a risk premium to the discount rate is that it assumes that the degree of risk is uniform over the life of the project. Due to the exponential nature of discounting, a uniformly higher discount rate (because of an add-on risk premium) substantially penalizes early cash flows and may not adequately reflect the risk in later periods.

Step 4. *Selecting an appropriate investment horizon and terminal value.* The final decisions to be made before undertaking a project analysis concern the likely time horizon of the project and the identification of any residual or terminal value. The time horizon of a project should be tied to the expected useful life of the asset or investment being purchased, whereas the terminal value should be determined with reference to rational assumptions regarding the value of the assets at the time of their disposal. In general, most professional analysts work with time horizons of five to seven years. Investment horizons longer than seven years are usually so difficult to predict with any reasonable degree of certainty that analysts try to avoid doing so. Moreover, adopting a shorter time horizon (e.g., three to five years) is another means to reflect additional risk exposure in one's analysis.

The terminal value of a project represents the expected cash flows, if any, to be received on termination or abandonment of a project. Terminal values are usually difficult to predict, particularly when the investment horizon exceeds five years, although we suggested the use of balance sheet–based approaches in the previous section.[19]

An Illustration

A U.S.–based trading company is considering the acquisition of Kaufmann & Hess, GmbH (K&H). With respect to this investment, the following facts have been gathered:

German tax rates	
Corporate income tax	40%
Withholding tax on dividends	15%
U.S. tax rates	
Corporate income tax (with credit given for foreign withholding taxes paid)	36%
Exchange rate	1.6 DM/$1 U.S.

To determine an appropriate purchase price, executives of the U.S. company have agreed on the following assumptions for purposes of preparing pro forma data regarding the investment:

- Sales dollar volumes will increase in response to new export markets at the rate of 10 percent per annum through 2001 and 7 percent per annum thereafter through 2004. Asset levels and cost structure assumptions are identical to those made earlier.

- The German DM is projected to depreciate 2 percent per annum against the U.S. dollar.

---

[18]This rate may actually be less than the parent's WACC if the funds can be borrowed elsewhere at a lower cost of capital.

[19]For those investments expected to continue in perpetuity, a terminal value can be estimated using any number of available growth models. For example, see F. J. Weston and T. E. Copeland, *Managerial Finance* (New York: Harcourt, Brace, Jovanovich, 1989), pp. 696–712.

- The residual value at the end of year 2004 is approximately 110 percent of the December 31, 2004, projected net worth. Since the U.S. company plans to hold K&H indefinitely, tax effects of the terminal value are ignored.
- In 2000, all excess cash will be used to pay down short-term debt. Thereafter, all excess cash will be remitted to the parent company in the form of dividends.

The U.S. executives have determined that they will be willing to pay a price equal to the present value of the project. For purposes of the analysis, the executives have decided to use a discounted cash flow approach over a five-year time horizon with a 14 percent discount rate. The risks of expropriation and of blocked funds were both considered to be negligible.

Analysis.   Exhibit 4–10 presents projected financial statements for K&H over the five-year time horizon. Note that, except for minor reformatting for the purpose of concise-ness, the first column of Exhibit 4–10 is identical to the projections in Exhibits 4–8 and

---

EXHIBIT 4–10

KAUFMANN & HESS, GmbH
Projected Financial Statements

	2000	*2001*	*2002*	*2003*	*2004*
Income Statement					
Sales	DM1,100.0	1,210.0	1,294.7	1,385.3	1,482.3
Cost of goods sold	605.0	665.5	712.1	761.9	815.2
Other operating expenses	220.0	242.0	258.9	277.0	296.4
Operating income	**DM 275.0**	**302.5**	**323.7**	**346.4**	**370.7**
Interest	21.2	26.1	21.7	22.2	22.6
Net income before taxes	**DM 253.8**	**276.4**	**302.0**	**324.2**	**348.1**
Taxes	101.5	110.6	120.8	129.7	139.2
Net income	**DM 152.3**	**165.8**	**181.2**	**194.5**	**208.9**
Balance Sheet					
Cash	DM 11.0	12.1	12.9	13.8	14.8
Accounts receivable	110.0	121.0	129.5	138.6	148.3
Inventory	55.0	60.5	64.7	69.2	74.0
Fixed assets, net	374.0	411.4	440.2	471.0	504.0
Total assets	**DM 550.0**	**605.0**	**647.4**	**692.7**	**741.2**
Accounts payable—trade	DM 49.5	54.5	58.3	62.4	66.8
Short-term debt	113.2	113.2	113.2	113.2	113.2
Long-term debt	50.0	50.0	50.0	50.0	50.0
Total liabilities	**DM 212.7**	**217.7**	**221.5**	**225.6**	**230.0**
Paid-in capital	30.0	30.0	30.0	30.0	30.0
Retained earnings	307.3	357.3	395.9	437.1	481.2
Total equities	**DM 550.0**	**605.0**	**647.4**	**692.7**	**741.2**
Statement of Cash Flows					
Net income	DM 152.3	165.8	181.2	194.5	208.9
Adjustments					
Change in net working capital	(10.5)	(11.5)	(8.9)	(9.5)	(10.1)
Change in fixed assets	(34.0)	(37.4)	(28.8)	(30.8)	(33.0)
Cash provided by operations	**DM 107.8**	**116.9**	**143.5**	**154.2**	**165.8**
Add. (dec.) in short-term debt	(96.8)	0.0	0.0	0.0	0.0
Add. (dec.) in long-term debt	0.0	0.0	0.0	0.0	0.0
Add. (dec.) in paid-in capital	0.0	0.0	0.0	0.0	0.0
Dividends	(10.0)	(115.8)	(142.6)	(153.3)	(164.8)
Net cash from financing	**DM (106.8)**	**(115.8)**	**(142.6)**	**(153.3)**	**(164.8)**
Change in cash	**DM 1.0**	**1.1**	**0.9**	**0.9**	**1.0**

EXHIBIT 4–11

KAUFMANN & HESS, GmbH
Valuation by U.S. Firm

	Total	2000	2001	2002	2003	2004
Dividends remitted by K&H		DM 10.0	DM 115.8	DM 142.6	DM 153.3	DM 164.8
Less: 15% withholding		1.5	17.4	21.4	23.0	24.7
Net dividends		DM 8.5	DM 98.4	DM 121.2	DM 130.3	DM 140.1
Foreign exchange rate		1.632	1.665	1.698	1.732	1.767
Dollar value of dividends net of German withholding taxes		$ 5.2	$ 59.1	$ 71.4	$ 75.2	$ 79.3
Less: U.S. taxes		1.9	21.3	25.7	27.1	28.5
Net cash flow from dividends		$ 3.3	$ 37.8	$ 45.7	$ 48.1	$ 50.8
Terminal net work						$ 511.2
Adjustment factor						1.1
						562.3
Net cash flows		$ 3.3	$ 37.8	$ 45.7	$ 48.1	$ 613.1
Interest factor		0.8772	0.7695	0.6750	0.5921	0.5194
Present value	$ 409.7	$ 2.9	$ 29.1	$ 30.8	$ 28.5	$ 318.4

4–9. Exhibit 4–11 illustrates the value calculation using Equation (10). The analysis reveals that the U.S. company should be willing to pay $409,700 U.S. (DM655,520) on December 31, 1999, to acquire the German operations.

Summary

Disaggregations of financial statement ratios are useful when they capture, or measure, in a convenient format, important factors of interest in managing a firm. A variant of the Du Pont formula described in this chapter captures in one equation the impact of both operating and financing decisions on financial statements.

Firm valuation concepts and pro forma financial statements are very closely linked. Reference to financial statement numbers are often a reference point for estimates of firm value (e.g., multiples of book assets, book net worth, operating income) and pro forma financial statements are an important way to explicitly consider the impact of future events on firm value.

Valuation of international investment opportunities are significantly more complex than domestic ones. Investors face additional sources of risk, including repatriation risk and foreign exchange risk.

Suggested References

Andriole, S. J., and G. W. Hopple. "An Overview of Political Instability Research Methodologies: Basic and Applied Recommendations for the Corporate Analysts." In Global Risk Assessment, ed. J. Rogers, vol. 3, 1988.

Copeland, T., T. Koller, and J. Murrin. Valuation: Measuring and Managing the Value of Companies. New York: John Wiley, 1990.

De la Torre, J., and D. H. Neckar. "Forecasting Political Risks for International Operations." International Journal of Forecasting (1988).

Haendel, D. Foreign Investment: The Management of Political Risk. Hartford, CN: Westview Press, 1979.

Heymann, H., R. Bloom, and R. Auster, "Cost-Volume-Profit Analysis Applied to Cash Management," Cashflow, July–August, 1984.

Li, R. P. "Investment and Political Risk Analyses: Framework and Strategies." In Global Risk Assessment, ed. J. Rogers, vol. 3, 1988.

Meek, G. "U.S. Security Market Responses to Alternate Earnings Disclosures of Non–U.S. Multinational Corporations." The Accounting Review, April 1983.

Rappaport, A. Creating Shareholder Value: The New Standard for Business Performances. New York: The Free Press, 1986.

Roll, R. "Industrial Structure and the Comparative Behavior of International Stock Market Indices." The Journal of Finance, March 1992.

Weston, F. J., and T. E. Copeland. Managerial Finance. New York: Harcourt Brace Jovanovich, 1989.

APPENDIX 4A
EXTENDING THE ROE MODEL

The development of modern financial management theory has focused increased attention on management's ability to generate returns to shareholders, and, consequently, managerial attention to financing decisions (e.g., the use of debt versus equity capital) is ever more intense. This led to the identification of a shortcoming in the Du Pont formula as a basis for modern financial statement analysis, namely the formula's inability to conveniently distinguish between the effects of management's operating decisions from those of its financing decisions on the return on invested capital.

For example, consider two firms that are identical in every respect, except that Firm A financed its asset acquisitions using only equity capital, while Firm B is financed with a debt to equity ratio of 25 percent. (In Commonwealth countries such as Australia, Canada, New Zealand, and Great Britain, the use of debt financing is referred to as *gearing;* in the context of these illustrations, we use the more common U.S. rubric of *leverage*.)[1] Although Firms A and B are equally profitable before considering interest expense, Firm A's ROA is higher than that of Firm B.[2] A refinement of ROA, **unleveraged ROA** (UROA), that overcomes this shortcoming and reflects the equality of operating performance for both firms, is given by the following:

$$\text{UROA} = \frac{\text{Net Income} + \text{Interest expense} \times (1 - \text{Incremental tax rate})}{\text{Average total assets}} \quad (1)$$

$$= \frac{NI + I(1 - TR)}{ATA}$$

where S refers to a company's net sales and ATA refers to its average total assets. Exhibit 4A–1 illustrates the deconstruction of UROA for Cray Electronics.

Now that ROA has been "deleveraged," a remaining refinement is to reinsert the effects of financial leverage in the Du Pont formula in such a way that it can be separately identified. The objective of this refinement is to develop an analytical framework that portrays some overall index of profitability as a multiplicative function of UROA and the effects of management's financing decisions on profitability. The general form of the framework should be as follows:

$$\text{Overall index of profitability} = UROA \times \text{Financial leverage} \quad (3)$$

---

[1]In general, $\text{Gearing} = \frac{\text{Interest-bearing debt}}{\text{Owners' equity}}$; $\text{Leverage} = \frac{\text{Total assets}}{\text{Owners' equity}}$.

[2]Implicit to this argument is that both debt and equity capital bear an opportunity cost. In the case of debt, this opportunity cost is explicitly captured by the deduction of "interest expense" on the income statement, whereas no parallel charge for equity capital is reflected in a firm's net income.

EXHIBIT 4A–1

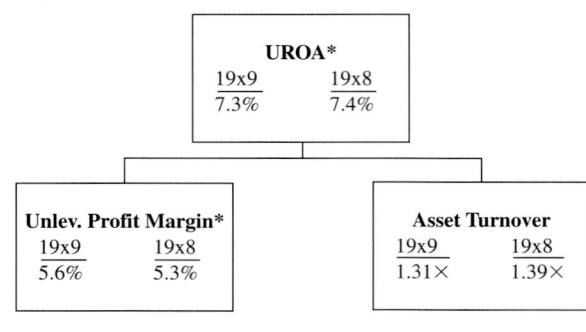

**Unleveraged ROA Analysis for
Cray Electronics Holdings Plc**

Although the ROA for Cray Electronics Holdings increased from 2.2 to 4.5 percent from 19x8 to 19x9, UROA can be seen to decrease slightly. The difference must be due to interest expense, generally viewed to be a nonoperating item. The data reveal that unleveraged profit margin improved but not sufficiently to offset the decline in asset turnover.

*A 33 percent incremental tax rate was used.

We begin extending the framework by designating the **return on common equity** (ROCE) as the new overall index of corporate performance:

$$\text{ROCE} = \frac{NI - PD}{ACEQ} \qquad (4)$$

PD in Equation (4) represents the dividends paid to preferred shareholders, and *ACEQ* is the average common equity for the period. The quantity (*NI* − *PD*) is referred to as *net income available to common shareholders*. Notice that since preferred dividend distributions are not tax deductible in the United States, there is no after-tax effect to consider. (In other countries such as Germany, preferred dividends are treated like interest expense for tax purposes, and thus the tax effect must be incorporated in Equation (3) by multiplying *PD* by 1 minus the incremental tax rate.) By excluding required distribution to preferred shareholders, ROCE reflects a measure of real returns to a company's true (i.e., voting) owners. It reflects the commonly held view that the principal goal of management should be to maximize shareholder wealth. Equation 3 can now be restated as follows:

$$\text{ROCE} = UROA \times \text{Financial leverage} \qquad (5)$$

Intuitively, financial leverage has the effect of magnifying operating results: a positive UROA should translate into an even higher ROCE when financial leverage is present. A useful ratio that portrays the extent of a company's financial leverage is the **common shareholders' capital structure leverage ratio** (CSL):

$$\text{Common shareholders' capital structure leverage ratio} = \frac{\text{Average total assets}}{\text{Average common equity}} \qquad (6)$$

CSL measures the extent to which common shareholders, as opposed to other suppliers of capital, have financed a company's investment in assets. In the context of this ratio, average common equity (ACEQ) is the average of total shareholders' equity excluding preferred shareholders' equity and minority interest.[3] CSL is commonly greater than or equal to 1 (so long as ACEQ is

---

[3]For simplicity, this section assumes "minority interest" of zero. If it were greater than zero, minority interest in earnings of subsidiaries would be treated as interest expense.

greater than zero) and can therefore be viewed as a leveraging factor; it has the effect of magnifying UROA.

CSL alone, however, does not fully explain the effects of financial leverage on the computation of ROCE. In the following equation, we develop the ROCE deconstruction further by (1) incorporating CSL into the ROCE analysis framework, (2) separating UROA into its unleveraged profit margin and asset turnover components, and (3) creating a new variable, Z, to denote the remaining unexplained multiplicative component of ROCE:

$$\text{ROCE:} = \frac{\text{Unleveraged}}{\text{profit margin}} \times \frac{\text{Asset}}{\text{turnover}} \times \frac{\text{Capital}}{\text{structure}} \times Z \qquad (7)$$

Substituting the formulas for ROCE, unleveraged profit margin, asset turnover, and capital structure leverage into equation (7), and then solving for Z, we obtain an expression for Z that we interpret as **common equity's share of operating earnings** (CSOE):

$$Z = \frac{NI - PD}{NI + I(1 - TR)} = \text{Common equity's share of operating earnings} = \text{CSOE} \qquad (8)$$

We then substitute CSOE in Equation (7) to obtain our completed ROCE analysis framework:

$$\text{ROCE} = \frac{NI + I(1 - TR)}{S} \times \frac{S}{ATA} \times \frac{ATA}{ACEO} \times \frac{NI - PD}{NI + I(1 - TR)} \qquad (9)$$

$$= \frac{\text{Unleveraged}}{\text{profit margin}} \times \frac{\text{Asset}}{\text{turnover}} \times \frac{\text{Capital structure}}{\text{leverage}} \times \frac{\text{Common equity}}{\text{share of}} \atop \text{operating earnings}$$

Common equity's share of operating earnings (CSOE) measures the proportion of a company's operating earnings (i.e., earnings before payments to creditors and preferred shareholders) allocable to the common shareholders. If net income after all payments to preferred shareholders—that is, the numerator in Equation (8)—is positive, the denominator of CSOE will be greater than its numerator. And, since the value of CSOE must range between zero and 1, the effect of CSOE on ROCE is to dampen the effect of capital structure leverage because the value of CSOE is similarly between zero and 1.

ROCE, like ROA and UROA, can be expressed by various levels of subcomponents, and this deconstruction is illustrated in Exhibit 4A–2 for Cray Electronics Holdings.

UROA: A Closer Look at Its Determinants

In general, two explanations for differences in UROA have been found to aid in the development of a coherent and succinct financial analysis, and they are the extent of a company's **operating leverage** and its **product life cycle.**[4]

Operating Leverage.   Firms operate with different mixtures of fixed and variable operating costs. Capital intensive companies, for example, incur relatively large amounts of depreciation expense, which is more or less fixed for any given period. Most retailers and wholesalers, by contrast, incur a high proportion of variable costs. Firms with a high proportion of fixed costs usually experience significant increases in operating income as their volume of sales increase. This occurs because fixed costs are being spread over a larger number of units sold, resulting in a decrease in the average unit cost.

The process of operating with a high proportion of fixed costs is referred to as **operating leverage.** Firms with high levels of operating leverage usually experience greater variability in their UROAs than firms with lower levels of operating leverage. The proportion of total assets composed

---

[4]Selling, T. and Stickney, C., "The Effect of Business Environment and Strategy on a Firm's Rate of Return on Assets," *Financial Analysts Journal,* Jan/Feb 1989, pp. 43–52.

EXHIBIT 4A–2

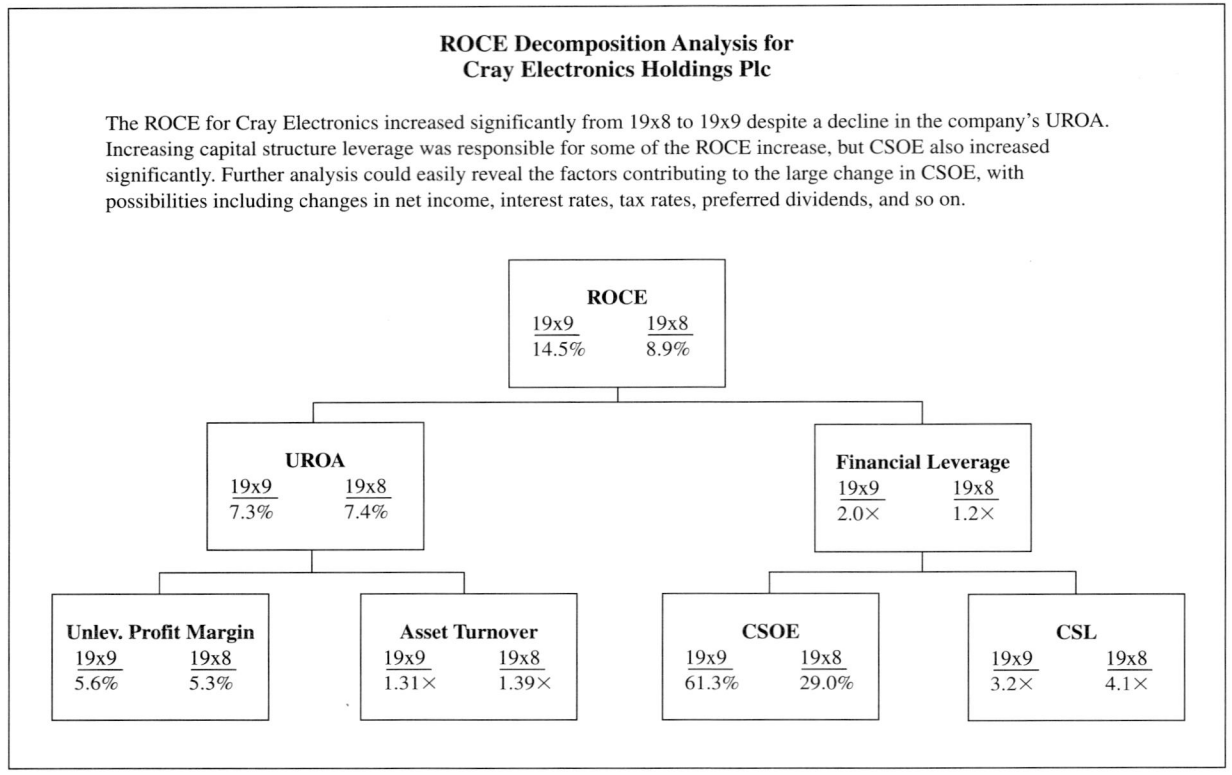

**ROCE Decomposition Analysis for
Cray Electronics Holdings Plc**

The ROCE for Cray Electronics increased significantly from 19x8 to 19x9 despite a decline in the company's UROA. Increasing capital structure leverage was responsible for some of the ROCE increase, but CSOE also increased significantly. Further analysis could easily reveal the factors contributing to the large change in CSOE, with possibilities including changes in net income, interest rates, tax rates, preferred dividends, and so on.

of fixed (or plant) assets—the **capital intensity ratio**—indicates the degree of a company's operating leverage. Higher levels of the capital intensity ratio are associated with high levels of UROA variability. Data also indicate that, consistent with modern financial theory, industries with high UROAs tend to have a high variability in UROAs, as measured by its standard deviation.

Product Life Cycle.   Product life cycle theory posits that products (and therefore the companies that produce them) move through four identifiable phases: introduction, growth, maturity, and decline. During the introduction and growth phases, a firm's focus is on product development (product R&D spending), market development (advertising and other promotional spending), and capacity enlargement (capital spending). The objective of these activities is to gain market acceptance and market share. During the maturity phase, as competition becomes more intense, emphasis shifts to reducing costs through improved capacity utilization (in gaining economies of scale) and more efficient production. During the decline phase, firms exit the market as sales decline and profit opportunities diminish.

During the introduction and early growth phases, expenditures on product development and marketing, coupled with relatively low sales levels, usually lead to negative ROAs and/or UROAs. As sales accelerate during the high-growth phase, operating income and UROAs turn positive. The rate of growth in UROAs is dampened during this phase, however, as extensive product development, marketing, and depreciation expenses moderate operating income, but heavy capital expenditures to build capacity for higher future sales increase the denominator of UROA. UROA usually increases significantly during the maturity phase because of the benefits of economies of scale and learning curve phenomena, as well as the general curtailment of capital expenditures. Finally, UROA deteriorates during the decline phase as operating income decreases, but it may remain positive or even increase for some time into this phase.

The concept of product life cycle can be applied most effectively to financial statements generated for a firms' **strategic business units** (SBUs)—independent, autonomous business segments that could be managed as viable and isolated concerns. The concept can be extended, however, to an entire firm by assessing the mix of products within the firm. For example, a computer firm often produces products that range from their introduction phase to their decline phase, although most computer firms are today probably in the later part of their high-growth phase. Other firms may be in a bipolar position: They have few mature products but many products in the other three categories. The food-processing industry is fully mature, although new products are continually being introduced. The U.S. steel industry might be viewed as being in the decline phase, although some companies have modernized production sufficiently to stave off decline. The Japanese steel industry, on the other hand, is generally viewed as being in the maturity phase.

Profit Margin–Asset Turnover Mix.   Possible explanations for differences in the profit margin–asset turnover mix also come from the disciplines of economics and business strategy. Economic theory helps to explain how capacity and competitive constraints affect the profit margin and asset turnover mix, and business strategy helps to explain how product differentiation and cost leadership strategies affect the mix.

Capacity and Competitive Constraints.   Figure 4A–1 depicts the ideas of capacity and competitive constraints in the context of UROA analysis. The two curves in Figure 4A–1 represent two levels of UROA; the curve farthest from the origin of the graph represents the higher of the two UROA levels. Both UROA levels depicted can be achieved by an infinite number of total asset turnover and unleveraged profit margin combinations. Managers seeking to maximize UROA (i.e., to be on a curve as far as possible from the origin) face constraints that limit the strategies that they can implement to increase their UROA.

Managers in industries that have heavy fixed capacity costs and require lengthy periods to add new capacity operate under a *capacity constraint.* As a consequence, there is an upper limit on the level of asset turnover that they can achieve. To attract sufficient capital, these managers must generate relatively high profit margins. The high profit margins usually are achieved through some form of entry barrier (e.g., large capital requirements, high risk, or regulation) and the attainment of economies of scale (i.e., spreading the fixed capacity costs over a large number of units sold). Examples of industries that operate under a capacity constraint are telecommunications, real estate, and oil exploration. These firms tend to operate in the area of section (A) of Figure 4A–1.

Managers in industries whose products are commodity like in nature, that have few entry barriers, and have intense competition operate under a *competitive constraint;* that is, there is an upper limit on the profit margin that they can achieve. To attract sufficient capital, these managers must strive for higher asset turnover. High asset turnover might be achieved by minimizing fixed costs, purchasing in sufficient quantities to realize discounts, or integrating vertically or horizontally to obtain cost savings. Such actions to control costs are also usually matched with aggressively low prices to gain market share and drive out marginal firms. Most retailers and wholesalers operate under a competitive constraint and thus are usually found to operate in section (C) of Figure 4A–1.

Managers of firms that operate in section (B) of Figure 4A–1 are not affected to a significant degree by either capacity or competitive constraints, at least as compared to those that operate in the tails of the curves. Thus, they have more latitude to take actions that will increase profit margin, asset turnover, or both, to achieve a higher UROA.

Product Differentiation versus Cost Leadership.   The thrust of a *product-differentiation strategy* is to create a product that is perceived industrywide to be unique and to therefore earn a higher profit margin by charging a higher price. The differentiation could relate to product capabilities, product quality, service, channels of distribution, or some other factor. The thrust of a *cost-leadership strategy* is to become the lowest-cost producer in a market to be able to charge the lowest prices and achieve the highest volume. The low-cost position can be achieved through

FIGURE 4A–1

Constraints on profit margin–asset turnover mix

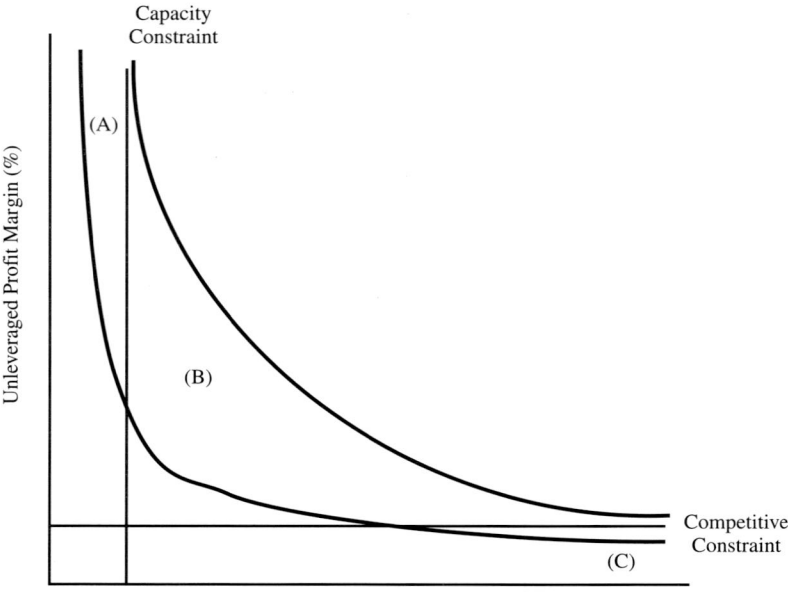

**Constraints on
Profit Margin–Asset Turnover Mix**

economies of scale, production efficiencies, outsourcing or similar factors, or asset parsimony (maintaining strict controls on investments in receivables, inventories, and plant and equipment).

The product-differentiation strategy may be viewed as profit-margin focused, whereas the cost leadership strategy is primarily asset-turnover focused. Note that movements toward (A) of Figure 4A–1 are product-differentiation oriented, and movements in the direction of (C) from any point along the UROA curves are cost-leadership oriented. Thus, although grocery stores will likely cluster around (C), some grocery stores will place heavy emphasis on specialty products (e.g., bakery, delicatessen, fresh flowers, VCR rentals, prescription drugs) that have higher profit margins than most grocery products.

Flexibility in trading off profit margin versus asset turnover is important when a firm considers its strategic alternatives (product differentiation versus cost leadership). Consider, for example, a firm with a profit margin–asset turnover mix marked as (A) in Figure 4A–1. This firm will have to give up significant profit margin to obtain a meaningful increase in asset turnover. To increase UROA, therefore, it should emphasize actions that increase profit margin. Firms in section (C), on the other hand, will have to give up considerable asset turnover to obtain much of an increase in profit margin. To increase UROA, these firms should emphasize actions that increase asset turnover. For firms operating in section (B), however, trade-offs of margin for turnover are more equal. Such firms would seem to have greater flexibility to design strategies that promote profit margin or asset turnover, or some combination (and/or some particular element[s] of these two components) when striving to increase UROA.

In summary, microeconomic and business strategy concepts are useful in understanding the behavior of UROA over time and across firms and industries. UROA variability differs across firms and industries, for example, according to their levels of operating leverage. UROA also differs across firms as products pass through different stages in their life cycles. Shortly we will investigate how forecasts of financial variables such as UROA can be transformed into pro forma financial statements.

The Du Pont Formula: A Final Comment

The Du Pont formula represents a powerful analytical framework to evaluate the financial health of most firms. A key assumption inherent in the formula is that financial accounting provides relevant and reliable measurements of management performance and changing business conditions. In countries such as Germany and Japan, where management strategies purportedly have much longer time horizons and where there is closer conformity between accounting and taxable income, the Du Pont formula may not so clearly capture the year-to-year financial effects of management performance and the dynamics of business environments. One modification to the framework used in this chapter to accommodate different time horizons is to compute ratios over longer time periods, say three to five years. For example, it may be more valid to compare ROCEs for a five-year period when comparing the ROCE of Cray Holdings to those of a Japanese firm in the same industry.[5]

In countries outside the United States, management objectives are explicitly different than simply maximizing common shareholder wealth. Consequently, alternative approaches may be superior to the Du Pont formula for evaluating management's progress toward achieving objectives that are not captured by ROA or ROCE. However, an investor's interest in the company may still remain simple: to choose a portfolio of investments that maximize return on investment given a target level of risk. Thus, a focus on ROA and ROCE may still be appropriate for the investor, even if management does not evaluate themselves the same way. Some alternatives to the Du Pont formula will be discussed in Chapters 7–13, as we consider the unique environmental setting of the individual countries.

---

[5]Comparing financial ratios over extended horizons is sometimes sufficient to overcome differences in cultural context as reflected in accounting methods; in other cases, it is not, and some restatement is necessary (see Chapter 6).

APPENDIX 4B
KAUFMANN & HESS, GMBH: DISPLAYED FORMULAS FOR EXCEL™ SPREADSHEET

	A	B	C	D
1	Interest rate on STD	0.1		
2	Interest rate on LTD	0.12		
3	Tax Rate	0.4		
4	Sales growth rate	0.1		
5				
6				
7		Historical Amounts		Projected
8	Income Statement			
9	Sales	1000		=B9*(1+$B$4)
10	Cost of goods sold	550	=B10/$B$9	=C10*$D$9
11	Other operating expenses	200	=B11/$B$9	=C11*$D$9
12	Operating Income	=B9-B10-B11		=D9-D10-D11
13	Interest	27		=B1*(B28+D28)/2+B2*(B29+D29)/2
14	Net income before taxes	=B12-B13		=D12-D13
15	Taxes	=B14*$B$3		=D14*$B$3
16	Net Income	=B14-B15		=D14-D15
17	Less: dividends	10		=B17
18	Change in retained earnings	=B16-B17		=D16-D17
19				
20	Balance Sheet			
21	Cash	10	=B21/$B$25	=B21/$B$25*$D$25
22	Accounts receivable	100	=B22/$B$25	=B22/$B$25*$D$25
23	Inventory	50	=B23/$B$25	=B23/$B$25*$D$25
24	Fixed assets, net	340	=B24/$B$25	=B24/$B$25*$D$25
25	Total assets	=SUM(B21:B24)	=SUM(C21:C24)	=B25/B9*D9
26				
27	Accounts payable—trade	45	=B27/B25	=C27*D25
28	Short-term debt	210		=D37-D38-D32-D29-D27
29	Long-term debt	50		=B29
30	Total liabilities	=SUM(B27:B29)		=SUM(D27:D29)
31				
32	Paid-in capial	30		=B32
33	Beginning retained earnings	41.2		=B36
34	Add: Net income	=B16		=D16
35	Less: Dividends	=B17		=D17
36	Ending retained earnings	165		=D33+D34-D35
37	Total equities	=B30+B32+B36		=D25

Exercises

4.1 Interpreting Ratios

One day at work at the Valley National Bank, a co-worker from the international lending division approaches you for assistance. This credit analyst has made a number of calculations and notes, but is obviously puzzled by what the results mean: "None of this makes any sense to me; I just don't understand what's going on with this British borrower!" Her numerical analysis included the following data:

	2000	1999
Return on equity	22%	19%
Working capital	£ 20,000	£ 5,000
Current ratio	1.25	1.07
Quick ratio	0.50	0.50
Average days' receivable outstanding	73	81
Inventory turnover	1.25×	1.69×
Times interest earned	3.75×	4.17×
Long-term debt to equity ratio	0.80	0.60
Dividends paid to shareholders' equity ratio	22%	19%
Shares outstanding	5,000,000	5,000,000

Required:

Try to help your co-worker develop an understanding of this borrower by identifying the important financial trends suggested by these data.

4.2 Ratio Analysis and Alternative GAAP

Ratios may be influenced by real changes in the operating performance of a company, as well as by artificial changes in a company's reported accounting numbers. Consider, for example, the case of FIFO Company and LIFO Company, which are identical in every respect except the method used to value inventory: LIFO Company uses the LIFO method, FIFO Company uses the FIFO method. The following are the most recent income statement data and balance sheets for the two Japanese companies:

Income Statement Data

	FIFO Company	LIFO Company
Sales	¥40,000,000	¥40,000,000
Less: Cost of sales	(18,400,000)	(22,560,000)
Gross margin	21,600,000	17,440,000
Less: Operating expenses	(10,000,000)	(10,000,000)
Net income	¥11,600,000	¥ 7,440,000

Balance Sheet Data

	FIFO Company	LIFO Company
Quick assets	¥18,000,000	¥18,000,000
Inventory	7,600,000	3,440,000
Total current assets	¥25,600,000	¥21,440,000
Noncurrent assets (net)	40,000,000	40,000,000
Total assets	¥65,600,000	¥61,440,000
Current liabilities	¥ 8,400,000	¥ 8,400,000
Noncurrent liabilities	18,000,000	18,000,000
Total liabilities	¥26,400,000	¥26,400,000
Total shareholders' equity	39,200,000	35,040,000
Total equities	¥65,600,000	¥61,440,000

Required:

Using the preceding financial data, calculate the following financial indicators for each firm:

- a. Current ratio.
- b. Inventory turnover ratio.
- c. Average number of days' inventory on hand.
- d. Return on total assets ratio.
- e. Total debt to total assets ratio.
- f. Long-term debt to shareholders' equity ratio.
- g. Gross margin ratio.
- h. Return on sales ratio.
- i. Return on equity ratio.
- j. Earnings per share (assume 2 million shares outstanding).

Based on these ratios, which company represents the following:

- k. The best investment opportunity?
- l. The best acquisition opportunity?
- m. The best lending opportunity?

4.3 Cash Flow Analysis

It was early 1999, and Pam Herberger was sitting at her desk staring at a set of financial statements. The statements, which follow, were those of the HFS Corporation, a British corporation. They represented the raw materials for Pam's first assignment as a credit analyst in the international lending division of Valley National Bank.

Herberger's immediate supervisor, Katherine Miller, had received the HFS statements as part of a loan application package. Because HFS was a privately held company, the statements did not have to conform to existing FASB or SEC disclosure standards; however, the only significant omission that Miller had noticed was the absence of a cash flow statement. Rather than ask the new customer to provide one, which might delay the loan review process, she decided to ask Pam to derive one from the available financial data.

Required:

- (a) Prepare a statement of cash flows for HFS for 1999.
- (b) On the basis of your answer to part (a), and any other analysis that you believe is necessary, prepare an evaluation of the creditworthiness of HFS, assuming that the company is interested in (1) a short-term loan of £15 million for working capital purposes and (2) a £75 million five-year loan for capital asset purchases.

HFS CORPORATION
Statement of Income
(in thousands)

	As of December 31	
	1999	*1998*
Net revenue	£22,733	£60,095
Less: Costs and expenses		
Cost of operations	28,250	13,818
General and administrative	5,777	2,541
Interest	9,901	5,389
Depreciation and amortization	22,708	7,118
	66,636	28,866
Net income before income taxes	56,097	31,229
Provision for income taxes:		
Current	203	
Deferred	24,266	12,804
Total	24,469	12,804
Net income after income taxes	31,628	18,425
Dividends paid	9,134	4,268
Transferred to retained earnings	£22,494	£14,157

HFS CORPORATION
Comparative Balance Sheets
(in thousands)

	As of December 31	
	1999	*1998*
Assets		
Current assets		
Cash	£ 14,696	£ 16,390
Receivables		
Trade	20,378	10,808
Other	324	866
Inventories	15,967	3,843
Prepaid expenses	197	2,414
Total current assets	£ 51,562	£ 34,321
Noncurrent assets:		
Property, plant, and equipment (at cost)	258,908	152,145
Less: Accumulated depreciation	(34,224)	(11,516)
Total noncurrent assets	224,684	140,629
Deferred charges and other assets	2,041	1,666
Total assets	£278,287	£176,616

Liabilities and Shareholders' Equity

Current liabilities		
Accounts payable	£ 20,160	£ 16,710
Accrued expenses payable	2,901	1,077
Income taxes payable	203	–0–
Current maturities on long-term debt	6,826	5,301
Total current liabilities	30,090	23,088
Long-term liabilities		
Convertible subordinated debentures	10,056	10,061
Notes payable	123,949	79,900
Deferred income taxes	44,730	20,464
Total long-term liabilities	178,735	110,425
Shareholders' equity		
Capital stock	1,380	912
Additional paid-in capital	19,949	16,552
Retained earnings	48,133	25,639
Total shareholders' equity	69,462	43,103
Total liabilities and shareholders' equity	£278,287	£176,616

4.4 Ratios Tell a Story

Corporate financial positions, results of operations, and cash flows vary substantially among companies. One of the principal reasons for the variation can be traced to the characteristics of the industries within which the companies operate. Some industries require large investments in property, plant, and equipment, whereas other industries do not. In some industries, the product-pricing structure allows companies to earn significant profit margins, while in other industries the profit margins are low. In most low-margin industries, however, companies often experience a relatively high volume of product throughput. Credit terms also vary among industries, with companies in some industries relying heavily on cash sales.

A second reason for corporate financial statement variation is due to different management philosophies and competencies. Some managements try to maintain a close relationship between production or service capacity and current demand, while others are more intent on building capacity in anticipation of demand. Some managements prefer a low debt-to-equity relationship, while others rely heavily on borrowed funds. Certainly the nature of the industry also affects managements' willingness to incur debt. Financial statement differences among competing companies that follow similar operating policies result, at least in part, from different management capabilities.

A third reason for corporate financial statement variation is attributable to the use of alternate accounting principles and to different estimates and judgments made in applying specific accounting principles. Comparisons of the financial statements of companies from different countries need to be made with the understanding that the generally accepted accounting principles used in their preparation are not uniform around the world.

This exercise was prepared by Robert M. Conroy and E. Richard Brownlee II. Copyright ©1992 by the Darden Graduate Business School Foundation, Charlottesville, Virginia.

These differences in industry characteristics, company policies, management philosophies and competencies, and accounting principles can be highlighted through the analysis of financial ratios. Exhibit 1 presents balance sheets, in percentage form, and selected ratios computed from the 1990 balance sheets and income statements of the following 11 companies:

A. Advertising agency (Europe).

B. Airline (North America).

C. Automobile manufacturer (Europe).

D. Commercial bank (North America).

E. Department store (North America).

F. Electronic game manufacturer (Asia).

G. Food and convenience stores (Asia).

H. Oil company—refining and production (Europe).

I. Pharmaceuticals (North America).

J. Public utility—gas (Asia).

K. Steel producer (Asia).

Using the data presented in Exhibit 1, identify each of the 11 companies represented. Give your reasons for associating a particular company with a particular column of data. The ratios in Exhibit 1 are based on the following formulae:

1. Current ratio $= \dfrac{\text{Total current assets}}{\text{Total current liabilities}}$

2. Acid test (quick ratio) $= \dfrac{\text{Quick assets (usually, Current assets} - \text{Inventory)}}{\text{Total current liabilities}}$

3. ROS (return on sales) $= \dfrac{\text{Net income}}{\text{Net sales}}$

4. Total asset turnover $= \dfrac{\text{Net sales}}{\text{Average total assets}}$

5. ROA (return on total assets) $=$ ROS $\times$ Asset turnover

   $= \dfrac{\text{Net income}}{\text{Average total assets}}$

6. Financial leverage $= \dfrac{\text{Average total assets}}{\text{Average total stockholders' equity}}$

7. ROE (return on equity) $=$ ROA $\times$ Financial leverage

   $= \dfrac{\text{Net income}}{\text{Average total stockholders' equity}}$

8. Long-term debt to capital $= \dfrac{\text{Long-term debt}}{\text{Long-term debt} + \text{Total stockholders' equity}}$

9. Inventory turnover $= \dfrac{\text{Cost of goods sold}}{\text{Average inventory during the period}}$

10. Receivables collection (days) $= \dfrac{\text{Average accounts receivable during the period}}{\text{Net sales/365 days}}$

EXHIBIT 1

Companies' Data

	1	2	3	4	5	6	7	8	9	10	11
Assets											
Cash & equivalents	1.0%	2.1%	27.7%	22.1%	10.0%	19.8%	6.4%	7.1%	17.2%	61.6%	14.9%
Accounts receivable	16.5	16.2	2.8	27.4	52.7	12.3	5.3	87.7	14.3	7.7	16.8
Inventory	23.7	11.3	6.3	11.7	1.8	3.4	0.5	0.0	19.5	15.9	11.1
Other current assets	1.7	1.4	2.3	2.6	0.5	2.5	1.7	0.0	1.0	1.9	4.1
Total current assets	42.9	31.0	39.1	63.8	65.0	38.0	13.9	94.8%	52.0	87.1	46.9
Net property & equip.	53.1	56.9	44.4	28.8	7.5	54.1	80.0	2.2	18.0	11.5	33.9
Other assets	4.0	12.1	16.5	7.4	27.5	7.9	6.1	3.0	30.0	1.4	19.2
Total assets	100.0%	100.0%	100.0%	100.0%	100.0%	100.0%	100.0%	100.0%	100.0%	100.0%	100.0%
Liabilities											
Notes payable	4.1%	5.6%	2.5%	17.2%	12.0%	7.4%	4.5%	2.0%	24.1%	0.0%	9.8%
Accounts payable	14.9	9.4	17.8	26.2	35.0	0.0	4.6	83.4	7.0	20.5	14.2
Accrued taxes	1.9	4.9	7.5	2.0	0.0	0.0	4.2	0.0	0.3	14.0	11.2
Other current liabs.	7.5	11.4	2.5	5.9	24.9	37.4	4.5	0.0	16.3	6.9	0.0
Total current liabs.	28.4	31.3	30.3	51.3	71.9	44.8	17.8	85.4	47.7	41.4	35.2
Long-term debt	43.2	17.0	7.8	10.0	1.7	18.5	31.7	3.3	6.4	0.0	1.5
Other liabilities	4.1	15.1	0.7	26.9	4.2	15.0	16.4	5.5	11.0	0.7	8.7
Total liabilities	75.7%	63.4%	38.8%	88.2%	77.8%	78.3%	65.9%	94.2%	65.1%	42.1%	45.4%
Equity											
Preferred stock	0.3%	0.0%	0.0%	0.0%	0.0%	0.0%	0.0%	0.6%	0.0%	0.0%	0.0%
Cap. stock & surplus	1.3	12.2	27.1	9.0	14.6	1.5	27.6	2.0	23.7	3.3	8.9
Retained earnings	22.7	24.4	34.1	2.8	7.6	20.2	6.5	3.2	11.2	54.6	45.7
Total equity	24.3%	36.6%	61.2%	11.8%	22.2%	21.7%	34.1%	5.8%	34.9%	57.9%	54.6%
Total liabs. & equity	100.0%	100.0%	100.0%	100.0%	100.0%	100.0%	100.0%	100.0%	100.0%	100.0%	100.0%
Ratios											
Current ratio	1.51	0.99	1.29	1.25	0.91	0.85	0.78	1.11	1.09	2.10	1.33
Acid test	0.68	0.63	1.08	1.02	0.88	0.77	0.76	1.11	0.68	1.72	1.02
ROS	4.83%	5.46%	6.75%	0.38%	2.20%	4.50%	2.15%	0.84%	−1.23%	16.60%	22.18%
Asset turnover	1.73	1.08	1.79	0.90	1.90	1.36	0.46	0.11	0.81	1.14	0.96
ROA	8.36%	5.87%	12.09%	0.35%	4.18%	6.11%	0.99%	0.09%	−1.00%	18.87%	21.96%
Financial leverage	4.11	2.73	1.64	8.45	4.50	4.60	2.93	17.18	2.87	1.73	1.83
ROE	34.37%	16.40%	19.77%	2.93%	18.79%	28.12%	2.00%	1.61%	−2.87%	32.59%	38.82%
Debt to capital	64.00%	31.70%	11.03%	45.80%	7.20%	46.00%	48.20%	36.10%	15.50%	0.00%	2.8%
Inventory turnover	5.28	7.04	18.89	6.40	—	—	—	—	3.46	4.09	1.71
Receivables collection	34.84	55.01	5.78	111.12	101.07	33.10	42.25	2875.96	64.29	24.87	64.00

4.5 Du Pont Formula Analysis

One day while at work at Venture Capitalists, Inc., a co-worker from the acquisitions department came to you for assistance. He was evaluating the financial results of two potential acquisition opportunities that were quite comparable in a number of respects. Both Japanese firms manufactured equivalent quality (and competing) products, controlled about the same market share, and earned the same ROE of 21 percent. His analysis had also identified the following financial differences:

	Firm X	Firm Z
ROS	2%	7%
ROA	7%	10.5%
Asset turnover	3.4×	1.5×
Total assets to shareholders' equity	3.0×	2.0×

Required:

Assist your co-worker in reaching a conclusion as to which company (X or Z) Venture Capitalists, Inc., should prefer to acquire.

4.6 Leverage Analysis

The following are condensed 1999 financial statement data for the Gear-Up Company Plc. Gear-Up's sales (or "turnover") have been as high as £60 million and as low as £40 million during the past five years; however, its interest coverage (i.e., times interest earned) has always been in excess of 4.5 during that same period. Gear-Up maintains an open line of credit with its lead lender, the Bank of Westminster, which would allow the company to borrow up to £10 million for a five-year term at 10 percent.

GEAR-UP CO., PLC
Condensed Balance Sheet
As of December 31, 1999
(in thousands of pounds)

Noncurrent assets	18,000
Current assets	9,000
Intangible assets	5,000
Total assets	32,000
Current liabilities	6,000
Debentures (8%)	16,000
Shareholders' equity	10,000
Total equity	32,000

GEAR-UP CO., PLC
Condensed Income Statement
For the Year Ended December 31, 1999
(in thousands of pounds)

Turnover	50,000
Less: Cost of sales	(32,500)
Selling and admin. expenses	(12,200)
Interest expense	(1,280)
Pre-tax net income	4,020
Less: Income taxes	(1,608)
Net income	2,412

Required:

(a) Using these data as a base, prepare at least four different sets of pro forma financial statements to demonstrate the effect of an increase in leverage on the company's ROE. Two of your pro forma presentations should assume the same sales and operating expenses but different levels of borrowing. The other pro forma presentations should assume an increase in debt and increased and decreased levels of sales. (You will need to make assumptions about the relationship between sales and the various expenses.)

(b) What can you infer from your analysis about the effect of leverage on shareholder returns, as measured by ROE?

4.7 Pro Forma Income Statements

HFS Corporation is in the latter stages of its principal product life cycle. The CEO has proposed that the company invest $10 million in a new product that has been under development for some time. Although the new product has received a good response in limited test markets, the board of directors is not convinced that this would be in the best interests of shareholders or the company. The following are HFS's income statements for 1997–1999.

HFS CORPORATION
Comparative Income Statements

	1997	1998	1999
Sales of old product	$ 10,000	$8,000	$7,000
Cost of sales—old product	6,000	5,000	4,550
Marketing costs—old product	1,500	1,280	1,225
Depreciation—old product	500	450	400
Interest—old product	200	180	150
Contribution—old product	$ 1,800	$1,090	$ 675
Sales of new product	$ 1,000	$3,000	$4,000
Cost of sales—new product	750	2,175	2,800
Marketing costs—new product	200	600	800
Depreciation—new product	100	110	150
Interest—new product	50	55	75
Contribution—new product	$ (100)	$ 60	$ 175
Corporate expense	$ 450	$ 475	$ 500
Income before taxes	1,250	675	350
Income taxes	$ 500	$ 270	$ 140
Net income	$ 750	$ 405	$ 210
Net assets employed—old product	$ 5,000	$4,800	$4,600
Net assets employed—new product	1,000	1,100	1,500
Owners' equity	3,600	3,800	3,900

Required:

Using these data, prepare two sets of pro forma income statements for HFS for 2000 and 2001, assuming that (1) $10 million will be invested in the new product, and (2) the new product is abandoned. List the assumptions that you made to prepare the pro formas. On the basis of your pro formas, what recommendation would you make to the board of directors?

4.8 Analysis of Unlevered Return on Assets

GTE Corporation is the fourth largest publicly owned telecommunications company in the world and is the largest local telephone company in the United States. GTE's two major product segments are Telephone Operations (Telephone) and Telecommunications Products and Services (Telecommunications).

Telephone provides a wide variety of communications services ranging from local telephone service for the home and office to highly complex voice and data services for industry. Telephone serves 17.1 million access lines in 33 states with the largest number of lines in California. Five million access lines are served in five foreign countries.

Results for 1993 include a one-time pretax restructuring charge of $1.8 billion provided to implement a reengineering plan to take place over the next three years. When fully implemented, the plan is expected to consolidate many areas of GTE and reduce the number of Telephone employees by 17,000.

Telecommunications develops and markets a wide variety of telecommunications systems and services, including mobile-cellular communications, government and defense communications systems and equipment, satellite and aircraft passenger communications (e.g., telephones for passengers in commercial aircraft), and yellow pages. Telecommunications revenues declined 5 percent in 1993; lower government communication sales resulting from the wind-down of a large contract more than offset higher revenues from the growth in mobile-cellular business. In 1993, 495,000 cellular telephone customers were added, an increase of 45 percent over 1992. Total cellular service revenues were $1.1 billion, a 27 percent improvement over 1992.

Exhibits 1, 2, and 3, present income statements, balance sheets, and statements of cash flow for GTE. Exhibit 4 presents additional segment data, and Exhibit 5 presents selected financial ratios for 1992.

Required:

(a) Compute the missing financial ratio amounts in Exhibit 5 for 1993. Assume that GTE's income tax rate for all years presented to be 34 percent. (*Note:* You must decide how to deal with 1993 restructuring and merger costs and extraordinary charge—early retirement of debt.)

(b) To the maximum extent possible given the data, interpret the change in GTE's unleveraged ROA from 1992 to 1993.

EXHIBIT 1

GTE CORPORATION AND SUBSIDIARIES
Consolidated Statements of Income
(millions of dollars)

	1993	1992
Revenues and Sales		
Telephone operations	$15,829	$15,862
Telecommunications products and services	3,919	4,122
Total	$19,748	$19,984
Costs and Expenses		
Telephone operations	$11,765	$11,828
Telecommunications products and services*	3,578	3,940
Restructuring costs	1,840	
Total	$17,183	$15,768
Operating income	$ 2,565	$ 4,216
Other (Income) Deductions		
Interest expense	1,197	1,332
Other	(190)	130
Total	$ 1,007	$ 1,462
Income before taxes	$ 1,558	$ 2,754
Income tax provision	568	967
Income from continuing operations	$ 990	$ 1,787
Discontinued operations		(48)
Extraordinary charge—early retirement of debt	(90)	(52)
Cumulative effect of accounting changes†		(2,441)
Net income (loss)	$ 900	$ (754)
Prefered stock dividends of parent	(18)	(26)
Net income (loss) applicable to common stock	$ 882	$ (780)

*Includes cost of sales as follows:	$ 3,036	$ 3,143

†A one-time noncash charge made on January 1, 1992, to adopt *SFAS 106* on postretirement benefits. *FAS 106* requires that these benefits be recorded during the years that employees render service.

EXHIBIT 2

GTE CORPORATION AND SUBSIDIARIES
Consolidated Balance Sheets
(millions of dollars)

	1993	1992	1991
Assets			
Current assets			
Cash and temporary investments	$ 322	$ 354	$ 517
Receivables	3,900	3,565	3,663
Inventories	659	814	910
Other current assets	1,067	1,563	2,476
Total	$ 5,948	$ 6,296	$ 7,566
Property, plant and equipment	28,720	29,820	29,323
Goodwill	2,102	2,167	2,180
Investment in unconsolidated companies	1,431	1,361	1,374
Deferred charges	2,462	1,683	1,114
Other non-current assets	912	817	880
Total	$35,627	$35,848	$34,871
Total assets	$41,575	$42,144	$42,437
Liabilities and Shareholders' Equity			
Current liabilities			
Short-term loans	$ 1,644	$ 2,692	$ 2,291
Accounts payable	1,968	1,917	1,895
Accrued taxes	1,108	571	621
Accrued restructuring costs	540		
Dividends payable	469	447	431
Other current liabilities	2,204	1,884	1,988
Total	$ 7,933	$ 7,511	$ 7,226
Long-term debt	13,019	14,182	16,049
Reserves and deferred credits			
Deferred taxes	2,808	3,071	3,184
Other	6,960	6,053	3,339
Total	$ 9,768	$ 9,124	$ 6,523
Total liabilities	$30,720	$30,817	$29,798
Minority interests in equity of subsidiaries	1,106	1,077	1,123
Preferred stock, subject to mandatory redemption	156	174	153
Shareholders' Equity			
Preferred stock	111	112	509
Common stock	48	47	46
Additional paid-in capital	7,309	7,134	6,232
Reinvested earnings	2,769	3,621	5,977
Guaranteed ESOP obligation	(644)	(657)	(673)
Treasury stock		(181)	(728)
Total	$ 9,593	$10,076	$11,363
Total liabilities and shareholders' equity	$41,575	$42,144	$42,437

EXHIBIT 3

GTE CORPORATION AND SUBSIDIARIES
Consolidated Statements of Cash Flows
(millions of dollars)

	1993	1992
Cash Flows from Operations		
Income from continuing operations	$ 990	$ 1,787
Depreciation and amortization	3,419	3,289
Restructuring costs	1,840	
Deferred taxes	(864)	37
Change in current assets and current liabilities, excluding the effects of acquisitions and depositions	(13)	(268)
Other—net	(95)	(13)
Net cash from operations	$ 5,277	$ 4,832
Cash Flows from Investing		
Capital expenditures	(3,893)	(3,909)
Acquisitions and investments	(46)	(84)
Sale of assets	2,267	662
Other—net	(66)	55
Net cash used in investing	$(1,738)	$(3,276)
Cash Flows from Financing		
GTE common stock issued	383	1,513
Long-term debt issued	2,325	590
Long-term debt and preferred stock retired	(4,836)	(2,002)
Dividends to shareholders of parent	(1,744)	(1,572)
Increase (decrease) in short-term obligations, excluding current maturities	304	(254)
Other—net	(3)	6
Net cash from (used in) financing	$(3,571)	$(1,719)
Change in cash and cash equivalents	$ (32)	$ (163)

EXHIBIT 4

GTE CORPORATION AND SUBSIDIARIES
Geographic and Operating Segment Data
(millions of dollars)

	1993	*1992*
Foreign Segment Data		
Revenues	$ 2,482	$ 2,369
Operating income	328	244
Total assets	6,096	5,963
Domestic Segment Data		
Revenues	$17,266	$17,615
Operating income	572	(998)
Total assets	35,479	36,181
Telephone Operations Data		
Revenues	$15,829	$15,862
Operations and maintenance	8,796	8,979
Depreciation and amortization	2,969	2,849
Restructuring costs	1,370	–0–
Operating income	2,694	4,034
Total assets	33,746	33,154
Access minutes of use (in millions)	55,616	51,976
Access lines (in thousands)		
Total	22,065	21,440
United States	17,073	16,819
Employees (in thousands)		
Total	95	104
United States	73	81
Telecommunications Data		
Revenues	$ 3,919	$ 4,122
Depreciation and amortization	450	440
Restructuring costs	398	
Other operating costs	3,128	3,500
Operating income	(57)	182
Total assets	5,973	6,204

EXHIBIT 5

GTE CORPORATION AND SUBSIDIARIES
Selected Financial Ratios

	1993	*1992*
Consolidated		
Unlevered rate of return on assets		6.3%
Profit margin for UROA		13.3%
Total assets turnover		0.47×
Depreciation and amortization expense percentage		16.5%
Other operating expenses percentage		62.4%
Income tax expense percentage (excluding tax effects of interest expense)		7.1%
Accounts receivable turnover		5.53×
Inventory turnover		3.65×
Fixed asset turnover		0.68×
Foreign Operations		
Rate of return on assets		4.1%
Profit margin		10.3%
Asset turnover		0.40×
Domestic Operations		
Rate of return on assets		−2.8%
Profit margin		−5.7%
Asset turnover		0.49×
Telephone Products Segment		
Rate of return on assets		12.2%
Profit margin		25.4%
Asset turnover		0.48×
Telecommunications Segment		
Rate of return on assets		2.9%
Profit margin		4.4%
Asset turnover		0.66×

4.9 Analysis of Return on Common Equity: Short- and Long-Term Risk Factors

Refer to the data for GTE Corporation in Exercise 4.8.

Required:

(a) Compute the missing financial ratio amounts in the following table for GTE for 1993.

(b) To the maximum extent permitted by the data, interpret the change in ROCE that occurred from 1992 to 1993. You need not explain reasons for the changes in UROA.

(c) Evaluate the changes in GTE's short-term and long-term risk factors.

GTE CORPORATION AND SUBSIDIARIES
Selected Financial Ratios

	1992	*1993*
Rate of return on common equity	16.4 %	_____
Common earnings leverage	0.66	_____
Capital structure leverage	3.95	_____
Current ratio	0.84	_____
Quick ratio	0.52	_____
Cash flow from operations to current liabilities	65.6 %	_____
Long-term debt to total assets	33.7 %	_____
Cash flow from operations to total liabilities	11.4 %	_____
Interest coverage	3.07	_____

4.10 Interpreting ROCE and Its Components

Listed below are five possible scenarios occurring during 1999 that may fully explain a change in ROCE and/or its components

Scenario 1

The interest rate on debt increased. Cash normally used to pay dividends is now used to pay the increased interest costs to lenders.

Scenario 2

A significant purchase of fixed assets was funded by debt. For the current period, incremental depreciation was exactly offset by reductions in the cost of sales. It is expected that cost savings in excess of incremental depreciation will occur in future years.

Scenario 3

Sales decreased. Operating expenses did not decrease at the same rate because of the presence of fixed costs. The diminished profitability is offset by reduced dividends.

Scenario 4

The company spun off a subsidiary to shareholders. The subsidiary made no contribution to operating revenues or expenses during either 1998 or 1999.

Scenario 5

The company purchased its own shares on the open market as a defense against a hostile takeover. The purchase was funded by issuing bonds.

Required:

Match each of these five scenarios with the five firms (i.e., A–E) in the following table. (Each case is based on actual company data, and there may be inaccuracies due to rounding.)

Changes in ROCE for Five Disguised Firms

	ROCE	=	ROA	×	Adjusted Leverage	=	Profit Margin	×	Asset Turnover	×	Common Earnings Leverage	×	Capital Structure Leverage
Firm A													
1998	15.5%		9.2%		1.7		5.4%		1.7		0.9		1.9
1999	13.5		9.2		1.5		5.4		1.7		0.8		1.9
Firm B													
1998	2.7		2.5		1.1		2.1		1.2		0.7		1.6
1999	0.5		0.9		0.6		0.9		1.0		0.4		1.6
Firm C													
1998	21.6		13.6		1.7		18.5		0.7		0.9		1.7
1999	23.0		13.6		1.7		18.5		0.7		0.8		2.0
Firm D													
1998	7.6		4.6		1.7		7.4		0.6		0.8		2.0
1999	3.3		0.6		5.5		7.4		0.1		0.8		6.7
Firm E													
1998	6.2		4.9		1.3		3.4		1.5		0.9		1.5
1999	8.1		6.0		1.3		3.4		1.8		0.9		1.5

4.11 Preparing Pro Forma Income Statements

Waterloo Furniture Components, Ltd. (WFC) is a manufacturer of office equipment and related products. The company is headquartered in Kitchener, Ontario, Canada, but is a wholly owned subsidiary of a U.S.-based conglomerate. WFC sells primarily to North American markets, and is increasing its sales to Asian and European markets.

Ron Simmons, president of WFC, is faced with a dilemma and requests your advice. Among the WFC product lines are office couches, whose markets have been steadily eroded by full-line U.S. furniture manufacturers selling similar products at significant price discounts. The markup on these products is, however, substantial and even at reduced volume levels make a significant contribution to WFC's pretax profits (in part because they absorb significant amounts of WFC's overhead).

In 1991, WFC was one of the first North American office equipment manufacturers to introduce a personal computer wrist rest in response to medical reports diagnosing large numbers of computer keyboard operators as having Carpal tunnel syndrome—an inflammation of the wrist apparently caused by extended computer keyboard use. Although the wrist rest product line had lost money in its first year, sales growth had been substantial, and by 1993, the new product line was showing a modest contribution to profit. Ron felt that the wrist rest product line had substantial profit opportunities in the short term (i.e., the next three to five years), but he was concerned about recent developments in the area of voice-activated computers, which would substantially reduce the amount of keyboard-related activities of computer users. According to recent computer industry surveys, voice-activated computers could be mass marketed as early as 1996. In the interim, however, industry sales of wrist rest type products were projected to exceed $200 million in each of 1994 and 1995. Analysts were reluctant to forecast 1996 sales due to uncertainties associated with the introduction of voice-activated personal computers.

Ron has been given the OK from holding company executives to invest up to $5 million in new plant and equipment for the wrist rest product line. He was concerned, however, that demand for the product could dramatically erode once voice-activated computers became available at reasonable prices. Ron's dilemma was as follows: Should he invest the available $5 million in an expansion of the wrist rest product line or instead ask headquarters for an increase in his R&D budget to begin the development of a new product line of office equipment compatible with voice-activated computers?

Required:

The following are selected income statement data for WFC for the period 1991–1993. To help you advise Ron, you should begin by developing pro forma income data for 1994–1996.

Clearly identify all assumptions used in preparing your pro formas. What recommendation would you make, and why?

WATERLOO FURNITURE COMPONENTS, LTD.
Selected Income Data
(000s omitted)

	Year Ended December 31		
	1991	*1992*	*1993*
Office couches			
Sales	$15,000	$12,000	$10,500
Less: costs of sales	(9,000)	(7,500)	(6,825)
depreciation	(750)	(675)	(600)
marketing costs	(2,250)	(1,920)	(1,838)
interest charges	(300)	(270)	(225)
Contribution to income	$ 2,700	$ 1,635	$ 1,012
Wrist rests			
Sales	$ 2,000	6,000	$ 8,000
Less: cost of sales	(1,500)	(4,350)	(5,600)
depreciation	(200)	(220)	(300)
marketing cost	(400)	(1,200)	(1,600)
interest charges	(100)	(110)	(150)
Contribution to income	$ (200)	$ 120	$ 350
Corporate overhead	$ 720	$ 760	$ 800
Income before taxes	$ 1,780	$ 995	$ 562
Less: Income taxes	(712)	(398)	(225)
Net income	$ 1,068	$ 597	$ 337
Contribution to cash flow*			
Couches	$ 3,450	$ 2,310	$ 1,612
Wrist rests	–0–	340	650
Net assets employed			
Couches	$ 5,000	$ 4,800	$ 4,600
Wrist rests	1,000	1,100	1,500
Owners' equity	3,600	3,800	3,900

*Contribution to cash flow = Contribution to income + Depreciation.

4.12 Pro Forma Financial Statements

SANTOS Ltd. is an oil and gas exploration and production company headquartered in Adelaide, Australia. SANTOS maintains exploration and/or production operations in Australia (principally South Australia, Queensland, and the Northern Territory), Southeast Asia (principally Cambodia, Papua New Guinea, and Indonesia), the United States (principally Texas, Oklahoma, and Louisiana) and Europe (principally in the North Sea and the Irish Sea).

During 1994, SANTOS expects to embark on a significant drilling program in the Pierce oil and gas field of the North Sea (blocks 22/22C, 22/27a, and 23/27). According to the company's managing director, SANTOS will drill 10 wells at an average cost of $4 million per well and that six of those wells will yield aggregate crude oil reserves (or gas equivalents) of approximately 10 million barrels. The remaining four wells are expected to be commercially unproductive.

The company's production plan calls for a maximum exploitation effort to earn the highest financial return. Consistent with this goal, the company's managing director developed the following production scenario:

Year	Number of Barrels (or gas equivalents thereof) to be Produced	Estimated Lifting Cost per Barrel*
1994	1,000,000	$5
1995	1,500,000	5
1996	1,500,000	6
1997	2,500,000	7
1998	3,500,000	8
	10,000,000	

*Excludes depreciation, depletion, and amortization costs.

Because of the relatively calm political atmosphere in the Middle East and expectations that conditions would remain so for the foreseeable future, oil and gas analysts have predicted substantial price increases in crude oil. The most recent projections call for an estimated selling price of $30, $30, $35, $50, and $45 per barrel in 1994 through 1998, respectively.

Because of the relatively low interest rates prevailing during 1993, SANTOS decided to seek syndicated bank financing for the exploration program. While organizing her presentation for bank representatives, the managing director realized that the perceived economic feasibility of the exploration program might appear different, depending on whether the company elected to use the full cost method or the successful efforts method. Consequently, she sent an immediate request to the controller: "Prepare pro forma statements showing the alternative accounting effects on cash flow, profit before tax, and financial position if we elect to use the successful efforts method or the full cost method."

For purposes of pro forma statement preparation, assume that the $40 million loan will be repaid as follows: (1) interest payments of 10 percent per year on the balance of the loan outstanding as of the beginning of the year and (2) $10 million principal repayment annually, to be paid at year end, beginning December 31, 1995.

Required:

Based on your pro forma statements for the period 1994 through 1998, what accounting method (successful efforts or full cost) recommendation would you make to the managing director, and why?

Special Issues in Financial Analysis

[E]arnings are distorted by accounting conventions that make it hard to compare values from one [securities exchange] to the next. But compare one must, if one has any hope of applying rationality to picking stocks.[1]

In the previous chapter, the fundamentals of financial statement analysis were considered. Implicit to that discussion was the important assumption of data comparability, both over time for a given firm, as well as between firms. As we will see in Chapters 7–13, however, this assumption is unlikely to be valid when comparing the financial data of companies from different countries and often within the same country. Even if a high degree of harmonization is achieved by the International Accounting Standards Committee (IASC), comparability concerns will continue to persist because of the inherent variability of financial data permitted under acceptable IASC reporting alternatives.

In this chapter, we consider a variety of data comparability issues, as well as some techniques that might be used to make adjustments to available data for the purpose of attaining improved comparability:

- Alternative revenue recognition policies.
- Alternative inventory valuation approaches.
- Alternative depreciation and amortization policies.
- Alternative asset capitalization policies.
- Asset impairment and revaluation.
- Off-balance sheet debt.
- Balance sheet reserves.

Alternative Revenue Recognition Policies

Generally accepted revenue recognition policies are likely to vary significantly within the various industries of a given country as well as between countries. Thus, the problem of alternative revenue recognition practices will be encountered when analyzing the finan-

---

[1]P. Fuhrman, "Parlez-vous P/E?" *Forbes,* June 27, 1988, p. 276.

cial results of almost any multinational company, regardless of the origin of the accounting principles used by the company in its financial statements. For example, consider the variability of revenue recognition practices among some typical industries within the United States:

- Retail concerns typically recognize revenue at the point of sale.
- Original equipment manufacturers (OEMs) frequently recognize revenue at the point of shipment.
- Oil and gas companies may recognize revenue from the sale of crude oil prior to its extraction. (This is accomplished through the sale of carved-out production contracts.)
- Companies producing goods or providing services under long-term contracts frequently recognize revenue on a percentage-of-completed work basis.

The following examples of non-U.S. revenue recognition practices illustrate some of the differences that can occur across countries:

- In Hong Kong, profit on installment sales contracts is generally recognized in proportion to cash payments received, whereas the more common practice in the United States is to recognize all revenues—except for amounts attributed to financing activities—at the point of sale.
- In Germany, the accepted practice is to delay revenue recognition until a right of return period has expired.
- Japanese companies rarely recognize revenue under long-term contracts on a percentage-of-completed work basis. Revenue recognition is usually delayed until a contract is completed.

When evaluating the revenue recognition policy of a given company, regardless of its national reporting origins, it is always wise to begin by comparing the policy in use to accepted industry norms. The use of an industry-accepted method, however, does not guarantee that a company's revenue streams will be risk free. Consider, for example, OEMs that recognize revenue at the industry-accepted norm of point of shipment. Because of highly competitive marketplaces, these companies frequently offer customers a right-of-return option that may last up to six months. As a consequence, the revenue (and cash) streams of such companies are often quite unpredictable, particularly when economic conditions are less than robust.

Aside from unexpected economic downturns that are usually accompanied by significant increases in sales returns and bad debts, the most often encountered concern with corporate revenue recognition policies is overly aggressive (or early) recognition, which is often referred to as front-end loading. **Front-end loading** occurs when sales are prematurely recognized, perhaps before a firm offer to buy is received or, if producing under a contract, before sufficient completion levels have been attained. The consequence of this is that revenues and net income, as well as receivables and total current assets, are overstated. These overstatements naturally are translated into somewhat overly optimistic assessments of corporate profitability, liquidity, and solvency.

Front-end loading has the effect of improving the appearance of current period results, usually at the expense of future periods. If front-end-loaded revenues are used as a basis for projecting future corporate revenues, there is some risk that an analyst's projections of revenues, earnings, and cash flow will be excessively optimistic. Of concern to the analyst, then, is the need to assess the reasonableness and riskiness of a company's revenue recognition policy.

In general, two types of risk are associated with revenues: (1) risk that the revenues have been booked too early and that a final sale will not be consummated and (2) risk that, once consummated, the sale will not yield the anticipated level of cash inflows. The first type of risk can be minimized by adopting a conservative revenue recognition policy (e.g., recognition at the point of sale) or when an aggressive recognition policy is adopted, by establishing a sufficient reserve to cover any future sales returns.

The second type of risk (i.e., cash collection risk) can be minimized by adopting a conservative credit-granting policy or by establishing a sufficient reserve to cover any future uncollectible accounts. The need for this reserve is estimated at the end of each accounting period, usually on the basis of a process known as **aging of accounts receivable,** which assumes that the older a receivable is, the lower the probability of collection. This process of estimating future uncollectible receivables enables management to deduct from current revenues an amount (i.e., the "provision for bad debts") representing the cost of extending credit during the current period. A parallel reserve account, the allowance for uncollectible accounts, appears on the balance sheet as a contra receivable account.[2]

When either type of risk is high, both the quality of the reported revenues and trade receivables will be low, and, as a consequence, the expected cash flows from operations uncertain. Evidence regarding the presence of these risks can be obtained in several ways:

- *Reviewing the footnote "Summary of Significant Accounting Policies" adopted by management in the preparation of the financial statements.* While the extent of accounting policy disclosure varies from country to country, a presentation of such information is required in most countries, as well as by *IAS No. 1.* This footnote can provide the analyst with information concerning just how and when revenues are being recognized. Hopefully, the adopted method will be an industry-accepted practice, and where it is not, the analyst should investigate whether special circumstances exist to warrant deviation from industry norms. Exhibit 5–1 (panel A), for example, presents the footnote disclosures of British Airways Plc (BA), American Airlines (AMR Corporation), and Lufthansa in regard to their accounting for operating revenues.

- *Comparing the cash collections from sales with sales recognized on the income statement.* Although there is frequently a lag between sale recognition and cash collection, the lag period should not exceed the normal cash collection cycle of a company or its industry (e.g., 30 to 90 days). However, when the lag period is excessive (or growing), it usually indicates the use of an aggressive revenue recognition policy, a substandard credit-granting policy, poor credit management, or some combination of these. Exhibit 5–1 (panel B) presents a comparison of accrual and cash revenues for British Airways Plc and two of its principal international competitors; that exhibit reveals that BA's cash sales lag its accrual sales in all but one year. Comparison to Lufthansa and American Airlines suggests, however, that BA's industry-accepted revenue recognition policy is not overly aggressive. The analysis could be extended further to include a time-series and cross-sectional comparison of bad debt allowances.

- *Examining such asset-based quality indicators as the average receivable collection period.* This ratio indicates the average time required to collect an outstand-

---

[2]It is always instructive to evaluate the reasonableness of a company's allowance for uncollectible accounts. Consider, for example, the case of Urcarco, Inc., which operates a chain of used car lots in the United States. According to the company's prospectus for its initial public offering, 22.7 and 18.4 percent of the cars sold in 1988 and 1989, respectively, were repossessed. For those same years, the allowance for uncollectible accounts relative to the outstanding receivable balance amounted to only 6.9 and 8.9 percent, respectively. In July 1990, two shareholder lawsuits were filed against Urcarco alleging that the company's financial statements were not prepared in conformity with GAAP on grounds that revenue recognition occurred prematurely and that allowances for sales returns and uncollectible accounts were inadequate.

EXHIBIT 5–1

Financial Statement Disclosures: Revenue Recognition

Panel A. Revenue Recognition Policy

British Airways

Operating revenues comprise the revenue from airline traffic carried during the year and revenue from other airline service and package holidays provided or delivered during the year. Operating revenues exclude sales based taxes and intragroup sales.

American Airlines

Passenger ticket sales are initially recorded as a current liability. Revenue derived from the sale is recognized at the time transporation is provided.

Lufthansa

No disclosure.

Panel B. Comparison of Cash and Accrual Sales for British Airways and Two Competitors

	19x9	*19x8*	*19x7*	*19x6*	*19x5*
British Airways					
Total operating revenues	£5,566	£5,224	£4,937	£4,838	£4,257
Add (subtract) decrease (increase) in trade receivables	(65)	(107)	138	(90)	(73)
Cash revenues	£5,501	£5,117	£5,075	£4,748	£4,184
Percentage difference	**1.2%**	**2.0%**	**−2.8%**	**1.9%**	**1.7%**
American Airlines					
Total operating revenues	$14,396	$12,887	$11,720	$10,480	$8,824
Add (subtract) decrease (increase) in trade receivables	(144)	148	(65)	(53)	(104)
Cash revenues	$14,252	$13,035	$11,654	$10,427	$8,720
Percentage difference	**1.0%**	**−1.2%**	**0.6%**	**0.5%**	**1.2%**
Lufthansa					
Total operating revenues	DM18,495	DM17,219	DM15,827	DM14,314	DM12,570
Add (subtract) decrease (increase) in trade receivables	(125)	(279)	(69)	(512)	(253)
Cash revenues	DM18,369	DM16,940	DM15,758	DM13,802	DM12,317
Percentage difference	**0.7%**	**1.6%**	**0.4%**	**3.6%**	**2.0%**

Panel C. Average Receivable Collection Period (365 ÷ Receivable Turnover)

British Airways	52.1 days	49.5 days	53.4 days	56.3 days	57.0 days
American Airlines	22.2	24.8	28.6	29.9	32.3
Lufthansa	48.1	47.3	47.5	45.1	40.3

Companies that fail to present a statement of cash flows or that present an indirect method statement of cash flows necessitate a calculation of cash revenues as above.

ing receivable and can provide important insights regarding not only the quality of receivables and the quality of the credit-granting policies employed by a company but also the quality of its revenue recognition policy. A growing or excessive receivable collection period is usually a very good predictor of pending cash flow problems.[3] Exhibit 5–1 (panel C) presents the average receivable collection period for the same three airlines. BA's collection period seems to be improving

---

[3]To illustrate the value of this tool, consider the case of Cardillo Travel Systems, Inc., a receivables-intensive travel service company. As of September 1985, Cardillo's receivables accounted for over 40 percent of the company's total assets. According to an SEC complaint issued on July 27, 1987, the company had experienced serious liquidity problems that had not been publicly disclosed. To the insightful analyst, however, Cardillo's liquidity problems could have been identified early in 1985 by examining the average receivable collection period, which had escalated to over 563 days.

slightly over time while Lufthansa's is eroding; however, BA still substantially lags Lufthansa. American's collection period may reflect a higher proportion of domestic service revenues in its sales mix, which may tend to include more cash sales.

Alternative Inventory Valuation Policy

The list of generally accepted inventory valuation approaches (or cost flow assumptions) varies greatly between countries. Although LIFO, FIFO, and weighted average are the most commonly used methods in the United States, LIFO is not permitted for use by companies in Great Britain or other British Commonwealth countries. Some countries (e.g., Australia, France, Hong Kong, Japan, and Germany) permit LIFO valuation for consolidated foreign subsidiaries but not for domestic company reports. Japan is one of the few countries permitting the use of highest-price-in, first-price-out (HIFO).

This diversity in accepted practice makes it essential for the financial analyst to carefully evaluate a company's chosen inventory valuation policy. The inventory valuation decision affects not only the inventory account on the balance sheet (and, thus a firm's liquidity and asset management indicators), but also the cost of goods sold on the income statement (and hence, a firm's reported profitability and solvency).

An analyst should consider a number of issues when evaluating the cost of goods sold and ending inventory. First, it is essential to remember that the various alternative inventory costing approaches are merely cost allocation methods. Each requires that a different assumption be made regarding the flow of costs from a firm's inventory of unsold goods to the cost of goods sold, and only one method (i.e., specific identification) attempts to pattern the flow of costs after the actual flow of products. When inventory prices vary over time, these methods produce very different effects on the balance sheet and the income statement. Consequently, they also produce (possibly substantially) different effects on the typical balance sheet and income statement ratios used by analysts.

Consider, for example, Exhibit 5–2, which presents the income statement and selected financial ratios for two economically identical multinational companies from Japan—FIFO Company and LIFO Company—which differ only in regard to the accounting method used to value the cost of goods sold and ending inventory. A review of these financial data reveals that since inventory costs are rising, FIFO Company appears to be financially better off than LIFO Company: Earnings are higher by ¥7.8 million, the liquidity indicators of working capital and the current ratio are higher, the borrowing capacity (as measured by the debt-to-equity ratio) is greater, and the profitability indicators of return on sales, return on equity, and return on assets are superior. Only the inventory turnover ratio appears to be better for the LIFO Company. But are these indicators really depicting economic reality?

Holding the question of taxes aside, the answer to this question is an emphatic "No!" The companies are economically identical, in spite of what the financial ratios indicate. In effect, the different cost allocation assumptions inherent in LIFO and FIFO mask the real economic performance of the two companies, which happens to be equivalent. If we now add the dimension of taxes and assume that each company uses the same costing approach for both tax purposes and financial statement purposes, the conclusion is even more startling: the LIFO company is actually superior in economic performance to the FIFO Company because greater cash flow is preserved in the LIFO Company due to its lower taxable earnings. Thus, contrary to the financial indicators, the LIFO Company would be a superior investment.

EXHIBIT 5–2
Inventory Costing Methods and Financial Statement Analysis

The following are the income statements and selected financial ratios for two Japanese companies that are identical in every respect except with regard to the method of inventory costing and the cost of goods sold:

	FIFO Company	*LIFO Company*
Sales	¥75,000,000	¥75,000,000
Less: Cost of goods sold	(34,500,000)	(42,300,000)
	¥40,500,000	¥32,700,000
Less: Other operating expenses	(15,000,000)	(15,000,000)
Net income before tax (NIBT)	¥25,500,000	¥17,700,000
Earnings per share	¥2.55	¥1.77
Current ratio	1.67:1	1.57:1
Working capital	¥10,800,000	¥ 3,000,000
Inventory turnover	2:1	3:1
Debt-to-equity ratio	1:5.17	1:4.91
Return on assets	10.8%	8.0%
Return on equity	14%	12.1%
Return on sales	34%	24%

A second analytical consideration concerns those companies using the LIFO method or other similar valuation methods (e.g., HIFO) that tend to or are designed to assign the highest costs to cost of goods sold and the lowest costs to ending inventory. One adverse outcome of these methods concerns the quality of the ending inventory valuation as reported on the balance sheet. Under LIFO and HIFO, the most recent (highest) inventory costs are assigned to the cost of goods sold, while the older, usually lower inventory costs are assigned to the ending inventory on the balance sheet. When inflation is present, the cost values reflected in the Inventory account may be substantially undervalued relative to their actual replacement cost. Thus, not only will the Inventory account be understated, but so also will be the level of working capital and such ratios as the current ratio, which includes the undervalued Inventory account.

The problem of inventory value misstatement is particularly prevalent among U.S. firms because of their propensity to use LIFO to obtain the income tax sheltering provided by this method. It is also a problem in Japan and, to a lesser extent, Germany, where higher-costing inventory is charged to net income in an effort to constrain taxable (and consequently book) income. In countries such as Great Britain and Italy, where asset revaluations are permitted and/or LIFO is not permitted, inventory value understatement is rarely encountered.[4]

To gain some perspective on the frequency with which LIFO accounting may be encountered worldwide, we conducted a study of the Compustat Global Vantage database of industrial companies. Exhibit 5–3 lists, by country,[5] the number of Global Vantage firms that report inventory, the number of those firms that disclose their method(s) of

---

[4]Some countries, such as the United States, do not permit the upward revaluation of inventories; these countries usually restrict inventory adjustments to write-downs under the lower-of-cost-or-market approach. Given the propensity for most economies to experience some degree of price inflation, the lower-of-cost-or-market adjustments for most companies tend to be relatively immaterial in amount. Occasionally, however, in commodity-related industries, such as the food, mineral, and oil and gas industries, these downward revaluations may be quite significant. Essentially every country in the world permits the downward revaluation of inventory, but only a few, such as Brazil, Italy, Great Britain, and those countries that require price-level adjusted financial statements, also permit the upward revaluation of inventory.

[5]We omitted countries that had relatively few industrial companies on the database.

Exhibit 5–3

Worldwide LIFO Inventory Valuation

Country of Incorporation	Firms with Inventory	Firms with Inventory Methods Disclosure	Firms with Inventory Valued at LIFO	Percentage of LIFO-Disclosed Firms
Belgium	56	22	6	27%
Canada	328	191	14	7
France	240	129	7	5
Germany	247	54	18	33
Great Britain	607	102	2	2
Italy	140	114	57	50
Japan*	698	553	53	10
South Africa	141	119	4	3
Switzerland	112	26	1	4
United States	2,582	1,965	753	38
Total	**5,151**	**3,275**	**915**	**28%**

*Global Vantage does not distinguish between HIFO and LIFO. Consequently, Japanese firms reported as LIFO in the database may actually measure their inventory using HIFO.

inventory valuation, and the number of firms that disclose that at least some of their inventory is valued using LIFO. The last column indicates, as expected, great variation in the incidence of LIFO firms across countries.

Concerned that the LIFO inventory values reported by companies listed on U.S. stock exchanges may be substantially undervalued, the FASB and the SEC adopted a requirement that audited financial statements using LIFO disclose the firm's LIFO reserve in the inventory footnote.[6] The **LIFO reserve** measures the difference between the current (or replacement) cost of ending inventory and its calculated LIFO cost. By adding the LIFO reserve to the LIFO cost of ending inventory, an analyst can obtain a more reliable assessment of the current cost of ending inventory. Similarly, a more realistic value for working capital and the current ratio may also be obtained. Finally, for those analysts interested in comparing LIFO earnings to FIFO earnings, the LIFO reserve is a useful tool for such comparisons. By adding the change in the LIFO reserve from one year to the next to the net income before tax (NIBT) under LIFO, the analyst can approximate FIFO NIBT.

A third analytical concern, also relating to companies using LIFO, involves LIFO liquidations. A **LIFO liquidation** occurs when inventory unit levels of a LIFO company decline below unit levels existing at the beginning of the fiscal period. When this occurs, cost of goods sold consists of two components: (1) cost of inventory acquired or manufactured during the period and (2) cost of inventory acquired or manufactured during past periods, going as far back in time possibly as the company's inception. These latter costs may be much lower than the current manufacturing costs, causing net income before tax to be overstated relative to non-LIFO liquidation periods. This increase in NIBT is purely a "paper profit" in that the cash flows from operations are not equivalently increased. In fact, the cash flows from operations are actually decreased under a LIFO liquidation in that the paper profits are usually subject to taxation. Consequently, in the eyes of most analysts, LIFO liquidation profits are of questionable quality.[7]

---

[6]*IAS No. 2,* as revised, permits the use of FIFO, weighted or average cost, specific identification, or LIFO for purposes of valuing inventories. Where LIFO is used, the impact on ending inventory, as compared to using either FIFO or weighted-average cost, should also be disclosed (i.e., the equivalent of the LIFO reserve).

[7]On the other hand, excess accumulations of inventory resulting from a desire to avoid the adverse tax consequences of LIFO liquidation are also undesirable and diminish the quality of liquidity ratios and turnover ratios that involve inventory.

The issues raised previously suggest that reported earnings and ratios based thereon can often be misleading. When inventory costs are rising, FIFO yields higher reported earnings than does LIFO, HIFO, or the weighted-average method. From a lender's or investor's perspective, however, higher earnings are not necessarily the most important performance criteria. Indeed, the level of cash flow is likely to be far more important to credit or investment analysts than are accrual earnings. Thus, when evaluating the financial health of a company, it is important to ascertain how the company is valuing its inventory for tax purposes, as well as for financial statement purposes.

Although it is always dangerous to make generalizations, particularly involving accounting methods, the following statement appears justified: During a period of rising materials and manufacturing costs, a company should, if possible, utilize the LIFO or HIFO inventory costing method for both taxes and financial statement purposes. Not only will the cash flows of the company be preserved, but the methods also permit superior managerial decision making. In spite of these obvious advantages, some managers nonetheless adopt the FIFO or weighted-average approach (perhaps because neither LIFO nor HIFO is permitted in their particular locale). When this is the case, the analyst should investigate any special circumstances (e.g., expiring tax credits, local accounting standards) that might justify this inventory costing decision. When no special circumstances exist, a lower quality of earnings may be implied.

Amortization and Depreciation Policy

Amortization (depreciation) refers to a company's current period allocation of intangible asset cost (fixed asset cost) against its revenues. Following the cost of goods sold and income taxes, depreciation and amortization often represent the next largest deduction against revenues on the income statement. Similarly, on the balance sheet, the capitalized values of property, plant, and equipment and of intangible assets frequently represent the largest categories of a company's total assets.

Most countries around the world permit the use of such traditional depreciation methods as straight line, double-declining balance, and sum-of-the-years' digits; whereas goodwill, if capitalized, is usually amortized on a straight-line basis (although other methods are permitted but are rarely used). Despite this worldwide consistency among accepted amortization and depreciation methods, the international financial analyst must be sensitive to the following considerations:

- In countries such as the United States and Great Britain where tax and book income may substantially diverge, the prevalent depreciation treatment for published financial statements is straight line; however, in countries such as Germany and Japan where tax and book income are substantially alike, the prevalent depreciation treatment is double-declining balance or sum-of-the-years' digits. Restatement for these systematic depreciation differences is difficult, if not impossible. Consequently, the analyst must look to comparisons of cash flow data to overcome these cost allocation differentials.
- Despite the presence of essentially identical assets, the depreciable life of assets may vary significantly between international companies. For example, Lufthansa,

the German airline, depreciates its fleet of aircraft over an average estimated life of 10 years, whereas British Airways, its British competitor, depreciates its fleet over an estimated life of approximately 17 years. This systematic difference in depreciation policy reflects the institutional setting faced by each firm (see Chapters 7 and 8). To obtain increased data comparability between such firms, the analyst needs to adjust the depreciation expense on the income statement and accumulated depreciation on the balance sheet for such estimate differences or alternatively focus principally on cash flow data, which inherently adjust for such cost allocation differentials. For example, in the case of Lufthansa and British Airways, to place the two airlines on a common depreciation basis, Lufthansa's depreciation charges could be reduced by an average of 41 percent (i.e., 1 minus (10/17)) to reflect that company's faster depreciation write-off schedule as compared to that of British Airways. Alternatively, since the cash flow from operations and EBITDA exclude depreciation charges, comparing the two airlines' performance on these financial indicators naturally overcomes any differences in reported profits attributable to such variances in cost allocation methods.

- The accounting for goodwill may vary not only in terms of method but also in terms of amortization period. Exhibit 5–4 (panel A), for example, reveals that Lufthansa amortizes its goodwill at a rate of 25 percent per year (i.e., over four years), whereas Cimentos de Portugal S.A., a Portuguese conglomerate, immediately charges off its (pre-1992) goodwill directly against its balance sheet reserves. Although most countries require that goodwill be capitalized to the balance sheet and then be amortized against earnings over the asset's expected economic life, in some countries (principally Germany, Italy, Japan, and the Netherlands), goodwill may be written off immediately against shareholders' equity (see Appendix 5A for an illustration of this approach). The charge-to-equity approach is preferred by some firms because it avoids the drag on future earnings caused by periodic goodwill amortization.[8] Analysts desiring to achieve greater data comparability between a firm using the charge-to-equity method and one using capitalization and amortization will find it easiest to restate the latter firm to a charge-to-equity basis (i.e., determine in which year restatement will be assumed to start and then write off the outstanding balance of goodwill against retained earnings, adjusting deferred income taxes for any tax effects).

- When goodwill is capitalized to the balance sheet, the acceptable period for amortization can vary dramatically. For example, most companies in Canada and the United States adopt a 40-year write-off, but in Japan and Korea, a 5-year write-off is the norm (see Exhibit 5–4, panel B). Restatement for alternative amortization periods is a relatively straightforward process, and it is usually easiest to restate from a longer period to a shorter one.[9] To execute the restatement, obtain $n + 1$ periods of

---

[8]While the charge-to-equity method is not considered GAAP in the United States, the practice is remarkably similar to the restatement procedures followed by most U.S. lending institutions. That is, because goodwill, unlike most tangible assets, lacks a readily accessible resale market, lending institutions usually reduce a borrower's "borrowing base" (i.e., collateralizable assets) by the quantity of its goodwill. This restatement is usually executed by writing off any goodwill (and other intangibles with questionable resale value) against the borrower's net worth. As a consequence, most lending institutions modify the debt-to-equity ratio to become the debt-to-tangible-equity ratio.

[9]Most analysts find it intuitively easier to restate from longer to shorter amortization periods, and there is another reason for doing so. Given the uncertainty associated with the expected life of most intangibles, the strong preference of most professionals is to write intangibles off over shorter periods of time. In essence, the quality of reported earnings is perceived to be higher when shorter amortization (depreciation) periods are in use.

EXHIBIT 5–4

Financial Statement Disclosures: Goodwill

Panel A. Alternative Accounting Approaches for Goodwill

Deutsche Lufthansa AG

Acquired concessions and similar rights are generally depreciated at a rate of 20 percent. Goodwill resulting from consolidation
   is depreciated at a rate of 25 percent.

Cimentos de Portugal, SGPS, S.A.

Acquisition of companies is accounted for using the purchase method. Goodwill arising on acquisition of a company represents the excess of
   the fair value of the consideration given over the fair value of the identifiable net assets acquired. On the first consolidation of the Group, in
   January 1, 1991, the difference between the cost of the investment and the relevant equity of each subsidiary or associated company were
   written off to consolidation differences reserve or adjustments on holding accounts in the Group's equity. Should such subsidiary or
   associated company be sold at a later date, the goodwill relating to the first consolidation will be transferred to retained earnings. Other
   goodwill is amortised over a period of five years or the investment's estimated useful economic life, up to a maximum of twenty years.

Panel B. Alternative Amortization Periods

AMR Corporation

The excess of the purchase price over the fair value of the net assets acquired (goodwill), aggregating $296.5 million at year-end,
   net of accumulated amortization of $22.4 million, is being amortized on a straight-line basis over 40 years.

Mitsui & Co. Ltd.

The consolidated financial statements include the accounts of the Company and its majority-owned domestic and foreign subsidiaries
   (together "the companies"). The excess of the cost of investments in subsidiaries over the equity in net assets at dates of acquisition is being
   amortized over periods of 5 to 20 years using the straight-line method.

Panel C. Negative Goodwill

Volvo

Acquisitions of companies are accounted for using the purchase method. Shareholders' equity in the subsidiaries at date of
   acquisition, including Equity in untaxed reserves, is eliminated in its entirety. Accordingly, only income arising after the date of
   acquisition is included in shareholders' equity. The difference between the cost of shares in a subsidiary and the shareholders'
   equity of the subsidiary at date of acquisition is, if the cost of the company's shareholding represents a higher amount (excess
   value), allocated to the assets to the extent considered appropriate. The remaining excess is included in the consolidated balance
   sheets as Goodwill. Negative goodwill is included in Shareholders' equity (Restricted reserves) or in Current liabilities. In the latter case,
   the negative goodwill is amortized over a maximum period of five years to cover losses and/or reconstruction costs in the acquired
   company.

---

historical data, where n equals the number of periods of comparative data desired
for analytical purposes (e.g., if $n = 5$, $n + 1 = 6$). Measure the change in the
goodwill balance from $n + 1$ to n to assess the quantity of periodic amortization and
average estimated life. (Be sure to review the footnotes to determine if there were
any additions to goodwill during this time frame.) Using the $n + 1$ balance of
goodwill, recalculate the amortization for the shorter write-off period and calculate
the increase to the expense account. It should be observed that this process is merely
an estimation process and likely to be imprecise. Depending on the availability of
historical data, a more accurate spreadsheet of the amortization process, and
adjustments thereto, can be developed. As always, the accuracy of the restatement
process is dictated by the availability of data and the desired level of accuracy.

• Regardless of the reporting origin of the company under analysis, the analyst must
   carefully review the accompanying footnotes and supplemental schedules to see if any
   amortization (depreciation) policy changes were effected during the period of comparison.
   For example, Union Camp, a large U.S. pulp and paper manufacturer, changed its estimate
   of the expected useful life of its mill equipment from 16 to 20 years. This policy change
   added $51 million to the company's net income in the year of the change and was
   disclosed in the footnotes. The comparability of Union Camp's financial data during this
   period relative to, say, Mitsubishi Paper Mills would have been dramatically altered

by this policy change, unless, of course, the change brought Union Camp's policies into greater conformity with those of Mitsubishi. Since Union Camp's cash flows were unaffected by this decision (it was not undertaken for tax purposes), the statement of cash flows represents a "safe haven" for analysts seeking a consistent source of reliable data for analytical purposes. In effect, analysts can safely circumvent the data comparability issues created by this type of policy change by focusing on a company's CFFO or discretionary cash flows. This strategy would be particularly useful in those cases in which the level of intangibles or fixed assets is large relative to total assets.

Alternative Asset Capitalization Policies

World accounting policies with respect to the capitalization of asset values differ dramatically. Consider, for example, the array of accounting practices regarding the capitalization of interest and for research and development costs as depicted in Exhibit 5–5.

For R&D costs, accepted policy runs the gamut from full expensing in the United States, to limited capitalization in Japan, to full capitalization in Brazil. Once capitalized, the period of amortization also varies from a fixed five-year period in Japan and Sweden to a variable period of "expected benefit" in Brazil. Similarly, accepted policy regarding the capitalization of interest for self-constructed assets varies from "not permitted" in Japan, to "optional" in Mexico, to "required" in Brazil and the United States.

These divergences raise a number of analytical issues. First, with the exception of companies domiciled in Germany and Japan, where accepted accounting policies are driven by tax policy, the analyst must always investigate for the presence of **rear-end loading.** A basic tenet of international GAAP, commonly referred to as the *matching principle,* stipulates that when revenues are recognized on the income statement, all expenses associated with generating those revenues also should be recognized. Some companies, however, elect to postpone the recognition of some of these expenses through a process of rear-end loading.

EXHIBIT 5–5

Asset Capitalization Policies

Country	R & D Costs	Interest on Borrowings
United States	Expensed currently (except for software development companies).	Capitalization required for self-constructed assets.
Great Britain	Research costs expensed, but some development costs capitalized.	Capitalization permitted but not widely practiced.
Germany	Expensed currently.	Capitalization permitted but not required.
Italy	May be expensed or, if capitalized, written off over five years; practice is dictated by tax laws.	Interest on debt obtained specifically for the acquisition or construction of an asset must be capitalized (as required by tax law).
Japan	R&D for existing products expensed currently, but capitalized for new products (with five-year write-off).	Capitalization not permitted (except for real estate development companies).
Korea	Should be capitalized if the costs (1) relate to specific products or technology, (2) are identifiable and (3) are reasonably expected to be recovered; otherwise they should be expensed.	Capitalization required.
Mexico	Expensed currently.	Capitalization permitted.
Sweden	Capitalization is permitted (with five-year write-off).	Capitalization permitted on self-constructed assets.

Under rear-end loading, an expenditure (which may involve either an actual cash out-flow or the incurrence of a liability for future cash outflows) is accounted for as an asset on the balance sheet rather than as an expense on the income statement. As a consequence, current period expenses are understated, causing net income and total assets to be overstated. Eventually, the deferred expenses pass through to the income statement and, when that occurs, future period expenses are overstated, causing net income to be understated. Thus, rear-end loading effectively involves trading off future earnings for higher current period earnings.

Identifying that a company has engaged in rear-end loading usually involves making a subjective assessment on the part of the analyst; in effect, the analyst must be willing to conclude that, contrary to management opinion, a higher level of costs should have been deducted against current and/or past earnings than in fact were.

To illustrate this problem, consider the case of America Online, Inc. (AOL), a leading provider of electronic interactive services. Under U.S. and IAS GAAP, the costs of obtaining new AOL customers may be either immediately expensed or deferred and amortized over the expected average life of an AOL account. AOL elected the latter approach and amortized its deferred subscriber acquisition costs over 24 months. By 1995, AOL's capitalized marketing costs of over $77 million exceeded the company's earned income to date by over $110 million (AOL had an accumulated deficit of $33 million). In late 1996, after considerable public criticism of its asset capitalization policy, AOL took a pretax write-off of $385 million. According to a *Wall Street Journal* writer, the large write-off "underscores just how massive the company's marketing efforts have been—and how illusory its profits really were." Investors were apparently pleased to see AOL adopt the more transparent and conservative accounting treatment as the company's share price was bid up considerably in the weeks following the write-off. The new treatment enabled analysts to predict the company's future permanent earnings with greater certainty.

A second analytical concern relates to the divergence of accepted practice regarding such high profile expenditures as interest costs. U.S. GAAP, as well as that of Mexico and many other countries, requires that all costs incurred in the acquisition of an asset and the preparation for its intended use be capitalized into the asset's balance sheet valuation. A natural extension of this general philosophy is to require the capitalization of interest on funds borrowed during the period of an asset's preparation or construction. Under this practice, the amount of interest to be capitalized is based on the interest charges actually incurred for a specific project or, if unknown, the firm's weighted average cost of capital and the average balance of debt associated with the asset. While the interest capitalized to the construction account will ultimately be written off in the form of higher future depreciation charges, the analyst should be concerned with the fact that current earnings will appear to be higher than anticipated because borrowing costs are being capitalized rather than expensed. Similarly, although earnings appear to be currently improved, actual cash flows are reduced by the current payments for debt service charges. Thus, under interest capitalization, current earnings and cash flows are moving in an opposite, rather than a parallel, direction.

Many professional analysts view the capitalization of interest to be an approved form of rear-end loading, arguing that since the cash outflow for interest charges occurs currently, it is inappropriate to defer the expense deduction until depreciation of the capitalized expenditure occurs at a later date. As a consequence, these professionals scan the footnotes to assess the level of currently capitalized interest[10] and then charge those amounts off against

---

[10]*SFAS No. 34* in the United States and *IAS No. 23* require that when interest is capitalized, the capitalized amount be disclosed in the footnotes to the financial statements.

retained earnings (net of the related deferred income tax effect under the assumption that the interest charges were probably immediately expensed for tax purposes).

Exhibit 5–6, for example, presents the financial statements of a (unnamed and figures scaled) real estate development company. The data reveal that in the absence of interest capitalization, the company would have reported a pretax loss of $16,577 (6,130-22,707) in 19x9, instead of a gain of $6,130. The company was so debt-laden that current debt service charges exceeded its total revenues, as well as its existing balance in cash and cash equivalents. A cash flow analysis would reveal that in spite of the positive accrual net earnings, the cash flow from operations was significantly negative. A second important distortion caused by the capitalization of interest involves the balance sheet valuation of "inventories of land." During the period 19x8 to 19x9, land values in the company's principal area of operations were substantially depressed and falling. Note, however, that as a consequence of the capitalization of interest to this account, the value of the land appears to be rising, contrary to reality. In fact, the company should have written down the value of its real estate holdings to their fair market value but had not as yet done so. Why the asset write-down (and the associated loss) had not yet been recognized in the financial statements is a topic we consider shortly.

EXHIBIT 5–6

Capitalization of Interest

	For the Six Months Ended June 30	
Panel A. Consolidated Statement of Income	*19x9*	*19x8*
Total Revenues	$19,538	$18,072
Cost and expenses		
Cost of land sold	5,592	3,325
Development service expense	3,712	9,145
Interest expense	22,707	19,569
Interest capitalized	(22,707)	(19,569)
Selling, general, and administrative expenses	4,104	3,216
Total	$13,408	$15,686
Income before taxes	$6,130	$2,386
Income taxes	2,820	1,098
Adjustment from parent company	(2,820)	(1,098)
Net income	$6,130	$2,386

Panel B. Consolidated Balance Sheet	*June 30, 19x9*	*December 31, 19x8*
Assets		
Cash and investments	$14,313	$29,877
Accounts and notes receivable	30,852	21,659
Inventories of land	519,197	500,115
Rental real estate	13,244	13,438
Property and equipment	2,812	3,127
Other assets	4,421	3,811
Total	$584,839	$572,027
Liabilities and Shareholders' Equity		
Accounts payable and accrued liabilities	$20,908	$23,817
Notes payable	420,047	410,455
Total liabilities	$440,955	$434,272
Common stock	100	100
Additional paid-in capital	30,475	30,475
Retained earnings	113,309	107,180
Total shareholders' equity	143,884	137,755
Total	$584,839	$572,027

A final analytical concern involves the divergence in practice relating to R&D costs. *IAS No. 9* prescribes that all R&D costs be expensed as incurred, with the exception of those development costs that must be capitalized if they meet the following criteria:

- The product or process is clearly defined, and attributable costs can be clearly identified therewith.
- The technical feasibility of the product or process has been demonstrated.
- Management has indicated its intention to produce, market, or use the product or process.
- There is clear evidence of the utility or marketability of the product or process.
- Adequate resources exist, or are reasonably expected to be available, to complete and market the product or process.

As Exhibit 5–5 reveals, however, existing GAAP for R&D varies greatly, with some countries permitting the capitalization of some (e.g., Japan) or all (e.g., Korea) of a company's research and development outlays, and others (e.g., Germany) not permitting capitalization. In the United States and Great Britain, the accounting for such intangibles is largely dictated by whether the "asset" was internally or externally developed. Internally developed intangible assets are expensed immediately, whereas those intangible assets acquired from other entities (i.e., externally developed) may be capitalized to the balance sheet. This treatment produces two concerns. First, for a company actively involved in research and development, little (if any) of this investment will ever appear on its balance sheet. Consequently, these companies may have significant unreported intangible asset values. Second, since little of the initial development cost is ever capitalized to the balance sheet, earnings in periods of intense R&D may be relatively understated due to R&D write-offs, with earnings of subsequent periods relatively overstated due to the absence of any R&D expenses to be matched with future revenues.

Several types of R&D costs have been exempted from general treatment in the United States. Computer software development companies, for example, are permitted to capitalize R&D costs once a commercially viable prototype has been developed; however, all original or new product development costs must be expensed as incurred. Similarly, the natural resource industry is permitted to capitalize exploration costs under the full cost method, as well as under the successful efforts method.

Asset Impairment and Revaluation

The capitalization of interest, deferred charges, and R&D costs permitted in some countries presents excellent examples of the large differences in accepted accounting practice that can exist between nations. It clearly reinforces the notion that restatement is often necessary to put financial analysis at the international level on a comparable basis. The extreme positions also raise doubts about the ability of international standard setters to achieve effective harmonization. These differences must be acknowledged as challenges to effective international financial analysis, and the analyst must respond to this challenge by equipping himself or herself with the necessary tools to overcome these impediments.

Thus far, the question of *which* expenditures should be capitalized (versus expensed) was considered. We now address the related issue of valuation adjustments, either upward (revaluation) or downward (**impairment**), of expenditures that were previously recognized as assets.

Impairment

It is widely accepted around the world that if the economic value of an asset has been permanently impaired, the value of the asset should then be written down by a charge against earnings to reflect the expected diminishment in future earnings and cash flows.[11] Just when an asset is "permanently" impaired, however, is a matter of professional judgment. And, in most cases, corporate management is reluctant to adjust the value of its corporate assets downward, hoping that the observed decline in value is only temporary. Asset write-downs are unpopular for two reasons: not only are total assets and net worth reduced but also current earnings are similarly reduced.

Consider, for example, the case of Trafalgar House Plc, a British property, construction, and transportation company. In 1993, Trafalgar concluded that the economic conditions in Great Britain had deteriorated sufficiently to place in jeopardy the recoverability of certain of the company's investments. As a consequence, Trafalgar booked a write-down of £397.3 million for property impairments and restructuring costs, declaring in effect the value of these assets to be "permanently" impaired.

Of concern to the analyst in regard to the question of permanent impairment is the vagueness inherent in existing international accounting standards, which effectively provide corporate management with considerable leeway in the timing and amount of asset write-downs. In the U.S., under *SFAS No. 121,* an asset impairment should be presumed to have occurred when any of the following conditions are found to exist:[12]

- A substantial reduction in the extent to which a plant (or other material asset) is used.
- A dramatic change in the manner in which an asset is used.
- A substantial drop in the market value of an asset.
- A significant change in the existing law or business environment, adversely affecting the utility of an asset or group of assets.
- A forecast indicating the lack of long-term profitability for an asset or group of assets.
- Costs capitalized in association with an asset, which exceed the cost to acquire or construct the asset.

If one or more of the above events or changes occurs, a company should estimate the future cash flows expected to result from the use of the impaired asset and its eventual disposition. If the sum of the (undiscounted) future cash flows from the asset is less than its carrying value, an impairment loss should be recognized. The amount of the loss should be the excess of the asset's carrying value over its fair value (i.e., the amount at which the asset could be bought or sold between willing parties).

Revaluation

The revaluation of assets is undertaken regularly by companies in Britain and other Commonwealth countries and periodically (i.e., when mandated by the government) in Italy (see Exhibit 5–7, panels A and B). In Mexico, asset values are revalued and indexed for that country's high rate of inflation (Exhibit 5–7, panel C), and in Germany and Sweden, revaluation is permitted, but only in unusual circumstances (see Chapters 8 and 10). In Japan and the United States, however, a strict application of the historical

---

[11]If an asset has been previously revalued upward using a revaluation reserve account, the write-down should first be taken against the reserve account; and in the event that the write-down exceeds the reserve balance, the excess should be charged against current earnings.

[12]Financial Accounting Standards Board, *SFAS No. 121,* "Accounting for the Impairment of Long-Lived Assets" (Stamford, CT, 1998).

EXHIBIT 5–7

Financial Statement Disclosures: Asset Revaluation

Panel A. British Airways Plc
Tangible fixed assets
(a) Basis

   Tangible fixed assets are stated at cost except for certain aircraft fleets and properties that are included at valuation. Depreciation is calculated to write off the cost or valuation, less residual value, on the straight-line basis.
(b) Fleet

   Cost/valuation. Apart from the Concorde fleet, which remains at a zero book value, the majority of the owned aircraft fleets were professionally valued on a market value basis, and are included in the financial statements on the basis of that valuation, with subsequent expenditure at cost, less depreciation.

Panel B. Fiat
Plant, property, and equipment are recorded at purchase or construction cost. These values are adjusted where specific laws of the country in which the assets are located allow revaluation to reflect, even if only partially, the changes in the purchasing power of the local currency or when a revaluation is obligatory. Plant, property, and equipment as of year-end, comprise the following (in billions of lire):

	Gross	Accumulated Depreciation	Net
Land and buildings	9,497	2,121	7,376
Plant and machinery	23,504	15,184	8,320
Other equipment	3,457	—	2,559
Construction in progress	39,017	19,431	19,586

Italian legislation (law 413/91) imposed on companies the compulsory revaluation of industrial and civil buildings and land to be developed by using coefficients established by the same law. The effect of the compulsory revaluations on consolidated fixed assets is approximately 1,600 billion lire. Depreciation on revalued amounts are calculated beginning in 1992.

Panel C. CIFRA S.A. DE C.V. and Subsidiaries—Property and Equipment
The subsidiary companies have recognized increase in the value of their property, equipment and installations, through the revaluation of their original cost, accumulated depreciation and amortization.

In accordance with the Fifth Amendment to Statement B-10 issued by the Mexican Institute of Public Accountants, as from January 1, 1997, nonmonetary assets must be restated solely using factors derived from the NCPI and no longer by the specific cost method used by the company up to December 31, 1996. It is not practical to determine the effect of the change in valuation method.

Property and equipment are summarized below:

	December 31 1997			1996
	Historical Cost	Revaluation Increment	Total	Total
Land	Ps 1,902,564	Ps 5,312,875	Ps 7,215,439	Ps 5,220,995
Buildings	Ps 2,223,074	Ps 3,738,752	Ps 5,961,826	Ps 3,687,064
Leasehold improvements and installations	1,336,661	1,189,251	2,525,912	1,928,196
	3,559,735	4,928,003	8,487,738	5,615,260
Less -				
Accumulated depreciation and amortization	371,477	1,596,300	1,967,777	1,686,217
	Ps 3,188,258	Ps 3,331,703	Ps 6,519,961	Ps 3,929,043
Furniture and equipment	Ps 3,000,440	Ps 3,307,500	Ps 6,307,940	Ps 4,520,476
Less -				
Accumulated depreciation	710,763	1,752,304	2,463,067	1,658,851
	Ps 2,289,677	Ps 1,555,196	Ps 3,884,873	Ps 2,861,625
Work in process			Ps 437,235	Ps 285,316
Total			Ps 18,017,508	Ps 12,296,979

cost rule is followed, and consequently revaluations are not permitted (except for marketable securities).

Although professional analysts applaud the efforts of Japan and the United States to secure *objective* asset values, they readily point out that the financial statements of companies from these countries can be very misleading, particularly in regard to long-lived, appreciating assets such as property and long-term investments. These analysts correctly observe that Japanese and U.S. financial statements often transfer the burden of obtaining up-to-date asset values from the reporting company (which presumably is in the best position to know those values) to the financial statement user, who may be ill-equipped to assess such information. At the extreme, this situation may lead to mispriced securities in the Japanese and U.S. stock markets.

The systematic revaluation of assets in some countries, and the absence of revaluation in others, is another source of data differentials. Unless an analyst has a particular vantage point that would permit him or her to know the underlying asset values of a U.S. or Japanese firm, it is usually best not to try to revalue those assets to achieve comparability with, say, a British firm. Instead, since the revaluation reserve is publicly disclosed in the shareholders' equity section of the balance sheet, it is a simpler task to readjust the British firm's asset values downward to achieve parity.

Off-Balance Sheet Debt

The problem of **off-balance sheet debt**—obligations not reported on the face of the balance sheet—plagues the accounting of every country in the world, to a greater or lesser extent. In this section, some common forms of off–balance sheet debt are considered, as well as techniques to compensate for their impact.

Unconsolidated Debt

Accepted practice with respect to the consolidation of controlled subsidiaries varies greatly between nations (see Appendix 5A). In the United States, all majority-controlled subsidiaries (except those in bankruptcy or in the process of being sold) must be consolidated with the financial results of the parent company; however, in Japan, controlled subsidiaries may remain unconsolidated and, instead, are accounted for by the equity method. This presents the anomalous situation in Japan (and other countries) that debt obligations legally attributable to the parent company may remain unconsolidated. Even in the United States, however, the debt of a joint venture that is guaranteed by the venture partners (i.e., the parent companies) may remain off-balance sheet to the partners because joint ventures are accounted for by the equity method.[13] As a consequence, the debt position of the parent, as revealed by its balance sheet, appears less highly leveraged than in fact it really is. To overcome this, it is a simple matter to adjust (increase) both the assets and the liabilities of the parent for the quantity of the debt, carried on the books of the

---

[13]In the United States, for example, *SFAS No. 94,* "Consolidation of All Majority-Owned Subsidiaries," does not cover joint ventures. Thus, if a parent company is involved in a number of joint ventures that have significant outstanding lines of credit guaranteed by the parent, the debt will appear only on the financial statements of the joint venture. In the view of many analysts, it is imperative to consider a worst-case scenario in which the joint venture fails and the parent is legally obligated to assume the guaranteed debt. Obviously, the worst-case scenario may never arise; however, if the investment or lending opportunity appears viable even under the worst-case conditions, the analyst can gain a certain degree of confidence through such information. Under *IAS No. 5,* the preferred accounting for joint ventures is proportionate consolidation, although the equity method is also allowed. When proportionate consolidation is adopted, the problem of unconsolidated off-balance sheet debt is avoided.

unconsolidated subsidiary or joint venture, but accruing to the parent by virtue of legal guarantees. This permits the analyst to obtain a truer assessment of the parent's effective level of gearing.

To illustrate, consider the case of General Motors, a large U.S. automaker, and its wholly owned financing subsidiary, General Motors Acceptance Corporation. Prior to 1988, GM accounted for GMAC on an unconsolidated basis using the equity method. Beginning in that year, as a consequence of the adoption of *SFAS No. 94* by the FASB, GM consolidated the operations of GMAC, and the effect of this accounting change can be illustrated by comparing the total debt-to-equity ratio for GM in 1992 both with and without the operations of GMAC:

	1992
Total debt-to-equity: without consolidation	18.5%
Total debt-to-equity: with consolidation	29.7%
Change	61%

These figures clearly illustrate the dramatic effect on solvency metrics that results when a parent is able to off-load debt to an unconsolidated subsidiary or joint venture.

Contingent Liabilities

Contingencies, or **contingent liabilities,** represent a category of potential liabilities. Whether a contingent liability is reported in the footnotes or not, however, is largely determined by management's assessment of the probability of the liability's expected occurrence. Under *SFAS No. 5* in the United States and *IAS No. 10,* if a contingent loss is "probable" and can be reasonably estimated, a liability should be formally accrued on the balance sheet, along with a loss on the income statement. If, on the other hand, the loss is only "reasonably possible" or if probable but the amount cannot be reasonably estimated, only footnote disclosure is required (see Exhibit 5–8, panels A and B). Finally, if realization of the loss and, hence liability, is judged only to be "remote," no disclosure whatsoever is required.

The "probable" threshold for purposes of applying *SFAS No. 5* or *IAS No. 10* is not explicit in the accounting literature. It is generally considered to be well above a 50 percent probability, somewhere between a probability of 70 to 90 percent, depending on the source. But just what conditions indicate a probable liability versus a reasonably possible liability vary between managers and often between auditors. More often than not, "probable" liabilities end up being reported only in the footnotes or, unfortunately, not at all.

Consider, for example, the case of Bristol-Myers Squibb, Dow Corning, and Merck, three international pharmaceutical companies involved in the manufacture of silicone breast implants. In the late 1980s, medical tests revealed that the implants were capable of leaking and that silicone could be linked to various health problems experienced by implant patients. Because of uncertainty regarding the extent of company liability associated with the defective implants, none of the companies accrued losses (or liabilities) for the class action lawsuits filed against them until early 1994, at which time the firms agreed to contribute various sums to a trust fund on behalf of the implant patients.

This case illustrates the all-too-often reluctance by management to recognize a loss and the related liability associated with contingent future events. Although the desire to avoid unpleasant news is quite natural, it suggests that analysts should be prepared to take

EXHIBIT 5–8
Financial Statement Disclosures: Commitments and Contingent Liabilities

Panel A. Mitsui & Co., Ltd.

The companies customarily enter into long-term purchase contracts for certain items, principally iron ore, copper ore, machinery and equipment, and aluminum ingots, either at fixed prices or at basic purchase prices adjustable to market. In general, customers of the companies are also parties to the contracts or by separate agreements are committed to purchase the commodities from the companies; such customers are large Japanese industrial companies. Long-term purchase contracts at fixed or basic purchase prices amounted to approximately ¥890,300 million ($5,634,810 thousand) at year-end. Scheduled deliveries are at various dates through 2001.

The companies had financing commitments totaling ¥68,985 million ($436,614 thousand) at year-end, principally for financing, on a deferred-payment basis, the cost of equipment to be purchased by their customers.

In the furtherance of their trading activities, it is a customary practice for the companies to guarantee, severally or jointly with others, indebtedness of certain of their customers and suppliers and of certain associated companies, as well as to guarantee the performance of contracts by such entities. At year-end, the aggregate amount of such guarantees was ¥256,584 million ($1,623,949 thousand) including ¥64,479 million ($408,095 thousand) relating to associated companies.

Various claims and legal actions are pending against the Company and its subsidiaries in respect of contractual obligations and other matters arising out of the conduct of the companies' business. Provision has been made for estimated liabilities under certain claims. In the opinion of management, based upon the advice of counsel, any additional liability will not materially affect the consolidated financial position or results of operations of the Company and its subsidiaries.

Panel B. Volvo

The amount shown for guarantees to customers and others pertaining to bank loans, 1,873 (1,804; 737) includes the unutilized portion of credit facilities, 11 (40; 88). Recourse obligations pertain to receivables that have been transferred (sales-financing operations), less reduction for recognized credit risks. Other contingent liabilities include 528 (940; 910) related to claims in connection with the tax audit of AB Volvo and its Swedish subsidiaries, for which provisions were not deemed necessary. In addition, a suit against Volvo Car Corporation in Puerto Rico pertaining to the model designations of passenger cars has been recorded as a contingent liability.

(000 SEK)	*1996*	*1995*	*1994*
Discounted bills	368	530	495
Guarantees:			
Bank loans and trade bills			
—associated companies	316	256	115
Bank loans—			
customers and others	1,873	1,804	737
Recourse obligations	515	1,252	1,746
Other contingent liabilities	3,116	3,608	4,488
Total	**6,188**	**7,450**	**7,581**

an aggressive stance in regard to restating published financial statements with respect to contingent liabilities.

Executory Contracts

A final category of off–balance sheet debt involves a group of contractual agreements called **executory contracts.** These contractual commitments are accounted for off the balance sheet because an exchange of something more than promises has not yet occurred. As a consequence, executory contracts are disclosed principally through the footnotes, much like a contingent liability. Examples include operating leases, purchase or supply agreements, loan guarantees on the borrowings of related companies, take-or-pay contracts, and working capital maintenance agreements, to name a few.

To illustrate the accounting conundrum created by these contracts, consider the following two contractual relationships:

1. A company borrows $1 million from a bank, agreeing to repay the borrowed amount, plus interest of $150,000 over a 12-month period.

2. A company signs a noncancellable, nontransferable lease on retail space, agreeing to pay $1.15 million in rent payments over the next 12 months.

In both cases, the company has incurred an economic liability of approximately equivalent amounts (i.e., $1.15 million over the one-year period, ignoring the small differential associated with the time value of money); however, only in the first relationship is the company obligated to record an accounting liability for future payments.

The second relationship depicts a typical operating lease, which in many countries (including the United States) requires no balance sheet recognition of the future lease payments. Instead, the lease payments are recognized only on the income statement as a lease expense, when paid. When operating leases are carried off-balance sheet, existing international GAAP (i.e., *IAS No. 17*) requires that the minimum future lease payments be disclosed in the company's footnotes.

It is often difficult for cash-flow minded analysts to understand why the accounting profession differentiates operating leases (and similar executory contracts) from other accounting liabilities. Perhaps the best explanation of this can be seen by examining the similarities and differences in the two preceding relationships. Although both contracts involve approximately equivalent cash outflows, they differ as to the amount of consideration received at contract signing. With the bank loan, consideration of $1 million was immediately received, and, thus, a liability for the repayment of that amount must be recorded. With the operating lease, however, only a *promise* of future consideration (i.e., the opportunity to utilize the retail space) was received.

For many analysts, this subtle distinction is irrelevant; what matters is that the company has a noncancelable obligation to make future cash payments. Similarly, in the eyes of many financial statement users, this condition alone is sufficient justification to merit inclusion of the economic liability in the accounting statements. Given this particular viewpoint, it is a simple matter to restate a company's financial statements for these unreported obligations if adequate information disclosures exist. As Exhibit 5–9 reveals, many countries (e.g., Italy and Japan) fail to capitalize any type of lease, and for those countries that do (e.g., Germany, Korea, and Sweden), the level of financial disclosures is quite limited. Thus, despite the IASC recommended treatment, only Great Britain and the United States appear to conform to the reporting expectations of *IAS No. 17*. Consequently, for both British and U.S. companies and those foreign companies that do provide adequate footnote disclosure, the restatement of financial statements to depict noncapitalized leases on the balance sheet is relatively straightforward.

To illustrate how this restatement can be undertaken, consider the financial data of Global Enterprises, Inc., (GE) a multinational company headquartered in the United States and presented in Exhibit 5–10.

Exhibit 5–10 reveals that GE leases substantial quantities of retail space, all via operating leases. To assess the impact of these leases on the financial statements of GE, we adopt an approach of treating all operating leases as capital leases, which involves capitalizing the present value of the future lease payments on GE's balance sheet as both a liability and an asset. Assuming that GE's incremental cost of borrowing at July 30, 1998, is 10 percent (the company's footnotes revealed that GE's short-term weighted average cost of capital was 9.3 percent and its long-term notes carried interest rates of approximately 9.75 percent), an estimate of the present value of the minimum future lease payments after 1998 total approximately $350.8 million. Using this estimated figure, the

---

EXHIBIT 5–9

Accounting for Leases

Country	Operating Leases	Capital Leases
Germany	Leases are carried off balance sheet but must be disclosed in footnotes if material.	Accounting treatment follows complex tax rules.
Great Britain	Treatment and criteria are similar to those in the United States.	Criteria are similar to those in the United States; however, capitalized leases are carried at face value.
Italy	All leases, regardless of economic substance, are treated as operating leases. No footnote disclosures required.	Not applicable.
Japan	Substantially all leases are treated as operating but no disclosures are required.	Not applicable.
Korea	Treatment and criteria are similar to those in the United States.	Treatment and criteria are similar to those in the United States. Present value of lease obligation is reported if significantly different from face value.
Mexico	Treatment and criteria are similar to those in the United States.	Treatment similar to that in the United States.
Sweden	Leases are carried off balance sheet unless the lease contract requires acquisition of the leased asset at some point during the lease period.	If a lease agreement provides for a deferred acquisition, at terms specified in the lease contract, balance sheet disclosure is recommended. Leases are valued at face value of obligation.
United States	Leases are carried off balance sheet, with footnote disclosure of future minimum, noncancelable lease payments.	Capitalized asset and liability are carried at present value of minimum future lease payments.

---

analyst then increases GE's long-term assets (i.e., leased property) by $350.8 million and its liabilities by an equivalent amount.[14]

Another executory contract deriving its existence from banking relations is the **working capital maintenance agreement.** Instead of guaranteeing the full performance of a debt contract, a parent company may guarantee only certain aspects of a contract. For example, since most debt contracts specify that the existing financial condition of a borrower be maintained, a working capital maintenance agreement (WCMA) may be negoti-

---

[14]More specifically, the accounting entry would appear as follows:

Dr. Leased assets	$350.8 million
Cr. Short-term lease obligation	$50.8 million
Cr. Long-term lease obligation	$300.0 million

The analyst should note that restating the balance sheet with this entry also requires a consideration of the effect of the restatement on the income statement. With capitalization, the lease expense needs to be replaced by depreciation expense (on the newly capitalized asset) and interest expense on the lease liability. Hence, capitalization requires that the analyst make certain assumptions regarding depreciation on the newly capitalized asset (i.e., method, salvage value, expected life).

EXHIBIT 5–10

Global Enterprises, Inc.

Panel A. Consolidated Balance Sheet (July 30, 1998)

Assets

Total current assets	$529,544
Net property, plant, and equipment	264,118
Excess of cost over net assets of subsidiaries acquired, less applicable amortization	60,597
Other assets and deferred charges, at cost less apllicable amortization	10,626
Total assets	$864,885

Liabilities and Stockholders' Equity

Total current liabilities	$271,293
Deferred federal and state income taxes	14,167
Long-term debt, excluding current installments	11,133
Stockholders' equity	
Common stock of $.10 par value. Authorized 100 million; issued 37,461,475	3,746
Capital in excess of par value	108,971
Retained earnings	455,575
Total stockholders' equity	$568,292
Total liabilities and stockholders' equity	$864,885

Panel B. Footnote Disclosures: Leases

The company conducts the major portion of its retail operations from leased store premises under leases that will expire within the next 25 years. Such leases generally contain renewal options exercisable at the option of the company. In addition to minimum rental payments, certain leases provide for payment of taxes, maintenance, and percentage rentals based upon sales in excess of stipulated amounts.

Total rental expense was as follows:	*1998*
Minimum rentals	$55,980
Percentage rentals	10,735
	$66,715

At July 30, 1998, minimum rental commitments under noncancellable leases were as follows:

Year	
1999	$ 55,892
2000	54,884
2001	53,434
2002	52,107
2003	50,606
2004–2008	210,166
2008–2012	129,807
2012–2016	54,572
after 2016	4,918
	$666,386

ated wherein a parent or affiliate company commits to maintaining the level of working capital of the borrower. Note the executory aspect of this agreement: In the event that the borrower's working capital falls below the level specified by the debt agreement, the guarantor is obligated to provide the necessary cash infusion to maintain the working capital level for the remaining life of the contract.

Most managers view a WCMA as a bottomless "black hole" in that there are seldom any limits (other than the life of the debt contract) on the required cash infusions. On more than one occasion, a guarantor has found it less costly to merely pay off the debt contract as a means to escape the perpetual cash flow drain created by a WCMA. Thus, analysts would be wise to note this view, and given that current GAAP disclosures for some countries require the presentation of the basic elements of an existing WCMA in the guarantor's footnotes, it is important to consider the impact of such commitments on the future cash flows of a company.

A final example is the **take-or-pay contract,** sometimes called a *thru-put contract.* Under a take-or-pay contract, one company agrees to make specific future cash payments to another for a predetermined minimum quantity of products or services. Payment for the minimum quantity is required regardless of whether a buyer desires, or is even able to accept, the product. Hence, if a buyer ceases operations, either temporarily or permanently, the cash outflow required by the take-or-pay contract must be maintained. Existing GAAP in the United States and elsewhere requires that a company disclose the existence of and the minimum cash flows required under such contracts, thereby enabling the financial statement user to project the future cash flows of a company under various operating scenarios. *IAS No. 10* requires only that when such contracts may lead to contingent losses, those losses be accrued if their occurrence is probable, or footnoted if occurrence is reasonably probable.

Balance Sheet Reserves

In the United States, the shareholders' equity section of the balance sheet is commonly segmented into three principal parts. *Contributed capital* includes the par or stated value of any issued common or preferred shares, as well as any contributed capital in excess of par or stated value. *Earned capital* includes retained earnings, both appropriated and unappropriated. Lastly, there are the *adjustments to shareholders' equity* that include any shares held in treasury, and Accumulated Other Comprehensive Income (to be discussed in Chapter 6).

In the financial statements of many non-U.S. companies, however, a fourth category is often observed as part of shareholders' equity, namely one or more "reserve" accounts.[15] These equity reserve accounts may arise for a variety of reasons, and some of the most common are as follows:

Account	*Purpose or Source of Origination*
Revaluation reserve	The cumulative (credit) balance resulting from the periodic (e.g., as in Italy and the U.K.) revaluation of noncurrent assets to reflect their changing market values, which is usually unavailable for distribution
Legal (or statutory) reserves	The cumulative balance of retained profits (usually 5–10 percent of annual earnings) that must be legally reinvested in the operations of a company and that is usually unavailable for distribution (e.g., as in Japan and Sweden)
Restricted reserves	The cumulative balance of retained earnings whose retention is required by a company's charter of association or incorporation and that is usually unavailable for distribution (e.g., as in Italy and Sweden)

[15]Usually, retained earnings is considered to be a reserve account (e.g., Profit and Loss Reserve).

From an analytical perspective, these reserves create a variety of financial effects, including these:

- Restricting the ability of a company to pay dividends.
- Preserving, on average, a higher portion of retained profits.
- Creating a form of legally enforced corporate reinvestment.

Not unexpectedly, one outcome of the use of equity reserves is a somewhat lower return on equity, at least as compared with the United States as the following data for 1998 reveal:

	Average ROE
United States	11.4
Germany	9.2
Italy	8.0
Japan	3.3

Available Reconciliations to U.S. GAAP

The U.S. Securities and Exchange Commission (SEC) grants foreign firms whose securities trade on national exchanges in the United States, and thus that are required to file financial statements with the agency, the alternative of presenting financial statements prepared in accordance with U.S. GAAP or of presenting financial statements according to the accounting principles of their home country. If the latter alternative is chosen, additional disclosures reconciling net income and shareholders' equity under home country GAAP to U.S. GAAP must accompany financial statements filed with the SEC. Arguably, the most famous of such reconciliations was made in 1993 by Daimler-Benz AG of Germany, which is reproduced in Exhibit 5–11.

Daimler-Benz, the largest manufacturer in Germany, was widely acknowledged to be experiencing financial problems in 1993. Despite these problems, Daimler had a long record of consistently healthy earnings under German GAAP. Due to its urgent need to gain access to U.S. financial markets, Daimler became the first German company to seek listing on a major U.S. stock exchange and, as a result, subjected itself to U.S. GAAP disclosure requirements. The reconciliation to U.S. GAAP revealed what many had expected: that German accounting techniques had effectively hidden Daimler's inability to generate a profit—Daimler's German GAAP net income for the first six months of 1993 was DM168 million versus a net loss of DM949 million under U.S. GAAP!

The Daimler disclosures effectively vindicated the SEC for its tough stance on foreign companies that were unwilling to disclose U.S. GAAP results in exchange for full access to U.S. investors. However, Exhibit 5–11 does contain one element of compromise: The reconciliation disclosures fail to facilitate a restatement of a foreign company's assets and liabilities to U.S. GAAP.

EXHIBIT 5–11

DAIMLER-BENZ AG
Notes to Unaudited Interim Condensed Consolidated Financial Statements
(in millions, except per share amounts)

The following is a summary of the significant adjustments to net income for the six-month periods, ended June 30, 1993 and 1992, and to stockholders' equity at June 30, 1993 and December 31, 1992, which would be required if U.S. GAAP had been applied instead of German GAAP.

	Six Months Ended June 30,	
	1993	*1992*
Net income as reported in the consolidated income statements under German GAAP	DM 168	DM1,073
Less: Income and losses applicable to minority shareholders	(51)	84
Adjusted net income under German GAAP	117	1,157
Add: Changes in appropriated retained earnings—provisions, reserves, and valuation differences	(1,615)	(169)
	(1,498)	988
Other adjustments required to conform with U.S. GAAP		
Long-term contracts	30	70
Goodwill and business acquisitions	(33)	(35)
Business dispositions		337
Pensions and other postretirement benefits	(135)	80
Foreign currency translation	(7)	161
Financial instruments	(293)	(199)
Other	67	(130)
Deferred taxes	920	(255)
Net income (loss) in accordance with U.S. GAAP before cumulative effect of a change in accounting principle	(949)	1,017
Cumulative effect of change in accounting for postretirement benefits other than pensions as of January 1, 1992, net of tax of DM33		(52)
Net income (loss) in accordance with U.S. GAAP	**(949)**	**965**
Earnings (loss) per share in accordance with U.S. GAAP	DM(20.37)	DM20.73*
Earnings (loss) per American depositary share in accordance with U.S. GAAP†	DM (2.04)	DM 2.07*

*Includes the negative effect of change in accounting for postretirement benefits other than pensions of DM 1.12 per share (DM 0.11 per American depositary share).
†Earnings per American depositary share are calculated on the basis of 10 American depositary shares for every ordinary share.

	At June 30, 1993	*At Dec. 31, 1992*
Stockholders' equity as reported in the consolidated balance sheets under German GAAP	DM18,938	DM19,719
Less: Minority interest	(1,260)	(1,228)
Adjusted stockholders' equity under German GAAP	17,678	18,491
Add: Appropriated retained earnings—provisions, reserves, and valuation differences*	8,316	9,931
	25,994	28,422
Other adjustments required to conform with U.S. GAAP		
Long-term contracts	161	131
Goodwill and business acquisitions	1,844	1,871
Pensions and other postretirement benefits	(1,347)	(1,212)
Foreign currency translation	203	(342)
Financial instruments	287	580
Other	(1,672)	(1,708)
Deferred taxes	761	(138)
Stockholders' equity in accordance with U.S. GAAP	**26,231**	**27,604**

*The adjustment to stockholders' equity of DM8,316 and DM9,931 would have reduced other provisions at June 30, 1993, and December 31, 1992, by DM5,945 and DM8,105, respectively. The remainder of the adjustments would have increased inventories and other receivables under U.S. GAAP.

A General Framework for Restatement

Given sufficient information for an informative restatement, how should one go about it? The approach taken in this section assumes that the analyst simulates an "opening" of a company's accounting ledger for a given period and debits and credits various accounts. The purpose is to achieve a cost-effective and preferable representation of financial results. The approach also retains the logic of the double-entry accounting model and thereby imposes a discipline on the analyst to fully consider the effects of restatement on financial reports.

To describe this restatement approach and to discuss some of the issues an analyst may encounter when attempting to achieve a useful restatement, we adapt an actual analyst's evaluation of a major German conglomerate, which we will call *Blauweiss AG.* Comparative balance sheets and an income statement for one recent year are presented in Exhibit 5–12.

The objective of the restatement is to reflect U.S. GAAP to the maximum extent practicable on the financial statements of *Blauweiss* to make them more comparable. The following is a summary of some important differences between German and U.S. GAAP identified by the analyst (see also Chapter 8). For some of these differences, the analyst has explicitly estimated their effects on a comparison of *Blauweiss'* financial statements with those of U.S. companies. For other differences, sometimes the best an analyst can do is merely note their existence and subjectively incorporate their impact on financial ratios and other measures of risk and return. For still others, the analyst may find it beneficial to undertake a partial restatement.

Excess Depreciation.   Most deductions claimed for tax purposes must also be booked for accounting purposes by German companies. Consequently, items such as accelerated depreciation claimed for taxes are also reported as expenses for shareholder reporting purposes. Had the straight-line method been used for book purposes, which is common in the United States and most other countries, the analyst estimated that the fixed assets would have been DM1,450 million higher as of the most recent balance sheet date. It is also estimated that straight-line depreciation was less than German tax basis depreciation in 19x9 by DM56 million.

The following journal entry gives recognition to these facts:

Ref.	Account Titles	Debit	Credit
a	Accumulated Depreciation	1,450	
	Depreciation and Amortization		
	(Retained Earnings)		56
	Retained Earnings		1,394

The effect on retained earnings is seen to consist of two components: the effect on the *current* period's earnings and the effect on *prior* periods' earnings. Thus, an entry similar to this one would be made for all periods that the analyst chose to restate.

Both U.S. and German GAAP provide for a proper matching of income tax expense to the book income before taxes for a period (however, the numerous book/tax conformity rules in the German tax code reduce the materiality of deferred taxes in that country). The following entry is made to capture the effect of the timing difference between book and tax income due to different depreciation methods:

Ref.	Account Titles	Debit	Credit
b	Taxes (Retained Earnings)	28	
	Retained Earnings	770	
	Deferred Taxes		798

EXHIBIT 5–12

Blauweiss AG

Panel A. Condensed German GAAP Balance Sheet, December 31, 19x9 (DM millions)

Current Assets

Cash and short-term investments	DM3,574	
Accounts receivable	4,704	
Inventories	2,898	
Total current assets		DM11,176

Current Liabilities

Debt	(607)	
Payables	(2,654)	
Accruals and provisions	(4,444)	
		(7,705)
Net Current Assets		3,471
Fixed assets	13,089	
Accumulated depreciation	(9,216)	
		3,873
Intangible assets	449	
Other assets	721	
		1,171
		8,515
Pensions provision		(3,472)
Other liabilities		(50)
		DM 4,993

Shareholders' Equity

Common ordinary capital	2,446	
Retained earnings	2,547	
Total shareholders' equity		**DM 4,993**

Panel B. German GAAP Income Statement, Year Ended December 31, 19x9 (DM millions)

Sales	DM22,330	
Inventory change/capitalized work	1,559	
Operating output	23,889	
Other operating income	688	
Cost of materials	(12,361)	
Staff costs	(7,830)	
Other operating expenses	(2,653)	
Income from participations	95	
Depreciation and amortization	(995)	
Value adjustments	(21)	
Net interest	292	
Profit on ordinary activities		**DM1,104**
Extraordinary results		(98)
Taxes		(501)
Net income		**DM 505**

Deferred Taxes is credited for the cumulative timing difference of DM1,450 multiplied by an assumed incremental tax rate of 55 percent.[16] The effects on income of current and prior periods is identical in concept to the adjustments made for excess depreciation.

Contingency Reserves.   Contingency reserves are a principal means used by German companies to smooth earnings. As evidence of the contingent nature of these reserves, the

---

[16]The normal German federal tax rate for corporations subject to unlimited tax liability is 50 percent. The incremental effect of local income taxes can vary widely.

other income caption in German profit and loss statements usually includes write-backs of prior year reserves no longer considered necessary. The analyst estimated that at least DM900 million of the amounts included in Accruals and Provisions would not be allowable under U.S. GAAP. New accruals in 19x9 are roughly estimated at DM50 million and are thought to be a component of Other Operating Expenses.

The following journal entries recognize these facts. It is assumed that the first entry creates a timing difference between book income before taxes and taxable income, thus necessitating the second entry.

Ref.	Account Titles	Debit	Credit
c	Accruals and Provisions	900	
	Other Operating Expenses (Retained		
	Earnings)		50
	Retained Earnings		850
d	Taxes (Retained Earnings)	28	
	Retained Earnings	467	
	Deferred Taxes		495

Goodwill. *Blauweiss's* present accounting policy is to capitalize and amortize goodwill from acquisitions over a period of four years. Considering that (1) common U.S. practice is to amortize goodwill over a 40-year amortization period and (2) *Blauweiss* has not recently acquired major subsidiaries, the analyst estimates that goodwill is understated as of December 31, 19x9, by DM285 million and that earnings for 19x9 are overstated by DM79 million.

The entry to record the adjustment to goodwill and shareholders' equity accounts is identical in concept to the depreciation adjustments made earlier:

Ref.	Account Titles	Debit	Credit
e	Intangible Assets	285	
	Depreciation and Amortization		
	(Retained Earnings)		79
	Retained Earnings		206

However, the recognition of deferred taxes on differences between the financial statement carrying amount and the tax basis of goodwill depends on whether (and over what period) the amortization of goodwill is deductible for tax purposes. For U.S. federal income tax purposes, amortization of goodwill is currently deductible, but only over an amortization period of 15 years. German tax law similarly provides for the deductibility of goodwill from taxable income but over much shorter periods. Thus, the after-tax effect of this restatement should give rise to recognition of a deferred tax liability:

Ref.	Account Titles	Debit	Credit
f	Taxes (Retained Earnings)	43	
	Retained Earnings	114	
	Deferred Taxes		157

Minority Interest. As is customary in Germany, *Blauweiss* considers minority interest to be part of shareholders' equity, and, consequently, there is no deduction in earnings for the minority interest's share in subsidiary earnings. In the United States, minority interest is classified separately from equity, and the minority interest's share of a subsidiaries' earnings are treated as a deduction from income. Minority interest in subsidiaries is estimated to be DM395 million as of the balance sheet date, and the income effect for the year is estimated to be DM41 million. The prior years' cumulative effect on income is estimated to be DM100 million.

The following entry accomplishes three things: (1) it reduces income of the current period by the amount of minority interest in earnings of consolidated subsidiaries; (2) it reduces retained earnings as of the beginning of the period by the effect of Minority Interest in Earnings from prior periods; and (3) it transfers the difference between DM395 million and the amounts from (1) and (2) from Common Ordinary Capital to a new balance sheet account titled Minority Interest in Subsidiary.

Ref.	Account Titles	Debit	Credit
g	Minority Interest in Earnings	41	
	Retained Earnings	100	
	Common Ordinary Capital	254	
	Minority Interest in Subsidiary		395

There is no deferred tax provision because minority interest in earnings is not deductible for tax purposes in Germany.

Provision for Pensions.   German pension plans are normally unfunded, and significant pension liabilities appear on the balance sheet. Pension expense, which is tax deductible, is based on changes in an actuarial pension obligation at the balance sheet date discounted at prescribed rates of interest. Income on pension assets is not separately identified because the pension assets themselves are not legally segregated from other company assets. Past service costs (i.e., retroactive grants of pension benefits to current or retired employees as a result of establishing a pension plan or "sweetening" an existing pension plan) are generally recognized immediately.

U.S. companies, on the other hand, fund their pension plans during periods of employee service (because if there is no funding, no tax deduction is permitted), and, in general, the company permanently forgoes access to plan assets. The pension plan is treated as a separate entity for accounting purposes and is not consolidated. Pension expense for financial reporting purposes is based on changes in actuarial liabilities (similar to the practice in Germany) but is reduced by actuarial estimates of income generated by pension plan assets. Past service costs are amortized over an extended period of time.

The most significant difference between U.S. and German plans is generally thought to relate to the issue of consolidation or, stated more plainly, whether the pension liability should be netted on the balance sheet against assets that will be used to pay retirees. To make German and U.S. financial statements more comparable, either reversing the offset on U.S. company financial statements or offsetting pension liabilities with pension assets could be appropriate.

In fact, neither solution is fully satisfactory because the divergence between U.S. and German GAAP in the area of pension accounting is in large part related to substantive differences in the pension plans themselves. Since German companies do not separately fund their actuarial pension liabilities, there is no legal segregation of pension plan assets, and the company determines how the assets will be utilized. Since U.S. companies establish separate legal entities for pension assets that are governed by trustees who are independent of the funding corporation, U.S. companies relinquish control of the assets.

Analysts may either make no restatement for pension accounting differences between the United States and Germany, or they may restate U.S. company balance sheets. Reasons to support the latter approach are the following:

- No information is available on German companies that would help an analyst identify which assets, if any, are earmarked to pay pension liabilities.
- Supplemental disclosures in U.S. company reports are usually sufficient to effect a disaggregation of pension assets and liabilities on the balance sheets of U.S. companies.
- U.S. companies do, in fact, have some control of pension plan assets: They select the plan trustees, and funding is usually not irrevocable. It is possible for any over funded pension plan assets to revert to the full control of the plan sponsoring company.

Extraordinary Results.   In Germany, extraordinary or unusual items that arise outside of ordinary operations are separately disclosed. The United States does not permit the segregation of extraordinary items from income from continuing operations unless the event that gave rise to the gain or loss recognition was both unusual and nonrecurring.

Since one objective of financial analysis is often to estimate a future stream of *permanent* income flows, an analyst frequently excludes extraordinary or unusual items from income. In doing so, however, a full restatement of both income statements and balance sheets is often not possible and/or desirable. For instance, the "extraordinary results" of DM98 million for *Blauweiss* probably resulted in a net outflow of cash or the incurrence of a future obligation. Although the analyst might want a better measure of permanent income than the net income reported, future profitability and riskiness are functions of the firm's level of cash and its future obligations, regardless of the type of event—unusual or ordinary—that gave rise to the change in assets and/or liabilities.

Ref.	Account Titles	Debit	Credit
h	Retained Earnings	98	
	Extraordinary Results (Retained Earnings)		98
i	Taxes (Retained Earnings)	54	
	Retained Earnings		54

The two entries taken together adjust the income statement for the after-tax effect of the extraordinary results on income. There is no balance sheet effect because retained earnings is both debited and credited for equal amounts.

Summary of *Blauweiss* Restatements.   The exercise of identifying areas of restatement can lead to actual changes in the appearance of financial statements in preparation for conducting an analysis or, as in the case of pension accounting, can alert the analyst to differences that are difficult to quantify but could be explicitly considered when evaluating accounting measures of profitability and financial position.

With respect to *Blauweiss,* the application of German GAAP has created a conservative bias that understates both net assets and earnings. Earnings trends likely tend to be very smooth because of the broad discretion of German financial statement issuers to manipulate provisions and reserves through valuation allowances and provisions for contingencies. The effect of restatement on the income statement and balance sheet are summarized in two worksheets that compose Exhibit 5–13. In general, restatement increases income dramatically. It also reduces liabilities and increases shareholders' equity, increasing the "strength" of *Blauweiss's* already strong balance sheet.

EXHIBIT 5–13

The Effect of Restatement for Blauweiss AG

Panel A. Restatement Worksheet for Balance Sheet, December 31, 19x9 (DM millions)

	Original	*Debit*	*Ref.*	*Credit*	*Ref.*	*Restated*
Current assets						
Cash and short-term investments	DM 3,574					DM 3,574
Accounts receivable	4,704					4,704
Inventories	2,898					2,898
Total current assets	DM11,176					DM11,176
Current liabilities						
Debt	DM (607)					DM (607)
Payables	(2,654)					(2,654)
Accruals and provisions	(4,444)	900	c			(3,544)
Total current liabilities	(7,705)					(6,805)
Net current assets	DM 3,471					DM 4,371
Fixed assets	13,089					13,089
Accumulated depreciation	(9,216)	1,450	a			(7,766)
	3,873					5,323
Intangible assets	449	285	e			734
Other assets	721					721
	1,171					1,456
	DM 8,515					DM11,150
Pension provision	(3,472)					(3,472)
Other liabilities	(50)					(50)
Deferred taxes				798	b	
				495	d	
				157	f	(1,450)
Minority interest in subsidiary				395	g	(395)
	DM 4,993					DM 5,783
Shareholders' equity						
Common/ordinary capital	DM 2,446	254	g			DM 2,192
Retained earnings	2,547	798	b	1,450	a	
		495	d	900	c	
		157	f	285	e	
		141	g			3,591
Total shareholders' equity	DM 4,993					DM 5,783

Exhibit 5–14 illustrates the effects of these restatements on selected financial ratios. Although liquidity and solvency ratios improve materially, the dramatic effect on profitability is reflected in the increased ROA, ROE, and ROS ratios.

A number of other German accounting differences limit comparability to U.S. companies and understate *Blauweiss's* shareholders' equity under German GAAP relative to U.S. GAAP:

- As is customary in Germany, *Blauweiss* classifies its income statement items by nature of expense (materials, personnel, and so on) rather than by function (cost of sales, advertising). Reformatting would be useful but extremely difficult. For example, we have no way of knowing how to allocate personnel expenses among product and period cost categories. As a result, normal U.S. profitability measures such as gross profit margin, the relationship of advertising to sales, and so forth are not calculable.

EXHIBIT 5–13 (continued)
The Effect of Restatement for Blauweiss AG

Panel B. Restatement Worksheet for Income Statement, Year Ended December 31, 19x9 (DM millions)

	Original	*Debit*	*Ref.*	*Credit*	*Ref.*	*Restated*
Sales	DM22,330					DM22,330
Inventory change/capitalized work	1,559					1,559
Operating output	DM23,889					DM23,889
Other operating income	688					688
Cost of materials	(12,361)					(12,361)
Staff costs	(7,830)					(7,830)
Other operating expenses	(2,653)			50	c	(2,603)
Income from participations	95					95
Depreciation and amortization	(995)			56	a	
				79	e	(860)
Value adjustments	(21)					(21)
Minority interest in earnings		41	g			(41)
Net interest	292					292
Profit on ordinary activities	DM 1,104					DM 1,248
Extraordinary results	(98)			98	h	–0–
Taxes	(501)	28	b			
		28	d			
		43	f			
		54	i			(348)
Net income	**DM 505**					**DM 900**

EXHIBIT 5–14
Effects of Restatement on Ratios for Blauweiss AG

Comparative Ratio Analysis

	Originally Reported	*Restated*	*Percentage Difference*
Current ratio	1.45	1.64	13.2%
Quick ratio	1.07	1.22	13.2
Debt to equity ratio	70.5%	60.9%	−13.7
Interest coverage ratio	4.78	5.27	10.3
Receivables turnover ratio	4.75	4.75	0.0
Total asset turnover ratio	1.38	1.24	−9.7
Return on assets ratio	3.1%	5.0%	61.0
Return on equity ratio	10.1%	15.6%	53.9
Return on sales ratio	2.3%	4.0%	78.2

- Asset write-downs (e.g., for inventory or fixed assets) are more conservative under German GAAP.
- Foreign currency translation losses are recognized, but gains are deferred under German GAAP. This approach is more conservative than either of the two permissible approaches under U.S. GAAP.
- Less overhead is generally included in inventory under German GAAP, and direct costing is permissible.

Summary

General-purpose financial statements satisfy some of the needs for financial information, but it is not infrequent for an analyst to be dissatisfied with some of the accounting methods that have a significant impact on objective analytical measures. Much of this dissatisfaction stems from a lack of comparability across companies being analyzed:

- Use of different, albeit permissible, accounting alternatives for similar circumstances. For example, one company may cost its inventory on a FIFO basis, but another may use a LIFO basis.
- Different accounting standards for the same economic events, as, for example, the difference in accounting for contingencies between the United States and Germany.
- Differences in economic circumstances that motivate a difference in accounting standards, as, for example, the difference in accounting for pensions between the United States and Germany.

It is extremely rare that financial statements perfectly match the needs of an analyst performing an in-depth evaluation of a company. Restatement connotes the ad hoc adjustments undertaken by an analyst to alter the content and appearance of company-prepared financial statements. The purpose is to enhance the comparability, relevance, and reliability of accounting information in a specific decision context. At least *some* restatement is almost always undertaken, ranging from as simple as rearranging and combining items to as complex as modifying accounting methods.

Suggested Readings

Comiskey, E., and C. Tritschler. "On or Off the Balance Sheet—Some Guidance for Credit Analysts." *Journal of Commercial Bank Lending, August 1984.*

Dawson, J. P., P. M. Neupert, and C. P. Stickney. "Restating Financial Statements for Alternative GAAP: Is It Worth the Effort?" *Financial Analysts Journal,* November/December 1980.

Ferris, K. R., K. L. Tennant, and S. Jerris. *How to Understand Financial Statements: A Nontechnical Guide for Financial Analyst Executives and Managers.* New York: Simon and Schuster, 1992.

Hector, G. "Cute Tricks on the Bottom Line." *Fortune,* April 24, 1989.

Heian, J., and J. Thies. "Consolidation of Finance Subsidiaries: $230 Billion in Off-Balance Sheet Financing Comes Home to Roost." *Accounting Horizons,* March 1989.

Means, K., and P. Kazenski. "SFAS 34: A Recipe for Diversity?" *Accounting Horizons,* September 1988.

Sannella, A. "The Capitalization of Operating Leases: The Discounted Cash Flow Approach." *Journal of Commercial Bank Lending,* October 1989.

Wang, P. "The Unlevel Accounting Field." *Forbes,* November 28, 1988.

APPENDIX 5A
A PRIMER ON CONSOLIDATED REPORTING PRACTICES

In many countries throughout the world, when one company obtains a "controlling" interest in another, the parent company is required to present the financial results of the subsidiary company on a consolidated or combined basis. The preparation of consolidated financial statements (i.e., statements reflecting the financial results of a parent company and its controlled subsidiaries) becomes, however, problematic when the parent company operates in one country and thus maintains its financial results in the currency of that country but its subsidiaries operate principally in other countries, maintaining their financial data in the currency of those other countries. It would be meaningless, for example, to consolidate the U.S. dollar-denominated results of a U.S.-based parent company with the Italian lira-denominated results of an Italian-based subsidiary. Thus, before the financial results of the combined entities can be prepared, the data of the foreign subsidiary must first be translated into U.S.-dollar equivalents. Following this translation process, which is the focus of Chapter 6, the consolidated financial results can then be tabulated.

But how are consolidated financial statements prepared? What accounting alternatives exist, and when are those alternative methods likely to be used? Unfortunately, the prevalent reporting practices used throughout the world are quite diverse, and the purpose of this appendix is to briefly overview those practices.

Control: Passive versus Active Investments.   A key determinant used to identify the appropriate consolidation practice involves the extent of *control* exercised by a parent company over its subsidiaries. Control is usually indicated by the quantity of voting shares held by the parent company and thus refers to the capacity of one entity to dominate the decision making of a second entity in regards to its operating policies. In most instances, a shareholding of less than 5 percent usually indicates a low degree of control, whereas a shareholding of 50 percent or more indicates a high degree of control. Between 5 and 50 percent, however, is a substantial gray area in which local accounting practices may differ dramatically. Even in those apparently clear-cut circumstances in which the level of ownership interest exceeds 50 percent, variation in consolidation practices may exist between countries, as will be seen shortly.

In the United States, for example, a shareholding of from 0 to 20 percent is generally interpreted as a low degree of control. For investments of this size, it is assumed (unless evidence to the contrary exists) that the parent company is unable (or unwilling) to exercise control over the operating policies of such subsidiaries. These *passive* investments are usually accounted for on a portfolio basis at their market value. Under this approach, an investment in a subsidiary is carried on the books of the parent company at its original cost, unless market fluctuations indicate the need for an upward or downward revaluation. Under U.S. GAAP (i.e., *SFAS No. 115*), the unrealized gains or losses due to revaluation are reflected in the income statement for portfolios of "trading" securities and on the balance sheet (in owners' equity) for portfolios of securities that are "available for sale." This treatment essentially parallels the accounting practice followed in such countries as Great Britain, wherein annual revaluation is the norm; however, in other countries, such as Germany and Japan, where assets are valued at historical cost applied conservatively, only downward revaluation (i.e., lower of cost or market) is permitted. *IAS No. 25* permits such investments to be valued at their original cost (without regard to market fluctuations), at the lower of cost or market, or at revalued amounts in excess of original cost.[1] Exhibit 5A–1 presents the footnote disclosures for several international companies illustrating the accounting treatment adopted for their investments.

When the level of parent shareholding exceeds 20 percent or when there is evidence that a parent company can exercise significant decision-making influence over the operations of a subsidiary (e.g., when the parent company has placed one or more of its executives or directors on the board of directors of the subsidiary), the parent will usually be required to account for its investment using the **equity method.**

Investments accounted for under the equity method are called *active* investments and usually involve associate or affiliate companies that may also be major suppliers to, or buyers from, the parent company or one of its various controlled subsidiaries. Although the equity method is a form of *un*consolidated reporting, it is often referred to as a *one-line consolidation*. To understand why this is the case, consider an illustration in which Global Enterprises S.p.A. (GE) purchases a 20 percent

---

[1]When an investment (or other long-term asset) is revalued above its original cost, the corresponding credit entry is usually to an equity reserve account carried under shareholders' equity on the balance sheet (e.g., Reserve for Asset Revaluations).

shareholding in Foreign Subsidiary, Inc. (FS), for L100,000. Immediately prior to this purchase, the balance sheets of the two companies appeared as follows:

	Assets	= Liabilities	+ Shareholders' Equity
GE S.p.A.	L1,000,000	= L0	+ L1,000,000
FS, Inc.	L700,000	= L200,000	+ L500,000

In the year following GE's investment in FS, FS earned net income of L25,000 and paid cash dividends of L10,000. In terms of FS's balance sheet, these events would appear as follows:

	Assets	= Liabilities	+ Shareholders' Equity
	L700,000	= L200,000	+ L500,000
Net income	+ 25,000		+ 25,000
Dividends	−10,000		−10,000
	L715,000	L200,000	L515,000

EXHIBIT 5A–1
Financial Statement Disclosures: Accounting for Investments

Panel A. Fiat
Investments

Investments in unconsolidated companies over which the group has significant influence (generally between 20 percent and 50 percent of voting capital) are stated on an equity basis. Less significant investments (generally companies in which the group holds less than 20 percent of voting capital) are valued at cost. Provision is made for the write-down of investments where there is a permanent loss in value.

Panel B. Mitsui & Co., Ltd.
Investments and marketable securities

Investments in associated companies (generally companies owned 20 percent to 50 percent and corporate joint ventures) are, with minor exceptions, stated at cost adjusted for the company's equity in earnings or losses since dates of acquisition, after appropriate adjustments for intercompany profits, dividends, and amortization (over periods of 5 to 20 years using the straight-line method) of differences between the cost of such investments and the equity in net assets at dates of acquisition.

The current and noncurrent portfolios of marketable equity securities (included in marketable securities and other investments, respectively, in the accompanying consolidated balance sheets) are each stated at the lower of aggregate cost or market.

Marketable securities and other investments (exclusive of marketable equity securities) are stated at the lower of cost or market and at cost or less, respectively.

Panel C. Volvo

The Volvo Group comprises the parent company, all subsidiaries—defined as companies in which AB Volvo holds more than 50 percent of the voting rights—and associated companies that are not subsidiaries but in which AB Volvo has long-term holdings equal to at least 20 percent of the voting rights.

Acquisitions of companies are accounted for using the purchase method. Shareholders' equity in the subsidiaries at date of acquisition, including equity in untaxed reserves, is eliminated in its entirety. Accordingly, only income arising after the date of acquisition is included in shareholders' equity. The difference between the cost of shares in a subsidiary and the shareholders' equity of the subsidiary at date of acquisition is, if the cost of the company's shareholding represents a higher amount (excess value), allocated to the assets to the extent considered appropriate. The remaining excess is included in the consolidated balance sheets as goodwill.

EXHIBIT 5A–1 (continued)
Financial Statement Disclosures: Accounting for Investments

Effective in 1989, holdings in associated companies are reported in accordance with the equity method.
The group's share of reported income in such companies, before allocations and taxes, is included in
the consolidated income statement, reduced in appropriate cases by amortization of excess values. The
group's share of reported taxes in associated companies and estimated taxes in allocations are included
in the group's tax expense.

As a consequence of these events, FS's total and net assets increased by L15,000; and, since GE
holds a 20 percent ownership interest in FS, it can be argued that the underlying value of GE's
investment in FS has increased by L3,000 (i.e., .20 × L15,000). This logic is inherent in the equity
method, and, consequently, GE values its year-end investment in FS as follows:

Original investment	L100,000
Ownership interest in	
Net income (.2 × L25,000)	5,000
Dividends (.2 × L10,000)	(2,000)
Year-end value	L103,000

The equity method is appealing in that it values the parent's investment in a subsidiary on a
basis consistent with the operations of the subsidiary. The parent's investment account is increased
(decreased) as a function of the subsidiary's earnings (losses). Similarly, the parent is entitled to
report its proportionate interest in the subsidiary's earnings (and losses) as part of its own net
income. Thus, the equity method provides a one-line summary of the operations-related activities of
the subsidiary on the financial statements of the parent company. *IAS No. 22* recommends the use of
the equity method for investments in associated companies except when they are held exclusively
for sale.

Consolidated Reporting.   In most countries, when a company obtains more than 50 percent of
the voting shares of another company, accepted accounting practice dictates the use of consolidated
reporting practices. In Germany and Japan, among others, however, this is not necessarily the case
(see Chapters 8 and 9); when a controlled subsidiary is not consolidated, the equity method is the
appropriate method of accounting for such investments.

Consolidated reporting may involve either a *full* or *partial* combination of financial data. When
a company acquires a 100 percent shareholding in another, the consolidated results under either full
or partial consolidation are exactly equivalent. When an acquired investment is less than 100 percent, however, full and partial consolidations yield different consolidated results.

To illustrate, consider a simple acquisition between two independent companies. Assume, for
example, that Global Enterprises S.p.A. purchased 90 percent of the voting stock of Foreign
Subsidiary, Inc., for L243,000.

Immediately prior to the acquisition, the balance sheets of the two companies appeared as follows:

	GE S.p.A.	**FS, Inc.**
Assets	L700,000	L312,000
Liabilities	L150,000	L100,000
Shareholders' equity	550,000	212,000
Total equities	L700,000	L312,000

Assume also that according to GE's financial analysts, the fair market value of FS's net assets was L267,000, or L55,000 more than its net book value of L212,000. This increase in value is attributable to several long-term assets whose reported book values were below current estimates of their fair market value. After considering this additional information, the analysts concluded that GE had purchased goodwill in the amount of L2,700 from FS as follows:

Fair Market Value of 90 Percent Shareholding in FS

L267,000 × .90 =	L240,300
Purchase price	L243,000
Less: Fair market value	(240,300)
Goodwill	L2,700

GE may have been willing to pay a premium in excess of the appraised value of FS's net assets for several reasons: the presence of a loyal customer base for FS's product, a competent management group, an efficient distribution system, or anticipated cost savings and other synergies between the operations of GE and FS.

Immediately following the acquisition, GE's balance sheet would appear as follows:

Assets	
Investment in FS	L243,000
Other assets	457,000
Total assets	L700,000
Liabilities	L150,000
Shareholders' equity	550,000
Total equities	L700,000

Full vs. Partial Consolidation.   At this juncture, GE's preparation of consolidated financial statements is predicated on the firm's decision to use full or partial consolidation. Under partial consolidation, only 90 percent of FS's reported values are transferred to GE's financial statements.[2] Thus, the journal entry to transfer the purchased net assets of FS to GE's consolidated books appears as follows:

Dr. Assets (from FS)	L280,800	
Dr. Revaluation of FS's Assets	49,500*	
Dr. Goodwill	2,700	
Cr. Liabilities (from FS)		L 90,000
Cr. Investment in FS		243,000

*.90 (L55,000) = L49,500. This represents GE's ownership share of the increase in the fair market value of FS's net assets.

In effect, GE's Investment in FS is replaced with the assets and liabilities from FS that GE now controls, which must also be revalued to reflect their acquisition cost (or fair market value), and the goodwill that GE purchased as part of the acquisition. GE's consolidated balance sheet then appears as:

---

[2]Partial consolidation is usually executed by taking a percentage of the subsidiary's assets and liabilities on a line-by-line basis. *IAS No. 31,* "Financial Reporting of Interests in Joint Ventures," specifically identifies the use of the partial (or proportionate) consolidation for jointly controlled entities.

Assets	
Assets (acquired from FS)	L330,300*
Other assets	457,000
Goodwill	2,700
Total Assets	L790,000
Liabilities (from GE)	L150,000
Liabilities (from FS)	90,000
Shareholders' equity	550,000
Total equities	L790,000

*(L280,800 + L49,500).

Partial consolidation assumes that the parent's consolidated balance sheet should reflect only its *proportionate* interest in the net assets of the acquired company. *Full consolidation,* however, assumes that since the parent company is the majority shareholder of the subsidiary, the parent effectively controls *all* of the subsidiary's net assets despite the fact that it might not own them all. Thus, under full consolidation, all of the subsidiary's net assets are consolidated with those of the parent. This practice, however, necessitates the creation of a new account—Minority Interest—to reflect the portion of the subsidiary's net assets not in fact owned by the parent company.

To illustrate, consider again GE's 90 percent acquisition of FS. Under full consolidation, the journal entry to transfer 100 percent of FS's net assets to GE appears as follows:

Dr. Assets (from FS)	L312,000	
Dr. Revaluation of FS's Assets	49,500	
Dr. Goodwill	2,700	
Cr. Liabilities (from FS)		L100,000
Cr. Minority Interest		21,200*
Cr. Investment in FS		243,000

*.10 (L212,000) represents the portion of FS's net assets not owned by GE.

Note that under this approach, 100 percent of the value of FS's assets and liabilities are transferred to GE's consolidated financial statements despite the fact that GE owns only 90 percent of FS. GE's consolidated balance sheet then appears as:

Assets	
Assets (acquired from FS)	L361,500*
Other assets	457,000
Goodwill	2,700
Total assets	L821,200
Liabilities (from GE)	L150,000
Liabilities (from FS)	100,000
Minority interest	21,200
Shareholders' equity	550,000
Total equities	L821,200

*(L312,000 + L49,500).

The Minority Interest account, which represents the value of FS's net assets *not* owned by GE, appears as a credit balance on GE's consolidated balance sheet, although it is neither a debt obligation nor a shareholders' equity account. It is merely a balancing account required under the full consolidation approach. As a consequence, this account is frequently ignored by financial analysts when calculating such ratios as the debt-to-equity ratio or the debt-to-total capitalization ratio.

As a concluding observation, it is noteworthy that the full consolidation approach results in a higher level of total (but not net) assets being reported by the parent company on its consolidated balance sheet (e.g., L821,200 versus L790,000). Since the consolidated net income of the parent may reflect only those earnings attributable to the parent and its ownership interest in its subsidiaries (i.e., the portion of the consolidated net earnings attributable to the minority shareholders are excluded and added to the Minority Interest account), some distortions in calculated ratios may result. For example, assume that in the year following GE's investment in FS, the consolidated net earnings before minority interest totaled L100,000, with L40,000 of that amount attributable to FS's operations. The calculation of GE's consolidated earnings *after* minority interest appears as follows:

Consolidated earnings before minority interest	L100,000
Less: Earnings attributable to minority interest	4,000*
Consolidated earnings	L 96,000

*.10 (L40,000).

GE's consolidated balance sheet appears as follows:

Assets	
Assets (acquired from FS)	L401,500
Other assets	517,000
Goodwill	2,700
Total assets	L921,200
Liabilities (from GE)	L150,000
Liabilities (from FS)	100,000
Minority interest	25,200
Shareholders' equity	646,000
Total equities	L921,200

Under full consolidation, GE's year-end assets total L921,200, whereas under partial consolidation, they total only L886,000 (i.e., L790,000 + L96,000). The return on total assets (ROA) ratio is calculated as follows:

Full Consolidation
$$\frac{L96,000}{(L821,000 + L921,200)/2} = 11.0\%$$

Partial Consolidation
$$\frac{L96,000}{(L790,000 + L886,000)/2} = 11.5\%$$

In this instance, GE's ROA is numerically higher under partial consolidation than under full consolidation (i.e., 11.5 versus 11.0, respectively). To avoid the analytical problems that may result if inappropriate comparisons are made, the analyst should always verify that comparable consolidation (and other accounting) practices have been used.

Goodwill.   A final consideration in our review of consolidated reporting practices involves goodwill. Goodwill arises when one entity acquiring another pays more than the fair market value of the acquired company. In the preceding illustration, GE was found to have paid L2,700 more than the appraised value of a 90 percent interest in FS:

Purchase price (of 90 percent shareholding)	L243,000
Fair market value	(240,300)
Goodwill	L 2,700

In accounting language, GE's acquisition of its 90 percent shareholding in FS is called a *purchase* because the transaction involved an exchange of one asset (i.e., cash) for another (i.e., the voting stock of FS). But not all acquisitions are executed in this manner. In some instances, the acquiror company may exchange its voting stock for the stock of another company. When such stock exchanges occur, IASC standards sometimes permit the acquiror to utilize the **pooling-of-interests method** of accounting.[3]

Under the pooling-of-interests method, the value assigned to the acquiror's shares exchanged in an acquisition is *not* their fair market value but the book value of the investment as carried on the acquiree's financial statements. For example, if GE had acquired 100 percent of FS's voting shares by exchanging its own shares for the voting shares of FS, the value assigned to GE's investment in FS would be L212,000. FS's book value would be used to value the GE investment even if the fair market value of the GE shares given up in the exchange exceeded L212,000. An important consequence of the pooling method is that goodwill *never* occurs. Thus, if goodwill is reported on the balance sheet of a company, it can be inferred that the company has engaged in various acquisition activities involving the purchase method.

Even if the purchase method is used to account for an acquisition, however, some local accounting practices enable the acquiror to avoid disclosing the amount of goodwill incurred in an acquisition. For example, in Germany, Italy, Japan, and the Netherlands, goodwill incurred as a consequence of an acquisition may be written off directly against various equity reserve accounts. To illustrate, consider again GE's acquisition of a 90 percent shareholding in FS, wherein goodwill in the amount of L2,700 was incurred. Assuming partial consolidation, GE's consolidated balance sheet following the acquisition appears as follows:

	Goodwill Capitalized to Balance Sheet	Goodwill Charged against Reserves
Assets		
Assets (acquired from FS)	L330,300	L330,300
Other assets	457,000	457,000
Goodwill	2,700	—
Total assets	L790,000	L787,300
Liabilities (from GE)	L150,000	L150,000
Liabilities (from FS)	90,000	90,000
Shareholders' equity	550,000	547,300
Total equities	L790,000	L787,300

Note that under the charge-to-equity approach of accounting for goodwill, GE's total and net assets are reduced by the amount of goodwill (i.e., L2,700) written off.

In most countries, if goodwill is capitalized to the balance sheet under purchase accounting, it must be periodically amortized against earnings, although the amortization period varies greatly

---

[3]*IAS No. 22* (revised 1998) requires that purchase accounting be used in all business combinations except when it is not possible to identify the acquiror firm, in which case the pooling-of-interests method should be used. *IAS No. 22* also requires that any goodwill inherent in the purchase price be capitalized to the balance sheet and amortized against earnings over a period of 5 years (with the possibility of extending the write-off period to 20 years). Around the world, pooling-of-interests accounting is sometimes referred to as merger accounting.

from country to country. In Canada and the United States, for example, the typical amortization period is 40 years, whereas in Japan and Korea, a 5-year amortization period is prevalent. In any case, the presence of goodwill on the consolidated balance sheet of the parent company represents a "drag" on the company's future earnings. In the case of GE, the reduction in earnings would be L540 per year (i.e., L2700/5) if a 5-year amortization period is used, or only L67.50 per year if a 40-year amortization period is adopted. (*Note:* Although straight-line amortization of goodwill is the most prevalent amortization approach, other methods are acceptable and vary by location.)

Companies that elect to write off goodwill immediately against existing equity reserve accounts do so primarily to avoid the reduction in future earnings associated with the amortization of goodwill. Why this election might be made by management can be explained with reference to existing stock market theories. As noted in Chapter 4, it is widely accepted in the financial community that a company's share price is a reflection of investor expectations regarding the company's future earnings. Hence, to maximize a company's share price, it follows that management should adopt those policies that maximize future earnings. One way to maximize the future accounting earnings of a company is to minimize the write-offs taken against future earnings (e.g., goodwill amortization). Whether in fact the charge-to-equity method of accounting for goodwill results in a higher share price is unclear.

Finally, although goodwill is most commonly found as an asset account on the balance sheet, on occasion an acquiror may find that its purchase price of an investment is *less* than the investment's recorded book value. When this occurs, **negative goodwill**—a credit balance—is said to arise (see Exhibit 5–4, panel C). Not surprising, the accounting for negative goodwill is quite diverse. In Germany, for example, negative goodwill is carried on the balance sheet as a credit balance and may be amortized to (i.e., an increase in) earnings over time. Under U.S. GAAP, however, negative goodwill may not be carried on a company's balance sheet and instead is usually written off against the remaining depreciable cost basis of an acquiree's long-term depreciable assets. Finally, in those countries such as Italy and the Netherlands where the charge-to-equity method is permitted, negative goodwill may be added immediately to the acquiror's equity reserves. Each of these approaches produces a different effect on the acquiror's balance sheet and income statement; however, whether the cash flow effect is equivalent is a function of local tax regulations regarding the tax deductibility of goodwill.

Summary

Consolidation accounting practices vary greatly from one country to the next. In most locations, the prevalent accounting treatment is the purchase method, although the pooling-of-interests method is also permitted by IASC standards. In some settings, despite a majority shareholding, a parent company may account for a controlled subsidiary using the equity method, which is essentially an abbreviated form of consolidated reporting. When an investment in a subsidiary is significant but does not constitute a controlling interest, the investment may be accounted for at its original cost, using the lower-of-cost-or-market method, at its revalued amount, or using the equity method. As always, the analyst should first identify accepted local accounting practice before embarking on any financial review.

Exercises

5.1   Alternative International GAAP and Financial Ratios

In a February 16, 1993, *Financial Times* article (p. 25), "Report Calls for Accounting Harmonisation," Andrew Jack notes that a NatWest Securities research report "warns that until standards are more uniform, investors need to be wary of differing accounting practices." He cites the report as highlighting several accounting practices of note that differ between countries including:

1. Revaluation upward of assets on the balance sheet (e.g., Olivetti and Philips).
2. Accelerated depreciation (e.g., Germany).
3. Substantial goodwill write-downs.
4. Long-term contracts.
5. Provisions and reserves used to help smooth profits.
6. Definition of extraordinary items.

Required:

Explain how each of these six items might affect the ROA, ROS, and ROE ratios.

5.2   Restating Financial Statements: Inventory

Following are the balance sheet and income statement of Global Enterprises, Inc. as of December 31, 1998. The footnotes to GE's financial statements included the following statement regarding inventories:

Inventories are valued on a FIFO basis. If LIFO has been used, inventories would have been valued at ¥889,000 on January 1, 1998, and at ¥1,270,000 on December 31, 1998.

Required:

(a) Assume that the tax rate is 50 percent and that Global Enterprises had been using FIFO for tax purposes. Restate the company's balance sheet and income statement for 1998 to reflect the use of LIFO instead of FIFO. (Would you recommend such a method change for income tax purposes also?)

(b) Calculate the following ratios for 1998 under both LIFO and FIFO:

  (1) Current ratio.

  (2) Inventory turnover.

  (3) Average number of days' inventory on hand.

  (4) Total debt-to-equity ratio.

(c) Which method do you think Global Enterprises should use, and why?

GLOBAL ENTERPRISES, INC.
Income Statement
For the year ended December 31, 1998

Sales revenue		¥4,950,000
Less: Cost of sales		
Beginning inventory	¥1,205,000	
Cost of production	3,665,000	
Goods available for sale	4,870,000	
Less: Ending inventory	1,720,000	
		(3,150,000)
Gross margin		1,800,000
Less: Research and development expenses	350,000	
Licensing fees	100,000	
Selling and administrative expenses	400,000	
		(850,000)
Net income before taxes		950,000
Less: Income taxes	475,000	
Investment and research tax credits	(60,000)	
		(415,000)
Net income after taxes		¥ 535,000

GLOBAL ENTERPRISES, INC.
Balance Sheet
As of December 31, 1998

Assets			*Equities*		
Current assets			Current liabilities		
Cash		¥ 436,000	Accounts payable		¥ 820,000
Trade receivables (net of allowance for			Accrued expenses payble		80,000
uncollectible accounts)		828,000	Total current liabilities		900,000
Inventories		1,720,000			
Prepared expenses		30,000			
Total current assets		3,014,000			
Noncurrent assets			Noncurrent liabilities		
Property, plant, and equipment		¥3,940,000	Notes payable		2,320,000
Less: Accumulated depreciation		(1,360,000)	Deferred federal Income taxes		800,000
		2,580,000	Total liabilities		4,020,000
Land		560,000	Owners' equity		
Deferred research and development cost		1,150,000	Common stock ¥ 1 par		2,000,000
Total assets		¥7,304,000	Retained earnings		1,284,000
			Total equities		¥7,304,000

5.3 Restating Financial Statements: Depreciation

The 1998 financial statements of Global Enterprises, Inc., included the following statement regarding the company's depreciation of property, plant, and equipment:

> Property, plant, and equipment is depreciated on a straight-line basis. If an accelerated method had been used, the depreciation expense for 1998 would have been ¥230,000 higher, and the end-of-year balance in Accumulated Depreciation ¥450,000 higher.

Required:

(a) Using the 1998 financial statements presented in Exercise 5.2 and assuming a 50 percent tax rate, restate Global Enterprises' financial statements for 1998 to reflect the use of accelerated depreciation (instead of straight line). GE reports all depreciation as a component of cost of goods sold. Would you recommend this policy change for income tax purposes?

(b) Calculate the following ratios for 1998 under both straight-line and accelerated depreciation:

   (1) Return on sales.

   (2) Return on total assets.

   (3) Noncurrent asset turnover.

   (4) Total asset turnover.

(c) Which method do you think GE should use, and why?

5.4 Restating Financial Statements: Research and Development Costs

The 1998 financial statements of Global Enterprises, Inc., included the following statement regarding the company's treatment of research and development costs:

The research and development expense for 1998 represented one-half of the actual R&D expenditure for 1998; the remaining balance had been capitalized. The company's policy is to begin amortization of these capitalized costs once a commercially productive asset has been developed. To date, no productive assets have resulted from the research program represented by the currently capitalized R&D costs.

Required:

(a) Using the financial statements presented in Exercise 5.2 and assuming a 50 percent tax rate, restate Global Enterprises' financial statements for 1998 to reflect the full current expensing of all R&D costs. (What recommendation would you make for income tax purposes?)

(b) Calculate the following ratios for 1998 under the old and new policies regarding expensing R&D expenditures:

(1) Return on sales.

(2) Return on total assets.

(3) Noncurrent asset turnover.

(4) Total asset turnover.

(c) Which method do you think Global Enterprises should adopt, and why?

5.5   Restating Balance Sheets: Leases

Global Telecommunications, Plc, leases a substantial portion of its noncurrent assets. For example, as of year-end 1998, GT had leased over one-third of its total noncurrent assets, and the capitalized obligations associated with those leases represented nearly 50 percent of the company's total reported long-term debt (see condensed balance sheet). In addition, the footnotes to the company's statements revealed that some of those leased assets were accounted for as "operating leases":

At December 31, 1998, the aggregate minimum rental commitments under noncancellable operating leases were as follows:

Year Ending 12/31	Amount
1999	£ 16,610,000
2000	15,443,000
2001	14,441,000
2002	12,669,000
2003	10,580,000
2004 and thereafter	49,220,000
Total minimum lease payments	£118,963,000

GLOBAL TELECOMMUNICATIONS, Plc
Condensed Balance Sheets
As of December 31
(in thousands)

	1998	1997
Assets		
Current assets	£228,428	£ 48,946
Noncurrent assets (net)	631,970	417,946
Total	£860,398	£466,892
Equities		
Current liabilities	£185,540	£ 23,729
Long-term debt	206,494	44,665
Capitalized lease obligations	227,582	250,451
Shareholders' equity	240,782	148,047
Total	£860,398	£466,892

Required:

(a) Assume that the implicit interest rate on GT's operating leases is 12 percent. Restate the balance sheet at year-end 1998, assuming that all of the operating leases should be capitalized.

(b) Calculate the following ratios both before and after your restatement in part (a):

(1) Long-term debt-to-shareholders' equity.

(2) Total debt-to-total assets.

(c) In an efficient marketplace, what should happen to GT's debt rating following the capitalization of all operating leases?

5.6   Alternative GAAP: FIFO versus LIFO

The following information is taken from the 19x9 financial statements of Cifra, SA, a major Mexican retailing company:

Inventories are valued on a LIFO basis; the year-end balances (in millions, new pesos) at 30 June were

	19x9	19x8
Inventory	3,158	3,029

If FIFO had been used, inventory would have been 2,152 million higher than reported on June 30, 19x9 (2,266 million higher on June 30, 19x8). During 19x9, net reductions in inventory levels resulted in liquidations of LIFO bases of 114 million in 19x9 (163 million in 19x8).

The condensed financial statements of Cifra are as follows:

CIFRA, SA
Balance Sheet
As of 30 June
(in millions, new pesos)

	19x9	*19x8*
Assets		
Quick assets	7,754	7,327
Inventories	3,158	3,029
Total current assets	10,912	10,356
Noncurrent assets	12,376	11,259
Total assets	23,288	21,615
Equities		
Current liabilities	8,688	8,153
Long-term liabilities	3,162	3,099
Total liabilities	11,850	11,252
Owners' equity	11,438	10,363
Total equities	23,288	21,615

CIFRA, SA
Statement of Earnings
For the year ended 30 June
(in millions, new pesos)

	19x9	*19x8*	*19x7*
Sales of products and services rendered	26,797	26,500	27,240
Cost of goods sold	(24,248)	(24,095)	(24,793)
Other income and expenses	450	312	167
Provision for income taxes	(975)	(900)	(962)
Net earnings	2,024	1,817	1,652

Required:

(a) If Cifra had used FIFO instead of LIFO in all prior years, how would the company's 19x8–19x9 financial statements differ? (Ignore income tax considerations.)

(b) Compare the income tax consequences of using LIFO instead of FIFO in 19x9 for Cifra.

(c) Assuming a tax rate of 33 percent, estimate the total tax savings received by Cifra in all years as a consequence of using LIFO instead of FIFO.

(d) Calculate the following ratios for 19x9 under both LIFO and FIFO:

(1) Current ratio.

(2) Quick ratio.

(3) Inventory turnover.

(4) Average number of days' inventory on hand.

5.7   Restating Financial Statements: Pooling versus Purchasing Accounting

In 1983, Carlton Brewing Co. (Melbourne, Australia) acquired the net assets of its chief competitor, the United Brewing Co., by issuing 1,891,678 shares of Carlton ordinary stock to the owners of United, forming the largest brewery in Australia (now the Carlton-United Brewing Co. or CUB). Carlton had accounted for the transaction as a pooling of interests and, accordingly, included in its consolidated balance sheet only $32 million of new net assets (i.e., the book value of United's net assets in 1983).

The merger was recorded on Carlton's books as follows:

Dr. Net assets (from United)	$32.0 million	
Cr. Ordinary capital		$3.0 million
Cr. Retained earnings		29.0 million

At the time of the merger, Carlton's shares traded on the Melbourne Stock Exchange at approximately $50 per share. Following are the consolidated financial statements for the Carlton-United Brewing Co. as of June 30, 1997 and 1998:

CARLTON-UNITED BREWING CO.
Consolidated Balance Sheet
As of 30 June, 1997 and 1998
(in millions)
December 31,

	1998	*1997*
Assets		
Cash and cash equivalents	$ 104	$ 147
Debtors	912	693
Inventories	1,750	1,670
Land	81	66
Building and equipment (net)	2,928	2,572
Long-term investments	103	85
Other assets and goodwill	220	146
Total	$6,098	$5,379
Liabilities and Shareholders' Equity		
Short-term creditors	$1,067	$ 790
Income tax payable	198	133
Notes payable	430	404
Deferred income tax	23	(24)
Long-term creditors (total)	948	1,011
Total	2,666	2,314
Ordinary capital	180	177
Retained earnings	3,252	2,888
Total	$6,098	$5,379

CARLTON-UNITED BREWING CO.
Consolidated Income Statement
For the Year Ended June 30, 1998 and 1997
(in millions)

	1998	*1997*
Turnover	$8,598	$7,613
Cost of goods sold	6,957*	6,172*
Other expenses (net)	844	715
Income taxes	232	234
Total expenses	8,033	7,121
Income	$ 565	$ 492
Note		
Depreciation for year	370	312
Dividends	201	182

*This figure includes depreciation allocable to cost of goods sold.

Required:

(a) Restate the CUB financial statements for 1997 and 1998 to reflect the use of purchase accounting instead of pooling of interests.

(b) How would CUB's reported net income change under purchase accounting? What conclusion, in general, would you draw from this about the effect of pooling versus purchasing accounting on reported net income?

(c) Calculate the following ratios for CUB in 1997 and 1998 under the two methods of consolidated reporting:

(1) Total debt-to-total assets.

(2) Book value per share. (Assume that 86.5 million shares are outstanding.)

(3) Earnings per share.

(4) Return on equity.

What conclusion, in general, would you draw about the effect of pooling versus purchasing accounting on ratio analysis?

5.8 Restating Financial Statements: Depreciation

The 1998 annual report of the Carlton-United Brewing Co. (CUB), headquartered in Melbourne, Australia, reported the following statement about the company's depreciation policy:

> Depreciation is computed principally using accelerated methods . . . for both income tax and financial reporting purposes. If the straight-line method had been in use, Buildings, machinery, and equipment (net) would have been $504 million, $430 million, and $370 million higher than reported at June 30, 1998, 1997, and 1996, respectively, and the depreciation expense for 1998, 1997, and 1996 would have been, respectively, $74 million, $60 million, and $48 million less.

Required:

(a) Using the CUB financial statements presented in Exercise 5.7 and assuming a 35 percent tax rate, restate the company's balance sheets for 1997 and 1998 to reflect the use of straight-line depreciation. Assume that straight line is used for both financial and tax reporting purposes.

(b) By how much would the company's reported net income change in 1997 and 1998 as a consequence of using straight-line depreciation?

(c) Calculate the following ratios for 1997 and 1998 under both depreciation methods:

  (1) Return on sales.

  (2) Return on total assets.

  (3) Noncurrent asset turnover.

  (4) Total asset turnover.

Under which method do the ratios look best?

5.9   Restating Financial Statements: Inventory

The 1998 annual report of the Carlton-United Brewery Co. (CUB), disclosed the following statement about the company's inventory (or "stock") policy:

> If FIFO had been in use, stocks would have been $1,960 million, $1,654 million, and $1,388 million higher than reported at June 30, 1998, 1997, and 1996, respectively. . . . The company has used LIFO for both tax and financial reporting purposes since 1983 when the merger of the Carlton and United companies occurred.

Required:

(a) Assume a tax rate of 35 percent and that CUB had adopted the FIFO method in 1983 and had been consistently used since that time. Restate the CUB balance sheets presented in Exercise 5.7 as of year-end 1997 and 1998 to reflect the use of the FIFO method.

(b) Assess the effect on net income in 1997 and 1998 assuming the use of FIFO instead of LIFO.

(c) Calculate the following ratios for 1997 and 1998 under both FIFO and LIFO:

  (1) Current ratio.

  (2) Inventory turnover.

  (3) Average number of days' inventory on hand.

  (4) Total debt-to-shareholders' equity.

Under which method do the ratios look best?

5.10   Accounting for Goodwill

During 1993, both QVC Network, Inc., and Viacom, Inc., made competitive acquisition bids for Paramount Communications, Inc. Both bids placed a value on Paramount of approximately $10 billion, and both offers involved a substantial amount of cash, as well as stock; thus, regardless of which firm won the bidding for Paramount, the acquiror would be required to account for the investment on a purchase method basis. Industry analysts speculated that Paramount's fair market value was approximately $7.5 billion, as compared to its book value of approximately $4.5 billion, at the time of the tender offers.

Required:

(a) How much goodwill is inherent in the acquisition bids for Paramount? Over what period of time would you recommend that the Paramount goodwill be written off? (*Hint:* Paramount is in the film production and sports business.) Calculate the annual "drag" on earnings caused by the goodwill, based on your estimate of the life of the Paramount goodwill.

(b) Why would QVC Network or Viacom be willing to pay in excess of the fair market value of Paramount?

(c) As we will see in Chapters 7–13, the accounting for goodwill differs dramatically around the world. In Japan, for instance, goodwill is written off over 5 years, and in Germany over 15 years. In the Netherlands, goodwill may be written off as a lump sum against retained earnings on the date of acquisition. Given the disparities of these practices, it is difficult to compare the performance of companies from different countries. What measure (or measures) of performance would you prefer to evaluate as a means to overcome this lack of comparability?

5.11   Restating Financial Statements

Global Electronics, Inc. (GE) produces airborne navigation systems, military and civilian communication systems, and multimedia systems and equipment that are marketed internationally largely to governmental customers. In early 1998, GE decided to modify several of its accounting and reporting policies to bring the company into closer compliance with existing IASC accounting proposals. This decision was reached because company executives felt that the company would have a better chance of winning governmental contracts around the world if GE were perceived to be more an international company and less a U.S. company. GE was headquartered in Chicago, Illinois.

Accounting Policy Changes

Since the company was founded in 1972, GE had used the LIFO method of accounting for its inventories. This decision was largely driven by GE's desire to minimize its current U.S. income taxes and the LIFO compliance regulation that required U.S. companies adopting LIFO for tax purposes to also use LIFO for financial reporting purposes. Consistent with a 1992 IASC proposal to eliminate the use of LIFO inventory accounting, GE had decided to switch to the FIFO method effective January 1, 1997. Company executives recognized that this accounting policy change would, of necessity, affect the company's tax position as well.

Prior to 1998, GE's policy with respect to research and development costs had been to capitalize all such costs applicable to specific product lines (or government contracts) to the extent that the costs were thought to be recoverable from existing or expected orders; all other R&D costs were charged to expense as incurred. Although company executives felt that this policy was substantially in compliance with IASC guidelines, they decided, nonetheless, to adopt a policy in which all R&D costs would be expensed when incurred. This change appeared warranted because of the changing environment of government contracting. Although in the past, GE could be certain that all R&D costs would be reimbursed by government clients, this was becoming less the case. Increasingly, government clients were expecting companies to spend their own risk capital on projects with little or no guarantee of reimbursement. GE decided to implement this policy change effective January 1, 1997.

Finally, prior to 1998, GE had followed an amortization policy for its various patents and license agreements under which these assets were amortized against earnings using a straight-line approach, with an estimated life of 15 years. GE executives realized, however, that with the de-escalation of the Cold War, many of their patented and licensed military products would face a rapidly declining marketplace. This fact, among others, suggested that patents and licenses be written off over a substantially shorter period. Thus, effective January 1, 1997, GE executives decided to amortize any remaining balances in those asset accounts over a five-year period.

The following Exhibits 1 and 2 are GE's comparative financial statements for 1996 and 1997. These statements do *not* reflect the accounting policy changes reached by GE executives in early 1998.

Required:

(a) Restate GE's 1997 statement of earnings to reflect the use of FIFO inventory accounting. If GE had used FIFO since 1972, by how much would the company's retained earnings have increased (relative to the use of LIFO) by year-end 1997? If GE had been using FIFO throughout all of 1997, what would the specific dollar effect have been on the company's net working capital?

(b) Restate GE's 1997 financial statements to reflect the new R&D policy effective January 1, 1997. Using an adjusting entry, illustrate how this change would be implemented. Should this policy be implemented for tax purposes also? Why or why not?

(c) Restate GE's 1997 financial statements to reflect the adoption of the new patents and licensing amortization policy. Using an adjusting entry, illustrate how this change could be implemented. Should this policy be implemented for tax purposes also? Why or why not?

(d) Explain how an efficient securities market should respond to these accounting policy changes vis-à-vis GE's stock price.

EXHIBIT 1

GLOBAL ELECTRONICS, INC.
Partial Consolidated Balance Sheets
(000s)

	As of December 31,	
Assets	*1996*	*1997*
Current assets		
Cash	$ 17,700	$ 21,416
Receivables (net)	56,532	58,114
Inventories—At current cost (approximates FIFO)	120,295	137,614
Less: Allowance to reduce value to LIFO basis	(28,052)	(31,261)
Total current assets	$ 166,475	$ 185,883
Investments in and advances to unconsolidated and		
50%-owned companies	21,144	23,524
Property, plant, and equipment	100,089	110,068
Less: Accumulated depreciation	(53,796)	(55,925)
Goodwill	9,950	9,000
Patent and license agreements	1,268,254	1,265,611
Less: Accumulated depreciation	(230,717)	(383,223)
Deferred research and development costs	1,061,726	2,140,445
Less: Accumulated amortization	(562,174)	(1,127,586)
Total assets	$1,780,951	$2,167,797

EXHIBIT 2

GLOBAL ELECTRONICS, INC.
Consolidated Statement of Earnings
(000s)

	As of December 31,	
	1996	*1997*
Revenues	$993,533	$1,070,990
Costs and expenses		
Cost of goods sold (including depreciation and amortization)	924,648	985,043
Selling and administrative	52,281	59,140
Interest and financing charges (net of interest earned)	8,187	12,424
	$985,116	$1,056,607
Earnings before taxes and extraordinary items	8,417	14,383
Provision for income taxes	(3,702)	(6,332)
	4,715	8,051
Equity in earnings of unconsolidated and 50%-owned companies	1,746	2,372
Earnings before extraordinary items	6,461	10,423
Extraordinary items	(1,266)	–0–
Net earnings	$ 5,195	$ 10,423

Accounting for Foreign Operations

[C]ross-border business has been driven forward by three main things: falling regulatory barriers to overseas investment; tumbling telecommunications and transport costs; and free domestic and international capital markets in which companies can be bought, and currency and other risks can be controlled.[1]

When a company operates exclusively within a single domestic market, it faces a set of conventional but nonetheless substantial business risks. These risks include those that characterize any competitive business situation and can typically involve new capital formation, product identity, quality, pricing, and obsolescence. When a company operates in a variety of marketplaces—domestic and foreign—representing diverse cultural, ethnic, and national contexts, however, its business risks are magnified both in number and in complexity. The question of how the Kellogg Company, a U.S. maker of breakfast cereals, can market a new product in the United States is far less complex than the question of how it can market Frosted Flakes™ or Cheerios™ in Italy or Japan. Kellogg must identify and respond to differences in language, consumer preferences, and issues relating to product distribution, manufacturing, packaging, and advertising. Without question, many new concerns and problems arise when a company expands its base of operations beyond its own domestic market and begins operating in international markets as well.

From an accounting perspective, the principal source of complexity relates to differences in a company's *local currency* (in accounting parlance, its **reporting currency**) and the other currencies in which it may transact its business. For example, Kellogg, as a U.S.-based corporation, uses the U.S. dollar for its reporting currency; however, Kellogg must translate currency in several situations:

- Contracts for sales and purchases of goods and services between Kellogg and other companies may specify that settlement is to be made in a foreign currency (e.g., the lira or the yen). To give accounting recognition to these transactions in its dollar-based accounting records, Kellogg must convert these foreign currency–denominated transactions into U.S. dollars using appropriate foreign currency exchange rates.

- Kellogg may hold or acquire foreign currency, or enter into a forward contract or option to sell or acquire foreign currency. Kellogg must translate the units of

---

[1] "A Survey of Multinationals," *The Economist,* March 27, 1993, p. 6.

foreign currency it holds in bank accounts into U.S. dollars using appropriate foreign currency exchange rates. This is also true for foreign currency futures and options contracts it is a party to.

- Kellogg may present its financial statements on a consolidated basis with one or more foreign subsidiaries whose accounting records are based in a foreign currency. To consolidate the financial statements of these foreign subsidiaries with Kellogg, they must first be translated into U.S. dollars.

The purposes of this chapter are to explore the role of foreign currency in business transactions and to consider how multinational companies account for international operations. Financial reporting policies with regard to foreign exchange can frequently have a material impact on financial statements—and related ratios—when exchange rates between a reporting currency (i.e., the U.S. dollar for Kellogg) and other currencies fluctuate. The following are just a few examples:

- In a case to be described more fully in the section on hedging, one analyst who was following Dell Computer Corp. claimed that deferred losses on investments in foreign currency options amounted to as much as 50 percent of Dell's net income in 1992. The analyst suspected that these losses were improperly deferred and should have been reflected in the income of the current period.
- Siemens, a German multinational company, reported foreign exchange losses of DM838 million for the year ended September 30, 1997. The firm reported net income of DM2.4 billion for the year. In this chapter, we will describe how foreign exchange accounting policies can affect net income.
- Michelin, the French tire manufacturer, reported reductions in shareholders' equity resulting from "cumulative translation adjustments" of FRF4 billion, roughly twice total shareholders' equity. In this chapter, we shall also describe the cause and nature of cumulative translation adjustments as a separate component of shareholders' equity.

The challenge to analysts in situations such as these is to evaluate the appropriateness of management's accounting policies with respect to investments in foreign currencies and foreign subsidiaries. This may entail distinguishing between the real effects of foreign currency movements on income for a period and what may be the result of income manipulation by management, or the application of "form-driven" accounting standards. The analyst must have sufficient technical knowledge of this complex area of accounting to gather relevant additional data to make appropriate assumptions and well-reasoned inferences. An intermediate product of the analysis may include a restatement of reported results.

Before discussing these analytical challenges, we begin with some background on foreign exchange. Foreign exchange presents a complex set of problems as companies and analysts try to determine the real effect of foreign exchange fluctuations on the earnings, cash flows, and net worth of a business.

Foreign Exchange

One principal source of complexity in conducting business across borders arises because almost every country in the world operates with its own form of currency or **exchange.** For example, the United States has the dollar ($), in Japan, the yen (¥); and in Great Britain, the pound (£). One potential simplification for at least some European countries results from the formation of the European Monetary Union in which some members of the European Union (EU) have adopted a single currency, the **European Currency Unit**

(Euro), for their business transactions beginning in 1999. This will surely make accounting for EU financial activities less complex.

Since the end of World War II, the level of international business activity by multinational firms has grown exponentially. Further, the increase of multinational companies (MNCs) and other publicly traded firms has created worldwide demand for financial reporting standards regarding the presentation of foreign operations in local currency. Generally accepted accounting principles (GAAP) governing foreign currency transactions and the translation of foreign currency financial statements in the United States are, for the most part, found in *SFAS No. 52.*[2] The existing world standard may be found in *IAS No. 21,* which is substantially consistent with *SFAS No. 52.* Current accounting practice in Korea, Sweden, and Great Britain is also substantially in compliance with *IAS No. 21,* while accounting treatment in Mexico, Germany, Italy, and Japan is not (although each of these four countries is likely to attain compliance in the near future).

Foreign exchange information is publicly available from a variety of sources. Exhibit 6–1, for example, presents a list of eight major currencies. The currency symbols in the exhibit are used as a quick method to indicate monetary denominations used by foreign exchange traders and information services and are part of a de facto world standard used to indicate over 100 currencies.

Exchange rates express the amount it costs to purchase one unit of currency with another currency. Rates can be quoted directly (i.e., in units of *local* currency) or indirectly (i.e., in units of a *foreign* currency). To illustrate the difference between direct and indirect quotation, consider the exchange rate between the USD as local currency and the DEM as the foreign currency. A direct quotation of the exchange rate indicates the number of USD it would cost to purchase one DEM, say [0.6045] USD on January 4, 1999. An indirect quotation is the reciprocal of this amount, or DEM [1.6543]. This is the number of DEM required to purchase one USD.

To promote economic stability, the major currencies of the world were at one time fixed. Occasionally, large changes (called **devaluations** or **revaluations**) in the exchange rates were required when substantial value changes occurred between two or more currencies. Today, value swings—appreciation or depreciation—caused by changes in the demand for, or in expectations regarding the value of, the various currencies occur so often that a floating exchange rate system has been adopted in which all major currencies are free to move against all other currencies according to market demand and expectations.[3] Not all

---

EXHIBIT 6–1

Selected Major Foreign Currencies

Country or Region	Currency	Symbol
Canada	Dollar	CAD
European Union	Euro	XEU
Germany	Deutsche mark	DEM
Great Britain	Pound sterling	GBP
Italy	Lira	ITL
Japan	Yen	JPY
Mexico	Nuevo peso	MXN
South Korea	Won	SKW
Sweden	Krona	SEK
United States	Dollar	USD

---

[2]*SFAS No. 52,* "Foreign Currency Translation" (Stamford, CT: FASB, 1981).

[3]Exceptions include Argentina and Hong Kong, which have pegged the value of their currency to the U.S. dollar.

exchanges of foreign currency take place, however, at market rates. Many countries still control the flow of capital over their borders by establishing "official" exchange rates. Frequently, official exchange rates for inflows (outflows) of foreign currency are more (less) favorable than market rates.

Foreign
Exchange Risk

Presented in Exhibit 6–2 are the prevailing market exchange rates (called **spot rates**) as of January 4, 1999, for several major currencies. These rates and those for a large number of currencies are quoted in the financial press on a daily basis and generally reflect the exchange rate among banks for amounts equivalent to 1 million USD or more. Rates for smaller transactions, such as when a traveler exchanges money at the airport when entering a new country, are usually less favorable.

Note that for some major currencies such as the pound sterling and Canadian dollar, rates **(forward exchange rates)** are also quoted for future delivery of currency in 30, 90, or 180 days. As we will soon see, most international trade involves a delay between setting the price of a transaction (e.g., the sale or purchase of goods between Kellogg and a foreign customer or supplier), and receiving (making) payment for those goods. Consequently, at least one of the participants in such a transaction faces the risk of losing some amount of local currency purchasing power because the exchange rate may fluctuate before payment is made or received; this type of risk is called *currency risk* or *foreign exchange risk*. Entering into a forward exchange contract to receive or pay foreign currency at a future date is one way for companies to limit or eliminate the risk associated with adverse fluctuations of exchange rates on commitments to pay or receive foreign currency. Put another way, a multinational company holding a receivable (payable) in a foreign currency can **hedge** all or part of its exposure to fluctuation in foreign exchange spot rates by entering into a forward contract to pay (receive) foreign currency at or around the due date of the receivable (payable).[4] The decision to hedge, however, involves real transaction costs and hence certain risks itself (to be discussed shortly).

In general, **foreign exchange risk** refers to the potential gain or loss that may arise from holding assets or liabilities whose values are sensitive to movements in foreign currency exchange rates. This exposure can be limited in some circumstances through the purchase of foreign exchange contracts (to be discussed shortly), as well as in other ways. One approach is for the counterparty to an exchange to agree on an effective price, as of a given day, that is *not* subject to exchange rate movements. This is normally accomplished by fixing or

EXHIBIT 6–2
Selected January 4, 1999 Foreign Currency Exchange Rates

Country (currency)	USD Equivalent	Currency per USD
Canada (CAD)	0.6553	1.5261
30-day forward	0.6553	1.5260
90-day forward	0.6554	1.5257
180-day forward	0.6611	1.5126
Great Britain (GBP)	1.6575	0.6033
30-day forward	1.6589	0.6028
90-day forward	1.6565	0.6037
180-day forward	1.6505	0.6059
Mexico (MXN)	0.1019	9.8160

---

[4]A *hedge*, or *hedging*, refers to the process of attempting to reduce or eliminate a firm's exposure to a particular type of risk (e.g., foreign exchange risk).

"denominating" the price of the goods or services in units of local currency of the company that does not wish to bear foreign exchange risk. For example, if Kellogg purchased goods from a German distributor, it could eliminate its exposure to foreign currency exchange rate fluctuations if the price of the goods were denominated in USD. In this way, all risk related to fluctuations in the DEM/USD exchange rate prior to settlement of the transaction would be borne by the German supplier. The USD to be received by the German supplier would be convertible into more or fewer DEM, depending on the movement of foreign exchange rates. In accounting parlance, risk of adverse foreign exchange movements as a result of the settlement of purchases or sales of goods and services is called **transaction risk.**[5]

Accounting versus Economic Foreign Exchange Transaction Risk

Transaction risk arises because receivables and payables that are denominated in foreign currencies are reported on balance sheets at their parent company's currency equivalents as of the balance sheet date. The restatement of these receivables and payables using balance sheet date exchange rates typically results in income statement gains and losses. For example, a receivable denominated in a foreign currency that was outstanding at the end of one period and settled sometime in the next period would give rise to a *transaction gain (loss)* on two income statements if the foreign currency appreciated (devalued) against the home currency.

To illustrate, consider a U.S. company that sold goods to a British customer for 100,000 GBP on December 15, 20x1. At the date of the transaction, the exchange rate was 2.00 USD. On December 31, 20x1, the end of the U.S. company's fiscal year, the exchange rate was 2.10 USD, and on January 15, 20x2, the date payment was received from the British customer, the exchange rate was 2.15 USD. Journal entries for the U.S. company (keeping its books in USD) related to this transaction follow:

12/15/x1	Accounts Receivable	200,000	
	Sales Revenue		200,000
12/31/x1	Accounts Receivable	10,000	
	Foreign Currency Transaction Gain		10,000
1/15/x2	Cash	215,000	
	Foreign Currency Transaction Gain		5,000
	Accounts Receivable		210,000

Under existing U.S. and IASC GAAP, these gains (or losses, as the case may be) are reported on the U.S. company's income statement in the period in which they arose. Note in the preceding example that the U.S. company's total transaction gain of 15,000 USD was spread between 20x1 and 20x2. Obviously, managers prefer to avoid any unpleasant surprises, such as a transaction loss, and thus regularly monitor their company's accounting transaction exposure or net receivable/payable position denominated in foreign currencies.

In order to evaluate the results of applying a particular accounting policy to foreign operations, it is helpful to distinguish between **accounting exposure** and **economic exposure.** Whereas accounting exposure is the risk of reporting income statement gains and

---

[5]*Transaction risk* (or *exposure*) refers to the likelihood that a company will experience a real cash flow gain (or loss) on an individual transaction as a direct consequence of an exchange rate movement. It is frequently distinguished from a second type of risk that results from currency movements, **translation risk,** which generally reflects the likelihood of experiencing an unrealized valuation gain (or loss) on the net assets of a company located in another country when exchange rate changes occur between balance sheet dates. Under both FASB and IASC accounting standards, the effects of transaction risk on shareholders' equity are reflected on the income statement, whereas the effects of translation risk are most commonly reflected on the balance sheet as a component of shareholders' equity.

losses or changes to shareholders' equity, economic exposure is the risk of real changes to the value of a business. The following are some examples of exchange rate movements when recognition of accounting gains or losses may not correspond to real economic gains or losses:

- The same economic events that caused a movement in exchange rates also affect the purchasing power of the reporting currency, and, hence, the price for various goods and services. Although accounting recognition is given immediately to changes in the fair value of foreign exchange and foreign currency–denominated receivables and payables, recognition of cost and revenue changes due to changing prices in the local currency are postponed until realized through actual transactions.

- A company does not intend to convert the foreign exchange received in settlement of a sale into cash of the home currency but will use it to purchase other goods and services in the foreign country. These goods and services are expected to generate revenues in the home currency.

- Inventory may be a natural hedge against foreign currency payables if the inventory is to be sold for foreign currency, yet the timing of income recognition on these items differ. Recognition of profits on investments in inventory is delayed until the period in which the inventory is sold; losses in foreign currency–denominated trade payables are recognized as soon as exchange rates fluctuate.

Forward Foreign Currency Contracts as Hedges

Strategies for reducing transaction risk or exposure are commonly referred to as **hedges,** as previously noted, and they can take many forms. One form just described is to agree to settle a transaction in one's home currency. In exchange for such an accommodation, however, the counterparty to the transaction is likely to charge a fee in the form of a less favorable price on the goods or services exchanged.

When a transaction is denominated in the home currency of one of the parties to a transaction, no additional hedging activity by the party receiving the accommodation is usually needed. However, the party granting the accommodation may wish to hedge its currency risk exposure. One way for the accommodating company to limit its foreign currency risk is by entering into a transaction with an exchange broker to purchase or sell foreign currency for future delivery at a fixed exchange rate. To illustrate, assume that on January 4, 1999, Alpha (a U.S. company) sells and delivers customized computer software to a Canadian company. The agreement between the two companies provides that Alpha will be paid 1,000,000 Canadian dollars (CAD) 180 days hence, at such time when it will be determined whether the product has met all of the buyer's specifications. To hedge its foreign currency exposure of 1 million CAD (or 655,300 USD = 1,000,000 CAD × .6553 USD), Alpha could enter into a forward contract that would require it to deliver 1,000,000 CAD on July 3, 1999. Given the forward exchange rates in Exhibit 6–2, such a contract would pay Alpha 661,100 USD (1,000,000 CAD × .6611) on that date.

The chart in Figure 6–1 plots the gains or losses that would result from changes in the value of (1) the CAD-denominated receivable, (2) the forward contract, and (3) their combination for possible July 3, 1999, exchange rates. The shaded area around exchange rates of .61 and .62 indicates that Alpha is exposed to a change in reported profits (and future cash flows) of ±10,000 USD with each ±.01 USD change in the July 3, 1999, exchange rate from its January 4, 1999, spot rate.

The effectiveness of the forward contract as a hedge of this exposure is derived from the fact that the rate of change in the value of the forward contract mirrors (i.e., is negatively correlated with) that of the receivable. The combined value of the receivable and the forward contract shows that if Alpha enters into the forward contract, the amount of U.S. dollars Alpha will realize from the combined sale and forward exchange transaction

Figure 6–1

Future gains and losses on a foreign currency receivable hedged with a forward exchange contract

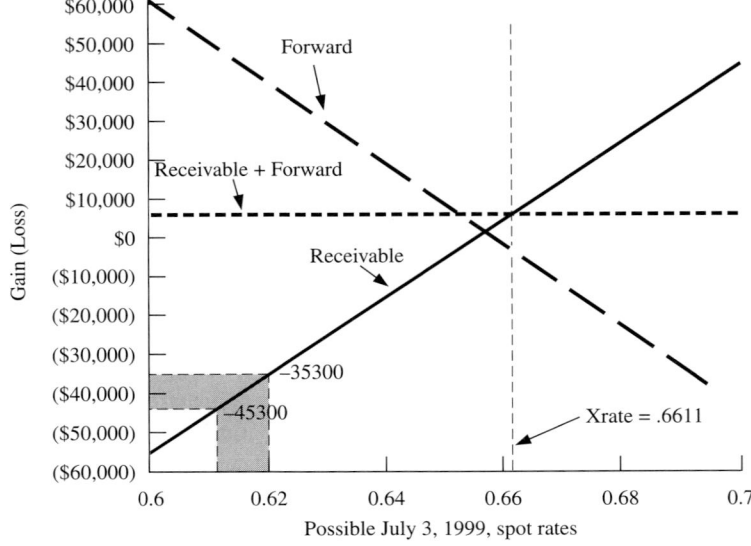

[6] In theory, the 5,800 USD (655,300 − 661,100) "premium" on the forward exchange contract contains two components. The first is a charge (or compensation, as the case may be) for interest gained (or lost) due to the difference between risk-free interest rates on the two currencies. In this case, the counterparty to Alpha pays Alpha to compensate for lower U.S. dollar interest rates over the period of the contract. The second component is the transaction cost, or fee, paid to the exchange broker.

is constant at $661,100.[6] But, *with hindsight,* the forward contract does not benefit Alpha unless the July 3, 1999, exchange rate is above .6611 USD (the 180-day forward rate that existed at the time that the foreign currency contract was negotiated).

Other Forms of Hedging

Foreign exchange risk can also be hedged by means of **option contracts.** The most fundamental difference between forward contracts and option contracts is that forward contracts require an exchange of currency at the settlement date. An option contract grants one party to the contract the right to choose whether (and sometimes when) an exchange will actually take place. Option contracts are often described as one-sided hedges because they are a form of "currency insurance." When structured properly, they pay a return only when foreign currency exchange rates move unfavorably relative to a company's unhedged position in a foreign currency. Using options to hedge foreign currency positions has one principal disadvantage, they cost significantly more than forward contracts, as illustrated by the following example.

Assume that the aforementioned Alpha Company would like to hedge the 1,000,000 CAD receivable by purchasing on December 15, 1998, a 180-day option contract to sell 1,000,000 CAD for 655,300 USD (i.e., an "at-the-money put option"). Using the Black-Scholes option pricing model, the price (or "premium") that will be paid for the option is 14,550 USD.[7]

The chart in Figure 6–2 tracks the gains and losses on changes in the value of the CAD-denominated receivable, the **put option** and their sum over various exchange rates. The solid line that depicts the value of the receivable over various possible January 15, 1999, spot exchange rates is identical to the corresponding line in Figure 6–1. However, changes in the value of the put option mirror the changes in the value of the receivable only for spot rates below .6553 USD, the exercise price of the put.

[7] Additional model inputs: Canadian dollar interest rate, 4.750 percent; U.S. dollar interest rate, 4.625 percent; standard deviation of daily spot rate, 8,000 percent; European-style exercise.

[8] Expansion into international markets *does* increase a firm's exposure to risk; however, it is noteworthy that such expansion may also represent a form of risk reduction through diversification into new markets.

FIGURE 6–2

Future gains and losses on a foreign currency receivable hedged with at-the-money put option

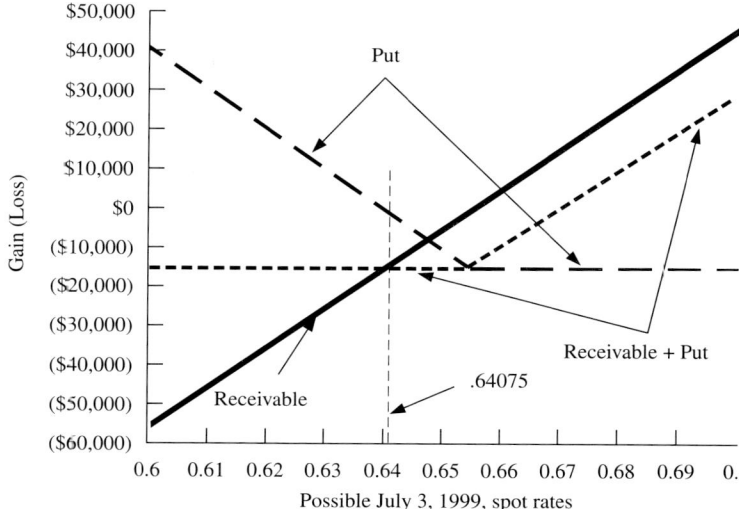

The put option will have added to Alpha's cash flows only when the January 15, 1999, CAD spot rate is less than .64075 USD (.6533 USD − .01455 USD). For all other outcomes, Alpha would have been better off without the put. In contrast, because of the smaller premium on the forward contract, greater downside protection is obtained by the forward contract, albeit by sacrificing any opportunity to profit from appreciation of the Canadian dollar.

U.S. accounting standards do allow *both* foreign currency forwards and options to receive special hedge accounting treatment. However, as the foregoing examples have illustrated, the decision to invest in a more costly put option instead of a forward contract implies a speculative intent on the part of management. This is because there must be some view or expectation that future movements in exchange rates will provide benefits that exceed the extra cost of investing in an option instead of a forward contract.

The final form of hedging considered here is *enterprise risk management*. As previously stated, certain operating assets and obligations that are the result of operating activities can be viewed as natural hedges of foreign currency positions. Some companies manage their multinational business by limiting their exposure to unfavorable movements in foreign currency exchange rates without incurring the cost of forward contracts or options. For example, a company might hold inventory to be sold in a foreign country as a **natural hedge** against its payables exposure. Or changes in the value of long-term debt denominated in a foreign currency may be naturally hedged by real estate investments in foreign countries.

The topic of risk management is quite broad and complex and deserves attention beyond the space available in this book. The interested reader is referred to the list of Suggested Readings at the end of this chapter.

Accounting for Foreign Exchange Transactions

When companies engage in international business operations, the nature and extent of the business risk faced changes.[8] For example, Exhibit 6–3 is an excerpt from the Management Discussion and Analysis section of Occidental Petroleum's recent SEC filing, which describes its view of the risks associated with its foreign operations.

EXHIBIT 6–3
Excerpt from the Management Discussion and Analysis of Occidental Petroleum Company's Annual Report

FOREIGN INVESTMENTS

Portions of Occidental's oil and gas assets are located in countries outside North America, some of which may be considered politically and economically unstable. These assets and the related operations are subject to the risk of actions by governmental authorities and insurgent groups. Occidental attempts to conduct its financial affairs so as to protect against such risks and would expect to receive compensation in the event of nationalization. At December 31, 1997, the carrying value of Occidental's assets in countries outside North America aggregated approximately $2.6 billion, or approximately 17 percent of Occidental's total assets at that date. Of such assets, approximately $950 million was located in the Middle East, approximately $950 million was located in Latin America, and substantially all of the remainder were located in the Netherlands and the Far East.

Accounting standards for reporting foreign currency transactions focus on the timing of recognition of foreign currency exchange gains and losses. The issues involve three classes of transactions:

1. Foreign currency–denominated receivables/payables arising from a company's operating activities.
2. Speculative investments in foreign currency spot markets, forward contracts, and options.
3. Hedges of future commitments that have created foreign currency risk.

Accounting for the first two classes of transactions is straightforward and noncontroversial. Investments in foreign currencies, foreign currency forward and option contracts, and foreign currency–denominated receivables/payables are measured at their fair values. Unrealized gains and losses are recognized as income/loss through the process of revaluing related balance sheet assets and liabilities. Accounting for hedges, on the other hand, is highly controversial and in a state of flux throughout the world. The nature of the controversy and its effects on financial statements is discussed in the next section.

Hedge
Accounting

Hedge accounting refers to methods that defer all or some of the gains or losses in the fair value of hedging instruments to a point in time when they can be offset by gains or losses on hedged items; in essence, it is a form of **income smoothing.** Most of the controversy in accounting for foreign currency transactions involves whether hedge accounting should be permitted and, if so, under what conditions. While the U.S. Financial Accounting Standards Board recently issued *SFAS No. 133*[9] as the first comprehensive standard on hedge accounting, the International Accounting Standards Committee is still actively trying to resolve problems presented by diverse worldwide practice.

Hedge accounting is an attempt to resolve measurement and recognition inconsistencies in accounting. The undesirable effects of the inconsistencies principally manifest themselves in income statement numbers that some argue do not adequately measure performance in a given period.

Measurement inconsistencies addressed by hedge accounting arise from differences in the bases of measurement applied to **hedged items** and **hedging instruments.** For example, the value of wheat held by a U.S. company for future sale creates exposure to fluctuations in the market price of wheat. A hedging instrument such as a futures or options contract is normally measured at fair value (which is, in turn, derived from the

---

[9]*SFAS No. 133,* "Accounting for Derivative Instruments and Hedging Activities" (Norwalk, CT: FASB, 1998). Effective for all fiscal quarter, beginning after June 15, 1999.

price of wheat). The wheat itself being held in inventory is usually measured at historical cost, lower-of-cost-or-market. Hedge accounting could consist of a policy for matching the gain or loss on the hedging instrument to the period in which any gain or loss on the wheat inventory is recognized.

Recognition inconsistencies addressed by hedge accounting arise when the hedged item is not recognized, or does not even come into being, until after the hedging instrument is acquired or created. Without some form of hedge accounting, changes in the value of the hedging instrument may occur and be recognized before the income effect of the hedged item is recognized. For example, a food processor desires to hedge its price risk from a firm purchase commitment to buy a fixed amount of wheat. Under hedge accounting, gains or losses in the market value of a hedging instrument designed to reduce price risk would be deferred until the wheat is physically delivered to the food processor.

Some of the most important questions to be resolved by standard setters and analysts are illustrated by a recent dispute between Dell Computer Corp. and David R. Korus, a computer industry analyst. The dispute was first publicized in *The Wall Street Journal* on November 30, 1992, and was also the subject of an investigation by the Securities and Exchange Commission into Dell's accounting practices. The dispute centered around Dell's accounting for losses on investing in foreign currency options. Dell's second quarter financial statements in 1992 disclosed deferred unrealized currency losses through hedge accounting of $38 million—more than half of Dell's pretax profits for the year to date. At the end of the 1991 fiscal year, Dell disclosed in its annual report that it had sold currency option contracts worth $435 million. In contrast, Dell's international sales for 1991 were only $200 million; it appears that many of these option contracts were accounted for as hedges of future, uncommitted sales.

While the SEC eventually conceded to Dell that extant accounting standards did not specifically preclude Dell's accounting practices, they expressed concern over the following issues:

1. *Is an option an appropriate hedging instrument?* As mentioned previously, some would argue that the decision to pay a larger premium for an option is irrefutable evidence that its purpose can only be speculative. (By definition, a gain or loss on a financial instrument held for speculative purposes is ineligible for special hedge accounting.)

2. *What proof should be required that an investment can be expected to be effective as a hedge?* A hedging instrument does not effectively reduce total enterprise risk if it duplicates, or undoes, a natural hedge. For example, a forecast of future expenses to be paid in a foreign currency could offset much of the foreign currency risk in forecasted future sales. Thus, an investment in a foreign currency option or forward could actually increase overall currency risk to a company such as Dell.

3. *Should transactions that are not given accounting recognition qualify as hedged items?* For example, firm commitments to purchase/sell goods or services are not given accounting recognition until performance by one or both parties to the commitment has occurred. *SFAS 52* allows gains and losses on foreign currency *forward* contracts to be deferred if management specifically designates the purpose of the contracts as hedges of *firm* commitments. However, some U.S. companies have applied hedge accounting to other less probable anticipated transactions by using foreign currency options as the hedging instrument. In Dell's case, the hedged item was not even a commitment, but a subjective forecast of future sales *and* their profitability. The SEC's position was that hedge accounting is taken too far when applied to highly uncertain future profits.

4. *What criteria should be used to distinguish between hedging and speculative activities?* If a Dell competitor entered into the exact same transactions and had the exact same prospects for sales in foreign currency *but* did not elect to designate the options as hedges, radically different measures of income could result for substantially identical economic circumstances.

The Dell investigation was just one of many cases that led the SEC to require new disclosures about foreign currency and similar forms of market risk (e.g., interest rates, commodities prices)[10] and also to encourage the FASB to develop more comprehensive rules on accounting for derivatives. Presented in Exhibit 6–4 are excerpts of these disclosures by Daimler-Benz in its 1997 annual report to the SEC on Form 20-F.

SFAS No. 133 *and Foreign Currency Hedges*

Born out of years of intense debate, *SFAS No. 133* formalized certain controversial hedge accounting practices and also established new methods of accounting for hedges. There can be no doubt that *SFAS No. 133* increased the rigor with which hedge accounting must be applied and added much greater transparency of the effects of hedge accounting on reported net income.

By many accounts, *SFAS No. 133* is the most complex standard yet created by the FASB and most of its details are well beyond the scope of this book.[11] It is nonetheless useful to review the major provisions and concepts of *SFAS No. 133* and their application to simple situations involving foreign currency. The basic provisions are summarized below:

- Derivative financial instruments—whether entered into for hedging or any other purpose—should always be measured and reported at fair value. For the most part, only derivatives may be designated as hedging instruments.
- Special hedge accounting should be available when a high degree of hedge effectiveness is demonstrated and documented at the inception of the hedge.
- No method of hedge accounting should result in reporting deferred losses or gains on the balance sheet.
- The method of hedge accounting to be employed will depend on the type of hedge.

With respect to this last provision, *SFAS No. 133* permits hedge accounting for the following classes of foreign currency transactions (discussed in greater detail below):

1. Foreign-currency-denominated firm commitments that have not been recognized as balance sheet assets or liabilities.
2. Foreign-currency-denominated forecasted transactions.
3. "Available-for-sale" securities whose prices are not quoted in U.S. dollars.
4. Net investments in foreign operations.

Interestingly, *SFAS No. 133* did not specify any particular type of hedge accounting for foreign-currency-denominated receivables or payables. This is because no recognition or measurement differences exist between the receivable or payable (the hedged item) and the forward or option (the hedging instrument). All of these assets and liabilities are already recognized on the balance sheet, revalued with changes in spot rates, and the changes in valuation are immediately reflected in income.

---

[10]U.S. Securities and Exchange Commission, "Quantitative and Qualitative Disclosures About Market Risk," Item 305 of Regulation S-K, and Item 9A of Form 20-F.

[11]The standard itself contains over 500 paragraphs, including 34 examples. A guide to the application of *SFAS No. 133* published by PriceWaterhouseCoopers contains almost 600 *pages.*

EXHIBIT 6–4

Excerpt from Daimler-Benz's 1997 Annual Report: Foreign Currency Hedging Activities

The Daimler-Benz Group is exposed to market risks from changes in interest rates and foreign currency exchange rates which may adversely affect its results of operations and financial condition. The Group seeks to minimize the risks from these interest rate and foreign currency exchange rate fluctuations through its regular operating and financing activities and, when deemed appropriate, through the use of derivative financial instruments. Any exposures of the Group to equity price risks are not material. The Group does not use financial instruments for trading or other speculative purposes.

Exchange Rate Exposure

Transaction Risk and Currency Risk Management

As a consequence of the global nature of Daimler-Benz' businesses, its operations and its reported financial results and cash flows are exposed to the risks associated with fluctuations in the exchange rates between the mark and the other major world currencies. The Group's currency risk exposure primarily occurs because the Group generates a substantial portion of its revenues in currencies other than the mark while a major share of the corresponding cost-of-sales is incurred in marks. This risk exposure primarily affects the Group's two largest business segments, Automotive and Aerospace. In the Passenger Car division, sales are denominated in the currencies of the countries in which cars are sold but manufacturing costs are denominated primarily in marks since manufacturing is concentrated in Germany. Similarly, Aerospace revenues resulting from the sale of aircraft, aircraft engines and certain other aerospace related products are principally denominated in dollars due to the requirements of the marketplace but the products are manufactured exclusively in Germany. An additional risk element associated with the operations of the Aerospace division is that the contracts for its products, especially aircraft, are generally entered into well in advance of the production and delivery of the products. As a result, Daimler-Benz Aerospace is exposed to fluctuations in the dollar/mark exchange rate between the date of the contractual order by the customer and the date of delivery and payment for the product, which may extend over a period of years.

In order to provide a natural hedge against potential currency exposures, the Group attempts to increase cash outflows in the same currencies in which the Group has a net excess inflow, where possible and appropriate. This is achieved mainly through increased procurement in foreign currencies and by increasingly producing in those countries which are primary markets for the Group's products. One example of these efforts is the M-Class manufacturing facility in Tuscaloosa, Alabama. See "Effects of Currency Translation" below.

In order to mitigate further the impact of currency exchange rate fluctuations, Daimler-Benz continually assesses its remaining exposure to currency risks and hedges a portion of such risks through the use of derivative financial instruments. Responsibility for managing the Group's currency exposures and use of currency derivatives is centralized within the Group's Currency Committee. The Currency Committee, which consists of two separate sub-groups, one for Daimler-Benz Aerospace and one for the Automotive business, is comprised of senior managers from each of the respective businesses as well as from the Finance Department of Daimler-Benz AG. Decisions concerning foreign currency positions taken by the Currency Committee are implemented by the Corporate Treasury Department. The Daimler-Benz Board of Management is regularly informed of the decisions of the Currency Committee as well as the actions of the Corporate Treasury. The Corporate Treasury is responsible for assessing, consolidating and managing foreign currency exposures through transactions with international financial institutions.

The principal derivative financial instruments used by the Group to cover foreign currency exposures are forward foreign exchange contracts and currency options. The maturity dates of forward contracts are established according to the anticipated cash flows of the Group. The policy of the Group is to use a proportional mixture of each instrument depending upon the Group's view of market conditions. At December 31, 1997 and 1996 the Group had entered into forward foreign exchange contracts and currency options with a nominal value, in terms of marks, of DM 40.3 billion and 34.1 billion, respectively. The currencies in which the Group's derivative financial instruments are denominated are in parallel with the currencies in which it is subject to transaction risk. See Note 23 to the Consolidated Financial Statements.

In 1997, the Group changed its policy for hedging transactions and began designating certain derivative financial instruments as hedges of foreign currency denominated assets, liabilities and firm commitments. To the extent a derivative financial instrument is designated as hedging a committed foreign currency transaction, unrealized gains and losses are deferred and recognized concurrently with the effect of the underlying business transaction. To the extent applicable accounting requirements do not permit hedge accounting, the Group marks the derivative financial instruments to market which results in unrealized gains and losses on financial instruments being recognized at each reporting date. See Note 23 to the Consolidated Financial Statements for further information with respect to the Group's foreign currency and financial instruments accounting policies.

During 1997 the Group's direct transaction risk (which is represented by the net imbalance between the currency in which its revenues were denominated and the currency in which the costs related to such revenues were denominated) was approximately DM 26.3 billion (using 1997 average exchange rates). This imbalance resulted from the net excess of non-mark denominated revenues over non-mark denominated costs—principally in dollars (DM11.3 billion), British Pounds (DM 3.7 billion), Italian Lire (DM 2.7 billion), Japanese Yen (DM 2.6 billion) and French Francs (DM 1.7 billion). As a result of significantly higher revenues in 1997 the Group's net transaction risk increased in 1997 by 16% compared to 1996.

During 1997 the major world currencies appreciated against the mark. This was primarily true for the dollar and the British Pound, the most significant sources of non-mark denominated revenues of the Group. Compared to 1996, the average exchange rates of the dollar and the

EXHIBIT 6–4 (CONTINUED)

British Pound increased by 15% and 21%, respectively. This development had a significant positive effect on the Group's operating results. Due to the smoothing effect of the Group's hedging activities, which in prior years significantly mitigated the negative impact of the high relative value of the mark, the beneficial effect on the Group resulting from the appreciation of the dollar and the British Pound was diluted to some extent. The average exchange rate of the Japanese Yen increased by 4% in 1997. Despite this development the Group's hedging rate exceeded the average exchange rate by a substantial margin.

The effective exchange rates for the major world currencies achieved for the Group through hedging transactions in contrast to the pure unhedged market average rates for these currencies in 1997 and 1996, respectively, were as follows:

		1997				1996		
Currency	*Effective[1]*	*% Change[2]*	*Market Average[3]*	*% Change[2]*	*Effective[1]*	*% Change[2]*	*Market Average[3]*	*% Change[2]*
U.S. Dollar	1.63	7.2	1.73	15.3	1.52	(1.9)	1.50	4.9
British Pound	2.41	6.6	2.84	20.9	2.26	(0.4)	2.35	4.0
Japanese Yen (JPY 100)	1.58	(0.6)	1.44	4.3	1.59	2.6	1.38	(9.8)
French Franc (FF 100)	29.32	1.6	29.71	1.0	28.85	0.8	29.41	2.4
Italian Lira (ITL 1,000)	0.97	5.4	1.02	4.1	0.92	7.0	0.98	11.4

[1]The effective rates shown represent the average of all hedging transactions for each specific currency which matured during the year shown including all hedging effects such as swap prices and the net premium revenue and expense resulting from option transactions.

[2]The percentage change shown is in comparison to the figure shown in the comparable column in the prior year, except that percentage changes for 1996 are as compared to the 1995 figures which are not shown.

[3]The rates for the foreign currencies shown are calculated based on the official rates fixed at the *Frankfurter Devisenbörse* (Frankfurt Currency Exchange).

Exchange Rate Sensitivity

Because the Group enters into foreign exchange transactions for a significant portion of its contracted and forecasted foreign exchange exposures, a significant increase or decrease in the exchange rate of the mark relative to other major world currencies should not, in the short term, materially affect the Group's cash flows. Over time, however, to the extent that such exchange rate movements are unable to be reflected in the pricing of the Group's products in local currency they could materially affect the Group's cash flows. In general, appreciation of the mark in relation to another currency has an adverse effect on the Group's reported revenues and results, and depreciation of the mark has a positive effect. The tables that follow provide information about the effect on the Group's pre-tax cash flow of a 10% appreciation of the mark against foreign currencies. The figures shown in the tables were calculated as of December 31, 1997.

1998	U.S. Dollar	Japanese Yen (JPY 100)	British Pound	French Franc (FF 100)[1]	Italian Lira (ITL 1,000)[1]	Others[1]	Total
				(DM equivalent in billions)			
Estimates of:							
Gross Amount of Foreign Currency Cash Inflows	17.7	3.4	4.0	3.1	3.5	7.6	39.3
Gross Amount of Foreign Currency Cash Outflows	6.5	0.4	0.4	0.6	0.3	3.0	11.1
Net Position from Underlying Transactions in Foreign Currency	11.2	3.0	3.6	2.5	3.2	4.6	28.2
Loss from a 10% Appreciation of DM After Hedging Activities[2]	0.21[3]	0.09[3]	0.08	0.04	0.06	0.06	0.54

[1]The net exposure of the Group in currencies of EU member states expected to participate in the single European currency amounts to approximately DM 8.0 billion.

[2]Sensitivity is calculated based on the net position from underlying transactions after consideration of the Group's derivative financial instruments entered into to offset such foreign currency exposure.

[3]In certain prior years, the U.S. Dollar and the British Pound fluctuated by more than 10%. Anticipated losses from a more than 10% appreciation of the DM against the U.S. Dollar and the British Pound would increase proportionately.

EXHIBIT 6–4 (CONCLUDED)

1999	U.S. Dollar	Japanese Yen (JPY 100)	British Pound	French Franc (FF 100)[1]	Italian Lira (ITL 1,000)[1]	Others[1]	Total
			(DM equivalent in billions)				
Estimates of:							
Gross Amount of Foreign Currency Cash Inflows	20.1	4.1	4.5	3.3	3.5	7.4	42.9
Gross Amount of Foreign Currency Cash Outflows	8.2	0.4	0.4	0.6	0.3	3.7	13.5
Net Position from Underlying Transactions in Foreign Currency	11.9	3.7	4.1	2.7	3.2	3.8	29.4
Loss from a 10% Appreciation of DM After Hedging Activities[2]	0.77[3]	0.32[3]	0.24	0.09	0.29	0.50	2.21

[1]The net exposure of the Group in currencies of EU member states expected to participate in the single European currency amounts to approximately DM 8.2 billion.

[2]Sensitivity is calculated based on the net position from underlying transactions after consideration of the Group's derivative financial instruments entered into to offset such foreign currency exposure.

[3]In certain prior years, the U.S. Dollar and the British Pound fluctuated by more than 10%. Anticipated losses from a more than 10% appreciation of the DM against the U.S. Dollar and the British Pound would increase proportionately.

The relatively lower sensitivity shown for 1998 is explained by the Group's policy to hedge relatively larger portions of short-term anticipated revenues. As a general rule, the longer the expected revenues extend into the future, the larger is the unhedged portion of such revenues. Derivative financial instruments with maturity dates after 1999 are not material to the Group. The Group's foreign exchange rate exposure will be significantly lower once a single European currency has been introduced.

Foreign-Currency-Denominated Firm Commitments. When a foreign currency derivative is used to hedge changes in the fair value of a firm commitment due to exchange rate movements, changes in the fair value of the derivative are reflected immediately in earnings. Accounting for the hedged item can be more complicated because *SFAS No. 133* requires that the balance sheet value of the hedged item be adjusted for changes in its fair value *due to the hedged risk only.* These changes in the balance sheet value of the hedged item are also reflected in earnings and will offset any loss (gain) recognized on the hedged item due to the hedged risk.

To illustrate, assume that Beta Company, on December 15, 2001, enters into a firm commitment to purchase equipment from a supplier in the country of Ham for 10,000 hocks (abbreviated **H**) 30 days later. On this same date, they enter into a forward exchange contract to purchase **H**10,000 for $1,000 in order to lock in the U.S. dollar price of the equipment. The following exchange rates apply:

30-day forward rate, December 15, 2001	$0.10:**H**
15-day forward rate, December 31, 2001	$0.13:**H**
Spot rate, January 15, 2002	$0.12:**H**

Exhibit 6–5 contains the journal entries to record the relevant transactions. The entries illustrate that the gain (loss) on the hedged item—the firm commitment—is offset by the loss (gain) on the hedging instrument—the forward contract—in both fiscal years. Perhaps more importantly, the method of hedge accounting constitutes an unprecedented development in the measurement of hedged assets and liabilities. In this case, an executory contract is recognized as an asset or liability that would never have been recognized prior to *SFAS No. 133.* Moreover, the measurement basis of the firm commitment is neither its historical cost (which is zero) nor any version of current value. The balance of the firm commitment on December 31, 2001, of $3,000 (a liability in this case) represents the change in the fair value of the firm

EXHIBIT 6–5

Accounting for a Hedge of a Foreign Currency Firm Commitment with a Forward Exchange Contract

		Debit	Credit
December 15, 2001	*(No entry is required as the forward-exchange contract's fair value is zero at the date of its initiation.)*		
December 31, 2001	Forward contract receivable	3,000	
	Gain on hedge activity		3,000
	(To recognize the change in fair value of the forward exchange contract.)		
	Loss on hedge activity	3,000	
	Firm commitment		3,000
	(To recognize the change in fair value of the firm commitment due to changes in exchange rates.)		
January 15, 2002	Loss on hedge activity	1,000	
	Forward contract receivable		1,000
	(To recognize the change in fair value of the forward exchange contract.)		
	Firm commitment	1,000	
	Gain on hedge activity		1,000
	(To recognize the change in fair value of firm commitment due to changes in exchange rates.)		
	Foreign currency	12,000	
	Forward contract receivable		2,000
	Cash		10,000
	(To record settlement of the forward-exchange contract.)		
	Equipment	10,000	
	Firm commitment	2,000	
	Foreign currency		12,000
	(To purchase equipment and close the firm commitment.)		
	Depreciation expense	2,000	
	Accumulated depreciation—equipment		2,000
	(To record depreciation for 2002, assuming a 5-year life and zero salvage value.)		

commitment from its inception to the balance sheet date *due only to changes in value attributed to the hedged risk.* The actual fair value of the firm commitment would take into account additional factors; for example, changes in the value of the equipment to be purchased and/or the ability of the manufacturer to fulfill its commitment to Beta.

Foreign-Currency-Denominated Forecasted Transactions.   Exhibit 6–6 contains the journal entries for the identical set of facts, except that the future purchase of equipment may only be characterized as a forecasted transaction and not as a firm commitment. Since the recognition of an asset or liability for the forecasted purchase cannot be justified under U.S. GAAP, no hedged item is recognized. Therefore, hedge accounting must provide some method for postponing the gains and losses to periods in which the hedged item affects income.

The *SFAS No. 133* solution to this accounting problem is to classify the gains and losses on the hedging instrument in a shareholders' equity account whose changes are not

EXHIBIT 6–6

Accounting for a Hedge of a Foreign Currency Forecasted Transaction with a Forward Exchange Contract

		Debit	Credit
December 15, 2001	*(No entry is required as the forward-exchange contract's fair value is zero at the date of its initiation.)*		
December 31, 2001	Forward contract receivable . . . . Other comprehensive income . . . . *(To recognize the change in fair value of forward exchange contract.)*	3,000	3,000
January 15, 2002	Other comprehensive income . . . . Forward contract receivable . . . . *(To recognize the change in fair value of forward exchange contract.)*	1,000	1,000
	Foreign currency . . . . Forward contract receivable . . . . Cash . . . . *(To record settlement of forward-exchange contract.)*	12,000	2,000 10,000
	Equipment . . . . Foreign currency . . . . *(To purchase equipment and close the firm commitment.)*	12,000	12,000
	Depreciation expense . . . . Accumulated depreciation—equipment . . . . *(To record depreciation for 2002, assuming a 5-year life and zero salvage value.)*	2,400	2,400
	Accumulated other comprehensive income . . . . Depreciation expense . . . . *(To transfer 1/5 of accumulated other comprehensive income to depreciation expense.)*	400	400

reported on the income statement: Accumulated Other Comprehensive Income (AOCI). When the hedged item affects the income statement, the related AOCI is transferred to retained earnings via the appropriate income statement category.[12] In Exhibit 6–6, the transfer from AOCI to depreciation expense offsets the extra depreciation recognized due to the decline in the value of the dollar.

Available-for-Sale (AFS) Securities. Under *SFAS No. 115,*[13] marketable securities are reported at their fair values. For those securities that management, through its own discretion, classifies as "available for sale" (as opposed to "trading") unrealized gains and losses are reported as Other Comprehensive Income. A hedging opportunity exists when a company invests in marketable securities that it designates as AFS, *and* whose prices are not quoted in the company's home currency. When a foreign currency derivative is acquired to offset gains or losses on these marketable securities due to movements in exchange rates,

---

[12]*SFAS No. 128,* "Reporting Comprehensive Income" (Norwalk, CT: FASB, 1998) requires that companies separately report Other Comprehensive Income (OCI) for the period and report AOCI as a separate component of shareholders' equity on the balance sheet. "Comprehensive income" is defined as all changes in shareholders' equity for a period from nonowner sources such as issuing stock, dividends, or treasury stock transactions. OCI is defined as comprehensive income less net income.

[13]*SFAS No. 115,* "Accounting for Certain Investments in Debt and Equity Securities" (Norwalk, CT: FASB, 1993).

the unrealized gain or loss on the AFS security *due to changes in exchange rates only* are recognized in net income of the current period. In this way, the gain or loss on the derivative hedging instrument serves to offset the unrealized gain or loss on the AFS security.

Net Investments in Foreign Operations.   Discussion of this aspect of hedge accounting is postponed until the next section of this chapter, when the accounting for investments in foreign operations themselves is considered.

Accounting for Foreign Subsidiaries

A significant problem for a multinational company is how to present its financial statements on a consolidated basis when one or more of its foreign subsidiaries maintain accounting records in a foreign currency. A significant problem for analysts is to evaluate the consolidated financial statements of companies with significant foreign subsidiaries. Considerable latitude is available to these companies, and that may lead to important differences in financial statement presentation.

To consolidate the financial statements of foreign subsidiaries with a parent company, the financial statements of the subsidiaries must first be translated into the reporting currency of the parent. To acomplish this process, two key translation method issues must be resolved:

1. Which assets and liabilities should be translated at the exchange rate existing at the balance sheet date (i.e., the *current* rate) versus the rates existing when the assets and liabilities were originally measured for financial statement purposes (i.e., *historical* rates)?

2. How should variances in the value of translated assets and liabilities (i.e., the effects of differences between the current and historical rates) be characterized on financial statements: as gains and losses on the income statement of the period or as some component of shareholders' equity on the balance sheet with no effect on net income?

SFAS No. 52 provides for two methods of foreign currency translation, which are in essence two sets of answers to the foregoing questions. That set of answers applied depends on the circumstances faced by a company. A description of these two methods will help to clarify just how these issues can have a significant and predictable impact on consolidated financial statements.

How **SFAS No. 52** *Works*

SFAS No. 52 provides a set of criteria that, when evaluated by management, allows a determination of the appropriate translation method to be used: the "temporal method" or the "current rate" method. Under the **current rate method,** all assets and liabilities are translated at the *current* exchange rate, or rate prevailing at the balance sheet date. Translation gains and losses must be excluded from income and instead classified as a separate component of shareholders' equity known as Accumulated Other Comprehensive Income. All revenues and expenses must be translated at the rate that prevailed when the revenue or expense was recognized. This rate can be approximated by using the weighted-average exchange rate for the period.

Under the **temporal method** of translating foreign financial statements, items quantified in terms of future events (e.g., receivables, payables, securities measured at fair value) are translated at the current exchange rate, whereas items quantified in terms of past events (e.g., inventory, equipment, common stock, depreciation, cost of goods sold) are translated at historical rates. This approach preserves the accounting logic of the original foreign-currency-denominated financial statements because if it is proper to quantify an item in terms of a past event, it would also seem proper to quantify that item at the exchange rate that existed when the past event took place. *SFAS No. 52* also specifies that if the temporal method is used, immediate recognition of translation gains and losses on the income statement is mandatory.

SFAS No. 52 introduced the concept of the *functional currency* to determine the appropriate method of converting foreign currency statements. In most cases, the functional currency is either the local currency of the foreign subsidiary or the U.S. dollar.

Management must designate a functional currency for each foreign subsidiary using the criteria suggested in *SFAS No. 52*. If the functional currency is determined to be the U.S. dollar, the temporal method is used and gains or losses resulting from translation are included in income for the period. Alternatively, if the functional currency is the local currency, the current rate method is applied; translation gains or losses are not recognized in the income statement but are included in shareholders' equity as a translation adjustment which is, in turn, included as a component of Other Comprehensive Income.

In general, the criteria for selecting a company's functional currency establish whether the foreign subsidiary is an independent, cash-generating center; if it is, the local currency is considered the functional currency. In coming to this determination, the following factors must be weighed:

- The degree to which cash flows related to the foreign entity's individual assets and liabilities are in the foreign currency or affect the parent's cash flows.
- The responsiveness of sales prices of the foreign entity's products on a short-term basis to changes in exchange rates.
- The existence of an active local market for the foreign entity's product, even though there may be significant amounts of exports.
- Whether labor, materials, and other costs for the foreign entity's products are incurred locally or elsewhere.
- The denomination of debt and the extent to which funds generated by the foreign entity's operations are sufficient to service existing and normally expected debt obligations.
- The volume of intercompany transactions and the extent of the interrelationship between the operations of the foreign entity and the parent company.

These criteria seek to assess the degree to which the exposure of cash flows from the foreign subsidiary to the parent are a principal source of foreign business risk for the parent. If so, the accounting exposure represented by the temporal method with immediate recognition of translation gains and losses would more closely match the economics of a situation in which the foreign subsidiary was not an independent generator of cash. The rationale underlying the current rate method is that it is merely an arithmetic procedure for restating the financial statements of the foreign subsidiaries, and any gain or loss has no economic interpretation; it is merely a *residual* of a mechanical arithmetic procedure.

Illustrating and Comparing the Methods

To illustrate the differences between the temporal and current rate methods in terms of their effects on reported earnings and financial position, consider an example in which the functional currency of the foreign subsidiary is identified as the local currency. We'll call this local currency the "grabule" (symbol ₵) and assume, for simplicity and with no loss in generality, that the exchange rate is fixed at $1:₵1 until January 19x1, the beginning of the current accounting period, and that the dollar devalues during 19x1 so that the exchange rate becomes $2:₵1 by the end of the period, December 31, 19x1.

EXHIBIT 6–7

Balance Sheet Translation

		Local Currency		Current Rate Method		Temporal Method	
		1/1/19x1	*12/31/x1*	*12/31/x1*	*Note*	*12/31/x1*	*Note*
Assets							
Cash	₲ or $	100	₲ 150	$ 300	(1)	$ 300	(1)
Inventory (FIFO)		500	750	1,500	(1)	1,125	(2)
Property, plant, & equipment (net)		800	700	1,400	(1)	700	(3)
Total assets	₲ or $	1,400	₲1,600	$3,200		$2,125	
Equities							
Payables	₲ or $	200	₲ 200	$ 400	(1)	$ 400	(1)
Common stock		900	900	900	(3)	900	(3)
Retained earnings		300	500	1,900		825	
Total equities	₲ or $	1,400	₲1,600	$3,200		$2,125	

Notes:

(1) Translated at current exchange rate of $2:₲1.

(2) Since the ending inventory was purchased ratably throughout the period, it is translated at the average exchange rate of $1.5:₲1.

(3) Translated at historical exchange rate of $1:₲1.

Balance Sheet Results. Exhibit 6–7 illustrates the differences in balance sheet amounts under the current rates and temporal translation methods. Only monetary items (cash and payables, in this case) are translated at the same rate under both methods. The current rate method calls for the translation of inventory and equipment at the current rate, whereas the temporal method requires the use of historical rates. Because FIFO inventory accounting is used and the cost of goods sold equals the beginning inventory balance (see Exhibit 6–8), the ending inventory value must consist of 100 percent of the period's purchases. The appropriate historical rate for inventories valued using FIFO is the average rate for the period (1.5), assuming that the purchases took place at a constant rate over the period. The retained earnings balances under both methods are, for now, "plug figures;" hence, we will ignore for the moment the translation adjustment disclosure required by the current rate method.

In general, the application of the current rate method results in higher (lower) values for assets (and hence net worth) if the U.S. dollar devalues (revalues) against a foreign currency (e.g., the grabule). The effect of this change on conventional financial ratios may increase the likelihood that some firms will become in technical default of certain indenture provisions. The dividend-paying ability of a firm may or may not be affected, depending on whether applicable laws consider the shareholders' equity account available for the payment of dividends.

The balance sheet (and income) numbers provided under the temporal method are easier to interpret. Under temporal method translation, a historical cost in grabules is multiplied by the exchange rate prevailing at the time of the transaction to yield a dollar-denominated amount that is simply a description of the actual cash flow that occurred to acquire the asset, translated to the dollar equivalent of that time period. In contrast, a local currency–denominated historical cost multiplied by the current exchange rate (per the current rate method) yields a number that defies interpretation: It is not a meaningful description of past cash flows, nor is it a description of future flows. Because changes in exchange rates are critically affected by comparative changes in prices, fluctuations in the exchange rate probably reflect some change in the underlying structure of asset prices. This, in turn, probably means that the mix and quantity of assets held has changed.

EXHIBIT 6–8

Income Statement Translation

	Local Currency	Current Rate Method		Temporal Method	
	12/31/x1	*12/31/x1*	*Note*	*12/31/x1*	*Note*
Sales	₵ 1,000	$1,500	(1)	$1,500	(2)
Cost of goods sold	(500)	(750)	(1)	(500)	(3)
Depreciation	(100)	(150)	(1)	(100)	(4)
Taxes	(200)	(300)	(1)	(300)	(1)
Operating income	₵ 200	$ 300		$ 600	
Translation gain (loss)				(75)	(5)
Net income	₵ 200	$ 300		$ 525	
Transation adjustment		$1,300	(5)		

Notes:

(1) Translated at average exchange rate for the period of $1.5:₵1.

(2) Same as (1), assuming sales occurred evenly throughout the period.

(3) Consists of beginning inventory acquired prior to December 31, 19x1, when exchange rate was $1:₵1.

(4) Translated at rate in effect when related assets were acquired—$1:₵1.

(5) See Exhibit 6-9 for derivation of these amounts.

Income Statement Results. Exhibit 6–8 shows how reported net income is significantly affected under the current rate method because of the omission of translation gains and losses, as well as other factors. Under the temporal method, the cost of goods sold (using FIFO) and the depreciation expense are translated at historical rates, whereas sales and other items are translated at the average rate for the period. The leverage provided by the fixed element of expense creates substantial variation in income—200 percent in our example—compared with the actual average foreign currency fluctuation for the period of only 50 percent.

Under the current rate method, all income statement items, including depreciation and the cost of goods sold, are translated at the average current rate. The fluctuation in income due to translation is thus 50 percent. Therefore, as this example illustrates, the fluctuation of operating income due to changes in the exchange rate is always less under the current rate method than under the temporal method.

Translation Adjustment. As Exhibit 6–9 indicates, the total translation adjustment under the current rate method is significantly larger than, and in the opposite direction of, the translation gain or loss under the temporal method. The fluctuation in income is significantly less under the current rate method because (1) the fluctuation of operating income is reduced (as described above) and (2) translation gains and losses are not reflected in income.

The current rate method leads to smaller fluctuations in operating income and much smaller fluctuations in net income in response to changes in exchange rates, but much greater changes in shareholders' equity because of translation adjustments. Everyone who uses financial ratios and income and equity numbers needs to be aware of those differences. For example, analysts may restate reported net income to include the change in the translation adjustment account. For this reason, *SFAS No. 133* allows companies to hedge those changes by taking a position in a foreign currency derivative. The gain or loss on the derivative in this case will be charged or credited, as the case may be, to the translation adjustment account.

EXHIBIT 6–9

Translation Adjustment versus Translation Gain (Loss)

	Local Currency	Current Rate Method	Temporal Method
		12/31/x1	
Beginning net assets	¢1,200	$1,200	$1,200
Ending net assets	1,400	2,800	1,725
Difference to be accounted for	¢ 200	$1,600	$ 525
Operating income	¢ 200	$ 300	$ 600
Translation gain (loss)	—	—	(75)
Net income	¢ 200	$ 300	$ 525
Translation adjustment	—	1,300	—
Change in owners' equity	¢ 200	$1,600	$ 525

EXHIBIT 6–10

Temporal versus Current Rate Methods: Key Financial Statement Ratios

	Dollar Devaluation	Dollar Revaluation
Current ratio	Increase	Decrease
Quick ratio	No change	No change
CFFO to current liabilities	Decrease	Increase
Debt to equity	Indeterminate	Indeterminate
Debt-to-total capitalization	Indeterminate	Indeterminate
Interest coverage*	Decrease	Increase
CFFO to interest expense	Decrease	Increase
CFFO to total liabilities	Decrease	Increase
Receivable turnover	No change	No change
Inventory turnover	Indeterminate	Indeterminate
Total asset turnover	Decrease	Increase
Average collection period	No change	No change
Average number of days' inventory on hand	Indeterminate	Indeterminate
Return on assets*†	Decrease	Increase
Return on equity	Indeterminate	Indeterminate
Return on sales*	Decrease	Increase

*Assuming that net income used in the ratio calculation excludes translation gains and losses; otherwise indeterminate.

†Assuming the numerator of the ratio is less than the denominator.

Systematic Ratio Effects

Exhibit 6–10 summarizes the effect on some key financial ratios as a result of financial statement translation using the temporal method versus the current rate method. For example, under a devaluation, operating income using the current rate method is lower than operating income under the temporal method because all expenses translated at the current rate are larger. (If revaluation occurs, the opposite result is produced.) Net income differences, including translation gains and losses, cannot be predicted, however. Although operating income under the current rate method is lower, a translation loss probably results under the temporal method if, as is likely, the firm is in a net translation liability position (i.e., total liabilities exceed its total monetary assets of cash, receivables, and marketable securities). The change in net income, therefore, depends on the relative magnitude of the decrease in operating income under the current rate method compared with the translation loss under the temporal method.

All asset categories and net worth are higher under the current rate method, which provides for the translation of all assets at the current devalued rate rather than under the

---
EXHIBIT 6–11

Risk Concepts

Currency risk: The degree of stability (or lack thereof) in the exchange rates between foreign currencies. Also known as **foreign exchange risk.**

Transaction risk: The likelihood of experiencing a cash flow gain or loss on an individual transaction as a direct consequence of an exchange rate movement.

Translation risk: The likelihood of experiencing an unrealized valuation gain or loss on the net assets of an entity located in a foreign country as a direct consequence of an exchange rate movement occurring between balance sheet preparation dates. Also known as **accounting risk.**

Political risk: The degree of stability (or lack thereof) among political groups and the established government in a given country; a significant contributor to currency risk.

Expropriation risk: The likelihood that a company's assets located in a foreign domain will be involuntarily appropriated by the government, with or without compensation.

---

temporal method, which requires that only some of these assets be translated at the current rate. All liability and debt items are translated at the same rate under both methods; hence, there is no change in liabilities and debt. The translation of sales is also unaffected.

Summary

Foreign operations, whether isolated transactions or those involving controlled foreign subsidiaries, possess attributes of risk that can be distinctly different from domestic operations. An important question for analysts to address is whether the accounting for foreign operations adequately portrays the impact of these risks on income and financial position.

Management has considerable latitude in its choice of accounting for foreign operations, and these choices often have a material impact on financial statements. Related issues include the following: (1) whether investments in foreign currency contracts (forward exchange contracts and options) should be accounted for as speculations or as hedges of other exposures to foreign currency fluctuations, (2) which asset and liability account balances should change as a result of foreign currency exchange rate movements, and (3) how such changes in asset and liability balances should be reflected in owners' equity and income of past, current, and future periods.

An important and pervasive theme of this chapter has been the identification of a company's exposure to various sources of international business risk, the measurement and subsequent reporting of that risk in a firm's consolidated financial statements, and ways to minimize the adverse consequences of those risk factors to the financial health and welfare of a company. Exhibit 6–11 summarizes the principal risk factors encountered by a business when conducting business on an international level.

In the next section of this book, we consider the specific business, cultural, and legal environments of seven different countries. Our goal is to become sufficiently familiar with the contextual environments of those countries so as to permit a fuller, more complete financial analysis of companies operating therein.

Suggested Readings

Agmon, T., and D. Lessard. "Investor Recognition of Corporate International Diversification." *Journal of Finance,* September 1972, pp. 1049–55.

Bierman, J., Jr., L. T. Johnson, and D. S. Peterson. *Hedge Accounting: An Exploratory Study of the Underlying Issues.* Norwalk, CT: FASB, 1991.

Brewer, T. L. "Political Risk Assessment for Foreign Direct Investment Decisions." *Columbia Journal of World Business,* Spring 1981, pp. 5–13.

Canto, Victor A. "Everything You Always Wanted to Know about the European Monetary System, the ECU and ERM, but Didn't Know Who to Ask." *Financial Analysts Journal,* November–December 1991, pp. 49–55.

Crawford, M. *One Money for Europe?* New York: Macmillan Press, 1993.

Doukas, J., and N. Travles. "The Effect of Corporation Multinationalism on Shareholders' Wealth: Evidence from International Acquisitions. *Journal of Finance,* December 1988, pp. 1161–76.

Errunza, V., and L. Senbet. "The Effects of International Operations on the Market Value of the Firm: Theory and Evidence." *Journal of Finance,* May 1981, pp. 401–17.

Fatemi, A. "Shareholder Benefits from Corporate International Diversification." *Journal of Finance,* December 1984, pp. 1325–44.

Fitzpatrick, M. "The Definition and Assessment of Political Risk in International Business: A Review of the Literature." *Academy of Management Review* 8, 1992, pp. 249–54.

Haner, F. T., and J. S. Ewing. *Country Risk Assessment: Theory and World-Wide Practice.* New York: Praeger, 1985.

Howell, L. D. "Political Risk in Southeast Asia: A Perspective through the Economist Model." *Journal of Asian Business,* Spring 1993, pp. 19–36.

Kohrin, S. J. "Political Risk: A Review and Reconsideration." *Journal of International Business,* Spring 1979, pp. 67–80.

Leavy, B. "Assessing Country Risk for Foreign Investment Decisions." *Long Range Planning* 17, 1993, pp. 141–50.

Marsh, D. "EMU Strain Begins to Show." *Financial Times,* January 17, 1995, p. 13.

Münchau, Wolfgang. "After the Fanfare, the Facts of Monetary Life." *Financial Times,* January 4, 1999, p. 9.

Wilson, A. C., G. Waters, and B. J. Bryan. "The Decision on Derivatives: FASB Statement No. 133 Establishes Comprehensive Accounting Requirements." *Journal of Accountancy,* November 1998, pp. 24–29.

APPENDIX 6A

The Euro   The European Union (EU) established the European Monetary System and created a composite currency unit, the European Currency Unit (ECU), on March 13, 1979. The ECU, renamed the "euro," combines a basket of currencies in fully equal weights. These weights are used daily by the European Union in Brussels together with the current exchange rates for individual currencies to yield a value for the euro. Exhibit 6A–1 illustrates this calculation to U.S. dollars for a set of exchange rates and weights as quoted in *The Wall Street Journal.* Column A represents the corresponding fixed unit of currency per each euro. Column B gives the indirect quote or exchange rate for number of dollars per fixed unit of currency for the listed countries. Column C is another indirect quote whereby the product of Column A and Column B results in the corresponding country's $/euro cross rate. The numbers in Column C are virtually identical because the small differences are due to rounding. The last line of the exhibit proves that when each country's cross rate is combined and then divided by the 11 member countries, it equals the same spot rate as quoted in *The Wall Street Journal.*

Intervention Mechanism.   A new exchange rate mechanism (ERM2) has replaced the former ERM as of January 1, 1999, and will help stabilize the currencies of the nonparticipating member

EXHIBIT 6A–1

The Euro and Its Components

Currency	(A) Fixed Unit per Euro	(B) Current Exchange Rate	(A*B) Specific Currency's $/Euro Cross Rate
Austrian schilling	13.7603	$0.08019	$ 1.103438
Belgian franc	40.3399	0.02736	1.1037
Dutch guilder	2.2037	0.5007	1.103393
Finnish markka	5.94573	0.1856	1.103527
French franc	6.5596	0.1682	1.103325
German mark	1.9558	0.5642	1.103462
Irish punt	0.7876	1.4012	1.103585
Italian lira	1936.2700	0.0005699	1.10348
Luxembourg franc	40.3399	0.02736	1.1037
Portuguese escudo	200.4820	0.005504	1.103453
Spanish peseta	166.3860	0.006632	1.103472
Actual Dollars per		**$1.1035**	12.13854/11
Euro Quote (WSJ)			**=$1.1035**

states. ERM2 categorizes EU member states as "ins" or "pre-ins." "Ins" are those 11 member states of the EU in Exhibit 6A–1, which adopted the euro from the outset on January 1, 1999. "Pre-ins" are those member states that did not adopt the euro from the outset, either because they did not fulfill the necessary conditions or because the Maastricht Treaty affords them the possibility of not adopting the new currency. The four countries falling into the "pre-in" category are Denmark, Great Britain, Greece, and Sweden. Great Britain and Sweden exercised opt-outs negotiated from provisions on Economic and Monetary Union of the Maastricht Treaty, but they may reconsider joining the other 11 member states at any time. Denmark and Greece, on the other hand, did not meet all the necessary convergence criteria (price stability, public deficits, exchange rate stability, long term interest rates) and will be reexamined every two years for possible acceptance. The Danish krone and the Greek drachma are linked to the euro through the ERM2. Great Britain and Sweden, both having declined joining the system, have sparked a debate between themselves and the others about whether participation in the new ERM2 is a prerequisite for membership of monetary union.

The main elements of ERM2, of which membership is voluntary, are:

1. The currencies of the participating "pre-ins" will have a central rate against the euro. By pursuing stability-oriented policies, these central rates will be the focus of economic management in the participating "pre-in" member states. Around each central rate, there will be relatively wide standard fluctuation margins of ±15 percent. However, narrower margins between the euro and the participating "pre-in" currencies will be possible.
2. Intervention support from the European Central Bank (ECB) will, in principle, be automatic and unlimited in the event of a "pre-in" currency reaching its standard fluctuation margin. Intervention support within the standard fluctuation margins will also be possible. In either case, intervention can be suspended if price stability is jeopardized. Credit and financing facilities for intervention activities will be available.
3. In the event of a central rate becoming unsustainable, realignment will take place. The ECB and any participant in the mechanism will have the right to trigger a confidential procedure, which may result in a realignment.

Why Use the Euro?   The euro is the proposed vehicle to create a single European currency. Currently, it is widely used in international bond issues and, to a lesser extent, in banking and hedging transactions. In most countries, its private use, except as a denomination currency for bond issues, has been very limited. In the first half of 2002, euro coins and notes will be introduced, but until that time the euro will coexist with national denominations.

Proponents of the single-currency concept believe that elimination of national currencies will create greater convenience for travelers and buyers of small amounts of goods. Small companies will recoup their competitive advantage as compared to larger companies that could engage in currency and banking transactions at lower rates. Some also believe that inflation will be more easily managed by a central bank than numerous national central banks, and politics will be a step removed from management of the economy through monetary means.

Others believe that universal adoption of the euro is too great a sacrifice for individual countries, which will lose the ability to stave off recessions through exchange rate intervention or, in general, through government management of monetary policy. The presence of a single currency administered by an independent central bank will not be a panacea for economic recession. Member countries will still make fiscal policy that will substantially affect the economies of other member countries.

Exercises

6.1   U.N. World Investment Report

In a July 21, 1993, *Financial Times* article (p. 3), "An Open Door Alone Is Not Enough to Attract Cash," David Dodwell cites the U.N.'s 1993 World Investment Report as stating that "governments keen to attract foreign investment '. . . should go beyond general, broad based efforts and focus on particular functions (e.g., regional headquarters, research and development, *accounting* [emphasis added]) for which they believe they have certain advantages'."

Required:

Discuss, being as specific as you can be, accounting principles that could be viewed by shareholders as providing a country with "a certain advantage" in attracting foreign direct investment. Do you perceive that the push toward the harmonization of accounting standards is conflicting with a nation's possible accounting "advantage"? Why or why not?

6.2   Foreign Currency Translation Effects

In mid-October, 1993, Digital Equipment Corporation reported a greater-than-expected loss and a 9 percent decline in revenue for the first quarter of its 1993 fiscal year (i.e., July 1–June 30). According to analysts familiar with the company, adverse foreign currency translations accounted for approximately half of the decline in sales for the period. In response to the adverse news, Digital's share price declined nearly 10 percent to $35.125.

According to a company spokesperson, Digital's revenues fell from $3.31 billion in 1992 to $3.0 billion in 1993. Currency translations apparently aided reported revenues in 1992 but reduced them in the first quarter of 1993 when the U.S. dollar strengthened against most foreign currencies. Digital generates approximately 50 percent of its sales in Europe.

Required:

(a) Did the decline in Digital's revenues that resulted from the adverse foreign currency movement represent a *real* economic loss to the company? If so, why? If not, why not?

(b) How could Digital's managers have avoided the revenue loss created by the adverse currency movement?

(c) Assuming that the stock market is efficient, what can we infer about the currency-related revenue loss from the movement of Digital's share price?

6.3   Foreign Currency Translation Adjustments

All developed countries in the world require that when a company conducts operations in a foreign location, the results of those foreign operations be included with those of the parent company.[1] What differs between each country is the specific mechanical process that is followed to translate the foreign operating results into the reporting currency of the parent company. Regardless of the mechanical process used, one account is common to the balance sheets of all countries: the Cumulative Currency Translation Adjustment account. This shareholders' equity account summarizes the unrealized foreign currency adjustments that occur from one period to the next.

The following are the account balances for the cumulative currency adjustment account taken from the financial data of four international companies:

Required:

Assume that the underlying balance sheets of the four companies' foreign subsidiaries have not materially changed from 19x8 to 19x9. Explain what might have happened to cause the changes in the cumulative currency translation adjustment account for each company.

6.4   Translating Foreign Financial Statements

Graham International, Inc. (GI), is a subsidiary of a Canadian-based conglomerate, The Graham Group, headquartered in Vancouver, Canada. GI, Inc., is headquartered in Mexico City, Mexico, although it represents the parent company worldwide.

	Cumulative Foreign Currency Translation Adjustment Account Balance	
	19x9	*19x8*
Company A	$ 564	$ 72
Company B	132	(189)
Company C	(456)	(309)
Company D	(39)	(474)

Exhibits 1 and 2 present GI's financial statements for fiscal year 19x9, expressed in new pesos. In late 19x8, the Mexican government replaced its old currency—the peso—with a new currency, the new peso; 1 new peso equals 1,000 old pesos.

GI had existed since 1987 when it was capitalized with an investment of 3,000,000 pesos (or 3,000 new pesos). At that time, the exchange rate was approximately 1,800 pesos to the Canadian dollar. Since then, the company has earned (after taxes and dividends) 15,000,000 pesos, with a translation value of $7,500 Canadian.

During 19x9, the exchange rate between the new Mexican peso and the Canadian dollar was as follows:

01/01/19x9	$.40 (1 new peso = $.40 Canadian)
12/31/19x9	.36
19x9 average	.38

---

[1]Not all countries require that the results of foreign subsidiaries be *consolidated* with those of the parent company and where consolidated reporting is not utilized, some other method of accounting (usually equity method accounting) is used. Thus, regardless of the specific method employed, the results of a company's foreign operations are reflected in some manner on the parent's financial statements.

Required:

(a) Prepare the translated (in Canadian dollar equivalents) financial statements of Graham International, Inc., at December 31, 19x9.

(b) Determine the balance (if any) required in the cumulative translation adjustment account for the owners' equity section of The Graham Group's 19x9 balance sheet.

(c) Prepare a translated statement of cash flows for Graham International, Inc., as of December 31, 19x9.

EXHIBIT 1

GRAHAM INTERNATIONAL, INC.
Statement of Income
For the Year Ended December 31, 19x9
(in new pesos)

Sales	82,000
Less: Costs and expenses	
Costs of sales	42,000
Depreciation	4,050
Selling, general and administrative expenses	7,250
Interest	2,500
	55,800
Net income before taxes	26,200
Less: Income taxes	13,300
Net income	12,900
Dividends paid to parent (12/31/x7)	1,500

EXHIBIT 2

GRAHAM INTERNATIONAL, INC.
Balance Sheet
As of December 31
(in new pesos)

	19x8	19x9
Assets		
Cash	2,000	3,000
Accounts receivable	6,000	7,400
Inventory	7,000	10,000
Total current assets	15,000	20,400
Plant and equipment	39,000	42,000
Less: Accumulated depreciation	(4,950)	(9,000)
Net plant and equipment	34,050	33,000
Total assets	49,050	53,400
Equities:		
Liabilities		
Accounts payable	6,050	4,000
Long-term debt	25,000	20,000
Total	31,050	24,000
Owners' equity		
Capital stock	3,000	3,000
Retained earnings	15,000	26,400
Total	18,000	29,400
Total equities	49,050	53,400

6.5   Translating Financial Statements Denominated in a Foreign Currency

Salem Electronics Company produces various types of household electronic equipment, which it sells primarily through retail store chains in the United States. On October 1, 19x0, Salem established a wholly owned subsidiary in South Korea, called Salem-Korea, for the purpose of assembling a small home version of a video arcade game that Salem had been licensed to produce. The Korean subsidiary sells its output directly to the U.S. retailers that carry the game (as opposed to selling its output to its U.S. parent for resale to U.S. retailers).

The following are the subsidiary's condensed balance sheets as of September 30, 19x1 and 19x2 (fiscal year-end) and an income statement for the year ended September 30, 19x2. Salem's controller, Marion Francis, asked a member of the accounting staff to translate these statements into U.S. dollars, following *FASB Statement No. 52*. The controller was particularly interested in how the choice of the functional currency—Korean or U.S.—would affect the translated financial statements.

The accounting staff person assembled the following information to assist in preparing the two sets of translated statements:

1. The South Korean unit of currency is the won. As of October 1, 19x0, the exchange rate was 1,000 won = $1.50; as of September 30, 19x1, the rate was 1,000 won = $1.30; as of September 30, 19x2, the rate was 1,000 won = $1.20.

2. All fixed assets were acquired on October 1, 19x0. All depreciation is considered a cost of producing inventory.

3. The video game has been so popular that Salem-Korea has been shipping them as fast as it can make them. As a result, no inventory was on hand at the end of either fiscal year.

4. The capital stock of Salem-Korea was issued to Salem Electronics on October 1, 19x0; no additional capital stock transactions had taken place. Dividends were paid by Salem-Korea for the first time in its history on September 30, 19x2.

SALEM-KOREA
Comparative Balance Sheets
(in millions of won)

Assets	9/30/19x1	9/30/19x2
Cash	800	1,176
Receivables	500	900
Fixed assets	1,800	1,600
Total assets	3,100	3,676

Equities		
Total liabilities	2,200	2,300
Capital stock	1,000	1,000
Retained earnings	(100)	376
Total equities	3,100	3,676

Income Statement
For the Year Ended 9/30/x2
(in millions of won)

Revenues	7,090
Cost of sales	4,415
Other expenses	1,399
Operating income	1,276
Translation gain (loss)	–0–
Net income	1,276
Less dividends	800
Change in retained earnings	476

Required:

    (a) Prepare translated year-end statements for Salem-Korea under the two functional currency assumptions.

    (b) Explain why the translation adjustment under the all-current method differs from the translation gain or loss under the temporal method.

6.6   Estimating the Effects of Accounting Exposure on Financial Statements to Foreign Currency Movements

Contessa Hotels is one of the larger hotel chains in the United States. Its wholly owned subsidiary, Contessa International, builds and operates hotel properties in Europe.

To establish a hotel in Europe, Contessa International typically obtains financing denominated in the new hotel's local currency for up to about 80 percent of the hotel's cost. The remaining start-up funds are obtained through equity financing and U.S. dollar–denominated intercompany loans. The hotel is built with materials and labor primarily sourced from within the country of operation. Hotel operating expenses are paid in the foreign currency of the country of operation, and hotel revenues are collected in the same currency. Net foreign currency operating flows above these amounts are used to repay the construction loan and intercompany loans and to pay dividends.

At the end of a recent fiscal year, the balance sheet of Contessa International was as follows:

Assets		
Cash and receivables		$ 2,777
Inventory		317
Plant and equipment, net		35,434
Deferred costs		1,490
Total		$40,018
Equities		
Short-term payables		$ 3,091
Long-term debt		
Swedish kronors	$ 5,465	
German marks	16,090	
French francs	2,751	
Belgian francs	5,026	
Total		29,332
Paid-in capital		7,595
Total		$40,018

Required:

    (a) Prior to *SFAS No. 52,* Contessa used the current/noncurrent method of foreign currency translation. Calculate foreign currency translation exposure under this method as well as for the two methods that *SFAS No. 52* comprises.

    (b) Assuming the average of all foreign currencies in which Contessa's European subsidiary has invested devalues 10 percent during the next year, approximate the translation gain/loss or translation adjustment that would occur under all three methods.

(c) Demonstrate the equivalence of the following two statements:

(1) Translation gain/loss on an account translated at the current exchange rate is equal to the balance of the account measured in *foreign* currency units at the beginning of the period multiplied by the change in exchange rates.

(2) Translation gain/loss on an account translated at the current exchange rate is equal to the balance of the account measured in *local* currency units at the beginning of the period multiplied by the *relative* change in exchange rates.

(d) Contrast the current/non-current method with the other two methods.

6.7   Accounting for Foreign Currency Risk Exposure

The January 5, 1995, issue of *The Wall Street Journal* carried a news piece with the following headline: "U.S. Firms Feel the Pain of Peso's Plunge." According to the article, because of the Mexican pesos' 37 percent decline in value relative to the U.S. dollar, many U.S. companies with significant operations in Mexico would be taking substantial asset write-downs. The following are examples:

• Ford Motor Co. executives reported that the cost of Ford autos "in peso terms has gone up enormously." In 1994, Ford exported over 27,000 vehicles to Mexico in addition to manufacturing some 200,000 vehicles there.

• Mattel, Inc., the toy maker, reported that it would take a "significant" charge against fourth quarter earnings because "the peso's decline has reduced the value of its Mexican inventory and receivables."

Prior to the pesos' devaluation, the exchange rate was $1.00: 3.45 NP (or new peso); following the devaluation, the exchange rate was approximately $1.00: 4.75 NP.

Required:

(a) Ignoring the specific dollar amounts involved, construct the journal entries for Ford and Mattel necessary to reflect the effects of the peso's decline in value.

(b) For both Ford and Mattel, explain why the fall in the peso necessitated an asset write-down.

6.8   Hedging and Accounting Effects

In April 1988, the Walt Disney Corp. entered into a series of transactions that, as a press release stated, "Effectively monetizes a substantial portion of the expected royalties from certain Tokyo Disneyland operations."

The company sold 20 years of Tokyo Disneyland royalties to a group of Japanese institutions for approximately 90 billion yen (about $725 million after conversion to U.S. dollars on foreign currency markets). The Japanese institutions have no recourse to Walt Disney Corp. if the actual royalty payments are less than expected. Likewise, Walt Disney Corp. does not participate in any royalty payments that are greater than expected.

"With this approach, we transferred some of the risk of the forecast for 20 years of revenues," said a Walt Disney Corp. executive. "Firms that have a series of identifiable flows from trademarks, royalties, license fees, franchises and the like might look at it."

Required:

    (a) What risks did Walt Disney Corp. hedge by this transaction? What did it cost the company to do it?

    (b) Describe the effect of the transaction on financial statements for 1988 and beyond.

    (c) If (a) the exchange rate today were ¥100:$1, (b) interest rates were substantially lower, and (c) royalty payments to date corresponded to expected amounts, which party to the transaction would have gained to date and which would have lost by this transaction?

6.9   Hedge Accounting

Easter Company is based in the United States and has historically sold most of its output domestically. However, on November 1, 19x2, Easter received a firm commitment to purchase a large quantity of merchandise from a Japanese company. The agreement between Easter and its new customer provided for delivery of merchandise on or before January 1, 19x3, for payment to Easter of ¥100 million at the earlier of January 31, 19x3, or 30 days from the date of delivery of the merchandise.

Easter had considered actions to limit its exposure to risk from fluctuations in the exchange rate between the Japanese yen and the U.S. dollar for a number of reasons. Primarily, this was a significant exposure given its cash situation. Second, it was believed that exchange markets could become particularly volatile around the time of a U.S. presidential election. Easter considered two hedging alternatives:

Alternative 1:   Enter into a forward contract on November 1, 19x2, to deliver ¥100 million 60 days hence (January 31, 19x3).

Alternative 2:   Purchase U.S. put options to sell an aggregate value of ¥100 million for $810,000 (price per yen of $0.008100). Easter would sell the option, which would expire on March 31, 19x3, on the open market on January 31, 19x3.

Easter has a calendar fiscal year-end. Relevant currency exchange data covering the period from the inception of the purchase commitment with the Japanese company and receipt of cash payment by Easter are as follows:

	Spot Rate	Forward Rate		Price of Put Option
November 1, 19x2	$0.008106	$0.008103	60 days	$0.0107
December 31, 19x2	0.008026	0.008020	30 days	0.0162
January 31, 19x3	0.008055	—	—	0.0057

Required:

    (a) Assume that the merchandise was delivered to the Japanese customer on January 1, 19x3. Provide journal entries to illustrate the financial statement impacts of both the forward contract and the put option if accounted for as hedges under *SFAS No. 133.*

    (b) Repeat part (a), assuming that the purchase of merchandise was a forecasted transaction instead of a firm commitment.

    (c) Provide at least three reasons why hedge accounting should, or should not be permitted under these and similar circumstances.

PART III

Financial Reporting Practices and Contexts in Selected Countries

In this section of the book, the unique contexts of and the financial reporting practices in seven major countries around the world are compared and contrasted. As you will see, despite all of the efforts directed toward harmonization, reporting practices remain widely divergent from country to country. This is all the more interesting because each of the seven countries has highly developed capital market. The cultural, business, and legal explanations for these divergences are also considered. Perhaps an alternative title for this section should be "a global guide to disharmony."

A principal objective of the following section is to compare and contrast not only the financial reporting practices of the seven countries but also the business, cultural, and legal setting of each country to identify the presence of any systematic effects that might be manifested in financial indicators. Consider, for example, the following 1993 fiscal-year data:[1]

Country	Quick Ratio	Interest Coverage Ratio	Inventory Turnover	Return on Assets
Great Britain	0.86	4.72	5.22	0.05
Germany	1.27	3.25	5.11	0.02
Japan	0.98	2.74	5.42	0.02
Sweden	0.99	1.56	2.58	0.01
South Korea	0.49	1.35	6.40	0.01
Italy	0.94	1.92	3.70	0.02
United States	1.00	2.90	4.84	0.03

[1]Data were obtained from the Compustat International file and reflects the median ratio of all listed firms.

Although it is tenuous to draw firm conclusions at this stage, some observations are nonetheless noteworthy. For example, German companies appear to maintain the highest quick ratios, with South Korean companies the lowest. For this latter group, liquidity appears to be enhanced by maintaining the highest inventory turnover. British companies appear to maintain the highest interest coverage ratio and, thus, appear somewhat debt averse as compared to South Korean or Swedish companies. These results, however, may be less related to debt aversion than to relative profitability—the return on assets is highest for British firms and lowest for South Korean and Swedish firms.

As you approach the next seven chapters, one of your educational missions is to focus on those institutional and cultural differences and similarities that may explain these data.

Great Britain[1]

The ASB's [Accounting Standards Board] proposals implicitly make the balance sheet the central plank of the financial statements, with the profit and loss account dependent upon it. The ASB appears to favor current valuations in preference to historical costs. Their approach seems to be to try to make the balance sheet more like a statement of wealth, with the movement in net assets being the primary measure of performance.[2]

The credibility of U.K. accounts could be undermined if the U.K. takes an independent approach to too many issues.[3]

Introduction

As the first great industrial power of the modern era, Great Britain has had a broad and enduring influence on financial reporting practices around the world. The historical importance and geographical reach of British financial reporting practices grow directly out of Great Britain's former role as a world power and pioneer of capitalism, and its continuing influence on international accounting standards is more that of an elder partner than a ruler. This shift in the dynamics of power is reflected in Great Britain's changing trade patterns, which have moved away from its colonies and dependencies of the 19th century to its current membership in the European Union (EU) and close ties with the United States.

Despite the dissolution of its empire, Great Britain continues to be a major factor in developing international financial reporting standards. It is not only a member of the European Union but also is prominently represented in other bodies that are attempting to develop workable international accounting standards, such as the Organization for

---

[1]In Chapter 1, Hofstede's cultural studies involving Great Britain were introduced. We have titled this chapter to be consistent with his focus. In fact, Great Britain includes England, Wales, and Scotland, whereas the United Kingdom includes Great Britain and Northern Ireland. We draw no distinctions for financial reporting purposes between Great Britain and the United Kingdom.

[2]R. Paterson, "In Support of the Profit and Loss Account—Balance Sheets Should Show the Results of the Company's Transactions," *The Financial Times,* September 16, 1993, p. 15.

[3]J. Kelly, "Accountants May Go It Alone on Global Issues," *The Financial Times,* January 27, 1997, p. 6.

Economic Cooperation and Development (OECD) and the International Accounting Standards Committee (IASC), of which the latter is headquartered in London. (For more information on these and other groups promoting harmonization of accounting standards, see Chapter 2.) Given the prominent role of Great Britain in international financial reporting circles, it is not surprising that British company law and reporting standards have exerted a heavy influence on EU directives affecting reporting practices. But Britain's influence comes from private sources as well: British multinationals are a major presence throughout the industrialized and developing world, and the international prestige of London's capital markets ensures that British financial reporting and disclosure requirements remain a prominent issue for major multinational firms around the world.

Environmental Factors

Cultural Environment

Although U.S. and British financial reporting have in some respects gone their own ways over the last 200 years, the exchange of ideas that has characterized Anglo-American relations has maintained a fundamental cultural bond between the two systems and the people that operate them. This bond can be illustrated by comparing the scores of U.S. subjects in Hofstede's study, introduced in Chapter 1, with those of their British counterparts. In three of the focal cultural dimensions, the scores of the two countries are separated by only five points or less. In power distance (PD), the British group registered a 35, and the U.S. group scored 40; in individualism (IDV), the British subjects scored 89, and the U.S. subjects 91; and in long-term orientation (LTO), the British scored 25 and Americans scored 29. In the only category in which the group scores were more than five points apart—uncertainty avoidance (UAV)—the British group scored 35 and the U.S. group 46.

In the context of Gray's analysis of the dimensions of the financial reporting subculture, also introduced in Chapter 1, the UAV scores reported for the British in fact reflect the slightly lower degree of conservatism found in British financial reporting as compared to practices in the United States. For example, the treatment of tangible fixed assets differs significantly between the United States and Great Britain: The United States requires the recording of these assets at cost whereas practice in Great Britain permits revaluation of these assets to market value. This reflects a more optimistic, less conservative approach in the measurement practices used in Great Britain versus those used in the United States. Other less conservative practices that differ between the United States and Great Britain, and that have a material effect on profit, include the treatment of inventories, deferred taxation, and the possibility of not amortizing goodwill carried as an asset. These and other financial reporting differences are discussed in detail in a subsequent section.

The 11-point spread in UAV, suggesting that the British have slightly more tolerance for ambiguity than do Americans, runs counter to a popular stereotype that contrasts a supposedly British love of order and propriety with a supposedly American love of unabashed freedom. No doubt it is true that the stereotype accurately reflects one side of the British national character.[4] However, it is equally true that the British have long cherished liberty as a distinctive feature of their society and culture—so much so that forms of social enforcement now taken for granted (e.g., police forces, standing armies) met

---

[4]See for example, C. Pearce and C. Osmond, "Metaphors for Change: the ALPs Model of Change Management," *Organizational Dynamics,* Winter 1996, pp. 23–35.

with vehement opposition on their introduction in England. Inevitably, the preservation of liberty has often entailed accepting a measure of disorder, a trade-off the British have been willing to make more often than is commonly appreciated. Perhaps, then, there is a cultural reason that the British output in the area of accounting regulation has lagged behind that of the United States. Prior to its demise in August 1990 the main British accounting regulatory body, the **Accounting Standards Committee,** issued only one pronouncement—these pronouncements were called **Statements of Standard Accounting Practice** (SSAPs)—for approximately every four issued by the Financial Accounting Standards Board in the United States. Another interesting observation recently made regarding the financial reporting subculture in Great Britain is that when British auditors were surveyed regarding their attitudes about the true and fair view audit opinion, several respondents volunteered that fair was more important than true; none suggested the reverse.[5] Such a response is perhaps not surprising given the British penchant for relatively small PD (e.g., all should have equal rights) and relatively low UAV (e.g., ambiguity of fair versus true is quite acceptable).

Whatever the cultural differences between Great Britain and the United States may mean, they should be kept in perspective. For example, they diminish considerably when we contrast U.S. and British scores with those of Latin America, the Far East, or even continental European groups in Hofstede's study. The cultural dimension scores for both Great Britain and the United States reflect a society characterized by flexible rules, the absence of an all-powerful hierarchy, and the solution of problems through negotiation. These characteristics seem a fairly accurate description of accounting policy formation and application in both Great Britain and the United States.

Legal and Political Environment

Corporation Law.   With very few exceptions, such as formation by Royal Charter, British companies are incorporated under the Companies Act currently in force. (The most recent one at this writing is the **Companies Act of 1985,** which consolidated all prior Companies Acts, and was amended by the Companies Act of 1989 to incorporate the EU's Seventh Directive.) The act requires all corporations to maintain accounting records that include sufficient information to give a **true and fair view** of a company's financial position and operations. The phrase *true and fair view,* first introduced in the 1947 Companies Act, is important in British accounting and auditing.[6] Even though its meaning is difficult to ascertain with precision (as is likely to be the case with any standard of "fairness"), it is the key phrase by which auditors express an opinion on a set of corporate financial statements. Companies must present audited financial statements in a stipulated format and a directors' report to shareholders at the annual meeting. In addition, they must file these documents with the Registrar of Companies. It is also important to note that the 1989 amendment "gave accounting standards legal definition for the first time; it defined them as statements of standard accounting practice issued by such body or bodies as may be prescribed by regulations. To date, the only body prescribed for this purpose is the Accounting Standards Board Ltd."[7]

In May 1997, Tony Blair became prime minister, ending 18 years of Conservative rule. Moreover, Mr. Blair's Labour Party won the largest majority in Parliament it has ever had.

---

[5]R. Parker and C. Nobes, " 'True and Fair': U.K. Auditors' View," *Accounting and Business Research,* Fall 1991, p. 353.

[6]See A. Cook, "Requirement for a True and Fair View—a U.K. Standard-Setter's Perspective," *The European Accounting Review,* 6, no. 4 (1997), pp. 693–704 for additional discussion.

[7]K. Wild and C. Goodhead, *Financial Reporting and Accounting Manual: Getting Reports Right* (London: Butterworth & Co./Touche Ross & Co., 1994), p. 4.

He has vowed that this is the "New Labour Party" and that he has no interest in returning to pre-Thatcher Labour Party years, rife with unemployment, inflation, corporate noncompetitiveness, and loss of British prominence. Specifically, he is on record as wanting to decentralize power to the regions, "supercharge Britain's entrepreneurial spirit," improve relations with continental Europe, pass a minimum wage, and have a newly independent Bank of England set monetary policy.[8] As the millennium nears, Mr. Blair has made progress toward his stated goals and has generally been a friend of business and investors.

One thorny issue that does exist for Great Britain, and Mr. Blair in particular, is the Economic Monetary Union (EMU). Great Britain, the U.K. more precisely, opted not to be a part of the January 1999 euro introduction and it is uncertain when they will join. British companies are split on the nature and magnitude of the costs/benefits of the country's participation. The split is generally along the lines of Britain's large, multinationals favoring monetary union, while its small and medium-sized companies are opposed.[9] Mr. Blair must manage his nation's move in this regard very carefully, with an eye to the most appropriate timing, the most favorable positioning of its benefits, and the articulation of the most confidence-building assurances of minimized negatives.

Individual Tax Law—Investor Incentives.   The investor orientation that has traditionally dominated British financial reporting is clearly reinforced by British tax law, which gives individuals several important incentives to invest in stocks. Although capital gains are taxable, they are eligible for tax breaks favoring small investors: Net gains are indexed to eliminate the effects of inflation and are subject to an annual exemption (as opposed to differential rates for short-term versus long-term capital gains as in the United States). The annual exemption amount has changed every year since 1980. The annual exemption, which in 1998 equaled £6,800, decreases the taxable portion of any capital gain. (At December 1998 exchange rates—$1.68 to £1—the exemption excluded the first $11,400 of capital gains from income.) Amounts in excess of the annual exemption are taxed at the regular marginal rate applicable to the highest portion of an individual's income. Tax rates on ordinary income range from 20 percent on the first £4,300 of taxable income, to a basic rate of 23 percent on income between £4,300 and £27,100, with a 40 percent rate applied to income over £27,100 (rates for 1998). Interest and dividend income is subject to a basic tax rate of 20 percent.

Under the imputation system in effect in Great Britain from 1973 to 1999, shareholders were granted partial relief from double taxation on corporate profits. When a British corporation paid dividends, it also made an advance payment on its income taxes for the year. The amount of this advance payment was 25 percent of the dividends paid. The advance payment, officially known as the **Advance Corporation Tax** (ACT), was paid by the company to the Inland Revenue Service and was imputed to shareholders as a tax credit to be applied against their personal income tax for the year. Thus, if a company paid a dividend of £100,000 and an advance tax payment of £25,000, a shareholder with a 1 percent holding would receive a dividend of £1,000 and a tax credit of £250 to be applied against his or her individual income tax obligation. The taxpayer must report £1,250 of income, which at a tax rate of 20 percent creates an additional £250 of tax liability. Thus, the imputed tax credit eliminated the marginal tax liability generated by the dividend payment—but only if the taxpayer was in the lowest income bracket. Taxpayers whose

---

[8]See S. Reed, "For Tony Blair, Ireland Will Be a Hard Act to Follow," *Business Week,* June 8, 1998, p. 60; S. Reed, "Britain: Each Reform Widens the Gap with Europe," *Business Week,* March 23, 1998, p. 55; and S. Reed, "Paying Court to Business," *Business Week,* May 19, 1998, pp. 50–51.

[9]R. King and N. Bray, "Coin Toss: Pan-European Currency Divides British Firms," *The Wall Street Journal,* April 24, 1997, p. A15.

income fell in a higher bracket owed a tax liability larger than the credit they received. For example, a taxpayer in the 40 percent bracket received the same £250 tax credit, but the dividend income generated an additional tax liability of £500 (£1,250 × 40 percent), creating a net tax liability of £250 (£500 − £250) from the £1,000 dividend payment—an effective tax rate of 25 percent on the dividend income. The corporation also received a credit of £25,000 which it could use, subject to certain limitations, to offset its income tax liability on its next return. The ACT was abolished in 1999, leaving many companies with ACT payment debits on their books because their regular income tax liabilities had been less (due to special capital expenditure allowances, large foreign profits, etc.) than their ACT payments which were based on dividends paid. The British government has said these companies will be able to offset these surplus ACT payments against future tax liabilities, if they would have normally expected to, otherwise they must write them off.[10]

Corporate Tax Law—Effects on Financial Statements. Great Britain is one of a number of nations in the world (like the United States) in which corporate tax law does *not* serve as the basis for financial reporting. In many countries, such as Germany, Japan, and Sweden, firms must keep their books of account in accordance with the dictates of tax regulations, a practice that subjects financial reporting standards to the actions of legislators and greatly hinders comparability across national boundaries. In Great Britain, however, the process is reversed. Income statements are prepared according to British GAAP and then are adjusted to arrive at taxable income. Typical adjustments include such items as substituting statutory "capital allowances" for financial depreciation and applying to current income any tax losses carried forward from a previous period. Because these adjustments are restricted to the tax return and are not entered on a company's books, readers of British financial statements escape the burdensome task of having to make adjustments and reclassifications to eliminate the effects of tax regulations to obtain more comparable measures of firm performance.

SSAP No. 15 requires companies to adopt for financial reporting purposes a modified version of the liability method of accounting for income taxes. Basically, this standard requires British companies to account for timing differences between tax and financial reporting only to the extent that management believes that a tax liability or asset will actually materialize. According to the standard, management should base its judgment on reasonable assumptions and on all relevant information available up to the date on which the financial statements are approved. Companies must also disclose the amount of the potential deferred tax liability that is not reflected on the balance sheet. Exhibit 7–1, extracted from the footnotes to the financial statements of Imperial Chemicals Industries, Plc., illustrates the typical disclosures for a firm's deferred tax liability, both recorded and unrecorded.

As can be seen from this schedule, accelerated tax depreciation (called *capital allowances*) and other timing differences account for a total of £233 million in deferred taxes. Of this, however, only £143 million is carried on the company's financial statements. This number is lumped into a balance sheet figure called *provisions for liabilities and charges* (not shown on this schedule). The directors of ICI have estimated that only the smaller (£143) amount is likely to materialize as a tax liability.

The corporate tax rate in Britain is 30 percent (effective April 1999); however, a "small companies rate" of 20 percent applies to companies that earn less than £300,000. Taxable profits between £300,000 and £1,500,000 are taxed at a slightly higher rate, but if a company's taxable profits exceed £1,500,000, all of it is taxed at 30 percent.

---

[10]R. Taylor, "Levy Reform Will End Anomolies for Companies," *Financial Times,* November 30, 1997, p. 5.

EXHIBIT 7–1

Imperial Chemicals Industries, PLC
Deferred Tax Disclosure

Taxation

The charge for taxation is based on the profit for the year and takes into account taxation deferred because of timing differences between the treatment of certain items, including post-retirement benefits, for taxation and for accounting purposes. However, no provision is made for taxation deferred by reliefs unless there is reasonable evidence that such deferred taxation will be payable in the future.

Deferred taxation

The amounts of deferred taxation accounted for at the balance sheet date and the potential amounts of deferred taxation are disclosed below.

	Group			Company		
	1997 £m	1996 £m	1995 £m	1997 £m	1996 £m	1995 £m
Accounted for at balance sheet date						
Timing differences on UK capital allowances and depreciation	213	189	193	68	61	63
Miscellaneous timing differences	(70)	(85)	(92)	25	9	(17)
	143	104	101	93	70	46
Not accounted for at balance sheet date						
Timing differences on UK capital allowances and depreciation	—	—	—	—	—	—
Miscellaneous timing differences	90	44	37	—	—	—
	90	44	37	—	—	—
Full potential deferred taxation	233	148	138	93	70	46

Business Environment

Form of Business.   The dominant business entity in Great Britain is the limited liability company, also referred to as a *company limited by shares.* A limited liability company may be incorporated as either a private or a public concern, the latter having the right to issue securities to the public. Both public and private companies must have at least two stockholders, and public companies must have at least two directors as well, but private companies need have only one director. For a limited liability company to be incorporated as a public entity, it must have a minimum share capital of £50,000 and include **Public Limited Company** (or **Plc**) in its name. A private company is subject to no minimum capital requirement and must include the word *Limited* (or *Ltd.*) at the end of its name.

Value Added.   British attitudes toward business and its social responsibilities are well documented. In a survey of corporate annual reports from nine countries, the British reports rated the best on disclosure of corporate social information.[11] Indeed, the belief that corporations must look beyond the maximization of profit has become a permanent if oft-debated element in British public opinion.

A by-product of this belief is the search for progressive ways to report the results of business operations—new methods that depict the corporation as a locus of cooperation rather than as a unit of competition. One of the most widespread and best known experiments in this direction is the **value-added statement,** which a significant minority of European firms began to include in their corporate reports in the 1970s. (See Exhibit 7–2 for an example of a value-added statement.) The popularity of value-added statements has declined in recent years because questions have been raised about their usefulness.

Devised by a U.S. Treasury official in the 18th century, the concept of value added has since been used by governments as a measure of national income. In the 1970s it was embraced by corporations—on the recommendation of the British government and the accounting profession—to provide additional information to shareholders, serve as the basis for employee incentive programs, and improve public and employee relations by

[11]A. Jack, "Survey Reveals Variety in Accounts," *The Financial Times,* October 5, 1992, p. 17.

EXHIBIT 7–2

IMPERIAL CHEMICALS INDUSTRIES PLC
Sources and Disposal of Value Added (Unaudited)
for the year ended 31 December 1997

	1997s	1996
	£m	£m
Sources of income		
Turnover	11,062	10,520
Royalties and other trading income	68	98
Less materials and services	(8,335)	(7,820)
Value added by manufacturing and trading activities	2,795	2,798
Share of profits less losses of associated undertakings	16	27
Value added related to exceptional items taken below trading profit	670	32
Total value added	3,481	2,857
Disposal of total value added		
Employees		
Employee costs charged in arriving at profit before tax	1,952	1,860
Governments		
Corporate taxes	210	158
Less grants	(9)	(6)
	201	152
Providers of capital		
Interest cost of net borrowings	251	89
Dividends to shareholders	232	232
Minority shareholders in subsidiary undertakings	49	65
	532	386
Re-investment in the business		
Depreciation	769	416
Profit retained	27	43
	796	459
Total disposal	3,481	2,857

showing what a company does with the wealth it creates. In short, a value-added statement provides a measure of wealth created by the operations that a company performs on inputs, and it shows the distribution of that wealth among major constituent groups: employees, investors, and the government. Such operations may involve constructing or manufacturing goods, assembling them, or simply making them more available.

The basic numerical definition of *value added* is sales less the cost of purchases. A refinement of this definition distinguishes gross value added (as just defined) from net value added, which subtracts depreciation as well as purchases from sales. Depending on who's doing the calculating, depreciation may be figured on a historical cost basis or a current cost basis. Governments typically attempt to calculate depreciation using the latter. The interest in value added has also spawned a variety of ratios, such as value added/payroll costs and operating profit/value added, designed to provide company planners with a new perspective on operations and to express the efficiency of a company in terms that are more easily understandable to the general public.

Accounting Profession and Policy Formulation.   The accounting profession in Great Britain is rich in tradition, well trained, and influential. Just as Great Britain is the cradle of modern capitalism, it is also the founding place of modern financial reporting and of the independent audit. The professional British title corresponding to certified public accountant in the United States is **chartered accountant,** and the best known professional associations are the English and Scottish and, in the larger context of the United Kingdom, the Irish Institute of Chartered Accountants. Along with the members of the Chartered Association of Certified Accountants, members of the three bodies just mentioned are recognized by the Department of Trade and Industry as qualified to carry out the required annual audit of British companies. The education and experience requirements for public practice include successful completion of special institute examinations, a minimum three years of training in an authorized training office, and two years of approved experience after completing the other qualification requirements.

These professional associations not only regulate entry into the profession but also governed the formulation of accounting and auditing standards until 1990. Although corporate financial statements must adhere to the basic requirements and format prescribed by national legislation, the promulgation of specific accounting and auditing standards was controlled by private committees formed by six associations of professional accountants (including the four bodies noted above). The Accounting Standards Committee (ASC) issued statements of standard accounting practice (SSAPs) in a manner similar to the process used by the Financial Accounting Standards Board in the United States on topics ranging from the accounting treatment of government grants to current cost accounting.

In 1990, however, responsibility for standard setting passed from the ASC to the newly formed **Financial Reporting Council** (FRC). The mission of the FRC, which is both better financed and more powerful than the ASC, is to tighten accounting rules in Great Britain and to develop a broader, more strategic outlook on financial reporting. In effect, the formation of the FRC streamlines and centralizes accounting policy formation, taking it out of the hands of Great Britain's numerous accountancy bodies and giving it to a council that includes industry and stock market representatives as well as professional accountants. The primary deliberative body of the FRC on accounting matters is its *Accounting Standards Board.* The key characteristic of the FRC is its radical expansion of the constituencies involved in the accounting standard-setting process: Users, preparers, and auditors are all involved.[12] The fundamental nature of the first several FRSs indicates the basic, hard look directed toward British financial reporting. For example, the FRC's first **financial reporting standard** (*FRS No. 1*) created the requirement for presentation of a statement of cash flows in lieu of a statement of sources and application of funds, *FRS No. 2* dealt with the accounting for subsidiaries, and *FRS No. 3* revisits the reporting of financial performance (i.e., income statement presentation issues), all but doing away with a previously overused income statement category—extraordinary items.

Within three years of its formation, informed observers of the ASB ascertained a clear orientation being articulated and pursued. Specifically, it appeared that a key aspect of the ASB's actions was a

> Desire to move the attention of readers of accounts away from a single number—earnings— towards a wider range of indicators of a company's performance.[13]

> [This] approach [, in the minds of some,] puts undue emphasis on the balance sheet. Financial reporting, from this standpoint, is essentially an exercise in valuation.[14]

---

[12]R. Dearing, "Accounting Standards the New Approach," *Accountancy,* June 1990, pp. 86–87.

[13]A. Jack, "Accounting Review Brings Mixed Results," *The Financial Times,* September 23, 1992, p. 19.

[14]Paterson, "In Support of the Profit and Loss Account," p. 15. See also M. Davies and P. Davies, "The ASB's New Principles for Old," *Accountancy,* March, 1996, p. 77 and N. Chesman, "The Politics of the True and Fair View," *Accountancy,* September, 1998, p. 73.

To this end, some of the ASB's more recent standards (e.g., *FRS Nos. 4–11*) also exhibited a very clear focus on the identification, recording, and valuing of balance sheet items. Consider also that in a 1993 published *statement* (as opposed to a published *standard*), the ASB set voluntary guidelines for companies for including an Operating and Financial Review (OFR) section in their annual reports. The OFR is similar to the Management Discussion and Analysis (MD&A) section found in U.S. annual reports. The OFR's aim is to provide a narrative of company performance "with analysis and a balance of good and bad while providing some element of a projection of the business into the future."[15] Such guidance is again evidence of the ASB's predilection to try to provide financial statement users with a multifaceted view of a company.

Capital Markets.   London has long been one of the financial capitals of the world, with a market capitalization that makes it Europe's largest equity market. The main securities exchange in Great Britain is officially designated as The International Stock Exchange of the United Kingdom and the Republic of Ireland, but it is traditionally and familiarly known simply as The Stock Exchange. Since 1973, The Stock Exchange has been electronically integrated with the securities exchanges of a number of other cities across England, Scotland, and Ireland, making it in fact not a single exchange but a network. Moreover, in 1998 the exchange began work on a single electronic trading system with the Frankfurt, Germany, exchange, whereby the shares of a selected group of European companies could be traded on either exchange. The Stock Exchange listed almost 3,000 companies at the end of 1997, over 500 of which are foreign companies.

Companies must fulfill a number of stringent requirements to be granted a full listing on The Stock Exchange. The securities to be listed must have a minimum initial capitalization of £700,000, and at least 25 percent of any class of issued equity capital must be held by the public. (In practice, the initial capitalization usually exceeds £5,000,000.) With its application for listing, the company must submit a variety of financial data, including audited financial statements. These should consist of the company's most recent balance sheet, its income statement, and a statement of cash flows. After it is granted a listing, the company must publish audited annual financial statements within six months of its year-end and unaudited interim statements semiannually. It must also release on a timely basis important ancillary information, such as preliminary profit announcements, details of major transactions, explanation of departures from standard accounting practices, and particulars concerning borrowings. The Stock Exchange reserves the right to publish information itself or to suspend a listing if it deems a company's public financial disclosures to be inadequate.

Since 1980 The Stock Exchange has provided an unlisted securities market (USM) whereby smaller, less established companies unable to meet the requirements for full listing may offer securities to the public. Companies seeking entry to this market need present only operating results from the last three years and place at least 10 percent of their securities in the hands of the public. No initial minimum capital requirement is stipulated, but most securities quoted on the USM are initially capitalized at £3,000,000 or more. In addition to full listing and USM, in 1987 The Stock Exchange opened the Third Market for capital-hungry new firms that did not have a sufficient trading history to qualify for the other two markets; however, the Third Market was subsequently absorbed into the USM.

---

[15]A. Jack, "Broad-Brush Approach for a Truer Picture," *The Financial Times,* July 8, 1993, p. 2.

Small companies may also offer their securities via over-the-counter (OTC) markets. Britain's OTC market provides capital for risk-oriented firms that desire greater flexibility than The Stock Exchange can provide. Requirements for entry into the OTC market are determined by the particular dealer handling the new issue.

In 1986, Great Britain began deregulating various aspects of its capital markets to encourage competition and broaden share ownership. The most profound alterations took effect in October of that year in what was popularly hearalded, with wry anxiety, as the "Big Bang." The Big Bang included a broad range of measures: abolishing minimum commission rates, admitting international firms to membership on The Stock Exchange, abandoning the mandatory separation of brokering and jobbing functions, and introducing an electronic trading system that allows off-floor trading. It was hoped that these changes would improve London's competitive edge as a trading center and that what the financial services industry would lose in lower commissions it would more than recoup in extra volume as small investors entered the market in larger numbers.

The Big Bang and subsequent changes have sparked an important debate over the best way to ensure that the markets remain fair. Traditionally self-regulating, The Stock Exchange is now overseen by a group of self-regulatory organizations (SROs) that must answer to the Securities and Investments Board (SIB), a watchdog agency with an ambiguous legal status. Observers expect, however, that the SIB will evolve into an extension of the national government with broad powers to regulate financial reporting as well as securities trading. Some commentators speculate that the SIB may even become directly involved in setting accounting and auditing standards. Paradoxically, the deregulation of the British capital markets has created the prospect of increased regulation of financial reporting. One remaining issue for the regulators is whether the system would function better with fewer regulatory bodies. Overlap between watchdogs creates confusion over who is responsible for what. It also increases the risk of a small, weak regulatory body becoming too close to those it is supposedly policing.[16]

At the close of 1997, 85 percent of the value of the U.K. stockmarket was held by institutions. Moreover, the vast majority of non-British money in the U.K. market was American. It is also interesting to note that 1997 witnessed the last of the British investment banks (Barclays' BZW unit) being put up for sale. It is clear that the U.K. market is not driven by, or the focus of, the British individual investor.

Labor Relations.   Organized labor exerts a significant if somewhat diminished influence over British society. Whereas membership in U.S. labor unions has never reached 40 percent and currently stands at less than 20 percent, British trade unions represent around 33 percent of the workforce, or about 9 million people (down from 60 percent of the workforce with 13.2 million members in 1979). Traditional union concerns, such as protection from arbitrary dismissal and the right to reasonable working conditions, are now institutionalized in the legislative framework in which British business operates.

Although labor relations have had little direct impact on accounting methods and conventions, they have undoubtedly affected several of the disclosure requirements

---

[16]"Regulatory Woes," *The Economist,* March 14, 1992, pp. 92, 94.

imposed on British corporations. For example, the Companies Act of 1985 requires certain disclosures pertaining to directors' fees and management salaries exceeding £30,000. Specifically, the company must reveal the amount paid to the chairman and (if not the same person) to the highest paid director, and it must indicate where remuneration paid to other directors and to management falls on a pay scale broken into £5,000 increments. The company must also disclose wage and salary expenses, social security costs, and pension costs paid to or on behalf of employees. All of this information may be of interest to union negotiators as well as investors. The Exhibit 7–3 footnote, taken from the 1996 financial statements of Grand Metropolitan Plc, illustrates the form that these disclosures typically assume.

British law does not mandate employee representation on company boards (as is the case in Sweden); however, a firm employing 250 or more workers must disclose its policy concerning employee consultation programs. Many individual companies and the Confederation of British Industry (an association of employers) have responded to the legal requirement by publicly supporting voluntary programs for employee participation at the firm level. In addition, many firms encourage share ownership among employees. Grand Metropolitan, for example, touches on these themes in its 1996 annual report (see Exhibit 7–4). Although Grand Metropolitan would undoubtedly like to be considered progressive, its policy statement is typical of those found in the annual reports of other British multinational firms.

EXHIBIT 7–3

GRAND METROPOLITAN PLC
Labor-Related Disclosures

Employees

The average number of employees during the year was:

	1996			1995		
	Full time	*Part time*	*Total*	*Full time*	*Part time*	*Total*
Continuing operations						
Food—Pillsbury	14,878	1,085	15,963	14,722	1,388	16,110
—Other European	5,715	116	5,831	5,589	416	6,005
—Burger King	17,378	12,549	29,927	17,104	9,711	26,815
Drinks—IDV	10,034	461	10,495	10,815	331	11,146
	48,005	14,211	62,216	48,230	11,846	60,076
Discontinued operations	2,834	649	3,483	3,018	733	3,751
	50,839	14,860	65,699	51,248	12,579	63,827

	1996	*1995*
	£m	*£m*
The aggregate remuneration of all employees comprised:		
Wages and salaries	982	948
Emploeyr's social security costs	117	111
Employer's pension costs	(30)	(33)
Other post employment costs	15	13
	1,084	1,039

EXHIBIT 7–4

Grand Metropolitan Employment Policies

GrandMet's employment policies are designed to ensure that the company is able to attract the highest calibre of employees from all sections of the communities within which it operates. The company values diversity in the work place and is committed to providing equality of opportunity to all employees and potential employees. It actively encourages continuous training and skills development in all its businesses.

Employment policies and training programmes have been developed to attract and retain the best people on the basis of their skills and abilities. This ensures that the company offers people with disability the same opportunities for employment, training and career progression as other employees. If an employee becomes disabled when in the company's employment, full support is given through the provision of training, special equipment or other resources to facilitate continued employment wherever possible.

To support the company's commitment to open communication with employees, a senior manager has been appointed to be responsible for designing management processes and media which encourage employee involvement and foster team working. At the same time, significant progress is being made to develop an intranet—'MetWeb'—from which all employees with access to a computer will be able to obtain timely and accurate news and information.

The company encourages the establishment of savings-related share option schemes for employees. A plan was launched in Germany during the year and the plans in the United Kingdom, United States, Canada, France and Ireland continued to be promoted.

Selected Financial Reporting Practices

Retrospectively, it has been argued that contemporary British financial reporting practices are the result of 20 years of two countervailing forces—preferences for and against the standardization of practice.[17] The pressure for standardization is attributed to senior members of the accounting profession, interested government agencies, and the financial press. General preferences for more accounting choice and flexibility tend to be articulated most consistently by corporate managers.

A case in point has to do with accounting for business combinations. The following chart is a summary of the swings in sentiment as expressed in various ASC and FRC statements. As noted by informed observers,

> The use of merger accounting [i.e., the pooling of interests method] will generally lead to higher reported group profits . . . than acquisition accounting [i.e., the purchase method]. Therefore, it can be said that to restrict the use of merger accounting is income-reducing. The [force for a high degree of standardized practice] is provided by senior policymakers supported by the Department of Trade and Industry and by criticism from the press. The force opposing standardization and the control of merger accounting, is provided by managers.[18]

Such a case in point is not all that different from certain U.S. experience (e.g., deferred taxes). The fact of the matter is that British accounting standards are the result of a process of debate, lobbying, and change just as U.S. standards are. As will be seen in subsequent chapters, however, this is not the predominant process in all countries (e.g., Japan and Germany).

---

[17]C. Nobes, "Cycles in U.K. Standard Setting," *Accounting and Business Research* 21, no. 83, (1991), pp. 265–74.

[18]Ibid., p. 269.

	Consolidation Accounting Sentiments	*Degree of Standardization Sought*
Late 1960s	Merger accounting is used for some large U.K. business combinations.	Low
1971	*ED 3* would demand merger accounting for mergers and acquisition accounting for acquisitions, although the rules might be avoidable.	High
1973	*ED 3* lapses after suggestions of illegality under the Companies Act 1948.	Low
1980	*Shearer v. Bercain.* This tax case held, *obiter dicta,* that merger accounting was illegal.	Low
1981	Companies Act grants merger relief (subsequently in s.131 of Companies Act 1985).	
1982	*ED 31* would impose standard practice similar to *ED 3.*	High
1985	*SSAP 23* allows acquisition accounting to be used for mergers and continues to have rules that can be evaded.	Low
1990	*ED 48* would demand merger accounting for mergers and acquisition accounting for acquisitions. Also the rules would be much tighter and mergers would be very rare.	High
1994	*FRS 6* adopts the intentions of *ED 48.*	High

ED = Exposure draft of a proposed accounting standard.
FRS = Financial reporting standard.

Source: C. Nobes, "Cycles in U.K. Standard Setting," *Accounting and Business Research* 21, no. 83 (1991), pp. 265–74. Modified and reproduced with permission.

Terminology

Several terms used in British financial statements may confuse or mislead unwary foreign readers. *Fixed assets,* for example, refers to *all* assets retained for continuous use in the business, not just to property, plant, and equipment (which the British call *tangible fixed assets*). The word *stocks,* on the other hand, generally refers to inventory, not shareholders' equity. Receivables are often lumped under the laconic heading "debtors," whereas payables of different sorts may simply be listed as "creditors." On the income statement, often called the *profit and loss account,* sales are referred to as *turnover* (see Exhibit 7–5, for example). Alternatively, *profit and loss account,* along with *reserves* or *retained profits,* may refer to retained earnings or some component thereof. As these examples suggest, the financial statement user must cultivate a judicious suspicion of familiar terminology; it may camouflage a distinctively British usage.

Format

Although the format of British financial statements varies in a number of ways from that used in typical U.S. statements, the most noticeable difference is in the arrangement of the balance sheet. Most British balance sheets follow a vertical format, running from low liquidity to high liquidity; hence, fixed assets appear above current assets. Companies adopting this format offset current assets against current liabilities and then offset total assets against current liabilities and long-term liabilities, balancing this figure against stockholders' equity. The balance sheet of Rolls Royce Plc (see Exhibit 7–6) provides an example of this format.

EXHIBIT 7–5

ROLLS ROYCE PLC
Group Profit and Loss Account
(for the Year Ended December 31, 1997)

	Continuing Operations £m	Discontinued Operations £m	1997 £m
Turnover	**4,216**	**118**	**4,334**
Cost of sales	(3,465)	(142)	(3,607)
Gross profit/(loss)	**751**	**(24)**	**727**
Commercial, marketing and product support costs	(142)	(2)	(144)
General and administrative costs	(131)	(13)	(144)
Research and development (net)	(215)	(1)	(216)
Share of profits of associated undertakings	13	—	13
Utilisation of provision for loss on sale/termination of businesses	—	40	40
Operating profit	**276**	**—**	**276**
Profit/(loss) on sale of business	1	(9)	(8)
Utilisation/(creation) of provision for loss on sale/termination of businesses	—	9	9
Profit/(loss) on ordinary activities before interest	**277**	**—**	**277**
Net interest payable			(1)
Profit/(loss) on ordinary activities before taxation			**276**
Taxation			(51)
Profit/(loss) on ordinary activities after taxation			**225**
Equity minority interests in subsidiary undertakings			(1)
Profit/(loss) attributable to ordinary shareholders			**224**
Dividends			(88)
Transferred to/(from) reserves			**136**

Consolidation

The Companies Act of 1985 requires companies with subsidiaries to prepare "group accounts." Under current practice, there is a substantial degree of subjectivity in the choice between accounting for a business combination via "acquisition accounting" (similar to the purchase method in the United States) versus "merger accounting" (equivalent to the pooling-of-interests method in the United States). Even though specific criteria exist for using merger accounting, managers can usually satisfy these criteria by careful structuring of a business deal. Similar to practice in the United States, *Financial Reporting Standard No. 6,* issued in 1994, restricts the use of merger accounting to those business combinations in which one party does not control another but in which the entities come together to equally share in future risks and benefits. The criterion set forth is that merger accounting be permitted only in those instances when acquisition accounting would not give a true and fair view of the nature of the business combination. The essence of this is to have the substance of a business combination rather than the particular details of its execution dictate the method of accounting for it.

Valuation of Assets

A British company may choose to value its assets according to historical cost principles or alternative valuation rules, or it may choose to use different methods for different assets. According to historical cost rules, current assets should be carried at the lower of cost or net realizable value; fixed assets should be carried at cost less accumulated depreciation (if applicable) and any permanent decline in value. (A permanent decline in value must be recognized as a loss on the income statement.) LIFO and the base stock method are generally considered unsuitable for inventory valuation.

EXHIBIT 7–6

ROLLS-ROYCE PLC
Vertical Format Balance Sheet
(as of December 31)

	1997 £m	1996 £m
Fixed assets		
Tangible assets	1,055	962
Investments—subsidiary undertakings	—	—
—other	102	85
	1,157	1,047
Current assets		
Stocks	959	798
Debtors—amounts falling due within one year	1,075	1,047
—amounts falling due after one year	332	262
Short-term deposits and investments	368	544
Cash at bank and in hand	511	231
	3,245	2,882
Creditors—amounts falling due within one year		
Borrowings	(302)	(88)
Other creditors	(1,898)	(1,571)
Net current assets	1,045	1,223
Total assets less current liabilities	2,202	2,270
Creditors—amounts falling due after one year		
Borrowings	(249)	(403)
Other creditors	(84)	(84)
Provisions for liabilities and changes	(407)	(458)
	1,462	1,325
Capital and reserves		
Called up share capital	296	295
Share premium account	522	519
Revaluation reserve	121	125
Other reserves	71	54
Profit and loss account	433	310
Equity shareholders' funds	1,443	1,303
Minority interests in subsidiary undertakings		
Equity interests	13	13
Non-equity interests	6	9
	1,462	1,325

The alternative valuation rules allow assets to be written up above historical cost as follows:

- Tangible and intangible fixed assets (except goodwill) may be written up to current fair market value.

- Long-term investments may be written up to market value as of the date of the last valuation (even if it differs from the balance sheet date).

- Investments of 20 percent or more in an affiliate's share capital may be accounted for under the equity method.

It is not uncommon for a firm to revalue its land and buildings periodically, taking the surplus to a revaluation reserve account in the shareholders' equity section of the balance sheet. This reserve is not available for distribution to shareholders.[19] Companies are required to disclose the bases of valuation for inventories, investments, and fixed assets. In light of the valuation options open to British companies and their possible impact on the balance sheet, a careful reader will surely want to check this information.

Goodwill

Purchased *goodwill* is defined as the difference between the fair value of consideration given and the aggregate fair values of the assets received in an acquisition. *FRS No. 10,* effective year-end 1998, requires that goodwill be capitalized to the balance sheet, and where its economic life is limited, to be amortized against earnings over a maximum period of 20 years. In some circumstances, however, *FRS No. 10* also allows companies to indefinitely carry forward goodwill (or any intangible asset). When goodwill is not being amortized, the company must justify the "durability" of the asset and annually review its carrying value for possible impairment. With respect to negative goodwill, the standard permits either an immediate credit to equity reserves or capitalization with a gradual credit to comprehensive income as the values of the identified net assets diminish.

Research and Development

Research expenditures are generally written off immediately against current earnings, whereas development costs may be capitalized to the balance sheet if they fulfill a number of requirements concerning the technical and commercial feasibility of the project to which they are related. Deferred development expenditures must be reviewed at the end of each period and be written off immediately if they no longer meet these feasibility requirements. Under *FRS No. 10,* capitalized development costs would be written off over their expected economic life or a maximum of 20 years, unless the capitalized asset's durability can be established, in which case no amortization may be required.

Leases

SSAP No. 21 distinguishes between operating and finance leases, requiring the latter to be capitalized by lessees in financial statements for years beginning on or after July 1, 1987. (Capitalization requirements for lessors came into effect three years earlier.) Finance leases are deemed to be those that essentially transfer the benefits and risks of ownership to the lessee (as evidenced by the fact that the present value of the minimum lease payments equals 90 percent or more of the leased asset's fair market value, evaluated at the inception of the lease agreement). Lessees should record an asset to be depreciated over the shorter of the lease term (including likely renewals) or the asset's useful life, record a liability for future payments to the lessor, and apportion lease payments between interest expense and repayment of principal. The lessor should record a receivable for the total minimum lease payments plus any residual value, less any provision for bad debts. The lessor should likewise apportion payments received between interest income and repayment of principal.

In 1995, *FRS No. 5,* "Reporting the Substance of Transactions," was adopted, requiring that transactions be reflected in the financial statements based on their substance and not form. Thus, even though a lease transaction might not satisfy the 90 percent criterion of *SSAP No. 21,* if the substance of the agreement indicated the presence of a financing lease, then the lease and the leased asset should be capitalized to the balance sheet.

---

[19]As the revalued amounts are written off (i.e., depreciated) against earnings, a proportionate transfer is made annually from the revaluation reserve account to retained earnings, at which time the revaluation reserve becomes distributable to shareholders.

Owners' Equity	In Great Britain, owners' equity is usually reflected under the heading Capital and Reserves on the balance sheet. The principal elements of this heading (and their U.S. counterpart in parentheses) include:

- Called-up share capital (common and preferred stock).
- Share premium account (paid-in capital in excess of par value).
- Revaluation reserve.
- Other reserves.
- Capital redemption reserve (treasury stock, at par).
- Reserves provided by the articles of association.
- Profit and loss account (retained earnings).

Under the Companies Act of 1985, dividends may be paid out of the Profit and Loss account only, although the Revaluation Reserve and the Capital Redemption Reserve may be used to issue additional share capital, for example, in the form of a share dividend.

Segment Reporting	Until 1990, British companies had only to disclose sales by geographic area. *SSAP No. 25*—one of the last issued by the ASC—requires companies to report sales, pretax profits, and operating assets by both geographic area and line of business.
Earnings per Share	Consistent with IAS practice, basic earnings per ordinary share is calculated using the weighted average number of ordinary shares outstanding, without regard to any potentially dilutive securities. The basis for calculating earnings per share must be disclosed in the footnotes.
Cash Flow Statements	One of the final acts of the ASC prior to its disbanding was the publication of *Exposure Draft No. 54,* "Cash Flow Statements." It proposed to replace *SSAP No. 10,* "Statements of Source and Application of Funds," with a statement of cash flows similar to what is now required in the United States. *SSAP No. 10* had long been criticized for its failure to define *funds* and for permitting a wide variety of formats. The new proposal tackled these criticisms head on, defining *cash* and *cash equivalents* and proposing a standard statement format. Indeed, the first act of the FRC was to issue *FRS No. 1,* which substantially adopted the ASC's cash flow exposure draft, and simultaneously brought British cash flow reporting into conformity with *SFAS No. 95* in the United States. The cash flow statement became mandatory for fiscal years ending after March 23, 1992. An example is presented in Exhibit 7–7.
Reconciliation of U.S. and British GAAP	Because British firms are frequently listed on U.S. securities exchanges,[20] some publish a reconciliation of net income and shareholders' equity calculated according to the accounting principles of the two countries.[21] Exhibits 7–8 and 7–9, excerpted

---

[20]*The Wall Street Journal* notes that over 50 British companies, more than from any other European country, were registered with the U.S. Securities and Exchange Commission and therefore had to file U.S. GAAP financial statements or provide a reconciliation of their results based on British GAAP to U.S. GAAP. See P. Gumbel and G. Steinmetz, "German Firms Shift to More-Open Accounting," *The Wall Street Journal,* March 15, 1995, pp. C1, C17.

[21]One study reveals that the reconciliation between U.S. and British GAAP provides investors with incremental information above and beyond the information content of just British GAAP–based financial results. Consequently, the finding supports the disclosure of such reconciliations for the benefit of foreign investors. See M. E. Barth (Harvard University) and G. Clinch (University of New South Wales), "International Accounting Differences and Their Relation to Share Prices: Evidence from U.K., Australian, and Canadian Firms," working paper, June 1993.

EXHIBIT 7–7

ROLLS ROYCE PLC
Group Cash Flow Statement
(for the Year Ended December 31, 1997)

	1997 £m	1996 £m
Net cash inflow from operating activities	308	166
Returns on investments and servicing of finance	(2)	(5)
Taxation paid	(30)	(26)
Capital expenditure and financial investment	(203)	(96)
Acquisitions and disposals	42	(21)
Equity dividends paid	(78)	(69)
Cash inflow/(outflow) before use of liquid resources and financing	37	(51)
Management of liquid resources	176	(387)
Financing	23	71
Increase/(decrease) in cash	236	(367)
Reconciliation of net cash flow to movement in net funds		
Increase/(decrease) in cash	236	(367)
Cash (inflow)/outflow from (decrease)/increase in liquid resources	(176)	387
Cash inflow from increase in borrowings	(19)	(53)
Change in net funds resulting from cash flows	41	(33)
New finance leases	—	(3)
Exchange adjustments	3	6
Movement in net funds	44	(30)
Net funds at January 1	284	314
Net funds at December 31	328	284

Analysis of net funds	At January 1, 1997 £m	Cash flow £m	Other non-cash changes £m	Exchange adjustments £m	At December 31, 1997 £m
Cash at bank and in hand	231	277	—	3	511
Overdrafts	(12)	(41)	—	—	(53)
Short-term deposits and investments	544	(176)	—	—	368
Other borrowings due within one year	(68)	(24)	(150)	—	(242)
Borrowings due after one year	(356)	(2)	150	—	(208)
Finance leases	(55)	7	—	—	(48)
	284	41	—	3	328

from the Hanson Plc annual report, present a reconciliation and explanatory notes that illustrate how the differences between U.S. and British accounting methods may affect net income and shareholders' equity. Notice that the treatment of goodwill is particularly important in Hanson's case, accounting for most of the difference between the shareholders' equity figures. The adoption of *FRS No. 10* will, in all likelihood, reduce the impact of the accounting for goodwill as a source of variance in the reported results of U.S. and British companies; however, for those British firms that opt to capitalize-but-not-amortize goodwill, considerable variance will still exist. Exhibit 7–10 presents a summary comparison of selected British and U.S. financial reporting standards.

EXHIBIT 7–8

HANSON PLC AND SUBSIDIARIES
Reconciliation to U.S. GAAP

The following is a summary of the estimated material adjustments to profit and ordinary shareholders' equity which would be required if U.S. Generally Accepted Accounting Principles (U.S. GAAP) had been applied.

Years ended October 1, 1996 and September 30, 1995

Profit Available for Appropriation	1996 £ million	1995 £ million	1996 $ million	1995 $ million
Profit available for appropriation as reported in the consolidated profit and loss account	**1,419**	966	**2,189**	1,490
Significant adjustments:				
Changes in accounting policy	**(3,296)**	49	**(5,084)**	76
Goodwill amortisation	**(142)**	(106)	**(219)**	(164)
Natural resources depletion	**(8)**	(13)	**(12)**	(20)
Pensions	**43**	55	**66**	85
Timberlands depletion and reforestation	**(24)**	(34)	**(37)**	(53)
Taxation	**103**	(45)	**159**	(69)
	(3,324)	(94)	**(5,127)**	(145)
(Loss) profit available for appropriation as adjusted to accord with U.S. GAAP	**(1,905)**	872	**(2,938)**	1,345
Arising from:				
continuing operations	**(2,227)**	(179)	**(3,435)**	(276)
discontinued operations —income from operations	**216**	1,089	**333**	1,680
—gain (loss) on disposals	**106**	(38)	**164**	(59)
	(1,905)	872	**(2,938)**	1,345

	Per share (p)		Per ADS ($)	
(Loss) profit				
Undiluted —continuing operations	**(42.9)**	(3.4)	**(3.31)**	(0.26)
—discontinued operations	**6.2**	20.2	**0.48**	1.56
—available for appropriation	**(36.7)**	16.8	**(2.83)**	1.30
Diluted —continuing operations	**(33.8)**	(3.4)	**(2.61)**	(0.26)
—discontinued operations	**4.9**	20.1	**0.38**	1.55
—available for appropriation	**(28.9)**	16.7	**(2.23)**	1.29

The cumulative effect of the changes in accounting policy on 1996 is £(2,338)mn for continuing and £(958)mn for discontinued. This represents undiluted earnings per ordinary share of (45.0)p for continuing and (18.4)p for discontinued and diluted earnings per ordinary share of (35.5)p and (14.5)p, respectively.

At October 1, 1996 and September 30, 1995

Ordinary Shareholders' Equity	1996 £ million	1995 £ million	1996 $ million	1995 $ million
Ordinary shareholders' equity as reported in the consolidated balance sheet	**2,535**	327	**3,964**	511
Significant adjustments:				
Changes in accounting policy	**—**	3,296	**—**	5,154
Goodwill	**3,204**	5,055	**5,010**	7,905
Revaluation of land and buildings	**(165)**	(165)	**(258)**	(258)
Natural resources	**202**	1,361	**316**	2,128
Pensions	**172**	322	**269**	504
Timberlands depletion and reforestation	**—**	(166)	**—**	(260)
Taxation	**(732)**	(2,079)	**(1,145)**	(3,251)
	2,681	7,624	**4,192**	11,922
Ordinary shareholders' equity as adjusted to accord with U.S. GAAP	**5,216**	7,951	**8,156**	12,433

The exchange rate used to translate the above profit and loss figures was the average rate for the year to October 1, 1996 of $1.5426 to £ and the rate used to translate the balance sheet figures above was the year-end rate of $1.5637 to £.

EXHIBIT 7–9

HANSON PLC AND SUBSIDIARIES
U.S. vs. British GAAP

The following are the main U.K. accounting principles as applied by Hanson in its financial statements which differ from those generally accepted in the USA:

Change in Accounting

Under U.K. accounting principles changes in accounting policies are dealt with as an adjustment to opening reserves. Under U.S. GAAP a change in accounting is recognised by a cumulative catch-up adjustment which is included in current year income in the year of the change. Prior year statements are not restated.

Goodwill

Goodwill arising on the acquisition of a subsidiary is carried within reserves from the year in which that subsidiary is acquired. Under U.S. GAAP such goodwill is capitalised and is amortised through the profit and loss account over its estimated useful life, not exceeding 40 years.

Revaluation of Land and Buildings

Periodically land and buildings are revalued on an existing use basis by professionally qualified external valuers and such assets are written up to the appraised value. Depreciation is, where applicable, calculated on these revalued amounts. When revalued properties are sold, the gain or loss on sale is calculated based on revalued carrying amounts and reflected in income and any revaluation surplus thus realised is reclassified directly to retained earnings. Under U.S. GAAP such revaluations would not be reflected in financial statements and the gain or loss on sale would be calculated based on original cost and reflected in income. The amount of additional depreciation charged in respect of the revalued properties is not material.

Pensions

Pension credits are only recognised when a refund of, or reduction in, contributions is likely. Under U.S. GAAP, a negative pension cost may arise where a significant unrecognised net asset or gain exists at the time of implementation. This is required to be amortised on a straight line basis over the average remaining service period of the employees.

Timberlands

Reforestation costs were charged to the profit and loss account as incurred and depletion of timberlands was only provided to the extent that the amount of timber harvested exceeded the estimated growth of standing timber. Under U.S. GAAP depletion on a unit of production basis is charged to the profit and loss account and reforestation costs are capitalised as part of the carrying cost of timberlands.

Taxation

Deferred taxation is not provided where, in the opinion of the directors, no liability is likely to arise in the foreseeable future. For U.S. GAAP disclosure purposes the group has adopted the provisions of the Financial Accounting Standards Board *SFAS No. 109,* "Accounting for Income Taxes." Under *SFAS No. 109,* the liability method is used in accounting for income taxes. Under this method, deferred tax assets and liabilities are determined based on differences between financial reporting and tax bases of assets and liabilities and are measured using the enacted tax rates. In adopting *SFAS No. 109* in 1994 for U.S. GAAP purposes Hanson increased the carrying amounts of certain natural resource assets acquired in previous years with a corresponding increase in the deferred tax liability.

Discontinued Operations

Discontinued operations are those which either ceased or left the group in the accounting period or soon thereafter. Under U.S. GAAP discontinued operations also include those which have been identified for discontinuance or sale, therefore under U.S. GAAP the profits in respect of Energy have been included in discontinued operations.

EXHIBIT 7–10

Comparison of Accounting and Reporting Standards

Item	Great Britain	United States
Asset valuation	Historical cost with revaluation adjustments permitted (either upward or downward)	Historical cost with selected revaluation (principally downward)
Inventory: valuation	Principally FIFO and average cost methods; LIFO not permitted for tax purposes, hence rarely used	Principally LIFO (because of tax considerations); also FIFO and average cost methods
Inventory: year-end	Lower of cost or net realizable value	Lower of cost or replacement cost
Depreciation	Principally straight line with accelerated methods permitted	Principally straight line with accelerated and production methods permitted
Goodwill	Capitalization to balance sheet, with amortization (principally straight-line) over a maximum of 20 years; amortization not required if durability (continued life) of goodwill is clearly established	Capitalized to balance sheet, with amortization (principally straight line) over a maximum of 40 years; negative goodwill not permitted (i.e., eliminated against noncurrent assets)
Research and development costs	Research costs expensed as incurred; development costs may be capitalized under limited situations	Research costs expensed currently; development costs expensed currently except in certain industries (i.e., software, oil and gas)
Capitalized interest costs	Capitalization permitted, but not widely practiced	Capitalization required for self-constructed assets
Intercorporate Investments:		
Marketable securities (current asset: trading securities)	Lower of cost or market value (portfolio basis) with revaluation permitted	Mark to market (on an individual security basis) with unrealized gains and losses taken to income
Long-term investments:		
0–20% ownership (available-for-sale securities)	Historical cost with revaluation permitted	Mark to market (on an individual security basis) with unrealized gains and losses taken to shareholders' equity
20–50% ownership	Equity method	Equity method
51–100% ownership	Consolidated, using pooling or purchase accounting	Consolidated, using pooling (until 2001) or purchase accounting
Debt valuation	All debt valued at face or settlement value	Long-term debt (except deferred income taxes) valued at present value; all other debt valued at face value
Leases	Financing leases capitalized to balance sheet; operating lease disclosed in footnotes	Capital leases reflected in balance sheet; operating leases disclosed in footnotes
Deferred income taxes	Computed under liability method, with management able to avoid its booking if not reasonable to assume it will be payable in foreseeable future (a partial provision method)	Computed under liability method
Pension liabilities	Reflected on balance sheet	Reflected on balance sheet
Discretionary reserves	Specific reserves permitted	Restricted to identifiable operational losses
Statement of cash flows	Required	Required

Analytical Considerations

The analysis of British financial statements can be problematic for foreign analysts, not only because of terminology and format differences but also because of significant method differences.[22] The reporting differences of principal concern include

- The revaluation of assets above historical cost.
- The treatment of goodwill in particular, and intangibles in general.

The revaluation of assets, along with the parallel creation of an equity revaluation reserve, causes a systematic upward bias in the balance sheet valuation (i.e., total assets and net worth) of British firms. Although revaluation leaves the statement of cash flows relatively unaffected, largely because revaluation is not permitted for tax purposes and the higher depreciation charges on the revalued assets are netted out, future reported earnings may nonetheless be somewhat depressed as a consequence of the additional depreciation charges resulting from any upward asset revaluation. These affects may also be manifested in financial ratios as follows:

Ratio	Effect on British Firm Relative to U.S. Firm
Profitability ratios (i.e., ROA, ROE)	Understated
Solvency ratios (i.e., debt-to-total assets, debt-to-equity)	Understated

Britain's adoption of *FRS No. 10* has the potential to reduce many of the reporting differences attributable to goodwill accounting that previously existed between U.S. and British GAAP. For many companies, any future differences will result simply from the shorter amortization period required by *FRS No. 10* (20 years maximum versus 40 years maximum under U.S. GAAP). Two aspects of the standard, however, will be the source of continued variance in company results. First, the transitional rules of *FRS No. 10* do not require British firms to retroactively adopt the standard. Thus, any goodwill previously written off can remain eliminated from the balance sheet. (Prior to the adoption of *FRS No. 10,* British firms predominantly used the charge-to-equity method; this method permits a company to immediately write off any acquisition-related goodwill against existing shareholders' equity, thereby avoiding any amortization against future earnings.) Second, capitalized goodwill may be carried on the balance sheet without any required amortization. Thus, the future earnings stream of a company is not burdened with the regular amortization charges that U.S. firms face. These two factors are likely to cause the following systematic ratio effects:[23]

---

[22]Despite these differences, a recent study reveals that the earnings disclosures by British companies are at least as informative and timely for investors as are U.S. corporate earnings disclosures. See A. Alford, T. Jones, R. Leftwich, and M. Zmijewski, "The Relative Informativeness of Accounting Disclosures in Different Countries," working paper, University of Chicago, July 1993.

[23]Despite the distortions caused by the charge-to-equity method, British investment analysts essentially use the same ratios as U.S. analysts for technical analysis purposes. See, for example, R. Pike, T. Meerjanssen, and L. Chadwick, "The Appraisal of Ordinary Shares by Investment Analysts in the U.K. and Germany," *Accounting and Business Research,* Autumn 1993, pp. 489–99.

Ratio	Effect on British Firm Relative to U.S. Firm
Profitability ratios (i.e., ROS, ROA, and ROE)	Overstated
Solvency ratios (i.e., debt to total assets, debt to equity, times interest earned)	Overstated

The distortive effects of the here-to-fore allowed charge-to-equity method of accounting for goodwill were sometimes partially offset when a company acquired a well-established brand name or trademark as part of an acquisition. When this occured, some British firms partially restored the written-off goodwill by capitalizing a portion of it as a brand or trademark on the balance sheet, usually under the account heading Other Intangible Assets. This practice, however, provided only partial relief: Since brands and trademarks need not be amortized under British GAAP, the earnings of such companies were not adversely impacted by the amortization of capitalized intangibles such as these.

In recent years, British accounting standard setters have taken significant steps to eliminate some of the previously material divergences between British and U.S. GAAP. For example, *Financial Reporting Standard (FRS) No. 1,* adopted in 1992, requires the presentation of a statement of cash flows along lines similar to *SFAS No. 95,* and *FRS No. 2* requires the consolidation of substantially all controlled subsidiaries in a manner similar to *SFAS No. 94.* This latter FRS effectively eliminated the off-balance sheet accounting of finance subsidiaries and their typically massive debt. Similarly the ASB adopted *FRS No. 3,* which

- Limits those items that are reported as "extraordinary" on the profit and loss statement.

- Requires that earnings per share be calculated *after* all exceptional and extraordinary items.

- Excludes any realized revaluation surplus (associated with the retirement of a revalued asset) from reported profits.

Finally, the recent adoption of *FRS No. 5* eliminates many of the off-balance sheet techniques previously employed by British companies by requiring that auditors consider the substance, not just the form, of financing contracts when evaluating whether an asset and liability should be recognized.

The efforts of the FRC to improve the disclosure practices in Great Britain already appear to have had a positive impact on securities prices. Projected price-earnings ratios, as reported by *The Wall Street Journal,* indicate increasing market efficiency among British securities as evidenced by the proximity of the average P-E ratios for the leading U.S. and British companies. The small discrepancy—it is less than for any of the other G-7 nations—is interpreted by financial economists as indicating an increasing availability of high-quality financial information in Great Britain.

Summary

Great Britain is a country of traditions, paradoxes, untapped possibilities, and interesting confluences. Consider the following:[24] Of Europe's 500 largest companies, 118 are based in London; of Europe's 11 busiest air routes, 9 involve London; the combined number of London workers involved in the financial, professional and business services sectors is greater than the population of Frankfurt, Germany; 1996 average compensation for a manufacturing worker in Germany, Sweden, and Italy was 2.2, 1.67, and 1.22 times as large, respectively, as that of a British manufacturing worker; in 1996 just over-half of Britain's 18-year-olds were engaged in some form of education or training compared to over 60 percent in Sweden and over 80 percent in Germany; in 1995 the output per capita in the British private sector was 40 percent less than in the United States and 20 percent less than in Germany; in 1996, there was more than three times as much direct investment made by the United States in the U.K. than in any other EU country; and in a late 1995 poll, nearly 60 percent of the British respondents were against a single European currency.

Against such a backdrop, consider these shareholder insights: According to a February 1990 survey conducted by the Confederation of British Industry, 60 percent of shareholders owned shares in only one company, with two in five respondents reported having no idea where to go to buy securities;[25] in a 1998 survey of Britain's top 100 companies, 89 percent reported not "feeling hampered by shareholders in taking the correct long-term strategy; and moreover, one respondent opined that U.S. investors are more concerned than U.K. investors to understand the business and want to meet people who run the individual divisions . . . they are less satisfied with the odd chat with the chief executive and finance director."[26] Such insights reveal a rather unsophisticated public involvement in the equity market and this is changing. Historically, financial reporting has not needed to be particularly responsive or even concerned with the investing public and this is now also changing.

Great Britain has become a major international business center creating growth *and* interdependencies. "One of the most encouraging things about Britain today is that people are asking questions. Nothing is off-limits."[27] Perhaps an increased international interdependency and a willingness to question long-standing thinking and ways of doing things may portend a reinvigorated opportunity for change and leadership in the world business community for Great Britain.

Suggested Readings

Arthur Andersen & Co. The Accounting Profession in the U.K. Chicago, IL: Arthur Andersen & Co., 1991.

Bruce, R. "The Analysts We Deserve." *Accountancy,* August 1994, p. 48.

Dearing, R. "Accounting Standards: The New Approach." *Accountancy,* June 1990, p. 86.

---

[24]See R. Chote, "Call for Focus on Management and Regulation," *Financial Times,* May 15, 1998, p. 11; "Compensation to Workers," *Financial Times,* November 7, 1997, p. 2; A. Pike, "Wealth, Deprivation Stand Side by Side," *Financial Times,* March 19, 1998, p. I; R. Waters, "U.S. Says Yes, Prime Minister," *Financial Times,* July 24, 1997, p. VI; "Britain: The Rogue Piece in Europe's Jigsaw," *Financial Times,* June 12, 1996, p. I; and "We Told You All Along," *The Economist,* January 27, 1996, p. 44.

[25]R. Waters, "Seeking a Nation of Shareholders," *The Financial Times,* March 23, 1990, p. 7.

[26]J. Martinson, "Shares in the Action," *Financial Times,* April 27, 1998, p. 17.

[27]"A Survey of Britain–In the Tracks of Nissan," *The Economist,* October 24, 1992, Survey 3.

Ernst & Young. U.S./U.K. GAAP Comparisons: A Comparison between U.K. and U.S. AccountingPrinciples. New York, NY: Ernst & Young, 1990.

Garside, L. "What Should We Tell Them?" Accountancy, August 1994, p. 83.

Nobes, C. "Cycles in U.K. Standard Setting." Accounting and Business Research, Summer 1991, pp. 265–74.

Porcano, T., and A. Tran. "Relationship of Tax and Financial Accounting Rules in Anglo-Saxon Countries." The International Journal of Accounting, 33, no. 4 (1998), pp. 433–54.

Price Waterhouse & Co. Doing Business in the United Kingdom. New York, NY: Price Waterhouse, 1998.

Smith, T. Accounting for Growth. London: Century Business, 1992.

Vieten, H. "Auditing in Britain and Germany Compared: Professions, Knowledge, and the State." The European Accounting Review 4, no. 3 (1995), pp. 485–511.

Exercises

7.1   Preparing Financial Statements under British GAAP

The following is the post-closing general ledger data from the accounts of Hanson Plc:

HANSON Plc
Pre-Closing Ledger Accounts
December 31, 1996
(millions of £)

	Dr.	Cr.
Short-term deposits and cash	4,147	
Debtors	3,129	
Stocks	661	
Investments—subsidiaries	200	
Investments—other (current)	19	
Tangible assets	6,370	
Creditors: due within one year		4,192
Other creditors: due within one year		1,577
Creditors: due after one year		2,988
Other creditors: due after one year		80
Provision for liabilities/charges		3,154
Called-up share capital		1,302
Share premium account		1,491
Revaluation reserve		165
Other reserves		(3,575)
Profit and loss account		3,188
Turnover		12,484
Dividends	1,455	
Exceptional items	(687)	
Cost of sales	10,958	
Interest expense (net)	407	
Taxation	387	
	27,046	27,046

Required:

Using the ledger account data, prepare an income statement and balance sheet (using vertical format) for Hanson for the year ended December 31, 1996.

7.2   Revaluation of Assets

Under British GAAP, the basic financial statements are normally prepared using the historical cost convention; however, the Companies Act of 1985 also permits the revaluation of certain assets:

- Intangible fixed assets (i.e., leased fixed assets) may be valued at current value, defined as the lower of an asset's net replacement cost or recoverable value.
- Tangible fixed assets (i.e., freehold property, leasehold property, plant and equipment) may be valued at current cost or market value (defined as the value as of the most recent revaluation date).
- Fixed asset investments (i.e., investments in controlled subsidiaries) may be reported at their market value as of their latest valuation or at a value determined by the board of directors if market values are not available (or are significantly out of date).
- Current investments (i.e., marketable securities) may be valued at current cost (i.e., current replacement cost or net realizable value).
- Stocks (i.e., inventory) may be valued at current replacement cost.

The following are selected excerpts from the footnotes of Dunlop Plc, a British manufacturer. The company follows British GAAP and annually revalues its assets by independent appraiser and/or by the company's officers and directors. Any changes in the asset values are credited to a shareholders' equity reserve account, Reserve for Asset Revaluations.

		19x9	*19x8*
Leased land, plant, and equipment	At cost	179,328	91,726
	(amortization)	(29,552)	(28,144)
		149,776	63,582
Plant and equipment	At cost	1,918,036	1,804,436
	Independent valuation	—	200
	Officer valuation	9,830	9,830
		1,927,866	1,814,466
	(depreciation)	(854,860)	(750,928)
		1,073,006	1,063,538
Freehold land	At cost	30,996	33,074
	Independent valuation	165,748	182,766
	Officer valuation	1,216	1,608
		197,960	217,448
Leasehold land and buildings	At cost	35,370	19,926
	Independent valuation	19,322	24,762
	Officer valuation	2,214	2,384
		56,906	47,072
	(amortization)	(8,968)	(6,890)
		47,938	40,182

The independent and officer valuations were reported as of June 30, 19x9.

Required:

(a) What are the advantages and disadvantages of the British practice of permitting annual revaluations of assets?

(b) Contrast this policy with that followed in the United States.

(c) Do you think the IASC should adopt the U.S. or British position? Why?

(d) Prepare the journal entry necessary to record

   (1) the revaluation of plant and equipment,

   (2) the annual transfer of depreciation on revalued amounts from the revaluation reserve to the profit and loss account, and

   (3) the retirement of revalued plant and equipment that has not been fully depreciated.

7.3   Accounting for Shareholder Accounts

Rolls-Royce Plc is one of the world's most recognized and respected manufacturers. According to the company's year-end 1997 annual report, the shareholders' equity section of its balance sheet appeared as follows (in millions of £):

The related footnotes to the company's capital and reserves were presented as follows:

	1997	*1996*
Capital and reserves		
Called-up share capital	296	295
Share premium account	522	519
Revaluation reserve	121	125
Other reserves	71	54
Profit and loss account	433	310
Shareholders' funds	1,443	1,303

Share Capital

	Special Share of £1	*Ordinary Shares of 20p Each*	*Nominal Value £m*
Authorized			
At January 1 and December 31, 1997	1	2,000,000,000	400
Issued and fully paid			
At January 1, 1997	1	1,475,671,585	295
Exercise of share options	—	2,536,272	1
In lieu of paying dividends in cash	—	1,816,905	—
At December 31, 1997	1	1,480,024,762	296

Subject to the provisions of the Companies Act 1985, the special rights redeemable preference share (special share) may be redeemed by the Treasury Solicitor at par at any time.

Reserves

	Non-distributable			
	Share Premium *£m*	*Revaluation Reserve* *£m*	*Other Reserves* *£m*	*Profit and Loss Account* *£m*
Group				
At January 1, 1997	519	125	54	310
Arising on share issues	3	—	—	—
Transfers between reserves	—	(4)	17	(13)
Profit for the year	—	—	—	136
At December 31, 1997	522	121	71	433
Company				
At January 1, 1997	519	109	167	318
Arising on share issues	3	—	—	—
Transfers between reserves	—	(2)	17	(11)
Loss for the year	—	—	—	79
At December 31, 1997	522	107	184	386

Goodwill, written off against other reserves, cumulatively amounts to £514m (1996 £514m).

The undistributed profits of overseas subsidiary and associated undertakings may be liable to overseas taxes and/or U.K. tax (after allowing for double tax relief) if remitted as dividends to the U.K.

Required:

(a) Using journal entries, explain the changes in Rolls-Royce's capital and reserve accounts during 1997.

(b) If Rolls-Royce followed U.S. GAAP, how would the company's capital and reserves accounts be different?

7.4   Valuation of the Firm: Accounting for Goodwill

In late 1994, Browning-Ferris Industries (BFI) launched a hostile takeover bid for Attwoods Plc, a British waste service company. The BFI offer of £364 million (or approximately $570 million) was flatly rejected by Attwoods' management on grounds that it was grossly underpriced. BFI executives, on the other hand, argued that the offer represented a premium of more than 115 percent above Attwoods' current value.

According to the BFI offer document, if Attwoods followed U.S. GAAP for goodwill, Attwoods' 1993 reported earnings of 5.3 pence per share would be halved to 2.5 pence per share. Based on average price-earnings multiples for waste companies in the United States, the value of one ordinary Attwoods share would be approximately 50 pence, or 19 times earnings. Hence, BFI's offer of 109 pence for each ordinary share could be seen to be quite generous. (Just prior to the BFI offer, Attwoods' ordinary shares had traded at 105 pence on the London Stock Exchange.)

BFI executives expressed concern that Attwoods' earnings were inflated when considered under U.S. accounting standards. In Great Britain, at this time, goodwill was written off directly against retained earnings, whereas in the United States it was capitalized to the balance sheet and typically amortized off against earnings over a 40-year expected life. Through 1993, Attwoods had written off against owners' equity over £179 million in goodwill.

Required:

Evaluate the merits of BFI's offer for Attwoods. Is it generous, as BFI executives claim, or grossly underpriced as Attwoods' management argue? Justify your position. Would your answer differ if the offer was made in 1999 following the adoption of *FRS No. 10?*

7.5   Acquisition Accounting

On November 30, 1993, Carlton Communications Plc announced a £624 million tender offer (or £26 per share) for the outstanding shares of Central Independent Television that it didn't already own. Carlton and Central were the two largest British independent television companies; the British government owned the largest broadcasting company, the British Broadcasting Corporation (or BBC). Together, Carlton and Central would represent about 22 percent of the British television ad revenue market.

Carlton, which already owned 19.1 percent of Central, agreed to pay £204 million in cash, with the remainder in ordinary and convertible preference shares for Central. For every 100 Central shares, Carlton indicated that it would pay £850.62 cash, 114 new Carlton ordinary shares, and 87.5 new Carlton preference shares. Carlton also agreed to retire all of Central's 6.5 percent convertible subordinated debentures due in 2008. The value of Carlton's bid was placed at 20 percent above Central's market value prior to the offer.

Required:

(a) How should Carlton account for its acquisition of Central, and why?
(b) If the fair market value of Central's net assets and shares not previously owned by Carlton were equivalent on the day *prior* to the Carlton tender offer, how much goodwill would be inherent in the transaction?
(c) How would the transaction be recorded on Carlton's financial records?
(d) How should Carlton account for the goodwill inherent in the tender offer?
(e) Why would Carlton be willing to pay a 20 percent premium for Central's shares?

7.6   Statement of Cash Flows

The Body Shop International Plc (TBS) produces and sells skin, hair care, and other health-related products through 727 stores worldwide. The company owns or has franchised 210 retail outlets in Great Britain and 517 retail outlets in 40 different countries.

TBS is headquartered in West Sussex. England, and consequently issues financial statements conforming to accepted accounting practice in Great Britain. Until 1994, the presentation of a statement of cash flows was not required under British GAAP.

Required:

The following are the group financial statements of TBS for the years ending February 29, 1994, and February 28, 1993. Using these data, prepare a statement of cash flows for 1994, identifying the cash flows from (for) operations, investing, and financing activities. What observations can be drawn from these data with respect to TBS during 1994?

THE BODY SHOP INTERNATIONAL Plc
Balance Sheets
As of February 1994

	Group	
	1994 *£000*	*1993* *£000*
Fixed assets		
Tangible assets	**56,359**	43,484
Investments	**2,298**	2,114
	58,657	45,598
Current assets		
Stocks	**38,457**	33,484
Debtors	**36,061**	26,895
Cash at bank and in hand	**483**	344
	75,001	60,723
Creditors: amounts falling due within one year	**54,060**	36,143
Net current assets	**20,941**	24,580
Total assets less current liabilities	**79,598**	70,178
Creditors: amounts falling due after more than one year	**(2,669)**	(2,924)
Provisions for liabilities and charges		
Deferred tax	**(2,459)**	(553)
Minority interests	**(292)**	(1,552)
	74,178	65,149
Capital and reserves		
Called up share capital	**9,361**	9,262
Share premium account	**33,502**	32,289
Profit and loss account	**31,315**	23,598
Shareholders' funds	**74,178**	65,149

THE BODY SHOP INTERNATIONAL Plc
Consolidated Profit and Loss Account
For the Year Ended February 29, 1994

	1994 *£000*	*1993* *£000*
Turnover	**147,441**	115,599
Cost of sales	**68,210**	50,393
Gross profit	**79,231**	65,206
Selling and distribution costs	**32,021**	27,494
Administrative expenses	**19,335**	15,725
	51,356	43,219
Trading profit	**27,875**	21,987
Interest receivable	**539**	541
	28,414	22,528
Interest payable	**3,211**	2,491
Profit on ordinary activities before tax	**25,203**	20,037
Tax on profit on ordinary activities	**8,688**	7,311
Profit for the financial year	**16,515**	12,726
Minority interests	**120**	623
Profit attributable to members of holding company	**16,395**	12,103
Dividends paid and proposed	**2,995**	2,261
Amount transferred to reserves	**13,400**	9,842
Earnings per ordinary share	**8.8p**	6.7p

THE BODY SHOP INTERNATIONAL Plc
Consolidated Statement of Source and Application of Funds
For the Year Ended February 29, 1994

	1994		*1993*	
	£000	*£000*	*£000*	*£000*
Source of funds				
Group profit before tax		**25,203**		20,037
Adjustments for items not involving the movement of funds:				
Group share of profit on acquisition of minority interest		**(1,380)**		(45)
Depreciation		**4,711**		3,500
Loss on disposal of fixed assets		**61**		4
Other goodwill written off		**(284)**		—
Exchange differences		**(240)**		257
Generated from operations		**28,071**		23,753
Proceeds on disposal of fixed assets		**398**		164
Issue of shares		**1,312**		29,623
		29,781		53,540
Application of funds				
Purchase of fixed assets		**18,213**		18,220
Purchase of investments		**184**		2,114
Corporation tax paid		**7,627**		5,723
Dividends paid		**2,570**		1,818
Purchase of goodwill		**5,439**		291
Redemption of variable rate loan stock		**1,000**		1,000
		35,033		29,166
Increase (decrease) in net working capital:				
Stocks	**4,973**		10,124	
Debtors	**8,718**		8,320	
Creditors	**(2,739)**		(2,319)	
		10,952		16,125
		45,985		45,291
Increase (decrease) in net liquid funds		**(16,204)**		8,249

THE BODY SHOP INTERNATIONAL Plc
Notes on the Accounts
For the Year Ended February 29, 1994

Accounting Policies

Basis of accounting

The accounts are prepared under the historical cost convention and in accordance with applicable Accounting Standards. The principal accounting policies which affect these accounts are as follows:

Consolidation

The consolidated accounts incorporate the accounts of the holding company and its subsidiary undertakings. All of these accounts have the same financial year-end. Where subsidiaries are acquired during the year their results are included in the consolidated profit and loss account from the effective dates of acquisition. The holding company's accounting policies have been applied consistently in dealing with items which are considered material in relation to the consolidated accounts.

Stocks

Stocks are included at the lower of cost and net realizable value. Finished stocks are usually valued at the cost of the raw materials, plus the cost of productive labour and with the addition of an appropriate proportion of factory overheads. However, where net realizable value is lower than cost then this lower figure is used. The cost of materials is calculated on the "first in, first out" basis whereby, as materials are used, the value of stock is adjusted by the cost of the oldest relevant materials. Net realizable value means the anticipated sale proceeds less the anticipated costs of selling the goods.

Depreciation and amortization

No depreciation is provided in respect of the cost of freehold land.
The cost of other fixed assets is written off by equal annual installments over their expected useful lives, using the following estimates of useful life:
Freehold buildings—Over 50 years
Leasehold property—Over the periods of the respective leases
Plant and equipment—Over 3 to 10 years

Accounting for finance leases

Gross earnings from finance leases are allocated to accounting periods on a straight-line basis over the lives of the respective leases, a basis which approximates to a constant periodic return on the net cash investment in finance leases.

Research and development

Research and development expenditure is usually charged to the profit and loss account in the year in which it is incurred. However, for development expenditure on future products, where the viability of the project is reasonably certain, the costs are carried forward as prepayments in the balance sheet to be written off within one year of the product launch.

Translation of foreign currencies

The trading results and balance sheets of foreign subsidiaries are converted into sterling at the rates of exchange ruling at the year-end. Any difference which arises as a result of converting the opening balance sheets at the year-end rate is taken straight to reserves. Other conversion differences are dealt with in the profit and loss account.

Deferred tax

Deferred tax is provided on differences arising from the inclusion of items of income and expenditure in taxation computations in periods different from those in which they are included in the accounts. The provision for deferred tax is provided at anticipated tax rates and to the extent that it is likely that a liability or asset will crystallize in the future.

Where advance corporation tax is expected to be recoverable it is deducted from the provision for deferred tax.

Goodwill

Purchased goodwill represents the amount by which the price paid for a business or company exceeds the fair value of the assets and liabilities acquired. Where goodwill arises it is written off immediately to reserves.

Turnover

Turnover represents the total amount receivable in the ordinary course of business for goods sold and services provided and excludes sales between companies in the Group, discounts given and Value Added Tax.

7.7   Financial Data and Security Prices

Just what type of information causes stock prices to move upward and downward, and why is it a subject of considerable debate among security analysts? Consider, for example, the case of Eurotunnel, the Anglo-French company that will operate the long-awaited tunnel (or "Chunnel") under the English Channel between France and Britain. During the period December 10, 1993, to January 10, 1994, the price of Eurotunnel shares rose about 40 percent, from 460 pence to 644 pence (or approximately $9.56) per share. During that same period, the following information was released to the public in regards to the Chunnel:

- On December 10, Eurotunnel took possession of the Chunnel from building contractors.
- In mid-December, the British government acted to lower interest rates.
- On December 20, the French and British governments jointly disclosed that they had extended Eurotunnel's right to operate the Chunnel for an additional 10 years.
- In early January, Eurotunnel's lead banking syndicate approved the company's funding plan, which included a commitment by the lenders to provide up to £500 million in new loans and paved the way for a long-awaited £500 million (or approximately $742.5 million) stock rights issue.
- On January 10, Eurotunnel started selling tickets for its "Le Shuttle" car transport service, at prices ranging from £160 to £300, depending on the season; at those prices, Chunnel travel would be slightly more expensive, although faster, than travel by ferry boat. The £10 billion project was scheduled to begin service on May 6, 1994.

Analysts familiar with the project were reportedly skeptical about its prospects for success, despite recent share price increases. Their concerns focused on the project's heavy debt load and its ability to generate sufficient revenues in an already highly competitive marketplace.

Required:

    (a) Explain why each of the preceding news events was associated with a positive share price movement.

    (b) What do these events and their related stock market response suggest about the anticipatory behavior of securities markets?

    (c) What kind of news or events would you expect to cause an adverse (or downward) share price reaction for Eurotunnel?

7.8   Accounting for Capital and Reserves

The following table contains selected financial information from the 19x9 annual report of British Communications Plc.

Required:

Using the available information, prepare journal entries to explain the changes in the company's Capital and Reserves accounts for 19x9.

	(£000)	
Selected Financial Information	*19x9*	*19x8*

Capital and Reserves		
Called-up share capital	18,190	18,143
Share premium account	7,880	3,228
Revaluation reserve	2,346	11,977
Other reserves	30,659	40,214
Profit and loss account	365,658	309,730
Total	424,733	383,292

Selected Footnote Information	**19x9**	*19x8*
Called up Share Capital	**£000**	*£000*
Authorized:		
272,000,000 Ordinary shares of 5p each (19x8—272,000,000)	**13,600**	13,600
170,000,000 6.5p (net) Cumulative Convertible Redeemable Preference		
shares of 5p each (19x8—170,000,000)	**8,500**	8,500
	22,100	22,100
Issued and fully paid:		
198,811,194 Ordinary shares of 5p each (19x8—197,844,477)	**9,941**	9,893
164,986,887 6.5p (net) Cumulative Convertible Redeemable Preference shares of		
5p each (19x8—164,993,528)	**8,249**	8,250
	18,190	18,143

The following changes have taken place in the issued share capital of the Company:

Share Premium Account, Revaluation and Other Reserves	*Share Premium Account £000*	*Revaluation Reserve £000*	*Other Reserves £000*
(a) The Group			
At 1 October 19x8	3,228	11,977	40,214
Premium on the issue of shares	4,652	—	—
Goodwill written off in the year	—	—	(9,839)
Share of associated undertakings' other reserve movements	—	—	284
Transfer to profit and loss account	—	(401)	—
Exchange differences	—	215	—
Revaluation in the year	—	(9,445)	—
At 30 September 19x9	**7,880**	**2,346**	**30,659**
(b) The Company			
At 1 October 19x8	3,228	9,479	993,374
Premium on the issue of shares	4,652	—	—
Transfer to profit and loss account	—	(289)	(179,480)
Revaluation in the year	—	(6,941)	—
At 30 September 19x9	**7,880**	**2,249**	**813,894**

At 30 September 19x9, other reserves of the Company, which were non-distributable, comprised (a) £369.1 million being the remaining balance of special reserves created on the cancellation of the share premium account in previous years, and (b) £272.2 million being the amounts arising on the application of section 131(2) of the Companies Act 1985 not yet realized. Transfers from other reserves to the profit and loss account represent section 131(2) amounts realized on disposals. The cumulative goodwill written off to Group reserves at 30 September 19x9 amounted to £1,026,640,000.

Profit and Loss Account	The Group £000	The Company £000
At 1 October 19x8	309,730	78,516
Retained profit for the year	46,091	443,575
Transfer from revaluation reserve	401	289
Transfer from other reserves	—	179,480
Goodwill reinstated on disposal of subsidiary	1,188	—
Exchange differences	8,248	—
At 30 September 19x9	**365,658**	**701,860**

Exchange differences in the Group are net of the movement on foreign currency borrowings and balance sheet hedging of £33,104,000. Included within the Company's profit and loss account at 30 September 19x9 was an amount of £507,485,000 which was not distributable at that date.

BRITISH COMMUNICATIONS Plc
Reconciliation of Movements in Shareholders' Funds

	19x9 £000	19x8 £000
Profit for the financial year	**94,028**	74,807
Ordinary and preference dividends	**(47,937)**	(45,564)
Other recognized gains and losses	**(982)**	587
New share capital issued	**4,699**	72,893
Goodwill written off	**(9,839)**	(71,569)
Goodwill reinstated in respect of disposal of business	**1,188**	—
Share of associates' other reserves movements	**284**	(96)
Net additions to shareholders' funds	**41,441**	31,058
Shareholders' funds at beginning of the year	**383,292**	352,234
Shareholders' funds at the end of the year	**424,733**	383,292

7.9   Great Britain Versus U.S. GAAP

SmithKline Beecham Plc (SKB) discovers, manufactures, and markets pharmaceuticals, over-the-counter (OTC) medicines, and other health-related products. The company manufactures its products in 27 different countries and markets them in most countries throughout the world. Although the company is headquartered in Middlesex, England, the vast majority of its sales occur in the United States, Italy, France, Germany, Japan, Spain, and Belgium.

SKB, a public limited company incorporated in 1989, was formed for the purpose of effecting the combination of the pharmaceutical and OTC medicine business of SmithKline Beckman Corporation, a Pennsylvania corporation, and Beecham Group Plc, a public limited company incorporated under the laws of England; Beecham also manufactured consumer health products.

Although the shares of SKB trade principally on the London Stock Exchange, they are also readily available to U.S. investors in the form of American depositary shares (ADRs), which trade on the New York Stock Exchange. Each ADR represents five ordinary SKB shares, which are held in trust for U.S. investors by Morgan Guaranty Trust Company of New York. Foreign companies issuing ADRs in the United States are required to file form 20-F with the Securities and Exchange Commission. This registration statement presents

EXHIBIT 1

SMITHKLINE BEECHAM Plc
Consolidated Profit and Loss Account
For the Year Ended December 31, 19x9

	19x9	£m	19x8
Sales			
Continuing operations	**4,501**		4,264
Discontinued operations	**263**		633
	4,764		4,897
Cost of goods sold	**(1,703)**		(1,889)
Gross profit	**3,061**		3,008
Selling, general and administrative expenses	**(1,701)**		(1,790)
Research and development expenditure	**(393)**		(400)
Trading profit of continuing operations	**938**		725
Trading profit of discontinued operations	**29**		93
Share of profits of associated companies	**3**		8
Profit before interest and taxation	**970**		826
Interest	**(110)**		(102)
Profit on ordinary activities before taxation	**860**		724
Tax on profit on ordinary activities	**(286)**		(244)
Profit on ordinary activities after taxation	**574**		480
Minority interests	**(9)**		(4)
Auction Rate Preference Share dividends	**(21)**		—
Profit before extraordinary items	**544**		476
Extraordinary items	**303**		(346)
Profit attributable to shareholders	**847**		130
Dividends payable	**216**		80
Earnings per Ordinary Share	**41·0p**		36·5p
Earnings per Equity Unit	**205·0p**		182·5p

the company's foreign financial statements prepared in accordance with U.S. GAAP or presents a reconciliation of the company's foreign GAAP statements to U.S. GAAP.

Required:

Exhibits 1 to 5 present the SKB 19x9 financial statements prepared in accordance with British GAAP, a statement of SKB's accounting policies, and a reconciliation of the SKB statements to U.S. GAAP. Using these data, prepare a comparative financial analysis of SKB for 19x9 using the British GAAP statements and the reconciliation data to U.S. GAAP. Calculate any financial ratios using both the British GAAP data and the reconciled data, and highlight any significant differences. As part of this analysis, construct a statement of cash flows from the SKB statements presented.

<u>**EXHIBIT 2**</u>

SMITHKLINE BEECHAM Plc
Balance Sheets
For the Year Ended December 31, 19x9

	£m	
	19x9	*19x8*
Fixed Assets		
Tangible assets	**1,433**	1,473
Investments	**45**	91
	1,478	1,564
Current Assets		
Stocks	**488**	515
Debtors	**1,150**	1,275
Assets held pending disposal	**—**	166
Investments	**459**	5
Cash	**314**	229
	2,411	2,190
Creditors: amounts falling due within one year		
Loans and overdrafts	**(1,108)**	(986)
Other	**(1,306)**	(1,556)
	(2,414)	(2,542)
Net current (liabilities) assets	**(3)**	(352)
Total assets less current liabilities	**1,475**	1,212
Creditors: amounts falling due after more than one year		
Loans	**(341)**	(999)
Other	**(31)**	(31)
Provisions for liabilities and charges	**(284)**	(457)
	(656)	**(1,487)**
Net Assets	**819**	(275)
Capital Employed		
Capital and reserves		
Called up share capital	**349**	351
Reserves	**939**	348
SB shareholders' equity before elimination of goodwill	**1,288**	699
Goodwill reserve	**(915)**	(995)
SB shareholders' equity after elimination of goodwill		
Auction Rate Preference Shares of subsidiary	**415**	—
Minority interests	**31**	21
Total Shareholders' Funds	**819**	(275)

EXHIBIT 3

SMITHKLINE BEECHAM Plc
Source and Application of Funds
For the Year Ended December 31, 19x9

	£m	
	19x9	*19x8*
Funds generated from trading		
Trading profit	**967**	818
Beecham trading profit for the first quarter 19x8	**—**	(143)
Depreciation	**151**	134
Miscellaneous items, including exchange	**(7)**	(16)
	1,111	793
Changes in working capital		
Stocks—(increase) decrease	**(19)**	4
Debtors—(increase)	**(53)**	(87)
Creditors and provisions—increase	**109**	96
	37	13
Changes in fixed assets		
Purchases of tangible assets	**(264)**	(209)
Sales of tangible assets	**30**	14
	(234)	(195)
Cash flow from operations	**914**	611
Interest	**(110)**	(113)
Tax paid	**(276)**	(199)
Dividends received from former SmithKline subsidiaries	**—**	56
Dividends paid	**(210)**	(203)
Free cash flow after financing costs and tax	**318**	152
Shares issued	**4**	191
Auction Rate Preference Shares issued, less expenses	**409**	—
Sale of investments	**3**	8
Acquisitions, including deferred payments	**(123)**	(34)
Disposal of business	**526**	95
Extraordinary items paid	**(246)**	(145)
Special dividend paid to former shareholders of SmithKline Beckman Corporation	**—**	(431)
Net inflow (outflow) of funds	**891**	(164)
Net funds		
Net (borrowings) at the beginning of the year	**(1,748)**	(163)
Exchange restatement	**181**	(87)
Issue of Loan Stock	**—**	(1,334)
Net inflow (outflow) of funds	**891**	(164)
Net (borrowings) at the end of the year	**(676)**	(1,748)
Net (borrowings) in continuing businesses	**(676)**	(1,751)
Net surplus funds in businesses in the course of disposal	**—**	3
	(676)	(1,748)

The movement in net borrowings for the year represents the difference between the amounts shown in the opening and closing balance sheets. Movements in other items do not correspond to the change in blanace sheet amounts primarily due to the effects of translating opening currency balances of overseas subsidiaries at closing exchange rates. Net borrowings comprise loans and overdrafts less cash and short-term investments.

EXHIBIT 4

SMITHKLINE BEECHAM Plc
Accounting Policies

The financial statements are prepared under the historical cost convention, modified for the revaluation of land and buildings. Certain comparative figures have been amended to reflect changes in presentation.

Basis of Consolidation
The consolidated accounts include the accounts of the Company and its subsidiaries to 31 December. The results of businesses sold are included up to the date of disposal. As permitted by the Companies Act of 1985, the Company has not presented its own profit and loss account.

Currency translation
Profit and loss accounts of companies operating outside Great Britain are translated to sterling using average rates of exchange for the period. The net assets of such companies are translated to sterling at the rates of exchange ruling at the balance sheet dates.

Exchange differences which relate to the translation of net assets of overseas companies and to foreign currency borrowings are taken directly to reserves. All other exchange differences are taken to the profit and loss account.

The costs and benefits arising from hedging arrangements to mitigate the effect of exchange rate fluctuations on profits are dealt with in the profit and loss account in the year in which the related exposure arises.

Research and development expenditure
Laboratory buildings and equipment used for research and development are included as fixed assets and written off in accordance with the Group's depreciation policy. Other research and development expenditure is written off in the year in which it is incurred.

Deferred taxation
Deferred taxation is provided on timing differences using the liability method where it is probable that tax liabilities or assets will crystallize within the foreseeable future.

Goodwill
Goodwill, representing the excess of the purchase consideration over the fair value of the net tangible assets acquired, is eliminated in the Group balance sheet against reserves in the year of acquisition.

Tangible fixed assets and depreciation
Tangible fixed assets are stated at cost (or professional valuation in the case of certain land and buildings) less depreciation. Depreciation is charged on the cost or valuation of fixed assets, except freehold land, in equal annual installments over their estimated useful lives. The range of average lives for each major asset category are:

Freehold buildings	20 to 50 years	Plant and equipment	10 to 20 years
Leasehold land and buildings	Term of lease	Vehicles	5 to 7 years

Stocks
Stocks are stated at the lower of cost or net realizable value. The cost of finished goods and work in progress comprises raw materials, direct labor and related production overheads.

Retirement benefits
The cost of providing pension benefits is charged to the profit and loss accounts over the periods benefitting from the employee's services. The difference between the charge to the profit and loss account and the contributions paid to the retirement plans is included as an asset or liability in the balance sheet. The costs of providing other retirement benefits is charged to the profit and loss account when paid.

EXHIBIT 5

SMITHKLINE BEECHAM Plc
Additional Information for U.S. Investors

The Group prepares its consolidated accounts with generally accepted accounting principles ("GAAP") in the U.K.

U.K. GAAP differs in certain respects from U.K. GAAP. The effect of such differences of a material nature is set out below. There is a fundamental difference between U.K. and U.K. GAAP in the accounting for the merger. Under U.K. GAAP the combination is accounted for using merger accounting principles, whereas under U.S. GAAP the transaction is accounted for using the purchase accounting method. For the purposes of this reconciliation to U.S. GAAP, it has been assumed that SmithKline is the acquiree.

	Year ended 31 December,	
	19x9 £m	19x8 £m
Income Statement Date		
Net income after extraordinary items per U.K. GAAP	**847**	130
U.S. GAAP adjustments (net of taxation):		
Elimination of SmithKline results prior to merger	**—**	(144)
Merger transaction and SmithKline restructuring costs	**—**	281
Goodwill—Beecham	**(88)**	(26)
Deferred taxation	**(3)**	(30)
Purchase accounting:		
Amortization of intangible assets	**(85)**	(60)
Amortization of goodwill	**(67)**	(28)
Depreciation and other	**(7)**	(42)
Other, net	**32**	6
Net income per U.S. GAAP	**629**	87
Represented by:		
Income before non-recurring charges and taxes on income	**680**	349
Non-recurring credits (charges)	**124**	(115)
Taxes on income	**(300)**	(162)
Income from continuing operations	**504**	72
Income from discontinued operations (net of taxes)	**125**	15
Net income per U.S. GAAP	**629**	87
Per Share Data		
Average number of A and B Ordinary Shares in issue	**1,326m**	952m
Per Ordinary Share per U.S. GAAP		
Income from continuing operations	**38-0p**	7-5p
Net income	**47-4p**	9-1p
Per Equity per U.S. GAAP		
Income from continuing operations	**190-9p**	37-5p
Net income	**237-0p**	45-5p
Balance Sheet Data		
Shareholders' equity per U.K. GAAP	**373**	(296)
U.S. GAAP adjustments:		
Goodwill—Beecham	**344**	461
Capitalization of interest	**38**	37
Dividends	**58**	50
Deferred taxation:		
due to timing differences	**(80)**	(66)
due to ACT	**14**	5
Revaluation reserve	**(140)**	(156)
Other, net	**20**	(13)
Purchase accounting:		
Property, plant and equipment	**52**	69
Intangible assets	**551**	754
Goodwill	**2,598**	2,665
Other, net	**27**	35
Shareholders' equity per U.S. GAAP	**3,855**	3,545

EXHIBIT 5   (continued)

Additional Information for U.S. Investors

(a) Goodwill

Under U.K. GAAP, goodwill may be amortised over its useful life through the profit and loss account or eliminated directly against reserves. Under U.S. GAAP, goodwill is capitalised and amortised by charges against income over the period which, it is estimated, is to be benefited. Goodwill eliminated directly against reserves in the U.K. accounts has been reinstated and amortised over a 40 year period, which is the estimated useful life for the purpose of U.S. GAAP.

(b) Capitalisation of interest

Under U.K. GAAP, the capitalisation of interest is not required and the Group does not capitalise interest in its financial statements. U.S. GAAP requires interest incurred as part of the cost of acquiring fixed assets to be capitalised and amortised over the life of the asset.

(c) Deferred tax

Under U.K. GAAP, provision is made for deferred tax under the liability method where it is probable that a tax liability will become payable or a tax asset will crystallise within the foreseeable future. In the U.S., Accounting Principles Board Opinion No. 11 requires deferred tax to be provided in full under the deferral basis.

Under U.K. GAAP, the Group writes off any Advance Corporation Tax ("ACT") which is not considered to be recoverable. However, if deferred taxation is provided, such ACT may be available for offset against the balance on the deferred taxation account. As deferred taxation is provided under U.S. GAAP on all timing differences, the deferred tax account has been reduced by the appropriate amount of ACT.

(d) Extraordinary items

Under U.K. GAAP, the costs or credits relating to the restructuring of the Group, including the disposal of operations, may be classed as extraordinary items. Under U.S. GAAP, such disposals and one-time charges are treated as non-recurring items or as discontinued operations.

(e) Discontinued operations

Under U.K. GAAP, income earned from both continuing operations and discontinued operations up to the date of sale is aggregated in the consolidated income statement; material gains and losses arising on the sale of discontinued operations may be shown as extraordinary items. Under U.S. GAAP, gains or losses on the sale of those activities which comply with the U.S. GAAP definition of discontinued operations are not shown as extraordinary items but are shown under the heading "discontinued operations," and income from continuing operations and discontinued operations normally is disclosed separately for each year presented.

(f) Ordinary dividends

Under U.K. GAAP, dividends are provided for in the fiscal year in respect of which they are declared by the Board of Directors. Under U.S. GAAP, such dividends are not provided for until formally declared by the Board of Directors.

(g) Property revaluation

Under U.K. GAAP, properties are carried either at original cost or a subsequent valuation, less related depreciation, calculated on the revalued amount where applicable. Any surplus on the revaluation of a property is taken directly to shareholders' equity. Under U.S. GAAP revaluations of properties are not permitted.

(h) Purchase accounting adjustments

Under U.K. GAAP, the combination is being accounted for using merger accounting principles, pursuant to which the assets and liabilities of the Group are the sum of the historical net assets of Beecham and SmithKline. Under U.S. GAAP, the combination has been accounted for using the purchase method. For the purposes of this reconciliation, SmithKline has been treated as the acquiree. Under the purchase method, the aggregate purchase price was allocated to the assets and liabilities of SmithKline based upon their independently appraised fair values, with the remainder allocated to goodwill. Goodwill arising of £2,693 million is being amortised over 40 years.

7.10 **Asset Valuation and the Fourth Directive**

The EU's Fourth Directive, passed in 1978, is generally viewed as *the* significant break-through in the harmonization of EU company accounting. It represented an important compromise between the legalistic approach to financial reporting typified by Germany and the professional judgment approach characterized by the British. This compromise is apparent in the flexibility that the Fourth Directive permits in the implementation of its articles.

Consider, for example, the valuation of assets. The Fourth Directive indicates that companies must use historical cost as the basis for asset valuation but also allows member-states to permit (or require) companies to revalue certain assets to reflect the effects of inflation, so long as the departure from historical cost is necessary to give a true and fair view and so long as the departure is disclosed in the financial statements. Examples of such departures include these:

- The valuation of property, plant, equipment, and inventories at replacement cost.
- The revaluation of tangible fixed assets and financial fixed assets (i.e., investments and loans) to fair market value.
- The valuation of *all* financial statement items by a method designed to recognize the effects of inflation.

An Illustration

To illustrate the functioning and effects of the Fourth Directive, the following information was excerpted from the financial statements of British Airways Plc:

- Footnote Disclosure of Accounting Policies

  Accounting Convention—The accounts have been prepared under the historical cost convention modified by the inclusion of certain assets at valuation as stated below and in accordance with all applicable British accounting standards.

  Tangible Fixed Assets—Tangible fixed assets are stated at cost except for certain aircraft fleets and properties that are included at valuation. Depreciation is calculated to write off the cost or valuation, less residual value, on the straight-line basis.

  Apart from the Concord fleet, which remains at nil book value, the majority of the owned aircraft fleets were professionally valued on a market value basis and are included in the accounts on the basis of that valuation, less depreciation.

  All properties, other than those of a specialized use nature such as hangars and aircraft maintenance buildings, were professionally valued at open market value for existing use and are included in these accounts on the basis of that valuation, less depreciation.

- Footnote Disclosure of Financial Effects
- Footnote Disclosure of Reconciliation to U.S. GAAP

	(£ Millions)		**Net Book Value**	
	Valuation	*Depreciation*	*19x9*	*19x8*
Revalued fleet and properties are included in the accounts at the following amounts:				
Property	100	27	73	63
Fleet	1,044	719	325	414
Total	1,144	746	398	477
If these assets had not been revalued they would have been included at the following amounts:				
31 March 19x9	955	684	271	—
31 March 19x8	1,066	706	—	300

Property and Fleet Valuation. Under U.S. GAAP, tangible assets must be stated at cost less accumulated depreciation. The valuation of properties and fleet incorporated by British Airways in its financial statements would not therefore have been included in financial statements prepared in accordance with U.S. GAAP and the subsequent charges for depreciation would have been correspondingly lower. When such assets are sold, however, any revaluation surplus thus realized would be reflected in income.

The estimated effect of the significant adjustments to net income and to shareholders' equity that would be required if U.S. GAAP were to be applied instead of accounting principles generally accepted in Great Britain are

	(£ millions)	
	19x9	*19x8*
Net income (after tax)		
Depreciation		
Fleet	61	83
Property	3	—
Surplus arising on disposal of revalued aircraft	33	28
Shareholders' equity		
Fleet	(264)	(299)
Property	(23)	(25)

Required:

Presented in Exhibits 1 and 2 are British Airways' 19x8 and 19x9 group profit and loss statements and balance sheets. Using this information and that contained in the case, consider the following questions:

(a) Under British and EU GAAP, are British Airway's net worth and net income overstated? If so, why (and by how much)? If not, why not?

(b) As an investment analyst, which data—the U.S. GAAP or the British/EU GAAP—would you prefer to use for your investment decisions? Why?

(c) When comparing the financial results for British Airways to a U.S.-based airline (e.g., American or Delta), how is your analysis likely to be affected? (*Hint:* Provide specific examples of ratios or other financial indicators that will be affected by the differences in GAAP.)

EXHIBIT 1

BRITISH AIRWAYS Plc
Group Profit and Loss Account
For the Year Ended 31 March
(in £ millions)

	Group	
	19x9	*19x8*
Turnover	4,937	4,838
Cost of sales	(4,653)	(4,339)
Gross profit	284	499
Administrative expenses	(117)	(115)
Operating Surplus	167	384
Other income and charges	112	18
Net interest payable	(29)	(57)
Profit before Exceptional Item	250	345
Exceptional item	(120)	
Profit on Ordinary Activities before Taxation	130	345
Taxation	(35)	(100)
Profit on Ordinary Activities after Taxation	95	245
Minority interests		1
Profit Attributable to Shareholders	95	246
Dividends paid and proposed	(64)	(64)
Retained Profit for the Year	31	182
Earnings per share		
—Basic	13.2p	34.1p
—Fully diluted	13.4p	31.2p
Dividends per share	8.85p	8.85p

EXHIBIT 2

BRITISH AIRWAYS Plc
Balance Sheet
As of March 31
(in £ millions)

	Group	
	19x9	*19x8*
Fixed Assets		
Tangible assets		
Fleet	2,513	1,917
Property	392	339
Equipment	229	208
	3,134	2,464
Investments	108	108
Current Assets		
Stocks	37	40
Debtors	795	923
Short-term loans and deposits	203	300
Cash at bank	22	32
	1,057	1,295
Creditors: amounts falling due within one year	(1,600)	(1,816)
Net Current Liabilities	(543)	(521)
Total Assets Less Current Liabilities	2,699	2,051
Creditors: amounts falling due after more than one year	(1,366)	(755)
Provisions for Liabilities and Charges	(55)	(64)
	1,278	1,232
Capital and Reserves		
Called up share capital	180	180
Reserves		
Revaluation	82	121
Other	(11)	(18)
Profit and loss account	707	629
	958	912
Convertible Capital Bonds 2005	320	320
	1,278	1,232

7.11 Annual Report Analysis

An interesting and important challenge for students of international financial reporting is to study the published annual reports of various companies from different countries. Your instructor will provide you with a recent copy of a British annual report. To facilitate your delving into the annual report, undertake the following endeavors.

Required:

(a) List the key differences between the British annual report and what you would expect to see for a U.S. company in the same industry.

(b) Calculate the following ratios for the British company, taking care to note the assumptions you found necessary to make and where you found the appropriate pieces of data in the annual report.

$$(1)\ \text{Current ratio} = \frac{\text{Total current assets}}{\text{Total current liabilities}}$$

$$(2)\ \text{Quick ratio} = \frac{\text{Cash + Marketable securities + Accounts receivable.}}{\text{Total current liabilities}}$$

$$(3)\ \text{Operating cash flow to current liabilities} = \frac{\text{Operating cash flow}}{\text{Average total current liabilities}}$$

$$(4)\ \text{Debt-to-equity ratio} = \frac{\text{Long-term debt}}{\text{Owners' equity}}$$

$$(5)\ \text{Debt-to-total capitalization ratio} = \frac{\text{Long-term debt}}{\text{Long-term debt + owners' equity}}$$

$$(6)\ \text{Interest coverage ratio} = \frac{\text{Net income before interest and income taxes}}{\text{Interest expense}}$$

$$(7)\ \text{Operating cash flow to interest charges} = \frac{\text{Operating cash flow}}{\text{Interest expense}}$$

$$(8)\ \text{Operating cash flow to total liabilities} = \frac{\text{Operating cash flow}}{\text{Average total liabilities}}$$

$$(9)\ \text{Receivables turnover ratio} = \frac{\text{Net sales}}{\text{Average accts. receivable}}$$

$$(10)\ \text{Inventory turnover} = \frac{\text{Cost of goods sold}}{\text{Average inventory}}$$

$$(11)\ \text{Asset turnover} = \frac{\text{Net sales}}{\text{Average total assets}}$$

$$(12)\ \text{Average collection period ratio} = \frac{365\ \text{days}}{\text{Receivables turnover ratio}}$$

$$(13)\ \text{Average number of days' inventory on hand ratio} = \frac{365\ \text{days}}{\text{Inventory turnover ratio}}$$

$$(14)\ \text{Return on assets (ROA)} = \frac{\text{Net income}}{\text{Average total assets}}$$

$$OR = ROS \times \text{Asset turnover}$$

(15) Return on equity (ROE) $= \dfrac{\text{Net income}}{\text{Average total owners' equity}}$

$$OR = ROA \times \text{Financial leverage}$$

(16) Return on sales (ROS) $= \dfrac{\text{Net income}}{\text{Net sales}}$

(17) Financial leverage $= \dfrac{\text{Average liabilities} + \text{average owners' equity}}{\text{Average owners' equity}}$

(18) Basic earnings per share (EPS) $= \dfrac{\text{NI applicable to common shareholders}}{\text{Weighted average common shares}}$

(19) Cash dividend yield $= \dfrac{\text{Cash dividend per common share}}{\text{Market price per common share}}$

(20) Cash dividend payout $= \dfrac{\text{Total cash dividend to common shareholders}}{\text{Net income}}$

(c) What do you conclude about the availability of the appropriate data in the annual report for calculating these ratios?

(d) What does this financial analysis tell you about the British company?

(e) What analytical metrics did this British company choose to report for itself? What do those choices say about the message the company is striving to tell and the audience it is addressing?

Germany

The German accounting "system is so flexible that it is easily abused."[1]

It is an illusion to believe that the financial statements of a German public limited company would be fully comparable with those of a U.S. corporation if both were drawn up under U.S. GAAP. The economic, social, and legal environment of those enterprises may be so different that the accounting figures can be assessed only taking into account the divergent environments.[2]

Introduction

Although the infrastructure of Germany[3] lay in ruins at the end of World War II, the country currently boasts the third largest economy in the Free World. With the help of the United States, Germany accomplished its *Wirtschaftwunder* (economic miracle) and has again taken a prominent place in the community of nations. Moreover, Germany maintains a powerful position in the European Union. Indeed, the European Central Bank (ECB) has its headquarters in Frankfurt, former chancellor Helmut Kohl's determination for a unified Europe is widely viewed as the engine for the 1999 realization of the European monetary union and the euro, and since the European Community was established in 1958, Germany has paid the "lion's share" of the cost.[4]

In spite of this country's remarkable economic resurgence and its wealth and power today, Germans as a group are not known for free-wheeling optimism (prior remarks notwithstanding). On the contrary, they are a highly prudential people with a tendency to

---

[1]G. Steinmetz, "German Shares Are Easy to Buy, But Analysts Warn of Pitfall," *The Wall Street Journal,* March 20, 1995, p. C1.

[2]H. Biener, "What Is the Future of Mutual Recognition of Financial Statements and Is Comparability Really Necessary?" *The European Accounting Review* 3, no. 2 (1994), pp. 335–42.

[3]This chapter primarily reflects the long-standing West German environment. With the 1990 unification of the two Germanies, experts believe the West German model of business will dominate; indeed, indications since unification are of a dramatic East German embrace of West German modes. The unification has, however, created certain challenges that are discussed later in this chapter.

[4]See D. Leonard, "The Price That Must Be Paid for Friendship," *Financial Times,* September 17, 1998, p. 14 and P. Norman, "EMU's Broody Hen," *Financial Times,* May 2, 1998, p. 7.

discourage or suppress excessive risk-taking and speculative behavior. Hostile corporate takeovers, for example, are virtually impossible in Germany in the face of restrictions on equity voting rights and the opposition of banks, which are themselves major corporate shareholders. Likewise, German financial reporting practices have become (along with Japanese financial reporting practices, which were influenced by German principles in the late 19th and early 20th centuries) some of the world's foremost examples of conservatism in measuring profits and valuing assets. Some of the reasons for this conservatism, historical as well as cultural, are discussed in the next section.

Environmental Factors

Cultural Environment

Hofstede's study of cultural attitudes recorded similar scores by German and U.S. subjects in the areas of power distance (PD) (35 by the Germans, 40 by the Americans) and long-term orientation (LTO) (31 by the Germans, 29 by the Americans). However, the scores in Hofstede's other two areas showed greater discrepancies: The German subjects' score of 67 in individualism (IDV) sharply contrasts with the Americans' score of 91, and the Germans' 65 in uncertainty avoidance (UAV) is considerably higher than the Americans' 46.

What light can these results shed on German financial reporting? The relatively low score in individualism highlights the German consensus-building tendencies. Indeed, "the concept of *Mitbestimmung* or co-determination is deeply ingrained in the national mentality" and constitutes the core of Germany's social-market economy.[5] Such a strong orientation to group consensus building often impedes change, slows decision making, and builds vast webs of rules and regulations. The relatively high score in uncertainty avoidance is manifested in the historical lack of venture capital and a predilection for investment safety.[6] Together, these two dimensions suggest that the German national culture places a premium on safety, predictability, and adherence to an established system of reasoned, somewhat entrenched, rules. The Germans' low score in the area of PD, which concerns the centralization of power, suggests that authority is primarily vested in systems rather than in individuals. The relatively low LTO score highlights a tendency for thrift, large savings, and a preference for slow and steady progress. Indeed, most German companies report interim financial results on a semiannual basis, not a quarterly basis as required in the United States. Based on this configuration of scores, Hofstede typifies German organizations in the cultural paradigm of the "well-oiled machine," which he describes as embodying a technocratic orientation that depends heavily on rules and established procedures instead of on personal command or individual initiative. In fact, German managers tend to believe that their authority with subordinates and their standing with colleagues is earned by their expertise, not their organizational position.[7]

Gray's framework (see Chapter 1) prompts the thought that such scores could also lead one to expect that German financial reporting systems tend to be more static and

---

[5]"Mighty Leap out of Recession," *Financial Times,* September 30, 1994, p. XXII. See also, "Is the Model Broken?" *The Economist,* May 4, 1996, pp. 17–19.

[6]See A. Fisher, "Afraid of a Flutter," *Financial Times,* November 21, 1994, p. V; J. Templeman, G. Edmondson, and L. Miller, "Finally, Germany Is Paring the Fat," *Business Week,* October 17, 1994, pp. 64–66; and "Scanty Charms," *The Economist,* May 24, 1997, p. 74.

[7]C. Lorenz, "Styles of Execution," *Financial Times,* February 23, 1994, p. 9. See also R. Stewart, "German Management: A Challenge to Anglo-American Managerial Assumptions," *Business Horizons,* May–June 1996, pp. 52–54.

rigid than U.S. systems. Indeed, German financial reporting practices tend to de-emphasize the role of professional judgment, which by its nature must entail a certain amount of individual creativity, subjectivity, and, hence, unpredictability. Most commentators would probably agree with this description, noting the higher degree of uniformity and the greater importance of rules in German financial reporting. This insight, useful as it may be, should not be allowed, however, to create the misconception that German financial reporting is therefore unsophisticated or unprofessional. On the contrary, it is highly sophisticated and requires considerable insight in its application. German accountants and auditors are among the world's most highly trained. The fundamental point is that their training and ability are channeled differently than those of accountants in Anglo-Saxon nations. German accountants are less likely (and, because of the legalistic nature of German accounting, less able) to experiment or innovate than their British or American counterparts. Historically, the German financial reporting system, characterized as it is by cultural and structural rigidity, changes less frequently than the U.S. or British systems, which are constantly evolving. Recently, however, foundations for change have been laid.

Given the cultural predispositions just described, it should not be a surprise that German accounting principles are essentially the product of legislation, created by specific provisions in both tax law and company law. (The legislative process creates the centralized system of rules to which all must adhere.) The cultural importance of this mode of accounting policy formation is that it concerns accountants and auditors primarily with correctness and compliance rather than fairness and disclosure. To illustrate this orientation, one need only examine the traditional German auditor's report, which has only recently been superseded in the pursuit of EU conformity. The orientation it reveals to a large extent persists today in German auditing and accounting. The accepted form reads: "According to our legally required audit, the accounting, the financial statements, and the annual report comply with statutory provisions and the Company's articles of association." The terseness of this statement suggests a rather simple situation: Either the law is being complied with or it is not. The sentence conveys little sense that professional judgment is being exercised in the audit or that these financial statements must communicate information to other people, such as investors. In fact, one German commentator succinctly noted that even though German audit opinions now refer to "true and fair," the fact remains that "the basic codified objective of commercial accounting [in Germany] is conformity with the regulations . . . [and] in short, the true and fair view concept is not applicable to German balance sheets."[8]

Whatever cultural biases German financial reporting (and social policy in general) may have in the direction of uniformity and stability, they have surely been reinforced by German history—specifically the interwar period, with its disastrously high rates of inflation and unemployment. (It is interesting to note that German accounting was in an important formative stage during this time with a uniform chart of accounts appearing for the first time in 1930.) Even now, Germany continues to be perhaps the most inflation-conscious nation in the world. Although inflation indices in Germany have rarely exceeded 5 percent per year in the last 20 years, even these relatively low rates are sometimes sufficient to trigger public anxiety and send officials scurrying to tighten the money supply. Indeed, one of the major reasons that the German business community has consistently and vehemently opposed any form of current cost accounting is its fear that such a scheme might reinforce inflationary expectations among businesspeople and the public at large.

---

[8]A. Haller, "The Relationship of Financial and Tax Accounting in Germany: A Major Reason for Accounting Disharmony in Europe," *International Journal of Accounting* 27 (1992), pp. 317 and 322.

*Legal and
Political
Environment*

Individual Tax Law.   Tax laws in Germany are currently designed to encourage individual investors to buy and hold equity shares. Although nominal rates on individual income range up to 53 percent and dividends are included in taxable income, the government has adopted an imputation system that grants partial relief from double taxation of corporate profits.[9] The individual taxpayer who receives dividends from a corporation is granted a credit amounting to 30 percent of the sum of the dividend payment plus the credit. For instance, shareholders receiving DM4,000 in dividends would also receive a credit of DM1,714 and would declare income of DM5,714 (4,000 + 1,714) on their tax return. For taxpayers in a 30 percent tax bracket, the credit would exactly offset the extra tax liability generated by the income (5,714 × 30 percent = 1,714). Those in a higher bracket would find the marginal liability attributable to the dividend payment somewhat higher than the credit.

Long-term capital gains on private assets are not taxed in Germany, and securities must be held only six months to qualify as long term. Exceptions to the capital gains exclusion include the sale of a significant interest (25 percent or more) in a business (in which case special rules apply) and the sale of securities held as business assets. Short-term capital gains, net of a DM1,000 exclusion, are included in taxable income.[10]

Corporate Tax Law.   Even though tax rates are relatively high, companies are permitted very generous deductions in reporting taxable income. Corporate tax is levied on individual entities (i.e., consolidation is not permitted) according to a split-rate system under which undistributed corporate profits are taxed at 45 percent and distributed profits at 30 percent.[11] In Germany, as in a number of other nations (such as Japan and Sweden), book and tax income are required to be substantially the same. This linkage between fiscal and financial reporting has the predictable effect of reinforcing the extreme conservatism with which German companies measure income. For example, the financial depreciation taken by most companies is generally the maximum allowable under tax law, which in some cases may be triple declining balance (or even more if special incentives apply).

Some differences between book income and taxable income are permitted, one of the most common being the accrual of losses or write-down of assets deemed appropriate for financial reporting purposes but not permissible as a tax deduction. (The willingness to write book income even lower than necessary to procure tax benefits indicates the powerful hold that conservatism has on the German psyche. Tax law is not its only motivation.) The liability method of deferred tax accounting must be employed when book income diverges from taxable income. If taxable income exceeds book income, giving rise to a potential deferred tax asset, a German company may record the asset on its financial statements only if it blocks an equivalent amount of retained earnings from distribution until the asset is reversed; however, it need not record the asset at all. If, on the other hand, book income exceeds taxable income, giving rise to a potential deferred tax liability, the company must record the liability on the books. In this regard, the financial statements of the Hoechst Group, a German chemicals concern, include a footnote stating that it is the policy of the company to record deferred tax liabilities but not deferred tax assets.

One also may locate untaxed reserve accounts on German balance sheets between shareholders' equity and long-term liabilities. These reserves allow firms to defer the recognition of income (i.e., income smoothing) for a stated period of time in accordance

---

[9]Beginning in 1999, it is anticipated that a series of tax rate cuts will be phased in such that the top rate will be 48.5 percent by the year 2002 (see R. Atkins, "Germany Coalition Agrees on Cut in Basic Tax Rate," *Financial Times,* October 12, 1998, p. 18).

[10]$1 U.S. = DM1.68 as of January 1, 1999.

[11]According to R. Atkins, "Germany Coalition Agrees on Cut in Basic Tax Rate," the corporate rate will decrease from 45 percent to 35 percent by 2002 and an array of generous deductions and loopholes will disappear.

with special tax provisions. One such provision encourages overseas investment by allowing German companies to defer the capital gains tax on assets transferred to certain foreign countries; another encourages takeovers of troubled companies by allowing the buyer to place up to 40 percent of the purchase costs in an untaxed reserve. For example, Hoechst includes a footnote in its financial statements (see Exhibit 8–1) regarding untaxed reserves of DM692 million that appear on the parent company's balance sheet.

The preponderance of obscure legal reference versus actual explanation in Exhibit 8–1 reveals what is perhaps the most important effect of tax law on German accounting: an orientation toward compliance instead of disclosure.

EU Membership.   As a founding member of the Common Market and the country with the largest economy in the EU, Germany has been a leader in the push for a broadening and deepening of the European Union. In particular, Germany is in favor of enlarging EU membership. Moreover, Germany strongly favors the euro and an elevated role for the European Parliament. Germany sees itself as the nexus of the European Union and indeed, some commentators have noted that "as Germany goes, so goes Europe."[12]

Germany has been deeply involved in the process of harmonizing financial reporting practices among EU member states. In December 1985, the government instituted wide-ranging reforms of the nation's accounting laws to bring them into compliance with both the Fourth and Seventh Directives, as well as with international standards issued by the International Accounting Standards Committee, making Germany one of the first nations to incorporate both directives in its national legal system.

*Business
Environment*

Form of Business.   German law recognizes two types of limited liability companies as legal entities in their own right: the *Aktiengesellschaft* (AG) and the *Gesellschaft mit beschränkter Haftung* (GmbH). The first of these, the AG, is analogous to the publicly held corporation in the United States and the Plc in Great Britain. It is the only business entity in

---

EXHIBIT 8–1

Hoechst AG Untaxed Reserves Note
Special Reserve Items Subject to Future Taxation

The special reserve items subject to future taxation in Hoechst AG include amounts under Article 6b EStG and section 35 EStR. These amount overall to DM55 million (DM26 million in the previous year, also including amounts under Article 52 para 8 EStG). In addition, the special reserve items subject to future taxation also include adjustments which arose under income tax regulations pursuant to Articles 6b, 7D EStG, Article 1 EntwHStG, Article 3 ZonenRFG, Articles 80, 82d EStDV, Article 14 BerlinFG, section 35 EStR, Article 4 FördergebietsG and the former provisions of Article 7C EStG and Articles 79, 82, 82de EStDV. Of the total adjustments of DM637 million (DM704 million in the previous year), DM567 million relates to tangible fixed assets (DM634 million in the previous year), DM67 million to investments (DM67 million in the previous year) and DM3 million to current assets (DM3 million in the previous year). Figures for the Hoechst Group are not required since adjustments allowable for tax purposes only and special reserve items subject to future taxation are not shown in the Group balance sheet.

The net income for the year of Hoechst AG increased by DM14 million (by DM45 million in the previous year), owing to measures taken solely in accordance with tax regulations. These measures, in the financial year or in previous years, were certain depreciation and write-offs of assets or the setting-up of special reserve items subject to future taxation.

As a result of tax measures, in subsequent years there will be earnings subject to an average tax burden of DM43 million.

---

[12]J. Templeman, "Not What the Doctor Ordered," *Business Week,* October 31, 1994, p. 60.

Germany whose shares may be traded on a stock exchange. The second, the GmbH, is analogous to a privately held corporation. It is generally selected by those owners, such as families, who wish to retain a measure of privacy and close personal control over their business.

An AG must have at least five shareholders at the time of its formation (although afterwards a smaller number of shareholders is permissible). It must possess a minimum share capital of DM100,000 (about $60,000) with at least 25 percent of this amount paid in. The AG is governed by two bodies: a *board of management,* which oversees the day-to-day operations, and a *supervisory board,* which advises company managers on behalf of the shareholders. Although the views of the supervisory board carry considerable weight with management, it usually does not possess the legal power to direct the company. All supervisory board members are appointed by the shareholders (unless a company has more than 500 employees, in which case employee representatives must be included on the board as well).

A GmbH need have only one shareholder at the time of its formation and share capital of at least DM50,000 (about $30,000), with the higher of 25 percent of the capital or DM25,000 paid in. Apart from these numerical differences, a GmbH differs from an AG in other important respects: Its shares are not freely transferable, and the responsibility for managing it is usually assumed by one or more individual directors instead of a management board. A GmbH employing fewer than 500 employees is not required to form a supervisory board.

Reporting and Audit Requirements.   German businesses must keep accurate and up-to-date business records designed in such a way that an audit may be performed with reasonable dispatch; however, German companies are not required to have their records audited. Firms may avoid the trouble and expense of an audit if they qualify as "small companies" by meeting two of the following three criteria: a balance sheet total of less than DM5.31 million (about $3.16 million), annual revenue of less than DM10.62 million (about $6.32 million), and fewer than 50 employees. (Note that these exemptions are as of 1997 and follow those set out by the European Union in the Fourth Directive.) All other companies must subject their records to examination by a statutory auditor. In Germany, a statutory audit must be performed by an independent auditor who is a professionally qualified member of the accounting profession. A statutory audit is therefore a good deal more than a mere formality.

In addition, firms that qualify as large companies must publish a complete set of financial statements, along with directors' and auditors' reports, in the *Federal Gazette.* A *large company* is deemed to be one that meets two of the following three criteria: total assets of more than DM21.24 million (about $12.64 million), annual sales of more than DM42.48 million (about $25.28 million), and more than 250 employees. Medium-sized firms (i.e., those that qualify neither as large nor as small companies) must file their audited financial statements with the *Trade Register* (where they are open to public examination) but are not required to publish them.

One important effect of EU harmonization has been the introduction of the true and fair view criterion into German accounting and auditing. (For more on this criterion, see Chapter 7.) Instead of merely ascertaining that financial statements comply with all relevant provisions of company and tax law, German auditors are now required to express an opinion on the fairness of the documents under examination, including the management report. Changes in the wording of the auditor's report reflect the evolving understanding of the auditor's role. Whereas earlier auditor's reports consisted only of a brief statement on the legality and propriety of the financial statements, since 1987 they have been suggesting that a more complex process of judgment is at work (see Exhibit 8–2).

EXHIBIT 8–2

German Audit Report: Lufthansa Group

The Consolidated Financial Statements which we have audited in accordance with professional standards comply with the legal regulations. The Consolidated Financial Statements present, in compliance with generally accepted accounting principles, a true and fair view of the net worth, financial position and results of the Group. The Group management report is in agreement with the Consolidated Financial Statements.

Dusseldorf, April 7, 1998

C & L Deutsche Revision
Aktiengesellschaft
Wirtschaftsprüfungsgesellschaft

Siepe   Dr. Vogelpoth
Wirtschaftsprüfer   Wirtschaftsprüfer

The movement away from legal compliance toward fair presentation as the proper standard of financial reporting is a direct result of EU negotiations on the Fourth Directive. Some commentators have questioned, however, whether the importation of the true and fair criterion will have much of a practical effect on the extremely conservative valuation and measurement habits of the Germans. As long as tax law continues to have a significant influence on financial reporting, the commentators argue that the role of professional judgment in auditing and accounting will be limited.

Accounting Profession.   The accounting profession in Germany is well trained and widely respected. The professional title that qualifies one to audit financial statements—*Wirtschaftsprüfer* (WP)—requires a university degree in economics, law, or a related subject, five years of experience in practice (four of which are in auditing), and successful completion of a rigorous examination. Few candidates manage to achieve full qualification before their early thirties. The stringent requirements for admission into the German accounting profession have kept the number of WPs relatively low.

Although accounting principles and the duties of auditors are closely legislated in Germany (at least as compared to U.S. standards), the accounting profession provides advice and acts as unofficial interpreter with regard to these areas. The profession also regulates entry into the main professional body, the *Institut der Wirtschaftsprüfer* (IDW), and it investigates and punishes violations of professional ethics and discipline. In addition, it bears primary responsibility for developing standards for audit fieldwork. IDW is not an accounting standard-setting body. It's interpretations do, however, from time to time become common practice via court referrals to a particular interpretation.

It is also interesting to note that, due in part to the accounting profession's historical absence in accounting standard setting, it can be said that the legalistic, tax-oriented nature of German accounting is void of a conceptual framework comparable to that promulgated in the United States by the FASB or in Britain by the ASB.[13] All of this, how-

---

[13]A. Holler, "International Accounting Harmonization: American Hegemony or Mutual Recognition with Benchmarks? Comments and Additional Notes from a German Perspective," *The European Accounting Review* 4, no. 2 (1995), pp. 235–47.

ever, may be changing in the near term. In the spring of 1998, the Law on Facilitation of Capital Acquisition (KapAEG) was passed in Germany. A primary objective of this was to make it easier for German-listed companies to raise capital in the international markets. In regards to accounting, this law permits German companies to prepare "consolidated financial statements according to internationally recognised principles for the first time, without additionally being obliged to prepare the group financial statements according to the German Commercial Code."[14] IAS or U.S. GAAP are noted as acceptable alternatives. The law will also affect the role of the WP in two ways. First, the financial statements prepared in accordance with internationally recognized alternative GAAP must be audited by an auditor appointed in the usual manner under the German Commercial Code. The auditor must attest to the fact that the company has met the criteria permitting it to utilize the alternative GAAP. Such criteria include an evaluation that: the alternative GAAP is "of a comparable standard to German regulations"; the alternative statements are in compliance with the EU's Seventh Directive; and the financial statement footnotes detail and comment on the GAAP applied as it deviates from German GAAP.

The second impact on the role of the WP is that this law "laid the foundation for a private sector standard-setting body."[15] Indeed, a German Accounting Standards Committee (GASC) has recently been established. It is initially being led by a former chairman of KPMG Germany and is comprised of six other members from the corporate sector, public accounting, academe, and the financial analysts' community. The German Ministry of Justice (MoJ) currently retains standard-setting authority, but the GASC's pronouncements will be published by the MoJ and thus, will be implicitly sanctioned by the MoJ. It remains to be seen what direct or indirect role the IDW will play in regards to the GASC, but it is hard to imagine that it will not have a significant role.[16]

Banks.   Historically banks have played a strong central role in providing capital to German companies, not only by granting loans but also by purchasing shares. When a German company seeks financing, its bank may lend money or buy shares, depending on the immediate financial position of the venture as well as its long-term outlook. Consequently, many German banks have built up sizable shareholdings in nonfinancial companies. In 1997, Deutsche Bank, for example, held equity interests of 5 percent or more in 11 German companies, 8 of those holdings equaling a 10 percent share or more and 3 of those exceeded a 20 percent share.[17] This includes a 21 percent interest in Daimler-Benz (it is now 12 percent after the Chrysler merger) and a 9 percent interest in Allianz. Even as Deutsche Bank talks about spinning some of these investments off, they plan to do so by creating a fully owned subsidiary that would hold such investments.

Needless to say, the extent of these equity holdings enable German banks to wield an unusual amount of influence over the policies of their clients. The degree of this influence is reflected in the composition of the supervisory boards of many companies. The supervisory board of a large German company typically includes at least one member from a major bank; many include more. A recent annual report of Daimler-Benz, for example, reveals that its supervisory board includes no less than four members from Germany's three major commercial banks: Deutsche Bank, Dresdner Bank, and Commerzbank. (The

---

[14]"International Briefing: Germany," *Accountancy,* June 1998, p. 63.

[15]L. Knorr, "In FASB's Footsteps?" *Accountancy,* July 1998, p. 62.

[16]It is interesting to note that, according to L. Knorr, "In FASB's Footsteps?", the GASC seeks to develop "one set of group accounting standards for all companies in about five years' time," replacing the current internationally recognized alternative GAAP deviations created by the KapAEG.

[17]G. Bowley, "Deutsche to Spin Off $24bn Assets," *Financial Times,* December 16, 1998, p. 1.

total membership of the board is 21, including about half a dozen employee representatives as required by law.)

The power of German banks and the presence of their representatives on the supervisory boards of major companies have important implications for financial reporting in Germany. Most important, banks have access to inside information on company operations and therefore do not have to depend on published financial statements as their major source of data. Because their largest shareholders also tend to be both their lenders and to some extent insiders, German companies have had relatively little incentive to develop the extensive—and expensive—financial reporting systems that Anglo-American firms find necessary to attract and hold investors. Indeed, German banks are prototypical relationship-oriented banks, whereas American banks are much more transactions/volume oriented. German banks have tended to focus on economies of scope, a stable employee pool with broad skills, information exchange with clients, and client cultivation.[18]

The disclosure standards governing German financial reporting are simply not as detailed and extensive as those in countries with strong public capital markets and a long tradition of financial stewardship (such as Great Britain). Given this situation, combined with the fact that in Germany "companies exercise prudence on behalf of stakeholders—which, in practice, thanks to Germany's weak equity culture, means on behalf of creditors and employees rather than shareholders," it is not surprising that banking concerns have had a prominent role in the development of German accounting practices.[19] This is starting to be tempered by two factors.

The first factor stems from existing and looming competitive pressures in the banking sector itself. The 1999 European Monetary Union, its prospects, and the growing number of non-German financial institutions seeking German business has prompted German banks to focus on getting more efficient, more profitable, and more aggressive in developing new markets and new business.[20] For example: In 1998 Deutsche Bank bought the U.S.'s Bankers Trust, creating the world's largest financial services company; in 1995, Deutsche Bank was the first German bank to fully adopt IASC GAAP as it sought to appeal to an international market; and Dresdner Bank, at the time of this writing, was planning to list its shares on the New York Stock Exchange.[21]

The second factor has to do with the beginnings of a rise in a heretofore miniscule equity culture. As a new generation of investors and entrepreneurs have come of age, Germany's renowned historical risk aversion and reliance on banks has begun to erode.[22] For example, consider: In 1998 the *Deutsche Börse* was the world's fourth largest stock exchange; in 1997 the *Neur Market* was created in the Deutsche Börse for smaller, high-tech, higher-risk companies to raise capital; in 1997 the percentage of Germans owning shares increased 16 percent from 1995 (7.6 percent to 8.8 percent, percentages far below those in Britain, the United States, and Sweden which are all 18 percent or more); and in 1996, the German public enthusiasticaly embraced Deutsche Telecom's initial public

---

[18]B. Keltner, "Relationship Banking and Competitive Advantage: Evidence from the U.S. and Germany," *California Management Review,* Summer 1995, pp. 45–72.

[19]"Bean Counters, Unite!" *The Economist,* June 10, 1995, p. 67.

[20]A. Fisher, "Streamlining Seems Inevitable," *Financial Times,* June 24, 1998, p. VI.

[21]See S. Ascarelli, "Deutsche Bank Says Net Jumped 24% in 1995, Discloses Big Hidden Reserves," *The Wall Street Journal,* March 29, 1996, p. A8; "The Battle of the Bulge Bracket," *The Economist,* November 28, 1998, pp. 73–74; and T. Barber, "Outsiders Eye the Market," *Financial Times,* November 10, 1998, p. IX.

[22]G. Bowley, "Corporate Germany Reaping the Rewards of Risk-Taking," *Financial Times,* August 11, 1998, p. 14.

offering of one-half billion shares.[23] All of this is not to say that German banks are about to witness a substantially reduced role in the overall German corporate sector—that is unlikely. What is happening, however, is that German banking is going through a metamorphosis, and those that adapt to monetary union, a growing equity culture, overseas competition, and the changing concerns of German corporate management will continue to have a powerful, but perhaps different, presence on the German business landscape.

Stock Exchanges.   Germany has eight stock exchanges. The Frankfurt exchange, with about 70 percent of the volume of all trading throughout Germany, is the largest, with the other seven operating as regional exchanges. In a move to create a world-class, primary exchange, the Deutsche Börse was created in early 1993. It serves as a holding company for the eight exchanges and has thrust the Frankfurt exchange to center stage. In spite of the global importance of the German economy, it is surprising that the total capitalization of the German stock market is only about 38 percent of its gross domestic product, as compared to 139 percent in the United States and 163 percent in the United Kingdom.[24] As late as 1997, fewer than 700 companies were listed on German exchanges (as compared to ten times that number in the United States and twice as many in Japan and the United Kingdom). It is also surprising to note that only as recently as 1994 did Germany make insider trading a criminal offense and set up its first Securities and Exchange Commission–like governing body, the Federal Supervisory Agency.[25]

Germany's commercial banks dominate the securities brokerage business, contributing to the lack of a heretofore strong equity culture in the country. To this end, the banks have historically focused on brokering for their large investors (e.g., institutions or other corporations), not small investors. Moreover, it is only recently, with a concern for investor fairness protection in mind, that the banks are required to establish "Chinese walls" between their trading and corporate finance departments.[26]

As a consequence of a historically secondary role, the German capital market has had little impact on financial reporting standards. The notion of shareholder value as a prime concern of German corporations traditionally has simply not existed.[27] Listed companies must supply the stock exchange with copies of their annual reports, but they need not fulfill any other substantial disclosure requirements. The influence of outside investors on financial disclosure is not likely to increase until small investors (or other outsiders) enter the German stock market in greater numbers or more German companies seek listings on overseas exchanges.[28] (In 1988, Bayer became the first German company to have its

[23]See S. Ascarelli, "Wary Germans Take a Chance on Stocks," *The Wall Street Journal,* October 9, 1996, p. A19; K. Miller and B. Bremner, "Europe's Sell-off to End All Sell-offs," *Business Week,* October 21, 1996, p. 54; "Germany's Capitalist Piglets," *The Economist,* December 6, 1997, p. 85; A. Fisher, "Looking Over Borders," *Financial Times,* March 24, 1998, p. II; A. Fisher, "New Era Dawns in Germany," *Financial Times,* February 28, 1997, p. III; A. Fisher, "Industry Comes of Age," *Financial Times,* June 24, 1998, p. III.

[24]A. Fisher, "Listening and Learning," *Financial Times,* June 24, 1998, p. III.

[25]A. Fisher, " 'Tally-ho' Sounds for an Elusive German Breed," *Financial Times,* December 23, 1994, p. 17.

[26]See "Commerzbank AG," *The Wall Street Journal,* November 15, 1994, p. A18; S. Ascarelli, "Germany's Law on Insider Trading Takes Effect Today," *The Wall Street Journal,* August 1, 1994, p. A12; and A. Fisher, "Perturbation in the Boardrooms," *Financial Times,* November 21, 1994, p. IV.

[27]See D. Waller, "Wooing the Shareholders," *Financial Times,* November 27, 1992, p. 15 and A. Fisher, "New Era Dawns in Germany."

[28]In 1994, the German government passed legislation recommending that publicly held companies lower the nominal value of their capital stock from the traditional DM50 (about $32.50) to DM5 (about $3.25). The purpose of the legislation was to lower the average per share price of German companies in an effort to increase share investments by small investors. Indeed, A. Fisher, "Afraid of a Flutter," reports a recent, slightly positive change in German's preference for investing in shares versus bonds, and A. Sharpe, "Germany Starts to Open Up," *Financial Times,* September 21, 1994, p. IV notes this may be a long-term trend.

shares quoted on the Tokyo exchange, and in 1993 Daimler-Benz became the first German company listed on the New York Stock Exchange, with Veba following suit in 1996.) The major change most likely to evolve if such a phenomenon were to occur (and it appears that it is), will be an increased level of corporate transparency (i.e., clearer, more extensive, and more timely financial disclosures).[29]

It is also worth noting that in Germany, equity holdings by a pension fund or an insurance company are restricted to 15 percent of their total investment portfolio. Moreover, to the extent that companies in these two industries do make equity investments, they are allowed to invest only in companies with "respectable" financial leverage. Many business leaders believe that these restrictions have created a German business environment that is more conducive to allowing companies to adopt long-term profit orientations rather than short-term profit policies and tactics.

The recent partnership of the Frankfurt and London exchange (see Chapter 7 for more on this), the monetary union's creation of the world's second largest equity market, the *Mittelstand* (medium-sized, family-owned) companies' opening up to outside equity, the huge domestic success of the Deutsche Telecom IPO, the need for Germany's largest companies to seek capital on a worldwide basis, and an onslaught of foreign investors entering Germany, have all contributed to an emerging German appetite for equity. Perhaps a vivid manifestation of this changing attitude is the *Neuer Market* alluded to earlier. In March 1997, the market came on stream with only a handful of companies. As of the end of 1998, it boasts 60.[30] An interesting aspect of the *Neuer Market* is some of its requirements, which include "quarterly and annual reports based on IAS or U.S. GAAP, issued in German and English, in addition to regular analyst and investor seminars."[31] Thus, a central tenet of the market is greater transparency to facilitate shareholder confidence, liquidity, and willingness to accept higher risks in exchange for higher-returns prospects.[32]

Labor.   Trade unions have long exerted a powerful influence on German politics and economics that appears in a variety of ways. For example, German industrial workers can boast of the world's highest wages and most restricted working hours.[33] But on the other hand, German industry has a solid commitment to employee consultation and participation; the works council (*Betriebsrat*), for example, is a permanent feature in most companies. In addition, the supervisory boards of companies with more than 500 employees must include employee representatives. For companies with 500 to 2,000 employees, one-third of the board members must be employee representatives; for companies with more than 2,000 employees, the proportion of employee representatives rises to one-half. Thus, German labor relations law grants a measure of real power to employee groups, an arrangement that both management and labor have praised publicly and privately.

Parallel with this commitment to employee consultation is the belief that employees (as stakeholders in an enterprise) are entitled to reasonably clear and complete information about their company. This belief (along with EU guidelines) has had some effect on the financial disclosures that companies must include in their annual reports. Firms are required to provide footnotes revealing total remuneration paid to management and supervisory board members, and they must disclose the average number of employees in each area of the business.

---

[29]See "Frankfurt's Role Consolidated," and A. Fisher, "Frankfurt Brushes Up Its Act," *Financial Times,* December 9, 1994, p. 12.

[30]See A. Fisher, "Corporate Germany Reaping Rewards of Risk-Taking," and A. Fisher, "New Era Dawns in Germany."

[31]See the Web site http://www.nevermarkt.de.

[32]G. Bowley, "Runaway Success Story," *Financial Times,* June 24, 1998, p. IV.

[33]See H. Banks, "Global Deregulation," *Forbes,* May 5, 1997, pp. 130–33. In this article it is noted that the western German average hourly industrial labor cost is about $32 (the eastern German cost is about $21) whereas it is about $20 in France, $15 in Britain, and $18 in the United States.

Exhibit 8–3 presents notes from the financial statements of the Mannesmann Group, an engineering and telecommunications company, illustrating a typical format for these disclosures.

In addition to these legally required disclosures, pressure from unions and various political groups has made German companies sensitive to public opinion and encouraged them to experiment with various types of social reporting. Although some companies have included value-added statements (see Chapter 7 on Great Britain) or social accounts statements in their annual reports, the most popular alternative usually involves some form of narrative presentation. The excerpts depicted in Exhibit 8–4 were taken from the annual report of Preussag Group, a transport and plant engineering company; they illustrate the way in which union pressure and public opinion have prompted German companies to provide some form of social reporting. As you examine these pages, be sure to notice the attention paid to issues such as leaves, fair employment practices, training, and changes in employees numbers. These are all common themes in German social reporting (another issue that frequently appears in German social reporting is protection of the environment).

EXHIBIT 8–3

Mannesmann Personnel Disclosures

Personnel Costs/Employees

	1997 in DMm	1996 in DMm
Wages and salaries	**8,123**	7,705
Social security and other pension costs	**2,017**	1,891
(of which for retirement pension)	**(163)**	(192)
	10,140	9,596

The other pension costs to not include the interest portion of the addition to provision for pensions in the amount of DM292 million (previous year: DM 252 million), which is shown under net interest.

Average Number of Employees by Division:

	Wage Earners	Salaried Staff	Trainees	1997	Total Workforce 1996
Demag	5,811	10,280	609	**16,700**	18,326
Dematic	5,477	6,204	387	**12,068**	11,678
Rexroth	9,645	8,901	652	**19,198**	19,018
Krauss-Maffei	2,473	3,805	292	**6,570**	6,646
Engineering	23,406	29,190	1,940	**54,536**	55,668
VDO	8,289	7,529	325	**16,143**	15,747
Sachs	12,656	4,438	473	**17,567**	19,421
Automotive	20,945	11,967	798	**33,710**	35,168
Mobilfunk	—	5,302	99	**5,401**	4,212
Arcor	1,746	5,575	—	**7,321**	—
Eurokom	—	244	10	**254**	181
Telecommunications	1,746	11,121	109	**12,976**	4,393
Tubes & Trading	11,335	3,781	185	**15,301**	20,885
Other companies	753	2,959	200	**3,912**	4,353
	58,185	59,018	3,232	**120,435**	120,467

Total Remuneration of the Board of Management, the Supervisory Board and Former Members of the Board of Management

The remuneration of the Board of Management for the 1997 financial year amounted to DM 9,542,954.00. A total of DM 5,840,431.00 was paid to former members of the Board of Management and their surviving dependants. An amount of

DM 48,660,897.00 has been set aside as a provision for pension obligations towards former members of the Board of Management and their surviving dependants. The remuneration of the Supervisory Board for the 1997 financial year amounts to DM 1,366,500.00.

Loans to Members of the Board of Management

As of 31/12/97, the loans to members of the Board of Management amounted to DM 273,403.00. The interest payable on the loans was four per cent; the agreed terms are between six and ten years.

As against the amount of DM 322,022.00 as of 31/12/1996, DM 48,619.00 have been repaid in 1997.

EXHIBIT 8–4

Preussag Group Employee Discussion

The development of the Preussag Group, with expansion of the growth areas, reduction of involvement in basic material fields and intensification of business in foreign markets, is reflected in changes in the structure of the workforce. The shift in emphasis has clearly affected the total workforce. At the end of the financial year 1996/97, the companies of the Group employed 62,601 people worldwide, approximately 5% less than in the previous year.

Workforce reduced by
changing Group structure

The reduction in the number of employees is largely due to the removal of the Metaleurop Group from the consolidation. About 3,350 employees, mostly in Germany and France, no longer number among the workforce. As a result of expansion in the building engineering division, approximately 1,450 new employees have been added to the workforce, mainly through acquisition of the French company Chaffoteaux et Maury S.A. Further changes result from continuation of the necessary cost management measures, particularly in the plant engineering division and mining-related activities.

80% of the jobs
in Germany

About 80% of the jobs were in German companies of the Group. Nonetheless, the personnel within Germany, with 49,563 employees, was about 7% lower than last year. The share of foreign workers remained constant at 9%, whereby the largest group, namely 50%, are Turkish, while 17% are from European Union countries.

Foreign companies in the Group employed 13,038 workers, about 3% more than last year. As before, employment was concentrated in the European Union, almost 50%, and North America, 17%.

Personnel
by division
in (%)

	1994/95	1995/96	1996/97	
Steel production	23	21	17	
Energy and commodities	18	16	16	
Trading and logistics	15	15	16	
Plant engineering and shipbuilding	26	26	26	
Building engineering and components	15	19	23	
Other companies	3	3	2	
	100	100	100	

Personnel costs
slightly up

Personnel costs were up by about 2% to DM5,534 million. Expenditure for wages and salaries increased by about 1%, to DM4,335 million. Contributions to social security and payments for pensions and assistance rose disproportionally to DM1,199 million and were 4% higher than last year. Altogether about 87% of the value added of the Preussag Group was used to cover personnel costs.

More than 30,000 former employees or their dependants received pensions and benefits from Group companies. In addition, approximately 40,000 employees have vested pension rights. This expenditure totalled DM277 million.

Personnel development aims
at international business

The progressive internationalisation of business makes ever new demands on personnel development as well as the initial and further training of our employees. The potential analysis system is an integral part of the personnel development programme, which is relevant for the entire Group. This system is aimed at filling management positions from the ranks. Thinking and acting internationally as well as understanding the behaviour of business partners and fellow-workers from other cultures are trained and encouraged in workshops. Periods of work abroad help to prepare for future assignments and increase language skills.

The Group's programme of further education and training is mainly directed at imparting and updating knowledge and skills. The 250 seminars and special courses offered created great interest and were attended by more than 3,000 employees.

---

[34]"The Economic Scene in Germany in Spring 1998," *Deutsche Bundesbank Monthly Report,* June 1998.

EXHIBIT 8–4   (concluded)

Additional training places created	Despite the reduced workforce, the German companies have further increased their number of training places. Trainees were recruited to 700 new jobs, an increase of 15% again. Over 1,700 young people are thus engaged in professional training in Preussag companies, an increase of 8% over last year. Besides the traditional areas of steel production, plant engineering and shipbuilding, training programmes are now also concentrated in the areas of trading and logistics and building engineering. The value of this strategy to ensure the next generation of employees is evidenced by over 500 successful examinations, often with very good results. Nearly all the young people trained have decided to remain in the Group's employment.
High participation in company suggestion scheme	Employees again proposed many improvements this year. About 3,900 proposals for improvements in production processes and for increased safety on the job demonstrated the considerable interest of the employees in their companies. Prizes worth DM1.2 million were awarded. The economic value of these improvement proposals has benefited both company and employees.
Health and safety programmes successful	Work in the area of safety and health protection has been given additional impetus by the amended employment protection law. For the Group, this meant the analysis and documentation of working conditions, in order to establish protective measures which conform to the new law. Meanwhile the safety standards described in the guiding principles of the Group continued to be upheld. The success of these can be seen in the number of accidents, which was clearly reduced again; accidents at work as well as on the way to and from work were at their lowest ever. The programme for health promotion with its goal to improve the situation at the work place and reduce absenteeism continues with the participation of the employees.
Preussag medical insurance scheme	Preussag's medical insurance scheme covered 47,000 members, an increase of about 4,200. A significant aspect here has been the institution of Preussag BKK Publik, extending participation in the medical health scheme to companies within the Group. Contributions—as required by law—were lowered by 0.4 percent points on 1st January, 1997. With contributions at 11% or 12%, according to region, Preussag BKK offers its companies and their employees a high standard of medical protection on favourable terms.
Acknowledgement	Preussag ended the financial year 1996/97 successfully. This is in large part due to the high level of commitment and performance of all our employees and management. For this, we wish to express our sincere thanks. We would also like to thank the elected employee representatives at the companies and also at Group level for their objective and conscientious cooperation.

Perhaps the most troublesome aspect of Germany's decade of unification involves labor. At mid-1998 total German unemployment stood at 11.2 percent while in the five former East German states, unemployment stood at 18.7 percent.[34] Predictions for the next several years forecast that these rates will increase. Moreover, the wage differentials between the two former Germanies are substantial. Actual earnings east of the former border are only about 70–75 percent of those west of the border.[35] Clearly, those in the former East Germany do not want such a second-class position and without large increases, they are likely to head west. But if wages go up too fast in the east, companies will lose a major incentive for investing there. Such is but one dilemma springing from unification.

Corporate Germany.   Germany's largest public corporations have recently entered the triple throes of restructuring operations, realigning foci, and redeploying investments. As of the start of 1999, they continue to do so, and there is every indication that it will be an ongoing issue for several more years. In some ways, Daimler-Benz's early 1990s divestures, New York Stock Exchange listing, and its 1998 merger with Chrysler have been the catalyst for much of what has followed in Germany. The verdict is still out as to whether corporate Germany's push to change has or will pay off. In two recent studies of national corporate competitiveness, Germany has actually lost ground or remains far behind the leaders.[36]

---

[35]F. Stüdemann, "Even a Downturn Can Have an Upside," *Financial Times,* October 13, 1998, p. IV.

[36]See G. Steinmetz, "Germans Falter in Struggle to Regain Competitive Edge," *The Wall Street Journal,* June 12, 1997, p. A14, and T. Barber, "Now Schröder and Germany Must Face the 1990s Productivity Test," *Financial Times,* October 1, 1998, p. 3.

Simply stated, international competition for customers and capital are the forces driving change. In response, and of late: Revolutionary (for Germany) flexible worker arrangements have been brokered with powerful unions; heretofore unheard-of hostile takeovers have surfaced; and previously forbidden corporate stock-option and stock-buyback plans have been cautiously tried by some.[37] One significant net result of the pressures on, and trends in, corporate Germany has been the strengthening and broadening of the shareholder value and corporate governance concepts.[38] Executives at some of the premiere German companies have been quoted as saying, "We need the international capital markets and, therefore, we inevitably need to meet international [financial reporting] standards."[39] "Satisfying the shareholders is the best way to make sure that other stakeholders are served as well."[40] "One could almost say we are a nonnational company [now]."[41] "Less social consensus, although it is important, and more value-added . . . this is the trend change in Germany."[42]

Such indications of profound fundamental changes in corporate Germany will necessitate a significant improvement in the informativeness of corporate financial reporting in Germany. In a recent study of the extent and nature of corporate financial reporting informativeness in 10 industrial nations, Germany was ranked last (the United States was ranked third behind Britain and France).[43] Indeed, in the same vein another study found that only 10 percent of Germany's approximately 600,000 *Mittelstand* (medium-sized or small) companies were publishing their financial accounts in contrast to 80 percent in the U.K. and France and 90 percent in Denmark.[44] In essence, 90 percent of Germany's *Mittelstand* were in violation of EU directives. With significant and new pressures for change butting against significant and entrenched tendencies in thinking and behaving, it remains to be seen what will emerge. Who would have predicted that one day the Germans would agree to replacing their beloved D-mark with a European currency? They have. Who would have predicted that one day Deutshe Telekom, Germany's state-owned telecommunications company until the mid-1990s, would be listed on the New York Stock Exchange and filing U.S. GAAP financial statements? They are. Who can predict what further changes will occur in regard to a shareholder-value orientation and in German corporate governance norms? We cannot.[45]

Selected Financial Reporting Practices

Succinctly stated, "the objectives of the German accounting system are to preserve equity, protect creditors, and facilitate the computation of taxable income."[46] In the pur-

---

[37]See G. Bowley, "Germany's New Shop Window," *Financial Times,* November 20, 1998, p. 15, and "Restructuring Corporate Germany," *The Economist,* November 21, 1998, pp. 63–64.

[38]See J. Templeman, C. Power, and W. Glasgall, "Revolution at Daimler," *Business Week,* February 5, 1998, pp. 56–57, and A. Fisher, "Companies Put Out the Welcome Mat," *Financial Times,* January 23, 1998, p. II.

[39]R. Atkins, "Jurassic Germany," *Financial Times,* January 14, 1998, p. 13.

[40]G. Steinmetz, "Satisfying Shareholders is a Hot New Concept at Some German Firms," *The Wall Street Journal,* March 6, 1996, p. A1.

[41]G. Steinmetz and M. Marshall, "How a Chemicals Giant Goes About Becoming a Lot Less German," *The Wall Street Journal,* February 18, 1997, p. A1.

[42]R. Atkins, "Jurassic Germany."

[43]M. Sesit, "Big Investors Bemoan Lack of Data on Overseas Firms," *The Wall Street Journal,* February 23, 1996, p. C1.

[44]J. Kelly, "Germany's Smaller Groups Told to Open Up Accounts," *Financial Times,* September 30, 1998, p. 17.

[45]See V. Hommel, "Regulating the Market for Corporate Control: Lessons from Germany," *International Journal of Business,* 3, no. 1 (1998), pp. 101–21 for a superb comparison of German and U.S. corporate governance norms.

[46]T. S. Harris, M. Lang, and H. P. Möller, "The Value Relevance of German Accounting Measures: An Empirical Analysis," *Journal of Accounting Research,* Autumn 1994, p. 190.

suit of these objectives, the dominant principle imbedded in German accounting practices is that of **prudence** (*Vorsichtsprinzip*) wherein assets (liabilities) may be recorded at values less (higher) than the amounts that would be acceptable under U.S. GAAP.[47] Even with the 1986 Accounting Directives Law, which integrated the EU's Fourth, Seventh, and Eighth Directives into German legislation and, thus, the EU notion of true and fair, it has been "difficult to change decades of established practice merely by changing the law."[48] A second and closely related principle is that of congruence (*Massgeblichkeitsprinzp*) wherein the treatment of transactions in the tax statements shall be consistent with that in the commercial statements.[49] In essence, with a few exceptions, what is reported to shareholders is what is reported to Germany's taxation authorities. Exhibit 8–5 presents a list of accounting principles taken from the Preussag Group's annual report and reflects the influence of tax-driven accounting practices common to many German corporations.

Perhaps the most noted German practice in this regard is the use of *hidden reserves* (see subsequent discussion) to smooth earnings via the buildup of liabilities and the decrease of earnings in good years and vice versa in so-called bad years. Such a practice has been linked to several contextual factors.[50] First, German law prohibits firms from retaining more than half of their annual earnings, thus, a sizable percent of earnings are potentially available for dividend payout. To minimize such outflows, companies have an incentive to minimize reported earnings in "good" years and to provide some stable level of dividends through "bad" years. Second, because of this dividend situation and given the banks' dominant role in financing and governing German companies, bankers' interests are protected by companies preserving cash (i.e., minimizing total dividend payouts) and, thus, preserving a strong debt-service capability. Third, because of the close link between tax and financial accounting, German management has an incentive to minimize reported financial earnings. Fourth, as previously noted, labor unions are a powerful force in the German economy. Many believe that smoothing reported earnings serves to mitigate labor's demand for ever-increasing wages. Last, the devout adherence to the prudence (i.e., conservatism) principle is consistent with the German psyche that is relatively high on uncertainty avoidance.

If Germany seeks to improve its ability to draw on the world's financial resources, it must heed the call for greater transparency (i.e., fuller disclosures) in its companies' financial statements. As of 1999, only three German companies, Daimler-Benz, Deutsche Telekom, and Veba AG, met the U.S. financial reporting requirements that allowed them to achieve NYSE listing. Thus, the world's most extensive equity market is virtually closed to German companies, in part, because of financial reporting practices that give "management the freedom to report what they want."[51] Since Daimler-Benz's 1993 financial reporting change of heart and NYSE listing, and Veba's in 1996, "there has hardly been a rush [by other German companies] to follow."[52]

[47]T. S. Doupnik, "Recent Innovations in German Accounting Practice through the Integration of EC Directives," *Advances in International Accounting* 5 (1992), pp. 75–103.

[48]C. L. Corbridge, W. Austin, and D. J. Lemak, "Germany's Accrual Accounting Practices," *Management Accounting,* August 1993, p. 46.

[49]A. Haller, "The Relationship of Financial and Tax Accounting in Germany: A Major Reason for Accounting Disharmony in Europe," *The International Journal of Accounting,* 27 (1992), pp. 310–323.

[50]See Harris et al., "The Value Relevance of German Accounting Measures," and Doupnik, "Recent Innovations in German Accounting Practice through the Integration of EC Directives."

[51]"Company News," *Financial Times,* November 22, 1993, p. 17.

[52]"More Capital, Less Privacy," *Financial Times,* March 29, 1995, p. 13.

EXHIBIT 8–5

Preussag Group Accounting Principles Disclosures

Notes on the Consolidated Financial Statements of the Preussag Group

The Consolidated Financial Statements of the Preussag Group and the Financial Statements of Preussag AG were prepared in accordance with the provisions of the Commercial Code, with due consideration of the supplementary regulations of the Companies' Act. In the balance sheets and the profit and loss statements of the Preussag Group and of Preussag AG, individual items have been grouped together for clarity of presentation; these items are referred to separately in these notes, together with the necessary explanations. The notes relating to the Consolidated Financial Statements and to the Financial Statements of Preussag AG are presented jointly.

The financial year of Preussag AG and of the Group runs from 1st October in any one year to 30th September of the following year.

Accounting and Valuation Methods

The same accounting and valuation methods as stipulated by Preussag AG were retained. Use was made of tax-related valuation options as in previous years.

Intangible and tangible assets were valued at cost of acquisition or manufacture, less scheduled depreciation. Manufacturing costs were determined on the basis of German tax regulations.

Depreciation was largely calculated on the basis of the following economic lives: 25–50 years for buildings; 5–20 years for plant and machinery including ships and railway cars; 3–10 years for other assets as well as for plant and office equipment.

Tangible fixed assets with a limited useful economic life were depreciated on the declining balance method, applying maximum rates allowable for tax purposes. Straight-line depreciation was then applied when the calculated amount based on this method exceeded that obtained by using the declining balance method. If use was made of tax-related extraordinary depreciation, assets were depreciated on the straight-line method. In accordance with tax simplification regulations, additions in the first half of the financial year were depreciated at the full rate for the year, whereas additions during the second half of the year were depreciated at half the annual rate. Low-value assets were written off in full in the year of acquisition.

For buildings and other real estate, depreciation was calculated either pro rata temporis on a straight-line basis, or, where permitted by tax regulations, on a declining balance basis.

If, at the financial year-end, the fixed asset was given a lower value, which was expected to be permanent, then the difference was offset by way of extraordinary depreciation expenses.

Use was made of tax-related options of depreciation methods and possibilities for transferring book profits. The resulting differences in relation to scheduled depreciation were included in the Financial Statements of Preussag AG under special non-taxed items. In the Consolidated Financial Statements, such special non-taxed items were dissolved and added to the revenue reserves while allowing for deferred taxation.

Investment allowances and subsidies received were absorbed without affecting results.

Fixed values have been established for reserve parts, factory equipment and rail installations. These accounted for 20–40% of the cost of acquisition or manufacture.

Successful crude oil and natural gas wells were generally depreciated on a declining balance basis, in accordance with the provisions of the State Ordinance (letter from the Federal Ministry for Finance dated 20th May 1980), whereas older wells were depreciated at reducing rates in line with the so-called Hanover Guidelines. Dry holes were written off in full.

Shares in Group companies and participation as well as other investments were valued at the cost of acquisition, or at the lower appropriate value. Non-interest or low-interest loans were discounted to their present values.

Inventories were valued on the basis of cost of acquisition or manufacturing costs, or at any lower appropriate value. Similar inventories were generally dealt with on the basis of the valuation simplification method (LIFO method).

Unfinished and finished goods and work in progress were valued on the basis of manufacturing costs, while observing the principle of the lower of cost or market value. They comprise direct material and production costs as well as proportions of indirect costs and depreciation as required by German tax laws and appropriate indirect cost surcharges for companies abroad. Coal stocks have been shown at the lower of production costs or the values determined in accordance with the guidelines of the Ruhr Mining Enterprises' Association. Where necessary, additional devaluation was applied. As far as risks in stock value were foreseeable, appropriate devaluations have been made. Advance payments received were fully offset against inventories.

In the case of receivables and other current assets, all identifiable individual risks and the general credit risk were taken into consideration by means of appropriate provisions.

Securities were shown at the rate of acquisition or the market rate as of the financial year-end, if lower.

Provisions for pensions, which also included coal-supply rights, early retirement and bridging payment rights, were itemized at the allowable value as per Section 6a of the Income Tax Law, calculated on actuarial principles based on an interest rate of 6%. In the case of personnel of foreign companies, the guidelines provided by national legislation have been observed.

Tax provisions and other provisions were valued in accordance with sound business principles.

Liabilities were shown at the repayable amount.

Consolidation

German companies with subsidiaries must prepare and publish audited financial statements if they meet two of the following three size criteria: have consolidated balance sheet total assets exceeding DM125 million (about $74.4 million), consolidated annual revenues exceeding DM250 million ($148.8 million), and more than 5,000 employees. If a German parent company is itself a subsidiary of another non-German, EU company that consolidates the German company according to EU directives, the German Commercial Code exempts the German parent from preparing consolidated financial statements. In preparing consolidated financial statements, both the purchase and pooling-of-interests methods are permitted; all domestic and foreign subsidiaries must be consolidated except if (1) a subsidiary is insignificant in relation to the group's net worth, total assets, and earnings; (2) the inclusion of the results of the subsidiary would be detrimental to a true and fair presentation of the group's results; or (3) the subsidiary is being held for sale. (Recall that under the 1998 Law on the Facilitation of Capital Acquisition, listed companies may prepare their consolidated statements according to U.S. GAAP, IASC GAAP, or the German Commercial Code.) The equity method of accounting for interests of 20 percent or more in affiliates is also practiced.

Valuation

German accounting is fundamentally committed to a highly conservative application of historical cost as the most appropriate basis for valuation. (As discussed, both cultural bias and tax policy support this orientation.) All prospective losses are to be recognized via accruals and write-downs, but prospective gains and appreciation of assets may not be recorded until realized. Historical cost for fixed assets is the cost of acquisition; thus, extraordinary write-downs (appropriate if an impairment in value is expected to be permanent) may be reversed in future periods if an asset recovers its original value. However, an asset may never be written up above historical cost or, in the case of depreciable assets, not above net book value as though "regular" depreciation had continued to be charged. Historical cost for current assets operates somewhat differently. Because the historical cost of a current asset is defined as its book value at the beginning of a period, write-downs are rarely reversed until the asset is disposed of. German companies are required to detail in their annual reports the increases and decreases to each of their long-term assets.

Inventories

Inventories are carried at the lower of cost or net realizable value. Manufacturing overhead costs may be treated as product costs or period costs. Cost must be allocated directly (i.e., specific identification), if possible; otherwise, the appropriate method is usually the moving weighted average. FIFO is acceptable only if the corresponding physical flow can be demonstrated, and LIFO has been accepted only since 1990.

Goodwill

The purchase price paid for the assets of a business must be allocated among the individual assets acquired on the basis of their fair market values. Any excess is considered goodwill, which generally is amortized over four years on a straight-line basis.[53] A longer period may be used if appropriate under the circumstances. Goodwill arising from consolidation may be, and often is, charged directly against retained earnings. Negative goodwill is reported on the consolidated balance sheet as the difference arising on capital consolidation, usually under the classification heading deferred income; it may be amortized to current income only under certain conditions.

---

[53]For tax purposes, the amortization period for goodwill is fixed at 15 years.

Research and Development

Research and development costs are expensed as incurred unless they are for a specific product and can be considered the beginning phase of that product's manufacturing process. In essence, few if any internally generated intangibles may be capitalized to the balance sheet. Patents that are purchased are capitalized and amortized over their useful lives on a straight-line basis. Organization costs may not be capitalized.

Pensions and Postretirement Benefits

Beginning January 1, 1987, German companies were required to accrue all pension and postretirement benefits earned after that date. No accrual was required for benefits earned prior to 1987, although most German companies did so to take advantage of existing tax benefits.

In Germany, most pension plans are not funded via a third-party trustee as in the United States; the plans are in-house and the plan assets are essentially all the company's balance sheet assets. Because of this fact, the typical German company pension obligation reflected on its balance sheet is an amount similar to the accumulated benefit obligation. This is in contrast to a U.S. company that would report the liability as the difference between the accumulated benefit obligation and the fair market value of the plan assets held by the trustee.

Contingencies

Company law permits German companies to provide for estimated *future* expenses or losses so long as they are possible (as opposed to the more stringent notion of probable) and reasonable. Thus, under the principle of prudence, German companies may, for example, record accruals that, over time, equalize the annual expenses for (1) anticipated major repairs that have not, as of year-end, been undertaken; (2) research and development projects not yet started; and (3) advertising and promotional campaigns not yet executed.[54] (See, for example, Exhibit 8–6, containing the provisions disclosures for The Hoechst Group.) Until the 1986 Accounting Directives Law, German law permitted an extreme application of the concept of prudence in which such liability reserves could be liberally used to stabilize earnings.[55] Although this activity was supposed to be attenuated beginning in 1986, traditional practice is often difficult to curtail, and as recently as 1993 (see Exercises 8.4 and 8.9), major German companies have publicly acknowledged the continued use of hidden reserves. Likewise, in 1996, Deutsche Bank AG disclosed that it had amassed nearly 21 billion marks ($12.5 billion) in hidden reserves.[56]

Shareholder Capital and Reserves

Shareholder equity generally comprises minority interests, share capital, and reserve accounts, which may be either capital or revenue reserves. Both ordinary and preferred shares may be issued, and details as to voting rights (particularly when multiple voting rights are involved) must be disclosed, along with a stock's nominal or par value. Capital reserves include amounts received for the issue of shares in excess of their nominal (or par) value, payments by shareholders with respect to subscribed shares, and amounts paid

---

[54]See Corbridge et al., "Germany's Accrual Accounting Practices."

[55]These reserves can be created by underreporting revenues and cash inflows or by overstating expenses and cash outflows. During periods of reduced profitability, such reserves can be reversed as a mechanism to increase (i.e., smooth) reported earnings. The use of such reserves is often referred to as the "creation of financial slack" and "hidden reserves."

[56]See S. Ascarelli, "Deutsche Bank Says Net Jumped 24% in 1995, Discloses Big Hidden Reserves," *The Wall Street Journal,* March 29, 1996, p. A8.

EXHIBIT 8–6

THE HOECHST GROUP
Provisions Disclosures

Panel A. Consolidated Balance Sheets

Assets	1997 DM million	1996 DM million
Intangible assets	15,200	10,868
Property, plant and equipment	15,861	16,975
Investments	7,562	3,867
Non-current assets	**38,623**	**31,710**
Inventories	6,739	7,863
Accounts receivable, trade	8,428	9,470
Other receivables and other assets	6,141	5,248
Receivables and other assets	14,569	14,718
Marketable securities	88	168
Cash and cash equivalents	547	382
Total liquid assets	635	550
Prepaid items	339	284
Current assets	**22,282**	**23,415**
Total assets	**60,905**	**55,125**
Stockholders' equity and liabilities		
Subscribed capital of Hoechst AG (587,953,690 shares outstanding in 1997 and 1996; nominal value DM5)	2,940	2,940
Additional paid-in capital	3,898	3,898
Hoechst AG reserve for own shares[1]	•	•
Retained earnings	8,063	6,600
Net income	1,343	2,114
Currency translation adjustments	−232	−1,044
Equity of Hoechst AG stockholders	**16,012**	**14,508**
Minority interests	3,097	3,574
Stockholders' equity	**19,109**	**18,082**
Provisions for pensions and similar obligations	6,910	6,842
Other provisions	9,476	9,435
Provisions	**16,386**	**16,277**
Corporate debt	16,615	11,819
Accounts payable, trade	4,083	4,509
Miscellaneous liabilities	4,610	4,338
Other liabilities	**25,308**	**20,666**
Deferred income	**102**	**100**
Total stockholders' equity and liabilities	**60,905**	**55,125**

[1]Amount below DM 0.5 million

EXHIBIT 8–6 (concluded)

Panel B. Footnote: Other Provisions

	Dec. 31, 1997	Dec. 31, 1996[1]
Taxes		
Current taxes	1,319	1,231
Deferred taxes	1,030	879
Restructuring	1,109	1,406
Damage and product liability claims	553	774
Environmental protection	814	749
Self insurance loss provisions	870	735
Employee-related commitments	666	718
Discounts, bonuses, sales commissions	406	437
Anniversary allowances	171	236
Purchase and sales contracts	38	65
Forward exchange contracts	5	13
Other	2,495	2,192
	9,476	9,435
Current portion	(5,679)	(5,658)

[1]Adjusted to improve comparability, see Note 4.

Provisions for taxes include amounts accrued for regular tax audits in Germany and abroad and for tax risks in connection with the realignment of the Group.

for conversion rights on debentures. Revenue reserves, on the other hand, are prescribed by the Commercial Code and include the following:

- Reserves required by a company's articles of incorporation (e.g., appropriations of earnings for various purposes—company officers can transfer up to 50 percent of annual net profit to reserves without shareholder approval).
- Reserve for treasury stock (equivalent to the value of treasury stock held).[57]
- Legal reserve (i.e., 5 percent of each year's profits must be allocated to this reserve until the reserve reaches 10 percent of the par value of share capital, net of any loss carryforwards).

Dividends may be distributed from retained earnings and the excess of revenue reserves over any capitalized expenses.

Special Items with an Equity Component

This potentially confusing account represents income that has not yet been subject to income taxes. It usually represents the excess (or "extraordinary") depreciation, permitted by German tax law, used to currently shelter otherwise taxable income. As the name implies, the account reflects both an equity component (i.e., income) and a debt component (i.e., the future taxes owing on the sheltered income.)

Exhibit 8–7 presents a summarized comparison of German and U.S. accounting and financial reporting standards.

---

[57]Treasury stock is usually accounted for as an asset under the account heading Temporary Investments.

EXHIBIT 8–7

Comparison of German and U.S. Accounting and Reporting Standards

Item	Germany	United States
Asset valuation	Historical cost, applied conservatively (i.e., downward revaluation)	Historical cost, with selected revaluation (principally downward)
Inventory valuation	Principally specific identification or moving weighted average method; FIFO and LIFO permitted, although rarely used	Principally LIFO (because of tax considerations); also FIFO and average cost methods
Inventory: year-end	Lower of cost or replacement cost	Lower of cost or replacement cost
Depreciation	Straight line, accelerated methods, and production based methods permitted; excess (or extraordinary) depreciation based on tax code permitted and frequently used	Principally straight line, with accelerated methods permitted
Goodwill	Goodwill either capitalized and amortized over (preferably) 4 years (15 years for tax purposes), or charged directly to reserves; negative goodwill reported as "difference arising on capital consolidation" on balance sheet and may be taken to income under certain conditions	Capitalized to balance sheet, with amortization (principally straight line) over a maximum of 40 years; negative goodwill not permitted
Research and development costs	Principally expensed as incurred	Research costs expensed currently; development costs expensed currently except in certain industries (i.e., software, oil and gas)
Capitalized interest costs	Capitalization permitted but not required	Capitalization required for self-constructed assets
Intercorporate investments: Marketable securities (current asset-trading)	Lower-of-cost-or-market value	Mark to market (on an individual security basis), with unrealized gains and losses taken to income
Long-term-investments: 0–20% ownership (available for sale)	Lower-of-cost-or-market value	Mark to market (on an individual security basis), with unrealized gains and losses reported on balance sheet (i.e., owners' equity)
20–50% ownership	Lower-of-cost-or-market value; equity method principally used when a company, included in the consolidated statements of a group, has a significant shareholding in another unconsolidated company.	Equity method
51–100% ownership	Consolidated except when controlled subsidiary is held for resale, when value is immaterial relative to the group, or when consolidation would be detrimental to a true and fair view of the group; both pooling and purchase accounting permitted	Consolidated, using pooling (until 2001) or purchase accounting
Debt valuation	Principally face or settlement value, although present value permitted	Long-term debt (except deferred income taxes) valued at present value; all other debt valued at face or settlement value
Leases	Financing leases capitalized to the balance sheet; significant operating lease commitments disclosed in footnotes	Capital leases reflected in balance sheet; operating leases disclosed in footnotes
Deferred income taxes	Largely unnecessary due to close conformity of book and taxable income; when present, often not disclosed	Computed under liability method
Pension liabilities	Reflected on balance sheet and likely to be an amount equal to the accumulated benefit obligation	Reflected on balance sheet and equal to the accumulated benefit obligation less the fair market value of the plan assets
Discretionary reserves	General-purpose reserves permitted	Restricted to identifiable operational losses
Statement of cash flows	Required (after 1998)	Required

Analytical Considerations

As noted, German financial reporting has an observable conservative bias that, not surprisingly, tends to understate the value of a firm's net assets and often its net earnings as well. The reasons for this, which are both cultural (historical) and institutional, include the following:

- *Legal requirements.* German accounting adheres strictly to company law, which results in an emphasis on legal form rather than economic substance.
- *Book-tax conformity.* Most deductions taken for tax purposes must also be recognized for accounting book purposes. As a consequence, excess depreciation claimed for tax purposes is also reflected in the accounting statements.
- *Creditor orientation.* German financial reporting tends to be principally oriented to creditor protection, rather than to investor returns.[58] As a consequence, greater attention is directed to provisions for asset write-downs and contingencies than would be found in, say, the United States or Great Britain.

The principal accounting factors causing the relative understatement of net worth and earnings of German companies include the following:

- *Excess depreciation of fixed assets.* German tax law permits accelerated depreciation at up to three times the straight-line rate; thus, German companies write off their fixed assets at a much faster rate than do U.S. companies. In addition, special tax allowances provided for investments in environmental protection equipment, R&D facilities, and equipment for R&D facilities effectively increase the tax basis, and thus, depreciation write-offs of these investments.
- *Contingency reserves.* Company law permits German companies to provide for estimated future expenses (or losses) so long as they are *possible* and *reasonable*. Under U.S. GAAP, the criteria to establish contingency reserves (i.e., a loss must be both *probable* and *measurable*) are more stringent. Thus, contingency reserves represent the primary means by which German companies smooth earnings. When general contingency reserves are created, they typically appear under the account rubric Other Provisions (see Exhibit 8–6), and, when reserves created in prior years are no longer considered necessary, they are reported under Other Income on the income statement. The use of hidden or off-balance-sheet reserves adds further conversatism to reported results.
- *Accounting for long-term contracts.* The predominant treatment of long-term contracts in Germany is the completed-contract method, by which substantially all profits are deferred until the provisions of a contract are essentially complete. In the United States, the prevailing accounting practice is the percentage-of-completion method. The completed-contract method tends to result in a lower reported earnings figure in all years except the year of contract completion. The method also causes substantial volatility in earnings (which may be controlled in German companies through the creation of general contingency reserves and hidden reserves).
- *Goodwill write-off.* Prior to 1987, the prevalent treatment of goodwill in Germany was the charge-to-equity method. Currently, prevalent practice is to capitalize

---

[58]Additional evidence of a noninvestor orientation is the absence of a requirement for German companies to report earnings per share data.

Exhibit 8–8
German versus U.S. GAAP: A Comparison of the Financial Statement Effects

Item	Financial Statement Effect	Financial Ratio Effect
Excess depreciation	Fixed assets, total assets, and shareholders' equity understated	ROS understated*
		Leverage overstated
	Depreciation expense overstated; net income understated	Total and noncurrent asset turnover overstated
Contingency reserves	Liabilities overstated; shareholders' equity understated	ROA and ROS understated*
		Leverage overstated
	Net income understated	
Completed-contract accounting	Total assets, shareholders' equity, and net income understated	ROS understated*
		Leverage overstated
Goodwill write-off	Total assets, shareholders' equity, and net income understated	ROS understated*
		Leverage overstated

*Since both net income and shareholders' equity are understated, the effect of these German accounting treatments on return on equity cannot be systematically predicted.

goodwill to the balance sheet and amortize it against earnings over a 4- to 5-year period (to a maximum of 20 years). In the United States, the capitalization of goodwill is required, and amortization is normally over 40 years.

The relative financial statement effects in general, and on selected financial ratios in particular, of these accounting differences are summarized in Exhibit 8–8. A related issue is the extent to which the capital markets of Germany and the United States compensate for these accounting differences when pricing equity securities. Recent market data reveal the average price-earnings ratio of U.S. stocks to be 28; for German stocks it is 21. These P-E averages reflect, in part, the presence of a "bull" market in the United States and a "bear" market in Germany. That fact aside, however, the relative equality of the two P-E averages suggests that German securities may be somewhat *underpriced* as compared to U.S. securities. In the absence of differences in investor expectations regarding the strength of the German and U.S. economies, we normally expect the average P-E ratio for Germany to be substantially higher than that for the United States as a consequence of conservative German accounting practices.

Summary

Mr. Gerhard Schröder was elected German chancellor on September 27, 1998. It was the first time in Germany's post–World War II history that a sitting chancellor (Helmut Kohl) was defeated. In addition, Mr. Schröder is the first German chancellor not to have lived through the experiences leading up to and during World War II. He takes office just as the D-mark begins to be phased out in favor of the new euro. Moreover, Mr. Schröder's new coalition government, between the left-leaning Social Democrats and the Free Democratic Party (the Greens) marks the first time in 16 years that the right-leaning Christian Democrats have not been in power. To top it all off, the seat of government will move from Bonn to Berlin. All of this change has created some excitement and uncertainty for Germany's leaders and people. Remember, this change is occurring in a country that in 1997 hotly debated whether retail shop owners should be required to extend their weekday hours from 6:00 P.M. to 8:00 P.M. and their Saturday hours into the afternoon—a debate and decision that one parliamentary leader declared was the "most stressful" of the then current parliament.[59]

The start of the new millennium will be a time of great change and adaptation in just about all sectors—industrial, economic, political, financial, and eurocentric. Not all of the necessary changes will be voluntarily imposed or widely embraced. The task is daunting. As one German observer recently noted:

> Germany's structural problems are legion. A rigid labour market, a generous but costly social welfare net, . . . a complex and inequitable income tax system, excessive red tape and an underdeveloped service sector, coupled with the costs of unification, have created a nation that finds it difficult to adapt quickly to change.[60]

A mere month after Mr. Schröder's election victory, newspapers were already reporting that: (1) his pledge to not change everything he inherited from Mr. Kohl is "far out of line with what he is now about to deliver," and (2) his pledge that everything he would propose would contribute to reducing unemployment "already appears Utopian."[61] Europe needs a strong, stable Germany. Germans want a strong, stable Germany. Change can be destablizing. It will be interesting to follow the fortunes and evolution of Germany during the next decade.

Suggested Readings

Alexander, D., and S. Archer. *The European Accounting Guide.* London: Academic Press, 1991.

Carson, I. "Accounting for Europe's Differences." *International Management,* June 1991, pp. 52–55.

Corbridge, C. L., W. W. Austin, and D. J. Lemak. "Germany's Accrual Accounting Practices." *Management Accounting,* August 1993, pp. 45–47.

Doupnik, T. S. "Recent Innovations in German Accounting Practices through the Integration of EC Directives," *Advances in International Accounting* 5 (1992), pp. 75–103.

Glaum, M., and U. Mandler. "German Managers' Attitudes Towards Anglo-American Accounting: Results from an Empirical Study on Global Accounting Harmonization." *The International Journal of Accounting* 32, no. 4 (1997), pp. 463–85.

Haller, A. "The Relationship of Financial and Tax Accounting in Germany: A Major Reason for Accounting Disharmony in Europe." *The International Journal of Accounting* 27, no. 4, 1992, pp. 310–23.

Harris, T. S., M. Lang, and H. P. Möller. "The Value Relevance of German Accounting Measures: An Empirical Analysis." *Journal of Accounting Research,* Autumn 1994, pp. 187–209.

Hommel, U. "Regulating the Market for Corporate Control: Lessons from Germany." *International Journal of Business* 3, no. 1 (1998), pp. 101–21.

---

[59]R. Atkins, "Longer Hours Leave Consumers Cold," *Financial Times,* November 2, 1997, p. 2.

[60]P. Norman, "Waigel Triumphs Against the Skeptics," *Financial Times,* March 23, 1998, p. IV.

[61]P. Norman, "Rebuilding the Castle," *Financial Times,* October 21, 1998, p. 15.

Ordelheide, D. "True and Fair View: A European and a German Perspective." *European Accounting Review* 1 (1993), pp. 81–90.

Orsini, L., L. McAllister, and R. Parish. *World Accounting.* New York: Matthew Bender, 1992.

Price Waterhouse. *Doing Business in Germany.* New York: Price Waterhouse, 1996.

Exercises

8.1   Change to a Core Level

In an April 29, 1993, *Financial Times* article (p. 18), "Daimler-Benz Gears Up for a Drive on the Freeway," author David Waller notes:

> German accounting differs from Anglo-American in a number of important areas. It is conditioned by tax laws and the requirement to put the interests of creditors above those of other users of accounts, for example shareholders. Although recent [EU] legislation has meant that group accounts have become more transparent, German accounting is still characterised by conservatism and a want of pertinent detail.
>
> The differences reflect contrasting styles of capitalism: the Anglo-American variety where the capital market plays an important role in the economy, and the Germanic, where there are only 665 listed companies and the stock market represents far smaller percentage of GDP than in the U.S. or the U.K.

As a partial but significant consequence of this fact, is the belief that:

> One of the ways in which the international investment community is ill-served [by German companies] is in the quality of accounting information.
>
> The poor quality of financial information available from many German companies makes it difficult for investors to buy a stock with confidence since valuations cannot be clearly established. . . . Few companies give any indication of divisional profits breakdown at the kind of level which would allow the investor to track margins over time and make comparison across companies.

Mr. Waller continues by noting that "just as important as the impact on reported profits [of an adoption of U.S. accounting practices by German companies] are the longer-term cultural changes which are likely to be induced by greater accounting transparency." He goes on to cite the examples of segmental reporting and a U.S.-style statement of cash flows.

Required:

    (a) How are these indicative of a "cultural change"?

    (b) Identify three other such changes likely to be experienced by German companies as a result of an entry into the U.S. capital markets.

8.2   Accounting for Shareholders' Equity

The following is the shareholders' equity section of the 19x9 balance sheet for Hoechst AG, a large German chemical and pharmaceutical company and parent company of the Hoechst Group.

Required:

Using journal entries, explain the changes in the company's shareholders' equity accounts from 19x8 to 19x9.

Selected Financial Information

Hoechst AG Stockholders' Equity

(DM, Millions)

	Notes	31 Dec. 19x9	31 Dec. 19x8
Subscribed capital	(9)	2,940	2,925
Capital reserves		3,898	3,880
Revenue reserves		3,243	3,226
Unappropriated retained earnings	(11)	412	527
Stockholders' equity	(8)	10,493	10,588

Selected Footnote Information
(8) Movement of equity

Hoechst Group	1.1.19x9	Capital Paid-In	Net Income for the Year	Dividend Payment	Currency Translation	Other Changes	31.12.19x9
Subscribed capital of Hoechst AG	2,925	15					2,940
Capital reserves of Hoechst AG	3,880	18					3,898
Other revenue reserves	5,033		466	527	202	−847	4,327
Equity of Hoechst AG stockholders	**11,838**	**33**	**466**	**527**	**202**	**−847**	**11,165**
Shares of minority interests	2,018	37	290	150	65	115	2,375
	13,856	**70**	**756**	**677**	**267**	**2732**	**13,540**

Hoechst AG		Capital Paid in	Net Income for the Year	Dividend Payment	Transfer of Net Income for the Year	
Subscribed capital	2,925	15				2,940
Capital reserves	3,880	18				3,898
Other revenue reserves	3,226				17	3,243
Unappropriated retained earnings	527	—	429	527	−17	412
	10,558	**33**	**429**	**527**	**—**	**10,493**

Goodwill of DM882 million was offset against the revenue reserves in the Hoechst Group under "other changes." Subsidiaries and associated companies consolidated for the first time have generated a credit difference of DM67 million. Owing to the nature of this item, DM25 million was allocated to the revenue reserves and DM12 million has been shown in the 19x9 income statement. A provision amounting to DM30 million has been set up for probable expenditures in the following years. The Group revenue reserves include the unappropriated retained earnings of Hoechst AG. In Hoechst AG, the increase in capital reserves by DM18 million relates to exercised option rights.

(9) Capital of Hoechst AG

The subscribed capital was increased by DM15 million (294,141 shares) from the unissued capital stock owing to the exercise of option rights .

Breakdown of the subscribed capital:

Number of Shares	Nominal Value in DM	Subscribed Capital in DM
38,215,369	50	1,910,768,450
1,115,000	100	111,500,000
545,000	200	109,000,000
399,000	500	199,500,000
609,000	1,000	609,000,000
		2,939,768,450

(10) Minority interests

This item comprises minority stockholders' interests in the equity of consolidated subsidiaries, in some cases after adjustment to the accounting principles of Hoechst AG.

(11) Unappropriated retained earnings of Hoechst AG

	DM
Net income for 19x9	428,567,583
Profit brought forward from the previous year	—
	428,567,583
Transfer to revenue reserves	17,000,000
Unappropriated retained earnings	411,567,583
Proposed dividend payment	411,567,583
Profit brought forward	—

The Board of Management and Supervisory Board of Hoechst AG transferred DM17 million from the net income for the year to the revenue reserves. Their proposal to the Annual General Meeting will be that DM411567583 from the unappropriated retained earnings to distributed as dividend.

8.3   Special Items with an Equity Component

Under German tax laws, companies in certain industries are permitted (but not required) to depreciate their fixed assets at a rate in excess of normal historical cost-based depreciation. This special (or "extraordinary") depreciation is granted as an investment incentive and enables a company to currently shelter otherwise taxable income.

The following is selected financial information from the 19x9 annual report of Deutsche Lufthansa, the national airline of Germany.

Required:

    (a) Using journal entries, explain the change in Lufthansa's "special items with an equity portion" account in 19x9.

    (b) Based on a statutory tax rate of 45 percent (for undistributed profits), calculate Lufthansa's tax benefit from special depreciation in 19x9 and in aggregate through year-end 19x9.

    (c) What comparable tax incentives exist for U.S. companies?

    (d) For purposes of ratio analysis, how should the special items with an equity portion be classified: debt, equity, or neither?

Selected Financial Information

	(DM, thousands)	
	31 Dec. 19x9	*31 Dec. 19x8*
Net loss	91,614	391,123
Shareholders' equity	2,136,512	2,280,857
Special items with an equity portion	1,555,822	1,473,035
Provisions	4,429,370	4,192,7575
Liabilities	9,288,373	8,923,193
Total equities	17,410,077	16,869,842

Selected Foonote Information

Special items with an equity portion

Group	Dec. 31, 19x9 (DM000)	Dec. 31, 19x8 (DM000)
Value adjustments to fixed assets in accordance with §82f EStDV, §7d EStG, §14 BerlinFG and §2 DDR-IG	1,555,822	1,471,685
Reserves in accordance with §52(5) EStG	—	1,350
	1,555,822	1,473,035

Company		
Value adjustments to fixed assets in accordance with §82f EStDV and §7d EStG	1,343,288	1,378,768
Reserves in accordance with §52 (5) EStG	—	1,227
	1,343,288	1,379,985

The difference between the financial depreciation allowed under commercial law and that permitted by tax regulations appears under special items with an equity portion. §82f EStDV makes it possible to claim depreciation up to 30 percent of the acquisition costs on new aircraft in addition to normal depreciation. §7d EStG allows higher depreciation for measures which benefit environment protection.

    The changes in special items with an equity portion have relieved the result from ordinary activities of the Company by DM37 million (previous year: DM476 million); Group's result has been charged with DM83 million (previous year: relief DM424 million). The tax on income resulting from the release of special items still existing will be spread over the course of the up to twelve-year release period (Group) or up to the ten-year release period (Company).

8.4   Analyzing Hidden Reserves

In December 1993, Volkswagen AG disclosed that the company was likely to report a consolidated loss of DM2.3 billion (or approximately $1.35 billion) for fiscal year 1993. Auto industry analysts in Europe, however, expressed skepticism that the company could achieve that level of earnings without drawing on hidden reserves. Analysts observed that the German auto market had steadily deteriorated in 1993, with VW sales down 24 percent.

In response to analysts' concerns, VW Chairman F. Piech denied that bookkeeping exercises would be used to enhance the company's profitability. Analysts familiar with German company accounting practices remained skeptical, however.

Required:

When analyzing a company's financial data, what information should be considered to help identify whether hidden reserves have been used to enhance reported results?

8.5   Analyzing Inventories

The last-in, first-out (LIFO) inventory valuation method is considered accepted accounting practice in only a few countries including Germany and the United States. According to the annual report of the BASF Group, a diversified German conglomerate, the company used LIFO to value a substantial portion of its inventory and average cost was used to value the remainder.

The following are selected financial data for the BASF Group as of year-end 19x9, as well as the company's inventory footnote as it appeared in the annual report.

Required:

(a) Calculate the current value of the Group's inventory at year-end 19x8 and 19x9. (The LIFO reserve at year-end 19x8 was DM534.3 million.)

(b) Calculate the Group's approximate net income (before tax) for 19x9 assuming that FIFO (instead of LIFO) had been used to value its inventory.

(c) Compare the Group's inventory turnover ratio for 19x9 under LIFO and FIFO.

(d) Comment on the decline in the Group's LIFO reserves from 19x8 to 19x9.

Selected Financial Data

	(DM, Millions)	
	31 Dec. 19x9	*31 Dec. 19x8*
Inventories	6,039.4	6,441.7
Sales (net)	40,568.4	41,932.8
Cost of sales	27,646.8	28,236.8
Net income (before tax)	1,057.6	1,239.4

Selected Footnote Information

Inventories

| | BASF Group | | BASF AG | |
	19x9	*19x8*	*19x9*	*19x8*
Raw materials and supplies			**305.9**	395.6
Work in process, finished goods and merchandise	**5,886.8**	6,293.8	**1,445.1**	1,627.0
Uncompleted contracts	**147.3**	136.7	**136.1**	190.5
Payment on account	**5.3**	11.2	**2.0**	0.3
	6,039.4	6,441.7	**1,889.1**	2,213.4

(DM, Millions)

For inventories valued on the LIFO basis, LIFO reserves approximated DM132 million for the BASF Group, and DM8 million for raw materials and DM72 million for work in process, finished goods and merchandise for BASF Aktiengesellschaft.

8.6   Accounting for Contingency Reserves

Under German GAAP, companies may provide for *future* expenses or losses currently, so long as the expenses or losses are *possible* and *reasonable*. When such events are provided for in the financial statements, they usually appear under the account Other Provisions and, when contingency reserves created in prior years are no longer considered necessary, they are usually reversed to Other Income on the income statement.

The following is selected financial information from the 19x9 annual report of the Hoechst Group, relating to its Other Provisions account.

Required:

(a) Review the company's data relating to Other Provisions. Under U.S. GAAP, how would the various components be accounted for? (*Hint:* See *SFAS No. 5.*)

(b) Based on your analysis in part (a), restate Hoechst's Operating Income for 19x9.

Selected Financial Information

(DM, Millions)

	31 Dec. 19x9	*31 Dec. 19x8*
Total assets	39,112	36,911
Shareholders' equity	13,540	13,856
Other provisions	6,414	5,366
Operating income (before income taxes)	1,476	2,152

Selected Footnote Information
Other provisions

	Hoechst Group		Hoechst AG	
	31.12.x9	*31.12.x8*	*31.12.x9*	*31.12.x8*
Taxes	1052	1096	353	505
Uncertain liabilities	4680	3687	1319	1090
Risks arising from transactions nct yet settled	637	536	244	267
Maintenance	45	47	21	21
	6414	**5366**	**1937**	**1883**

The item "uncertain liabilities" includes many different types of provisions. These relate in particular to expenditure on restructuring measures, holiday remuneration, compulsory social security contributions, environmental protection, anniversary allowances, discounts, bonuses and commissions.

The risks arising from transactions not yet settled are mainly risks arising from purchase and sales contracts, damage claims, plant engineering business and guarantees.

8.7   Statement of Cash Flows

Under German company law, corporations are required to present a balance sheet, an income statement, and relevant footnotes. Prior to 1999, neither a statement of changes in financial position nor a statement of cash flows was required, although occasionally such information was presented as part of the report of the board of management and supervisory board to shareholders.

The following is the statement of changes in financial position of the Hoechst Group as it appeared in the company's 19x8 annual report. Also presented are the company's balance sheet and statement of income.

Required:

Recast the 19x8 statement of changes in financial position of the Hoechst Group into a statement of cash flows. What conclusions can you draw about the company from the cash flow data?

HOECHST GROUP
Statement of Changes in Financial Position

In DM Million				19x8		19x7
Net income for the year	+			**756**		**1,182**
Depreciation and write-offs of fixed assets and investments	+			3,322		3,180
Disposals of fixed assets and investments	+			414		369
Appreciation of fixed assets and investments	−			6		7
Increase in long-term provisions	+			899		699
Cash flow				5,385		5,423
Dividend payments (previous year and advance payments on dividends)	−			677		819
Funds from internal financing				4,708		4,604
Capital expenditure on tangible fixed assets	−	3,597			3,779	
Investments in particpating interests	−	1,572			764	
Other additions to fixed assets and investments	−	222	5,391		315	4858
Change in inventories	−	−237			−7	
Change in receivables	−	1,174	937		115	108
Balance resulting from internal financing				−1,620		−362
Capital increases	+	70			127	
Change in long-term liabilities	+	1,424	1,494		576	703
Balance resulting from long-term financing				−126		341
Change in accounts payable, trade	+	31			−218	
Change in other liabilities	+	−331			−544	
Other changes	+	103	−197		−138	−900
Change in liquid assets				−323		−559

HOECHST GROUP
Statement of Income

		19x8 DM (m)	19x7 DM (m)
Net sales		**46,047**	**45,870**
Cost of sales	−	30,497	29,807
Gross profit from sales		**15,550**	**16,063**
Distribution/selling costs	−	9,969	9,973
Research costs	−	3,039	2,904
General administration costs	−	1,842	1,890
Other operating costs	+	1,004	1,057
Other operating expenses	−	228	201
Operating profit		**1,476**	**2,152**
Income from investments	+	87	396
Net interest	−	449	488
Other financial income	+	113	48
Profit from ordinary activities/profit before taxes on income		**1,227**	**2,108**
Taxes on income	−	471	926
Net income for the year		**756**	**1,182**

HOECHST GROUP
Balance Sheet

Assets	31 Dec. 19x8 DM (m)	31 Dec. 19x7 DM (m)
Intangible fixed assets	323	300
Tangible fixed assets	15,778	14,794
Investments	3,188	2,839
Fixed assets and investments	**19,289**	**17,933**
Inventories	7,081	7,210
Accounts receivable, trade	8,212	7,452
Other receivables and other assets	1,943	1,742
Receivables and other assets	10,155	9,194
Marketable securities	564	1,198
Cheques, cash on hand, in the Bundesbank, the Postbank and in other banks	1,024	713
Liquid assets	1,588	1,911
Prepaid and deferred items	999	663
Current assets	**19,823**	**18,978**
	39,112	**36,911**

Stockholders' equity and liabilities		
Subscribed capital of Hoechst AG	2,940	2,925
Capital reserves of Hoechst AG	3,898	3,880
Revenue reserves	4,327	5,033
Minority interests	2,375	2,018
Stockholders' equity	**13,540**	**13,856**
Provisions for pensions and similar obligations	6,084	5,621
Other provisions	6,414	5,366
Provisions	**12,498**	**10,987**
Corporate debt	7,280	6,765
Accounts payable, trade	2,715	2,637
Miscellaneous liabilities	3,009	2,597
Other liabilities	**13,004**	**11,999**
Deferred income	**701**	**69**
	39,112	**36,911**

8.8 Accounting for Negative Goodwill

Goodwill refers to the difference between the fair value of the identifiable net assets acquired in a business combination and the purchase price paid. On occasion, the purchase price paid for a company (or its net assets) may be less than its (their) current reported value. This might occur if a company is struggling financially or if the securities market perceives the future of the company to be limited or in doubt. Under these conditions, *negative goodwill* may arise as part of a business combination.

Under U.S. GAAP, negative goodwill may not be carried on the consolidated statements of the parent company, and instead is written off against the value of the noncurrent assets acquired in the combination. Under German GAAP, however, negative goodwill may be carried on the liability side of the consolidated balance sheet, usually under the account Difference Arising on Capital Consolidation.

The 19x9 annual report of the BASF Group revealed the following information:

	DM, Millions	
	31 Dec. 19x9	*31 Dec. 19x8*
Goodwill (net)	17.8	88.0

In addition to amortization, the footnotes revealed that "a difference of DM37.6 million on the liabilities side arising from the capital consolidation has been offset under goodwill."

Required:

(a) Prepare a hypothetical journal entry to show how negative goodwill might arise on the consolidated balance sheet of the BASF Group.

(b) Prepare a journal entry to illustrate how the company offset its negative goodwill against its (positive) goodwill. What was the impact of this offset on the company's earnings?

8.9   Accounting for Reserves

On March 25, 1993, *The Wall Street Journal* carried an article with the following headline: "Daimler-Benz Discloses Hidden Reserves of $2.45 Billion, Seeks Big Board Listing." According to the article, Daimler-Benz AG, Germany's largest industrial company, would report $2.45 billion U.S. (or DM4 billion) as an unexpected addition to its 1992 balance sheet. The disclosure apparently came as part of Daimler's efforts to become the first German company to list its shares on the New York Stock Exchange (NYSE).

According to U.S. Securities and Exchange Commission representatives, many foreign companies would like to gain access to the huge U.S. equity and debt markets; however, a major stumbling block for those companies is complying with U.S. reporting and disclosure practices designed to protect investors. In a statement to financial analysts, Gerhard Liener, Daimler's chief financial officer, reported that the company had already adopted some U.S. accounting practices: It had been reporting quarterly data to shareholders for the past two years and its method of reporting cash flows had conformed to U.S. practice since 1992.

With respect to the previously undisclosed reserve of $2.45 billion, financial analysts observed that German companies "were notorious for squirreling away cash that never appears on their balance sheet." According to a Daimler spokesperson: "This is money that we've had in the back room, but it will be visible now. The company will continue to retain the cash as an internal cash reserve."

Analysts familiar with German accounting practice note that companies can create hidden or "silent" reserves in a variety of ways: understating revenues, overstating expenses, and overstating charges for "provisions for contingencies," among others.[1] With respect to Daimler's reserve, the $2.45 billion resulted from an inconsistent application of pension valuation methods throughout the company. Daimler's operating companies apparently discounted their pension fund commitments at 6 percent, whereas the holding company discounted those same commitments at 3.5 percent.

Daimler-Benz officials stated that they hope that the recent disclosures will help the company attain NYSE listing by year-end 1993. A remaining problem, however, may be the company's accounting for goodwill. Under U.S. practice, goodwill arising from a merger or acquisition must be capitalized to the balance sheet and then amortized off against earnings over the asset's expected useful life (but not to exceed 40 years). In recent years, Daimler acquisitions have produced over $2.0 billion in goodwill, which under German accounting practice has been charged off against retained earnings.

Required:

Exhibits 1 and 2 present the Daimler-Benz consolidated balance sheet and consolidated statement of income as of December 31, 1991. Recast the company's 1991 financial statements to reflect the previously hidden reserves and the goodwill charged to equity. Consider the ways that companies reporting their financial results under U.S. GAAP can smooth their reported earnings (e.g., create hidden reserves). List these methods and the reasons that a company might want to smooth their earnings.

---

[1]The provision for contingencies is analogous to the creation of a loss (or expense) reserve in the United States. The principal difference, however, is that in Germany, provisions for normally occurring expenses (e.g., maintenance) may be created often with the explicit purpose of smoothing reported earnings. Under U.S. practice, the creation of reserves is limited to specifically identifiable and estimable expected losses.

EXHIBIT 1

DAIMLER-BENZ AG
Consolidated Statement of Income

	In Millions of DM	
	1991	*1990*
Sales	**95,010**	**85,500**
Increase in Inventories and Other Capitalized In-House Output	3,556	2,840
Total Output	**98,566**	**88,340**
Other Operating Income	3,545	3,598
Cost of Materials	(49,456)	(44,477)
Personnel Expenses	(29,372)	(26,890)
of which for Old-Age Pensions DM1,511 million		
(1990: DM1,347 million)		
Amortization of Intangible Assets, Depreciation of Fixed Assets		
and of Leased Equipment	(5,977)	(5,169)
Other Operating Expenses	(13,824)	(12,016)
Income from Affiliated, Associated and Related Companies	56	4
Net Interest Income	623	989
Write-Downs of Financial Assets and of Securities	(134)	(158)
Results from Ordinary Business Activities	**4,027**	**4,221**
Extraordinary Result	(544)	—
Income Taxes	(1,039)	(1,814)
Other Taxes	(502)	(612)
Net Income	**1,942**	**1,795**
Profit Carried Forward from Previous Year	8	5
Transfer to Retained Earnings	(1,275)	(1,124)
Income Applicable to Minority Shareholders	(99)	(145)
Loss Applicable to Minority Shareholders	29	34
Unappropriated Profit of Daimler-Benz AG	**605**	**565**

EXHIBIT 2

DAIMLER-BENZ AG
Consolidated Balance Sheet

	In Millions of DM	
Assets	*December 31, 1991*	*December 31, 1990*
Non-Current Assets		
Intangible Assets	774	304
Fixed Assets	16,574	15,057
Financial Assets	3,758	1,569
Leased Equipment	8,092	6,518
	29,198	23,448
Current Assets		
Inventories	20,732	18,855
Advance Payments Received	(5,827)	(5,727)
	14,905	13,128
Receivables	12,370	11,321
Other Assets	9,783	9,019
Securities	5,725	5,154
Cash	2,010	3,786
	44,793	42,408
Prepaid Expenses and Deferred Taxes	1,723	1,483
	75,714	67,339

Stockholders' Equity and Liabilities		
Stockholders' Equity		
Capital Stock	2,330	2,330
Paid-In Capital	2,117	2,117
Retained Earnings	13,182	11,934
Minority Interests	1,214	881
Unappropriated Profit of Daimler-Benz AG	605	565
	19,448	17,827
Provisions		
Provisions for Old-Age Pensions and Similar Obligations	10,790	10,831
Other Provisions	17,239	16,536
	28,029	27,367
Liabilities		
Accounts Payable Trade	7,015	6,469
Other Liabilities	20,713	15,312
	27,728	21,781
Deferred Income	509	364
	75,714	67,339

8.10   Accounting for Leases

Deutsche Lufthansa AG is the parent company of the German national airline, Lufthansa. For most airlines, the largest single asset account is the investment in flight equipment. For example, at year-end 19x3, nearly 60 percent of Lufthansa's total asset value was reflected in its fleet of over 200 aircraft. Comparable figures for American Airlines and British Airways were 52 and 64 percent, respectively.

Financing for the acquisition of fleet equipment is frequently provided externally in the form of leases. This case concerns the accounting for leases in Germany, the United Kingdom, and the United States.

Lease Accounting.   Most developed countries recognize the existence of two types of leases, capital and operating, but how that information is disclosed in financial statements and the extent to which capital leasing is utilized vary considerably between countries.

EU directives do not specify any required accounting treatment for leases, but IAS No. 17 requires that the accounting for leases follow from the *substance* of the lease agreement. If a lease transfers substantially "all of the risks and rewards incident to ownership" to the lessee, it is considered to be a *capital* (or finance) *lease* under which the leased asset and a lease liability should be recognized on the lessee's balance sheet. The value assigned to the capitalized asset and liability is the lesser of the asset's (or liability's) fair market value or the present value of the minimum lease payments. If, on the other hand, a lease does not transfer substantially all of the risks and rewards of asset ownership to the lessee (i.e., those risks and rewards are retained by the lessor), the lease is considered to be an *operating lease* under which no balance sheet disclosure is required, but a lease expense should be reflected on the lessee's income statement.[1]

The fundamental concepts of *IAS No. 17* are likewise reflected in the generally accepted accounting practice of Germany, Great Britain, and the United States, but important differences nonetheless exist. In Great Britain, for example, a lease is usually considered to be a capital lease only when, as of the lease inception, the present value of the minimum lease payments equals (or exceeds) 90 percent of the fair market value of the leased asset. In the United States, however, a capital lease may exist when *any one* of the following four criteria is satisfied:

1. The lease agreement transfers ownership of the property to the lessee.
2. The lease agreement contains a bargain purchase option.
3. The lease term is at least 75 percent of the leased asset's useful economic life.
4. The present value of the minimum lease payments is at least 90 percent of the leased asset's fair market value.

---

[1]*IAS No. 17* requires that, for both capital and operating leases, the footnotes to the financial statements disclose (1) the amount of assets held under capital or operating leases; (2) commitments for minimum lease payments under capital leases and noncancelable operating leases with a term of more than one year, giving the amounts and periods in which the payments are due; and (3) any significant financing restrictions, renewal or purchase options, and contingent rental payments arising from the lease agreement.

In Germany, the primary criterion for determining the existence of a capital lease is the lease term in relation to the economic life of the leased asset: If the lease term is 90 percent or more of the leased asset's economic life, capitalization of the lease is required. Leases that are, in effect, installment sales, under which title passes after the final payment, are always considered to be capital leases.

The institutional setting in each country, however, may also influence prevalent GAAP. In Great Britain and the United States, for example, accounting standards and tax regulations rarely coincide. In Germany, however, prevailing GAAP is largely derived from the German Commercial Code, which in turn is dictated by tax court rulings and company law. Thus, lease accounting in Germany generally follows complex tax laws, and since depreciation deductions generally remain with the lessor, there is significant disincentive for German companies to use lease financing at all.

Required:

Exhibits 1–3 present selected financial data from the published annual reports of American Airlines, British Airways, and Lufthansa, respectively. Review these data and consider the following:

(a) Compare the amount of leasing, in total, and the proportion of capital to operating leases undertaken by each of the airlines. Also evaluate the extent of the financial statement disclosure regarding leases. What can you conclude from this regarding the institutional or cultural setting of each respective country?

(b) Calculate the total debt to total assets ratio and the total debt-to-equity ratio for the data in Exhibits 1–3. Restate Exhibits 1 and 2 to reflect the capitalization of operating leases for both American Airlines and British Airways and then recalculate these ratios. (Assume a discount rate of 8 percent.)

(c) Does the use of operating leases increase the ability of a company to lever itself? If so, are German companies at a competitive disadvantage in the world capital markets when competing for borrowed funds?

Exhibit 1

AMERICAN AIRLINES
Selected Financial Disclosures

Condensed Balance Sheet (31 December 19x3)

	($ millions)
Current assets	2,657.8
Equipment and property (net)	7,852.6
Equipment and property (net) under capital leases	1,295.0
Other assets	1,548.2
Total assets	13,353.6
Current liabilities	4,824.7
Long-term debt	1,674.2
Capital lease obligations	1,597.7
Other liabilities	1,529.6
Stockholders' equity	3,727.4
Total equities	13,353.6

Income Statement Data

Operating lease costs	580.5
Income before taxes	(33.3)

Footnote Disclosure: Lease Commitments

The future minimum lease payments required under capital leases (together with the present value of net minimum lease payments) and future minimum lease payments required under operating leases that have an initial or remaining non-cancelable lease term in excess of one year as of December 31, 19x3 were as follows (in millions):

Year ending December 31,	*Capital Leases*	*Operating Leases*
19x4	$ 185.1	$ 580.5
19x5	184.7	612.1
19x6	181.3	598.2
19x7	179.4	584.9
19x8	190.2	565.0
19x9 and subsequent	2,275.6	11,817.0
	3,196.3[a]	14,757.7[a][b]
Less minimum sublease rentals	—	143.6
		$14,614.1
Less amount representing interest	1,539.5	
Present value of net minimum lease payments	$1,656.8[c]	

[a]Future minimum payments required under capital leases and operating leases include $451.1 million and $4.3 billion, respectively, guaranteed by AMR relating to special facility revenue bonds issued by municipalities. Minimum sublease rentals relative to capital leases are $26.0 million.

[b]American has 226 aircraft under operating lease. Other AMR subsidiaries operate 129 regional aircraft under operating leases. During 19x3, 36 Boeing 727-100s, 20 Boeing 727-200s, 2 Boeing 747SPs and 6 Fairchild Metro IIIs which were previously owned were sold and leased back.

[c]Includes $140.5 million guaranteed by American.

The aircraft leases can generally be renewed at rates based on fair market value at the end of the lease term for one to five years. Most aircraft leases have purchase options at the end of the lease term at fair market value, but generally not to exceed a stated percentage of the defined lessor's cost of the aircraft. Of the aircraft American has under operating lease, 15 Boeing 767-300ERs and 25 Airbus A300-600Rs are cancelable upon 30-days' notice during the initial 10-year lease term. At the end of that term, the leases can be renewed for periods ranging from 10 to 12 years.

Rentals and landing fees for 19x3, 19x2 and 19x1 include rent expense of $788.2 million, $621.9 million and $441.7 million, respectively.

EXHIBIT 2

BRITISH AIRWAYS Plc
Selected Financial Disclosures

Condensed Balance Sheet (31 March 19x3)

	(£ millions)
Current assets	1,295
Fixed assets	
Fleet	3,438
Property and equipment	943
	4,381
Less: Accumulated depreciation	(1,917)
	2,464
Investments	108
Total fixed assets	2,572
Total assets	3,867
Current liabilities	1,816
Long-Term liabilities (excluding leases)	943
Finance lease obligations	132
Provisions for liabilities	64
Shareholders' equity	912
Total equities	3,867

Income Statement Data

Depreciation on finance-leased aircraft	30
Operating least costs:	
Aircraft	179
Property and equipment	54
Income before taxes	345

Footnote Disclosure: Operating Lease Commitment

At March 31, 19x4 future minimum rental payments under noncancelable operating leases were as follows:

	Fleet	*Property and Equipment (£ millions)*	*Total*
Within one year	220	46	266
Between one and two years	178	27	205
Between two and three years	172	25	197
Between three and four years	137	24	161
Between four and five years	30	20	50
Over five years	2	231	233
	739	373	1,112

BRITISH AIRWAYS Plc
Selected Financial Disclosures

Amounts payable within one year related to commitments expiring as follows:

Within one year	35	13	48
Between one and two years	14	6	20
Between two and three years	14	8	22
Between three and four years	102	12	114
Between four and five years	50	—	50
Over five years	5	7	12
	220	46	266

The fleet leasing commitments include the balance of rental obligations under operating leases in respect of 13 Boeing 747-400, seven Boeing 767-300, five Boeing 747-200, seven Boeing 757, 20 Boeing 737 and eight BAe ATP aircraft, but exclude nine Boeing 737 and three Boeing 757 aircraft which were converted from operating leases to finance leases with effect from March 31, 19x4. In the case of most of these obligations, British Airways may be required to meet a small share of any loss on resale if options to renew the leases or convert them into finance leases are not exercised.

British Airways has extendible operating leases with two companies, which are affiliates of British Airways, for eight Boeing 747-400 and seven Boeing 767-300 aircraft.

EXHIBIT 3

DEUTSCHE LUFTHANSA AG
Selected Financial Disclosures

Condensed Balance Sheet (31 December 19x3)

	(DM millions)
Current assets	3,139,483
Aircraft	7,828,706
Other assets	2,210,232
Total assets	13,178,421
Current liabilities	1,616,035
Long-term liabilities	3,636,729
Provisions	2,623,673
Special items with an equity portion	2,113,626
Shareholders' equity	3,186,535
Total equities	13,178,421

Income Statement Data

Income before taxes (DM millions)	142,446

Footnote Disclosure: Other Financial Commitments

The payments for long-term leasing contracts for aircraft amounted to DM105 million in the Group in 19x3 (DM52 million in the AG). These contracts will involve payments in subsequent years of up to DM165 million (DM78 million in the AG).

8.11   Annual Report Analysis

An interesting and important challenge for students of international financial reporting is to study the published annual reports of various companies from different countries. Your instructor will provide you with a recent copy of a German annual report. To facilitate your delving into the annual report, undertake the following endeavors.

Required:

(a) List the key differences between the German annual report and what you would expect to see for a U.S. company in the same industry.

(b) Calculate the following ratios, taking care to note the assumptions you found necessary to make and where you found the appropriate pieces of data in the annual report.

$$(1)\ \text{Current ratio} = \frac{\text{Total current assets}}{\text{Total current liabilities}}$$

$$(2)\ \text{Quick ratio} = \frac{\text{Cash + Marketable securities + Accounts Receivable}}{\text{Total current liabilities}}$$

$$(3)\ \begin{array}{l}\text{Operating cash flow to}\\ \text{current liabilities}\end{array} = \frac{\text{Operating cash flow}}{\text{Average total current liabilities}}$$

$$(4)\ \text{Debt-to-equity ratio} = \frac{\text{Long-term debt}}{\text{Owners' equity}}$$

$$(5)\ \text{Debt-to-total capitalization ratio} = \frac{\text{Long term debt}}{\text{Long term debt + owners' equity}}$$

$$(6)\ \text{Interest coverage ratio} = \frac{\text{Net income before interest \& income taxes}}{\text{Interest expense}}$$

$$(7)\ \begin{array}{l}\text{Operating cash flow to interest}\\ \text{charges}\end{array} = \frac{\text{Operating cash flow}}{\text{Interest expense}}$$

$$(8)\ \begin{array}{l}\text{Operating cash flow to total}\\ \text{liabilities}\end{array} = \frac{\text{Operating cash flow}}{\text{Average total liabilities}}$$

$$(9)\ \text{Receivables turnover ratio} = \frac{\text{Net sales}}{\text{Average accts. receivable}}$$

$$(10)\ \text{Inventory turnover} = \frac{\text{Cost of goods sold}}{\text{Average inventory}}$$

$$(11)\ \text{Asset turnover} = \frac{\text{Net sales}}{\text{Average total assets}}$$

$$(12)\ \text{Average collection period ratio} = \frac{365\ \text{days}}{\text{Receivables turnover ratio}}$$

$$(13)\ \begin{array}{l}\text{Average number of days'}\\ \text{inventory on hand ratio}\end{array} = \frac{365\ \text{days}}{\text{Inventory turnover ratio}}$$

$$(14)\ \text{Return on assets (ROA)} = \frac{\text{Net income}}{\text{Average total assets}}$$

$$OR = \text{ROS} \times \text{Asset turnover}$$

(15) Return on equity (ROE) $= \dfrac{\text{Net income}}{\text{Average total owners' equity}}$

$$OR = \text{ROA} \times \text{Financial leverage}$$

(16) Return on sales (ROS) $= \dfrac{\text{Net income}}{\text{Net sales}}$

(17) Financial leverage $= \dfrac{\text{Avg. liabilities} + \text{Avg. owners' equity}}{\text{Avg. owners' equity}}$

(18) Basic earnings per share (EPS) $= \dfrac{\text{NI applicable to common shareholders}}{\text{Weighted average common shares}}$

(19) Cash dividend yield $= \dfrac{\text{Cash dividend per common share}}{\text{Market price per common share}}$

(20) Cash dividend payout $= \dfrac{\text{Total cash dividend to common shareholders}}{\text{Net income}}$

(c) What do you conclude about the availability of the appropriate data in the annual report for calculating these ratios?

(d) What does this financial analysis tell you about the company?

(e) What analytical metrics did the company choose to report for itself? What do those choices say about the message the company is striving to tell and the audience it is addressing?

Japan

[Japanese] financial accounting information is oriented towards the needs of other corporations, financial institutions, and the government rather than the individual stockholder.[1]

We don't give a hoot about things like return on equity.[2]

Introduction

When reviewing the major geopolitical developments of the latter half of the 20th century, historians will surely include among them the collapse of communism in eastern Europe, the formation of the European Union, and the establishment of Japan as an international economic power. In spite of its relatively small population (126 million people), tiny land mass, and relatively meager natural resources, Japan has developed the world's second largest economy and has become a dominant force in international trade. The country's spectacular post–World War II successes probably owe as much to Japanese discipline and social cohesiveness as to its unique government-regulated form of "free market capitalism." Indeed, the Japanese have shown a remarkable ability to accommodate Western economic theory to traditional Japanese values, creating a unique way of conducting business and accounting for the results. The Japanese have a phrase to describe their ability to adapt foreign methods to their own needs and purposes: *wakon yosai,* which means "Japanese spirit, Western techniques." Yet, it is perhaps this hybrid form of capitalism, a form that served the nation well in the latter half of the 20th century, that must be reformulated if the first half of the 21st century is to be as successful and prosperous for Japan.

Financial reporting practices, like so much else in modern Japan, represent a dynamic combination of foreign influence with indigenous attitudes and behavior patterns. Japanese law includes two major codes governing the preparation of financial statements: the German-influenced **Commercial Code,** the history of which dates back to 1899, and the **Japanese Securities and Exchange Law of 1948,** based on the U.S. Securities Exchange Acts of 1933 and 1934. Consequently, contemporary Japanese

---

[1]M. Darrough, H. Pourjalali, and S. Saudagaran, "Earnings Management in Japanese Companies," *International Journal of Accounting* 33, no. 3 (1998), p. 316.

[2]A January 1998 quote attributed to K. Aikawa, Chairman of Mitsubishi Heavy Industries. See J. Rohwer, "Japan's Quiet Corporate Revolution," *Fortune,* March 30, 1998, p. 82.

reporting practices consist of a curious amalgamation of Germanic conservatism and Anglo-American investor orientation, with the whole adapted to the distinctive cultural and economic structures governing Japanese business.

Like financial reporting in many other countries, Japanese reporting is moving toward a new internationalism as it responds to the development of global financial markets. Japanese multinationals are increasingly providing restated results for use by overseas investors. However, even as Japan's financial reporting practices move toward greater technical conformity with U.S. and international practices, well-informed interpretations of Japanese financial statements still require familiarity with its relevant cultural, legal, and economic contexts. For example, although differences in accounting rules are partly responsible for the low net income historically reported by most Japanese companies, a reader must bear in mind such confounding factors as the existence of the closely allied, legally independent corporate group known as *keiretsu;* the nature of Japanese capital markets; the relatively modest expectations of Japanese investors; and the often-cited long-run view that trades off short-term profitability in exchange for survival and ultimately market dominance.

Environmental Factors

*Cultural
Environment*

Much has been written in recent years about the effect of Japanese culture on Japanese business practices, an influence that has created a striking contrast between the values and habits of Western capitalism and those of Asian capitalism. One may begin to grasp something of this cultural chasm by referring to Hofstede's series of indexes (introduced in Chapter 1) designed to measure the basic cultural attitudes: power distance (PD), individualism (IDV), uncertainty avoidance (UAV), and long-term orientation (LTO). In the first area, PD, the score for Japan indicated a high acceptance of power distance: 54 compared to 40 for the United States. In the area of IDV, Japan scored 46, and the United States had the highest score of any group included in the study, 91. In the area of UAV, the scores were reversed: the United States scored 46, and the Japanese registered a much higher 92. Finally, in the area of LTO, the Japanese scored 80, the third highest ranking in the group studied, and the United States scored a moderately low 29. Thus, we see dramatic divergences in the three categories of individualism, uncertainty avoidance, and long-term orientation, as well as a marked difference in power distance.

The difference between the U.S. and Japanese scores in IDV probably does not surprise anyone acquainted with Japanese culture. One of its most pervasive and influential features—one that has received extensive attention in the Western press and academic literature—is *dantai ishiki,* or group consciousness, and its related social values of interdependence and harmony. Group consciousness has been described as a *frame* orientation rather than an *attribute* orientation that sees the self in terms of affiliations with others in a reference group rather than as a discrete individual with qualities and attributes all one's own.[3] This can be traced to the teachings of Confucius, specifically that the family is the model for all social organizations and a person is foremost a member of a family, not an individual.

In Japan, as well as in other East Asian societies influenced by Confucianism, the boundaries of freedom are defined much differently than in the West. Public duty, not

---

[3]J. McKinnon, "Cultural Constraints on Audit Independence in Japan," *International Journal of Accounting,* Fall 1984, pp. 17–43.

individual rights, is the highest value. "Loyalty to the master," filial piety, and deference to authority—not freedom of expression or personal liberty—form the ethical foundations of society.[4] This cultural value profoundly affects the nature of Japanese business relationships and conditions attitudes toward external reporting of financial results.

It is often remarked in the West that Japanese group consciousness creates a level of loyalty within business organizations rarely seen in other cultures that results in extraordinary efforts by each individual for the good of the whole group. Although westerners can certainly appreciate the importance and potential effectiveness of well-directed, cooperative action, they nevertheless place a high value on psychological (and, if possible, financial) independence and hence are not well equipped to understand the web of emotional and financial dependency that holds Japanese society together. It is normal and expected for Japanese workers to attach their careers—even their identities—to that of a corporate or personal patron. The West tends to stigmatize dependency, but the Japanese take it for granted as the natural and necessary condition of social existence.

Group membership is quite simply the dominant fact of Japanese economic life: People belong to companies, companies belong to groups, and everyone belongs to the nation.[5] This fact has resulted in some important alterations in economic practices imported from the West. Capitalism is still highly competitive in Japanese culture but is less a matter of creating individual opportunity than of fostering group security and harmony. Alliances and affiliations are not entered into lightly and are meant to last a very long time. These characteristics of Japanese business and culture are supported by the relatively high score for LTO. Within groups and alliances, the Japanese expect business relationships to proceed on the basis of mutual trust; as a result, disclosures tend to be personal and informal rather than routinized and mandatory. Thus, traditional Japanese managers may not see the point of creating and reviewing the kind of internal control systems that are so important for U.S. financial reporting. Moreover, because group membership involves a major emotional commitment, Japanese managers feel an unusually strong compulsion to screen corporate affairs—the routine as well as the potentially scandalous—from the view of outsiders. They are more disposed to maintain harmony and stability within the corporate household than to worry about the "rights" of outside parties, including small investors.

Although the scores for IDV support the cultural differences discussed, the divergence of scores on the LTO index is equally supportive in explaining cultural differences between the United States and Japan. The divergence of scores on the LTO index, like that of IDV, probably does not surprise anyone acquainted with Japanese culture. Recall from Chapter 1 that LTO values—perseverance, ordering relationships by status and observing this order, thrift, and having a sense of shame—are associated with the teachings of Confucius, teachings that are considered to be the roots of Eastern ethics and culture. Confucius was a teacher of practical ethics without any religious content—he dealt with virtue and harmony, but left the question of truth open. Hofstede posits that for this reason, questions concerning truth seem to be insignificant to Eastern cultures.[6] This cultural attitude toward truth may help to explain why true and fair accounting practices

---

[4]N. Gardels, "East Beats West: Transforming Cultural Values into Economic Gains; The New World Order May Be Asian, Not Western, Replacing Liberalism With Conformity, Discipline," *The Washington Post,* January 5, 1992, p. C3.

[5]B. R. Schlender, "Japan: Is It Changing for Good?" *Fortune,* June 13, 1994, pp. 124–34. See also, H. Schutte, "Asian Culture and the Global Consumer," *Financial Times,* September 21, 1998.

[6]G. Hofstede, *Cultures and Organizations: Software of the Mind,* London: McGraw-Hill (U.K.), 1991, p. 164.

differ between Japan and, say, the United States or Britain. It may also help to explain why Japanese companies are allowed to have reserve accounts (not allowed in the United States) and how they may use these reserves. If in a given year a Japanese company expects a loss or extraordinarily low net income (compared to other years), it can, for example, draw from reserves to create a smoother, more consistent pattern of net income (financial reporting). This would seem to be supported by the idea that maintaining harmony, a key principle in Confucius's teachings, is more important than what is true and fair according to a Western mind-set.

Japanese long-termism is also the result of several other embedded cultural needs and norms. For example, relationships and the exchange of favors foster a long-term orientation regarding one's indebtedness to another. Similarly, the pursuit and preservation of market share, a key indicator in providing access to Japan's governmental industrial policy makers, also fosters a long-term view over a short-term profit-focused view. And, in a general sense, Japanese resistance to change and strong desire to avoid embarrassment of oneself or others also undergirds Japan's high LTO score.[7]

Perhaps Japan's relatively high UAV is best epitomized by the following: "venture capital is an oxymoron in Japan," and as of the end of 1996, only 6 percent of individuals' total financial assets were in equity stocks whereas over 50 percent were in demand or time deposits.[8] Indeed, a predilection for tradition, for predictability, for constancy has led to an inculcation of cautious conservatism.[9] With one of the world's most proportionately elderly populations, it will be interesting to see if such a propensity for UAV fades away as the older generation steps aside for the younger.

Recall from the discussion of Gray's framework in Chapter 1 that a high UAV score and a low IDV score would support, in the case of Japan, a financial reporting subculture with a high degree of secrecy and low degree of professionalism. With respect to a professionalism versus statutory control orientation to financial reporting, it is true that changes in accounting standards or reporting requirements rarely work their way up from the professional grass-roots level in Japan; instead, the government acts as primary initiator and facilitator, not individual companies or the accounting profession.[10] As for secrecy, Japan's high UAV score and low IDV score, relative to those of the United States, explain, at least in part, a lower degree of disclosure in Japanese financial reporting than U.S. financial reporting.

Cultural attitudes, as described, may help to explain the remarkable reticence that characterizes the annual reports of Japanese companies: firms fulfill disclosure requirements, but they rarely volunteer information. Even Canon, Inc., one of the world's premier manufacturers of cameras and copying machines and a company that publishes an annual report espoused to be in accordance with U.S. GAAP, preferred to accept a qualified opinion from its auditor in 1997 rather than provide segment information (see Exhibit 9–1). Other disclosures that U.S. or European investors may take for granted— information concerning investments in subsidiaries and affiliates, employee and director

---

[7]For more discussion on such drivers of Japan's long-term orientation, see N. Yoshimura and P. Anderson, *Inside the Kaisha* (Boston, MA: Harvard Business School Press, 1997).

[8]D. Hamilton, "Entrepeneur Brings 'Vision' to Japan, Tries to Teach Bankers to Embrace Risk," *The Wall Street Journal,* October 7, 1996, p. A19 and *Tokyo Stock Exchange Fact Book,* Tokyo, Japan: Tokyo Stock Exchange, 1998.

[9]See G. Baker, "On a Collision Course," *Financial Times,* January 18, 1996, p. 17, and R. Neff, "Why Japan Won't Act to Save Itself," *Business Week,* May 18, 1998, p. 144.

[10]For example, most Japanese companies have a fiscal year-end of March 31, which coincides with the end of the Japanese government fiscal year.

EXHIBIT 9–1

Report of Canon, Inc.'s Independent Accountants

The Board of Directors
Canon Inc.:

We have audited the accompanying consolidated balance sheets (expressed in yen) of Canon Inc. and subsidiaries as of December 31, 1997 and 1996, and the related consolidated statements of income, stockholders' equity and cash flows for each of the years in the three-year period ended December 31, 1997. These consolidated financial statements are the responsibility of the Company's management. Our responsibility is to express an opinion on these consolidated financial statements based on our audits.

We conducted our audits in accordance with generally accepted auditing standards. Those standards require that we plan and perform the audit to obtain reasonable assurance about whether the financial statements are free of material misstatement. An audit includes examining, on a test basis, evidence supporting the amounts and disclosures in the financial statements. An audit also includes assessing the accounting principles used and significant estimates made by management, as well as evaluating the overall financial statement presentation. We believe that our audits provide a reasonable basis for our opinion.

Canon Inc. and subsidiaries have not applied Statement of Financial Accounting Standards No. 115 ("SFAS 115") in accounting for certain investments in debt and equity securities but have provided the disclosures required by SFAS 115. The effects on the consolidated financial statements of not adopting SFAS 115 are summarized in note 4 of the notes to consolidated financial statements.

The segment information required to be disclosed in financial statements under United States generally accepted accounting principles is not presented in the accompanying consolidated financial statements. Foreign issuers are currently exempted from such disclosure requirement in Securities Exchange Act filings with the United States Securities and Exchange Commission.

In our opinion, except for the effects of the departure from SFAS 115 in accounting for certain investments in debt and equity securities, as discussed in the third paragraph of this report, and except for the omission of the segment information, as discussed in the preceding paragraph, the consolidated financial statements referred to above present fairly, in all material respects, the financial position of Canon Inc. and subsidiaries at December 31, 1997 and 1996, and the results of their operations and their cash flows for each of the years in the three-year period ended December 31, 1997, in conformity with United States generally accepted accounting principles.

The accompanying consolidated financial statements have been translated into United States dollars solely for the convenience of the reader. We have recomputed the translation and, in our opinion, the consolidated financial statements expressed in yen have been translated into United States dollars on the basis set forth in note 2 of the notes to consolidated financial statements.

KPMG Peat Marwick

Tokyo, Japan
February 9, 1998

Source: Canon Inc. Annual Report, 1997.

---

remuneration, outstanding convertible debt, nonmonetary transactions, to name a few—rarely appear in Japanese reports. Although the Japanese government and the globalization of capital markets have been pressuring Japanese corporations toward greater disclosure, progress has been slower than many foreign investors would like. But some change is in the making. For example, beginning in 1999, full industrial and geographic segment disclosure is required, as is diluted earnings per share and a consolidated statement of cash flow. Other changes are stipulated to occur in 2000 or 2001 and are detailed in a later section.

Legal and Political Environment

Individual Tax Law.   Japanese combined national and local individual tax rates range from 15 to 65 percent on taxable income of ¥5,300,000 ($46,100)[11] to ¥37,000,000 ($322,000) and above, respectively. Gains on the sale of corporate shares and convertible debentures are taxed at a preferential flat national plus local rate of 26 percent. The familiar notion of classifying capital gains as short term or long term is not applicable to gains on sales of securities, but it is a classification scheme imposed on the sale of real estate.

Corporate Tax Law.   Japanese company law links financial income to taxable income by requiring that expenses claimed on a company's tax return be recorded on its books of account. With a statutory income tax rate of 37.5 percent on undistributed corporate income (and frequently an effective tax rate over 50 percent due to additional local income taxes that results in Japan placing one of the heaviest tax burdens in the world on its corporations), companies have a strong incentive to keep reported earnings down, chiefly by taking advantage of tax-deductible reserves and favorable depreciation provisions allowed by the Ministry of Finance. A few examples follow.

Many expense allowances familiar to U.S. managers, which are calculated on the basis of historical experience rates in the United States, must be recorded in Japanese financial statements at percentages provided by tax authorities and are usually calculated to be the maximum allowed by law irrespective of actual or expected experience rates. As a consequence, the amount deducted on a Japanese company's income statement as bad debts, sales returns, or sales warranties may have little to do with the actual economic conditions or prior experience of the firm. Other Japanese allowances, not so familiar to U.S. financial statement readers, are also the product of tax regulations, even though that fact may never be disclosed. Kawasaki Steel's financial statements, for example, include an allowance of ¥45 billion for special repairs in the long-term liability section of its balance sheet. A characteristically laconic Japanese note "explains" the allowance without mentioning that it essentially represents a special tax benefit (see Exhibit 9–2).

This yearly special repair deduction is taken in addition to regular depreciation on equipment and allows the company to reap tax benefits before such costs are actually incurred. When the work is actually done, the account is zeroed out, with any variation between actual and estimated repair costs treated as current income or loss. Other allowances of this sort include employee retirement benefits and product warranty costs.

EXHIBIT 9–2

**Footnote Excerpt from Kawasaki Steel's
Annual Report**

Allowance for special repairs

Blast furnaces and hot blast stoves, including related machinery and equipment, periodically require substantial repairs and replacement of components. Such work normally occurs approximately every 7 to 10 years for blast furnaces and every 14 to 20 years for hot blast stoves. The estimated future costs of such maintenance are provided and charged to income on a straight-line basis over the periods to the respective dates of such anticipated replacements and repairs. Difference between the estimated costs and actual costs are charged or credited to income as incurred.

Source: Kawasaki Steel Annual Report, 1997.

---

[11]At February 1, 1999, $1 = ¥115.

In addition, companies may create special reserves from retained earnings to secure special tax deferrals. For example, a company may obtain a tax deduction in the year that it books a reserve as an appropriation of retained earnings; in some future period, the entry would be reversed, thereby restoring the amount to taxable income. The most common reserves of this type are for special depreciation (bonus or accelerated depreciation allowed in addition to regular depreciation), inventory price fluctuations, and overseas investment losses. All of these reserves and their related deductions are contingent on meeting specific Ministry of Finance requirements that are calculated to promote the Japanese national interest. Exhibit 9–3 presents a footnote from Kawasaki Steel's financial statements that illustrates and explains the nature of these reserves.

These reserves are often buried in retained earnings, with little or no reference to them on the financial statements themselves. Reserves of this sort do not conform to U.S. GAAP and result in a relative understatement of net income in Japanese financial statements vis-à-vis U.S. financial statements.

In addition, corporations must create a legal reserve, which is not a tax-deductible reserve; it is a requirement imposed by the Japanese Commercial Code. Corporations must appropriate to the legal reserve an amount of retained earnings equal to at least 10 percent of the cash dividends paid each period until the reserve equals 25 percent of stated capital (the par value of capital stock). The reserve (as well as surplus capital) is not available for dividends but may be used to reduce a corporate earnings deficit by a resolution of the shareholders or may be transferred to stated capital by a resolution of the board of directors. This legally mandated appropriation effectively requires corporations to maintain a proportionate level of capitalization by reinvesting a portion of earnings in the business; the deficit reduction provision allows companies to smooth income and create at least an appearance of stable, "harmonious" earnings over the long term.

Linking tax policy to financial reporting practices inevitably distorts the presentation of corporate performance in financial statements by encouraging managers to maximize tax benefits or requiring them to follow tax guidelines rather than striving to achieve a broader reporting objective akin to a true and fair representation of the business's economic substance. Predictably, the effect of tax law on Japanese financial statements has created some confusion among international investors. The artificially low earnings reported by Japanese companies and the relatively strong performance of Japanese stocks

---

EXHIBIT 9–3

FOOTNOTE EXCERPT FROM KAWASAKI STEEL
Annual Report

Retained earnings

Retained earnings include the reserves under the Special Taxation Measures Law. The schedule was as follows:

	Millions of Yen		Thousands of U.S. Dollars
As of March 31	*1997*	*1996*	*1997*
Reserve for accelerated depreciation	¥ 4,271	¥ 5,445	$34,416
Reserve for losses on overseas investments	66	78	532
Reserve for advanced depreciation of property	52,183	47,831	420,499
Total	¥56,521	¥53,355	$455,447

The Special Taxation Measures Law permits the Company to deduct for income tax purposes, transfers to certain reserves that are not required for financial accounting purposes, if recorded on the books as profit appropriations or charges to income, and to restore them to taxable income in future years.

Source: Kawasaki Steel Annual Report, 1997.

on the Tokyo market during, for example, 1995 resulted in an extremely high price-earnings (P-E) ratio for the Tokyo stock exchange companies of about 80 times earnings. This was about four times the P-E ratio for the U.S. S&P 500 in 1995.[12] Even with the decline in Japanese stocks since 1995, as of January 1997, the Tokyo Stock Exchange average P-E ratio was about 40, still twice that of the S&P 500.[13] Some Western analysts point to the effect of tax law on financial reporting as an explanation for these high P-E ratios and suggest that the price/net cash flow ratio is a more appropriate tool for comparing Japanese and U.S. equities. Indeed, one recent analysis put this ratio between a 10 to 12 multiple for U.S., U.K., and Japanese stocks.[14]

National Economic Policy.   Japanese firms also tend to report lower earnings than their U.S. counterparts because their managers are less interested in short-term profitability than in continuous long-term growth. (One reflection of this emphasis on the long run is Japanese managers' freedom from the quarterly earnings reports that publicly held U.S. companies must issue.) In this respect, they practice the macroeconomic strategy pursued by the nation's political and financial leaders. Market share, technological progress, and corporate harmony have, heretofore, been the top priorities of Japanese managers and Japanese political culture. The sacrifice of immediate rewards and comforts for the sake of greater economic power in the future is still a central tenet of the national consensus that made possible the country's remarkable economic progress in the 1970s and 1980s. Such an outlook fits well with the historical, and still strong although lessening, Japanese commitment to lifetime employment, the fulfillment of which would naturally depend on continued economic growth and faith in the future. One could say, then, that the historically low net income reported by Japanese firms can be attributed in part to a social-political ethos that is less interested in short-term results than in long-term rewards. The depth of Japans' late 1990s recession has certainly shaken some of these long-held paradigms. It remains to be seen if it is of such a duration that a real change in mind-set occurs.

Business Environment

Form of Business.   The dominant form of business organization in Japan is the *Kabushiki Kaisha* (KK), a type of limited liability company similar to a U.S. corporation. The Japanese Commercial Code requires that a KK elect at least one statutory auditor to examine the performance of its directors and report to shareholders annually. There is no requirement, however, that the statutory auditor be a certified public accountant.[15] A large KK—one with stated capital of ¥500 million (about $4.4 million, based on February 1999 exchange rates) or liabilities of ¥20 billion (about $1.74 million)—is required to appoint three statutory auditors (one of whom is an outsider) and is required to hire an independent outside auditor. The statutory auditors principally examine the managerial behavior of the directors and the performance of the independent auditor. The duties and powers of the independent auditor are limited to an examination of the accounting records.

One reason that Japanese managers have historically been able to focus on long-term objectives without having to worry about takeovers is the pattern of stable shareholding established by the corporate families, or ***keiretsu,*** which dominate the Japanese economy. One might consider the *keiretsu* (literally, headless combines) a manifestation of group consciousness at the organizational level. These giant alliances of technically unaffiliated companies grew out of the U.S. attempt in the late 1940s to break up the great industrial

---

[12]R. Steiner, "Japanese Stock Values Near Global Levels," *The Wall Street Journal,* January 31, 1997, p. A14.

[13]Ibid.

[14]W. Dawkins, "Corporate Japan Suffers Split Personality," *Financial Times,* April 22, 1997, p. 21.

[15]Coopers & Lybrand, *International Accounting Summaries,* New York: John Wiley & Sons, Inc., 1993, p. J-3.

conglomerations (known as ***zaibatsu***) of prewar Japan. When the Allied Occupation ended in 1948, companies quietly and informally began to form new ties—generally under the aegis of a major bank or a large trading company—by lending each other money, establishing interlocking directorates, buying each other's stock, and creating helpful patterns of trade within the group.

Six large *keiretsu* dominate the Japanese business landscape. The Mitsui, Mitsubishi, and Sumitomo groups are the powerful trading company *keiretsu;* Fuji, Sanwa, and Dai-ichi Kangyo are the dominant banking groups. One estimate places 12,000 companies, with sales equivalent to 25 percent of Japan's GNP, in the web of related companies headed by these six associations.[16] *Keiretsu* tend to be highly diversified, each attempting to form within itself an economic microcosm to minimize risk and maximize benefit to individual members. One writer has summarized the principal characteristics of the *keiretsu* as follows:

- The members are all "independent" major firms in their own oligopolistic industries.
- The confederation pursues the one-set formula (i.e., excluding competitors but aimed at representing all lines within the confederation).
- Service firms (e.g., banking, trading, insurance, and shipping companies) from within the *keiretsu* perform special functions for industrial member firms in varying degrees (not usually to the complete exclusion of outsiders).
- Between the firms there are several cross-ties (e.g., borrowing from the same banks, mutual shareholdings, interlocking directors, using the same trademark and the same trading company, and liaison planning by presidents' clubs).
- Much interfirm business, horizontal and vertical, is done within the group of firms.
- Holding companies at the top (as in the prewar *zaibatsu*) have been eliminated so that the relationship between these groupings is now more cooperative than controlled.[17]

As Exhibit 9–4 illustrates, a vast number of group members typically do not purchase large enough blocks of stocks to trigger financial reporting consolidation requirements

---

EXHIBIT 9–4

MITSUBISHI GROUP: MAJOR SHAREHOLDERS
in the Group's Financial Core
(percentage of outstanding shares)

	Bank of Tokyo-Mitsubishi	*Mitsubishi Trust & Banking*	*Tokio Marine & Fire Insurance*
Bank of Tokyo-Mitsubishi	—	3.1	4.6
Mitsubishi Trust & Banking	2.0	—	2.9
Tokio Marine & First Insurance	4.1	1.8	—
Meiji Life Insurance	5.7	3.8	4.4
Mitsubishi Electric	1.4	1.7	—
Mitsubishi Heavy Industries	3.0	2.7	1.8
Asahi Glass	1.4	2.2	1.7
Dai-ichi Life Insurance	3.5	—	1.5
Total	21.1	15.3	16.9

Source: *Japan Company Handbook, First Section* (Tokyo: Toyo Keizai Inc., 1996).

---

[16]"Inside the Charmed Circle," *The Economist,* January 5, 1991, p. 54.

[17]D. F. Henderson, *Foreign Enterprise in Japan: Law and Policies* (Chapel Hill, NC: University of North Carolina Press, 1973), pp. 131–32.

under Anglo-American rules. *Keiretsu* involve no holding company and no controlling board of directors as would be typical in European conglomerates, for example. The group as a whole often owns a significant percentage of the voting stock of each of its core members, but that ownership is dispersed among a number of companies. The quantitative aspect of share ownership is less important than the qualitative aspects of these relationships: planning and coordination, special trade and credit relationships, information sharing, and even occasionally rescuing a distressed firm.

Keiretsu influence the capital structure of Japanese corporations by altering the relationship between debt and risk, and hence changing the way in which analysts should interpret a Japanese balance sheet. Until recently, when Japanese firms ventured more strongly into international equity markets, many of them carried a debt loading that would prove fatal to most U.S. or European businesses. Nippon Oil's balance sheet, for instance, recently reflected that shareholders' equity accounted for only about 20 percent of its total assets. (By way of comparison, shareholders' equity in Shell was nearly 60 percent of total assets in the same year.) Commentators have offered a variety of explanations for this phenomenon: Equity costs more and is scarcer in smaller Asian markets; Japanese workers tend to save rather than invest in stocks; and Japanese banks historically have played a central role in the economy because they were the primary sources of capital for post-war reconstruction. All of these explanations are valid, although some of the national characteristics they describe may be changing: The rise of investment trusts suggests that Japanese investors may be looking for equity investment vehicles, and the liquidity created by success in export markets has made some large trading companies less dependent on home-country banks for working capital. But such factors address necessities and constraints rather than the reasons that debt financing has worked well in Japan for so many years. In fact, many debt-laden Japanese corporations have survived and prospered because of the uniquely cooperative patterns of behavior between members of *keiretsu*.

Much of the debt on a typical Japanese corporate balance sheet has been provided by other members of its *keiretsu*—banks, insurance companies, trading companies—which means that less risk is attached to high levels of debt than would be the case elsewhere. Under normal circumstances, much of a firm's short-term bank debt is automatically rolled over, making it in fact a type of long-term debt. Trade credit, by virtue of extremely favorable terms of payment, also serves as a kind of semipermanent financing provided by major trading companies to its friends. And when a group member runs into financial difficulty, its creditor affiliates—if it has properly maintained its alliances—will in fact extend additional credit, buy stock, and, if necessary, lend managerial expertise rather than abandoning it. What else would one expect since about two-thirds of the shares traded on the Tokyo exchange are in the hands of related firms?[18]

This kind of cooperative behavior, which would be difficult to characterize as strictly arm's length, not only changes the meaning and function of debt but also raises questions about the applicability of Western concepts of consolidated reporting to Japanese business. It has been argued rather persuasively that customary Anglo-American assumptions about stock ownership and legal control simply do not adequately explain the complexity of corporate relationships in Japan.[19] McKinnon suggests that there may be cultural limits

---

[18]J. Sapsford, "Japanese Stocks Tumble as Huge Insurer Bucks Clubby Shareholding Practices," *The Wall Street Journal,* July 25, 1996, p. A8.

[19]J. McKinnon, "Application of Anglo-American Principles of Consolidation to Corporate Financial Disclosure in Japan." In *Frontiers of International Accounting,* ed. F. D. S. Choi and G. G. Mueller (Ann Arbor, MI: UMI Research Press, 1985), pp. 31–52.

to harmonization of accounting principles between countries, even though a measure of technical conformity to Western methods may be adopted by the Japanese. In essence, even if Japanese corporations prepare statements in accordance with U.S. GAAP, one's reading of them may yet be distorted simply by virtue of differing social and cultural factors. In spite of such questions, though, Japan continues to move toward consolidated financial statement guidelines similar to those practiced in the United States. For example, in 1991, the Ministry of Finance added disclosure requirements, some of which are very similar to those required by U.S. GAAP. Annual reports are now required to disclose related-party transactions among business entities belonging to the same financial group. The definition of *related parties* is similar to that adopted in the *Statement of Financial Accounting Standards No. 57* in the United States.[20]

Capital Markets.   The liberalization of Japanese financial markets and the explosive growth of the Tokyo Stock Exchange (TSE), (second in size in the world, albert a distant second in 1998 behind the New York Stock Exchange, using total market value as a measure) has made Tokyo a major global financial center. The TSE is not the only stock exchange in Japan—there are eight others—but it is by far the largest, routinely handling more than 80 percent of all shares traded. Although as recently as the early 1980s Japanese markets were reputed to be resistant to analysis and too geared to inside information, those opinions have become much less common as a wave of foreign involvement in the Japanese markets has dispelled misconceptions and lessened the likelihood of real abuses. The pressure exerted by an internationalized capital market may well turn out to be the single most effective agent for change in the evolution of Japanese accounting standards.

The securities markets in Japan are governed primarily by the Securities and Exchange Law of 1948, under the direction of the Ministry of Finance (MOF). Public offerings of more than ¥100 million (about $0.9 million) require the offering company to file with the MOF a report including audited consolidated and parent-company financial statements for the last two fiscal years. Also, after an offering is completed, the company must file a report with the MOF, again including audited consolidated and parent-company financial statements, within three months of each fiscal year-end. In addition, eligibility for the TSE requires that a firm list at least 6 million shares if its main offices are located in or around Tokyo; if the company's main business is outside of Tokyo, companies must list at least 20 million shares. The number of shares held by the 10 largest and other specially related shareholders must not exceed 70 percent of the shares listed.

It is interesting to note that in Japan the "principal reason for holding shares is not to secure a financial return, but to further a business relationship."[21] Indeed, analysts estimate that "between 60 percent and 70 percent of listed shares in Japan are held by long-term investors for strategic purposes"[22] and that industrial companies hold about 25 percent of all shares while banks account for roughly 22 percent.[23] So, even though Japan has one of the world's highest household savings rates (about 12 percent of disposable income versus 3 for the United States), less than 7 percent of individuals' financial assets are directly invested in equities.[24] Such conditions create a situation in which freely traded and available shares are limited and trading volumes are far short of other major

---

[20]The Japanese Institute of Certified Public Accountants, *Corporate Disclosure in Japan* (Tokyo: JICPA, 1991), p. 68.

[21]G. Baker, "Trapped in Stagnant Waters," *Financial Times,* February 22, 1995, p. 19.

[22]J. Sapsford, "Cross-Holding System in Japan Shows Strains," *The Wall Street Journal,* August 25, 1994, p. A8.

[23]Baker, "Trapped in Stagnant Waters."

[24]See G. Tett, "Tokyo Has a Fit of the Sulks," *Financial Times,* November 10, 1997, p. 13, and Tokyo Stock Exchange. *Fact Book 1998,* p. 87.

securities exchanges. For example, the 1993 value of securities traded in Japan totaled 21 percent of total capitalization; the same values for London, Paris, and New York were 60 percent, 56 percent, and 45 percent, respectively.[25] Stated in a slightly different way, the average daily trading volume in the foreign section of the exchange during the first quarter of 1995 was a mere 145,000 shares as compared to 2,750,000 shares in 1987.[26] Indeed, such circumstances, combined with the high cost of maintaining a Japanese listing have prompted a substantial number of foreign firms to exit the Japanese exchanges.[27] In fact, one recent account notes only 60 foreign companies listed on the Tokyo Exchange in 1997 as compared to 110 at the end of 1993.[28] Among those exiting were General Electric, Scott Paper, Hewlett-Packard, and British Gas.

Generally, filing requirements similar to those applicable to Japanese companies apply to foreign companies desiring to make a public offering of shares in Japan. However, they need not file financial statements audited by Japanese auditors if the statements were examined by auditors deemed to be their equivalent. This provision has created an interesting situation: The Ministry of Finance will accept a U.S. audit report, but the U.S. SEC will not necessarily accept a Japanese audit report. If the SEC is not familiar with the Japanese auditing firm providing the report, it will investigate the quality of the audit report before deciding whether to accept it.[29]

To stem the exodus of foreign companies from the Tokyo Exchange, a number of listing rules were relaxed effective January 1, 1995. Quite significantly, one change is that foreign companies will no longer have to translate full annual reports into Japanese; they may issue an abbreviated translated report for their Japanese investors.[30] It remains to be seen whether Tokyo can make enough changes quickly enough to solidify and build its potential as a major international equity center.

During the 1980s, experts noted that the most dramatic growth in the TSE was not in original offerings but in the secondary stock market. This phenomenon suggests that the Japanese public has become more willing to invest in shares than they used to be. During the 1980s, individual investors and investment trusts (which get 80 percent of their funds from individuals) were undoubtedly encouraged to invest in the stock market by a variety of factors: the continuing gains posted by Japanese shares, the belief that the government would step in to support the market should that prove necessary, and the tax breaks available to individual investors in Japan. The 1990s proved that Tokyo's stock market is not immune from drastic downturns. Although some individuals—as well as institutions—have realized substantial losses from investments in the stock market, others refuse to sell. In any case, the trend of increasing numbers of individual investors that began in the 1980s is not necessarily over. Perhaps what is over is the individual investor's complete dependence on brokers' advice and tolerance for little disclosure.[31] Recent events in the Japanese stock market may have initiated a basic shift in the financial habits of Japanese investors and, perhaps, in some of the reporting and disclosure habits of Japanese corporations.

---

[25]Ibid.

[26]G. Baker and R. Waters, "Tokyo Exchange Hit by Departures of U.S. Companies," *Financial Times,* March 26, 1995, p. 1.

[27]According to Baker and Waters, "Tokyo Exchange Hit by Departures" and Baker, "Trapped in Stagnant Waters," the costs of being listed on a U.S. exchange are between $1 and $6 per 1,000 shares traded and between $6 to $10 on European exchanges. In Japan it is much more than the average cost on European exchanges. Moreover, investors in Japan must pay purchase fees eight times higher than the world's other major exchanges.

[28]Tokyo Stock Exchange, *Fact Book 1998.*

[29]An attorney at the SEC International Affairs Department, August 5, 1992.

[30]W. Dawkins, "Tokyo Relaxes Listing Conditions," *Financial Times,* December 21, 1994, p. 15.

[31]Comments by H. Ogasawara, a Japanese researcher visiting the University of Virginia, June 16, 1992.

The foregoing should not be construed, however, as a suggestion that the power of Japan's banks and financial institutions has been or is likely to be wrested away by individual equity investors with major consequences for financial reporting just around the corner. Japanese shareholders are generally less demanding than their U.S. counterparts. Today, even though loan defaults are up sharply and the stock market losses that have accrued to the banks' investment portfolios are inhibiting domestic lending, Japanese companies as a group still raise far more money from bank loans than from domestic equity markets. Change is happening, but it seems to be more attributable to the efforts and demands of foreign fund managers and analysts than to the requirements of a collection of individual Japanese investors. Nevertheless, a Japanese public that is slowly becoming increasingly savvy in the ways of equity investment may create internal pressures for increased disclosure, if only by calling traditionally accepted roles and attitudes into question.

An increasing number of large Japanese corporations, primarily those that have aggressively pursued international financing in the past and that have become cash rich because of their success in export markets, are looking away from the traditionally powerful banks and placing more emphasis on foreign equity markets for meeting their capital needs. Sony, perhaps the most progressively international firm in Japan, was the first Japanese company to be listed on the New York Stock Exchange and often has more shares traded in New York than in Tokyo. The tendency of these companies to seek less expensive foreign capital, most recently in European markets, necessarily subjects them to more stringent disclosure requirements than would be the case at home. Consequently, internationally listed companies such as Sony, Sanyo, and Honda are becoming accustomed to the reporting practices of the West. As noted in Exhibit 9–5, many of these companies now provide results restated in accordance with U.S. GAAP for the use of U.S. investors.

Foreign investors and analysts have, in the past, characterized the Tokyo market as being too clubbish and susceptible to manipulation by insiders. The increasing involvement of foreign brokers and investment banks, however, has circumscribed the ability of anyone to "manage" the market or to conduct business as an insider. In addition, the Japanese government enacted tougher rules in January 1989, making insider trading a criminal instead of a civil offense. In late 1990, new regulations came into effect requiring investors with stakes of 5 percent or more in listed companies to file public reports detailing such holdings. Such moves are intended to make the market more transparent and less intimidating for small investors.

EXHIBIT 9–5

**Footnote Excerpt from Sony Corp.
Annual Report**

Summary of Significant Accounting Policies

The parent company and its subsidiaries in Japan maintain their records and prepare their financial statements in accordance with accounting principles generally accepted in Japan while its foreign subsidiaries maintain their records and prepare their financial statements in conformity with accounting principles generally accepted in the countries of their domicile. Certain adjustments and reclassifications, including those relating to the tax effects of temporary differences, capitalization of stock purchase warrants, deferral of insurance acquisition costs, the accrual of certain expenses and the accounting for foreign currency translation, have been incorporated in the accompanying consolidated financial statements to conform with accounting principles generally accepted in the United States of America (U.S. GAAP). These adjustments were not recorded in the statutory books of account.

Source: Sony Annual Report, 1998.

As Japan's stock exchanges grow and continue to attract foreign investment, power will inevitably be diffused among more sophisticated and heterogeneous investors who cannot be counted on to join in any informal collaboration. In addition, as more and more acquisitions of Japanese corporations are undertaken by Western companies (e.g., Goodyear's late 1990's takeover of Sumitomo Rubber and Daimler-Chrysler's discussions with Nissan Diesel), greater transparency of Japanese accounts and more Western-like capital structures are likely to infiltrate and spread throughout the Japanese financial reporting world. Moreover, as foreign fund managers observe and participate in the TSE over time, many are coming to understand it on its own terms rather than simply concluding that any apparently inexplicable quirk is the result of behind-the-scenes skulduggery. It is interesting to note that, "a tenth of all Japanese shares, or about 60 percent of those that are freely traded, are owned by foreign investors."[32] Indeed, foreign analysts are creating higher standards for securities analysis in Tokyo, and by doing so, they implicitly (and often explicitly) reiterate the case for fuller and fairer disclosure by companies. As these analysts and managers find their way, their successes encourage the Japanese to reexamine their accounting methods and disclosure practices and to improve them.

Up to now, and still in large measure, "The status of a shareholder ranks slightly behind the person who serves the tea."[33] This is perhaps most dramatically evident in the fact that the return on equity for the Nikkei 300 industrial companies in 1997 was only about 4 percent (compared to 20 percent for U.S. industrial stocks), and on average only once since 1990 have Japanese companies not destroyed shareholder value—that is, had returns in excess of their very low cost of capital.[34] But times are slowly changing. For example, the large Japanese cosmetics company, Kao, recently publicly embraced EVA™ (economic value added) and in 1997, during the first two months following the legalization of corporate stock options, 35 companies (including Toyota Motor Co.) initiated stock option plans for their managers.[35]

Banking.   Modern Japanese banks were created by government fiat at the end of World War II to raise and distribute relatively inexpensive capital for Japan's industrial reconstruction. With such a mission, they have traditionally sought and earned very modest returns, and in turn have paid depositors a marginal return on savings (of late, 1 to 3 percent). Because Japan has one of the world's highest personal savings rates, it is not surprising to note that Japanese banks hold a higher proportion of their debt in the form of short-term demand deposits than most banks in Europe or the United States.[36] But after 50 years of such an environment and central role in "Japan, Inc.," the banking system finds itself overpopulated, uncompetitive, underdeveloped, saddled with huge bad loan portfolios, and gradually losing ground to the bond and stock markets as providers of capital.[37]

The latter half of the 1990s bore witness to a major (albeit slow) reconfiguration of the banking sector in Japan. The changes that began were inevitable if the banks were to survive as viable, robust players in the world's financial sector. For example, in 1995 Sumitomo Bank wrote off $8 billion in bad loans, providing the most profound insight to

---

[32]"Swapping Parts," *The Economist,* April 27, 1996, p. 85.

[33]P. Gawith, "The Picture Is Complicated," *Financial Times,* July 14, 1998, p. III.

[34]Ibid.

[35]See P. Abrahams, "Kao Puts on a New Face for Investor Relations," *Financial Times,* October 22, 1998, p. 17 and see also B. Spindle, "Corporate Japan Embraces Stock Options," *The Wall Street Journal,* July 30, 1997, p. A10.

[36]Baker, "The Appeal of Foreign Climes."

[37]G. Tett, "A Bang or a Whimper," *Financial Times,* April 1, 1998, p. 15.

date of the extent of nonperforming loans the banks possess.[38] Moreover, a merger between the Bank of Tokyo and Mitsubishi Bank was announced in 1995, thus setting the stage for creating the world's largest private bank.[39] The merger also ignited the start of winnowing down the number of banks in Japan that will ultimately remain in business, leaving only the truly strong ones that can compete on a global basis. The 1998 deregulation moves by Japan have opened the doors for commercial banks to enter the mutual fund market, allow the creation of financial holding companies to facilitate bank mergers, and permit banks and insurance companies to engage in other's industries via subsidiaries.[40] Banks have recently been allowed to fail, heretofore unheard of and unthinkable in Japan.[41] Finally, of note, the Japanese Bankers Federation has proposed two bank accounting rule changes that would seek to provide greater transparency: report all loans with interest 90 days in arrears (rather than 180 days) and report all loans that have been restructured.[42] These moves are intended to make the banks more globally competitive and transparent, something badly needed since the official estimate of bad loans held by Japanese banks is around ¥75 billion, twice the size of Australia's economy, while nongovernmental estimates are twice that figure.[43]

These and other changes portend some fundamental changes in the Japanese financial system. A traditional avoidance of uncertainty and a clear preference for long-term relationships may not be manageable in competing for a prominent position in the global financial market. Moreover, as industrial Japan shifts from market share goals toward a "more western-style stress on profitability and return on equity," banks will have to more carefully assess the creditworthiness and profit potential of their would-be customers.[44] Likewise, as the banks seek to be a more global source of funds, they will not be able to rely on relationships for garnering comfort regarding a customer's creditworthiness. Instead, more careful credit analysis will be necessary with an increased need for and reliance on financial disclosures. It is probable that Japanese banks will emerge as real consumers of financial information and thus catalysts for increased transparency in Japanese corporate financial reports.

Accounting Profession and Policy Formulation.   Japanese accountants, like other Japanese professionals and workers, are highly educated and well trained. The enactment of the Certified Public Accountants Law in 1948 requires that Japanese accountants be as qualified as those of the United States and the United Kingdom; their status is comparable with Japanese lawyers.[45] To earn the designation of certified public accountant and to become eligible for membership in the Japanese Institute of Certified Public Accountants (JICPA), a candidate must pass three examinations covering mathematics, language competency, accounting, auditing, management, economics, business law, and other topics. After passing the second examination, the candidate may register as a junior CPA and

---

[38]R. Neff and W. Glasgall, "An $8 Billion Write-Off and a Celebration," *Business Week,* February 13, 1995, p. 56.

[39]J. Sapsford and R. Steiner, "Huge Japanese Merger Could Revitalize the Financial Sector," *The Wall Street Journal,* March 29, 1995, p. A1.

[40]"Big Bang Schedule," *Financial Times,* March 26, 1998, p. III.

[41]"And It Finally Came to Tears," *The Economist,* November 29, 1997, pp. 77–79.

[42]G. Tett, "Japan's Banks To Tighten Bad Debt Rules," *Financial Times,* March 25, 1998, p. 8.

[43]See G. Tett, "A Bang or a Whimper," *Financial Times,* April 1, 1998, p. 15, and J. Rohwer, "Yikes! Japan's Bank Debt Bomb Is Scarier Than You Think," *Fortune,* November 9, 1998, pp. 124–26.

[44]"Japanese Corporate Strategy: New, Improved," *The Economist,* March 21, 1992, p. 72.

[45]JICPA, *The CPA Profession in Japan,* July 1987.

begin to fulfill a two-year work experience requirement. Before applying for the third examination, a candidate must also complete a one-year course that covers all aspects of a CPA's duties. These stringent requirements have greatly limited the size of the profession in Japan. Basic accounting principles and auditing standards are dictated by code law (specifically, the Commercial Code and the Securities and Exchange Law) or by the Business Accounting Deliberation Council (BADC), an agency of the Ministry of Finance. The BADC is increasingly considering IASC standards and some see Japanese GAAP dramatically moving that way in the future.[46] JICPA may issue supplementary guidelines for auditors.

Under the requirements of the Securities and Exchange Law of 1948, the auditors report expresses an opinion as to the fairness of presentation of a company's financial statements in accordance with Japanese GAAP. The opinion also refers to the consistent application of GAAP.

Selected Financial Reporting Practices

As noted earlier, tax accounting and financial reporting in Japan have a very close connection. Indeed, such a fact is but one manifestation of the dominant role that government ministries play in determining financial reporting practices. In sum, the essential difference between U.S. and Japanese GAAP is that the latter is determined in the public sector (principally by the Ministry of Finance), whereas the former is determined in the private sector (primarily the FASB).[47] Such a phenomenon has been described as the natural manifestation of the Japanese cultural belief in the moral basis of government and the belief in government's "superior ability to formulate and implement the law."[48] Moreover, group consciousness (i.e., low IDV) may be considered responsible for a Japanese corporate reluctance to make public disclosure of corporate financial activities.[49]

Given such a backdrop, it is useful to consider that:

> Japanese accounting in the 1990s is descended from native medieval bookkeeping, overlaid by a commercial code modeled on late 19th century Franco-German precedents, rounded off with U.S.-inspired securities laws of the late 1940s.[50]

In particular, some of the German influence is manifested in a strict application of the historical cost concept, no provision for proposed dividends, and the dominance of form over substance (e.g., leases tend not to be capitalized). On the other hand, the U.S. influence can be seen in the preparation of a statement of cash flows, the amortization of goodwill, the sequence of balance sheet items (e.g., most to least liquid), and the disclosure of basic and diluted earnings per share. A number of other similarities and nuances

---

[46]E. Sawa, "The Standard-Setting Process in Japan," *IASC INSIGHT,* June 1997, pp. 13–14. See also, "Fallen Idol," *The Economist,* June 20, 1998, p. 23.

[47]T. Cooke, "The Impact of Accounting Principles on Profits: The U.S. versus Japan," *Accounting and Business Research,* Autumn 1993, pp. 460–76.

[48]W. L. Harrison and J. L. McKinnon, "Culture and Accounting Change: A New Perspective on Corporate Reporting Regulation and Accounting Policy Formulation," *Accounting, Organizations and Society* 11, no. 3 (1986), pp. 233–52.

[49]Ibid.

[50]C. Nobes, "Japanese Practices Embody Radical Approach," *Financial Times,* February 14, 1991, p. 14.

in Japanese reports are interesting, however, and important to note. These include valuation, consolidated reporting, doubtful accounts, liabilities, leases, deferred income tax, deferred charges, business enterprise tax, retirement and severance benefits, warrant bonds, director bonuses, depreciation expense, and shareholder capital and reserves.

Valuation

Japanese companies adhere closely to the historical cost principle applied conservatively. Inventories are valued at cost or at market if it is significantly lower and not expected to recover. Cost is determined by the following methods: individual cost, FIFO, LIFO, HIFO (i.e., highest price in), moving average, and/or adjusted selling price.

Property, plant, and equipment are stated at cost less accumulated depreciation. (Current cost information is not used, even on a supplementary basis.) Depreciation, which is not applicable for land, is generally computed by the declining-balance method using rates prescribed under tax regulations, although the straight-line method may also be used. Special accelerated depreciation allowed under the tax laws is recorded either as a charge to income or as an appropriation of retained earnings.

In the case of marketable equity securities (other than shares in a subsidiary), Japanese GAAP closely parallels that of the United States. Trading securities are marked-to-market, with any unrealized gains and losses recorded in income. For fiscal years beginning after April 1, 2001, available-for-sale securities will also be marked-to-market, with any unrealized gains and losses taken to shareholders' equity until realized. As most Japanese companies classify their marketable securities as available-for-sale, most revaluation adjustments are expected to be disclosed on the balance sheet.

Consolidated Reporting

As in the United States, in Japan the financial results of majority-controlled subsidiaries must be consolidated with those of the parent unless (1) the voting control over the subsidiary is temporary (i.e., a sale is pending), (2) control is not effective (e.g., due to bankruptcy or reorganization), or (3) inclusion of the subsidiary's results would be misleading to shareholders. Consolidation may also be avoided if a subsidiary represents less than 10 percent of the consolidated group's total assets or sales (i.e., a materiality exclusion). Consolidation may be effected using either pooling-of-interests or purchase accounting, depending on how a parent's investment in a subsidiary was obtained. For investments representing ownership interest of 20 to 50 percent, the equity method is commonly used.

Doubtful Accounts

A bad debt allowance is calculated in accordance with percentages of outstanding receivables as specified by tax law (e.g., retail companies—1%; manufacturing—0.8%; financial—0.3%; other—0.6%). It is considered generally accepted to charge the allowance to the legal limit, regardless of the dictates of sound business judgment and expected or actual past experience. In contrast, U.S. accounting practice stresses net collectible amounts in valuing accounts receivable—a long-standing tradition in accounting, stemming from the days when creditors were the major users of financial statements. In Japan, where a company's creditors are often members of the firm's own business group (and thus are privy to the group's detailed financial information), making the effort to determine and report exact or realistic collectible amounts has little significance because if the timely payment of an account is doubtful, it is likely to be given an extension or perhaps even forgotten.

Liabilities

Liabilities, both current and noncurrent, are recorded on the balance sheet at face value (as compared to present value under U.S. GAAP). Certain expenses (e.g., employee bonuses and repairs) and losses (e.g., sales returns and rebates) relating to future periods may be charged against current income by creating a reserve in the liabilities section of the balance sheet. Contingent losses on future sales, purchases, or product warranties must be accrued in the balance sheet if the liability is both probable and reasonably estimable.

Leases

Most leases are accounted for as operating leases by both the lessor and the lessee. Although in practice leases are rarely capitalized, a guideline issued by JICPA suggests the capitalization of some leases that contain a bargain purchase clause, those involving machinery that was built specifically for the lessee and cannot be leased to others, and those in which the leased property is land or buildings. Additionally, finance leases that are deemed to transfer ownership of the leased asset to the lessee should be capitalized, while other finance leases may be accounted for as an operating lease if certain "as if capitalized" information is disclosed in the footnotes. As mentioned earlier, the general absence of lease capitalization is often cited as an example of one of several German-style features in Japanese accounting; it has been described as an example of the dominance of form over substance and the lack of an overriding fair principle.[51]

Deferred Income Tax

Because differences between taxable and financial income in Japan are minor, the deferral of income taxes is not as commonly found as it is in the United States. For example, in the United States, accelerated depreciation methods are frequently used for tax purposes, whereas straight-line depreciation is most commonly used for financial reporting purposes. This is not the case in Japan, where accelerated methods are typically used for both tax and reporting purposes. Japanese companies that restate results in accordance with U.S. GAAP, however, usually must make some provision for deferred income taxes. Beginning in 1999, it became permissible to recognize deferred tax assets in the consolidated balance sheets; previously, recognition was prohibited because deferred tax assets did not satisfy the legal definition of an asset.

Deferred Charges

Deferred charges permitted to be capitalized under the Japanese Commercial Code are as follows:

Deferred Charge	Maximum Amortization Period
Organization costs	5 Years
Preoperation costs	5 Years
New share issuance costs	3 Years
Bond issuance costs	3 Years or the redemption period, whichever is shorter
Bond discounts	The redemption period of debt

[51]C. Nobes and S. Maeda, "Japanese Accounts: Interpreters Needed," *Accountancy,* September 1990, pp. 82–84.

Goodwill may be recorded as a deferred charge only when it is acquired for consideration or through merger and consolidation and, if deferred, it is normally amortized against earnings over a five-year period. Prior to 1999, the capitalization of research and development costs, with amortization over five years, was also permitted. For fiscal years beginning after April 1, 1999, such costs must be expensed as incurred.

Business Enterprise Tax

The local business enterprise tax (BET) is a tax that is normally about 12 percent of total corporate income. The BET is one of three corporate taxes and is the only one expensed on a cash basis. Thus, if net income and/or the BET rate increases year to year, the effective total Japanese corporate income tax rate for a given year will be several points lower than that year's combined nominal rate.

The BET is a cost-of-doing-business tax. Its rate schedule is determined by each prefecture (a local political subdivision) in which an entity operates. It has been observed that the BET is reported as a part of selling, general, and administrative costs in the statutory accounts filed in accordance with Japan's commercial code, but it is frequently aggregated with income tax expense in the convenience-translation financial statements issued for public consumption. As a result, the reported income before taxes differs for each of the two types of reports.[52]

Retirement and Severance Benefits

Japanese companies generally follow the terminal funding approach, making lump-sum payments to retiring employees, the amount of which is calculated according to salary history and length of employment. Beginning in 2000, however, any unfunded pension liabilities must be recognized in the consolidated balance sheet. Pension liabilities will be measured at their present value, and any unfunded balance calculated with reference to the pension assets measured at fair value. Amortization of any unfunded balance will occur over 15 years. Exhibit 9–6 illustrates the pension disclosures for the Wacoal Corporation.

Director Bonuses

Bonuses to directors and statutory auditors must be voted on by a company's shareholders and are treated as a distribution of profits rather than an expense. They are charged directly to retained earnings and are not tax deductible. In contrast, under U.S. GAAP, director bonuses are treated as an expense. This difference in treatment may explain, in part, the difference between the salaries of CEOs in the United States as compared to those in Japan: Executive compensation in Japan is substantially less than that in the United States.

Depreciation Expense

Depreciation expense is based on the accelerated depreciation method for both financial and tax reporting as required by Japanese tax regulations.

Shareholder Capital and Reserves

Owners' equity on the balance sheet is usually segmented into four accounts: Capital Stock, Capital Reserve, Legal Reserve, and Retained Earnings. Capital stock includes both common and preferred shares issued, with or without par value.[53] When shares are issued without a par value, not less than 50 percent of the proceeds of the sale price must be recorded as capital stock.

---

[52]Ibid.

[53]When common stock is issued with a par value, that value is most commonly ¥50.

EXHIBIT 9–6

Wacoal Corp. and Subsidiaries

Termination and Retirement Plans

The Companies sponsor termination and retirement benefit plans which cover substantially all employees. Benefits are based on the employee's years of service and certain other factors. If the termination is involuntary or caused by death, the employee is usually entitled to greater payments than in the case of voluntary termination. The Companies fund a portion of the obligations due under these plans. The general funding policy is to contribute amounts computed in accordance with actuarial methods accepted by Japanese tax law.

Contributory Retirement Plan

The Company has a contributory retirement plan that is interrelated with the Japanese government social welfare program which consists of a basic portion requiring employee and employer contributions plus an additional portion established by the Company.

Periodic pension payments required under the basic portion are prescribed by the Japanese Ministry of Welfare, commence at age 60 and continue until the death of the surviving spouse. Benefits under the additional portion are usually paid in a lump sum at the earlier of termination or retirement, although periodic payments are available under certain conditions.

The following table summarizes the financial status of the contributory retirement plan and the amounts recognized in the consolidated balance sheets at March 31, 1998 and 1997:

	Millions of Yen		Thousands of U.S. Dollars
	1998	1997	1998
Actuarial present value of benefit obligations:			
Vested	¥23,639	¥19,684	$177,470
Nonvested	920	603	6,907
Accumulated benefit obligation	24,559	20,287	184,377
Effect of projected future salary increases	6,161	5,448	46,254
Projected benefit obligation for service rendered to date	30,720	25,735	230,631
Less trusteed fund assets at fair value (cash equivalents, bonds and stocks)	19,999	17,641	150,143
Projected benefit obligation in excess of plan assets	10,721	8,094	80,488
Unrecognized net loss	(4,450)	(2,798)	(33,408)
Remaining unrecognized net transition asset	707	825	5,308
Liability recognized in consolidated balance sheets	¥ 6,978	¥ 6,121	$ 52,388

The pension expense recorded for the contributory retirement plan included the following components for the years ended March 31, 1998, 1997 and 1996:

	Millions of Yen			Thousands of U.S. Dollars
	1998	1997	1996	1998
Service cost, less employees' contribution	¥2,396	¥2,101	¥2,210	$17,988
Interest cost on projected benefit obligation	1,029	1,162	877	7,725
Actual return on plan assets	(807)	(591)	(1,148)	(6,059)
Net amortization and deferral	116	247	850	871
Net expense	¥2,734	¥2,919	¥2,789	$20,525

EXHIBIT 9–6   (concluded)

The actuarial present value of the projected benefit obligation at March 31, 1998, 1997 and 1996 was determined using discount rates of 4.0%, 4.5% and 4.5%, respectively, and rates of increase in future compensation levels of 2.0%, 2.0% and 3.0%, respectively. The expected long-term rates of return on plan assets at March 31, 1998, 1997 and 1996 were 3.5%, 4.0% and 4.0%, respectively. The unrecognized net loss is being amortized utilizing an accelerated method, and the remaining unrecognized net translation asset is being amortized on a straight-line basis over 15 years.

Noncontributory Termination Plans
The Companies have several partially funded plans administered by independent trustees and one unfunded termination plan administered by the Company. These plans provide lump-sum termination benefits and are paid at the earlier of the employees' termination or the mandatory retirement age except for payments to directors and corporate auditors which require approval by the shareholders before payment.

Domestic subsidiaries record provisions for termination benefits sufficient to state the liability (net of plan assets) equal to the plans' vested benefits, which exceed the plans' accumulated benefit obligations.

A summary of these obligations at March 31, 1998 and 1997 is as follows:

	Millions of Yen		Thousands of U.S. Dollars
	1998	*1997*	*1998*
Vested benefits	**¥4,694**	¥4,533	**$35,241**
Less plan assets at fair value, primarily cash equivalents	**1,615**	1,560	**12,125**
Pension liability recognized in the consolidated balance sheets	**¥3,079**	¥2,973	**$23,116**

The net expense for noncontributory termination plans for the years ended March 31, 1998, 1997 and 1996 was ¥452 million ($3,393 thousand), ¥500 million and ¥510 million, respectively.

The Capital Reserve account reflects any paid-in surplus from the sale of stock and any gain on the repurchase of treasury stock. The Legal Reserve account reflects appropriated retained earnings; an amount equal to at least 10 percent of each cash dividend must be credited to the Legal Reserve account until the reserve equals 25 percent of the capital stock account. Finally, retained earnings is usually composed of both unappropriated and appropriated balances. Exhibit 9–7 illustrates the shareholders' equity disclosures for Kajima Corporation. Exhibit 9–8 presents a summary comparison of Japanese and U.S. accounting and reporting practices.

EXHIBIT 9–7

KAJIMA CORPORATION
Shareholders' Equity Disclosures

Panel A. Balance Sheet Excerpt

	Millions of Yen		Thousands of U.S. Dollars
	1998	*1997*	*1998*
Stockholders' equity (Notes 12, 13):			
Common stock, authorized, 1,920,000,000 shares, ¥50 par value; issued and outstanding, 961,312,022 shares	64,071	64,071	485,386
Additional paid-in capital	32,147	32,147	243,538
Legal reserve	16,178	16,167	122,561
Retained earnings	254,050	270,719	1,924,621
Total	366,466	383,104	2,776,106
Treasury stock—at cost	(1)	(2)	(8)
Total stockholders' equity	366,445	383,102	2,776,098
TOTAL	**¥2,684,328**	**¥2,868,379**	**$20,335,818**

Panel B Footnote Excerpts

12. SPECIAL RESERVES

The Japanese Special Taxation Measures Law permits companies to take as tax deductions certain reserves which are not required for financial reporting purposes. Under Japanese tax law, these reserves must be recorded in the books to be tax deductible and must be reversed into taxable income in future years. The effect of such reserves is the deferral of tax payments. Retained earnings as of March 31, 1998 included ¥18,693 million ($141,614 thousand) of such reserves.

13. STOCKHOLDERS' EQUITY

The Code provides that retained earnings in an amount equal to at least 10% of any amount paid by the Company as an appropriation of retained earnings, including dividends and bonuses to directors and corporate auditors, be appropriated to a legal reserve until such reserve equals 25% of the stated capital. This reserve is not available for dividends but may be used to reduce a deficit by resolution of the stockholders, or may be capitalized by resolution of the Board of Directors.

Under the Code, at least 50% of the issue price of new shares, with a minimum of the par value thereof, is required to be designated as stated capital. The portion which is to be designated as stated capital is determined by resolution of the Board of Directors.

Proceeds in excess of the amounts designated as stated capital have been credited to additional paid-in capital. The Company may transfer, by resolution of the stockholders, a portion of retained earnings available for dividends to a common stock account, and the Company may issue new shares of common stock to the existing stockholders without consideration by resolution of the Board of Directors, to the extent that the amount calculated by multiplying the number of outstanding shares after the issuance by par value per share shall not exceed the stated capital, and that the amount calculated by dividing the total amount of stockholders' equity by the number of outstanding shares after the issuance shall not be less than ¥50. These issuances of the new shares are treated as stock splits.

Cash dividends at the fiscal year-end must be approved by the stockholders at an annual meeting to be held subsequent to the year-end, while interim dividends may be paid after the half-year end upon resolution of the Board of Directors.

As of March 31, 1998 and 1997, the number of shares of common stock of the Company held by unconsolidated subsidiaries and affiliates was 4,878 thousand shares.

EXHIBIT 9–8

Comparison of Japanese and U.S. Accounting and Reporting Standards

Item	Japan	U.S.
Asset valuation	Historical cost (applied conservatively) with selected revaluation (principally downward)	Historical cost, with selected revaluation (principally downward)
Inventory valuation	Specific identification, moving and weighted average, LIFO, FIFO, HIFO (i.e., highest purchase price)	Principally LIFO (because of tax considerations); also FIFO and average cost methods
Inventory: year-end	Lower of cost or replacement cost	Lower-of-cost or replacement cost
Depreciation	Principally accelerated methods, although production-based methods and straight-line also permitted	Principally straight line, with accelerated and production-based methods permitted
Goodwill	Capitalized and amortized, normally over 5 years; negative goodwill permitted	Capitalized to balance sheet, with amortization (principally straight-line) over a maximum of 40 years; negative goodwill not permitted
Research and development costs	Expensed as incurred: (in 1999 and thereafter)	Research costs expensed currently; development costs expensed currently except in certain industries (i.e., software, oil and gas)
Capitalization of interest costs:	Generally not practiced except for real estate development companies	Capitalization required for self-constructed assets
Intercorporate investments		
Marketable securities (current asset–trading)	Market value (on an individual-security basis) with unrealized gains and losses to income statement	Market value (on an individual-security basis) with unrealized gains and losses to income statement
Long-term investments:		
0–20% ownership (available for sale)	Market value (on an individual-security basis) with unrealized gains and losses to balance sheet (i.e., owners' equity)	Market value (on an individual-security basis) with unrealized gains and losses to balance sheet (i.e., owners' equity)
20–50% ownership	Equity method	Equity method
51–100% ownership	Consolidated, unless the subsidiary (1) composes less than 10% of total group assets or sales, (2) control is temporary, (3) is not a going concern, or (4) consolidation produces misleading results; unconsolidated subsidiaries equity method accounted; pooling and purchase accounting permitted	Consolidated, using pooling (until 2001) or purchase accounting
Debt valuation	All debt valued at face or repayment value	Long-term debt (except deferred income taxes) valued at present value; all other debt valued at face value
Leases	Most leases treated as operating leases; finance leases which transfer ownership are capitalized.	Capital leases reflected in balance sheet; operating leases disclosed in footnotes
Deferred income taxes	Generally unrecorded due to close proximity of book and taxable income	Computed under liability method
Pension liabilities	Reflected on balance sheet	Reflected on balance sheet
Discretionary reserves	Specific reserves permitted	Restricted to identifiable operational losses
Statement of cash flows	Required	Required

Analytical Considerations

The Center for International Financial Analysis and Reporting recently concluded that the accounting practices of Japan (and Germany) were the furthest removed from global norms and that this departure from global norms was manifested in substantially under-reported earnings. Consider, for example, the average price-earnings ratio data for listed stocks reported in Exhibit 9–9. On the surface, these data appear to suggest that

EXHIBIT 9–9
Average Price-Earnings Ratio Data of Companies Listed on the
Tokyo Stock Exchange and the New York Stock Exchange

	*Tokyo Stock Exchange**	*New York Stock Exchange†*
1988	58.4	14.2
1989	70.6	13.8
1990	39.8	14.7
1991	37.8	20.1
1992	36.7	25.4
1993	64.9	23.3
1994	74.5	15.1
1995	86.5	19.1
1996	79.3	15.7
1997	37.6	17.4

*Tokyo Stock Exchange, *Fact Book, 1998.*
†*New York Stock Exchange Fact Book*—1998.

Japanese stocks are substantially overpriced relative to U.S. securities; however, when one considers the institutional setting in Japan, the high P-E multiple afforded Japanese securities can be seen to reflect, to a large extent, the underreporting of earnings characteristic of that country. Recall that conservative accounting practices in Japan are driven, in large part, by the legal requirement that expenses claimed for tax purposes correspond to those claimed for book purposes.[54] Thus, unlike their U.S. counterparts, Japanese managers are unable to effectively pursue the dual objectives of minimizing taxable income while maximizing book income. But what are the principal causes of income underreporting in Japan, and how are those factors likely to be manifested in financial indicators of performance? What are the key differences on the balance sheet under Japanese versus U.S. GAAP? With respect to the income statement, the primary determinants of income underreporting in Japan involve the use of discretionary tax-deductible reserves and higher depreciation provisions. With respect to the balance sheet, the key differences involve the valuation of liabilities, in general, and consolidation practices in particular.

As noted in Exhibit 9–8, Japanese companies value debt at its face, repayment, or settlement value. This treatment dramatically contrasts with U.S. practice by which long-term liabilities (except deferred income taxes) are valued at discounted (or present) value. All other things being constant, this difference in reporting practice generally causes Japanese companies to carry a lower book value (or net worth) than U.S. companies carry, since the repayment value of debt generally exceeds its present value. This practice may particularly distort financial analysis involving Japanese companies when one also considers the propensity of Japanese companies to finance via debt (versus equity). The lower book value of Japanese companies caused by their higher valuation of debt would, however, be partially offset by two other reporting considerations. First, many Japanese subsidiaries that would otherwise be consolidated under U.S. GAAP (i.e., *SFAS No. 94*) are equity accounted in Japan. An important consequence of this is that the debt of many unconsolidated Japanese subsidiaries is not reflected on the books of the consolidated

---

[54]This Japanese tax-book compliance requirement is somewhat akin to the LIFO tax-book compliance regulation that exists in the United States, although the origins of each are substantially different.

entity, thereby causing the relative debt levels of U.S. conglomerates to exceed those of comparable Japanese companies. A final consideration relates to the treatment of leases. In Japan, few leases are capitalized to the balance sheet, suggesting that, *ceteris paribus,* there should be less leasing debt reported on the books of Japanese companies when compared to U.S. companies.

All in all, the conservative valuation of debt and the propensity to finance debt tend to cause Japanese companies to appear to be substantially less solvent than their U.S. counterparts. Recognizing that this may hurt their chances of obtaining foreign investment, many Japanese companies issue financial statements prepared according to U.S. GAAP, thereby enabling analysts and investors to make a more informed comparison of Japanese versus U.S. company results.

Profitability

A review of Japanese GAAP reveals that, relative to U.S. GAAP, numerous current income-reducing practices abound. For example, deductions for bad debts in Japan are prescribed by income tax regulations (usually about 1 percent of receivables) rather than actual corporate experience. In addition, interest costs relating to debt associated with the self-construction of assets cannot be capitalized and must be expensed as incurred. Of greater significance than either of these policies are the depreciation and reserve policies followed by Japanese companies.

In general, for purposes of calculating book depreciation, Japanese companies use the shorter estimated lives for depreciable assets specified by Japanese tax law, and declining-balance depreciation is the most prevalent method used. In contrast, most U.S. companies use straight-line depreciation and asset lives that exceed those permitted under the U.S. tax code. Not surprising, the net effect of these differences is that Japanese companies appear less profitable as a consequence of the larger depreciation deductions taken against earnings. This outcome is compounded by the fact that Japanese GAAP permits a company to establish contingency accounts for a variety of general future expenses, such as product warranties and various other business risks. In the United States, GAAP relating to the creation of contingent reserves is considerably more stringent, permitting reserves only for identifiable operating losses. Further, U.S. managers have little incentive to aggressively anticipate such charges against income, given the securities market's preference for higher (not lower) reported earnings and the preponderance of executive compensation plans linked to security prices.

The net effect of these practices is a relatively understated assessment of firm profitability. As a consequence of the understatement of profitability and the overstatement of debt, the average ROE for Japanese publicly listed companies consistently runs approximately 300 percent less than for U.S. publicly held companies. This distortion in reported financial indicators makes comparative cross-national financial analysis involving Japan a challenging exercise.

Analyzing Japanese Financial Data

It is widely acknowledged that significant accounting, economic, and cultural differences exist between Japan and the United States (and most other non-Asian countries) and that these differences should, and apparently are, reflected in security prices and such market-derived indicators as P-E ratios. But what are the implications of this for financial analysis? Should analysts, for example, attempt to restate Japanese financial data to conform to U.S. GAAP or should they evaluate less traditional financial indices, perhaps ones unique to the Japanese setting?

Until recently, the answers to these questions seemed clear. The preponderance of available evidence indicated that a majority of the difference between Japanese and U.S. financial measures could be reconciled by adjusting for the differences in accounting and business practices between the two countries.[55] More recently, however, the notion that analysts should attempt to restate Japanese financial data has been called into question. A recent study found that adjusting for different accounting principles explained very little of the difference in P-E ratios or rates of return on assets and common equity.[56] Subsequent research has revealed that neither country appeared to generate *systematically* higher profitability but that across time and for most industries, the ROA of U.S. companies exceeded those of Japanese companies primarily because of consistently higher asset turnover rates for U.S. firms.[57] The observed differences in profitability and rates of return have been primarily attributed to cultural (e.g., credit-granting policies and inventory management techniques) and structural (e.g., governmental controls over the supply of money) factors.

These findings appear to closely dovetail with the prevailing practice of professional mutual fund managers in the United States: Instead of trying to restate foreign earnings to compare such traditional market indices as the P-E ratio for purposes of investment decisions, many mutual fund managers have opted for less traditional financial indexes, particularly those that are less sensitive to the differences in accounting practices that may exist between companies from different countries.[58] Consider, for example, the cash flow from operations (CFFO); this measure inherently removes many of the differences (e.g., depreciation accounting and other noncash or cost-allocation related factors) that exist between the accounting practices in different countries. Thus, some mutual fund managers now use the price-cash flow ratio and/or cash flow per share instead of the traditional P-E ratio as a benchmark to compare investments across national boundaries.

Summary

It would be unfair not to acknowledge that Japan is undergoing significant changes. During the early 1990s, the Nikkei stock average hit a 12-year low, consumers experienced a nine-year high in inflation, a rise in Tokyo housing costs to a level 10 to 12 times the average homebuyer's annual income, record levels of bankruptcies, a sharp decline in banks' capital ratios necessitating many to market subordinated debt to their large corporate customers to replenish capital, an increase and then a drastic decrease in interest rates, credit tightening by the Bank of Japan, saddling of the nation's financial institutions with billions of newly acknowledged bad debt, a decline in corporate profits by as much as 50 percent, a decrease in corporate capital spending by as much as 30 percent, and the slowing of GNP growth to about 2 percent. Some analysts believe that these facts portend a serious, although not hopeless, situation. Indeed, "Japan, Inc." is reported by astute observers to be in the throes of a major economic shift—one where the *keiretsus* are less insular and less prevalent, one where jobs for

[55]See, for instance, K. R. French and J. M. Poterba, "Were Japanese Stock Prices Too High?" *Journal of Financial Economics* 29 (1991), pp. 337–63; and R. Officer and G. Isgro, "The Relative Behavior of Price-to-Earnings Ratios in Australia, Japan, the U.S., and the U.K., and Implications Thereof," working paper, the University of Melbourne, Australia, 1990.

[56]P. Brown, V. Soybel, and C. Stickney, "Achieving Comparability of U.S. and Japanese Financial Statement Data," *Japan and the World Economy* 5 (1993), pp. 51–72.

[57]P. Brown, V. Soybel, and C. Stickney, "Comparing U.S. and Japanese Corporate-Level Operating Performance Using Financial Statement Data," *Strategic Management Journal,* January 1994, pp. 75–83.

[58]Morningstar Mutual Funds newsletter, December 10, 1993, p. 2; see also P. Martin, "Good Buys, but a Risky Business," *Financial Times,* August 22, 1992, p. 6.

life are not automatic, and one where government's main role is to let a market-based economy truly take root.

Hard work, loyalty, education, and respect for traditional ways of doing things are still the foremost Japanese traits. The trend is clear, however, Japan enters the 21st century more open to Western imports and investment than ever before, but with a realism that the 1970's and 1980's formula for success needs serious modification. In many people's minds, Japan's government-regulated capitalism must give way to market-based capitalism. Currently, considerable concern exists in the West that Japan's recent bad economic trends will cause the Japanese government to become more insular (as before), not less, as a way to work out of this recession.

Change is occurring. Perhaps indicative of a subtle change in domestic priorities is the Ministry of International Trade and Industry's industrial policy paper for the 1990s. In lieu of the usual opening discussion of industrial goals, the paper dealt first with issues of worker vacations, increased consumer protection, higher imports, and better child care facilities.[59] Indicative of a not so subtle change in the Bank of Japan's recent hiring of the U.S. consulting firm McKinsey & Co. to help improve the Bank's operations and information systems.[60] Another example of change can be found in Japanese corporate goals. Japanese firms are being compelled to reconsider their traditional strategy of seeking maximum sales and market share. The nation's number two automaker, Nissan, has formally abandoned its policy of giving top priority to increasing market share and has instead adopted a policy that emphasizes improving profitability.[61] Another avenue for change may come as a result of its prior economic successes and growing sense of economic confidence: Japan appears to be more willing to cooperate with other industrialized countries than to go its own way. Faced with a recently achieved economic maturity, Japan now finds itself needing to tend to issues previously subordinated to the one goal of world-class economic leadership.

More and deeper change is needed, however. Historically, "Japanese companies have existed first for their employees, then the pensioners, third for business partners (suppliers and dealers), fourth for the main bank, and fifth for the shareholders."[62] These priorities are being reevaluated. Moreover, "better accountancy, tougher auditing standards, and improved corporate governance are an urgent priority in [Japan's move to] a more market-oriented environment."[63]

Suggested Readings

Bildersee, J., J. Chek, and C. Lee. "The International Price-Earnings Ratio Phenomenon." *Japan and the World Economy* 4 (1990), pp. 263–82.

Bloom, R., S. Long, and M. Collins. "Japanese and American Accounting: Explaining the Differences." *Advances in International Accounting* 6 (1994), pp. 265–84.

Bremmer, B. "Japan's Real Crisis," *Business Week,* May 18, 1998, pp. 136–42.

Campbell, N. "The Role of Japan's Top Managers." *Journal of General Management,* Winter 1994, pp. 20–28.

---

[59]"How the Japanese are Changing," *Fortune,* September 24, 1990, pp. 15–22.

[60]G. Tett, "Bank of Japan Turns to Overseas Consultant," *Financial Times,* January 21, 1999, p. 1.

[61]P. Blustein, "When This Recession Is Over, Japan May Never Be the Same," *The Washington Post,* June 22, 1992, p. A1.

[62]A. Harney and P. Abrahams, "Death of a Salaryman?" *Financial Times,* November 12, 1998, p. 15.

[63]"Wonderland Accounting," *Financial Times,* November 26, 1997, p. 15.

Cooke, T. E., and M. Kibruya. *Financial Reporting in Japan: Regulation, Practice, and Environment.* New York: Oxford Press, 1992.

Coopers & Lybrand. *Executive Summary of Principal Differences between Accounting Principles in the United States and Japan,* New York: Coopers and Lybrand, 1989.

Darrough, M., H. Pourjalali, and S. Saudagaran, "Earnings Management in Japanese Companies," *The International Journal of Accounting* 33, no. 3 (1998), pp. 313–34.

Dawkins, W. "Loosening of the Corporate Web." *Financial Times,* November 30, 1994, p. 13.

"Fallen Idol." *The Economist,* June 20, 1998, pp. 21–23.

Fallows, J. "How the World Works." *The Atlantic Monthly,* December 1993, pp. 61–87.

Grant, C. "Information Sources for U.K. Investors and Financial Analysts Working in the Japanese Market." *Asian Review of Accounting* 1 (1992), pp. 12–30.

Ide, M., "Corporate Profitability and Stock Valuation in Japan." *Financial Analysts Journal,* March/April 1996, pp. 40–55.

"Japan Looks Ahead to the Millennium." *Accountancy,* December 1997, p. 13.

Lowe, H. D. "Shortcomings of Japanese Consolidated Financial Statements." *Accounting Horizons,* September 1990, pp. 1–9.

McDonald, J. "The *Mochiai* Effect: Japanese Corporate Cross-Holdings." *Journal of Portfolio Management* 9 (1989), pp. 90–94.

Rohwer, J., "Japan's Quiet Revolution." *Fortune,* March 30, 1998, pp. 82–88.

Schieneman, G. S. "Japanese P/E Ratios: Myth and Reality." *International Investment Review,* March 30, 1989.

Price Waterhouse & Co. *Doing Business in Japan.* New York: Price Waterhouse, 1995. *The Spicer and Oppenheim Guide to Financial Statements around the World.* New York: Wiley, 1989.

Yoshimura, N. and P. Anderson. *Inside the Kaisha.* Boston, MA, Harvard Business School Press, 1997.

Exercises

9.1   Japanese Credit Analysis: Qualitative Aspects

In a January–February 1994 *Bankers Magazine* article (pp. 56–59), "Commercial Loan Decisions: The Japanese Way," S. Gupta, H. Roehm, and J. Castellano identify four important qualitative dimensions to Japanese bankers' commercial loan decisions: (1) the extent to which the applicant manages for the long term, (2) the applicant's commitment to employees, (3) the applicant's commitment to their community, and (4) the quality of the applicant's management.

Required:

Comment on the ways in which you see these considerations as consistent with or in contrast to what you understand to be the cultural context of doing business in Japan.

9.2   Stricter Disclosure

In a September 21, 1994 *Financial Times* article (p. V), "Overseas Investors Wooed," E. Terazono reports a Nippon Telegraph and Telephone official's rationale for its planned New York Stock Exchange listing: "By listing in the U.S., where the disclosure rules are stricter than in Japan, we hope to win trust from investors."

Required:

Identify several ways in which you believe the U.S. financial disclosure rules are stricter than those in Japan. Comment on whether meeting those stricter disclosures is likely to "win trust from investors."

9.3   Japanese Accounting Policies

Kajima Corporation is one of Japan's leading construction companies. It maintains operating subsidiaries in North America, Europe and Asia and is active in construction and real estate development around the world. The company's activities encompass railway construction, electrical power development, highrise structures, nuclear power plants and maritime-related projects.

Required:

Presented below is Kajima's "Summary of Significant Accounting Policies." Identify any differences between Kajima's accounting policies and (a) International Accounting Standards and (b) U.S. Accounting Standards.

Kajima Corporation
Summary of Significant Accounting Policies

a. *Recognition of Revenues and Related Costs*—Revenues from and related costs of construction contracts are recorded using the completed-contract method.

b. *Foreign Currency Transactions*—Short-term receivables and payables denominated in foreign currencies are translated into Japanese yen at the current exchange rates as of each balance sheet date. Long-term receivables and payables denominated in foreign currencies are translated into Japanese yen at historical exchange rates. However, when there is a significant unrealized exchange loss related to long-term receivables and payables derived from foreign currency fluctuations, such receivables and payables are translated into Japanese yen at the exchange rates in effect at the balance sheet date. Assets and/or liabilities which are converted at the foreign exchange rate or swap rate are translated using the exchange rates set forth in the applicable exchange contract and the relevant currency swap agreement. The exchange gains and losses are deferred and recognized as income ratably over the term of the contract period. Other exchange gains and losses are recognized in the fiscal periods in which they occur.

c. *Inventories*—Inventories other than materials and supplies are stated at cost as determined on a specific project basis. Related general and administrative expenses and financial charges are excluded from such costs. Materials and supplies are stated at cost determined by a moving-average method.

d. *Marketable Securities and Investments in Securities*—Securities listed on stock exchanges included in marketable securities and investments in securities are stated at the lower of cost or market value, cost being determined by the moving-average method. Other securities are stated at cost, determined by the moving-average method.

e. *Investments in Subsidiaries and Affiliates*—Investments in subsidiaries and affiliates (20% to 50% owned) are stated at cost. Profits of these companies are reflected in the Company's books only to the extent dividends are received.

f. *Property and Equipment*—Property and equipment are stated principally at cost. Depreciation has been computed using a declining-balance method based upon the estimated useful lives for buildings and structures ranging from 2 to 65 years and for machinery and equipment ranging from 2 to 20 years.

g. *Costs of Research and Development and Debenture Issuance*—All research and development costs and debenture issuance costs are charged to income as incurred. Costs of research and development totaled ¥18,465 million ($139,886 thousand) and ¥19,567 million for the years ended March 31, 1998 and 1997, respectively.

h. *Allowance for Doubtful Accounts*—The Company provides for possible losses due to uncollectibility of notes, accounts, and loans receivable at the higher of either management's estimate or the maximum amount allowable for tax purposes.

i. *Retirement Benefits*—The Company has two types of retirement benefit plans to cover severance payments that would be required if all employees voluntarily terminated their services with the Company at each balance sheet date. The Kajima Pension Fund, the assets of which are administrated by the board of trustees composed of management and employee representatives, covers approximately 60% of the total amount of the severance payments and the remaining 40% is covered by an unfunded plan. In respect to the unfunded plan, the Company provides for the liability for severance payments at 40% of the amounts payable if all eligible participants were to terminate their employment at each balance sheet date, which is the maximum amount allowable for tax purposes. Normal costs of the pension plan are funded and currently charged to income. Past service costs are amortized and charged to income over a period of 20 years. The Company provides for officers' retirement allowances at 100% of the amount that would be required if all directors and corporate auditors voluntarily terminated their office as stipulated in the retirement regulations.

j. *Leases*—All leases are accounted for as operating leases. Under the Japanese accounting standards for leases, finance leases that deem to transfer ownership of the leased property to the lessee are to be capitalized, while other finance leases are permitted to be accounted for as operating lease transactions if certain "as if capitalized" information is disclosed in the notes to the lessee's nonconsolidated financial statements.

k. *Income Taxes*—The Company provides for income taxes at the amounts currently payable for each year, and deferred income taxes are not recognized.

l. *Appropriations of Retained Earnings*—Appropriations of retained earnings are accounted for and reflected in the accompanying nonconsolidated financial statements when approved by the stockholders.

9.4   Consolidated Reporting

Kajima Corporation is one of Japan's leading construction companies. The company prepares two sets of financial statements for its shareholders—one on an unconsolidated basis and a second on a consolidated basis. Both presentations are generally accepted under the Japanese Commercial code.

Required:

Presented below are Kajima's consolidated and unconsolidated financial statements for 1998.

1. How profitable were Kajima's unconsolidated subsidiaries?

2. Contrast the company's debt position on a consolidated versus unconsolidated basis.

KAJIMA CORPORATION
Statement of Income (1998)
(in millions of yen)

	Consolidated	*Unconsolidated*
Total revenues	¥ 1,938,933	¥ 1,512,804
Cost of sales	(1,778,719)	(1,376,468)
Gross profit	160,214	136,336
S,G&A	(136,832)	(106,494)
Operating income	23,382	29,842
Other income (expense)	(20,803)	(17,339)
Income before taxes	2,579	12,503
Income taxes	(8,559)	(6,500)
Minority interests	(4,907)	—
Equity in losses of unconsolidated subsidiaries	(6,531)	—
Net income	¥ (7,604)	¥ 6,003

Balance Sheet (1998)
(in millions of yen)

	Consolidated	*Unconsolidated*
Current assets	¥1,784,265	¥1,515,530
P,P&E (net)	564,381	380,798
Investments and other	335,682	367,968
Total assets	¥2,684,328	¥2,264,296
Current liabilities	¥1,662,009	¥1,398,169
Long-term liabilities	646,539	460,886
Minority interest	9,335	—
Stockholders' equity	366,445	405,241
Total equities	¥2,684,328	¥2,264,296

9.5   Account Analysis

The Daiei, Inc., is one of Japan's leading retailers. The company's product mix is approximately:

Foodstuffs	42%
Clothing and personal-care products	19%
Household items	15%
Hobbies, sporting goods, and other	8%
Wholesale	16%
Total	100%

A review of the company's 1998 annual report revealed the following:

Consolidated Balance Sheet
(in millions of yen)

	1998	*1997*
Current assets	¥ 667.787	¥ 446,320
P,P&E (net)	573,229	701,155
Investments and other	888,029	1,044,338
Goodwill	—	4,511
Translation adjustment	21,390	—
Total assets	¥2,150,435	¥2,196,324
Current liabilities	¥1,262,685	¥1,301,957
Long-term liabilities	738,162	759,285
Goodwill	1,884	
Translation adjustment		1,440
Minority interest	35,042	11,951
Shareholders' equity	112,662	121,691
Total equities	¥2,150,435	¥2,196,324

Required:

1. Why is goodwill carried as an asset in 1997 but as an equity item in 1998?
2. Why is the translation adjustment carried as an equity item in 1997 but as an asset in 1998? How would the account be reported under U.S. GAAP?
3. Calculate the long-term debt-to-equity ratio for 1997 and 1998, using a consistent treatment (i.e., U.S. GAAP) for the translation adjustment account.

9.6   Lease Accounting

Minolta Co., Ltd. is a leading manufacturer of photocopiers, printers, cameras, and other optical products. The company's annual reports discloses the following footnote information with respect to its treatment of leases:

> The company and various consolidated subsidiaries lease certain equipment under noncancelable lease agreements referred to as finance leases. Finance leases, other than those which transfer the ownership of the leased property to the lessee, are accounted for as operating leases.

Under Japanese GAAP, finance leases that deem to transfer ownership of leased property to a lessee are to be capitalized, whereas other finance leases are permitted to be accounted for as operating leases if certain "as if capitalized" information is disclosed in the notes to the lessee's consolidated financial statements.

Minolta's footnotes revealed the following information:

Lease Transactions:

Information on the lease payments of the company and its subsidiaries is summarized as follows:

(a) *For finance leases, exclusive of those which transfer the ownership of the leased equipment to the lessee:*

At March 31, 1998	*Millions of Yen*
Unexpired lease payments:	
1 year or less	¥ 6,619
Over 1 year	7,509
	¥14,128

(b) *For operating leases:*

At March 31, 1998	*Millions of Yen*
Unexpired lease payments:	
1 year or less	¥ 2,225
Over 1 year	6,144
	¥ 8,369

Presented below is the abbreviated balance sheet for 1998 for Minolta Co., Ltd. Using the above information, recast the company's balance sheet to reflect the capitalization of all leases. What assumptions did you make for your analysis? What assumptions would be necessary if you also wanted to restate the company's income statement? Does restatement make a difference?

MINOLTA CO., LTD.
Abbreviated Consolidated Balance Sheet
(in millions of yen)

	1998
Current assets	¥316,188
Investments	48,026
P,P&E (net)	82,652
Other	8,224
Total assets	¥455,090
Current liabilities*	¥308,843
Long-term liabilities*	64,961
Minority interests	736
Shareholders' equity	80,550
Total equities	¥455,090

*The annual interest rates on short-term bank loans ranged from 1% to 22% in 1998.
The annual interest rates on long-term bank loans ranged from 1% to 13% in 1998.

9.7   Pension Accounting

The accounting for employee benefits, such as pensions and other postretirement benefits varies greatly around the world. Much of this variance can be linked to the alternative funding schemes permitted to satisfy these future corporate obligations.

In the United States, for example, current funding is required, under which companies must expense and fund (or accrue a liability for) the present value of all retirement benefits earned in a period. Elsewhere, the pay-as-you-go approach is common. Under this method, no current funding of earned benefits is required; instead, benefits are funded only to the extent that current cash outflows are expected to occur. Finally, terminal funding is the norm in Japan and Asia in general. Under this approach, the present value of all earned benefits is funded as a lump sum when an employee retires.

Since Japanese tax law allows retirement benefits to be deducted in an amount equal to 40 percent of a company's total future obligation, regardless of funding status, retirement benefit expensing and liability accrual for most Japanese companies is equal to this amount. In a study of Japanese companies, Morgan Stanley Dean Witter concluded that many Japanese firms under expense and only partially fund their pension funds.[1] For example, Morgan Stanley estimated that Japan Air Lines' cumulative underexpensing of its pension obligation equaled 68 percent of shareholders' equity (as compared to that under U.S. GAAP), while the amount of pension underfunding equaled 32 percent of its reported debt.

[1] Morgan Stanley Dean Witter, *Apples-to-Apples: Japan Accounting* (1998).

Required:

Presented below is the abbreviated balance sheet of Sumitomo Corporation for 1998. Assume that the results of the Morgan Stanley Dean Witter study are applicable for all Japanese companies. Using those results, restate Sumitomo's financial results to bring them into compliance with U.S. GAAP. (The company's effective tax rate in 1998 was 41 percent.)

SUMITOMO CORPORATION
Abbreviated Balance Sheet
(in millions of yen)

	1998
Current assets	¥3,813,168
Investments	1,095,167
P,P&E (net)	807,905
Total assets	¥5,716,240
Current liabilities	¥3,389,817
Long-term debt	1,676,948
Liability for severance payments (note 7)	29,353
Minority interests	44,235
Shareholders' equity	575,887
	¥5,716,240

Employees' Retirement Benefits:

Under most circumstances, employees terminating their employment are entitled to severance payments based on the rate of pay at termination, years of service and certain other factors. A portion of the payments due under this plan is being funded.

The liability for severance payments is stated at the amount that would be required if all employees eligible for severance payments should voluntarily terminate their employment at the balance sheet date, less assets of the pension fund.

The Company also has a non-contributory pension plan covering substantially all employees. Normal cost is charged to income and funded currently. The full amount of unfunded prior service cost is included in liabilities. The Company amended the expected return rate on assets from 5.5% to 4% in the year ended March 31, 1998, as actual return rates on pension assets had been lower than that. As a result of this amendment, ¥8,857 million ($67,098 thousand) was additionally recognized as prior service cost. This amount is amortized over four years equally and ¥2,216 million ($16,788 thousand) was included in other expenses for the year ended March 31, 1998. In addition, the Company recognized ¥2,132 million ($16,151 thousand) as prior service cost due to tri-annual reassessment by actuaries. This amount was also included in other expenses.

9.8   Marketable Securities and Investments

Wacoal Corp. is Japan's leading creator of intimate apparel for women. Like most Japanese companies, Wacoal maintains a significant investment in marketable securities:

	Percent of 1998 Assets
Marketable securities: current	7.6
Marketable securities: noncurrent	6.6
Total	14.2%

Under current Japanese GAAP (until 2000), such investments are commonly reported on the historical cost basis. Beginning in 2000, however, Japanese companies are expected to report current marketable securities on a market value basis. Under U.S. GAAP (i.e., *SFAS No. 115*), such investments must first be classified as trading, available-for-sale, or held-to-maturity (for debt securities). Securities classified as trading or available-for-sale are accounted for on a marked-to-market basis.

According to Wacoal's footnotes, if the company had applied the provisions of *SFAS No. 115,* all of the company's marketable securities would have been classified as available for sale; and their fair market values would have been as follows:

	Millions of Yen			
	Historical Cost	*Unrealized Gain*	*Unrealized Loss*	*Fair Value*
Marketable securities				
Current	¥15,535	¥ 446	¥ 58	¥15,923
Noncurrent	12,995	22,250	1,715	33,530
Total	¥28,530	¥22,695	¥1,773	¥49,453

Required:

The following are the abbreviated financial statements for Wacoal Corp. as of year-end 1998. Recast the company's financial statements, assuming the implementation of *SFAS No. 115.*

WACOAL CORP.
Consolidated Statement of Income
(in millions of yen)

	1998
Operating income	¥13,165
Other income (expense)	4,129
Income before income taxes	17,294
Income taxes	
(Current: 7,841; Deferred: 1,103)	(8,944)
Net income	¥ 8,350

WACOAL CORP.
Consolidated Balance Sheet
(in millions of yen)

	1998	
Current assets		
Cash and others	¥114,582	
Marketable securities	15,535	
Total		¥130,117
P,P&E (net)		52,878
Other assets		
Marketable securities	¥ 12,995	
Other	14,499	
Total		27,494
Total assets		¥210,489
Current liabilities		
Long-term liabilities		¥ 42,319
Long-term debt	¥ 13,739	
Deferred income taxes	1,563	
Total		15,302
Shareholders' equity		152,868
Total equities		¥210,489

9.9   Valuation of the Firm

In 1989, Sony, the Japanese consumer electronics company, paid $3.4 billion for Columbia Pictures. At the time of the acquisition, the price paid was approximately 340 times Columbia's 1989 net earnings of $10 million. Columbia Pictures was subsequently renamed Sony Pictures Entertainment (SPE).

In late 1994, Sony announced that it would write off ¥265 billion (or approximately $2.65 billion U.S., based on then-current exchange rates) of SPE's net worth. This disclosure followed a previous announcement that, for the first half of 1994, SPE's operations had lost ¥310 billion (or approximately $3.1 billion). Analysts familiar with Sony concluded that the SPE write-down was precipitated by a realization on the part of Sony executives that the original purchase price paid for SPE was significantly overvalued. According to Sony insiders, the original SPE acquisition price had been calculated on the basis of undiscounted future earnings.

Required:

(a) Comment on Sony's valuation approach used in the acquisition of Columbia Pictures. If you disagree with Sony's method, what approach would you use?

(b) On the basis of your approach, estimate how much Sony should have paid for Columbia Pictures.

9.10   Identifying Industry Characteristics Through Financial Statements

Analyzing a company's financial statements requires an understanding of the environment in which a firm operates. Many characteristics of this environment are common to all firms in an industry and, to some extent, influence reported financial data. In addition, differences in accounting across countries may affect the power of accounting data to reflect industry characteristics.

Exhibit 1 presents condensed financial statement information for nine Japanese firms with principal operations in nine different industries. Balance sheet and income statement items are expressed as a percentage of total net revenues. To improve "resolution" of these items, they have been calculated as four-year averages instead of annual figures.

The companies represented in the exercise operate primarily in the following industries:

Advertising agency services	Insurance underwriting
Automobile manufacturing	Metals mining
Consumer electronics	Pharmaceutical manufacturing
Discount retailing	Utilities
Distilling	

Required:

Using the data in Exhibit 1, match the companies (numbered 1 thru 9) with the industries listed above.

EXHIBIT 1

Common-Size Four-Year Average Financial Statements
(net sales or revenue = 100)

	1	2	3	4	5	6	7	8	9
Cash and cash equivalents	13.12	19.64	40.71	17.52	11.16	165.50	6.57	4.57	11.99
Net accounts receivable	9.87	24.64	41.00	39.17	29.07	16.70	7.27	11.81	12.56
Inventories	19.80	24.62	9.97	18.56	4.03	11.36	2.14	14.82	49.35
Total current assets	42.79	68.91	91.68	75.24	44.25	193.56	15.98	31.20	73.91
P,P&E at cost	36.58	66.89	81.83	125.97	20.08	39.58	401.62	74.02	69.63
Accumulated depreciation	10.91	39.78	34.16	48.84	4.57	17.60	134.04	29.35	31.75
Net property, plant, equipment	25.67	27.11	47.67	77.13	15.51	21.98	267.58	44.67	37.88
Other assets (net)	(1.74)	20.11	3.02	20.39	3.27	0.77	17.45	15.47	11.24
Total assets	66.72	116.13	142.37	172.76	63.04	216.31	301.02	91.34	123.03
Total current liabilities	16.05	62.40	29.47	60.56	20.16	144.20	173.55	32.07	62.62
Long-term debt	9.81	21.88	21.81	44.71	0.00	3.77	56.99	13.20	5.77
Other noncurrent liabilities	5.67	7.07	12.95	3.88	0.61	2.45	6.21	0.94	6.76
Total liabilities	31.53	91.35	64.22	109.14	20.77	150.42	236.75	46.21	75.15
Owners' equity	35.19	24.78	78.15	63.61	42.27	65.89	64.27	45.13	47.88
Total liabilities and equity	66.72	116.13	142.37	172.76	63.04	216.31	301.02	91.34	123.03
Net sales or revenue	100.00	100.00	100.00	100.00	100.00	100.00	100.00	100.00	100.00
Cost of goods sold	89.30	76.89	48.00	78.16	74.89	35.84	66.91	68.56	60.18
Depreciation expense	1.70	5.57	4.91	4.73	0.20	0.00	13.41	4.19	3.02
SG&A expense	0.57	1.08	1.11	3.98	19.66	7.92	10.72	0.97	4.22
R&D expense	0.00	6.64	13.20	0.00	0.00	0.00	0.00	4.65	0.00
Interest expense	7.62	2.64	13.54	9.11	0.00	23.35	0.00	24.33	32.50
Income taxes	0.48	1.91	8.00	2.86	1.66	1.56	3.09	1.30	1.21
Other (net)	(0.10)	1.34	2.46	(0.42)	1.96	30.94	1.91	(5.23)	(1.57)
Net income	0.43	3.92	8.79	1.57	1.63	0.38	3.96	1.24	0.46

9.11   Annual Report Analysis

An interesting and important challenge for students of international financial reporting is to study the published annual reports of various companies from different countries. Your instructor will provide you with a recent copy of a Japanese annual report. To facilitate your delving into this annual report, undertake the following endeavors.

Required:

(a) List the key differences between that report and what you would expect to see for a U.S. company in the same industry.

(b) Calculate the following ratios for the Japanese company taking care to note the assumptions you found necessary to make and where you found the appropriate pieces of data in the annual report.

(1) Current ratio $= \dfrac{\text{Total current assets}}{\text{Total current liabilities}}$

(2) Quick ratio $= \dfrac{\text{Cash + Marketable securities + Accts. receiable}}{\text{Total current liabilities}}$

(3) Operating cash flow to current liabilities $= \dfrac{\text{Operating cash flow}}{\text{Average total current liabilities}}$

(4) Debt-to-equity ratio $= \dfrac{\text{Long-term debt}}{\text{Owners' equity}}$

(5) Debt-to-total capitalization ratio $= \dfrac{\text{Long-term debt}}{\text{Long-term debt + Owners' equity}}$

(6) Interest coverage ratio $= \dfrac{\text{Net income before interest and income taxes}}{\text{Interest expense}}$

(7) Operating cash flow to interest charges $= \dfrac{\text{Operating cash flow}}{\text{Interest expense}}$

(8) Operating cash flow to total liabilities $= \dfrac{\text{Operating cash flow}}{\text{Average total liabilities}}$

(9) Receivables turnover ratio $= \dfrac{\text{Net sales}}{\text{Average accts. receivable}}$

(10) Inventory turnover $= \dfrac{\text{Cost of goods sold}}{\text{Average inventory}}$

(11) Asset turnover $= \dfrac{\text{Net sales}}{\text{Average total assets}}$

(12) Average collection period ratio $= \dfrac{365 \text{ Days}}{\text{Receivables turnover ratio}}$

(13) Average number of days' inventory on hand ratio $= \dfrac{365 \text{ Days}}{\text{Inventory turnover ratio}}$

(14) Return on assets (ROA) $= \dfrac{\text{Net income}}{\text{Average total assets}}$

$$OR = \text{ROS} \times \text{Asset turnover}$$

$$(15)\ \text{Return on equity (ROE)}\ =\ \frac{\text{Net income}}{\text{Average total owners' equity}}$$

$$OR = \text{ROA} \times \text{Financial leverage}$$

$$(16)\ \text{Return on sales (ROS)}\ =\ \frac{\text{Net income}}{\text{Net sales}}$$

$$(17)\ \text{Financial leverage}\ =\ \frac{\text{Average liabilities} + \text{Average owners' equity}}{\text{Average owners' equity}}$$

$$(18)\ \text{Basic earnings per share (EPS)}\ =\ \frac{\text{NI applicable to common shareholders}}{\text{Weighted average common shares}}$$

$$(19)\ \text{Cash dividend yield}\ =\ \frac{\text{Cash dividend per common share}}{\text{Market price per common share}}$$

$$(20)\ \text{Cash dividend payout}\ =\ \frac{\text{Total cash dividend to common shareholders}}{\text{Net income}}$$

(c) What do you conclude about the availability of the appropriate data in the annual report for calculating these ratios?

(d) What does this financial analysis tell you about the company?

(e) What analytical metrics did the company choose to report for itself? What do those choices say about the message the company is striving to tell and the audience it is addressing?

CHAPTER 10

Sweden

The interest in international accounting within Sweden seems to have increased over the last few years.[1]

Sweden, being a small country with several large international companies, has much to gain from harmonizing accounting standards with international practice, as far as the law permits.[2]

Introduction

The Kingdom of Sweden has long occupied a paradoxical place in the community of nations. One of the oldest continuous democracies in the world, it has carefully protected its autonomy politically by adhering to a policy of neutrality since 1815. However, the Swedes' insistence on their independence has hardly resulted in national isolation. Sweden has historically been a symbol of a progressive global order, of the need for non-violent resolution of conflicts, and for international cooperation. Its leaders and politicians have always been active in promoting the cause of world peace.

The 1990s were a tale of two stories. During the first part of the decade, dramatic changes occurred in Sweden.[3] Between 1989 and 1992, industrial production dropped 15 percent. Unemployment, never over 3.5 percent during the 1970s and 1980s, hit 14 percent in 1993. In 1992, the **krona** (the Swedish currency, frequently abbreviated as SEK) was floated and within six months had depreciated 21 percent against the European currency unit (ECU) and a year later had depreciated 30 percent against the German mark. In 1990, Sweden ran a budget surplus, but by the middle of 1993, a budget deficit equal to 13.8 percent of gross domestic product (GDP) existed, the worst in the industrialized world. Real estate prices dropped 50 percent in two years. An aggressive privatization

---

[1]N. Hellman, "A Comparative Analysis of the Impact of Accounting Differences on Profits and Return on Equity," *European Accounting Review,* December 1993, pp. 495–96.

[2]R. Rundfelt, "Standard Setting in Sweden," *European Accounting Review,* December 1993, p. 589.

[3]For this background see "Sweden: A Survey," *Financial Times,* December 21, 1993, pp. I–V; "Ask the Devil," *The Economist,* March 13, 1993, p. 62; "Join the Club," *The Economist,* February 22, 1992, pp. 44–45; "This May Hurt," *The Economist,* January 16, 1993, p. 50; "Worse and Worse," *The Economist,* October 9, 1993, pp. 58–59; and P. Klebnikov, "The Swedish Disease," *Forbes,* May 24, 1993, pp. 78–79.

program of Swedish companies had stalled due to a falling stock market, and the banking system was in need of a government bailout. In November 1994, Sweden's populace voted to join the European Union (EU). In 1995, Sweden became the 15th country to join the EU, marking the beginning of a new era for Sweden.

As the 20th century comes to a close, Sweden's inflation rate is one of Europe's lowest (around 2 percent compared to about 10 percent in 1991), interest rates are down from a 1992 high of 500 percent to an attractively low level of around 5 percent, exports are healthy, the banking bailout has been successfully and virtually painlessly completed, and unemployment is down to single-digit levels.[4] All is not perfect, however. Unemployment is still too high in the minds of most Swedes, as is the tax burden. Although Sweden was one of the first EU countries to meet the European monetary union (EMU) criteria, it chose not to be a part of the 1999 euro launch. The state still employs more than 30 percent of the workforce, and the September 1998 elections saw support for the Social Democratic Party, the ruling party for nearly all of the post World War II era, fall to its lowest level.[5]

The desire to balance national independence with international cooperation characterizes Sweden's place in the globalization of business. Although becoming more open, its capital markets restrict international influence and ownership. Comparatively few Swedish concerns are well known to foreign investors. Historically, the most important factor in determining financial reporting practices has been national tax and economic policy, not international capital markets. Yet Sweden's economy depends heavily on foreign trade; its exports account for approximately one-third of the nation's GDP. Swedish business and accounting professionals are active in the cause of harmonization: They participate in the activities of the International Accounting Standards Committee (IASC), award a prize each year to the Swedish company that produces the best annual report, and (in the case of large multinationals) pursue foreign investors by providing excellent and clear financial statements. Not too long ago, a columnist for *The Wall Street Journal* even suggested that the way to improve international financial reporting was to emulate Volvo's.[6] The Swedish, however, do not (overtly, at least) claim for themselves the leading role in developing international financial reporting guidelines that others have sometimes cast them in. The attitudes and ideals that characterize Swedish society in general do shape the Swedish approach to the formulation of international financial reporting policy. Those attitudes are: a self-effacing pragmatism, a respect for technical expertise, a perspective that combines global awareness with a realistic assessment of national constraints, and a desire to build consensus through negotiation rather than to impose it through fiat.

Environmental Factors

*Cultural
Environment*

Social Mandate and Individual Freedom.   One of the most intriguing and attractive aspects of Swedish culture is its ability to mediate between social welfare and individual privacy. On the one hand, Sweden is involved in one of the most far-reaching collectivist

---

[4]See S. Reed, "Will Stockholm Give Away the Store?," *Business Week,* February 18, 1997, p. 54; "Faces Lengthen," *The Economist,* April 12, 1997, pp. 49–50; see also the "Sweden Survey Section," *Financial Times,* April 14, 1998.

[5]T. Burt and G. McIvor, "Social Democrats' Battering Sends a Shudder through Swedish Business," *Financial Times,* September 22, 1998, p. 2.

[6]J. N. Slipkowsky, "The Bottom Line in European Accounting," *The Wall Street Journal,* August 24, 1987, p. 22.

experiments ever attempted by a Western democracy. In recent times, between 60 and 70 percent of its GDP has gone for public expenditures, far more than any other OECD nation. On the other hand, Sweden is internationally famous as a bastion of individual freedom in which one's personal convictions and private morality are allowed considerable latitude. This concern for personal freedom may explain why a group of Swedish subjects in Hofstede's study of cultural attitudes scored a rather high 71 in individualism (compared to a score of 91 for U.S. subjects and 46 for the Japanese) in spite of the strongly collectivist elements in Swedish society. In business, "Swedes are used to an open system in which small teams [do exist but] are largely left on their own. [When it is time to make high-level decisions], executives prefer to [then] get the whole group's approval . . . not handing down orders. *Alla aer i baten,* the Swedes call it: 'Get everyone in the boat.' "[7]

It is important to remember this dual perspective of Swedish culture—the interplay between a strong tendency for individual preference and a genuine, pervasive social consciousness—to understand the place of financial reporting policy formation and regulation in Sweden. Even though financial reporting policy in Sweden is heavily influenced by the requirements of macroeconomic policy and tax law (more about this below), Swedish businesses and the national government nevertheless rely a great deal on the judgment of professionals in formulating and administering policy pronouncements. A well-regarded study of accounting regulation in Sweden found widespread agreement that auditors are a leading group in the process of policy formation and elaboration, indicating a healthy respect among the business community for auditor professionalism.[8] The study also found that although legislation is very important in setting boundaries, considerable debate takes place in the private sector about matters of method and theory. The professional judgment of private individuals and corporations does carry weight in Sweden. Impetus for discussion and change may be generated by a single firm's adoption of an innovation in its annual report or even by a single writer pursuing an issue in the press.

The willingness to engage in debate over policy rather than regarding it as engraved in stone implies a significant amount of tolerance for ambiguity on the part of the Swedish. Interestingly enough, the Swedish subjects in Hofstede's study scored low in the areas of uncertainty avoidance (29) and power distance (31), lower than the United States (46, 40) and Great Britain (35, 35) in both categories. It has been argued that low scores in these areas, combined with a high score in individualism, indicate a bias toward professionalism in a national culture.[9] Indeed, the important role of the *Föreningen Auktoriserade Revisorer* (FAR), Sweden's counterpart to the U.S. American Institute of CPAs, in spearheading the creation in 1989 of a new standard-setting body, the *Redovisningsrådet* (Financial Reporting Council), suggests that this hypothesis is borne out in the case of the Swedish accounting establishment.

Similar to the United States (29) and Great Britain (25), but in contrast to Japan (80) and Korea (75), Sweden scored a 33 on the long-term orientation cultural dimension. Such a relatively low score highlights a tendency for doing things the way they have always been done, a deemphasis of thrift, and a desire for more immediate results. Perhaps indicative of these traits is the historical role of global neutrality that Sweden has adopted and that was initially manifested in a fairly widespread opposition to joining the

---

[7]R. Frank and T. Burton, "Cross-Border Merger Results in Headaches for a Drug Company," *The Wall Street Journal,* February 4, 1997, p. A1, A13.

[8]S. Jönsson, *Accounting Regulation and Elite Structures* (Chichester, England: Wiley & Sons, 1988).

[9]S. J. Gray, "Towards a Theory of Cultural Influence on the Development of Accounting Systems Internationally," *Abacus* 24, no. 1 (1988), pp. 1–15.

EU and in more recent times, an opposition to joining the EMU. Moreover, in recent history there has not been a need for personal savings and investment because the social welfare system provides unemployment and retirement incomes almost equal to one's working wages.

Auditor reports from a recent Swedish annual report depicts something of the commitment to tradition, a concern for the common good, the role for professional judgment, and a desire to embrace an EU sense of community. Exhibit 10–1 presents the 1997 auditor report for Electrolux. It reflects a very Swedish orientation of the common good by attesting to the financial statement's conformity to the Annual Accounts Act and the Swedish Companies Act. The auditors explicitly express no opinion that the financial statements give a true and fair view of the company's income and financial position.

The Corporation in Society.   Europeans in general have a highly developed sense of the corporation as a public entity with social responsibilities, and nowhere is this more true than in Sweden. The Swedish people accept the need for corporate profitability, as long as the profits generated are reinvested in economic growth or otherwise used for the public good. The very nature of an extensive welfare state demands such an outlook. Beyond the immediate political imperatives, however, Hofstede's study suggests that there may be a more deeply rooted cultural basis in Sweden (and the other Nordic countries, for that matter) supporting a socially oriented view of business entities. On Hofstede's axis of masculinity, designed to measure the role of gender expectations in a society, Sweden scored the lowest of the 40 countries included in the survey.[10] In Hofstede's terms, Sweden has the most feminine culture of the countries surveyed (employing the term *feminine* in this context purely as a social construct). In other words, Hofstede's research indicates that Swedish culture elevates those values traditionally associated with femininity above those traditionally associated with masculinity—nurturance above competition, relationships above money, quality of life above public achievement.

Because of its emphasis on building and maintaining relationships, one might call it an *aptitude for solidarity,* this basic feature of Swedish culture may help to explain the relative importance of cooperation and conflict resolution in Swedish national culture. Likewise, it has undoubtedly contributed to certain features of Swedish corporate reporting, such as the required disclosure of employment and compensation information with potential ramifications for labor relations. Many firms publish value-added statements as a social-reporting supplement to traditional financial statements. (See Exhibit 10–2 for a copy of Electrolux's value-added statement; for more on the value-added statement, see Chapter 7.) Moreover, it is not unusual for Swedish annual reports to focus at length on cooperative alliances with major competitors, the firm's sensitivity to the environment, and good relationships with workers.

Legal and Political Environment

Tax Law—General.   Corporate income, in Sweden as in the United States, is subject to double taxation. After income is taxed at the corporate level, cash dividends paid to shareholders are taxed again as ordinary income, or what is called *income from capital* in Sweden. (Companies not listed on the stock exchange, however, may deduct 70 percent of their dividends paid during the tax year.) Stock dividends are not taxable, and dividends received by a Swedish corporation from a second Swedish corporation in which it has a minimal holding of 25 percent are also not taxable. Interest expense is fully deductible, and capital gains on the sale of equity shares are taxable at a flat rate of 28

---

[10]In the other country-specific chapters included in this book, we have chosen not to address this cultural dimension, but because Sweden's score is so extreme, it is highlighted here.

EXHIBIT 10–1

Illustrative Swedish Audit Report

AB Electrolux

To the Annual General Meeting of the shareholders
of AB Electrolux (Reg. no. 556009-4187)

We have audited the parent company and the consolidated financial statements, the accounts and the administration of the Board of Directors and the President of AB Electrolux for the 12-month period ending December, 1997. These accounts and the administration of the Company are the responsibility of the Board of Directors and the President. Our responsibility is to express an opinion on the financial statements and the administration based on our audit.

We conducted our audit in accordance with Generally Accepted Auditing Standards in Sweden. Those Standards require that we plan and perform the audit to obtain reasonable assurance that the financial statements are free of material misstatement. An audit includes examining, on a test basis, evidence supporting the amounts and disclosures in the financial statements. An audit also includes assessing the accounting principles used and their application by the Board of Directors and the President, as well as evaluating the overall presentation of information in the financial statements. We examined significant decisions, actions taken and circumstances of the Company in order to be able to determine the possible liability to the Company of any Board member or the President or whether they have in some other way acted in contravention of the Companies Act, the Annual Accounts Act or the Articles of Association. We believe that our audit provides a reasonable basis for our opinion set out below.

In our opinion, the parent company and the consolidated financial statements have been prepared in accordance with the Annual Accounts Act, and, consequently we recommend

> *that* the income statements and the balance sheets of the Parent company and the Group be adopted, and
> *that* the profit of the Parent Company be dealt with in accordance with the proposal in the Administration Report.

In our opinion, the Board members and the President have not committed any act or been guilty of any omission which could give rise to any liability to the Company. We therefore recommend

> *that* the members of the Board of Directors and the President be discharged from liability for the financial year.

Stockholm, March 10, 1998

Ernst & Young AB
GUNNAR WIDHAGEN
Authorized Public Accountant

---

percent. Income tax is levied on individual companies—there is no such thing as consolidated tax returns in Sweden.

Individual income tax rates in Sweden have been notoriously high. In recent times, the marginal tax rate reached as high as 85 percent, with most taxpayers falling into a bracket in the 40 to 50 percent range. The early 1990s, however, were a period of significant legislative reform for the Swedes, and currently the maximum individual municipal plus national income tax rate is 59 percent on earned income over SEK240,000 ($29,600), and 30 percent on taxable unearned income (e.g., interest, dividends, and capital gains).[11] In

---

[11]As of January 1, 1999, $1 = SEK 8.11.

EXHIBIT 10–2

Electrolux 1997 Value-Added Statement

Added value represents the contribution made by a company's production, i.e. the increase in value arising from manufacture, handling, etc. within the company. It is defined as sales revenues less the costs of purchased goods and services.

Sales revenues for the Electrolux Group in 1997 totalled SEK 113,000m (110,000). After deduction of purchases of goods and services, the value added by the Group amounted to SEK 32,977m (35,309), a decrease of 7% (−4) from the previous year. The decrease refers mainly to the provision for the restructuring program. During the past five years, added value has increased at an average annual rate of 4.5% (5.8).

In 1997, SEK 3,628m (5,536) of the value added remained within the Group and was utilized among other things for capital expenditure as well as product development and marketing. Dividend payments to shareholders accounted for 3% (3) of added value in 1997, or 4% (3) of the Group's total payroll costs.

The added value generated within the Group over the past two years and its distribution are shown in the tables below.

Calculation of Added Value	1997 SEKm	%	1997 per Employee, SEK '000	1996 SEKm	%
Total revenues	113,000	100	1,067	110,000	100
Cost of purchased goods and services	−80,023	−71	−756	−74,691	−68
Added value	32,977	29	311	35,309	32

Distribution of Added Value

	1997 SEKm	%	1997 per Employee, SEK '000	1996 SEKm	%
To employees					
Salaries	19,883	60	188	20,249	58
Employer contributions	6,185	19	58	6,174	17
	26,068	79	246	26,423	75
To State and municipalities					
Taxes	944	3	9	1,237	3
To credit institutions					
Interest, etc.	1,422	4	13	1,198	3
To shareholders					
Dividend payments (1997: Proposed)	915	3	9	915	3
	3,281	10	31	3,350	9
Retained in the Group					
For wear on fixed assets (depreciation)	4,255	13	40	4,438	13
Other	−627	−2	−6	1,098	3
	3,628	11	34	5,536	16
Added value	32,977	100	311	35,309	100

addition, however, Swedes pay a value-added tax (VAT) of 25 percent on most goods and services (although the rate is only 12 percent for food and beverages, passenger transportation, and hotel and restaurant services) as well as a 1.5 percent wealth tax on the aggregate value of certain year-end net assets they possess (including shares of stock).

Tax Law—Corporate.   As is the case in Japan, Swedish tax law prescribes essentially the same method of accounting for both tax and financial reporting. This requirement inevitably skews key figures on the financial statements because legalities and economic incentives built into the Swedish tax code take precedence over financial reporting practices that are generally accepted elsewhere. In 1994 the corporate income tax rate was lowered to 28 percent and as of 1998, it is still 28 percent.

In the early 1990s, the most important effect of Sweden's tax law on the financial statements of Swedish corporations was the creation of an untaxed reserve account called the *Special Tax Equalization Reserve* (SURV). Corporations were able to lower their effective tax rate by allocating a portion of net income to the SURV account, which was designed by the Swedish government to encourage the reinvestment of corporate earnings. The allocation was figured as either a percent of net equity or payroll. Not surprising, this opportunity created an inherent fiscal conservatism, or fiscal bias, to the results of most Swedish companies.

Beginning with fiscal years ending in 1994, SURV allocations were no longer permitted. In fact, from that point on, companies were given seven years to reverse the SURV reserves, taking any remaining balance into taxable income. However, in 1994, an income adjustment reserve (*periodiseringsfond,* or IAR) was authorized that works in essentially the same way as the SURV. Unlike the SURV, the IAR permits an annual tax-deductible allocation of up to 25 percent of pretax profit. Moreover, any year's allocation must be reversed to taxable income within five years of its original creation.[12] Thus, as subsequent years have higher levels of pretax profits than prior years, new IAR allocations will exceed old IAR allocation reversals, and assuming a constant tax rate, companies will have been able to permanently lower their effective tax rate.

In this latter regard, consider the fact that a company makes a reserve allocation by recording an increase (i.e., a credit) to the untaxed reserve account and a decrease (i.e., a debit) to the net income account. Because allocations to the untaxed reserve are eventually reversed and consequently increase income in later years, the reserve account essentially enables companies to defer a portion of their tax liabilities. As long as a company is able to make new allocations to the reserve to offset the reversal of previous allocations, it can continue to postpone a portion of its tax burden. However, to qualify for the tax deductions afforded by the use of untaxed reserves, companies must record allocations on their financial reports as well as on their tax returns. Conceptually, then, one could say that the untaxed reserve account is a hybrid account, containing elements of both debt and equity. Because it is a deferral of income that would have been taxed at a rate of approximately 28 percent, part of its balance represents a deferred tax liability, and the other represents stockholders' equity (specifically, retained earnings).

Untaxed reserves not only allow Swedish companies to reduce income in profitable years but also allow companies in cyclical industries to smooth income and maximize tax benefits over time. If a company records a net loss in one year, its management may elect in a later year to reverse a portion of its earlier allocations and include the reversal in income to avoid reporting the loss on its financial statements. Thus, the company gains a permanent tax advantage since no tax liability is created by reversing prior untaxed reserve allocations to cancel out a net loss. In effect, a company in this situation has been able to shift taxable income from a high-income period (in which income is taxed at 28 percent) to a low-income period (in which it is not taxed at all). The following table shows how a Swedish corporation can use untaxed reserves to allocate income between periods to maximize its tax benefits:

	Year 1	*Year 2*
Income before allocations & taxes	1000	(300)
Allocations to untaxed reserve	(400)	—
Reversal of reserve	—	300
Income before taxes	600	—
Taxes (28 percent)	168	—
Net income	432	—

[12]Price Waterhouse, *Doing Business in Sweden* (New York: Price Waterhouse, 1995).

By making a SEK400 allocation to its untaxed reserve in Year 1, the company defers SEK112 (400 × 28 percent) of its tax liability. By using SEK300 of the reserve in Year 2 to cancel out a net loss, the company avoids reporting the net loss and eliminates SEK84 (300 × 28 percent) of its deferred tax liability. SEK100 remains in the reserve account, representing SEK28 of deferred tax liability and SEK72 of stockholders' equity.

Exhibit 10–3 presents data from Volvo's 1997 financial statements and provides an overview of the activity in the company's reserve accounts. Notice that Volvo's unrestricted reserves are equivalent to a U.S. company's retained earnings. It should also be noted that the SEK9,262 in the Net Income line is the company's 1997 net income that is being closed to unrestricted reserves. Last, the restricted reserves are synonymous with the statutory reserves described above and noted in Volvo's narrative disclosures also presented in Exhibit 10–3.

Prior to the 1994 creation of the IAR and the SURV's creation in 1991, Sweden already had a long history of similar tax reserve allocations. At one time, tax reserves were permitted that pertained to property, plant, and equipment investment, depreciation, payroll, and inventory. Because of the dramatic effect that allocations to untaxed reserves may have on net income, Swedish corporations argue, understandably, that consolidated net income under Swedish GAAP does not provide them with a useful basis for measuring financial performance and calculating per share data. As a consequence, they often prepare a reconciliation of their Swedish net income with net income as it would appear under U.S. GAAP, using the latter as the basis for calculating earnings per share. Exhibit 10–4 presents such a reconciliation from the 1997 Electrolux annual report. The exhibit reveals that the principal differences in Electrolux's equity relate to the accounting for acquisitions, pensions, and income tax timing differences, which refer mainly to untaxed reserves. The company's 1997 net income was most impacted by differences relating to these tax-timing differences: the accounting for fixed assets and certain investments.

Business Environment

Form of Business.   The most common form of business organization in Sweden is the limited liability company (*Aktiebolag,* abbreviated AB), which is regulated by a national companies act. An AB may issue shares that carry voting or ownership restrictions. Class A shares carry greater voting power than class B shares: 10, 100, or even 1,000 times in some cases. Effectively, this equity structure concentrates voting power in the hands of a few investors and has created spheres of influence among Swedish multinationals. For example, the prominent Wallenberg sphere, controlled by Peter Wallenberg, controls 94 percent of the voting rights in Electrolux and 22 percent of the voting rights in Ericsson, while having provided under 4 percent of both companies' capital.[13] Moreover, it is estimated that the Wallenberg sphere accounts for 40 percent of the entire Stockholm exchange's market capitalization while holding only 4 percent of the capital.[14] Other spheres play a similar but relatively smaller role in the Swedish economy.

The Swedish spheres resemble Japanese *keiretsu* in the mutual loyalty shown by member companies and in the protection they afford from hostile takeover. They also serve as a buffer against "excessive" foreign influence since most unrestricted shares—those that may be purchased or held by overseas investors—tend to be class B shares. Management teams among major Swedish multinationals have consequently been able to adopt long-term strategies with comparatively little regard for short-term profits, a behavior pattern

---

[13]G. McIvor, "Electrolux Vote Reform Puts Swedish Equality to the Test," *Financial Times,* March 11, 1998, p. 18.

[14]T. Burt, "Reform from Above at Investor," *Financial Times,* January 28, 1998, p. 18.

EXHIBIT 10–3

Volvo: Untaxed Reserves

Allocations, deferred tax liability, untaxed reserves

Tax laws in Sweden and certain other countries allow companies to defer payment of taxes through allocations to untaxed reserves.

The individual Group companies (including AB Volvo) report untaxed reserves as a separate balance sheet item. In the income statements, allocations to and withdrawals from untaxed reserves are reported under the heading Allocations. The reported tax expense is based on income after allocations.

In the consolidated balance sheet, untaxed reserves are divided into deferred tax liability in untaxed reserves, which is reported as deferred taxes among Provisions, and Equity in untaxed reserves, which is included in Restricted equity. The deferred tax liability in untaxed reserves is calculated based on the anticipated tax rate for the immediately following year in each country. Calculation of the amount of tax liability takes into account that a portion of the untaxed reserves may be withdrawn without tax consequences by utilizing tax-loss carryforwards. Deferred tax receivables resulting from future tax-loss carryforwards exceeding deferred tax liability are not reported.

No allocations to untaxed reserves are reported in the consolidated statements of income. Group tax expense is calculated as the sum of reported tax expense for each Group company, adjusted for the effects of allocations to, and withdrawals from, untaxed reserves. This adjustment corresponds to the annual change in the item deferred tax liability in untaxed reserves included in Deferred taxes in the consolidated balance sheet. Group tax expense is also affected by the Group's share of tax expenses in associated companies and by consolidated adjustments, primarily the elimination of internal profits. The Group's reported tax expense thereby becomes attributable mainly to reported income after financial items.

Change in Shareholders' Equity	Share Capital	Restricted Reserves	Unrestricted Equity	Total Equity
Balance, December 31, 1995	**2,318**	**14,264**	**34,618**	**51,200**
Cash dividend	—	—	(1,854)	(1,854)
Distribution of shareholding in Swedish Match	—	—	(4,117)	(4,117)
Net income	—	—	12,477	12,477
Effect of equity method of accounting[1]	—	373	(373)	—
Transfer between unrestricted and restricted equity	—	439	(439)	—
Translation differences	—	(222)	87	(135)
Exchange differences on loans and futures contracts[2]	—	—	40	40
Other changes	—	52	213	265
Balance December 31, 1996	**2,318**	**14,906**	**40,652**	**57,876**
Cash dividend	—	—	(1,993)	(1,993)
Redemption of shares	(113)	—	(5,694)	(5,807)
Bonus issue of shares	441	(113)	(328)	—
Net income	—	—	10,359	10,359
New issue of shares	3	113	—	116
Effect of equity method of accounting[1]	—	(34)	34	—
Transfer between unrestricted and restricted equity	—	92	(92)	—
Translation differences	—	1,396	(528)	868
Exchange differences on loans and futures contracts[2]	—	—	(665)	(665)
Accumulated translation difference on the Renault holding[3]	—	—	(552)	(552)
Other changes	—	113	116	229
Balance, December 31, 1997	**2,649**	**16,473**	**41,309**	**60,431**

[1]Mainly associated companies' contributions to net Group income, reduced by dividends received.

[2]Hedge net assets in foreign subsidiaries and associated companies.

[3]Difference pertains to Renault shares sold and, in connection with the sale, has affected consolidated capital gains.

that is changing as Swedish companies tap foreign capital markets. Even so, the spheres are likely to remain a dominant factor in the Swedish economy for some time to come.

The Swedish Companies Act requires that the annual report of an AB—which must include a balance sheet, an income statement, a statement of changes in financial position, notes, an auditor's report, and various other management disclosures—be audited. The auditor must be either a *Godkand Revisor* (GR), a junior qualification requiring a two-year course of study in a university and five years of professional experience, or an

EXHIBIT 10–4

Electrolux Consolidated Financial Statements Reconciled to U.S. GAAP

The consolidated accounts have been prepared in accordance with Swedish accounting standards, which differ in certain significant respects from American accounting principles (U.S. GAAP). The most important differences are described below:

Adjustment for acquisitions

In accordance with Swedish accounting principles, the tax benefit arising from application of tax-loss carryforwards in acquired companies is deducted by the Group from the current year's tax costs. According to U.S. GAAP, this tax benefit should be booked as a retroactive adjustment of the value of acquired intangible assets.

Pensions

According to the American recommendations for pensions known as FAS 87 (Employers' Accounting for Pensions), computation of the projected benefit obligation and pension costs for the year must take account of such factors as future salary increases and inflation. The computed Swedish provision for PRI pensions is not adjusted for future salary increases, but this is offset by the lower discounting rate applied for computation of the provisions for PRI pensions in comparison with FAS 87. The initial difference arising from the first application of FAS 87 is amortized over the future average employment period, so that the effect on net income is insignificant.

Securities

According to Swedish accounting principles, holdings of debt and equity securities should be reported according to the lowest-value principle. According to FAS 115 (Accounting for Certain Investments in Debt and Equity Securities), these holdings should be classified with respect to intention, i.e. if they are to be traded, if they are to be retained until maturity, or if they are in an intermediate category. Valuation and reporting of income differ according to the classification of the securities. For Electrolux, this means that certain securities must be reported at market value in the balance sheet, while the difference between market and acquisition value must be taken directly to equity, according to U.S. GAAP. In connection with the sale of these securities, the change in value previously reported directly against equity is reported in the income statement.

Deferred taxes

Taxation and financial reporting are affected during different periods by certain items. Electrolux reports deferred taxes on the most important timing differences, which refer mainly to untaxed reserves, with due consideration in certain cases for the future fiscal effects of tax-loss carryforwards. U.S. GAAP requires reporting of fiscal effects for all significant differences and tax-loss carryforwards, with the proviso that deferred tax assets may be reported only if it is probable that the tax benefit will be utilized.

Timing differences

According to Swedish accounting principles, provisions for costs referring to a shutdown are booked when the decision is made to shut down the plant. U.S. GAAP rules require meeting additional criteria before provisions can be made for severance pay and other costs related to shutdowns. Therefore, compliance with U.S. GAAP requires that provisions for these and similar costs be made at a later date.

Write-ups on assets

In certain situations, Swedish accounting principles permit write-ups of fixed assets in excess of acquisition cost. This does not normally accord with U.S. GAAP.

Distribution of Gränges

In accordance with the decision by the Annual General Meeting in April 1997, all shares in Gränges AB were distributed to Electrolux shareholders on May 20, 1997. In accordance with Swedish accounting principles, Gränges has been removed from the Group's financial statements for 1997, but is included in the comparative figures for 1996.

According to U.S. GAAP, Gränges should be included in the Group's balance sheet and income statement up to the date that the decision to distribute the shares was made, and should be reported in the income statement as a divested operation. Gränges is not included in the Group's net sales for 1997, but is included for 1996 in the amount of SEK8,444m.

A. Consolidated Net Income (SEKm)

	1997	1996
Net income as reported in the consolidated income statement	352	1,850
Adjustments before taxes:		
Acquisitions	6	−71
Timing differences	669	−315
Other	19	−3
Taxes on above adjustments	−191	149
Other taxes	−39	58
Gränges AB	—	−206
Approximate net income according to U.S. GAAP, excluding divested operation	816	1,462
Divested operation	61	206
Approximate net income according to U.S. GAAP	877	1,668
Approximate net income per share in SEK according to U.S. GAAP, excluding divested operation	11.10	20.00
Approximate net income per share in SEK according to U.S. GAAP (no. of shares in 1997 and 1996 = 73,233,916)	12.00	22.80

EXHIBIT 10–4 (Concluded)

B. Equity (SEKm)

	1997	1996
Equity as reported in the consolidated balance sheet	20,565	22,428
Adjustments:		
Revaluation of fixed assets	−45	−45
Acquisitions	−1,090	−1,074
Pensions	−127	−244
Securities	123	187
Timing differences	971	330
Taxes on the above adjustments	−247	−55
Other taxes	182	236
Approximate equity according to U.S. GAAP	20,332	21,763

C. Balance sheet (SEKm)

The table below summarizes the consolidated balance sheets prepared in accordance with Swedish accounting principles and U.S. GAAP.

	According to Swedish Principles		According to U.S. GAAP	
	1997	1996	1997	1996
Intangible assets	3,517	3,558	2,546	2,624
Tangible assets	22,519	24,118	22,442	24,037
Financial assets	1,744	1,270	1,876	1,457
Current assets	51,860	56,223	55,710	59,831
Total assets	79,640	85,169	82,574	87,949
Equity	20,565	22,428	20,332	21,763
Minority interests	913	1,952	913	1,952
Provisions for deferred taxes	—	893	—	712
Provisions for pensions and similar commitments	6,247	5,974	6,461	6,322
Other provisions	4,656	2,161	3,685	1,831
Financial liabilities	28,479	31,342	32,403	34,950
Operating liabilities	18,780	20,419	18,780	20,419
Total liabilities and equity	79,640	85,169	82,574	87,949

Auktoriserade Revisor (AR), a senior qualification requiring a bachelor of commerce degree and five years of professional experience.

Capital Markets. Sweden has only one securities exchange, located in Stockholm (the Stockholm Fondbörs). In this, as in other matters, the Swedish have shown their flair for technical innovation and their penchant for orderliness: recently replacing vocal bidding with a computerized trading system that has made Stockholm's securities exchange one of the calmest trading arenas in the world. Although the Stockholm Exchange has generally performed impressively in the last decade (both in terms of prices and volume) and can trace its roots back more than 200 years, historically, protectionist measures have restricted foreign access to Sweden's capital markets and prevented Stockholm from becoming a truly significant international financial center.

Securities listed on the Stockholm exchange are divided into two lists, AI and AII. The AI list, which accounts for more than 90 percent of the volume of equity trading, includes shares of the largest companies, those with more than SEK10 million (approximately $1.2 million) in share capital and more than 1000 shareholders. An AII listing requires SEK4 million (approximately $.5 million) in capital and more than 400 shareholders. A company wishing to list its shares on the exchange must file an application with the council of the exchange and submit audited annual reports for the last five years. Companies wishing to issue debt securities must provide financial statements for only the last two years.

The Swedish government has historically regulated the scope and manner of foreign involvement in Swedish securities markets to limit foreign competition for Swedish capital and foreign control of Swedish companies. Sweden recently, however, abolished a 1991 law limiting the number of shares available to foreign investors. Moreover, as of January 1, 1993, the last of the ownership restrictions limiting the kind and extent of shares foreigners may purchase and own was removed. In fact, the Companies Act now prohibits Swedish companies from designating certain types of shares (with certain types of rights) as restricted to Swedish citizens. Indicative also of Sweden's opening up of its capital markets are the regulations, effective January 1, 1994, that permit foreign companies (e.g., Credit Lyonnais of France and Unibank of Denmark) to become members of the Stockholm Stock Exchange. Clearly, Sweden is trying to open its financial markets so that it can become a global financial center.

As a consequence of the Swedish government's historical insulation of its capital markets, international competition for capital does not yet exert the same kind of pressure on financial reporting in Stockholm as it does in New York, London, or Tokyo. Only a few large Swedish multinationals that have chosen to list on foreign exchanges—Volvo, Electrolux, and Ericsson are examples—have shaped their reporting methods and practices to attract foreign investors. The recently created Financial Reporting Council has, however, expressed an intention to promulgate Swedish accounting standards that are harmonious with IASC practices to the extent that the companies act allows.[15] Moreover, the progressive attitude adopted by the major Swedish-based international companies has affected the Swedish business community in general and has given Swedish companies a deserved reputation for high quality in international financial reporting. In particular, Volvo, which is listed (among other places) in London, Tokyo, and on the U.S. NASDAQ system, has provided leadership in promoting high accounting standards among Swedish companies. Another factor stimulating an increased international financial reporting orientation is the growth of outside shareholders. As non-Swedish investors' stakes in Sweden's publicly traded companies has risen from 10 to 30 percent, between 1993 and 1998, more and more companies are finding it necessary to satisfy the information needs of a diverse shareholder constituency.[16] Likewise, as Europe's financial markets consolidate, partly in response to the euro, Sweden is actively looking to extend its presence and expand its influence. In fact, the Stockholm Exchange announced in the spring of 1998, a cooperative arrangement with the Danish exchange. This created Europe's first cross-border trading market and in some protagonists' minds, it was an initial step toward creating a "pan-Nordic share market."[17]

[15]Price Waterhouse, *Doing Business in Sweden.*

[16]T. Burt, "Special Partners Sought," *Financial Times,* April 14, 1998, p. III.

[17]T. Burt, "Alliances Are Just the Beginning," *Financial Times,* March 24, 1998, p. V.

Relations with the European Union.   In May 1994, the European parliament voted in favor of admitting Sweden, Norway, Finland, and Austria into the European Union (EU). In November 1994, the Swedish populace voted its approval to join the European Union and Sweden officially joined in 1995. Membership in it has already had a considerable impact on the Swedish economy. Fear of EU retaliatory power prompted the Swedish government to deregulate banking and the capital markets. Swedish multinationals, determined not to be left behind by EU competitors, have increased their investment in member nations and are locating an increasing proportion of their manufacturing operations within EU borders. To date, however, Sweden has opted not to join in EMU.

Labor.   Sweden's strongly developed sensitivity to the social role of business is, to a large degree, reflected in the nation's approach to labor relations. Although membership in trade unions is not legally required of workers, Sweden is a highly unionized nation. In early 1998, 90 percent of the employed workforce belonged to a union—far more than in the United Kingdom, Germany, or the United States. Even so, relationships between management and employees are generally cooperative, and a number of labor relations laws in force since 1977 have tended to formalize attitudes and approaches that were already common. Employees participate in the operation of businesses; in companies with more than 100 employees, they have the right to place two members on the board of directors, one representing blue-collar employees and one representing white-collar employees. Management has praised this arrangement as an effective way for labor leaders to share responsibility for difficult personnel decisions.

This is by no means to say, of course, that labor-management friction is nonexistent. In a recent Volvo annual report, the letter to shareholders referred to a three-week strike by white-collar workers that cost the company an estimated SEK1.1 billion, for which it received SEK395 million in compensation from the Swedish Employers' Confederation and the Swedish Metal Trades Employers' Association. Nevertheless, Volvo's desire to depict itself publicly as a partner, not as an antagonist of labor, even in times of adversity, appeared throughout the letter. The chairman noted that in spite of the strike, the group increased its earnings thanks to "a special and extraordinary effort on the part of all Volvo employees acting as a team." The chairman also stressed the company's commitment to providing employees with a pleasant and dignified work environment. Such a positive tone is all the more interesting because it came in a strike year.

Although there is no evidence of a significant, direct union influence on Swedish accounting practices, it would be naive to conclude that labor has no effect on Swedish financial reporting.[18] Even if unions themselves do not contribute directly to the formation of accounting policy, their relative prominence in Swedish politics and society affects the tone of management public relations (as we have just seen) and the ways in which government regulates the private sector. In fact, Swedish companies are required by law to disclose potentially sensitive employment information such as the average number of employees in each Swedish municipality and each foreign country, and total wages and salaries for the year with separate figures for senior management and other workers. (A copy of Volvo's 1997 personnel financial statement footnote is presented in Exhibit 10–5.) Such information could be particularly important in future management-labor disputes.

---

[18]Jönsson, *Accounting Regulation and Elite Structures.*

EXHIBIT 10–5

Volvo Personnel Disclosures

In accordance with a resolution adopted at the Annual General Meeting, the fee paid to the Board of Directors is a fixed amount of SEK2,260,000, to be distributed as decided by the Board. The Chairman of the Board, Håkan Frisinger, receives a fee of SEK850,000.

During 1997, Leif Johansson, President and Chief Executive Officer since April 23, 1997, received $5,164,383 in salary and other benefits amounting to SEK121,106. His bonus for 1997 is SEK692,300 (SEK1,000,000 on an annual basis). Leif Johansson is eligible to take early retirement on pension at age 55. A pension is earned gradually over the years up to the employee's retirement age and is fully earned at age 55. During the period between the ages of 55 and 65, he would receive a pension equal to 70% of his pension-qualifying salary, and a pension amounting to 50% of his pension-qualifying salary after reaching the age of 65. Leif Johansson has a twelve month notice of termination from AB Volvo and six months on his own initiative. If Leif Johansson's employment is terminated by AB Volvo, he is entitled to a severance payment equal to two years' salary, plus bonus.

During 1997, Sören Gyll, President and Chief Executive Officer up to and including April 22, 1997, received SEK6,158,506 in salary and other benefits amounting to SEK432,783. A payment of SEK3,180,000 was also made to a pension fund on behalf of Sören Gyll, equal to the bonus to which Sören Gyll was entitled. Sören Gyll continued to serve the Group until December 31, 1997, and then retired on pension. During the period between the ages of 57 and 65, he will receive a pension amounting to 70% of his salary, and upon reaching the age of 65 he will receive a pension amounting to 50% of his salary.

The Group Executive Committee, members of the executive committees of subsidiaries and a number of key persons receive bonuses in addition to salaries. Bonuses are based on the performance of the Volvo Group and/or of the executive's company, in accordance with the bonus system established by the Volvo Board

in 1993 and revised in 1996 and 1997. A bonus may, in principle, amount to a maximum of 50% of an executive's annual salary.

The employment contracts of certain senior executives contain provisions for severance payments when employment is terminated by the Company, as well as rules governing pension payments to executives who take early retirement. The rules governing early retirement provide that, when employment is terminated by the Company, an employee is entitled to severance pay equal to the employee's monthly salary for a period of 12 or 24 months, depending on age at date of severance. In certain contracts, replacing contracts concluded earlier, an employee is entitled to severance payments amounting to the employee's monthly salary for a period of 30 to 42 months. In agreements concluded after the spring of 1993, severance pay is reduced, in the event the employee gains employment during the severance period, in an amount equal to 75% of income from new employment. An early-retirement pension may be received when the employee reaches age 60. A pension is earned gradually over the years up to the employee's retirement age and is fully earned at age 60. From that date until reaching the normal retirement age, the retiree will receive 70% of the qualifying salary.

In February 1996, Skandia and Trygg-Hansa (insurance companies) offered approximately 100 senior executives in the Volvo Group an opportunity to acquire call options on AB Volvo's Series B shares. At the close of the subscription period approximately 90% of the executives had accepted the offer. The call options, which expire March 3, 2001, entitle the holder to acquire one Volvo Series B share for each option held. The option price, based on a market valuation, was fixed at SEK21.15 and the exercise price is SEK200. Members of the Group Executive Committee were offered an opportunity to acquire 6,000 or 10,000 options each. Other senior executives could acquire 4,000 or 6,000 options each. A total of 514,000 options were subscribed.

	1995		1996		1997	
Average Number of Employees	*Number of Employees*	*of Whom Women %*	*Number of Employees*	*of Whom Women %*	*Number of Employees*	*of Whom Women, %*
AB Volvo						
Sweden	409	39	448	37	318	56
Subsidiaries						
Sweden	41,133	18	43,293	18	43,682	17
Western Europe	13,168	12	14,681	14	14,664	17
Eastern Europe	185	13	308	15	524	13
North America	6,525	18	6,937	22	7,870	19
South America	2,229	7	1,819	10	2,030	11
Asia	1,684	10	2,003	11	2,065	12
Other countries	616	11	687	13	679	15
Automotive operations	**65,949**	**21**	**70,176**	**19**	**71,832**	**18**
Operations being divested	14,420	40	1,729	50	6	33
Group total	**80,369**	**21**	**71,905**	**18**	**71,838**	**18**

EXHIBIT 10–5   (Concluded)

Wages, Salaries and Other Remunerations, SEKm	1995 Board and President	of Which, Bonuses	Other Employees	1996 Board and President	of Which, Bonuses	Other Employees	1997 Board and President	of Which, Bonuses	Other Employees
AB Volvo									
Sweden	17.5	3.7	154.3	20.7	5.4	172.1	28.3	6.2	127.8
Subsidiaries									
Sweden	42.9	7.5	9,671.5	51.6	6.6	10,774.7	98.4	43.9	10,864.6
Western Europe	128.9	22.3	3,797.8	134.6	19.5	3,883.5	166.0	34.7	4,421.5
Eastern Europe	0.7	—	12.6	1.5	—	22.0	1.6	—	38.7
North America	42.9	2.5	1,831.5	42.2	0.7	1,787.6	85.2	2.4	2,116.7
South America	15.0	0.3	394.1	18.9	0.6	343.2	20.1	0.4	376.9
Asia	22.9	0.9	333.0	25.5	0.9	328.5	53.0	2.1	533.0
Other countries	2.5	—	112.0	4.2	0.2	127.2	11.0	0.4	134.2
Automotive operations	**273.3**	**37.2**	**16,306.8**	**299.2**	**33.9**	**17,438.8**	**463.6**	**90.1**	**18,613.4**
Operations being divested	112.0	38.5	2,672.2	18.8	6.9	272.5	0.3	—	4.6
Group total	**385.3**	**75.7**	**18,979.0**	**318.0**	**40.8**	**17,711.3**	**463.9**	**90.1**	**18,618.0**

Wages, Salaries, Other Remuneration and Social Costs	1995 Wages, Salaries, Remuneration	Social Costs	of Which, Pension Costs	1996 Wages, Salaries Remuneration	Social Costs	of Which, Pension Costs	1997 Wages, Salaries, Remuneration	Social Costs	of Which, Pension Costs
AB Volvo[1]	171.8	99.9	74.7	192.8	131.4	101.8	156.1	128.1	106.0
Subsidiaries	19,192.5	7,783.4	2,955.2	17,836.5	7,835.9	3,343.9	18,925.8	7,740.7	3,554.1
Group total[2]	**19,364.3**	**7,883.3**	**3,029.9**	**18,029.3**	**7,967.3**	**3,445.7**	**19,081.9**	**7,868.8**	**3,660.1**

[1]Of the **Parent Company's** pension costs, 43.0 (29.9; 30.0) pertains to Board members and the President. The Company's outstanding pension obligations to these persons amount to 275.0 (244.4; 214.2).

[2]Of the **Group's** pension costs, 94.5 (87.9; 74 9) pertains to Board members and the President. The Group's outstanding pension obligations to these persons amount to 360.9 (326.7; 284.3).

Selected Financial Reporting Practices

The primary objective of Swedish financial statements has historically been compliance with the law. Of late, and certainly now that Sweden must conform to the EU directives, true and fair financial reporting is the focus for listed companies. One aspect of the compliance objective that continues. however, is the:

> [r]equirement that financial reporting should be in conformity with tax accounting. [Therefore,] in order to be able to show a more realistic profit figure, not totally destroyed by tax considerations, most [individual] Swedish companies account for deductions which are specifically made for tax purposes under the special heading of appropriations, with a corresponding entry under untaxed reserves in the balance sheet. For foreign readers this has proved to be confusing. The *Redovisningsrådet* therefore took the decision to abolish [this approach] in group accounts. Instead it introduced deferred tax accounting based on the U.S. system [and this practice] is limited to [only] group accounts.[19]

The *Redovisningsrådet,* often referred to as the Financial Reporting Council (FRC), is charged with establishing accounting standards. It includes nine, part-time members representing the accounting profession, industry, and the government. As a body, it has

---

[19]Rundfelt, "Standard Setting in Sweden," p. 586.

no enforcement mechanism; corporate compliance is voluntary. To date, compliance has been generally high.

The underlying principles of Swedish GAAP are the widely embraced notions of historical cost, going concern, conservatism, and accrual accounting. Moreover, with an eye toward becoming a real player in the European Union and on the world corporate scene, the FRC work has exhibited a "strong influence from IASC standards."[20]

Bad Debts

Receivables must be stated at the amount the company actually expects to collect (i.e., net realizable value). Bad debts are recorded by direct write-off or by creation of a reserve that reduces the asset; Swedish tax law does not permit bad debt deductions based on management estimates of uncollectible accounts.

Intercorporate Investments

Marketable securities considered to be current assets are valued at the lower-of-cost-or-market method applied individually or on a portfolio basis. Write-downs are included in current income, and reversals of previous write-downs are permitted. Long-term investments are carried at cost and written down only for permanent declines in value. Reversals of previous write-downs are not permitted, although in some cases, a write-down may be offset by the write-up of another noncurrent asset. Investments in 20 to 50 percent owned companies are usually valued using the equity method (sometimes referred to as "the capital interest method"). If equity method accounted, the undistributed earnings of such affiliate companies should be classified as a restricted reserve (i.e., not available for distribution). A 50 percent share in a subsidiary (or an agreement that gives one company substantial control over another) requires the preparation of consolidated financial statements.

Inventories

As mentioned previously, inventories are carried at the lower of cost or net realizable value. (Obsolescence deductions at a standard rate of 3 percent of cost are frequently taken.) Prior to 1991, inventories were frequently reported at an amount less than that permitted under the lower of cost or market due to existing tax incentives (i.e., ending inventory could be written down by as much as 50 percent to an *inventory reserve*); however, those incentives were rescinded effective January 1, 1991. Cost is principally determined using FIFO; use of the LIFO method is not permitted.

Fixed Assets

Fixed assets (defined as those for continuous use in or possession by the business) with values higher than net book value may be written up to reflect appreciated value if an offsetting entry is credited to a nondistributable shareholders' equity reserve or used to write down another fixed asset whose value has declined permanently. The current assessed value of real estate must be disclosed in the notes to the financial statements.

Long-Term Contracts

Construction contracts covering more than one accounting period are generally accounted for under the completed-contract method, although the percentage-of-completion method is also permitted.

Research and Development Costs

Under the Swedish Accounting Act (1974), R&D may be capitalized to the balance sheet and amortized to income over a period not to exceed five years. More recently, the *Redovisningsrådet* has recommended (in Swedish Accounting Standard R1) that research costs be expensed as incurred but development costs be capitalized when the expenditure is recoverable with a high degree of certainty, the new product or process is technically feasible, and adequate resources exist to complete the project (and bring it to market if resale is intended). The new standard brings Swedish GAAP into conformity with *IAS No. 9.* (See, for instance, Exhibit 10–6.)

---

[20]Ibid., p. 590.

EXHIBIT 10–6

Active Biotech AB

Panel A. Consolidated Balance Sheet: Capitalized R&D

Amounts in SEK Thousand	1997	1996
Assets		
Research and development	193,780	1,219
Goodwill	29,569	20,657
Other	400	400
Total intangible fixed assets	**223,749**	22,276
Buildings and land	144,511	47,926
Machinery and other technical facilities	763,928	574,170
Equipment, tools, and other technical fixtures and fittings	40,536	7,912
Total tangible fixed assets	**948,975**	630,008
Shares in associated companies		
Other long-term receivables	250	6,839
Total financial fixed assets	**250**	6,839
Total fixed assets	**1,172,974**	659,123
Total inventories	**70,274**	20,796
Accounts receivable—trade	75,714	22,295
Short-term interest-bearing receivables	—	8,731
Other receivables	25,709	30,979
Total short-term receivables	**101,423**	62,005
Other short-term investments	169,000	190,388
Cash and bank balances	169,737	347,030
Total short-term investments	**338,737**	537,418
Total current assets	**510,434**	620,219
Total Assets	**1,683,408**	1,279,342

Panel B. Footnote Excerpts

Research and development

The Group capitalises development costs that meet the capitalisation requirements in accordance with the Swedish Accounting Standards Board's R1 and IAS 9 (International Accounting Standards) recommendations. Capitalisation pertains to development costs for which a specific application is envisaged and clearly confined to specific projects. Costs pertaining to basic research are charged against profit for the year in which they occur.

Fixed assets and depreciation

Fixed assets are reported at acquisition cost less accumulated depreciation according to plan. Calculation of depreciation according to plan is based on the estimated life and the actual acquisition cost. Depreciation according to plan is reported at the following percentage rates:

Machinery	10–20%
Computer equipment	20–30%
Buildings	2–14%
Land improvements	3–14%
Vessels	4%
Aircraft*	3–10%
Helicopters**	10,9%
Goodwill	10%
R&D costs***	7%

*Aircraft acquired in 1990 and later are depreciated at 3 per cent annually. Aircraft acquired before 1990 are fully depreciated. Engines are depreciated at SEK 900–1,000 per flying hour, depending on plane type.

**The depreciation period for helicopters is 4 years for 1/3 of acquisition value and 25 years for 2/3 of acquisition value. Helicopters subject to depreciation were acquired in 1997.

***Amortisation of R&D costs commences when the product becomes available for sale or use. Amortisation is according to plan, and amortisation periods are determined individually, depending on the respective product's economic life. The amortisation period does not exceed the patent period for the product, however.

Debt

The general accounting treatment applied to both current and long-term liabilities is the same; they are carried on the balance sheet at face or settlement (nominal) value.

Leases

Effective January 1, 1997, the Swedish Accounting Standards Council adopted a new leasing standard, Recommendation RR6—"Accounting for Leasing Contracts," intended to bring Swedish practice more into conformity with IASC GAAP. Under the new standard, leases are segmented into operational and financial leasing contracts, with non-cancelable financial leases capitalized to the balance sheet and operational leases carried off-balance sheet as a commitment/contingency.

Interest Costs

Interest cost on debt associated with the construction of fixed assets is rarely capitalized, although the practice is permitted under Swedish GAAP.

Consolidations

Business combinations are usually accounted for under the purchase method, with any goodwill capitalized and amortized, normally over a period of 5 years but in any case not to exceed 20 years. Negative goodwill is permitted to be carried on the consolidated balance sheet and is usually classified as a current liability or as a restricted reserve in shareholders' equity. The pooling-of-interests method, permitted but rarely used, applies only if the acquiring company issues shares, the companies are approximately the same size, and both companies continue their particular business activities following the combination.

Extraordinary Items

Extraordinary items are defined more loosely by Swedish companies than is allowed under U.S. GAAP and may include such items as gains or losses on the sale of fixed assets, costs associated with plant closures, and foreign currency exchange gains or losses.

Segment Reporting

The Swedish Companies Act requires companies engaged in diverse lines of business to separately disclose the operating income (or loss) of each independent line of business, either on the income statement or in the footnotes. The Companies Act, however, does not require the disclosure of earnings per share data, although basic EPS can be calculated because disclosure of the number of shares outstanding is required.

Shareholders' Equity

Shareholders' equity is segmented into two categories: restricted and nonrestricted. Restricted equity (i.e., untaxed and unavailable for dividend distribution) includes capital stock, legal reserves, and revaluation reserves, whereas nonrestricted equity includes unrestricted reserves (principally retained earnings). Legal restricted reserves include the equity portion of the untaxed reserve, foreign currency exchange reserves,[21] and any amounts received in excess of the nominal value of issued shares. Revaluation reserves, on the other hand, arise in those rare circumstances when fixed assets are written up in excess of cost. Exhibit 10–7 presents a comparison of Swedish and U.S. accounting and reporting standards.

---

[21]This is a special situation in which unrealized foreign currency exchange gains arising from long-term receivables and payables are recorded (net of unrealized exchange losses) in an untaxed reserve.

Exhibit 10–7
Comparison of Swedish and U.S. Accounting and Reporting Standards

Item	Sweden	United States
Asset valuation	Principally historical cost, although revaluations are permitted under special circumstances	Historical cost, with selected revaluation (principally downward)
Inventory valuation	Principally FIFO, which is prescribed by tax law	Principally LIFO (because of tax considerations); also FIFO and average cost methods
Inventory: year-end	Lower of cost or net realizable value	Lower of cost or replacement cost
Depreciation	Principally straight line, but any "appropriate depreciation plan" permitted; excess depreciation permitted	Principally straight line, with accelerated and production-based methods permitted
Goodwill	Capitalized and amortized usually over 5 years but in any case not in excess of 20 years; negative goodwill permitted and reported as either current liability or as shareholders' equity (restricted reserves)	Capitalized to balance sheet, with amortization (principally straight line) over a maximum of 40 years; negative goodwill not permitted (i.e., eliminated against noncurrent depreciable assets)
Research and development costs	Research costs expensed currently; development costs may be capitalized, with amortization commencing when the product becomes available for sale or use (but the amortization period may not exceed the patent period for the product)	Research costs expensed currently; development costs expensed currently except in certain industries (i.e., software, oil and gas)
Capitalized interest costs	Permitted but rarely practiced	Capitalization required for self-constructed assets
Intercorporate investments: Marketable securities (current asset trading)	Lower of cost or net realizable value, preferably on a portfolio basis	Market value (individual security basis), with unrealized gains and losses to income statement
Long-term investments: 0–20% ownership (available for sale)	Historical cost, adjusted for any permanent declines in value; upward revaluations permitted in rare cases	Market value (individual security basis only), with unrealized gains and losses to balance sheet (i.e., owners' equity)
20–50% ownership	Equity method	Equity method
51–100% ownership	Consolidated, using principally purchase accounting (although pooling permitted)	Consolidated, using pooling (until 2001) or purchase accounting
Debt valuation	Face or settlement (nominal) value	Long-term debt (except deferred income taxes) valued at present value; all other debt valued at face value
Leases	Financial leases capitalized to balance sheet; operational leases disclosed in footnotes	Capital leases reflected in balance sheet; operating leases disclosed in footnotes
Deferred income taxes	Provided for in the balance sheet for (principally) untaxed reserves; otherwise generally unneeded because of book-tax consistency	Computed under liability method
Pension liabilities	Accrued on the balance sheet if not fully funded	Reflected on balance sheet
Discretionary reserves	Fully permitted under Swedish tax laws but limited to excess depreciation and a special tax reserve	Restricted to identifiable operational losses
Statement of cash flows	Not required, although statement of changes in financial position required and often presented on a cash basis (principally using indirect method)	Required

Analytical Considerations

In Sweden, like Germany and Japan, the financial statements of domestic companies tend to be systematically downwardly biased as compared to U.S. corporate financial data. As noted previously, the explanation for this is straightforward: Swedish tax law stipulates that taxable income be determined by reference to a taxpayer's accounting (or book) income. As a consequence, only those expenses appearing on a Swedish company's published financial statements may appear on its tax return (except for those additional deductions allowed under Swedish tax law). Given management's overriding desire to shelter income and cash flows from taxation, it stands to reason that Swedish companies would tend to report lower earnings than U.S. firms, on average. This expectation appears supported by the following country composite data for 1998:

	Return on Equity	Price-Earnings Ratio
Sweden	13.9%	49.8
United States	19.5	20.0

Source: Global Vantage.

Despite Sweden's lower composite return on equity, the Swedish securities market appears to have compensated for the institutionalized downward income bias of that country as reflected in the relatively higher price-earnings multiples afforded Swedish companies.

What are the principal factors responsible for this downward biasing? Although there are many differences between U.S. and Swedish GAAP, the most important factors appear to be the following:

• *Depreciation.* In Sweden (as in the United States), fixed assets are normally valued at their acquisition cost less any depreciation taken to date. In certain circumstances, however, fixed assets may be written up to a higher carrying value if the assets are considered to have an "enduring value" in excess of acquisition cost. Assets whose values have been written up are then depreciated over their normal expected useful life, thereby creating depreciation deductions in excess of original historical cost. In any case, depreciation may be determined using either book or planned depreciation methods. Under *book depreciation,* the amount of depreciation claimed for tax purposes is equivalent to that taken for financial reporting (or book) purposes. Under *planned depreciation,* depreciation is limited to a deduction equivalent to straight-line amortization of the asset over its planned service life. Planned service lives, however, are determined by reference to the *minimum* service lives provided by Swedish tax law: machinery, 5–10 years; equipment, 3–5 years; and vehicles, 5 years. As a consequence, many Swedish firms depreciate their assets over the shortest lives permitted by Swedish law. In the United States, most firms adopt asset depreciation periods for book purposes that substantially exceed those permitted for tax purposes.

Swedish corporate managers may thus select whatever depreciation policy they so desire, subject to certain ceiling tests to avoid writing long-lived assets off too rapidly.[22] One outcome of this situation is that Swedish companies rarely deduct an amount that would be considered systematic under U.S. GAAP. More often than not, the amount deducted exceeds the systematic deduction, and, thus, a situation of excess depreciation is said to exist. As a consequence, the reported earnings of Swedish companies appear understated relative to their U.S. counterparts.

- *Untaxed Reserves.* Prior to 1991, Swedish companies were permitted to take reserve deductions against pretax operating income for a variety of purposes such as inventory, investment, and payroll. In 1991, however, a major tax reform eliminated most of these reserves in exchange for a substantial reduction in Sweden's corporate tax rate from 52 to 30 percent (28 percent beginning in 1994). As part of this reform effort, Swedish corporations were granted the right to allocate a portion of pre-tax earnings to a special tax equalization reserve (SURV), to a maximum of 30 percent of equity capital. In 1991, for example, Procordia, Sweden's fifth largest corporation (based on asset size), allocated SEK600 million, or 17 percent, of pretax income to its SURV. Beginning in 1994, however, a seven-year phaseout of the SURV began. Shortly thereafter, a new income adjustment reserve (the IAR) was implemented. The IAR permits an annual tax-deductible allocation of up to 25 percent of pretax profit to the untaxed reserve account. Each annual allocation, however, must be reversed and included in taxable income within five years. These reserves may not be distributed as dividends until they are reversed to the income statement and included in taxable income. Swedish GAAP also provides that the untaxed reserves be segmented into its two components: a restricted equity reserve account (72 percent) and a deferred tax liability account (28 percent).

  A significant consequence of the use of untaxed reserve accounts is the understatement of reported earnings and a parallel overstatement of assets and shareholders' equity (restricted reserves) relative to U.S. companies. With respect to traditional ratios, the profitability indicators of Swedish companies appear uniformly less positive than those of comparable U.S. companies. The liquidity and solvency indicators for Swedish companies, however, should (correctly) appear relatively more positive than for comparable U.S. firms. Finally, since the IAR is granted for tax purposes as well as book purposes, Swedish companies appear to be better cash flow generators than their U.S. counterparts. In effect, the IAR represents an interest-free loan, with a five-year payback period, from the Swedish government to its domestic corporations. For those Swedish companies whose profits continually increase, the payback period for these reserves can be effectively postponed almost indefinitely.

- *Capitalization of Asset Values.* Despite the fact that Swedish GAAP permits the capitalization of certain expenditures to the balance sheet as assets, most firms rarely avail themselves of this option. For example, while the capitalization of interest during the self-construction of assets is permitted in Sweden, most firms expense such interest costs to obtain current tax deductibility. Similarly, although most betterment expenditures are capitalized in the United States, they are expensed in Sweden, largely due to tax considerations. And despite the fact that

---

[22]Book depreciation is subject to two ceiling tests: (1) a 130 percent declining-balance rule and (2) a 20 percent straight-line provision. At the end of each year, a corporation has the option to select which of the two tests yields the highest depreciation charge. In all cases, however, the ceiling test selected must be consistently applied to all of a company's fixed assets.

under Swedish GAAP, some development cost outlays can be capitalized, the practice is not widespread among Swedish firms. The consequence of this prevalent propensity to expense, rather than to capitalize, is a somewhat more conservative presentation of reported earnings.

Summary

Sweden is one of the most affluent countries in the world. It has had no significant under-class, virtually full employment (until recently), and relatively well-off retirees. It has the largest public service sector in the Western world: Over half of its voters get their income from the government through jobs or welfare and the bulk of its GDP is devoted to public service expenditures. Such circumstances spring from the deeply held belief that the purpose of employers is to provide the financial resources that the state can use for the improvement of all citizens' standard of living via the provision of public services. During the first half of the 1990s, the vehicles for this welfare state—high tax rates and a dominant Social Democrat Party—have been in flux. Recently tax rates have been lowered; Swedish companies have pursued a number of European alliances, some successfully (e.g., ASEA AB and BBC Brown Boveri Ltd.), some not (e.g., Volvo and Renault); and the Social Democrat Party governs with its lowest support in half a century. It is generally conceded, however, that the "Swedish welfare state will be cheaper, leaner, and hopefully more efficient, but it will not disappear."[23] Time will tell how successful the Swedes will be in maintaining an enviable domestic prosperity and becoming a full-fledged player in a robustly dynamic global and European community. As Swedish corporate boardrooms abandon the Swedish language for English, and in the wake of Ikea and Tetra Laval moving their headquarters offshore for tax reasons (Ericsson is toying with the same idea because of the difficulty in attracting top talent due to Sweden's high personal tax rates), Sweden's proclivity for proactive positive change cannot afford to be lessened.[24]

Suggested Readings

Cooke, T. E. "Disclosure in the Corporate Annual Reports of Swedish Companies." *Accounting and Business Research,* Spring 1989, pp. 113–24.

——. "Voluntary Corporate Disclosure by Swedish Companies." *The Journal of International Financial Management and Accounting,* Summer 1989, pp. 171–95.

Coopers & Lybrand. *Executive Summary of Principal Differences between Accounting Principles in the United States and Sweden.* New York: Coopers & Lybrand, 1989.

Hellman, N. "A Comparative Analysis of the Impact of Accounting Differences on Profits and Return on Equity: Differences between Swedish Practice and United States GAAP." *European Accounting Review* 3(1993), pp. 495–530.

---

[23]D. Milbank, "Sweden's Welfare State Stares Down Reform Efforts," *The Wall Street Journal,* January 30, 1995, p. A15.

[24]See T. Burt, "Swedish Goes by the Board," *Financial Times,* March 11, 1998, p. 15; G. McIvor, "Swedish Tax Exodus Threatens," *Financial Times,* May 9, 1997, p. 2; and "The Luddites Are Coming," *The Economist,* August 22, 1998, p. 44.

Price Waterhouse. *Doing Business in Sweden.* New York: Price Waterhouse, 1995.

Rundfelt, R. "Standard Setting in Sweden." *European Accounting Review* 3 (1993), pp. 585–91.

Slipkowsky, J. N. "The Volvo Way of Financial Reporting." *Management Accounting,* October 1988, pp. 22–25.

Weetman, P., and S. J. Gray. "A Comparative Analysis of the Impact of Accounting Principles on Profits: The U.S.A. versus the U.K., Sweden, and the Netherlands." *Accounting and Business Research,* Autumn 1991, pp. 363–79.

Exercises

10.1   Swedish versus U.S. GAAP

In a December 1993 *European Accounting Review* article (pp. 495–530), "A Comparative Analysis of the Impact of Accounting Differences on Profits and Return on Equity: Differences between Swedish Practice and U.S. GAAP," N. Hellman reports that "the adjustments for U.S. GAAP requirements, on average, caused *lower* profits under U.S. GAAP, compared with profits in accordance with Swedish accounting practice. . . . These results were *not* in line with expectations."

Required:

(a) Obtain a copy of this article and report on the rationale for the initial expectations that Swedish GAAP would be more conservative than U.S. GAAP.

(b) Summarize the author's rationale for the contrary results and comment on whether you see merit in that rationale or not.

10.2   Financial Analysis: Swedish versus U.S. GAAP

AB Electrolux, a Swedish company, is one of the world's leading producers of household appliances. The company's shares trade in Stockholm, London, and on the NASDAQ over-the-counter exchange in the United States in the form of American Depositary Receipts. Each Electrolux ADR equals one share of Class B stock. As of December 31, 1997, the company's share capital was composed of:

	Par Value (SEK million)
2,000,000 A-Shares, par value SEK 25	50
71,233,916 B-Shares, par value SEK 25	1,781
73,133,916	1,831

In 1998, the company increased the voting rights of each B-share from 1/1,000 to 1/10 of a vote (each A-share possessed one full voting right) and reduced the par value of both the A and B shares from SEK25 to SEK5.

The company's 1997 annual report provided summary financial results under both Swedish and U.S. GAAP to assist its foreign shareholders. Over 60 percent of Electrolux's shareholders were foreign:

Shareholders by County	*Percentage of Share Capital*
U.S.A.	33%
U.K.	15%
Other	12%
	60%

AB ELECTROLUX
Summary Financial Results
(SEK millions)

1. Income Statement Data

	1997	*1996*
Consolidated net income		
As per Swedish GAAP	352	1,850
As per U.S. GAAP	877	1,668

2. Balance Sheet Data

	According to Swedish GAAP		According to U.S. GAAP	
	1997	*1996*	*1997*	*1996*
Intangible assets	3,517	3,558	2,546	2,624
Tangible assets	22,519	24,118	22,442	24,037
Financial assets	1,744	1,270	1,876	1,457
Current assets	51,860	56,223	55,710	59,831
Total	79,640	85,169	82,574	87,949
Equity	20,565	22,428	20,332	21,763
Minority interests	913	1,952	913	1,952
Provision for deferred taxes		893		712
Provisions for pensions	6,247	5,974	6,461	6,322
Other provision	4,656	2,161	3,685	1,831
Financial liabilities	28,479	31,342	32,403	34,950
Operating liabilities	18,780	20,419	18,780	20,419
Total	79,640	85,169	82,574	87,949

Required:

(a) How would Electrolux account for the 1998 change in voting rights and par value of its A and B shares?

(b) Using the data above, prepare a comparative financial analysis of Electrolux under Swedish versus U.S. GAAP. What generalities can you draw from your analysis?

(c) Explain why Electrolux's provision for deferred taxes was nonexistant in 1997 under both Swedish and U.S. GAAP.

10.3 Lease Capitalization

Volvo was founded in 1915 and has grown to be the largest industrial company (as measured by sales) in the Nordic area, including Sweden, Norway, Denmark, Finland, and Iceland. The company began assembling cars in 1926 and trucks in 1928. Today Volvo is engaged in a broad range of activities in the automotive and related industries (e.g., cars, trucks, and buses complemented by marine and industrial engines, aircraft engines, and construction equipment). The company also has substantial shareholdings in companies with operations in the branded consumer products field, as well as the pharmaceutical and biotechnology fields.

Volvo or its consolidated subsidiaries lease a significant number of assets. Under Swedish GAAP, consistent with IASC GAAP, leases are divided into operating and finance leases, with finance leases capitalized to the consolidated balance sheet.

In December 1984, Volvo shares began trading in the United States over the NASDAQ exchange in the form of American depositary shares (or ADSs). Each ADS represents one Class B Volvo share; each Class B share confers one-tenth (1/10) of one vote, whereas each Class A share confers one full vote. Accordingly, Volvo files an annual set of financial statements (form 20-F) with the U.S. Securities and Exchange Commission.

Volvo's year-end 1997 form 20-F revealed the following information:

1. Accounting Principles

Leasing contracts

Effective in 1997, Volvo is applying the Recommendation of the Swedish Financial Accounting Standards Council pertaining to leasing contracts, which came into force January 1, 1997. In accordance with this Recommendation, leasing contracts are divided into operational and financial leasing contracts. The change represents an adaptation to international standards. Volvo's sales-financing operations have been reported earlier in accordance with international standards. The Recommendation is otherwise being applied only to transactions following the date when the Recommendation came into force and has had only a limited effect on Volvo's consolidated income statement and balance sheet.

Leasing

Effective in 1997, Volvo is applying Recommendation RR6, "Accounting for leasing contracts," of the Swedish Financial Accounting Standards Council.

At December 31, 1997, future rental costs related to noncancellable leases amounted to 6,356 (7,269; 7,122), of which 2,548 (2,170; 1,173) in sales-financing companies. Rental expenses in 1997 amounted to 2,002 (1,782; 1,401).

Future rental payments are distributed as follows:

	Rental Payments
1998	1,861
1999	1,404
2000	1,029
2001	832
2002	687
2003 or later	543
Total	**6,356**

The company's long-term debt carries a weighted average cost of capital of 10 percent.

Required:

    (a) Assume that all leases are capitalized to a company's balance sheet. What value would be assigned to Volvo's outstanding lease commitments on the company's balance sheet as of December 31, 1997?

    (b) Volvo's total assets at December 31, 1997, amounted to SEK 163,295 million and its long-term debt, excluding operating leases, was SEK 23,135 million. Calculate the company's long-term debt to total assets ratio *both* with and without the capitalization of Volvo's leases.

    (c) Are companies like Volvo able to leverage themselves to higher debt levels than would otherwise be the case as a consequence of accounting standards that permit operating leases to be carried off-balance sheet?

10.4   Converting Funds Flows to Cash Flows

In Sweden, limited companies are required to provide shareholders with an annual report containing an administration report, a balance sheet, an income statement, and a statement of changes in financial position. An increasing trend among Swedish companies is to present the statement of changes in financial position in the context of cash flow data. The statement of changes in financial position for Esselte, as presented in the company's 1996 annual report and a brief description of that statement from the company's footnotes are presented here as an example. Esselte, headquartered in Solna, Sweden, is a worldwide supplier of office products.

Required:

    (a) Recast Esselte's statement of changes in financial position into a statement of cash flows (indirect method) as it would appear under U.S. GAAP.

    (b) Comment on Esselte's financial health vis-à-vis its cash flows.

Excerpt from Esselte's Footnotes
STATEMENT OF CHANGES IN FINANCIAL POSITION

The Statement of Changes in Financial Position has been revised to better reflect cash flow, as well as the effects of exchange rate fluctuations, acquisitions and divestments. Accordingly, the terms used in the Statement of Changes in Financial Position correspond better to those used internally for controlling the divisions.

Cash flow after dividend is the same as operating income, financial income and expense, taxes and dividends, as well as the change in capital employed in local currency translated into Swedish kronor using the average exchange rate for the period.

The translation effects of exchange rate fluctuations during the year which have affected capital employed translated into Swedish kronor are shown as a separate item. Capital employed in the Group is defined as operating assets less operating liabilities. Capital employed includes tax receivables and tax liabilities, as well as appropriations for future costs.

Unallocated capital employed includes mainly tax receivables and liabilities, certain real estate properties, as well as a reserve for future higher rental costs for the office building in Solna.

The Group's net financial liabilities are defined as financial liabilities less financial assets.

ESSELTE
Statement of Changes in Financial Position
31 December, 1996 and 1995

SEK Millions	1996	1995
Operating income before depreciation	**1,149**	1,219
Change in working capital	**71**	−225
Cash flow before investments and acquisitions/divestments	**1,220**	994
Capital expenditures on property, plant, equipment and intangible assets	**−254**	−246
Sales of property, plant and equipment	**17**	21
Acquired/divested capital employed	**−341**	5
Cash flow from investments and acquisitions/divestments	**−578**	−220
Cash flow from business areas	**642**	774
Nonallocated expenses before depreciation	**−71**	−93
Change in nonallocated capital employed	**104**	74
Cash flow from nonallocated items	**33**	−19
Cash flow from operations	**675**	755
Financial income and expense	**−30**	−119
Taxes paid	**−253**	−237
Cash flow from financial items	**−283**	−356
Cash flow before dividends	**392**	399
Dividends	**−137**	−103
Cash flow after dividends	**255**	296
Exchange differences in capital employed	**−22**	330
Change in net financial liabilities	**233**	626
Specification of change in net financial liabilities		
Change in liquid assets and short-term notes	**65**	−66
Change in long-term financial assets	**−15**	−1
Change in financial assets	**50**	−67
Change in short-term borrowings	**−97**	−584
Change in long-term borrowings	**−89**	−108
Change in pension liabilities	**3**	−1
Change in financial liabilities	**−183**	−693
Change in net financial liabilities	**233**	626

10.5   Statement of Cash Flows

Under Swedish GAAP, public companies are required to provide shareholders with an annual report containing an administration report, balance sheet, income statement, and statement of changes in financial position (usually presented in terms of sources and uses of funds). There is an increasing tendency, however, for companies to present cash flow statements using the indirect method.

The following are the consolidated income statement and consolidated balance sheet for Active Biotech AB for the year ended 31 December 1996 and 1997. Active Biotech is headquartered in Malmo and is one of Europe's leading suppliers of vaccines and pharmaceuticals that prevent and cure diseases.

ACTIVE BIOTECH AB
Consolidated Income Statement

	SEK million	
	1997	*1996*
Net sales	456,679	292,611
Cost of goods sold*	−335,083	−184,543
Gross Profit	**121,596**	108,068
Selling expenses	−50,794	−39,466
Administrative expenses	−39,773	−41,805
Research and development costs	−15,943	−524
Items affecting comparability	12,285	—
Other operating income	9,631	—
Operating Profit	**37,002**	26,273
Result from financial investments		
Result from share in subsidiaries	—	396,593
Result from participations in associated companies	—	—
Interest income and similar income items	59,702	16,738
Interest expense and similar expense items	−54,621	−43,801
Operating Profit after Financial Items	**42,083**	395,803
Minority interest	−3,344	−4,036
Profit before Tax	**38,739**	391,767
Tax on profit for the year	−8,317	−4,686
Profit for the Year	**30,422**	387,081

*Depreciation expense in 1997 amounted to 52,926.

ACTIVE BIOTECH AB
Consolidated Balance Sheet

Assets				*Liabilities and Shareholders' Equity*		
	SEK Million				**SEK Million**	
	1997	*1996*			*1997*	*1996*
Assets				*Restricted shareholders' equity*		
Research and development	193,780	1,219		Share capital	139,150	138,150
Goodwill	29,569	20,657		Restricted reserves	52,421	21,014
Other	400	400			**191,571**	159,164
Total intangible fixed assets	**223,749**	22,276		*Unrestricted shareholders' equity*		
Buildings and land	144,511	47,926		Unrestricted reserves	324,826	20,255
Machinery and other technical facilities	763,928	574,170		Profit for the year	30,422	387,081
Equipment, tools, and other technical fixtures and fittings	40,536	7,912			**355,248**	407,336
Total tangible fixed assets	**948,975**	630,003		**Total shareholders' equity**	**546,819**	566,500
Shares in associated companies	—	—		**Minority interests**	**23,561**	40,805
Other long-term receivables	250	6,839		Provision for pensions	33,661	17,205
Total financial fixed assets	**250**	6,839		Provision for taxes	42,487	20,036
Total fixed assets	**1,172,974**	659,123		Structural reserve	32,658	48,334
Total inventories	**70,274**	20,796		**Total allocations**	**108,806**	85,575
Accounts receivable—trade	75,714	22,295		Interest-bearing long-term liabilities	528,929	461,123
Short-term interest-bearing receivables	—	8,731		Convertible loan	32,834	34,937
Other receivables	25,709	30,979		Other long-term liabilities	138,854	
Total short-term receivables	**101,423**	62,005		**Total long-term liabilities**	**700,617**	496,060
Other short-term investments	169,000	190,388		Accounts payable—trade	61,817	13,569
Cash and bank balances	169,737	347,030		Tax liabilities	46	10,850
Total short-term investments	**338,737**	537,418		Interest-bearing current liabilities	141,867	22,183
Total current assets	**510,434**	620,219		Other current liabilities	99,875	43,800
Total Assets	**1,683,408**	1,279,342		**Total current liabilities**	**303,605**	90,402
				Total Shareholders' Equity and Liabilities	**1,683,408**	1,279,342
				Assets pledged and contingent liabilities Note 17		

Note 17 Assets Pledged and Contingent Liabilities

	Group	
SEK Thousand	*1997*	*1996*
Assets pledged		
For liabilities to credit institutions	1,521,233	620,679
FPG/PRI pensions	18,000	18,600
Other	4,849	4,818
	1,544,082	644,097
Contingent liabilities		
Guarantees	—	—
Warranties	21,104	13,222
	21,104	13,222
Of which, to Group companies		
Total assets pledged and contingent liabilities	1,565,186	657,319
Assets pledged for liabilities to credit institutions		
Real estate mortgages	53,415	3,415
Chattel mortgages	44,600	2,000
Ship mortgages	614,391	497,257
Aircraft mortgages	14,560	12,709
Helicopter mortgages	131,949	41,479
Net value of assets in subsidiaries	552,453	60,309
Other shares	46,658	3,510
Blocked bank funds	63,207	—
	1,521,233	620,679
Assets pledged for FPG/PRI pensions		
Chattel mortgages	18,000	18,600
Blocked bank funds	4,849	4,818
	22,849	23,418

Required:

(a) Using Active Biotech's financial data, construct a statement of cash flows for 1997. Comment on the company's financial health vis-à-vis its cash flows.

(b) Of what use is the information on pledged assets and contingent liabilities presented in footnote 17?

10.6   Accounting for Appropriations and Reserves

Atlas Copco AB is an international industrial company with operations in construction, mining, and the manufacture and sale of industrial tools and equipment. Although founded and headquartered in Stockholm, over 95 percent of the company's sales occur outside Sweden. Atlas Copco AB is the parent company of the Atlas Copco Group.

The following are the company's income statements and balance sheets for the years ended 31 December 19x8 and 19x9, as well as several excerpts from the notes to the financial statements.

Required:

(a) Using the following information, reconstruct the journal entries for 19x8 and 19x9 involving the Appropriations account.

(b) Calculate the company's return on investment (1) with and (2) without the use of the Appropriations and the Untaxed Reserves accounts.

ATLAS COPCO AB
Income Statement
(SEK, millions)

	19x9	*19x8*
Operating income	238	173
Operating expense	−85	−116
Operating profit before depreciation	153	57
Cost depreciation (NOTE 3)	−7	−8
Operating profit after depreciation	146	49
Financial income and expense	461	282
Profit after financial income and expense	607	331
Appropriations (NOTE 5)	−177	−12
Profit before taxes	430	319
Taxes	—	0
Net Profit	**430**	**319**

ATLAS COPCO AB
Balance Sheet
(SEK, millions)

Assets		*19x9.12.31*		*19x8.12.31*	
Current assets	Cash, bank and short-term investments	**1,038**		1,174	
	Receivables	**1,673**	**2,711**	1,676	2,850
Fixed assets	Shares and participations	**3,816**		3,541	
	Other fixed assets	**415**	**4,231**	790	4,331
Total Assets			**6,942**		7,181
Liabilities and Shareholders' Equity					
Current liabilities	Non-interest-bearing liabilities	**326**		198	
	Interest-bearing liabilities	**1,692**	**2,018**	2,318	2,516
Long-term liabilities	Interest-bearing liabilities		**446**		436
Total Liabilities			**2,464**		2,952
Convertible debenture loan (NOTE 22)			**—**		137
Untaxed reserves (NOTE 23)			**450**		458
Shareholders' equity	Share capital (36,703,184 shares, par value SEK 25)	**918**		855	
	Legal reserve (NOTE 25)	**1,737**		1,522	
	Retained earnings	**943**		908	
	Net profit	**430**	**4,028**	319	3,634
Total Liabilities and Shareholders' Equity			**6,942**		7,181
Assets pledged			**44**		5
Contingent liabilities			636		548

Excerpts: Notes to Financial Statements

3. Depreciation

The Atlas Copco Group uses three depreciation concepts: cost depreciation, book depreciation and current cost depreciation.

Cost depreciation is based on original cost and is applied according to the straight-line method over the economic life of the asset. Goodwill is amortized in accordance with a plan established for each specific case.

Book depreciation is used in each individual company in accordance with the maximum amount permitted by tax legislation in each country. The difference between book depreciation and cost depreciation is reported under "Appropriations" in the Income Statement. The total value is reported in the Balance Sheet among untaxed reserves under the heading "Accumulated additional depreciation." In the case of the Group, untaxed reserves and appropriations are eliminated.

5. Appropriations

Tax legislation in Sweden and in other countries allows companies to retain untaxed profits through tax-deductible allocations to untaxed reserves. By utilizing these regulations, companies can dispose and retain earnings within the business without being taxed. The untaxed reserves created through this means may not be used for dividends.

The untaxed reserves first become subject to tax when they are withdrawn. Should the company report a loss, certain untaxed reserves can be used to cover the loss without being taxed.

	Parent Company	
	19x9	*19x8*
Difference between book depreciation and cost depreciation (NOTE 23)	8	4
Allocation to tax equalization reserve	—	−206
Group contributions, net	−185	190
	−177	−12

Under certain circumstances, the transfer of earnings, in the form of Group contributions can be made between Swedish companies within the same Group. The contribution is a tax deductible expense for the donor and taxable income for the receiver. During 19x9, the Parent Company received contributions from Atlas Copco Tools AB and made contributions to Atlas Copco Construction and Mining Technique AB and Uniroc AB.

23. Untaxed reserves

Untaxed reserves are reported in the Parent Company balance sheet as a compounded item. The distribution is shown below. These are totally eliminated in the consolidated accounts.

	Parent Company	
	19x9	*19x8*
Accumulated additional depreciation		
Machinery and equipment	12	20
Buildings	10	10
Tax equalization reserve	428	428
	450	458

	Accumulated Additional Depreciation	
	Machinery and Equipment	*Buildings*
Opening value, Jan. 1, 19x9	20	10
Dissolutions	−8	—
Closing value, Dec. 31, 19x9	12	10

25. Restricted reserves

	Group	Parent Company
Restricted reserves, Dec. 31, 19x8	3,429	1,522
Premium on conversion and non-cash issue	226	226
Less taxes	−11	−11
Transfers between restricted and unrestricted capital	773	
Restricted reserves, Dec. 31, 19x9	4,417	1,737

The increase in restricted reserves for the Atlas Copco Group relates primarily to translation differences and the portion of shareholders' equity in allocations made to untaxed reserves in individual companies.

10.7 Accounting for Fixed Assets

The accounting for fixed assets in Sweden differs from that in the United States in two important respects. First, in certain circumstances (i.e., if an asset can be shown to have "enduring value" in excess of its acquisition cost), Swedish accounting principles permit fixed assets to be written up to values in excess of their historical cost, which in turn affects the depreciation that is charged on such revalued assets. Second, regardless of whether a company's fixed assets have been revalued or not, Swedish GAAP permits the level of reported (or "booked") depreciation charges to exceed normal cost-based depreciation. Under U.S. GAAP, fixed asset write-ups are not permitted and depreciation deductions are limited to the historical cost of an asset allocated over its expected economic life.

The Sandvik Group, headquartered in Sandviken, Sweden, is one of the world's leading manufacturers of specialty machine tools. Presented below are the income statement and balance sheet for the years ended 31 December, 19x8 and 19x9, for the parent company of the Sandvik Group. Also presented are selected excerpts from the company's notes to financial statements.

Required:

(a) Using journal entries, explain the change in the Buildings account (see balance sheet) from SEK 312 in 19x8 to SEK 304 in 19x9.

(b) Explain Sandvik's 19x9 year-end valuation of SEK 304 for buildings.

(c) In 19x9, Sandvik incurred SEK 24 million in interest charges in connection with the financing of newly constructed fixed assets. Why wasn't this amount included in the valuation of the company's fixed assets (see Note 13, Fixed Assets)?

SANDVIK
Income Statement

		Amounts in SEK Millions	
		19x9	*19x8*
Invoiced sales		**8,197**	7,047
Costs of production, selling and administration		**−6,932**	−6,403
OPERATING PROFIT BEFORE DEPRECIATION		**1,265**	644
Scheduled depreciation	Note 4	**−343**	−300
OPERATING PROFIT AFTER DEPRECIATION		**922**	344
Financial items:			
Dividends received from subsidiaries		**603**	2,972
Interest received from subsidiaries		**19**	13
Other interest received		**128**	171
Interest paid to subsidiaries		**−120**	−235
Other interest paid		**−84**	−99
Exchange differences on loans		**−10**	−78
PROFIT AFTER FINANCIAL INCOME AND EXPENSES		**1,458**	3,088
Non-recurring earnings		**7**	1,017
Non-recurring expenses		**−128**	−256
PROFIT BEFORE APPROPRIATIONS AND TAXES		**1,337**	3,849
Appropriations:			
Difference between book and scheduled depreciation	Note 18	**104**	124
Change in transitional reserve for inventory reserve, etc.	Note 19	**600**	300
Change in tax equalization reserve	Note 19	**−1,790**	−400
Other appropriations	Note 19	**−3**	14
Group contributions		**−33**	−115
PRE-TAX PROFIT		**215**	3,772
Accrued taxes		**−75**	-0-
Estimated future taxes		**79**	39
NET PROFIT		**219**	3,811

SANDVIK
Balance Sheet

Assets	Amounts in SEK Millions	
	19x9	*19x8*
CURRENT ASSETS		
Cash and bank balances	**70**	77
Short-term placements	**1,374**	935
Receivables from subsidiaries	**1,395**	1,320
Trade accounts receivable	**498**	394
Prepaid expenses and accrued income	**177**	210
Other current receivables	**139**	118
Inventories	**1,906**	1,864
	5,559	4,918

SANDVIK
Balance Sheet
(continued)

		Amounts in SEK Millions	
		19x9	*19x8*
FIXED ASSETS			
Shares and participations in subsidiaries		**5,675**	5,288
Shares and participations in other companies		**419**	461
Receivables from subsidiaries		**171**	171
Other long-term receivables		**15**	15
Construction in progress		**78**	63
Machinery and equipment	Note 13	**1,671**	1,688
Buildings	Note 13	**304**	312
		8,333	7,998
TOTAL ASSETS		**13,892**	12,916
Assets pledged		**596**	581
Liabilities and Equity Capital			
CURRENT LIABILITIES			
Owed to suppliers		**423**	315
Tax debts		**152**	96
Accrued expenses and prepaid income		**672**	559
Short-term loans		**6**	93
Other current liabilities to subsidiaries		**1,189**	1,035
Other current liabilities		**168**	133
		2,610	2,231
LONG-TERM LIABILITIES			
Long-term loans		**7**	13
Provision for pensions		**787**	858
Latent tax liability		**12**	91
Other long-term liabilities		**—**	42
		806	1,004
UNTAXED RESERVES			
Accumulated depreciation above schedule	Note 18	**1,129**	1,233
Tax equalization reserve	Note 19	**2,190**	400
Transitional reserve for inventory reserve, etc.	Note 19	**—**	600
Other untaxed reserves	Note 19	**8**	5
		3,327	2,238
EQUITY CAPITAL			
Restricted equity capital:			
Share capital (278,476,380 shares of SEK 5 nominal)		**1,392**	1,366
Statutory capital reserve		**291**	286
Proposed new issue		**—**	25
		1,683	1,677
Unrestricted equity capital:			
Retained earnings		**5,247**	1,955
Net profit		**219**	3,811
		5,466	5,766
Total equity capital		**7,149**	7,443
TOTAL LIABILITIES AND EQUITY CAPITAL		**13,892**	12,916
Contingent liabilities		**629**	1,005

SANDVIK
Excerpts from Footnotes

Valuation Principles

Fixed assets

Fixed assets are shown in the Accounts after the deduction of accumulated scheduled depreciation. Scheduled depreciation charges in the industrial operations are based on the historical cost of the assets and their estimated economic lives; for machinery and equipment this means normally between five and fifteen years, for buildings between ten and fifty years, and for site improvements twenty years. Degressive depreciation based on a life of from three to five years is applied to computer equipment. The difference between book and scheduled accumulated depreciation is shown as an untaxed reserve at the individual company.

Depreciation on the undepreciated portion of accumulated write-ups on buildings is charged at 2% of the original write-up.

NOTE 4. Depreciation

GROUP

	Goodwill and Other Intangible Assets		Machinery and Equipment		Industrial and Residential Buildings		Site Improvements		Total	
	19x9	*19x8*	*19x9*	*19x8*	*19x9*	*19x8*	*19x9*	*19x8*	*19x9*	*19x8*
Scheduled depreciation	**−82**	−48	**−874**	−741	**−146**	−86	**−2**	−2	**−1,104**	−877

PARENT COMPANY

	Machinery and Equipment		Industrial and Residential Buildings		Site Improvements		Total	
	19x9	*19x8*	*19x9*	*19x8*	*19x9*	*19x8*	*19x9*	*19x8*
Scheduled depreciation	**−327**	−286	**−15**	−13	**−1**	−1	**−343**	−300
Difference between book and scheduled depreciation	**93**	115	**11**	9	**—**	—	**104**	124
Book depreciation	**−234**	−171	**−4**	−4	**−1**	−1	**−239**	−176

NOTE 13. Fixed assets

Machinery, equipment, buildings, land, site improvements and agricultural and forest properties are entered at their net value after scheduled depreciation and after accumulated write-ups not yet written off. Accumulated excess depreciation reported by the individual companies is entered among untaxed reserves under the heading "Accumulated depreciation above schedule."

GROUP	Machinery and Equipment		Industrial and Residential Buildings		Agricultural and Forest Properties		Land and Site Improvements	
	19x9	19x8	19x9	19x8	19x9	19x8	19x9	19x8
Historical cost[1]	**11,689**	10,601	**3,545**	3,031	**1**	1	**548**	466
Accumulated scheduled depreciation	**−7,475**	−6,552	**−1,583**	−1,289	**—**	—	**−34**	−28
Scheduled remaining values	**4,214**	4,049	**1,962**	1,742	**1**	1	**514**	438
Accumulated write-ups not yet written off	**5**	8	**187**	186	**10**	10	**132**	130
Remaining values	**4,219**	4,057	**2,149**	1,928	**11**	11	**646**	568
Assessed valuations[2]	**—**	—	**916**	913	**34**	34	**135**	134
PARENT COMPANY								
Historical cost	**4,465**	4,166	**408**	403	**1**	1	**27**	27
Accumulated scheduled depreciation	**−2,794**	−2,478	**−177**	−164	**—**	—	**−5**	−5
Scheduled remaining values	**1,671**	1,688	**231**	239	**1**	1	**22**	22
Accumulated write-ups not yet written off	**—**	—	**—**	—	**10**	10	**40**	40
Remaining values	**1,671**	1,588	**231**	239	**11**	11	**62**	62
Accumulated depreciation above schedule	**−1,104**	−1,198	**−19**	−29	**—**	—	**−6**	−6
Book values	**567**	490	**212**	210	**11**	11	**56**	56
Assessed valuations	**—**	—	**197**	198	**34**	34	**42**	43

[1]The acquisition value of assets in acquired companies is based on the company's historical cost, regardless of whether the assets were acquired before or after the date when consolidation arose.

[2]The figures apply to the Swedish part of the Group. The book value of real estate held by foreign subsidiaries amounted to SEK 1,716 m. (1,658).

NOTE 18. Parent Company's accumulated depreciation above schedule

	Machinery and Equipment	Industrial and Residential Buildings	Site Improvements	Total
Reported at end of 19x8	1,198	29	6	1,233
Difference between book and scheduled depreciation	−94	−10	—	−104
Reported at end of 19x9	**1,104**	**19**	**6**	**1,129**

10.8   Accounting for Untaxed Reserves

Sandviken, Sweden, is the parent company of the Sandvik Group, which comprises over 200 companies operating in 60 countries worldwide. In 19x9, the group had sales of approximately SEK 22 million, or about $165 million.

One of the unique features of generally accepted accounting practice in Sweden is the presence of untaxed reserves. Under Swedish GAAP, a company can smooth currently reported earnings by either appropriating a portion of pre-tax income (i.e., to lower current pre-tax profits) or by restoring to income appropriations from prior periods (i.e., to raise current pre-tax profits). Sandvik AB's income statement for 19x8 and 19x9 (see Exercise 10.7) reveals that both of these actions were undertaken by the company's management. The following excerpt from the company's income statement details those actions:

Additional information is available from the company's balance sheet (see Exercise 10.7):

	Amounts in SEK Millions	
	19x9	*19x8*
Profit before appropriations and taxes	1,337	3,849
Appropriations:		
• Difference between book and scheduled depreciation	104	124
• Change in transitional reserve for inventory	600	300
• Change in tax equalization reserve	(1,790)	(400)
• Other appropriations	(3)	14
• Group contributions	(33)	(115)
Pre-Tax Profit	215	3,772

Finally, the company's footnotes provided additional detail:

	Amounts in SEK Millions	
	19x9	*19x8*
Untaxed Reserves		
• Accumulated depreciation above schedule	1,129	1,233
• Tax equalization reserve	2,190	400
• Transitional reserve for inventory	—	600
• Other untaxed reserves	8	5
	3,327	2,238

NOTE 19. Parent Company's other untaxed reserves

	Tax Equalization Reserve (K)	*Transitional Reserve for Inventory*	*Other Untaxed Reserves*
Reported at end of 19x8	400	600	5
Change during the year	1,790	−600	3
Reported at end of 19x9	**2,190**	—	**8**

In compliance with a legal enactment concerning the reversal of untaxed reserves an allocation was made in 19x7 to a transitional reserve for inventory reserve, etc. During 19x9 the amount outstanding has been reversed to taxation.

Required:

   (a) Using journal entries, explain the changes in Sandvik's untaxed reserves for 19x8 to 19x9.

   (b) How much in income taxes did the company save in 19x9 as a consequence of its large contribution to the tax equalization reserve?

10.9   Special Tax Reserves

Based on asset values, Volvo is the largest industrial company in Sweden. Founded in 1927 as a manufacturer of passenger cars, today the company's products include cars, trucks, buses, marine and industrial engines, and aerospace engines.

As is true in the United States and most other industrialized countries, the government of Sweden uses its tax laws to help achieve a wide variety of national goals. Unlike the United States, however, the effects of Sweden's tax laws and, by extension, its national goals can be observed in the financial statements of Swedish companies in that Swedish tax law stipulates that taxable income be assessed from a taxpayer's accounting statements. In essence, revenues and expenses may appear on a Swedish corporation's tax return only to the extent that they appear in the published financial statements. Thus, it is possible to examine the external financial statements of Swedish companies with the goal of identifying in what ways and to what extent the Swedish government has instituted economic incentives for its domestic companies.

In recent years, the use of tax incentives by the Swedish government has undergone a number of reforms. Prior to 1991, for example, companies could take significant pre-tax deductions from operating income by creating inventory, payroll, depreciation, and investment reserves.[1] Most of these untaxed reserves, however, were eliminated in 1991 in exchange for a significant reduction in Swedish corporate income tax rates (i.e., from 52 to 30 percent, effective January 1, 1991). The 1991 tax reform did not eliminate the excess depreciation allowance enjoyed by most companies and, in addition, created a special tax equalization reserve (SURV) that could not exceed 30 percent of a corporation's equity capital. Further tax reform was enacted effective January 1994, lowering the corporate income tax rate to 28 percent and phasing out the SURV. Beginning in 1994, a new tax reduction reserve (the IAR) was introduced that permitted annual tax deductible allocations of up to 25 percent of pretax profits.

Exhibit 1 presents the 1996 and 1997 income statements and balance sheets for AB Volvo, the parent company of the Volvo Group. Exhibit 2 contains selected footnote disclosures regarding those financial statements. Use these data to complete the following:

Required:

   (a) What advantages and disadvantages arise for those firms that choose to employ (and most do!) the Swedish system of special reserves?

   (b) What are the potential benefits of the system of untaxed reserves to the Swedish government?

   (c) In what ways does the existence of the Swedish tax reserves system affect the

---

[1] The charge (a debit) against operating income was also credited to a nondistributable shareholders' equity reserve account.

ability of a financial statement user to evaluate a Swedish firm vis-à-vis a non-Swedish firm?

(d) Determine the financial effect of Sweden's untaxed reserve on AB Volvo's financial statements for 1997. Show the journal entry used to create the 1997 reserve. If the untaxed reserve did not exist in 1997, how would AB Volvo's key profitability ratios (ROA, ROE, and ROS) have changed?

EXHIBIT 1

AB VOLVO
1997 Financial Statements

Panel A. Statement of Income (SEK, millions)

		1996	1997
Net sales		559	**520**
Cost of sales		(559)	**(520)**
Gross income		—	**—**
Administrative expenses		(340)	**(426)**
Other operating income		11	**47**
Other operating expenses		(41)	**(24)**
Operating income before nonrecurring items		(370)	**(403)**
Nonrecurring items		—	**—**
Operating income		(370)	**(403)**
Income from investments in Group companies		685	**15,360**
Income from investments in associated companies		23	**39**
Income from other shares and participations		156	**(137)**
Interest income and similar credits		233	**218**
Interest expenses and similar charges		(1,048)	**(788)**
Other financial income and expenses		239	**(594)**
Income after financial items		(82)	**13,695**
Allocations	Note 9	978	**4,354**
Taxes		2	**—**
Net income		898	**18,049**

EXHIBIT 1   (continued)

Panel B. Balance Sheet (SEK, millions)

		Dec. 31, 1996	Dec. 31, 1997
Assets			
Non-current assets			
Property, plant and equipment		97	30
Total tangible assets		97	30
Shares and participations in Group companies		46,893	39,868
Long-term receivables with Group companies		—	628
Other shares and participations		7,025	1,051
Other long-term receivables		105	100
Total financial non-current assets		54,023	41,647
Total non-current assets		54,120	41,677
Current assets			
Short-term receivables from Group companies		1,971	5,309
Other short-term receivables		64	57
Short term investments in Group companies		—	5,178
Cash and bank accounts		6	5
Total current assets		2,041	10,549
Total assets		56,161	52,226
Shareholders' equity and liabilities			
Shareholders' equity			
Share capital (441,520,885 shares, par value SEK 6)		2,318	2,649
Legal reserve		7,241	7,241
Total restricted equity		9,559	9,890
Retained earnings		17,228	10,111
Net income		898	18,049
Total unrestricted equity		18,126	28,160
Total shareholders' equity		27,685	38,050
Untaxed reserves	Note 15	758	481
Provisions			
Provisions for pensions		280	296
Other provisions		104	126
Total provisions		384	422
Non-current liabilities			
Liabilities to Group companies		8,606	10,951
Other loans		1	—
Total non-current liabilities		8,607	10,951
Current liabilities			
Loans from Group companies		7,067	—
Other loans		2	1
Trade payables		36	37
Other liabilities to Group companies		11,322	2,162
Other current liabilities		300	122
Total current liabilities		18,727	2,322
Total shareholders' equity and liabilities		56,161	52,226
Assets pledged		1,217	—
Contingent liabilities		64,650	72,287

EXHIBIT 2

AB VOLVO
Selected Disclosures from 1997 Financial Report

9 Allocations

	1996	*1997*
Group contributions received	2,578	**5,655**
Group contributions granted	(1,581)	**(1,578)**
Reversal of tax equalization reserve	89	**89**
Reversal of/allocation to exchange reserve	(108)	**172**
Allocation to extra depreciation	0	**16**
Total	978	**4,354**

15 Untaxed reserves

The Composition of, and Changes in, Untaxed Reserves:	*Value in Balance Sheet 1996*	*Allocations 1997*	*Value in Balance Sheet 1997*
Tax equalization reserve	354	(89)	265
Exchange reserve	375	(172)	203
Accumulated extra depreciation Machinery and equipment	29	(16)	13
Total	**758**	**(277)**	**481**

10.10   Annual Report Analysis

An interesting and important challenge for students of international financial reporting is to study the published annual reports of various companies from different countries. Your instructor will provide you with a recent copy of a Swedish annual report. To facilitate your delving into this annual report, undertake the following endeavors.

Required:

(a) List the key differences between the Swedish annual report you were given and what you would expect to see for a U.S. company in the same industry.

(b) Calculate the following ratios, taking care to note the assumptions you found necessary to make and where you found the appropriate pieces of data in the annual report.

$$(1)\ \text{Current ratio} = \frac{\text{Total current assets}}{\text{Total current liabilities}}$$

$$(2)\ \text{Quick ratio} = \frac{\text{Cash} + \text{Marketable securities} + \text{Accounts Receivable}}{\text{Total current liabilities}}$$

$$(3)\ \text{Operating cash flow to current liabilities} = \frac{\text{Operating cash flow}}{\text{Average total current liabilities}}$$

$$(4)\ \text{Debt-to-equity ratio} = \frac{\text{Long-term debt}}{\text{Owners' equity}}$$

(5) Debt-to-total capitalization ratio $= \dfrac{\text{Long-term debt}}{\text{Long-term debt} + \text{Owners' equity}}$

(6) Interest coverage ratio $= \dfrac{\text{Net income before interest and income taxes}}{\text{Interest expense}}$

(7) Operating cash flow to interest charges $= \dfrac{\text{Operating cash flow}}{\text{Interest expense}}$

(8) Operating cash flow to total liabilities $= \dfrac{\text{Operating cash flow}}{\text{Average total liabilities}}$

(9) Receivables turnover ratio $= \dfrac{\text{Net sales}}{\text{Average accts. receivable}}$

(10) Inventory turnover $= \dfrac{\text{Cost of goods sold}}{\text{Average inventory}}$

(11) Asset turnover $= \dfrac{\text{Net sales}}{\text{Average total assets}}$

(12) Average collection period ratio $= \dfrac{\text{365 days}}{\text{Receivables turnover ratio}}$

(13) Average number of days' inventory on hand ratio $= \dfrac{\text{365 days}}{\text{Inventory turnover ratio}}$

(14) Return on assets (ROA) $= \dfrac{\text{Net income}}{\text{Average total assets}}$

$$OR = \text{ROS} \times \text{Asset turnover}$$

(15) Return on equity (ROE) $= \dfrac{\text{Net income}}{\text{Average total owners' equity}}$

$$OR = \text{ROA} \times \text{Financial leverage}$$

(16) Return on sales (ROS) $= \dfrac{\text{Net income}}{\text{Net sales}}$

(17) Financial leverage $= \dfrac{\text{Average liabilities} + \text{average owners' equity}}{\text{Average owners' equity}}$

(18) Basic earnings per share (EPS) $= \dfrac{\text{Net Income applicable to common shareholders}}{\text{Weighted average common shares}}$

(19) Cash dividend yield $= \dfrac{\text{Cash dividend per common share}}{\text{Market price per common share}}$

(20) Cash dividend payout $= \dfrac{\text{Total cash dividend to common shareholders}}{\text{Net income}}$

(c) What do you conclude about the availability of the appropriate data in the annual report for calculating these ratios?

(d) What does this financial analysis tell you about this Swedish company?

(e) What analytical metrics did this Swedish company choose to report for itself? What do those choices say about the message the company is striving to tell and the audience it is addressing?

Mexico

The Instituto Mexico de Contadores Publicos has made harmonization with International Accounting Standards its top priority.[1]

Introduction

The United Mexican States share more with the United States of America than a similar name. Mexico shares a 2,000-mile border and a partnership in the North American Free Trade Association (NAFTA). Moreover, in 1996, 85 percent of Mexico's exports were *to* the United States and 75 percent of its imports were *from* the United States. There are Mexican short-term debt instruments linked to the U.S. dollar (called *Tesobonos*), and there is serious talk by Mexican economists and businesses regarding the merits of linking the value of the Mexican peso to the U.S. dollar.[2] Like the United States, Mexico has a generally well-educated workforce, a bicameral national Congress, an unemployment rate of around 4 percent, and a quickly growing number of Wal-Mart Supercenters.

Even with so many connections to and similarities with the United States, Mexico has many different and unique challenges. For example, inflation rates during 1987–1996 ranged between 7 and 131 percent. The peso experienced a 25 percent devaluation in 1994. The banking system has been fraught with cronyism, massive bad debts, interest rates as high as 45 percent, and heated debates about restructuring. Such factors have all contributed to an economic picture that has been extremely volatile.[3] Consider also that Mexico's economy has historically been heavily dependent on the price of oil. One commentator recently noted that government oil revenues comprise about 40 percent of total government revenues and each US$1 drop in oil prices reduces Mexico's budgeted income by US$1 billion.[4] And finally, although Mexico generally has a well-trained, fully

---

[1]G. Jeffrey, "Down Mexico Way," *Accountancy International,* March 1999, p. 90.

[2]See J. Friedland, "Mexicans Quietly Mull Tying Peso to Dollar," *The Wall Street Journal,* September 28, 1998, p. A20; H. Tricks, "Calls for Mexico to Adopt U.S. Dollar," *Financial Times,* September 24, 1998, p. 9; and H. Tricks, "Dangers of Dollarisation," *Financial Times,* October 7, 1998, p. III.

[3]See J. Blake and P. Wraith, "Management Accounting in Latin America," *Management Accounting,* April 1998, pp. 56–57; H. Tricks, "Mexican Opposition Takes Aim at Country's Crony Capitalism," *Financial Times,* August 10, 1998, p. 4; and H. Tricks, "Chauffeur-Driven to Despair," *Financial Times,* October 7, 1998, p. IV.

[4]H. Tricks, "Hurt by the Global Pinch," *Financial Times,* October 7, 1998, p. III.

employed workforce, it is a workforce whose labor rates are sometimes one-tenth those in the United States.[5]

As the new millennium dawns, Mexico finds itself at a crucial crossroads. President Zedillo must step down in the year 2000 after finishing his six-year term. He has worked diligently to implement reforms that he hopes will put the government and the budget in good order so that a presidential election will not be disruptive. Yet as the millennium comes to a close, Mexico's leading private-sector economists are not generally optimistic. In a recent survey, Mexican analysts noted the five significant factors causing them concern: international financial stability, inflationary pressures, uncertainty over the foreign exchange rate, declining oil prices, and congressional delays in approving a bank rescue package.[6]

The financial reporting world in Mexico has also not been divorced from the country's topsy-turvy environment. For example, the recent banking crisis led to government-imposed action in the banking sector: As of January 1, 1997, Mexican banks were to adopt more informative, conservative financial reporting practices regarding nonperforming loans, largely patterned after U.S. and IASC GAAP. Likewise, with an increasing world-wide interest in the Mexican stock exchange *(Bolsa Mexicana de Valores),* and as Mexico privatizes more and more heretofore government-owned businesses, investors have demanded more informative and extensive financial information. In response, Mexico has tended to embrace U.S. or IASC standards where none exist under Mexican GAAP.

Environmental Factors

Cultural Environment

The group of Mexican subjects in Hofstede's study of cultural attitudes scored relatively low in individualism (30), high in power distance (81), high in uncertainty avoidance (82), and were not scored on the long-term-orientation dimension. (Recall that the U.S. scores, respectively, were 91, 40, and 46.) The low score in individualism is not atypical for a country historically struggling to emerge from poverty and with a strong centralized government—Mexico has only recently embraced a market-based economy. Most Mexicans have simply never enjoyed the wealth or personal freedoms/possibilities that characterize highly individualistic cultures.

The high scores in power distance and uncertainty avoidance place Mexico (along with Japan and other Latin American countries) in Hofstede's paradigm of the "pyramid." Organizations in pyramid cultures, according to Hofstede, tend to take the form of bureaucracies characterized by hierarchical personnel relations and codified work flow. Power tends to be centralized. This description seems to offer some insight into the Mexican economy, major features of which have been, until only recently, constant supervision by the central government and its agencies and massive public monopolies in key industries.

Gray has drawn on Hofstede's findings to suggest that national cultures registering high scores in uncertainty avoidance and power distance and a low score in individualism tend to prefer rigid, codified financial reporting systems that leave relatively little room for the exercise of professional judgment.[7] Mexico, however, seems to contradict Gray's hypothesis. In Mexico, as in Canada and the United States (and unlike Japan and many

---

[5]R. Lapper, "Unhappy Trade-off," *Financial Times,* October 7, 1998, p. II.

[6]L. Conger, "Mexico Sees Harder Times for Economy," *Financial Times,* September 8, 1998, p. 9. See also G. Smith, "A Torpedo That Could Cripple the Economy," *Business Week,* June 22, 1998, p. 62.

[7]S.J. Gray, "Towards a Theory of Cultural Influence in the Development of Accounting Systems Internationally," *Abacus* 24, 1 (1988), pp. 1–15.

European countries), financial reporting standards are primarily propagated by a private-sector board, the Accounting Principles Board of the Mexican Institute of Public Accountants (*Instituto Mexicano de Contadores Publicos*—the IMCP), not a central government or quasi-governmental authority. The IMCP's prominent role is a function of the National Banking and Securities Commission (*Comision Nacional Bancario y de Valores*—the CNBV) giving it to them. The CNBV has legal authority to establish accounting standards for those companies listed on the Mexican Stock Exchange. It might be concluded that Gray's hypothesis is accurate in its application to Mexico in one unique way. In particular, if Mexican GAAP is

> . . . silent on a particular subject, Mexican accountants and companies must look to IASC pronouncements for guidance. If neither Mexican GAAP nor IASC pronouncements cover the subject, GAAP in other countries may be followed. In such circumstances, U.S. GAAP is the most common source for supplementing Mexican GAAP.[8]

Thus, rather than being free to exercise judgment and some entrepreneurial creativity, Mexican accountants must turn to the IASC or the United States, or some other country's GAAP for specific guidance—a rather unique, but nonetheless specific, directive.

Legal and Political Environment

Government Ownership.   Much of Mexico's infrastructure has been government held and run. Of late, banks, airports, railroads, oil and gas distribution, ports, and telecommunications have been opened to private investment. There are, however, significant parts of the economy still under state control, not the least of which is Pemex, the petroleum monopoly created in 1938. By law, Mexico has six categories of investment that dictate the nation's investment patchwork quilt of private/public and domestic/foreign ownership of business and industries. These categories are:[9]

1. Activities exclusively reserved to the Mexican state (e.g., oil, electricity, and satellite communications).
2. Activities exclusively reserved to Mexican nationals and to Mexican companies in which foreign investment cannot participate (e.g., domestic land transportation, services for passengers, radio broadcasting, and television services).
3. Activities in which foreign investment is limited to specific percentages (e.g., domestic air transportation, commercial banks, and basic telephone services).
4. Activities requiring permission to obtain more than 49 percent foreign ownership (e.g., legal services, insurance brokers, cellular telephones).
5. International land transportation, to be phased in, allowing foreign ownership up to 100 percent by January 1, 2004.
6. Acquisition of existing corporations by a foreign entity to an extent greater than 49 percent requiring approval of the Foreign Investment Commission, regardless of the industry sector.

Thus, even though Mexico wants to think and behave as if it maintains a pure market economy, there are significant aspects to its governmental economic policy that cause it to be a blended economy.

Banking.   In the early 1980s, Mexico nationalized the country's private banks in an attempt to turn around a floundering economy. For a decade, the government was both

---

[8]Ernst & Young, *Doing Business in Mexico* (Mexico City: Ernst & Young Intl., Ltd., 1997), p. 61.
[9]Price Waterhouse, *Doing Business in Mexico* (NY: Price Waterhouse, 1995), pp. 48–52.

the banks' owner and biggest customer, a situation not conducive to the development of astute banking professionals. In the early 1990s, the government privatized the banks, and many of the buyers were wealthy businessmen, not experienced bankers. These buyers retained many of the managers accustomed to the state-owned banking environment.

> The combination of imprudent lenders, inexperienced borrowers, weak supervision, and a booming economy proved fatal. By the end of 1993 [after just two years], banks were carrying on average, three times the proportion of past-due loans that they had at privatization.[10]

To make matters worse, the peso was devalued in 1994 by 25 percent and inflation rose to around 40 percent. Under these conditions, many small borrowers joined ranks and refused to repay their loans. Add to this roaring confluence for disaster the fact that Mexico's bankruptcy laws make it difficult to seize assets that have supposedly securitized a loan. In the end, *Fobaproa,* the government agency established to save the banks, spent the equivalent of nearly US $70 billion in buying up bad loans from the troubled banks. This amounted to nearly 15 percent of Mexico's GDP (the U.S.'s 1989–1991 bank bailout bill had cost about 6 percent of U.S. GDP).[11] The question before the government was, "Who pays the *Fobaproa's* tab?" Three views existed: (1) Convert *Fobaproa's* 10-year promissory notes used to bail out the troubled banks into public debt, payable over many years; (2) allow the government to default on the notes; or (3) some blend of public debt and absorption of costs on the part of the banks. To some extent, and at different times, Mexico's major political parties have embraced all three options. In December 1998, the third option was embraced. The fragile nature of Mexico's economy, currency, and private/public blend all suggest that this compromise resolution will be crucial. Hopefully, it will not undermine the economic progress Mexico has achieved of late.[12]

Individual Tax Law.   As of 1999, the highest marginal tax rate for individual taxpayers was 40 percent. Several specific tax breaks exist for individuals who are investors.[13] First, gains from the sale of securities on the Mexican Stock Exchange are not taxable. Second, there is a break for those individuals earning interest on savings accounts with Mexican banks and on publicly issued bonds or debentures. The payer of the interest must withhold and remit tax equal to 20 percent of the first 10 percent of interest earned. The remaining net interest proceeds to the recipient are tax exempt.

Dividends also receive special tax treatment. Generally, individuals receiving dividends need not include them in taxable income if the paying corporation has paid corporate income tax on the underlying earnings from which the dividends emanated. Individuals may, however, elect to include an amount in their taxable income equal to the dividends received plus the corporate tax paid (at a 35 percent rate) on that proportion of underlying earnings. The corporate tax equivalent may then be claimed as a tax credit against the individual's total tax liability. Thus, if an individual's marginal tax rate is less than the corporation's rate of 35 percent, the individual is able to increase the after-tax amount of the dividend received.

---

[10]"No End to the Burden," *The Economist,* July 25, 1998, p. 73.

[11]Ibid. See also "Time to Settle Up," *The Economist,* September 5, 1998, p. 30.

[12]It is also interesting to note that at the time of this writing, the Mexican Supreme Court had a case before it testing the efficacy of banks charging compound interest. Moreover, in December 1998, Mexico opened up its three largest banks to 100 percent foreign ownership.

[13]See the Ernst & Young and Price Waterhouse, *Doing Business in Mexico* books noted earlier.

Corporate Tax Law.   In Mexico, there are a number of differences between tax accounting and financial reporting. Consider, for example, the following:[14]

- Inventory-related costs are deductible when incurred (i.e., there is no notion of inventory as an asset on the tax books).
- Fixed asset depreciation is set at predetermined, annual straight-line rates or at a predetermined, immediate, one-time percentage equal to the present value of the future straight-line rates and lives discounted at 3 percent.
- Amortization of goodwill is not permitted for tax purposes.
- Provisions for employee retirement are deductible only if paid into an irrevocable trust.
- The inflation adjustment procedures on certain items are different under the tax code versus GAAP.

Unlike individuals, corporations must pay tax on the gains obtained from the sale of another company's shares that it held. The cost basis of the investment is adjusted for inflation in a prescribed manner before determining the ultimate taxable gain. Capital losses from such sales may be carried forward five years against capital gains.

As of 1999, the corporate income tax rate was 35 percent. This rate applies to net gains after a host of monthly inflationary adjustments are applied, aimed at deriving the constant purchasing power gain. Loss carryforwards are permitted. There is also a 10 percent value-added tax (VAT) in effect in Mexico. Moreover, companies are required to distribute to employees 10 percent of adjusted taxable income (as defined in the tax code) as employees' share of corporate profits. Distributions to employees must occur within five months of year-end, and the amount individuals receive is a function of days worked during the year and their salary.

*Business
Environment*

Form of Business.   The business entity in Mexico analogous to a U.S. corporation is known as the *sociedad anónima* (S.A.). A special form of a S.A. is the *sociedad anónima de capital variable* (S.A. de C.V.). A minimum of two shareholders is required to form an S.A., as is a permit from the Department of Foreign Affairs. The minimum capital required is 50,000 pesos (about $5,500 as of early 1999).

All Mexican companies must have a statutory auditor who is charged to:

> maintain an overview of the company's operations at all times, without restrictions as to scope, and to submit an annual report on the correctness, adequacy and fairness of the financial statements and other representations of the board of directors. In fulfilling this responsibility, the statutory auditor may use the services of independent professionals. Audits by external auditors are required for [companies listed on the Mexican Stock Exchange and other companies meeting certain size requirements].[15]

Exhibit 11.1 presents the statutory auditor's report for Cifra, S.A. de C.V.

Moreover, all corporations must allocate 5 percent of their net income to a legal reserve account in the owners' equity section of their balance sheet until that account equals 20 percent of the value of the outstanding capital stock. This legal reserve is tantamount to an appropriation of retained earnings and is intended to represent an ongoing minimum capital base.

The other main forms of businesses in Mexico are the *sociedad de responsabilidad limitada* (S.R.L.) and the *sociedad en nombre colectivo* (S. en N.C.). The former is a limited liability partnership, whereas the latter is a general partnership often used by professional firms.

---

[14]Ibid.

[15]Price Waterhouse, *Doing Business in Mexico*, p. 33.

EXHIBIT 11–1

Cifra, S.A. de C.V.
Statutory Auditor's Report

To the General Meeting of Shareholders of Cifra, S.A. de C.V.

In my capacity as statutory auditor and in compliance with Article 166 of the Mexican Corporations Act and the bylaws of Cifra, S.A. de C.V. and subsidiaries, I am pleased to submit my report on the consolidated financial statements for the year ended December 31, 1998, presented to you by the board of directors.

I attended the shareholders' and the board of directors' meetings to which I was summoned and I obtained from the board members and the Company's officers the information on the Company's operations, documentation and records that I considered necessary for examination. I conducted my review in accordance with auditing standards generally accepted in Mexico.

In my opinion, the accounting and reporting policies and criteria observed by the Company in the preparation of the consolidated financial statements that are being presented to the shareholders are adequate and sufficient and were applied on a basis consistent with that of the prior year. Consequently, it is also my opinion that the abovementioned consolidated financial statements present fairly, in all material respects, the consolidated financial position of Cifra, S.A. de C.V. and subsidiaries at December 31, 1998, and the consolidated results of their operations, changes in their shareholders' equity and changes in their financial position for the year then ended, in conformity with accounting principles generally accepted in Mexico.

Alberto Tiburcio
Statutory Auditor
Mexico City, February 8, 1999

Accounting and Audit Requirements.   As noted earlier, all companies listed on the Mexican Stock Exchange are required to have an annual external audit. Moreover, companies must publish an annual set of financial statements that include a balance sheet, an income statement, a statement of changes in owners' equity, and a statement of changes in financial position (a statement somewhat similar to a statement of cash flows). Within these financial statements, all nonmonetary assets, owners' equity, and income statement accounts must be adjusted for inflation to reflect a peso of constant purchasing power (see a later section for specifics on this issue). Exhibit 11.2 presents the inflation-adjusted consolidated balance sheet and income statement of Cifra, S.A. de C.V., Mexico's largest retailer.

Accounting Profession.   Although relatively small, "the Mexican accounting profession is mature, independent, well organized, and well regarded by the business community."[16] A *contador público* (C.P.) is a university-awarded degree. To practice professionally, a C.P. must register with the Federal Ministry of Education. In 1995, it was estimated that there were only about 8,000 C.P.'s in public practice.[17]

The Mexican Institute of Public Accountants (IMCP) is the governing body of the profession. Through its Accounting Principles Board, it issues accounting standards. The National Banking and Securities Commission (CNBV), which has authority over the companies listed on the Mexican Stock Exchange, has generally deferred its accounting rule authority to the IMCP. Mexico has long had an interest in furthering global accounting issues. The IMCP was a founding member of the IASC in 1973, and its active membership role has continued. As a bit of evidence of the IMCP's favorable attitude toward the work of the IASC, the IMCP has decreed that companies under its auspices must use IASC accounting standards in areas where there are no Mexican guidelines.

---

[16]Ibid, p. 115.
[17]Ibid.

Exhibit 11–2

Cifra, S.A. de C.V.

Panel A. Consolidated Balance Sheets

Thousands of Mexican pesos with purchasing power at December 31, 1998

	December 31	
	1998	*1997*
Assets		
Current assets:		
Cash and cash equivalents	Ps 7,543,399	Ps 7,701,676
Accounts receivable	683,353	1,413,855
Inventories	5,239,511	5,678,608
Prepaid expenses	127,536	106,399
Total current assets	13,593,799	14,900,538
Property and equipment-net	21,930,344	21,370,566
Total assets	**Ps 35,524,143**	**Ps 36,271,104**
Liabilities and Shareholders' Equity		
Current liabilities:		
Accounts payable to suppliers	Ps 7,735,719	Ps 8,511,693
Other accounts payable	1,250,792	737,149
Total current liabilities	8,986,511	9,248,842
Reserve for seniority premiums	81,834	76,221
Total liabilities	9,068,345	9,325,063
Shareholders' equity		
Historical capital stock	4,718,417	4,873,600
Restatement	3,546,195	3,555,763
Restated capital stock	8,264,612	8,429,363
Legal reserve	948,778	752,497
Retained earnings	18,843,346	17,230,827
Reserve for repurchase of shares	1,118,186	2,001,983
Accumulated result of restatement	(3,856,612)	(2,969,610)
Premium on sale of shares	1,500,981	1,500,981
Employee stock option plan	(363,493)	—
Total shareholders' equity	26,455,798	26,946,041
Total liabilities and shareholders' equity	**Ps 35,524,143**	**Ps 36,271,104**

Panel B. Consolidated Statement of Income

Thousands of Mexican pesos with purchasing power at December 31, 1998

	December 31	
	1998	*1997*
Net sales	Ps 51,474,544	Ps 39,032,819
Cost of sales	(41,409,756)	(31,086,655)
Operating expenses	(8,144,779)	(6,055,360)
Operating income	1,920,009	1,890,804
Comprehensive financing income:		
Financial income-net	1,443,997	1,186,417
Exchange gain	281,274	83,269
Monetary position loss	(92,986)	(135,872)
	1,632,285	1,133,814
Other income-net	32,499	63,576
Income before income tax, employee profit sharing and extraordinary items	3,584,793	3,088,194
Income tax and employee profit sharing	(1,026,968)	(749,042)
Income before extraordinary items	2,557,825	2,339,152
Benefit derived from carryforward of tax losses from prior years	223,106	603,822
Net effect on labor obligations	—	1,186,346
Net income	**Ps 2,780,931**	**Ps 4,129,320**
Earnings per share (in pesos):		
Before extraordinary items	Ps 0.539	Ps 0.626
Extraordinary items	0.047	0.479
Total	**Ps 0.586**	**Ps 1.105**

Stock Markets. The Mexican Stock Exchange, the *Bolsa Mexicana de Valores* (the *Bolsa*), is the primary market for Mexico's publicly traded companies. By 1997, the *Bolsa* had 165 listed companies, of which only 20 were actively traded, with another 45 modestly so.[18] The 1996 price/earnings ratio for the *Bolsa* was 21.6 (18.2 for the United States).[19] There is another market, the *Mercado Intermedio,* which was recently established for small and midsized companies, but there is little activity on it. Mexico has no over-the-counter market for listed companies.[20]

In 1997, the *Bolsa* rose over 50 percent. By September 1998, it was down by 50 percent. Such has been the roller-coaster ride of Mexican shareholders. As one observer noted, "Mexico has done everything to ensure a stable currency, reasonable growth, and lower inflation, and it's getting whacked just the same."[21] Until inherent, chronic inflationary pressures, oil dependency, a weak peso, the narrowness of the stock market, and political unrest *all* dissipate, the *Bolsa* is not a place for the timid investor.

NAFTA. In 1994, the North American Free Trade Association (NAFTA) became a reality. The benefits to Mexico have been enormous.[22] NAFTA has ameliorated the economic impact on Mexico of the decade-ending Asian financial crisis and the free fall in oil prices. In 1997, it helped fuel an all-time record level of direct investment in Mexico and fostered a much-needed diversification of Mexico's export base. It has helped create and solidify long-term relations with U.S. importers. Because of NAFTA, for example, Mexico is now the world's leading exporter of clothing to the United States. In addition, NAFTA transformed the *maquila* program—a production-for-export program established by Mexico in 1965— which allowed foreign companies to establish wholly owned subsidiaries in Mexico. Under NAFTA, beginning January 1, 1994, roughly half of the U.S. exports began entering Mexico duty-free.

Much of these exports went to assembly plants in the northern cities (e.g., Cuidad Juárez), where in turn, the finished goods were then exported back to the United States. Hewlett-Packard, IBM, and the U.S.'s "Big Three" automakers are major players in utilizing this northern *maquila* section. (*Maquiladoras* may locate anywhere in Mexico.) In 1999, two thirds of the U.S. exports into Mexico became duty free, and Mexican tariffs on all other NAFTA-country industrial goods are scheduled to dissipate in 2004. Under NAFTA, the *maquila* businesses have become Mexico's single largest provider of export revenues. Moreover, at the outset of NAFTA, the *maquila* businesses were allowed to sell up to 50 percent of their output domestically—each year thereafter the percentage is allowed to increase by 5 percent.[23] This feature of the agreement has helped diffuse the economic benefits of the hearty *maquiladora* northern region throughout Mexico. As noted previously, as tariffs dissipate on NAFTA-country imports, the *maquila* sector of the Mexican economy "will lose much of its uniqueness" because NAFTA goods will be duty free "regardless of whether the importing company in Mexico is organized as a *maquiladora*."[24]

NAFTA has not been a boon for all concerned. U.S. trade unions believe NAFTA has directly led to a loss of jobs for American workers. Even though more than half of the

---

[18]Ernst & Young, *Doing Business in Mexico.*

[19]Ibid.

[20]Price Waterhouse, *Doing Business in Mexico.*

[21]I. Katz, "Latin America: More Where That Came From," *Business Week,* September 14, 1998, p. 73.

[22]See R. Lapper, "Unhappy Tradeoff"; R. Lapper, "The Cracks Keep on Spreading," *Financial Times,* October 7, 1998, p. I; E. Malkin, "Holding Off Asia's Assault," *Business Week,* April 13, 1997, pp. 44–45; and D. Bottorff, "Reaping the Rewards of NAFTA," *Management Accounting,* August 1997, pp. 37–40.

[23]R. Lapper, "Manufacturing a Marked Improvement in Sales," *Financial Times,* October 7, 1998, p. II.

[24]Ernst & Young, *Doing Business in Mexico,* p. 24.

Mexican labor pool is unionized, Mexican companies are legally required to provide employee training programs. Mexico's labor pool has a high literacy rate (about 80 percent), although Mexican manufacturing wages are a mere fraction of the U.S.'s.[25] As long as that wage differential exists, the *maquiladoras* can be assured of a certain measure of U.S. assembly and product work.

Selected Financial Reporting Practices

The Accounting Principles Committee of the IMCP publishes bulletins, interpretations, and occasionally amendments to previously issued bulletins. The bulletins themselves are organized into four series as follows:

- Series A—Basic accounting principles (e.g., materiality, realization, etc.)
- Series B—Principles related to financial statements (e.g., inflation, interim financial statements)
- Series C—Specific items or concepts (e.g., inventories, prepayments, liabilities, etc.)
- Series D—Special problems in the determination of income (e.g., income taxes, leases, etc.).

The single most important and distinctive influence on Mexico's system of accounting is inflation, which is principally covered by Bulletin B-10. In this text, the concepts and mechanics behind accounting for inflation are covered in Appendix 11A of this chapter. The discussion of Mexico's financial reporting practices to follow presumes that the reader is familiar with the terminology and general procedures of inflation accounting.

Effects of Inflation

Companies may either use the "general price index method" (i.e., historical cost/constant currency in the terminology of Appendix 11A) or the "specific cost method" (i.e., current cost, constant currency). The following important provisions apply:

- Specific costs can be any of the following:

  –specific price indexes published by the Bank of Mexico

  –Specific indexes developed internally

  –Replacement costs

  –Expert appraisals

  –Other values readily available, if they are similar to replacement costs:
  FIFO for inventories, LIFO for cost of sales, or updated standard costs.

  A recent amendment to Bulletin B-10 requires that machinery and equipment values be based only on the National Consumer Price Index (NCPI). (See Exhibit 11–3, for example.) For imported machinery and equipment, the company may elect to apply the general inflation index of the country of origin and the currency exchange rate as of the end of the year.
- Public companies filing reports with the national securities commission are required to use the specific cost method.

---

[25]Ernst & Young, *Doing Business in Mexico.*

EXHIBIT 11–3

Cifra, S.A. de C.V.
Inflation Accounting

Note 3—Property and Equipment

Cifra and its subsidiaries have been restating their property, equipment and facilities as follows:

Through the year ended December 31, 1996, the Company restated its fixed assets based on appraisals made by independent experts.

Since January 1, 1997, the Company has restated its fixed assets using the constant-peso-value method. Fixed assets owned at December 31, 1996, were restated by applying the NCPI to the appraised values determined by independent expert appraisers at such date, as specified by the fifth amendment to accounting Bulletin B-10 issued by the Mexican Institute of Public Accountants.

An analysis of property and equipment is as follows:

	December 31	
	1998	*1997*
Land	**Ps 8,697,818**	**Ps 8,558,232**
Buildings	7,513,216	7,071,322
Facilities and leasehold improvements	3,357,894	2,995,984
	10,871,110	10,067,306
Less:		
Accumulated depreciation	2,788,630	2,333,980
	Ps 8,082,480	**Ps 7,733,326**
Furniture and equipment	Ps 8,041,360	Ps 7,481,848
Less:		
Accumulated depreciation	3,395,441	2,921,444
	Ps 4,645,919	**Ps 4,560,404**
Construction in progress	**Ps 504,127**	**Ps 518,604**
Total	Ps 21,930,344	Ps 21,370,566

Rental expense for the years ended December 31, 1998 and 1997 amounted to Ps. 521,518 and Ps 417,061, respectively.

- The purchasing power gain or loss for the period is included in the income statement as a component of "integral cost of financing" or a similarly descriptive title. This caption also includes interest expense and revenue, and foreign exchange gains and losses. The specific components may be displayed on the face of the financial statements or in a note.
- Unrealized holding gains or losses bypass the income statement and are reported in shareholders' equity as "gain or loss from holding nonmonetary assets" or "surplus or deficit in stockholders' equity." Realized holding gains and losses are usually not separately displayed but are combined with related expense captions on the income statement.

Intercorporate Investments

All marketable securities are stated at fair value with unrealized gains and losses taken directly to income. Nonmarketable investments are measured at lower-of-cost-or-market. Write-downs are taken only when declines in value are judged to be permanent.

The equity method is applied to investments of more than 25 percent of outstanding shares. Investors have a legal right in Mexico to appoint at least one board member when their shareholdings exceed 25 percent.

Consolidations

Majority-owned subsidiaries are consolidated unless the activities of the subsidiary are significantly different from those performed by other members of the group. Presentation of minority interest is flexible and is usually displayed as a component of consolidated shareholders' equity. Pooling-of-interests accounting is not permitted.

Goodwill is amortized over a maximum of 20 years. Negative goodwill is classified as a deferred credit and amortized over a period not exceeding five years.

Financial statements of consolidated foreign subsidiaries are restated for inflation in their functional currency based on the subsidiary country's inflation rate, and subsequently translated to Mexican pesos by using the currency exchange rate at the balance sheet date. The effect of translation on shareholders' equity bypasses the income statement to be recorded directly in the cumulative translation adjustment account.

Inventories

In addition to FIFO, LIFO, average cost, and specific identification, use of the most recent price for measuring cost of goods sold is allowed.

Cost Capitalization

Interest and other integral costs of financing *may* be capitalized during the periods of asset construction. Although policies and practices for capitalization of financing costs do vary widely, disclosures must state the amount of interest capitalized during the period, and the periods over which capitalized interest is being applied to income. Promotional costs related to new product launches may be deferred.

Extraordinary Items

There are no specific definitions of extraordinary or unusual items in Mexican GAAP, with the only exception being that utilization of tax loss carryforwards must be separated from other captions. In practice, operations and gains or losses on fixed asset sales that are different from normal activities are considered extraordinary items.

Deferred Taxes

Bulletin D-4 of Mexican GAAP establishes the "partial liability method" of measuring deferred tax assets, liabilities, and expense. This method limits the recognition of deferred tax liabilities to significant timing differences for which reversal is reasonably assured within a defined period of time. Deferred tax assets may not be recognized unless their realizability is virtually certain. Measurement of deferred tax liabilities is similar to U.S. GAAP: based on tax rates expected to be in effect at the time of reversal.

Stockholders' Equity

In addition to contributed capital and earned surplus, Mexican law requires that 5 percent of income be appropriated to a legal reserve until the reserve is equal to 20 percent of capital stock.

Pensions and Other Employee Compensation

The accounting for defined-benefit pension plans is similar in concept to U.S. standards. However, for company-sponsored postretirement benefits such as health care common in Mexico, no recognition of the expense is made until the services are actually provided to employees. Seniority premiums paid upon termination or layoffs are accrued, as are legally required employee profit sharing costs.

Statement of Cash Flows

Mexican GAAP requires the presentation of a "statement of changes in financial position," with funds defined as cash and temporary investments (see, for example, Exhibit 11–4). The following items are classified in investing or financing that would be classified in operations as adjustments to net income under U.S. standards:

- An unrealized foreign exchange gain or loss is displayed as a financing item.
- A gain or loss on monetary position is displayed as a financing item.

EXHIBIT 11–4

CIFRA, S.A. de C.V.
Consolidated Statement of Changes in Financial Position
Thousands of Mexican Pesos with Purchasing Power at December 31, 1998

	Year Ended December 31	
	1998	*1997*
Operating activities		
Income before extraordinary items	Ps 2,557,825	Ps 2,339,152
Charges not requiring use of resources:		
Depreciation	1,099,438	842,175
Reserve for seniority premiums	24,121	20,346
	3,681,384	3,201,673
Changes in:		
Accounts receivable	730,502	(318,711)
Inventories	(192,858)	(1,360,126)
Prepaid expenses	(21,137)	3,494
Accounts payable to suppliers	(775,974)	1,579,733
Other accounts payable	513,643	(10,709)
Seniority premiums	(18,508)	(13,307)
Resources provided by operating activities before extraordinary items	3,917,052	3,082,047
Extraordinary items	223,106	1,790,168
Resources provided by operating activities	4,140,158	4,872,215
Financing activities		
Repurchase of shares	(1,855,928)	
Cash dividends paid		(3,307,716)
Cash refund of employee pension fund-net		111,123
Premium on sale of shares		239,094
Decrease in capital stock	(164,751)	
Resources used in financing activities	(2,020,679)	(2,957,499)
Investing activities		
Purchase of property and equipment	(1,914,263)	(1,526,238)
Employee stock option plan—net	(363,493)	56,535
Resources used in investing activities	(2,277,756)	(1,469,703)
Net (decrease) increase in cash and cash equivalents	(158,277)	445,013
Increase in cash and cash equivalents due to merger of subsidiaries		1,608,049
Cash and cash equivalents at beginning of year	7,701,676	5,648,614
Cash and cash equivalents, end of year	**Ps 7,543,399**	**Ps 7,701,676**

- A change in investments due to application of the equity method is displayed as an investing item.
- A gain or loss on the retirement of fixed assets is displayed as an investing item.

Exhibit 11–5 presents a summary comparison of Mexican and U.S. generally accepted accounting practices.

EXHIBIT 11–5

Comparison of Mexican and U.S. Accounting and Reporting Standards

Item	Mexico	United States
Asset valuation	Historical cost/constant currency, or specific cost based on specific price indexes or appraisals	Historical cost with selected revaluation (principally downward)
Inventory valuation	FIFO, LIFO, moving average, specific identification, or most recent purchase price	Principally LIFO (because of tax considerations); also FIFO and average cost methods
Inventory: year-end	Historical cost, constant currency, or specific cost based on specific price indexes or appraisals	Lower of cost or replacement cost
Depreciation	Principally straight-line. If the asset is revalued, depreciation based on the revalued amount	Principally straight-line with accelerated and production-based methods permitted
Goodwill	Capitalized to the balance sheet and amortized over expected useful life; negative goodwill permitted	Capitalized to balance sheet, with amortization (principally straight-line) over a maximum of 40 years; negative goodwill not permitted
Research and development costs	Expensed as incurred	Research costs expensed currently; development costs expensed currently except in certain industries (i.e., software, oil and gas)
Capitalized interest costs	Elective, along with other integral financing costs, for self-constructed assets	Capitalization required for self-constructed assets
Intercorporate investment: Marketable securities (current asset trading)	Market value, with unrealized gains and losses to income	Market value (individual security basis), with *unrealized* gains and losses taken to income
Long-term investment: (0–10% ownership) (available for sale)	Market value, with unrealized gains and losses to income	Market value (individual security basis) with *unrealized* gains and losses taken to owners' equity.
10–50% ownership	25%–50% ownership, equity method	Equity method
51–100% ownership	Consolidated (with exceptions); pooling not permitted	Consolidated, using pooling (until 2001) or purchase accounting
Debt valuation	Amount originally agreed to plus accrued interest when applicable	Long-term debt (except deferred income taxes) valued at present value; current debt valued at face value
Leases	Capitalized only when related to the financing of an asset acquisition	Capital leases reflected in balance sheet; operating leases disclosed in footnotes
Deferred income taxes	Partial liability method	Computed under liability method
Pension liabilities	Reflected on balance sheet	Reflected on balance sheet
Discretionary reserves	Permitted if repetitive in nature, and can be measured with reasonable accuracy. If isolated in occurrence, may estimate the probable outcome within reasonable limits	Restricted to identifiable operational losses
Statement of cash flows	Required, with funds defined as cash and short-term investments	Required

Analytical Considerations

The key differences between Mexican and U.S. accounting relate to the Mexican accounting for inflation, and it pervasively affects measures of profitability, performance, and risk in significant and unpredictable ways. For example, the higher asset and equity balances that accompany revaluation via indexing or specific price adjustments tend to depress (correctly) such profitability measures as ROA and ROE by increasing their denominators and reducing their numerators. Income and gross profit margin tend to be lower due to inflation-indexed depreciation on older assets and higher measures of the cost of materials.

On the other hand, higher asset and equity values tend to result in lower leverage indicators (e.g., debt to assets and debt to equity), thereby suggesting an apparently superior solvency position. This effect of inflation adjustments on solvency and liquidity ratios is also affected by the common practice of denominating debt in a more stable currency, usually the U.S. dollar. The accounting effect of this financial strategy is to grow the book value of the debt largely in tandem with the increases in assets and equity. Thus, the magnitude, and sometimes the direction, of these ratio differences are difficult to predict, but are directly tied to the age of assets, the denomination of debt, the correlation of exchange-rate movements to inflation rates, and asset revaluations.

ROE can be particularly unstable due to the variability and unpredictability of the integral cost of financing. To illustrate, consider the data in Exhibit 11–6 for Cemex, S.A. de C.V., one of the three largest cement companies in the world. Most of the decrease in pretax ROE for 1997 is due to the decreased amount of "net comprehensive income," which occurred principally because lower inflation in 1997 led to a smaller "monetary position gain" on the company's net monetary-liability position. This was only partially offset by lower foreign exchange losses and interest costs because the Mexican peso did not devalue as much against the currencies in which Cemex borrows.

In contrast, pretax ROE *before* comprehensive financing income increased for Cemex. Most analysts will focus on this measure of performance for at least two reasons. First, it is very difficult, if not impossible, to adequately unravel the various causes for changes in the net integral financing cost. Second, the year-to-year changes in integral financial costs provide little indication of effective risk-management strategies and/or operating performance. Better information on liquidity risk can be obtained through cash-flow and capital-structure analysis.

Aside from inflation accounting, other significant differences tend to enhance the reported results of Mexican companies relative to U.S. companies. Use of the partial liability method for deferred taxes will tend to result in lower tax expense, and nonaccrual of certain employee benefits will increase income and measures of leverage. The greater flexibility of consolidation and leasing policies create greater opportunities for off–balance-sheet financing.

EXHIBIT 11–6

SELECTED DATA FOR CEMEX, S.A. DE
(Millions of Constant Mexican Pesos as of December 31, 1997)

	1997	*1996*
Operating Income	$ 7,224	$ 6,734
Comprehensive financing income:		
Financial expenses	(4,116)	(5,605)
Financial income	835	689
Foreign exchange loss, net	(95)	(846)
Monetary position result	4,657	10,203
Net comprehensive financial income	$ 1,281	$ 4,441
Other expenses, net	(1,829)	(2,141)
Income before taxes	6,676	9,034
Income taxes and employees' statutory profit sharing	(536)	(833)
Net income	$ 6,140	$ 8,201
Total stockholders' equity	$28,367	$28,010
ROE	22%	29%
Pretax ROE	24%	32%
Pretax ROE before comprehensive financing income	19%	16%

Summary

For Mexico, the new millennium is uncertain—full of possibilities and hope, yet rife with factors over which the country may have little control. It is widely expected that Mr. Zedillo's ruling parting, the Institutional Revolutionary Party (PRI), which has held the presidency for 70 years, will lose it. Skeptics doubt whether the newly empowered central bank will be able to provide a steady rudder through a change in government. In addition, it is estimated that for every percentage point decline in U.S. economic growth, Mexico's declines almost as much.[26] Who knows what will become of oil prices, and as a third of the Mexican government's revenues are derived from oil sales, who knows what resources it will have available and when? Add to this uncertain recipe pressures of a free-floating peso, historically high inflation, yo-yoing interest rates, and increasing real wages, and Mexico's prospects may be a roll of the dice. On the other hand, times have seldom been better than recently. In 1997, Mexico's stock market was the strongest in all of Latin America.[27] The bank bailout debate was settled in late 1998. NAFTA has been extremely beneficial to and widely embraced by Mexico. Foreign direct investment continues to increase. Merger and acquisition activity in Mexico doubled in 1997, and the prospects of more synergies and more corporate improvements loom on the horizon.[28]

There is no question that Mexico's commitment to shareholders and their information needs is sincere and likely to continue. Fiercely proud, yet not foolishly so, Mexico has developed its own generally accepted accounting principles while also explicitly embracing the IASC's, or even the U.S.'s, in those areas that it has not, and may never, address. Moreover, as a number of Mexico's largest, most global, growing companies seek U.S. ADR listings, greater financial transparency and increased disclosures will be required and will likely become the Mexican standard because of such companies' prominence at home. Perhaps the bottom line for all of those interested and involved in Mexico's international fronts at this important time is best summed up by a U.S. business executive heavily involved in Mexico:[29]

Expect setbacks, but remember that perseverance pays off.

APPENDIX 11A
ACCOUNTING FOR THE EFFECTS OF INFLATION

According to the *Surabaya Post* of Indonesia, one kilogram of coconut oil cost 1,475 rupiah in February 1995 and had increased to 4,850 rupiah by January 1999. On the same dates, the rupiah-per-dollar exchange rates were approximately 2,200 and 8,000, respectively. In essence, what tran-

---

[26]H. Tricks, "New Meaning for Millennium Bomb," *Financial Times,* October 2, 1998, p. XXIX.
[27]Ibid.
[28]*Crossborder Monitor.* (London, The Economist Intelligence Unit Ltd., 1998) website as of December, 1998.
[29]D. Bottorff, "Reaping the Rewards of NAFTA," p. 38.

spired over a few short years was a massive loss of purchasing power (i.e., "inflation") of the rupiah for nearly all goods and services available to Indonesian consumers.

The economic and political factors contributing to the rupiah inflation were many. However, the impact of inflation on Indonesian prices can be thought of either in terms of the similar impact on *all* goods and services (changes in general prices levels) or the specific impact on the price of *one* product or service. For example, while the prices of virtually all goods and services in Indonesia increased over the period 1995–1998 (an example of general price-level inflation), gasoline prices in Indonesia were relatively more stable. Government-produced oil and gas is sold on domestic markets at subsidized prices (an example of specific price-level inflation).

Inflation affects the wealth of individuals and the value of businesses, and germane to the topics of this text, inflation also impairs the quality of information reported in financial statements. For an Indonesian company reporting in rupiahs using "traditional" accounting methods:

- Book values of long-lived assets have little meaning if a significant portion were acquired in prior years.
- Revenues and expenses are not comparable to corresponding amounts from prior years.
- Cash and other *monetary items* are not comparable to corresponding amounts from prior years.
- The significant economic effects of inflation on a business entity are not explicitly identified from the other activities of the business.

Remeasuring Financial Statements for the Effects of Changing Prices

Because inflation can distort reported financial data, it is often advisable to consider a remeasurement approach to eliminate the distortive effects. For example, financial analysts can incorporate the effects of inflation in financial data on an ad hoc and/or piecemeal basis. Alternatively, financial statement issuers can adjust complete sets of financial statements for the effects of inflation, or simply provide supplemental disclosures about the effects of inflation on the financial statements. Regardless of the approach, the remedies to inaccurate financial reporting when inflation is present are usually considered worse than the disease when only moderate inflation exists. But when inflation rates are high, traditional historic cost financial statements are so distorted as to render them meaningless.

International Accounting Standard IAS No. 29, *Financial Reporting in Hyperinflationary Economies,* contains guidance for adjusting historic cost financial statements for the effects of inflation when hyperinflation exists.[1] In the United States, where there has been no hyperinflation for decades, accounting standards do not permit adjustments to company financial statements for inflation. Statement of Financial Accounting Standards No. 89, *Financial Reporting and Changing Prices,* does, however, permit certain supplementary disclosures of financial statement items to illustrate the effects of general price-level or specific price changes. Application of this standard is voluntary, and consequently, few companies have elected to provide SFAS No. 89 disclosures.

---

[1]According to IAS No. 29, the existence of hyperinflation is a matter of judgment. Indicators include a tendency of the general population to keep its wealth in nonmonetary assets or in a relatively stable foreign currency, prices quoted in a relatively stable foreign currency, interest and wage rates linked to a price index, and cumulative inflation rates over three years aggregating more than 100 percent.

The Accounting Choices.   There are two fundamental choices that must be made when attempting to remeasure accounting data to remedy the distortive effects of changing prices:

1. The *attribute* to be measured: "historic" cost (HC) or "current replacement" cost (CC).[2]
2. The *unit of measure:* "nominal" monetary units at the date of a transaction (N$) or units of "constant" purchasing power (C$).[3]

The choice among the two attributes to be measured and two types of measurement units yields four possible combinative accounting alternatives:

1. Historic cost, nominal currency units (HC/N$)—traditional accounting.[4]
2. Historic cost, constant currency units (HC/C$)—historic cost financial statements adjusted for changes in general price levels. This method is frequently referred to as "general price level accounting" (GPLA).
3. Current cost, nominal currency units (CC/N$)—assets and liabilities are measured by changes in their specific prices, but the economic effects of general price inflation are disregarded.
4. Current cost, constant currency units (CC/C$)—assets and liabilities are measured by changes in their specific prices, *and* the economic effects of general price inflation are explicitly measured.

The fourth of these alternatives, CC/C$, is the most comprehensive and most frequently encountered around the world when high levels of inflation are present. We derive all four alternatives in the examples to follow because (1) hybrid methods are frequently encountered, and (2) discussing them in sequence facilitates a systematic development and understanding of the relevant concepts.

A Simple Example.   To illustrate the derivation and interpretation of financial statements that recognize the effects of general and specific price changes, we begin with a Mexican company, Muestra, S.A. de C.V., established on December 31, 1997. The company used contributed capital of M$1,100, to acquire land at a cost of M$1,000 with the remainder left in a bank account earning 40 percent interest. During the year, the company generated sales of M$1,900 and incurred operating expenses of M$1,200 evenly throughout the year (all for cash). General price inflation for 1998 was 30 percent and the recently acquired land had a specific replacement cost of M$1,400 on December 31, 1998. Exhibit 11A–1 displays the comparative financial statements under each of the four accounting alternatives.

Notice that the 12/31/97 balance sheets have been restated to units of constant purchasing power (in columns 2 and 4) to reflect the general price inflation of 30 percent for 1998. Consequently, it now becomes apparent that the *real* increase in the company's cash position is only M$850 (M$980 − M$130) even though the *nominal* increase in cash is M$880 (M$980 − M$100). The detailed discussion of the derivation of columns 2 through 4 (to follow) will demonstrate, among other things, that:

- The company's purchasing power gains and losses result from remeasurement from nominal currency units to units of constant purchasing power.
- The company's unrealized holding gains and losses result from recognized changes in the current replacement cost of assets held at the end of the period.

---

[2]Other attributes, such as "present value of future cash flows" or "net realizable value" are also possible. Current replacement cost (or "current cost," for short) is most prevalent, and our discussion will be limited to it.

[3]To illustrate the difference between N$ and C$, assume an inflation rate of 10 percent for the current year. A machine purchased one year earlier for $1,000 (N$) would have required a sacrifice of $1,100 (C$) one year ago, if measured in today's units of purchasing power.

[4]It is somewhat of an oversimplification to refer to HC/N$ financial statements as "traditional" accounting because they are almost never encountered in pure form. Nearly all accounting conventions require that at least *some* assets or liabilities be measured by some attribute other than historic cost. For example, in the United States, inventories are measured at the "lower of historic cost or market" and marketable securities are "marked-to-market."

Exhibit 11A–1

MUESTRA, S.A. de C.V.
Comparative Financial Statements for Years Ended December 31

	(1) HC/N$		(2) HC/C$		(3) CC/N$		(4) CC/C$	
	1997	*1998*	*1997*	*1998*	*1997*	*1998*	*1997*	*1998*
Income Statement								
Sales revenue		M$1,900		M$2,185		M$1,900		M$2,185
Operating expenses		(1,200)		(1,380)		(1,200)		(1,380)
Interest revenue		180		207		180		207
Operating income		880		1,012		880		1,012
Purchasing power gains (losses)				(162)				(162)
Unrealized holding gains (losses)						400		100
Net income		M$ 880		M$ 850		M$1,280		M$ 950
Statement of Retained Earnings								
Retained earnings, beginning of year		M$ —		M$ —		M$ —		M$ —
Net income		880		850		1,280		950
Dividends		—		—		—		—
Retained earnings, end of year		M$ 880		M$ 850		M$1,280		M$ 950
Balance Sheet								
Cash	M$ 100	M$ 980	M$ 130	M$ 980	M$ 100	M$ 980	M$ 130	M$ 980
Land	1,000	1,000	1,300	1,300	1,000	1,400	1,300	1,400
Total assets	M$1,100	M$1,980	M$1,430	M$2,280	M$1,100	M$2,380	M$1,430	M$2,380
Contributed capital	M$1,100	M$1,100	M$1,430	M$1,430	M$1,100	M$1,100	M$1,430	M$1,430
Retained earnings	—	880	—	850	—	1,280	—	950
Total equities	M$1,100	M$1,980	M$1,430	M$2,280	M$1,100	M$2,380	M$1,430	M$2,380

Historic Cost, Constant Currency (HC/C$). The year-end HC/C$ amounts in column 2 of Exhibit 11A–1 may be best seen as derived from the 1998 HC/N$ year-end financial statements in column 1. This is indeed how these financial statements are frequently derived in practice. Exhibit 11A–2 presents a worksheet for deriving the amounts in column 2 of Exhibit 11A.1 by "adjusting" column 1.

Revenues and expenses occurring more or less evenly throughout the year are usually remeasured as if they all occurred in the middle of the year. Since the general rate of inflation was 30 percent for all of 1998, inflation from the middle to the end of the year is assumed to be 15 percent. Hence, these revenues and expenses are adjusted by 15 percent to reflect their historical amounts expressed in terms of end-of-year purchasing power.

Land and contributed capital are expressed in units of purchasing power as of the beginning of the year. To reflect these historical amounts in terms of end-of-year purchasing power, they must be increased by 30 percent, which corresponds to inflation for the year. Spending M$1,000 on December 31, 1997, to acquire the land is equivalent in sacrifice of purchasing power to spending M$1300 on December 31, 1998. Similarly, receiving MS$1,100 on December 31, 1997, from investors is equivalent to receiving MS$1,430 on December 31, 1998.

The cash balance as of the end of the year is not remeasured, because its balance is already stated in units of purchasing power as of the end of the year.[5]

Deriving and interpreting the purchasing power gain (loss)—Economically and intuitively, wealth is lost when a monetary asset such as cash is held during inflationary periods. Quite simply,

---

[5]Other monetary items, if they existed for Muestra, would be treated similarly. Examples could include accounts receivable, accounts payable, and debt.

cash buys less at the end of the year than it did at the beginning. Similarly, wealth is gained when a monetary liability can be settled with currency of lesser purchasing power than the currency borrowed. The accounting entries in Exhibit 11A–2 capture the effects of inflation on Muestra's only monetary item, cash, albeit through a very nonintuitive process: reflecting the remeasurement of the *nonmonetary* items in the purchasing power gain (loss) account.

Exhibit 11A–2

MUESTRA, S.A. de C.V.
Worksheet for Restating 1998 fromHC/N$

	HC/N$	Adjustments		HC/C$
		Dr.	Cr.	
Income Statement				
Sales revenue*	M$1,900		a285	M$2,185
Operating expenses	(1,200)	b180		(1,380)
Interest revenue	180		c27	207
Purchasing power gain (loss)	—	a285	b180	(162)
		c27	d300	
		e330		
Net income	M$ 880			M$ 850
Statement of Retained Earnings				
Retained earnings, beginning of year	M$ —			M$ —
Net income	880			850
Dividends	—			—
Retained earnings, end of year	M$ 880			M$ 850
Balance Sheet				
Cash	M$ 980			M$ 980
Land**	1,000	d300		1,300
Total assets	M$1,980			M$2,280
Contributed capital	1,100		c330	1,430
Retained earnings	880			850
Total equities	M$1,980			M$2,280

*M$2,185 = M$1,900 × 1.15
**M$1,300 = M$1,000 × 1.30

December 31, 1997, to aquire the land is equivalent in sacrifice of purchasing power to spending M$1,300 on December 31, 1998. Similarly, receiving MS$1,100 on December 31, 1997, from investors is equivalent to receiving MS$1,430 on December 31, 1998.

The cash balance as of the end of the year is not remeasured, because its balance is already stated in units of purchasing power as of the end of the year.[5]

Deriving and interpreting the purchasing power gain (loss)—Economically and intuitively, wealth is lost when a monetary asset such as cash is held during inflationary periods. Quite simply, cash buys less at the end of the year than it did at the beginning. Similarly, wealth is gained when a monetary liability can be settled with currency of lesser purchasing power than the currency borrowed. The accounting entries in Exhibit 11A–2 capture the effects of inflation on Muestra's only monetary item, cash, albeit through a very nonintuitive process: reflecting the remeasurement of the *nonmonetary* items in the purchasing power gain (loss) account.

---

[5]Other monetary items, if they existed for Muestra, would be treated similarly. Examples could include accounts receivable, accounts payable, and debt.

Understanding how the remeasurement process illustrated in Exhibit 11A–2 corresponds to economic principles is best accomplished analytically. Our approach is to review the accounting process for measuring the purchasing power gain/loss in algebraic terms.

First, define the following terms:

- PIC, R/E, Land, Cash, PPG/L are the symbols for contributed capital, retained earnings, land, cash and the purchasing power gain (loss) respectively; and all measured under HC/N$.
- The subscript "1" denotes an account balance as of the beginning of the year, and the prefix "Δ" denotes the change in an account balance for the year.

We begin by rearranging the fundamental accounting equation as of the beginning of the year to segregate monetary and nonmonetary items:

$$\text{Cash}_1 = \text{PIC}_1 + \text{R/E}_1 - \text{Land}_1 \tag{1}$$

Since this equation holds for a point in time, it must also hold for changes over time:

$$\Delta\text{Cash} = \Delta\text{PIC} + \Delta\text{R/E} - \Delta\text{Land} \tag{2}$$

We can also see from the worksheet debit and credit entries in Exhibit 11A.2 that the purchasing power gain (loss) may be expressed as:

$$\text{PPG/L} = -.3\text{PIC}_1 - .3\text{R/E}_1 + .3\text{Land}_1 - .15\Delta\text{PIC} - .15\Delta\text{R/E} + .15\Delta\text{L} \tag{3}$$

Or simplifying, our equation is:

$$\text{PPG/L} = -.3(\text{PIC}_1 + \text{R/E}_1 - \text{Land}_1) + -.15(\Delta\text{PIC} + \Delta\text{R/E} - \Delta\text{L}) \tag{4}$$

From equations (1) and (2), we can substitute the expressions for Cash_1 and ΔCash in equation (4) and obtain:

$$\text{PPG/L} = -.3(\text{Cash}_1) - .15(\Delta\text{Cash}) \tag{5}$$

And finally, inserting our known values for Cash_1 and ΔCash from our HC/N$ balance sheets, yields:

$$\text{PPG/L} = -.3(\text{M\$100}) - .15(\text{M\$880}) = -\text{M\$162} \tag{6}$$

Thus, we can explain Muestra's reported purchasing power loss in economic terms: Muestra held cash as the purchasing power of cash declined due to inflation of the Mexican peso. In this specific case, M$100 was held for an entire year, and the M$880 cash flow for the year was held, on average, for half a year.

While the analysis of Muestra's purchasing power gain (loss) is relatively straightforward, more complicated examples will yield the same general result. For example, companies tend to hold other monetary assets and liabilities in addition to cash. The more general result for Muestra can be stated as:

$$\text{PPG/L} = -.3(\text{net monetary position}_1) - .15(\Delta\text{net monetary position}) \tag{7}$$

Presentation of the Purchasing Power Gain/Loss in Financial Statements—We stated earlier that wealth is gained when a monetary liability can be paid off with currency of lower purchasing power than when it was originally borrowed. Lenders realize this and attempt to set interest rates that anticipate future inflation as well as provide them with a "real" rate of return. Therefore, purchasing power gains and losses are best interpreted together with other financial revenues and expenses. Recognizing this, IAS No. 29 encourages, but does not require, that other financial revenues and expenses be presented together with the gain or loss on net monetary position.

For Muestra, the purchasing power loss of M$162 can be compared to the reported interest revenue of M$207. The net revenue difference can be seen as a function of the difference between the nominal interest rate on its cash balances less actual inflation ($40\% - 30\% = 10\%$). M$45 is equivalent to 10 percent interest on M$100 for a full year (M$10), plus a half year's interest on sales revenue less operating expenses ([M$1,900 − M$1,200] × 10% × 0.5 years = M$35). If inflation for 1998 were perfectly anticipated, 10 percent would be the risk-adjusted, real rate of interest paid by Muestra for its borrowings.

Interpretation of the purchasing power gain/loss is practically never as clean as the foregoing example. Lenders rarely perfectly anticipate inflation in their nominal interest rates. Perhaps more important is that neither accounting systems nor lenders explicitly recognize or measure interest on most trade receivables and payables—they are reported on financial statements as if they were interest free (which, of course, they are not!)

Current Cost, Nominal Currency (CC/N$).   The case of Muestra is so simple that only one adjustment is required to restate the financial statements from HC/N$ to CC/N$ (column 3 in Exhibit 11A–1):

> Dr. Land   M$400
>   Cr. Unrealized holding gain   M$400

Thus, the land account is stated at its current cost at each balance sheet date. IAS No. 29 does not allow the presentation of CC/N$. However, it is included in our discussion because it facilitates the analysis and understanding of other methods.

Current Cost, Constant Currency (CC/C$).   Under this last alternative in column 4 of Exhibit 11A–1, the December 31, 1997, amounts for assets and liabilities are their current costs expressed in units of purchasing power as of December 31, 1998. To derive the 1998 financial statements, the constant currency adjustments to the HC/N$ balances are made. These are identical to those illustrated in Exhibit 11A–2 and have the effects of recognizing the same purchasing power gain/loss. The additional entry to recognize the unrealized holding gain on the land is now:

> Dr. Land   M$100
>   Cr. Unrealized holding gain   M$100

Thus, the unrealized gain on Land is only the "real" change in the value of Land for the period: M$1,400 less the beginning-of-year current cost measured in units of end-of-year purchasing power (M$1,300). Therein lies the conceptual superiority of CC/C$: simultaneously controlling for changes in the unit of measure due to general price inflation and recognizing only real, as opposed to nominal, gains and losses.

A More Detailed Example

The foregoing example was used to explain the essential concepts of remeasurement for changing prices in as straightforward a manner as possible. To that end, frequently encountered and more technical, important details have been omitted. For example, it is difficult to provide a general interpretation of unrealized gains and losses when assets that are never used up—like land—are the only ones considered. Therefore, we now consider the case of depreciable assets and inventory.

Detalle, S.A. de C.V. is exactly the same as Muestra, except:

- M$500 of contributed capital is replaced with U.S.-dollar-denominated debt of $50, bearing interest at a rate of 10 percent. Interest is payable at the end of the year, and the entire principle is due in five years. At the beginning of the year, the exchange rate was M$10.00:US$1.00, and at the end of the year it was M$12.00:US$1.00.[6]
- M$400 of land is replaced with 4 identical units of inventory. Unrealistically, but for ease of calculation, we will assume that the current cost of the inventory increased to M$120 on the first day of 1998. Two of the inventory units were then sold on that first day for M$250 per unit. The current cost of the units remaining in inventory at the end of 1998 was $150 per unit.

---

[6]A frequent method for coping with the uncertainty of future inflation by both cross-border and home-country lenders is to denominate loans in a more stable currency, such as the U.S. dollar. In so doing, a cross-border lender can insulate itself from exchange rate risk and a home-country lender can protect itself from unanticipated inflation.

EXHIBIT 11A–3

DETALLE, S.A. DE C.V.
Comparative Financial Statements for Years Ended December 31

	(1) HC/N$ 1997	(1) HC/N$ 1998	(2) HC/C$ 1997	(2) HC/C$ 1998	(3) CC/N$ 1997	(3) CC/N$ 1998	(4) CC/C$ 1997	(4) CC/C$ 1998
Income Statement								
Sales revenue		M$ 500		M$ 650		M$ 500		M$ 650
Cost of inventory sold		(200)		(260)		(240)		(312)
Depreciation		(100)		(130)		(150)		(195)
Operating income		M$ 200		M$ 260		M$ 110		M$ 143
Realized holding gain—inventory						40		52
Realized holding gains—equipment						50		65
Realized operating income		M$ 200		M$ 260		M$ 200		M$ 260
Comprehensive Financing Cost:								
Interest revenue		240		276		240		276
Interest expense		(55)		(63)		(55)		(63)
Foreign exchange gains (losses)		(105)		(121)		(105)		(121)
Purchasing power gains (losses)				(42)				(42)
		80		50		80		50
Realized income		M$ 280		M$ 310		M$ 280		M$ 310
Unrealized holding gain—inventory						100		40
Unrealized holding gains—equipment						250		100
Net income		M$ 280		M$ 310		M$ 630		M$ 450
Statement of Retained Earnings								
Retained earnings, beginning of year		M$ —		M$ —		M$ —		M$ —
Net income		280		310		630		450
Dividends		—		—		—		—
Retained earnings, end of year		M$ 280		M$ 310		M$ 630		M$ 450
Balance Sheet								
Cash	M$ 100	M$ 780	M$ 130	M$ 780	M$ 100	M$ 780	M$ 130	M$ 780
Inventory	400	200	520	260	400	300	520	300
Equipment	600	600	780	780	600	900	780	900
Accumulated depreciation	—	(100)	—	(130)	—	(150)	—	(150)
Total assets	M$ 1,100	M$ 1,480	M$ 1,430	M$ 1,690	M$ 1,100	M$ 1,830	M$ 1,430	M$ 1,830
Dollar-denominated debt	500	600	650	600	M$ 500	M$ 600	M$ 650	M$ 600
Contributed capital	600	600	780	780	600	600	780	780
Retained earnings	—	280	—	310	—	630	—	450
Total equities	M$ 1,100	M$ 1,480	M$ 1,430	M$ 1,690	M$ 1,100	M$ 1,830	M$ 1,430	M$ 1,830

- The remaining M$600 of land is replaced with equipment. The equipment is to be depreciated on a straight-line basis over six years with no salvage value. Again, solely for ease of calculation, we will assume that the current cost of the equipment increased to M$900 on the first day of 1998. As of the end of 1998, the current cost of identical new equipment was M$900; the current cost of identical one-year-old equipment was M$750.

Exhibit 11A–3 displays the comparative financial statements for Detalle under each of the four bases of accounting. The format of the income statements in Exhibit 11A–3 is designed to present separately the results of operations, holding gains and losses, and the effect on income of financial decisions.

Operating income reported under current cost accounting (column 4) is viewed by some to be more informative than under historic cost accounting (column 1). This is because positive operating income under current cost accounting requires that revenues for a period must cover the costs of *replacing* the resources used for the period. Historic cost accounting only requires that revenues exceed the *allocated portion of the amounts paid* for resources under the matching principle to report positive operating profit.

Observe that realized incomes are equal between historic cost accounting and current cost accounting when the unit of measure is held constant (i.e., column 1 vs. column 3 and column 2 vs. column 4). This is because current cost accounting reports a new element of bad news that is exactly offset by a new element of good news. The bad news is that prices for resources used during the period have increased during the period. If those prices do not change again, Detalle will have to pay more to replace the resources than they paid to acquire them in the first place. This bad news is reflected in higher cost of sales and depreciation relative to historic costs.

The good news reported by current cost accounting is that resources used by Detalle in 1998 were acquired before their price increased. This is reflected in the *realized holding gains* reported— for an amount that exactly offsets the difference between historic cost operating expenses and current cost operating expenses.

Unrealized holding gains are the results of changes in the current costs of assets and liabilities held as of the end of the period. They are excluded from operating income, because like realized holding gains, they are normally viewed as apart from ordinary operating activities. Frequently, unrealized and realized holding gains and losses are not separately disclosed, although we do so in this example.

As mentioned earlier IAS No. 29 encourages, but does not require, that related financial items such as interest revenue and expense, purchasing power gain/loss, and foreign exchange gains/losses be presented together. The format of Detalle follows this recommendation. The terminology "comprehensive financing costs" is that used by Mexican accounting standards (*Costo integral de financamiento*), which *do* require that these items be presented together.

Foreign-Currency-Denominated Receivables and Payables.   *HC/N$*—The change in the exchange rate between the peso and the dollar requires a remeasurement of the dollar-denominated debt from M$500 to M$600. This explains M$100 of the reported M$105 foreign exchange loss. The additional M$5 can be derived from the following analytical journal entries (all dated 12/31/98):

> Dr. Interest expense   M$55
>   Cr. Interest payable   M$55
> To accrue interest at the average exchange rate for 1998,
> calculated as follows: US$50 × 10% × 11.0*
> *(average exchange rate of 11.0)
> Dr. Foreign exchange loss   M$5
>   Cr. Interest payable   M$5
> To remeasure interest payable to the current
> exchange rate of 12.0: US$50 × 10% × 12.0 = M$60
> Dr. Interest payable   M$60
>   Cr. Cash   M$60
> To pay interest of US$5 on its due date.

HC/C$—Since the nominal interest expense was measured in midyear currency units, it must be inflated by 15 percent to convert it to year-end units of purchasing power: M$55 × 1.15 = M$63.25.

Inventory.   *HC/C$*—Cost of sales is remeasured from the HC/N$ amount to units of purchasing power at the end of the period. Since the sale occurred on the first day of the year, the HC/N$ amount reported is in units of purchasing power as of the first day of the year. Therefore, we use an inflation factor for one year: M$200 × 1.3 = M$260. The ending balance of inventory is remeasured to constant units of purchasing power as well. Since the inventory was acquired by the beginning of the period, we use an inflation factor for one year: M$200 × 1.3 = M$260. Note that the same relationship between inventory and cost of sales holds regardless of the unit of measure:

	HC/N$	HC/C$
Beginning inventory	M$400	M$520
Purchases	0	0
Less: ending inventory	200	260
Cost of inventory sold	M$200	M$260

CC/N$—The cost of inventory sold is the current cost of the inventory at the time it was sold. For Detalle, the realized holding gain on inventory is the difference between the current cost at the time it was sold and its balance at the beginning of the period: 2 units × (M$120 − M$100) = M$40. The unrealized holding gain is the difference between the current cost of the unsold inventory at the end of the period and its current cost at the beginning of the period: 2 units × (M$150 − M$100) = M$100.

CC/C$—The cost of inventory sold is the current cost of the inventory at the time it was sold, and remeasured to units of purchasing power as of the end of the year by using an inflation factor for one year: M$260 × 1.3 = M$312. The unrealized holding gain on inventory is M$60 less, which is the amount of the change in the current cost of inventory due to inflation. This leaves only the "real" unrealized holding gain to be reported: 2 units × (M$150 − M$100 (1.3)) = M$40. Detalle's realized holding gain on inventory under CC/N$ is "real" because all of the gain occurred on the first day of the year. However, under CC/C$ it must be remeasured to units of purchasing power as of the end of the year: 2 units × (M$120 − M$100) (1.3) = M$52.

Equipment.   *HC/C$*—Depreciation expense is remeasured to units of constant purchasing power by multiplying the historic depreciation cost by the inflation factor: M$100 × 1.3 = M$130. Although depreciation occurs evenly throughout a period, it was measured in beginning-of-year currency units. For Detalle, the interest factor is for only one year of inflation, but in the general case, a factor representing more than one year of inflation would be used when depreciation is expressed in units of purchasing power of earlier years.

CC/N$—Deriving an amount for depreciation is one of the most difficult aspects of accounting for current costs because it requires rules for distinguishing the natural decline in a long-lived asset due to use (i.e., depreciation) from changes in the current cost due to changing market conditions for the asset. Yet, separating depreciation from other changes in current cost is an integral component in measuring operating income.

Detalle's policy for measuring depreciation is that annual depreciation is equal to one sixth of the current cost of new equipment. Since the current cost of new equipment was M$900 throughout 1998, M$150 is the amount of depreciation for the year. The total holding gain of M$300 (M$900 − M$600) is allocated as follows: M$50 (1/6 × M$300) to realized holding gains because one sixth of the equipment was used during 1998. The remainder is the unrealized holding gain.

*CC/C$*—Since depreciation under CC/N$ was based on beginning-of-year units of purchasing power, it must be remeasured to end-of-year units: M$150 × 1.3 = M$195. The unrealized holding gain is the amount by which the current cost of the "unused" portion of the equipment exceeded its current cost as of the beginning of the year and remeasured in end-of-year units of purchasing power: (M$900 − M$150) − (5/6)M$600(1.3) = M$100. The realized holding gain is the CC/N$ realized holding gain multiplied by the inflation factor for one year, since, as with inventory, the price change took place on the first day of the year: M$50(1.3) = M$65.

Weighing the Costs and Benefits of Accounting for Changing Prices

The fact that inflation-adjusted financial statements are only required when inflation is extremely high attests to a consensus view that the remedy they promise may be worse than the disease— except in extreme circumstances. While most financial executives concede the conceptual superiority of inflation adjustments and current costs, they are quite skeptical of the ability of most financial analysts to understand them sufficiently. Also, there is concern that their additional costs may not be worth the sacrifice of objectivity and reliability.

Selected Readings

Bottorff, D. "Reaping the Rewards of NAFTA." *Management Accounting,* August 1997, pp. 37–40.

Ernst & Young. *Doing Business in Mexico.* Mexico City: Ernst & Young International, 1997.

Financial Reporting North America: Highlights of Joint Study. Norwalk, CT: Financial Accounting Standards Board, 1994.

Fitzsimmons, A., Levine, M., and Siegel, J. "Comparability of Accounting and Auditing in NAFTA Countries." *The CPA Journal,* May 1995, pp. 38–44.

Martinez, J. D. *Compared Financial Accounting Standard.* Instituto Mexicano de Contadores Publicos, A.C., 1996.

Mexico: Building for the Future. Coral Gables, FL: Latin Finance Special Projects, 1997.

"Mexico: *Financial Times* Survey." *Financial Times,* October 1, 1998.

Poole, C. "Mexican Accounting." *Mexico Business,* June 1996, pp. 37–39.

Exercises

11.1 Mexican versus U.S. GAAP

One of the key differences between the established accounting standards in Mexico versus the United States concerns consolidation accounting. Under Mexican GAAP, for example, negative goodwill is capitalized to the balance sheet as a deferred credit and amortized to income over a 5-year period. Under U.S. GAAP, negative goodwill is charged off against the value of any acquired noncurrent assets and is rarely capitalized. Moreover, under U.S. GAAP, consolidation is normally required where a parent maintains a controlling ownership interest in a subsidiary. Under Mexican GAAP, the criteria for consolidation is "control."

Required:

Prepare a brief essay evaluating the strengths and weaknesses of (a) capitalizing negative goodwill, and (b) consolidating subsidiaries where control exists regardless of the actual level of ownership.

11.2 Accounting Policies for Inflation and Foreign Currency

Fomento Económico Mexicano, S.A. de C.V. (FEMSA), is the largest integrated producer of beer and soft drinks in Mexico, as well as a major bottler of soft drinks in Argentina. Among FEMSA's 1998 annual report disclosures of significant accounting policies is the following on recognition of the effects of inflation in the financial statements:

> The consolidated financial statements have been prepared in accordance with Bulletin B-10, "Recognition of the Effects of Inflation in the Financial Information," as amended. Bulletin B-10 requires that all Mexican entities:
>
> 1. Restate nonmonetary assets such as inventories and fixed assets, including related costs and expenses when such assets are consumed or depreciated. On January 1, 1997, the Fifth Amendment to Bulletin B-10 went into effect, which establishes (a) options to restate inventories by using either the National Consumer Price Index ("NCPI") or replacement cost and (b) options to restate fixed assets by either (i) applying the NCPI to all fixed

assets, or (ii) for domestic fixed assets applying the NCPI, but for imported equipment, applying the inflation rate of the country of origin, then translating such amounts at the year-end exchange rate. The value of property, plant and equipment as of December 31, 1996, as well as the useful lives assigned according to appraisals, were the basis of the restatement and calculation of depreciation beginning in 1997.

2. Restate capital stock, additional paid-in capital and retained earnings by the amount necessary to maintain the purchasing power equivalent in Mexican pesos on the dates such capital was contributed or income generated, through the use of NCPI.

3. Include in stockholders' equity the cumulative effect of holding nonmonetary assets (net difference between charges in the replacement cost of nonmonetary assets and adjustments based upon the NCPI).

4. Include in the cost of financing the purchasing power gain or loss from holding monetary items.

The Company restates its consolidated financial statements in terms of the purchasing power of the Mexican peso as of the most recent balance sheet date by using for Mexican subsidiaries the NCPI, and by using for foreign subsidiaries the inflation rate plus the latest year-end exchange rate of the country in which the foreign subsidiary is located.

The Company restates its income statement using NCPI factors determined from the month in which the transaction occurred to the date of the most recent balance sheet.

Financial information for Mexican subsidiaries for prior years was restated using the NCPI, and for foreign subsidiaries and affiliated companies included in the consolidated financial statements, the financial information was restated using the inflation rate of the country in which the foreign subsidiary or affiliated company is located, then translated at the year-end exchange rate of the Mexican peso. Accordingly, the amounts are comparable with each other and with the preceding years since all are expressed in the purchasing power of the respective currencies as of the end of the latest year presented.

Required:

(a) Which of the four bases of accounting that are described in Appendix 11A does FEMSA appear to be using in 1998?
(b) Assume that the inflation rate in Argentina and countries from which FEMSA imports its fixed assets has been lower than Mexico. How did the choice of method of accounting for inflation and translation under Bulletin B-10 affect FEMSA? Construct a simple example to demonstrate that your answer to this question is correct.
(c) Evaluate the quality of the Mexican accounting standards upon which FEMSA bases its accounting policy.

11.3 Restatement and Interpretation of Funds Flow Information

Presented on this page is the consolidated statement of financial position for FEMSA as presented in its 1998 annual report, and the information necessary to reconcile this statement to a statement of cash flows in accordance with U.S. GAAP. All amounts are expressed in millions of constant Mexican pesos as of December 31, 1998.

FEMSA
Consolidated Statement of Changes in Financial Position
For years ended December 31

	1998	1997	1996
Resources Generated by (Used in):			
Operations:			
Consolidated net income for the year	Ps 2,038	Ps 2,805	Ps 2,996
Depreciation	1,315	1,225	1,166
Amortization and other	1,014	1,043	852
	4,367	5,073	5,014
Working capital:			
Accounts receivable	243	(288)	219
Inventories	(321)	(361)	(627)
Prepaid expenses	109	(92)	(13)
Suppliers and other liabilities	457	307	118
Recoverable taxes, net	(167)	47	28
Net resources generated by operations	4,688	4,686	4,739
Investments:			
Investment in shares	(176)	72	
Property, plant, and equipment, net	3,093	2,893	2,779
Deferred charges	1,062	840	595
Fixed asset write-offs	(183)	(95)	
Acquisition of Emprex minority interest	375		
Acquisition of new territories Coca-Cola FEMSA		1,082	147
Other assets, net		319	(836)
Net resources used in investing activities	4,171	5,111	2,685
Net resources (used in) generated after investing activities	517	(425)	2,054
Financing Activities:			
Bank loans, notes and interest payable	(1,270)	1,553	(294)
Amortization in real terms of long-term liabilities	(1,321)	(1,273)	(2,132)
Dividends paid	(461)	(153)	(102)
Noncash dividends	(118)		(1,059)
Increase in capital stock	1,138		1,157
Minority contribution of capital stock in:			
FEMSA Cerveza	2,106		
Amoxxo	68	159	88
Labor liabilities	(150)	(306)	(58)
Merger effect in subsidiaries			16
Translation adjustment of Coca-Cola FEMSA Buenos Aires			
investment	45	372	299
Net resources generated by (used in) financing activities	37	352	(2,085)
Net increase in cash and cash equivalents	554	(73)	(31)
Cash and cash equivalents at the beginning of the year	1,657	1,730	1,761
Cash and cash equivalents at the end of the year	Ps 2,211	Ps 1,657	Ps 1,730

FEMSA
Reconciliation of funds flow to cash flow under U.S. GAAP
For the years ended December 31

	1998	1997	1996
Resources generated by operations under Mexican GAAP	Ps 4,688	Ps 4,686	Ps 4,739
Gain on monetary position	(930)	(1,153)	(2,490)
Unrealized foreign exchange loss	1,053	276	328
Loss on retirements of property, plant and equipment	183	95	
Cash flow generated by operations under U.S. GAAP	Ps 4,994	Ps 3,904	Ps 2,577
Resources used in investing activities under Mexican GAAP	Ps 4,171	Ps 5,111	Ps 2,685
Loss on retirements of property, plant, and equipment	183	95	
Noncash dividends			1,058
Restatement of investments	(362)	50	404
Cash flow used in investing activities under U.S. GAAP	Ps 3,992	Ps 5,256	Ps 4,147
Resources generated by (used in) financing activities under Mexican GAAP	Ps 37	Ps 352	Ps (2,085)
Gain on monetary position on financing assets and liabilities	2,049	1,523	3,270
Noncash dividends			1,058
Foreign exchange loss	(1,860)	(279)	(300)
Cash flow generated by financing activities under U.S. GAAP	Ps 226	Ps 1,596	Ps 1,943

Required:

(a) To the maximum extent permitted by the data, convert the statements of changes in financial position to statements of cash flows in accordance with U.S. GAAP.

(b) To the maximum extent permitted by the data, identify FEMSA's principle sources and uses of cash, and evaluate its financial health.

11.4 Differences between Mexican and U.S. GAAP

U.S. securities laws require that FEMSA provide supplemental U.S. GAAP information since it is traded on a U.S. stock exchange. Note 27 of FEMSA's 1997 annual report contains the following reconciliations of Mexican GAAP to U.S. GAAP. All amounts are expressed in millions of constant Mexican pesos as of December 31, 1998.

FEMSA
Reconciliation of Net Majority Income to U.S. GAAP
For the years ended December 31

	1998	1997	1996
Net majority income under Mexican GAAP	Ps 1,360	Ps 1,174	Ps 1,434
Approximate U.S. GAAP adjustments:			
Restatement of prior year's financial statements			11
Restatement of machinery and equipment	(17)	(15)	
Noncash dividends valued at market value			(198)
Deferred income tax (1)	(579)	(397)	177
Deferred employee profit sharing	(1)	8	192
Pension plan cost	(11)	(18)	(27)
Capitalization of interest expense	17	(19)	(20)
Minority interest in U.S. GAAP adjustments	88	104	(34)
Goodwill generated by the minority interest acquisition	(103)		
Monetary gain on labor liabilities			(221)
Impairment of long-lived assets			(283)
Deferred promotional expenses		(1)	11
Total Adjustments	(606)	(338)	(392)
Approximate net majority income under U.S. GAAP	Ps 754	Ps 836	Ps 1,042

(1) The available tax loss carryforwards in each year were offset against the deferred tax expense.

FEMSA
Reconciliation of Majority Stockholders' Equity
As of December 31

	1998	1997
Majority stockholders' equity under Mexican GAAP	Ps 14,735	Ps 5,798
Approximate U.S. GAAP adjustments:		
Restatement for prior year financial statements		(23)
Restatement of machinery and equipment	414	584
Deferred income tax	(3,499)	(2,920)
Deferred employee profit sharing	(1,274)	(1,273)
Accumulated pension plan liability	112	120
Capitalization of interest expense	435	418
Minority interest in U.S. GAAP adjustments	1,198	1,713
Goodwill generated by the minority interest acquisition	11,344	
Deferred promotional expenses	(5)	(5)
Total Adjustments	8,725	(1,386)
Approximate majority stockholders' equity under U.S. GAAP	Ps 23,460	Ps 4,412

Required:

(a) Specify the adjusting journal entries to FEMSA's 1998 financial statements that would convert them from Mexican to U.S. GAAP.

(b) To the maximum extent permitted by the data, identify the probable causes of these differences between Mexican and U.S. GAAP.

11.5 Accounting for the Effects of Inflation

This problem is a continuation of the Muestra, S.A. de C.V. example in Appendix 11A. The historical cost, nominal dollar financial statements contain the 1999 results in addition to 1998 and 1997 repeated from the text.

MUESTRA, S.A. de C.V.
Comparative Financial Statements for Years Ended December 31

	1997	*1998*	*1999*
Income Statement			
Sales revenue		M$ 1,900	M$ 2,200
Operating expenses		(1,200)	(1,500)
Interest revenue		180	294
Operating income		880	994
Purchasing power gains (losses)		—	—
Unrealized holding gains (losses)		—	—
Net income		M$ 880	M$ 994
		—	—
Statement of Retained Earnings		—	—
Retained earnings, beginning of year		M$ —	M$ 880
Net income		880	994
Dividends		—	(200)
Retained earnings, end of year		M$ 880	M$ 1,674
Balance Sheet			
Cash	M$ 100	M$ 980	M$ 1,474
Accounts receivable			300
Land	1,000	1,000	1,000
Total assets	M$ 1,100	M$ 1,980	M$ 2,774
Contributed capital	M$ 1,100	M$ 1,100	M$ 1,100
Retained earnings	—	880	1,674
Total equities	M$ 1,100	M$ 1,980	M$ 2,774

Additional information:

1. Revenues and operating expenses were incurred evenly throughout the year. Some sales were made on account, but it can be assumed that cash collections occurred evenly throughout the year.
2. Dividends were declared and paid on January 1, 1999.
3. The replacement cost of the land was $1,700 on December 31, 1999. Inflation for the year was 25 percent and interest on bank deposits was 30 percent.

Required:

(a) Prepare Muestra's comparative 1998 and 1999 financial statements under the following three additional bases of accounting: (1) historical cost, constant currency; (2) current cost, nominal currency; (3) current cost, constant currency.

(b) Explain the purchasing power gain or loss for 1999 in terms of inflation and monetary position.

(c) To the maximum extent permitted by the data evaluate Muestra's performance for 1999.

11.6 Accounting for the Effects of Inflation

Restituto S.A. de C.V. was established on January 1, 19x1 by issuing M$1,000 in common stock and US$200 bonds requiring annual interest payments of 10 percent.

Additional Information:

1. Equipment costing M$1,000 was purchased January 1, 19x1. It has a useful life of five years, with no salvage value. The replacement cost of new and six-month-old equipment on July 1, 19x1, was M$1,200 and M$1,100, respectively. The replacement cost of new and one-year-old equipment on December 31, 19x1, was M$1,500 and M$1,300, respectively.
2. Five identical units of inventory were purchased on January 1, 19x1, for M$80 per unit. Due to a hurricane that destroyed one of the two factories that manufacture this item, the replacement cost increased to M$200 on July 1, 19x1.
3. The company sold four units of inventory for M$2,500 on July 1. Three units of inventory were purchased at a cost of M$200 on December 31, 19x1.
4. Inflation in Mexico was 40 percent during 19x1. At January 1, 19x1, the exchange rate was M$8.00:US$1.00, and at the end of the year it was M$10.00:US$1.00.
5. Restituto deposits all cash on hand in a noninterest-bearing account.

Required:

(a) Prepare Restituto's comparative 19x1 financial statements under each of the following four bases of accounting: (1) historical cost, nominal currency; (2) historical cost, constant currency; (3) current cost, nominal currency; (4) current cost, constant currency.

(b) Explain the purchasing power gain or loss for 19x1 in terms of inflation and monetary position.

11.7 Annual Report Analysis

An interesting and important challenge for students of international financial reporting is to study the published annual reports of various companies from different countries. Your instructor will provide you with a recent copy of an annual report from a Mexican company. To facilitate your delving into this annual report, undertake the following endeavors.

Required:

(a) List the key differences between the Mexican annual report and what you would expect to see in the annual report of a similar U.S. company.

(b) Calculate the following ratios, taking care to note the assumptions you found necessary to make and where you found the appropriate pieces of data in the annual report.

$$(1) \text{ Current ratio} = \frac{\text{Total current assets}}{\text{Total current liabilities}}$$

$$(2) \text{ Quick ratio} = \frac{\text{Cash} + \text{Marketable securities} + \text{Accounts Recievable}}{\text{Total current liabilities}}$$

$$(3) \text{ Operating cash flow to current liabilities} = \frac{\text{Operating cash flow}}{\text{Average total current liabilities}}$$

(4) Debt to equity ratio $= \dfrac{\text{Long-term debt}}{\text{Owners' equity}}$

(5) Debt to total capitalization ratio $= \dfrac{\text{Long-term debt}}{\text{Long-term debt} + \text{Owners' equity}}$

(6) Interest coverage ratio $= \dfrac{\text{Net income before interest and income taxes}}{\text{Interest expense}}$

(7) Operating cash flow to interest charges $= \dfrac{\text{Operating cash flow}}{\text{Interest expense}}$

(8) Operating cash flow to total liabilities $= \dfrac{\text{Operating cash flow}}{\text{Average total liabilities}}$

(9) Receivables turnover ratio $= \dfrac{\text{Net sales}}{\text{Average accounts receivable}}$

(10) Inventory turnover $= \dfrac{\text{Cost of goods sold}}{\text{Average inventory}}$

(11) Asset turnover $= \dfrac{\text{Net sales}}{\text{Average total assets}}$

(12) Average collection period ratio $= \dfrac{365 \text{ days}}{\text{Receivables turnover ratio}}$

(13) Average number of days' inventory on hand ratio $= \dfrac{365 \text{ days}}{\text{Inventory turnover ratio}}$

(14) Return on assets (ROA) $= \dfrac{\text{Net income}}{\text{Average total assets}}$

$$OR = \text{ROS} \times \text{Asset turnover}$$

(15) Return on equity (ROE) $= \dfrac{\text{Net income}}{\text{Average total owners' equity}}$

$$OR = \text{ROA} \times \text{Financial leverage}$$

(16) Return on sales (ROS) $= \dfrac{\text{Net income}}{\text{Net sales}}$

(17) Financial leverage $= \dfrac{\text{Average liabilities} + \text{average owners' equity}}{\text{Average owners' equity}}$

(18) Basic earnings per share $= \dfrac{\text{NI applicable to common shareholders}}{\text{Weighted average common shares}}$

(19) Cash dividend yield $= \dfrac{\text{Cash dividend per common shares}}{\text{Market price per common share}}$

(20) Cash dividend payout $= \dfrac{\text{Total cash dividend to common shareholders}}{\text{Net income}}$

(c) What do you conclude about the availability of the appropriate data in the annual report for calculating these ratios?

(d) What does this financial analysis tell you about the Mexican company?

(e) What analytical metrics did the Mexican company choose to report for itself? What do those choices say about the message the company is striving to tell and the audience it is addressing?

Republic of South Korea

Close liaison between government and business, in which the government picked industrial winners, promoted them with cheap bank loans, and pushed them down the path of exporting, transformed Korea into an industrial powerhouse . . . [this approach] is clearly incompatible with the more open, democratic government the country now enjoys.[1]

In Korea, the accounting is used to hide lots of things.[2]

Introduction

The Republic of South Korea emerged at the end of the 1980s as one of the fastest growing economies in the world. In contrast, the late 1990s were a time of great turbulence and of a search for ways to ease the pain of a shift from a government-driven economy to a market-based economy. Indeed, Korea is entering a new stage of maturity that promises to transform the way in which the country does business. Historically, South Korea's prosperity has depended on exports and relatively low wages. Koreans have recently seen foreign demand for their products sag while domestic consumption rose, the result of unprecedented levels of wealth among the country's working and middle classes. Leading Korean multinationals, once content to provide low-cost products based on foreign technology and designs, are attempting to increase investments in research and development to develop their own reservoir of technical expertise and record of innovation. North American protectionism and steep increases in Korean labor costs have prompted Korean manufacturers to begin to move some of their operations overseas to ensure access to the North American market and to tap the less expensive labor pools available in eastern Europe and less developed areas of Asia.

The maturation of the Korean economy, as well as the nation's emergence into democracy, is certain to place new, more sophisticated demands on its financial markets and the role that financial reporting plays in those markets. Indeed, Korean financial reporting practices and disclosure requirements have remained considerably less developed than

[1]"Learning from South Korea," *Financial Times,* November 7, 1995, p. 15.
[2]B. Condon, "Dónde está earnings?" *Forbes,* June 15, 1998, p. 234.

those in the Western economies, largely because of an underdeveloped securities market and the government taking a leading role in capital allocation by formally and informally directing bank loans to selected enterprises. In addition, foreign direct investment in Korea has historically been severely restricted: Prior to January 1992, foreign investors were not allowed to trade directly on the Seoul stock exchange and even prior to 2000 they were allowed to do so to only a limited extent. Even more of a hindrance is the belief among corporate managers and bankers from around the world that Korea is

- The most nationalistic country in Asia.
- One of the most bureaucratic countries in Asia.
- An economy dominated by cartels and state-owned companies.
- The most protectionist nation in Asia.
- The Asian country with the highest potential for labor unrest.[3]

As Korean multinationals seek to develop new overseas markets and to tap new sources of financial capital and as the Korean government attempts to liberalize the nation's financial markets, the pressures for more detailed financial disclosure will undoubtedly guide Korean financial reporting to a new level of sophistication and transparency.

Environmental Factors

Cultural Environment

A variety of religions and world views exert an influence on the South Korean people (20 percent of whom are Christian), making the country a complex mix of old and new that resists convenient generalization. Korean culture has been most deeply affected by the Confucian ethic, which became the officially sanctioned state philosophy in the late 14th century and has been dominant since. With its emphasis on hierarchy, conformity, and social cohesiveness, Confucianism teaches Koreans to depend on social and communal institutions, especially the family, for their sense of identity. This attitude has been labeled a *frame* orientation (as opposed to Americans' *attribute* orientation), in which the self is conceived primarily in terms of affiliations and loyalties rather than personal achievements and character traits. Such a frame is manifested by Korea's score of 18, one of the lowest recorded, on Hofstede's individualism (IDV) dimension. Not even Japan, traditionally viewed as one of the most collectivist societies, scored as low as Korea on the IDV dimension.

The sense of group membership, of who is an "insider" and who is an "outsider," looms significantly in Korean culture and takes precedence over more abstract values such as fairness. Outsiders may gradually earn only a small measure of acceptance, with proper introductions often being required for what an American would consider a casual interaction. Within the group, relationships (ideally, at least) are conducted on the basis of a scrupulous and finely honed sense of rank and a mutual trust that is less a sign of personal regard than a cultural norm. (This trust, of course, may be forfeited by serious misbehavior.) Each member is expected to subordinate his or her desires to the collective welfare of the group and the preservation of harmonious cooperation. The authority of the leader, who is usually something of a father figure in Korea, is not to be questioned (Koreans scored a relatively high 60 on Hofstede's power-distance dimension); Koreans, unlike Americans, tend

---

[3]P. Abrahams, "Uphill Battle for Investors," *Financial Times,* June 23, 1994, p. III.

to place the prerogative of rulers above the desires and interests of the ruled. This Korean ideal of group consciousness not only permeates organizations and institutions within Korean society, including corporations, but also provides a model for society as a whole.

Social reality is inevitably more complex and ambiguous, however, than social ideology. The Confucian vision of harmony (a notion consistent with Korea's relatively high scores in uncertainty avoidance of 85 and long-term orientation of 75 as reported by Hofstede) and hierarchical order is being seriously challenged in Korea by the imperatives of capitalism, which generally celebrates individual freedom and views social control as unnecessarily restrictive and counterproductive. Moreover, capitalism sees society and social institutions in rather fluid terms as constantly evolving entities driven by conflicts and tensions. A free market economy, in traditional versions of capitalism, is less a harmonious household than a system of contending and dynamic forces that, given the space to operate properly, stimulates economic growth and provides the opportunity for social mobility.[4]

The ideological tension between traditional Korean values and modern consumer capitalism has been aggravated by the material effects of the country's steep growth rate. Far from fulfilling the Confucian ideal of a harmonious society modeled after the patriarchal family, Korea's rapid industrialization has eroded traditional values and brought in its wake a number of social problems: severe labor unrest, housing shortages caused by urbanization and rampant land speculation, and widespread resentment over the concentration of wealth and the power of big business. Unlike other east Asian peoples, Koreans express anger openly and vociferously rather than masking it behind a facade of formality. After sharp drops in the Korean Stock Exchange in 1990, for example, gangs of investors—reportedly including middle-aged women—signified their displeasure by smashing furniture in brokerage offices. Strikes often turn violent, as do protests against government repression. While the inevitable dislocations of rapid growth have fueled dissension in Korean society, even its recent material success has caused problems as Koreans struggle to reconcile their newfound wealth with a traditional suspicion of luxury. Regardless of a people's cultural predispositions, the development of a full-fledged industrial economy does not occur without painful dislocations—both economic and ideological—and Korea is proving no exception to the rule.

Korean cultural values affect financial reporting practices and the economic environment in several ways. Confucianism tends to centralize authority in a single father figure or a small ruling elite, a pattern reflected in the pyramidal management structure of the 30 or so business groups (known as *chaebol*) that dominate the economy. This penchant for autocratic power structures has posed something of a problem as the country struggles to transform itself from an underdeveloped nation with an authoritarian regime and a protected economy into a modern liberal democracy with open markets. Although a democratic constitution was adopted and free elections held in 1987, and the government promised to liberalize the financial markets, Koreans have found that old authoritarian habits die hard.

Likewise, the promulgation of financial reporting policy is a highly centralized process in Korea. Policy formation and reporting requirements are controlled by two agencies of the national government, the Securities Supervisory Board and the Ministry of Finance. The accounting profession has little influence on the standard-setting process other than assisting the board in formulating particular pronouncements. The Ministry of Finance is responsible for administering Korea's professional accounting examination,

---

[4]For an interesting discussion of a Confucian approach to capitalism see, Y. Paik and J. Derick Sohn, "Confucius in Mexico: Korean MNCs and the Maquiladoras," *Business Horizons,* November–December 1998, pp. 25–33.

granting certificates, and regulating Korean CPAs, but it has delegated the authority to set auditing standards and procedures to the Korean Institute of Certified Public Accountants.

Education is highly valued for its own sake in the Confucian tradition, and Koreans also know that the quality of their training will affect their ability to compete in the world market. As a result, Korea boasts a well-trained workforce and a high rate of literacy. Korean education diverges from Western methods in its centralization—the textbooks and curriculum being dictated by the national government—and its greater emphasis on conformity, discipline, and technical training. In other words, Korean education stresses socialization and preparation for group membership rather than personal growth and development of independent judgment. Innovation, originality, and independence—the values on which British and American accounting professionals pride themselves—are not encouraged in Korea's educational system and may seem presumptuous and unnecessarily risky to a Korean. Individual initiative—and, hence, personal responsibility—takes a backseat to the needs of the group and the desire for consensus.

Westerners must also realize that the concept of accountability occupies a different place in the context of Korean group consciousness. In a homogeneous and tightly knit society in which most organizations are controlled centrally, "the public's right to know" carries considerably less weight than in the relatively open societies of the West. Financial data that are routinely shared with the press and the public in the United States may be considered company property in Korea and held in confidence. Given Koreans' habitual distrust of foreigners and their inexperience with international capital markets, Western investors and analysts seeking financial information from Korean enterprises should expect to meet with a degree of reticence, even suspicion, that may seem unreasonable by the standards to which Westerners are accustomed.

Even the largest, most sophisticated Korean firms release extremely sketchy financial data for overseas consumption, not because they are unaware of the benefits of global publicity but because they are cautious about giving potential weapons to outsiders. Convenience translations of recent annual reports for such companies as Samsung, Sunkyong, and Daewoo often include few or no footnotes even though such notes are required for domestic reporting. For example, in its English-language 1997 annual report, Samsung presents a combined balance sheet, income statement, and statement of changes in cash flow in three different currencies—the Korean won, the U.S. dollar, and the European currency unit—but it presents no footnotes detailing the basis on which these financial statements were constructed. Eventually, the reluctance of Korean multinationals to share detailed data may be overcome as they begin to compete for foreign capital; in the meantime, however, foreign investors must expect lower levels of disclosure than they are accustomed to in domestic company statements.

Legal and Political Environment

Tax Law—Individual Shareholders. In spite of its autocratic habits and its history of directing capital flows, the Korean government has recognized the importance of developing a vigorous domestic market for Korean equities and, consequently, has structured tax laws to encourage companies to list their shares on the Korea Stock Exchange and to encourage investors to buy them. As evidence of this, any capital gain from the sale of stocks listed on the Korean Stock Exchange is tax exempt. Moreover, dividends received from a Korean corporation are taxed at a 15 percent rate, and a tax credit equal to 19 percent of the dividends received may be available. Income tax rates are 10 percent on taxable income up to W10 million ($8,200), with a top rate of 40 percent on taxable income over W80 million ($65,300).[5]

---

[5]The basic unit of currency in Korea is the ***won,*** denoted W, which was trading at about W1225 = US$1 as of April 1999. This exchange rate has been retained throughout the chapter.

Tax Law—Corporations.   Book income, although not required, is generally equal to taxable income in Korea. For instance, tax law prescribes methods of depreciation (straight line or double-declining balance in most cases) and useful lives for assets. Most companies claim the same amount of depreciation on both their financial statements and their tax returns, resulting in an overstatement of expenses and an understatement of net income on the financial statements.

Tax law also allows Korean companies to set up various tax-deductible reserves for a variety of purposes, such as overseas market development, export losses, and overseas investment. Although these reserves appear in the retained earnings section of the balance sheet, they do not affect book income, only taxable income. The note shown in Exhibit 12–1, taken from the financial statements of Daewoo Corporation, provides an illustration of these reserves and a characteristically laconic explanation.

The tax rates on corporate income are 16 percent on taxable income less than W100 million (about $81,600) and 28 percent on income exceeding W100 million. Corporations must also pay the 7.5 percent resident surtax on all corporate tax payments.

Business Environment

Form of Business.   The Korean Commercial Code recognizes four kinds of business entities: the limited partnership, the unlimited partnership, the limited liability company (similar to the GmbH in German company law, used for closely held businesses with 50 or fewer stockholders), and the joint stock company (known as the ***chusik hoesa***). A joint

---

EXHIBIT 12–1
Daewoo Corporation Reserves Disclosures

Appropriated retained earnings are summarized as follows:

	Millions of Won	*Thousands of U.S. Dollars*
Legal reserve	20,221	25,023
Reserve for business rationalization	51,470	63,693
Reserve for improvement of financial structure	68,709	85,025
Reserve for overseas market development	180,451	223,303
Reserve for export loss	44,367	54,903
Reserve for loss on overseas operations	14,500	17,943
Reserve for loss on overseas investments	26,750	33,102
Reserve for redemption of long-term debt	—	—
	406,468	502,992

(a) Legal Reserve, Reserve for Business Rationalization, and Reserve for Improvement of Financial Structure
The Korean Commercial Code requires the Company to appropriate as a legal reserve an amount equal to at least 10 percent of cash dividends for each accounting period until the reserve equals 50 percent of stated capital. Under the Tax Exemption and Reduction Control Law, the Company is allowed to make certain deductions from taxable income for overseas operations. The Company is, however, required to appropriate from retained earnings the amount of tax benefit obtained and transfer such amount into reserve for business rationalization. The Financial Control Regulations for listed companies require the company to appropriate as a reserve for improvement of financial structure an amount equal to at least 50 percent of the net gain on sale of property, plant, and equipment and 10 percent of the net earnings for each year until the company's net worth equals 30 percent of total assets. The above reserves may be used to reduce a deficit or they may be transferred to stated capital in connection with a free issue of shares.
(b) Reserves Set Up for Tax Purposes
Under the Tax Exemption and Reduction Control Law, the Company is allowed to make certain deductions from taxable income and set up reserves for overseas market development, export loss, loss on overseas operations and overseas investments, by appropriating retained earnings. The unused portion of the reserves is generally added back to taxable income over two to seven years after certain grace periods.
(c) Voluntary Reserves (Reserve for redemption of long-term debt)
The voluntary reserve included in the appropriated retained earnings was established by a stockholders' resolution for the purposes of redemption of long-term debt and may be restored to unappropriated retained earnings by a future stockholders' resolution.

stock company may be formed by seven or more investors with a minimum capitalization of W50 million (about $40,800). It must also establish a legal reserve for the protection of shareholders and creditors by annually allocating a sum equal to 10 percent of annual cash dividends to the reserve account until it equals 50 percent of issued capital.

Every joint stock company must retain a statutory auditor who is directly elected by the shareholders and charged with reviewing the company's financial statements and general operations. Although the statutory auditor may not be an officer or director of the company, he or she is not required to be independent or professionally qualified to fill this role. In addition, joint stock companies listed on the Korean Stock Exchange or with W6 billion (about $4.9 million) in total assets must be audited by an independent CPA.

Accounting Profession.   As mentioned, the accounting profession in Korea exerts relatively little influence on the formation of accounting policy. One reason is that it is relatively young; Korea's Certified Public Accountants Law was passed in 1950, and CPA examinations have been administered by the Ministry of Finance only since 1955. The profession remains small, consisting of approximately 2,000 licensed practitioners to serve a country of 46 million. The main professional association in Korea is the Korean Institute of Certified Public Accountants, which the Ministry of Finance has authorized to establish auditing guidelines.

Chaebol.   Korea's economy is dominated by 30 large, diversified conglomerates known as *chaebol,* whose ranks include such familiar names as Samsung, Hyundai, and Lucky-Goldstar, as well as lesser-known groups such as Sunkyong and Daewoo. Together, the combined sales of the 30 *chaebol* equal about 90 percent of Korea's GDP. These groups, like the Japanese *keiretsu,* are bound together by intricate and extensive cross-guarantees, cross-subsidies, and cross-holdings of stock among a large number of companies and usually include a general trading company as the flagship member.[6] Exhibit 12–2 provides information concerning some of Korea's larger *chaebol.*

EXHIBIT 12–2

South Korea's Largest *Chaebol*

	Sales	Net Profit	Total Debt	Debt as % of equity
	Trillion of Won			
Hyundai	68.0	.2	43.3	439
Samsung	60.1	.2	37.0	268
Lucky-Goldstar	46.7	.4	28.8	346
Daewoo	38.2	.4	26.4	337
Sunkyong	26.6	.3	18.0	385
Ssangyung	19.4	(.1)	12.7	409
Kia	12.1	(.1)	11.9	524
Hanwho	9.7	(.2)	9.7	778
Hanjin	8.7	(.2)	11.8	557
Hyosung	5.5	.0	3.3	373

Source: *Financial Times Graphics.*

---

[6]L. Nakarmi, "A Flying Leap toward the 21st Century?" *Business Week,* March 20, 1995, pp. 78–80.

The corporate structure of the *chaebol* tends to follow a brother-sister rather than a parent-subsidiary pattern, an arrangement that raises questions about the usefulness of Anglo-American consolidation rules in the Korean context. The Korean government has issued rules requiring consolidation of majority-owned subsidiaries, but implementation and enforcement of these requirements has been slow. Thus, it is not unusual to encounter annual reports that present financial statements for the flagship company only. For example, Daewoo Corporation's annual report states that "the financial statements include only the accounts of Daewoo Corporation. Investments in subsidiaries are accounted for on the cost basis." (The equity method is not required under Korean GAAP unless consolidated financial statements are prepared.) Although Sunkyong lists its major investments in subsidiaries and affiliates by company, it does not indicate its percentage of ownership of these enterprises, a common omission in Korean annual reports.

For all their size and sophistication, the *chaebol* have not yet distinguished themselves for detailed and helpful financial reporting. In fact, their financial statements are notable primarily for their terseness. The 14 pages of notes accompanying Hyundai's 1997 financial statements appear rather forthcoming by Korean standards, although they seem quite reticent to the U.S. or British reader. The most immediate reason for this is the lack of an experienced and sophisticated investing public in Korea, one that needs and demands detailed financial information. Rather than depending on large numbers of individual investors, the *chaebol* have depended largely on government-guided loans from Korea's tightly controlled banking system to meet their capital needs, creating an altogether different sense of corporate accountability and disclosure than one expects from Ford or General Motors. Recently, at a time when small businesses were being charged interest rates of 30 percent on borrowed funds, the *chaebol* were receiving rates of around 18 percent. It is no wonder that they have tended to opt for borrowings rather than shareholder funds to fuel their diversification and growth. This phenomenon is attested to by the whopping debt-to-owners' equity ratios noted in Exhibit 12–2. As a result of this extensive and favorable borrowing, capital has not been efficiently allocated across the Korean market, and, according to one noted expert, the large and powerful *chaebol* heavy debts "have made hostages of the commercial banks."[7]

Collectively, the *chaebol* exert an enormous influence over the Korean economy (too much, in fact, according to many Koreans who want a more equitable distribution of the nation's wealth). Many observers openly wonder whether the *chaebol* and the rest of Korea with them will be able to make the transition from cheap labor, low value-added manufacturing into the more capital-intensive and higher value-added industries in which they will achieve full citizenship in the global marketplace. To do so, they will have to attract enough money to raise their historically low levels of research and development expenditures and capital investment. To attract that money, they will have to broaden their ownership base and eventually will address the information demands of an increasingly sophisticated cadre of international equity investors.[8]

Toward these ends, the Korean government in late 1993 began allowing banks to charge small and large borrowers market interest rates,[9] thus creating the need for banks to become more sophisticated in credit analysis. Moreover, in January 1994, the government announced the agreement to its 1993 request that the *chaebol* prepare to restructure by concentrating on a limited number of core businesses. In particular, as part of its 1993–1997 economic plan, the Korean government requested the 10 largest *chaebol* to

---

[7]J. Burton, "Industrial Empires Still Dominate," *Financial Times,* November 18, 1992, p. 14.

[8]J. Burton, "Protection for a Tiger's Cubs," *Financial Times,* May 2, 1995, p. 15.

[9]"Role Reversal," *The Economist,* November 13, 1993, pp. 37–38.

identify the three business sectors they wished to remain in (at the time of the request they were operating in an average of 11 sectors), and the next 20 largest *chaebol* were instructed to identify the two sectors they would remain in (a reduction from their average of seven). The government promised continued favorable state-backed financing to those who reduce the diversity in their business activities and who also reduce the ownership interest of the controlling families. With such a move, the government has sparked a new era for business in Korea that aims to

- Encourage competition and foster small business.
- Wrestle power from the old industrial dynasties and hand it over to professional managers.
- Stem the "octopus-like growth" of the *chaebol* into unrelated areas.[10]

By the end of 1997, progress along this restructuring path had been virtually nonexistent. With the economic woes of Korea climbing and the unprecedented bankruptcies in 1997 of the Hanbo and Sammi *chaebols,* the 14th and 26th largest Korean *chaebols,* 1998 ended with Korea's top five *chaebol* agreeing to "halve the number of subsidiaries they have between them to 130, . . . swapping subsidiaries between the groups [to reduce] the number of Korean competitors to only two in critical export industries, [and] to reduce their debt burdens from 5.5 times equity to twice equity in the next year."[11] It remains to be seen whether these behemoths can change their focus from size to lean, from market share to profits, and from privileged access to low-cost debt to owners' equity. In addition, accounting reforms have begun (e.g. a new requirement for consolidated balance sheets) but they must continue because, "the big *chaebol* are riddled with cross subsidies and guarantees and with obscure accounts that render their affairs impenetrable to outsiders."[12]

Capital Markets.   Although the Korea Stock Exchange, located in Seoul, is among the 10 largest exchanges in the world with about 700 listed companies and a market capitalization in excess of $10 billion, many Korean companies are not accustomed to selling securities as a major avenue of financing. As mentioned, companies have traditionally depended on government-guided bank loans for their financial needs. In 1989, however, the government sought to strengthen the market by requesting, under the Capital Market Development Law, nonpublicly held firms to list on the exchange after (1) accumulating paid-in capital of W5 billion (about $4.1 million) or net equity of W10 billion ($8.2 million); (2) operating, on a continuous basis, over three years; (3) achieving a debt-to-owners' equity ratio not more than 1.5 times the average for other listed companies in the same industry; and (4) achieving a ratio of profit to paid-in capital higher than the prevailing interest rate for one-year deposits.[13] Listed firms are required to file an independently audited annual report with the Korean SEC no later than 60 days after the end of their fiscal year, and they must file unaudited mid-year statements.

Foreign direct investment in Korean companies listed on the Seoul exchange was first allowed in January 1992. Such investment, however, was restricted. Initially, foreign ownership was not allowed to exceed 10 percent of a company's shares.[14] Within weeks

---

[10]See "Taming the *Chaebol*" and Nakarmi, "A Flying Leap toward the 21st Century?"

[11]J. Burton, "S. Korea's Top Five Conglomerates Agree to Reform," *Financial Times,* December 18, 1998, p. 1.

[12]J. Burton, "Won-upmanship," *Financial Times,* February 25, 1999, p. 15.

[13]*Doing Business in the Republic of Korea,* Price Waterhouse, New York, 1996.

[14]For a select few companies, the ceiling is 25 percent. See "A Door Creaks Open," *The Economist,* January 4, 1992, p. 72; and P. Montagnon and J. Burton, "The Burden of Membership," *Financial Times,* May 29, 1995, p. 12. The 12 percent limit was raised to 15 percent in July 1995.

after this tentative step toward capital market liberalization, the 10 percent ceiling had been reached in 72 companies.[15] Such restrictions led to the following situation:

> Once the ceiling is hit, a foreigner can buy stock only from another foreigner. The result is a two-tier market—one price for Koreans, another for foreigners. As an example, consider Korea Mobile Telecommunications, the country's cellular phone monopoly. For Koreans, it [traded] at W120,100 a share. But, for foreigners, the price is W210,175, a 75 percent premium.[16]

The government has permitted the creation of *Korea funds,* investment trusts traded on major stock exchanges around the world. In addition, it has allowed a handful of Korean companies to issue convertible bonds on overseas markets, a move suggesting that foreign bondholders will at some point be allowed to hold equity shares. In fact, foreign participants in the first of these issues, floated by Samsung in 1985 and originally scheduled for conversion in 1987, were finally allowed to convert their bonds in early 1990. Thus, these investors became the first foreign owners of Korean equities with the right to sell them and purchase others with the proceeds. Historically, the fact remains that due to the government's role of allocating capital across corporate Korea, combined with the dominance of the *chaebol* in the Korean economy, there has not been the need for or development of efficient public capital markets.[17] As the tumultuous 1990s came to a close, Korea had migrated to fully open bond and stock markets. It will be interesting to observe the evolution of Korean corporate governance and financial reporting as foreigners become an ever larger source of corporate capital.

Selected Financial Reporting Practices

Korean GAAP is a mixture of decrees and regulations issued by the Ministry of Finance and the Securities and Exchange Commission as well as a blend of practices espoused by a variety of miscellaneous laws, tax principles, and general conventions. At a root level, the historical cost principle, with some exceptions, is one of the core concepts adhered to as is the accrual basis of accounting, the going-concern assumption, and the consistent application of GAAP. As Korea emerges from its isolationist financial markets cocoon and as the equity market, in particular, becomes a more viable and important source of domestic and international capital, Korean financial reports must become more illuminating of the financial position of the companies they purport to portray. For example, a fundamental issue pertaining to the definition of the most appropriate reporting entity is yet to be resolved. Moreover, Korean companies have historically had a government safety net that is now being withdrawn in some measure, thus giving rise to a recent local corporate and financial market challenge of understanding and assessing financial risk. With a strong historical role in government industrial and tax policy, Korean financial reporting practices are making their debut on the world stage. The following is a review of key Korean financial reporting practices and accounting principles. Exhibit 12–3 provides a comparison of Korean and U.S. GAAP. Where significant differences are noted to exist between Korean GAAP and that of other major financial markets, one must realize that enormous pressure exists for Korea to change as Korean companies search for global capital.

---

[15]"Past the Worst," *The Economist,* January 30, 1993, p. 71.

[16]D. Darlin, "A Half-Open Door," *Forbes,* February 5, 1993, pp. 188–90.

[17]M. E. Porter, *The Competitive Advantage of Nations* (New York: The Free Press, 1990).

EXHIBIT 12–3

Comparison of South Korean and U.S. Accounting and Reporting Standards

Item	*South Korea*	*United States*
Asset valuation	Historical cost with selected revaluation (e.g., fixed assets under the asset revaluation law)	Historical cost with selected revaluation (principally downward)
Inventory valuation	Specific identification, FIFO, LIFO, weighted average, or "retail pricing"	Principally LIFO (because of tax considerations); also FIFO and average cost methods
Inventory: year-end	Lower-of-cost-or-market value on an item-by-item basis	Lower of cost or replacement cost
Depreciation	Straight-line, declining balance, or unit-of-production methods; additional depreciation permitted and separately identified	Principally straight line with accelerated and production-based methods permitted
Goodwill	Capitalized to the balance sheet, with amortization (principally straight line) over a maximum of 5 years; negative goodwill added to capital surplus on balance sheet	Capitalized to balance sheet with amortization (principally straight line) over a maximum of 40 years; negative goodwill not permitted
Research and development costs	Capitalized and amortized over expected useful life if (a) incurred in relation to a specific product or technology, (b) costs are clearly identifiable, and (c) future benefits are reasonably expected; otherwise, expensed as incurred	Research costs expensed currently; development costs expensed currently except in certain industries (i.e., software, oil and gas)
Capitalization of interest costs	Capitalization required for debt directly related to the manufacture, purchase, or construction of fixed assets	Capitalization required for self-constructed assets
Intercorporate investments: Marketable securities (current asset trading)	Cost or market value	Market value (individual security basis only) with *unrealized* gains and losses taken to income
Long-term investments: 0–20% ownership (i.e., available for sale)	Cost or market value, with unrealized gains and losses reported as an adjustment to shareholders' equity.	Market value (individual security basis only) with *unrealized* gains and losses reported on balance sheet in owners' equity
20–50% ownership	Cost or equity method	Equity method
51–100% ownership	Consolidated (required after 1993), principally using purchase accounting (although some regulations require the use of pooling)	Consolidated, using pooling (until 2001) or purchase accounting
Debt valuation	All debt valued at face value unless present value is significantly different, in which case present value is used	Long-term debt (except deferred income taxes) valued at present value; current debt valued at face value
Leases	Financing leases capitalized (e.g., when ownership is transferred, lease contains a bargain buyout option or the lease term approximates the estimated life of the leased asset); operating leases disclosed in footnotes	Capital leases reflected in balance sheet; operating leases disclosed in footnotes
Deferred income taxes	Computed under deferral method (effective April 1998).	Computed under liability method
Pension liabilities	Private pension plans rare, but when present and unfunded, liability reported on balance sheet	Reflected on balance sheet
Discretionary reserves	Provisions for future expenses not permitted, except for severance pay, repairs and maintenance, product warranties, and others that can be reasonably estimated	Restricted to identifiable operational losses
Statement of cash flows	Not required (although statement of changes in financial position required)	Required

Valuation

Assets are generally valued at historical cost, with certain exceptions. Inventories, for example, must be written down if replacement value has declined below cost. Marketable equity securities may be valued at market value or cost (where cost approximates market value). Long-term equity investments in publicly traded companies are reported at market value, with unrealized gains and losses treated as a component of shareholders' equity.

Under the provisions of the Asset Revaluation Law, certain tangible fixed assets may be written up to market value when the Bank of Korea wholesale price index has risen 25 percent from the date they were acquired (or from the date they were previously revalued). The amount of the revaluation is based on a certified appraisal of the assets, and the resultant gain is subject to a revaluation tax of 3 percent. The gain is not treated as income nor the tax as an expense; instead, the net amount of the two figures is shown as a separate capital reserve in the stockholders' equity section of the balance sheet. Although the revaluation reserve may not be appropriated for cash dividends, it may be used to issue stock dividends by transferring an amount equal to the par value of shares issued to the common stock account.

Depreciation

Depreciation rates and useful asset lives generally follow Korean income tax law and may not reflect the true business judgment of management. In certain cases (i.e., plant and equipment acquired on or before December 31, 1994), special depreciation in addition to normal depreciation may be charged against income on a company's financial statements. Special depreciation due to excess equipment usage is considered to be a manufacturing cost; special depreciation for any other reason is classified as an extraordinary loss.

Bad Debts

Reserves for doubtful accounts are generally calculated in accordance with Korean income tax law and may not reflect actual economic experience. A reserve of 1 percent (2 percent for financial institutions) is allowed under tax law. Estimating the allowance on the basis of prior years' experience is also permitted.

Goodwill

Purchased goodwill, or the excess of the acquisition price paid for a business over the fair market value of the net assets acquired, is capitalized and amortized over five years using the straight-line method. Negative goodwill, on the other hand, is treated as a "gain on business combination" and recorded as capital surplus on the balance sheet.

Income Taxes

Although Korean tax law causes both timing and permanent differences between book and tax income, interperiod tax allocation is not required, nor is it commonly practiced. Effective April 1, 1998, however, the use of deferred tax accounting became recommended. Previously, there were no requirements, hence the income tax expense shown in the financial statements reflected the actual tax due for operations during the year (i.e., the flow-thru approach).

Leases

Korean GAAP provides for the classification of leases as either operating or financing leases. Because of differing criteria for classification, however, many leases that would be capitalized under U.S. GAAP are treated as operating leases. Under Korean GAAP, leases that meet the following criteria are considered to be financing leases: (1) title is transferred from lessor to lessee, (2) the lease contains a bargain buyout option, or (3) the lease life is approximately equal to the leased asset's remaining useful life.

In the case of a financing lease, the lessor reports a receivable on its balance sheet, with payments being divided between interest income and a reduction of the receivable. The lessee carries the asset at its fair market value at the time of its acquisition and discloses a capital liability, with payments being divided between interest expense and a reduction of the liability. In the case of an operating lease, the lessor may calculate depreciation based on the term of the lease rather than the asset's useful life. In general, the lessee must provide a description of the lease arrangements for both financing and operating leases in its financial statements.

Prior Period Adjustments

Changes in accounting method are applied only prospectively, not retroactively. Prior period adjustments are accounted for by adjusting the beginning balance of unappropriated retained earnings or are reported as an extraordinary item in the income statement.

Capital and Reserves

Shareholders' equity is generally composed of four types of accounts: share capital, capital surplus, retained earnings, and capital adjustments. Share capital consists of the par value of any common or preferred shares issued. Capital surplus consists of Paid-in Capital in Excess of Par Value, the asset revaluation surplus account, and any other specific reserve accounts that may arise as a result of a gain on the retirement of share capital, a gain on business combination (i.e., negative goodwill), and various government subsidies. Retained earnings includes various legal reserves, discretionary reserves, and unappropriated retained earnings or undisposed deficit. Finally, capital adjustments include treasury stock, any discounts on share capital issued, prepaid dividends, gains (losses) on valuation of equity investment securities, and outstanding stock rights and warrants. Cash dividends may be declared only from unappropriated retained earnings; stock dividends, on the other hand, may be declared from unappropriated retained earnings, capital surplus, or any legal reserves.

Other Disclosure

Korean accounting principles do not require disclosure of industry segment information, nor are pension or postretirement liabilities required to be disclosed (although many companies now do so). Earnings per share disclosures (based on the weighted-average number of common shares actually issued and outstanding) are now required. Beginning in 1998, an entity's environmental standards and policies, including environment-related investments, should be disclosed.

Analytical Considerations

Only in the last decade has the importance of South Korea as an economic entity become widely acknowledged. As a consequence, comparative financial data for Korea and the United States are somewhat limited. Nonetheless, the following country composite ratio data are quite revealing.[18]

Financial Indicator	*Korea*	*United States*
Current ratio	1.13	1.94
Quick ratio	.46	1.10
Times-interest earned ratio	1.80×	6.50×
Inventory turnover ratio	6.60×	6.80×
Return on assets ratio	2.8%	7.4%
Return on equity ratio	13.1%	13.9%

[18]F. Choi, H. Hino, S. K. Min, S. O. Nam, J. Ujiie, and A. Stonehill, "Analyzing Foreign Financial Statements: The Use and Misuse of International Ratio Analysis," *Journal of International Business Studies,* Spring 1983, pp. 113–31.

These data present a relatively stark comparison of Korean and U.S. businesses: Korean companies appear less liquid, solvent, efficient, and profitable as compared to U.S. companies while also being more highly leveraged. This generalization is both a function of doing business in Korea and a consequence of the prevalent accounting and reporting practices of Korea.

A review of Exhibit 12–3 suggests that accepted practice in Korea is frequently more conservative than that commonly followed in the United States. Consider, for instance, the following:

- *Depreciation expense.* The revaluation of fixed assets produces higher levels of depreciation; in addition, additional special depreciation is permitted.
- *Amortization expense.* Intangible assets are generally amortized over no more than 5 years (versus 40 in the United States).
- *Deferred income taxes.* Deferred taxes are rarely needed because of the parallel between reported accounting income and taxable income; however, beginning in 1998, where book-tax differences arise, they will be accounted for using the deferral method.

Just how material these various differences in accounting practices may be can best be analyzed in relation to actual corporate data. For example, with respect to the revaluation of property, plant, and equipment, Daewoo Corporation reported that its total assets increased by approximately 10 percent while shareholders' equity increased by 8 percent relative to the values that would have been reported under U.S. GAAP.

Where capital markets are efficient, which is substantially true (but to varying degrees) for the countries profiled in Chapters 7–13, reporting differences like those noted above should be largely compensated for in security prices. And this appears to be the case in the following 1998 market data:

Country	Average Price-Earnings Multiple	Average Price-Book Value Multiple	Average Price-EBITDA Multiple
Britain	19.5	3.8	12.7
Germany	31.2	3.7	9.8
Italy	29.1	3.1	10.1
Japan	43.3	1.8	9.9
Mexico	16.6	2.3	9.6
S. Korea	110.7	0.7	3.7
United States	26.6	4.6	15.6

Source: Morgan Stanley Capital International

A comparison of average price-earnings multiples for Korean and U.S. companies (110.7 vs. 26.6) reveals how conservative reported results can be under Korean GAAP. A comparison of average price-EBITDA multiples, on the other hand, reveals the severity of Korea's recent economic recession versus the relative prosperity experienced in the United States, as well as investor expectations regarding the near-term economic climate of those two countries.

Summary

As the 20th century draws to a close, Korea finds itself a nation pulled by contrasting forces. For example, Korea can boast of improved labor relations, yet up to 10,000 workers a day are losing their jobs. There has been a steady growth of an affluent middle class, yet 3,000 businesses are going bankrupt a month. Korea's adolescent democracy has opened and liberalized the nation's economy, yet it needs International Monetary Fund loans and is very slow in creating an effective social welfare system for its displaced workers. It has one of the world's highest savings rates yet one of the world's worst performing stock markets.

Upon recently becoming the 29th member of the Organization for Economic Cooperation and Development (OECD) and with a renewed dedication to develop a market-based economy, Korea's future harbors positive prospects. Once known as the "hermit kingdom" because of its isolationist preferences, Korea is striving to be among the world's leading industrialized nations. As one commentator noted, "To achieve that exalted status, Korea must open both markets and minds."[19] Moreover, as one renowned Korean economist recently noted:

> We think we are changing very rapidly because we only compare ourselves to our own past. What people don't realize is that the rest of the world is changing just as quickly, and we are in danger of being left out.[20]

Suggested Readings

"An Open and Shut Market." *Euromoney*, February 1992, pp. 62–64.

Bremmer, B. and M. Ihlwan. "Korea: Rage and Despair." *Business Week*, August 17, 1998, pp. 47–49.

Choi, F. D. S. et al. "Analyzing Foreign Financial Statements: The Use and Misuse of International Ratio Analysis." *Journal of International Business Studies*, Spring 1983, pp. 113–31.

Clifford, M. and J. Lim. "Meltdown in Seoul." *Business Week*, February 10, 1997, pp. 50–51.

Darlin, D. "A Half-Open Door." *Forbes*, February 15, 1993, pp. 188–90.

Han, D., and K. Ojah. "Evidence on Managers' Perceptions of Effects of Government Control of the Business Environment: A Study of the Republic of Korea." *International Executive*, January/February 1995, pp. 61–79.

Herd, R., and R. S. Jones. "Spotlight on Korea." *The OECD Observer*, June/July 1994, pp. 32–35.

"Korea: A Survey." *Financial Times*, April 23, 1998, pp. I–IV.

Kraar, L. "Korea's Tigers Keep Roaring." *Fortune*, May 4, 1992, pp. 108–10.

Montagu-Pollock, M. "Overtaking the West." *Asian Business*, January 1990, pp. 48–51.

Paik, Y. and J. Derick Sohn. "Confucius in Mexico: Korean MNCs and the Maquiladoras." *Business Horizons*, November–December 1998, pp. 25–33.

"South Korea." *The Times*, March 8, 1995, special report.

Weinberg, N. "Symptom Therapy." *Forbes*, January 11, 1999, pp. 88–90.

Exercises

12.1 *Chaebol* Capital Structure Changes

One of the reforms being pushed in Korea is for the *chaebol* to lower their debt-to-equity ratios to around 200 percent. Using the data in Exhibit 12–2, characterize the magnitude of the capital restructuring required to bring this about. In addition, opine as to the most efficacious way to bring about this restructuring.

---

[19]J. P. Lehmann, "Asian Tigers Make Way for the Bamboo Network," a *Mastering Global Business* special section in the *Financial Times*, April 3, 1993, p. 4.

[20]G. deJonquieres, "The Tigers Face a Challenge," *Financial Times*, October 17, 1994, p. 19.

12.2 Revaluation of Assets

Under the provisions of the Korean Asset Revaluation Law, corporations are permitted to revalue certain qualifying tangible assets above historical cost. For example, Daewoo Corporation's "summary of significant accounting principles" makes the following statement:

> The Company, and its domestic affiliated companies have, to some extent, recognized the loss of purchasing power of the won by upward restatement of the cost of property, plant and equipment with a corresponding credit to capital surplus. Revaluation taxes paid are offset against the revaluation surplus. Such surplus may be offset against exchange losses, a deficit, or may be transferred to stated capital in connection with a free distribution of shares.

In addition the company footnotes revealed:

> Had assets not been revalued, the consolidated financial statements would have been increased (decreased) as follows for the year:

Accounts	(Won, millions)
Net property, plant, and equipment	(55,758)
Investments and advances	(65,034)
Common stock	(14,343)
Capital surplus	(37,290)
Retained earnings	(47,025)
Minority interest—surplus	(22,134)
Net earnings	1,665

The company's financial statements also revealed the following data as of year-end:

Accounts	(Won, millions)
Net property, plant, and equipment	2,124,752
Investments and advances	341,567
Common stock	440,285
Capital surplus	418,267
Retained earnings	302,036
Minority interests—surplus	(418,368)
Net earnings	50,476

Required:

(a) On the basis of the information contained in Daewoo's footnote, what journal entries were made in regard to the company's revaluation of assets? (Ignore amounts.)

(b) Assess the impact of the asset revaluation on Daewoo's financial results.

12.3 Accounting for Equity Reserves

Founded in 1967, the Daewoo Corporation is the parent company of the Daewoo Group, Korea's fourth largest *chaebol*. *Fortune* magazine rated Daewoo as the world's 45th largest industrial corporation.

Generally accepted accounting practice in Korea encourages eligible corporations to create tax-deductible reserves for a variety of qualifying purposes as a means to reduce otherwise taxable corporate earnings. The "qualifying purposes" usually reflect sectors of the Korean economy that the government desires to economically stimulate or to particular macrolevel economic objectives of Korea's Ministry of Finance.

Exhibit 12–1 in this chapter lists the equity reserve accounts for the Daewoo Corporation.

Required:

(a) Using journal entries, explain the change in each of Daewoo's eight reserves listed in Exhibit 12–1. Why do some reserves increase, while others decrease? Based on a statutory tax rate of 28 percent, how much income tax did the company save under the system of tax-deductible reserves?

(b) Compare and contrast Korea's system of tax reserves to that used in Japan (Chapter 9) and in Sweden (Chapter 10).

(c) Write a one-sentence explanation regarding the role or purpose of each of Daewoo's equity reserves. What observations can you draw from your analysis?

12.4 Analyzing Financial Trends

The following are the balance sheets and income statements for Sunkyong Industries for 19x7 to 19x9.

Required:

Prepare common-size financial statements for the three-year period and identify any significant financial trends of the company.

SUNKYONG INDUSTRIES
Income Statement

	Won (millions)		
Revenue	*19x9*	*19x8*	*19x7*
Sales revenue	**578,637**	539,031	509,725
Nonoperating revenue	**34,976**	24,347	28,957
Interest income	**15,095**	8,578	10,593
Other nonoperating income	**19,881**	15,769	18,364
Total revenue	**613,613**	563,378	538,682
Expense			
Cost of sales	**469,202**	452,941	455,400
Selling & administrative expense	**57,726**	45,252	47,888
Nonoperating expense	**78,107**	63,320	31,956
Financial expense	**59,057**	48,045	23,618
Other expense	**19,050**	15,275	8,338
Total expense	**605,035**	561,513	535,244
Ordinary income	**8,578**	1,865	3,438
Extraordinary items	**244**	285	1,413
Net profit before tax	**8,822**	2,150	4,851
Income tax	**1,999**	415	2,216
Net profit after tax	**6,823**	1,735	2,635

SUNKYONG INDUSTRIES
Balance Sheets

	Won (millions)		
Assets	*19x9*	*19x8*	*19x7*
Current assets			
Cash on hand & in banks	**159,436**	100,935	14,744
Marketable securities	**19,437**	19,548	18,193
Accounts receivable—trade	**101,345**	90,733	82,579
Accounts receivable—others	**8,118**	5,540	8,406
Finished goods	**48,734**	35,806	33,237
Work in process	**9,884**	9,240	8,746
Raw materials & supplies	**27,990**	21,614	30,431
Prepaid expense	**2,940**	2,945	2,846
Other current assets	**25,327**	27,745	45,853
Total current assets	**403,211**	314,106	245,035
Investment & other assets			
Investment assets	**42,636**	9,198	2,659
Other assets	**27,365**	32,461	25,780
Total investment & other assets	**70,001**	41,659	28,439
Fixed assets			
Land	**30,999**	29,506	29,790
Buildings & structure	**94,649**	92,494	60,851
Machinery & equipment	**308,136**	303,560	132,990
Construction in progress	**27,819**	66,427	214,810
Other tangible assets	**21,750**	40,625	90,956
Intangible assets	**629**	662	664
Total fixed assets	**483,982**	533,274	530,041
Deferred charges	**16,888**	9,742	2,092
Total assets	**974,082**	898,781	805,607
Liabilities			
Current liabilities			
Accounts payable—trade	**102,022**	80,338	96,714
Short-term borrowings	**245,974**	175,292	126,751
Accounts payable—others	**12,771**	16,872	31,470
Accrued expenses	**6,418**	5,122	7,167
Current portion of long-term debt	**66,982**	99,145	32,235
Other current liabilities	**4,572**	856	2,825
Total current liabilities	**438,739**	377,625	297,162
Long-term liabilities			
Long-term debt	**94,756**	162,463	184,433
Bonds	**227,653**	141,301	122,847
Reserve for retirement	**42,016**	38,709	34,080
Total long-term liabilities	**364,425**	342,473	341,360
Deferred liabilities	**1,365**	3,345	5,522
Total liabilities	**804,529**	723,443	644,044

SUNKYONG INDUSTRIES
Balance Sheets (continued)

	19x9	*19x8*	*19x7*
Shareholders' Equity			
Total paid-in capital	**53,418**	50,440	43,992
Capital surplus	**88,978**	96,809	85,722
Retained earnings			
Reserves—legal & others	**19,293**	23,480	23,801
Other retained earnings	**1,041**	2,874	5,413
Net profit for the period	**6,823**	1,735	2,635
Total retained earnings	**27,157**	28,089	31,849
Total shareholders' equity	**169,553**	175,338	161,563
Total liabilities & shareholders' equity	**974,082**	898,781	805,607

12.5 Analyzing Cash Flows (Direct Method)

The following are selected financial data from The Lucky-Goldstar Group for 19x8 and 19x9.

Required:

(a) Using the available information, prepare a direct method statement of cash flows for 19x9.

(b) What conclusions can you draw from these data about the company's financial health?

THE LUCKY-GOLDSTAR GROUP
Statements of Income
For the Years Ended December 31, 19x9 and 19x8

	Millions of Won	
	19x9	*19x8*
Revenue		
Export sales	**5,447,868**	4,763,580
Domestic sales	**9,720,814**	8,602,381
Other income	**1,030,244**	94,984
	16,198,926	13,460,945
Costs and expenses		
Costs, excluding items below	**13,253,947**	11,177,715
Depreciation	**540,181**	349,936
Accrual of severance benefits	**141,244**	141,899
Selling, general, and administrative expenses	**1,346,277**	1,119,311
	15,281,649	12,788,861
Operating income	917,277	672,084
Other expenses		
Interest expense, net of interest income	**480,685**	383,617
Others, net	**121,063**	(29,653)
	601,748	353,964
Income before income taxes	**315,529**	318,120
Income taxes currently payable	**155,557**	125,609
Net income	**159,972**	192,511

THE LUCKY-GOLDSTAR GROUP
Statement of Changes in Financial Position
For the Years Ended December 31, 19x9 and 19x8

	Millions of Won	
	19x9	*19x8*
Sources of working capital		
From operations		
Net income	₩159,972	₩192,511
Items not affecting working capital		
Depreciation and amortization	690,808	493,644
Accrual of severance benefits	141,244	141,899
Foreign exchange translation loss	26,501	118
Loss on valuation of investments and others	(33,708)	—
Working capital provided from operations	984,817	828,172
Increase in long-term debt	1,970,643	1,447,172
Disposition of property, plant, and equipment	175,876	189,172
Issuance of capital stock for cash	633,426	971,475
Decrease in investments and other assets	330,771	280,638
Total sources of working capital	4,095,533	3,716,629
Uses of working capital		
Additions to property, plant, and equipment	1,408,467	1,624,110
Current maturities of long-term debt	752,143	363,087
Decrease in long-term payables and other	89,460	189,787
Increase in investments and other assets	840,754	654,304
Cash dividends	81,508	87,971
Payment of severance benefits	40,304	33,605
Increase in deferred charges	194,903	T104,126
Payment of revaluation tax and others	38,052	232
Total uses of working capital	3,445,591	3,057,222
Increase in working capital	₩649,942	₩659,407

Changes in components of working capital elements:

Increase (decrease) in current assets:		
Cash and bank deposits	64,121	241,247
Marketable securities	(300,744)	401,043
Accounts and notes receivable	930,634	481,903
Inventories	406,602	137,014
Short-term loans	474,925	35,032
Advance payments	59,051	12,244
Other current assets	1,153,392	1,633,830
Increase in current assets	2,787,981	2,942,313
Increase (decrease) in current liabilities:		
Accounts and notes payable	1,111,474	384,062
Short-term borrowings	950,079	148,947
Current maturities of long-term debt	365,622	14,362
Income taxes payable	17,609	(5,040)
Advances received	36,142	2,062
Withholding taxes	460,493	12,695
Other current liabilities	(803,380)	1,725,818
Increase in current liabilities	2,138,039	2,282,906
Increase in working capital	649,942	659,407

12.6 Korean versus U.S. GAAP

The following is the summary of significant accounting policies from the 1998 annual report of Samsung Electronics Co., Ltd. Samsung is a leading manufacturer and distributor of electronic consumer goods, communication facilities, semiconductors, and telecommunication equipment. The company's shares trade on the Korean Stock Exchange, as American Depository Receipts in the United States, and as Global Depository Shares in the U.K.

Required:

Review the accounting policies used by Samsung and identify those policies that deviate from generally accepted accounting practice in the United States.

SAMSUNG ELECTRONICS CO., LTD.
Selected Annual Report Excerpts
Summary of Significant Accounting Policies

The significant accounting policies followed by the Company in the preparation of its financial statements are summarized below.

Transitional Presentation of Comparative Financial Statements
In accordance with the transition clause of the addendum to the revised financial accounting standards generally accepted in the Republic of Korea effective January 1, 1997, the Company has not presented financial statements for the year ended December 31, 1996 for comparative purposes.

Basis of Financial Statement Presentation
The official accounting records of the Company are maintained in Korean Won in accordance with the laws and regulations of the Republic of Korea. For the convenience of the reader, the accompanying financial statements have been condensed, restructured and translated into English from the statutory Korean language financial statements, with certain expanded descriptions. Certain supplementary information included in the statutory financial statements, not required for a fair presentation of the Company's financial position or results of operations, is not presented in the accompanying financial statements.

Marketable Securities
Marketable securities are stated at cost, which approximates market value.

Allowance for Doubtful Accounts
The Company provides an allowance for doubtful accounts and notes receivable based on the aggregate estimated collectibility of the amounts receivable.

Inventory Valuation
Inventories are stated at the lower of cost or market, cost being determined by the average cost method, except for materials in transit which are stated at actual cost as determined by the specific identification method.

Property, Plant and Equipment and Related Depreciation
Property, plant and equipment are stated at cost, except for certain assets subject to upward revaluation in accordance with the Asset Revaluation Law. The revaluation presents production facilities and other buildings at their depreciated replacement cost, and land at the prevailing market price, as of the effective date of revaluation. The revaluation increment, net of 3% tax, is first applied to offset accumulated deficit, if any, and the remainder may either be credited to capital surplus or may be transferred to common stock. A new basis for calculating depreciation is established for revalued assets.

Depreciation is computed using the straight-line method, based on the estimated useful lives of the assets as described below.

	Estimated Useful Lives (Years)
Buildings and auxiliary facilities	7–60
Machinery and equipment	2–8
Tools and fixtures	2–10
Structures and other	2–40

In 1997, the Company extended the estimated useful lives of property, plant and equipment to improve the matching of revenue and expenses in recognition of the changes in the Company's business environment. Pursuant to revised Korean Corporate Income Tax Law, the residual value of assets acquired on or before December 31, 1994, is depreciated over three years following the year in which 90% of the cost is fully depreciated. If 1997 depreciation had been computed on the same basis as that of the prior year, depreciation expense for the year ended December 31, 1997, would be greater by approximately ₩23,910 million. As a result of this change, net income for the year ended December 31, 1997, is approximately ₩458,517 million greater than that which would have been reported under the previous accounting method.

In conformity with Korean accounting practices, the Company recognizes special accelerated depreciation expense on certain plant and equipment acquired on or before December 31, 1994, which are used in operations more than 12 hours a day on average. During 1997, the Company recognized special depreciation of ₩2,650 million.

The Company capitalizes interest as part of the cost of constructing major facilities and equipment. Interest costs of ₩62,325 million were capitalized in 1997.

Maintenance and Repairs

Routine maintenance and repairs are charged to expense as incurred. Expenditures which enhance the value or extend the useful life of the related assets are capitalized.

Investments in Subsidiaries and Affiliated Companies

Investments in subsidiaries and affiliated companies are reported at cost, except where market value or net book value declines significantly compared to acquisition cost and is not expected to recover, in which case the investment is reduced to the market value or net book value.

Under generally accepted financial accounting standards in the Republic of Korea, neither consolidation of subsidiaries nor the equity method of accounting for minority owned companies is applied in the primary financial statements of the Company.

Pursuant to the revised generally accepted financial accounting standards effective January 1, 1997, equity investments in publicly traded companies excluding subsidiaries and affiliated companies, classified as noncurrent deposits and other assets, are reported at market value and the differences between the market value and the acquisition cost are treated as gains or losses on the valuation of investments in equity securities, a component of shareholders' equity. As a result of this change, shareholders' equity as of December 31, 1997, is approximately ₩909 million less than that which would have been reported under the previous accounting method.

The company is required to prepare, in addition to these unconsolidated financial statements, audited financial statements that are consolidated with those of certain domestic and overseas subsidiaries as defined by Consolidation Financial Accounting Standards. Such audited consolidated financial statements for 1997 are required to be prepared by April 30, 1998.

Deferred Charges

Research and development costs, as well as stock and debenture issuance costs are charged to operations as incurred.

Deferred foreign exchange losses are amortized over the terms of the related debt using the straight-line method.

Deferred discounts or premiums related to debentures are amortized to interest expense over the terms of the related debentures using the straight-line method.

Accrued Severance Benefits

Employees and directors with more than one year of service are entitled to receive a lump-sum payment upon termination of their employment with the Company, based on their length of service and rate of pay at the time of termination. Accrued severance benefits which would be payable assuming all eligible employees terminated their employment as of December 31, 1997, are ₩777,358,321 thousand.

Severance pay expense is calculated based on the net change in the accrued severance benefit liability assuming the termination of all eligible employees as of the beginning and end of the accounting period.

Under prevailing generally accepted accounting standards, as of December 31, 1990, accrued severance benefits were underaccrued by approximately ₩42,254 million. The Company is adjusting the underaccrued severance benefits over 10 years beginning in 1991 in accordance with the provisions of the Addendum of the Financial Accounting Standards of the Republic of Korea. Accordingly, for the year ended December 31, 1997, the Company deducted ₩4,225 million from retained earnings for additional accrued severance benefits.

Accrued severance benefits are funded approximately 45% at December 31, 1997, through a group severance insurance plan with Samsung Life Insurance Company, Ltd. The amounts funded under this insurance plan are classified as noncurrent deposits and other assets. Subsequent accruals are to be funded at the discretion of the Company.

In accordance with the National Pension Act, a certain portion of accrued severance benefits is deposited with the National Pension Fund and deducted from the accrued severance benefits liability. The contributed amount shall be refunded from the National Pension Fund to employees on their retirement.

Foreign Currency Translation

Monetary assets and liabilities denominated in foreign currencies are translated into Korean Won at the rates prevailing at the balance sheet date (in the case of US Dollars, US$1 = ₩1,415.20). Resulting exchange losses and gains are included in operations.

However, in accordance with the revision of financial accounting standards in 1997, net unrealized losses and gains arising from long-term foreign currency assets and liabilities are recorded as deferred charges or liabilities. Foreign exchange losses from long-term foreign currency liabilities, previously charged to shareholders' equity as a foreign exchange debit have been transferred to deferred charges. As a result of this change, 1997 net income is approximately ₩306,242 million less and shareholders' equity is approximately ₩3,176,319 million greater than that which would have been reported under the previous accounting method.

Income Taxes

The provision for income taxes is comprised of corporate tax, resident tax and agriculture and fishery development special tax surcharges, payable for the current year. In conformity with accounting practices prevailing in the Republic of Korea, the Company does not recognize deferred income taxes arising from temporary differences between amounts reported for financial accounting and income tax reporting purposes.

Investment tax credits are recognized as a reduction of income tax expense in the year in which they are utilized.

Earnings Per Share

Earnings per share are computed, after deduction of dividends declared on preferred stock, using the weighted average number of common shares outstanding during the period.

Product Warranties and Performance Guarantees

In conformity with accounting practices prevailing in the Republic of Korea, costs related to repairs, service and other work required in accordance with product warranties and performance guarantees are charged to expense when incurred.

12.7 Accounting for Foreign Currency Translation

Following are the financial statements for Samsung Electronics Co., Ltd. as of year-end 1997. According to the company's footnotes, the method of foreign currency translation is as follows:

> Monetary assets and liabilities denominated in foreign currencies are translated into Korean Won at the rates prevailing at the balance sheet date. Resulting exchange gains and losses are included in operations.
>
> However, in accordance with the revision of financial accounting standards in 1997, net unrealized losses and gains arising from long-term foreign currency assets and liabilities are recorded as deferred charges or liabilities.

Required:

(a) What method of foreign currency translation accounting is being used by Samsung? How does that approach compare to U.S. GAAP?

(b) Assume that Samsung is using the temporal method as per U.S. GAAP, how would its financial statements differ?

(c) Assume that Samsung is using the current rate method as per U.S. GAAP, how would its financial statements differ?

SAMSUNG ELECTRONICS CO. LTD.
Statement of Income
for the year ended December 31, 1997

	In Thousands of Korean Won
Sales:	
Domestic	8,013,718,934
Export	10,451,640,507
	18,465,359,441
Cost of sales	12,701,065,224
Gross profit	5,764,294,217
Selling, general, and administrative expenses	2,908,073,790
Operating profit	2,856,220,427
Nonoperating income:	
Interest and dividend income	171,182,036
Gain on foreign currency transactions	1,869,713,309
Other	411,715,036
	2,452,610,381
Nonoperating expenses:	
Interest expenses	759,045,307
Amortization of deferred charges	1,581,287,365
Loss on foreign currency transactions	2,092,372,147
Other	720,061,983
	5,152,766,802
Ordinary profit	156,064,006
Extraordinary income	65,610
Extraordinary loss	2,508,902
Net income before income taxes	153,620,714
Income taxes	30,115,805
Net income	123,504,909
Earnings per share (in Korean Won and U.S. Dollars)	1,232

SAMSUNG ELECTRONICS CO. LTD.
Balance Sheet
December 31, 1997

In Thousands of Korean Won

ASSETS

Current assets:

Cash and bank deposits	1,367,157,250
Marketable securities	44,365,620
Accounts and notes receivable,	
less allowance for doubtful accounts of ₩29,871,528 thousand	3,308,507,239
Inventories	2,341,451,639
Guarantee deposits	331,116,907
Other	388,714,910
Total current assets	7,781,313,565
Property, plant and equipment,	
including revalued portion, net of accumulated depreciation	7,159,313,067
Investments in subsidiaries and affiliated companies,	
less valuation allowance of 5,584,116 thousand	2,509,654,756
Noncurrent deposits and other assets	2,438,895,146
Deferred charges	3,176,340,631
	23,065,517,165

LIABILITIES AND SHAREHOLDERS' EQUITY

Current liabilities:

Accounts and notes payable	1,946,117,338
Short-term borrowings	1,311,944,971
Current maturities of long-term debt	1,383,898,185
Accrued expenses	836,591,876
Dividends payable	59,969,415
Income taxes payable	8,981,053
Other	322,053,208
Total current liabilities	5,869,556,046
Long-term debt, net of current maturities	8,394,519,378
Foreign currency notes and bonds	2,278,904,464
Accrued severance benefits,	
net of W MACRO72,107,419 thousand transferred to national pension	692,574,539
Deferred liabilities	21,757
Total liabilities	17,235,576,184
Commitments and contingencies	
Shareholders' equity:	
Capital stock:	
Common stock	490,350,200
Preferred stock	119,467,135
Revaluation surplus	24,400,991
Other capital surplus	1,451,541,645
Retained earnings:	
Appropriated	4,030,347,930
Unappropriated	31,881
Capital adjustments:	
Treasury stock	(427,838,371)
Consideration for conversion rights	142,549,059
Loss on valuation of investments in equity securities	(909,489)
Total shareholders' equity	5,829,940,981
	23,065,517,165

12.8 Accounting for Retained Earnings

Presented below is the Statement of Retained Earnings for Samsung Electronics Co. Ltd. as of year-end 1997. Also presented is the company's explanatory footnote for its various equity reserves. Samsung's shareholders' equity section of its 1997 balance sheet appeared as follows:

Shareholders' Equity *(Thousands of Won)*	
Capital stock:	
Common stock	490,350,200
Preferred stock	119,467,135
Revaluation surplus	24,400,991
Other capital surplus	1,451,541,645
Retained earnings (See note 12):	
Appropriated	4,030,347,930
Unappropriated	31,881
Capital adjustments:	
Treasury stock	(427,838,371)
Conversion rights	142,549,059
Valuation allowance for equity securities	(909,489)
Total	5,829,940,981

Required:

(a) Write a brief explanation of the role or purpose of each of Samsung's equity reserves.

(b) Why is there such a disparity in size between Samsung's appropriated versus unappropriated retained earnings?

(c) At a statutory tax rate of 28 percent, how much income tax has Samsung saved through Korea's system of tax-deductible reserves?

SAMSUNG ELECTRONICS CO. LTD.
Statement of Retained Earnings
for the year ended December 31, 1997

	In Thousands of Korean Won
Date of appropriation: March 27, 1998 for 1997	
Unappropriated retained earnings,	
end of the year:	
Carried forward from prior year	31,611
Additional accrued severance benefits (Note 2)	(4,225,454)
Net income for the year	123,504,909
	119,311,066
Transfers from voluntary reserves (Note 12):	
Reserve for overseas market development	15,609,315
Reserve for overseas investment losses	21,799,899
Reserve for technology development	90,000,000
Reserve for export losses	18,631,016
	146,040,230
Appropriations (Note 12): Legal reserve	10,000,000
Reserve for business rationalization	100,000,000
Reserve for improvement of financial structure	30,000,000
Reserve for technology development	65,350,000
Cash dividends	59,969,415
(Common stock: 10%) (Preferred stock: 11%)	
	265,319,415
Unappropriated retained earnings to subsequent year	31,881

12. RETAINED EARNINGS

Retained earnings at December 31, 1997, comprise the following:

	Reference	Thousands of Won
Appropriated:		
Legal reserve	(A)	187,789,000
Reserve for business rationalization	(B)	712,100,829
Reserve for improvement of financial structure	(C)	204,815,000
Reserve for overseas market development	(D)	655,941,108
Reserve for overseas investment losses	(D)	353,782,252
Reserve for technology development	(D)	1,428,186,683
Reserve for export losses	(D)	353,118,058
Reserve for facilities	(E)	134,615,000
		4,030,347,930
Unappropriated:		31,881
		4,030,379,811

(A) The Korean Commercial Code requires the Company to appropriate as a legal reserve an amount equal to a minimum of 10% of annual cash dividends declared until the reserve equals 50% of capital stock. This reserve is not available for the payment of cash dividends but may be transferred to capital stock or used to reduce accumulated deficit, if any.

(B) Pursuant to the Tax Exemption and Reduction Control Law, the Company is required to appropriate as a reserve for business rationalization, an amount equal to the exemption of income taxes resulting from investment tax credits and certain deductions from taxable income specified by such law. This reserve may be used for the reduction of accumulated deficit, if any, or transferred to capital stock.

(C) The Financial Control Regulations for listed companies require the Company to appropriate as a reserve for improvement of financial structure an amount equal to at least 50% of the net extraordinary gain on disposal of property, plant and equipment and 10% of net earnings for each year until the Company's net worth equals 30% of total assets. This reserve is not available for payment of cash dividends, but may be transferred to capital stock or used to reduce accumulated deficit, if any.

(D) Pursuant to Korean tax laws, the Company is allowed to claim the amounts of retained earnings appropriated for reserves for overseas market development, overseas investment losses, technology development and export losses as deductions in determining taxable income. These amounts are not available for dividends until used for the specified purposes or reversed.

(E) The reserve for facilities represents amounts appropriated by the Company for capital expenditures and may be used for any purpose through shareholders' resolution.

12.9 International Accounting Standards and Security Prices

Presented on the next page are comparative market-based data for seven countries as of May 1998. Assume that the capital markets in these countries are relatively efficient. Review these data and then comment on the following questions:

Required:

(a) Sequence the countries from highest to lowest using the average price-earnings multiple. Which countries appear to have the most conservative GAAP? The least conservative GAAP? Based upon your reading in this text, is the ordering about what you expected? If not, what explanation can you offer?

(b) Sequence the countries from highest to lowest using the average price/book value multiple. Which countries appear to have the most conservative GAAP? The least conservative GAAP? Is this sequence consistent with your ordering from question 1? If not, why not?

(c) Sequence the countries from highest to lowest using the average price/EBITDA. Which countries appear to have the highest average valuations? The lowest average valuations? If you were a "momentum investor," in which countries would you be most likely to invest? If you were a "value investor," in which countries would you be most likely to invest?

Country	Average Price-Earnings Multiple	Average Price/EBITDA Multiple	Average Price/Book Value Multiple
Britain	19.5	12.7	3.8
Germany	31.2	9.8	3.7
Italy	29.1	10.1	3.1
Japan	43.3	9.9	1.8
Mexico	16.6	9.6	2.3
S. Korea	110.7	3.7	0.7
United States	26.6	15.6	4.6

12.10 Annual Report Analysis

An interesting and important challenge for students of international financial reporting is to study the published annual reports of various companies from different countries. Your instructor will provide you with a recent copy of a Korean annual report. To facilitate your delving into this annual report, undertake the following endeavors.

Required:

(a) List the key differences between the Korean annual report you were given and what you would expect to see for a U.S. company in the same industry.

(b) Calculate the following ratios taking care to note the assumptions you found necessary to make and where you found the appropriate pieces of data in the annual report.

(1) Current ratio $= \dfrac{\text{Total current assets}}{\text{Total current liabilities}}$

(2) Quick ratio $= \dfrac{\text{Cash} + \text{Marketable securities} + \text{Accounts Receivable}}{\text{Total current liabilities}}$

(3) Operating cash flow to current liabilities $= \dfrac{\text{Operating cash flow}}{\text{Average total current liabilities}}$

(4) Debt-to-equity ratio $= \dfrac{\text{Long-term debt}}{\text{Owners' equity}}$

(5) Debt-to-total capitalization ratio $= \dfrac{\text{Long-term debt}}{\text{Long-term debt} + \text{Owners' equity}}$

(6) Interest coverage ratio $= \dfrac{\text{Net income before interest and income taxes}}{\text{Interest expense}}$

(7) Operating cash flow to interest charges $= \dfrac{\text{Operating cash flow}}{\text{Interest expense}}$

(8) Operating cash flow to total liabilities $= \dfrac{\text{Operating cash flow}}{\text{Average total liabilities}}$

(9) Receivables turnover ratio $= \dfrac{\text{Net sales}}{\text{Average accounts receivable}}$

(10) Inventory turnover $= \dfrac{\text{Cost of goods sold}}{\text{Average inventory}}$

(11) Asset turnover $= \dfrac{\text{Net sales}}{\text{Average total assets}}$

(12) Average collection period ratio $= \dfrac{\text{365 Days}}{\text{Receivables turnover ratio}}$

(13) Average number of days' inventory on hand ratio $= \dfrac{\text{365 Days}}{\text{Inventory turnover ratio}}$

(14) Return on assets (ROA) $= \dfrac{\text{Net income}}{\text{Average total assets}}$

$OR = \text{ROS} \times \text{Asset turnover}$

(15) Return on equity (ROE) $= \dfrac{\text{Net income}}{\text{Average total owners' equity}}$

$OR = \text{ROA} \times \text{Financial leverage}$

(16) Return on sales (ROS) $= \dfrac{\text{Net income}}{\text{Net sales}}$

(17) Financial leverage $= \dfrac{\text{Average liabilities + Average owners' equity}}{\text{Average owners' equity}}$

(18) Basic earnings per share (EPS) $= \dfrac{\text{NI applicable to common shareholders}}{\text{Weighted average common shares}}$

(19) Cash dividend yield $= \dfrac{\text{Cash dividend per common share}}{\text{Market price per common share}}$

(20) Cash dividend payout $= \dfrac{\text{Total cash dividend to common shareholders}}{\text{Net income}}$

(c) What do you conclude about the availability of the appropriate data in the annual report for calculating these ratios?

(d) What does this financial analysis tell you about this Korean company?

(e) What analytical metrics did this Korean company choose to report for itself? What do those choices say about the message the company is striving to tell and the audience it is addressing?

Italy

Inadequate disclosure requirements and insufficient safeguards for minority shareholders . . . may have slowed down the development of the securities market.[1]

Italian accounting is now devoting much energy to the public financial statement.[2]

Introduction

For a variety of reasons, Italy found the going difficult as it sought to harmonize its financial reporting standards with those of other European Union members. Despite being a founding member of the EU, Italy did not implement the Fourth and Seventh Directives until 1991. The reasons for this delay included the magnitude of the required change and the lack of accounting experience and expertise on crucial topics such as consolidations. Among the more deeply rooted reasons were the relative insignificance of the country's equity markets, the prominence of family-controlled companies in the Italian economy, and the incentive to suppress or distort financial information caused by the traditional association of accounting income with tax collection. The former set of problems has confronted legislators and accounting professionals with procedural obstacles as they devise and implement changes; the latter continues to raise questions about the purpose of financial reporting in Italy as the nation's economy moves from semi-industrialized insularity toward international integration.

Change is proceeding in Italy, regardless of how difficult and incremental the steps may be. The status of the accounting profession is increasing as government and business alike realize the necessity of a sophisticated corps of experts to develop and operate financial reporting systems. During the 1970s, a new agency modeled on the U.S. Securities and Exchange Commission, the ***Commissione Nazionale per le Societá e la Borsa*** (*CONSOB*), was created to regulate Italy's securities markets. And even though Italy does not have a formidable contingent of internationally traded companies resolutely leading the private sector toward international reporting (as Germany and Sweden

---

[1]A. Goldstein and G. Nicoletti, "Italy: Corporate Governance," *The OECD Observer,* February/March 1995, p. 48.

[2]E. Viganò, "Accounting and Business Economics Traditions in Italy," *European Accounting Review* 7, no. 3 (1998), p. 395.

do), high visibility firms such as Fiat and Pirelli are finding it advantageous to adopt international accounting standards and to prepare consolidated statements. As a charter member of the EU, a major industrial power, and a nation whose economy depends on international trade, Italy has no intention of being left out as the rest of the industrialized world lays the groundwork for a new global economic order.

Environmental Factors

*Cultural
Environment*

Generally speaking, the results of Hofstede's study of cultural attitudes suggests that groups of subjects scoring high in uncertainty avoidance can be found in countries with accounting systems based on statutory law: Germany, Japan, France, Brazil, and others. (It should be noted that Sweden provides a notable exception to this generalization for reasons that are discussed in the chapter on that country.) Because he is more concerned with organizational behavior than financial reporting practices, however, Hofstede never attempts to establish a correlation between national culture and financial reporting. Other researchers, though, have drawn on his research to do so. Gray, for example, advances the hypothesis that a country with high scores in uncertainty avoidance and power distance and a low score in individualism is likely to have a financial reporting environment characterized by uniformity (i.e., one that is legislated by a central power rather than negotiated by contending parties).[3]

Italy seems to bear out this tentative generalization, at least in part. Italian financial reporting is characterized by a high degree of legal prescription, and the Italian subjects surveyed in Hofstede's study scored high in uncertainty avoidance: a 75, compared to a 46 for the United States. This score, along with a score of 50 in power distance, places Italy in the organizational paradigm that Hofstede calls the "pyramid of people." Hofstede describes this paradigm as hierarchical, held together by unity of command and adherence to rules. Employees operating under the pyramid paradigm are more likely to settle a disagreement by referral to higher authority than by negotiation. The strong appeal of hierarchical authority in Italian culture is evident in a number of the nation's traditional social structures such as the patriarchal structure of Italian families, the dominance of Roman Catholicism, and the influence of authoritarianism on the nation's political history and public discourse. (Although Italy and the rest of Continental Europe have attempted to shed the heritage of fascism, splinter groups still garner more than token support. In the case of Italy, the neofascist party has been capturing a noticeable percentage of the voters in recent national elections.) Even though the general tenor that Italian politics has taken since World War II could hardly be labeled authoritarian, it is still characterized by relatively strong central government initiatives and relatively weak local and regional control. Moreover, while political power in Italy is split among numerous parties, discipline within parties is strong, and voters do not change their allegiances easily.

Nevertheless, the reality of Italian organizational and political culture is predictably complex. It cannot be adequately described merely by appealing to the authoritarian and hierarchical elements mentioned. The Italians in Hofstede's survey also registered a high score in individualism (76), which suggests a very different side of the national character, one that is reflected in the popular stereotype of the passionate and rebellious Mediterranean temperament. If many Italians have been and continue to be attracted by

---

[3]S. J. Gray, "Towards a Theory of Cultural Influence on the Development of Accounting Systems Internationally," *Abacus* 24, no. 1 (1988), pp. 1–15.

the stability offered by hierarchical authority, others are repelled by the restrictions it places on individual freedom. More than 90 percent of the population calls itself Roman Catholic, but few actually attend worship services, and Italians are not noted for docile submission to papal pronouncements. Likewise, Italian families, both domestic and political, are justly reputed for the frequency and vehemence of their internal disagreements. Italians, it might be said, enjoy more than most societies the emotional support and emotional release that social structures such as family, religion, and regionalism may provide, but they do not necessarily want such institutions to assert excessive control over their personal actions.[4] As one veteran reporter observed, there is a "battle which is waging perpetually in the Italian character between the forces of self-destructive irresponsibility and those of responsible pragmatism."[5]

The peculiar ambivalence that marks the Italians' attitude toward authority results in notoriously inefficient social administration, a problem that affects financial accounting as well as other areas of Italian business. Although the rules governing Italian financial reporting practices are prescribed by a central authority, the resulting system is neither orderly nor particularly effective (at least by Anglo-American standards). Historically, a lack of coordination among tax law, company law, and securities law has created a plethora of rules and made compliance a nontrivial process. Businesses must exercise caution, lest in fulfilling one set of requirements, they violate another. Moreover, since 1991 "virtually all of the previous regulation dealing with the technical and professional side of accounting has been swept away,"[6] introducing an era of new debate and a fresh focus on the purpose and role of financial reporting in Italy. Such a catalyst is needed if Italy is ever to address the informational needs of an international financial constituency.

Legal and Political Environment

EU Membership.   The most effective impetus for change in Italian financial reporting is Italy's membership in the European Union. As mentioned in Chapter 3, the EU has issued two directives that bear directly on financial reporting: the Fourth Directive, concerning the format and content of financial statements, and the Seventh Directive, concerning the preparation of consolidated statements. The requirements of these directives do not impose a prefabricated system on member nations; rather, each country must revise its laws within a certain time period so that they conform to the directives in all essential points. (Some flexibility is built into the requirements of the directives.) Both directives have necessitated substantial change in Italian accounting practices.

In late 1991, Italy formally adopted both directives by revising its civil code. (All other EU members at the time had previously adopted and implemented the Fourth Directive.) The detailed principles being developed by the Italian accounting profession (discussed subsequently) are, for the most part, now fully consistent with the requirements of the directives. The Fourth Directive took effect for fiscal years ending December 31, 1993; the Seventh Directive's consolidation requirements took effect one year later.[7] Until the Seventh Directive took effect, only companies listed on stock exchanges were

---

[4]See "Vox Populi," *The Economist,* June 26, 1993, pp. Survey 6–12 and "Great Expectations," *The Economist,* June 26, 1993, pp. Survey 21–22.

[5]J. Wyles, "Dynamic but Deadlocked," *Financial Times,* April 17, 1990, p. I. Italy was not a part of Hofstede's studies involving the LTO cultural dimension and as a result, it is not discussed here. It is useful to note, however, that Italians have a relatively high savings rate, comparable to the Japanese, who score relatively high on the LTO dimension. See "Northern Grit," *The Economist,* June 26, 1993, pp. Survey 12–15.

[6]S. Zambon and C. Saccon, "Accounting Change in Italy," *European Accounting Review* September 1993, pp. 245–84.

[7]C. Nobes and S. Zambon, "Piano, Piano: Italy Implements the Directives," *Accountancy,* July 1991, pp. 84–85.

required to prepare and publish consolidated statements, and there was no formal requirement that such statements be independently audited (though in practice most large companies have this done). Now, consolidation accounts are required for groups meeting two of the following three size tests: (1) total assets of more than L10 billion ($5,583,000), (2) sales of more than L20 billion ($11,167,000), and (3) more than 250 employees.[8] For the years prior to the directives' implementation, the *CONSOB* directed companies to follow International Accounting Standards Committee (IASC) pronouncements, and that is why a company such as Fiat explicitly states in its annual report that it adhered to IASC standards when most large international companies from around the world make no reference to IASC standards.

Political Instability.   The volatility of Italian politics is well known. Since World War II, Italy has experienced more than 56 governments, with few administrations lasting more than a year (the longest was that of Bettino Craxi in the 1980s—1,058 days). The frequent changes can be attributed to the multiparty structure of Italian politics (over 40 parties were active in recent elections), because any single party is unlikely to achieve an outright parliamentary majority, much less maintain one. Thus, cabinets are forced to rely on coalitions (usually tenuous ones) to muster sufficient support to stay in power. Administrations topple when disgruntled coalition members decide to switch allegiance or walk out. The advantage of such a system, of course, is that it allows considerable room for active dissent, and, consequently, minority groups often exercise real power. The disadvantage is equally obvious: Achieving and maintaining effective governance is difficult. Indeed, corporate managers often lament, "We want stability. We need a government that can last long enough to make the changes that are needed."[9]

Paradoxically, the very volatility of this system has hampered accounting reform in Italy. Changing a nation's legal infrastructure requires deliberation, resolution, and, above all, a government strong enough to see the job through. Because Italian accounting practices are based on statutory law, the process of major reform is complex and beset with political pitfalls. Under Italy's parliamentary system, cabinets are simply too weak to initiate and push through reform measures by themselves. Although reform measures do not disappear when a cabinet is relieved of office, administrative shuffles routinely delay their approval and implementation by months or even years. Such delays were the reason that important stock exchange regulations were bottled up in the Italian parliament (see the following discussion) and that Italy was among the last EU member nations to incorporate the requirements of the Fourth Directive in its company law.

Taxation of Shareholders.   Dividend and interest income are both taxed as ordinary income under Italian tax law. (Tax rates on individuals run from 10 percent to 51 percent. An additional "local" tax rate of 16.2 percent does not apply to dividends and interest.) Under the imputation system now in effect, however, recipients of dividends from Italian companies are entitled to a tax credit designed to provide at least partial relief from double taxation of corporate profits. The credit, available to corporate as well as individual shareholders, is currently set at 56.25 percent of dividend payments received, and the amount of the credit is included in income along with the amount of the dividend received.

---

[8]Zambon and Saccon, "Accounting Change in Italy." The Italian *lire* is often noted as Lit or L. As of April 12, 1999, $US1 = L1,791.

[9]B. Coleman, "Italy's Economic Backbone, the North, Is Heeded in Search for New Leadership," *The Wall Street Journal,* December 29, 1994, p. A6.

Hence the recipient of L10,000,000 (US$5,583) in dividends from an Italian corporation also receives a tax credit of L5,625,000 ($3,140) and is required to show L15,625,000 ($8,729) of income on his or her tax return. If the taxpayer were in the 36 percent bracket, the dividend income would generate no extra tax liability (15,625,000 times 36 percent, less the credit of 5,625,000, equals zero). Of course, if the taxpayer were in a bracket higher than 36 percent, the marginal tax liability generated by the dividend income would exceed the tax credit. Because the basic national tax rate for corporations is 37 percent, the imputed credit is obviously designed to enable corporate shareholders to receive dividends substantially tax free.

Capital gains on the sale of shares are included in the ordinary income of business enterprises. Prior to September 1993, however, they were not taxable to individuals. Since that date, capital gains have been taxable to individuals at preferential rates between 20 and 30 percent, depending on various parameters.

Corporate Tax Law.   As mentioned, the basic national corporate tax rate in Italy is 37 percent. Nondeductible regional taxes raise the effective tax rate to approximately 53 percent, however. Taxable income is calculated by adjusting book income to reflect tax law. Such adjustments generally include adding back expenses that are nondeductible for tax purposes or that exceed statutory allowances (such as excess depreciation, bad debt allowances, and maintenance costs) and applying tax losses carried forward from a previous period. Book income is not required to equal taxable income, although it frequently closely approximates it.

Because financial statements provide the basis for tax returns, tax rules do affect book income. Most costs and expenses are not deductible for tax purposes unless they are also shown on the income statement; hence, tax considerations often induce Italian corporate management to record a larger expense than is required under accepted financial accounting principles. For example, fixed assets with a unit cost of less than L1 million (about $558) may be fully written off for tax purposes but only if they are also fully written off for accounting purposes. Moreover, most companies adopt the maximum depreciation allowable for tax purposes as their depreciation expense on the financial statements. This propensity to conservatively measure reported earnings is commonly referred to as *fiscal bias* and creates a significant challenge for those analysts and investors interested in comparing the financial results of Italian companies with counterparts from other countries.

Most Italian companies accrue income taxes payable based on an estimate of their tax liability when the next return will be filed (i.e., a flow-thru approach). Although interperiod tax allocation is not widespread, some companies adopt a form of it in accordance with international accounting standards in which they account for deferred taxes only to the extent that an actual liability is expected to arise within the next three years. Accordingly, an Italian company can avoid a deferred tax charge if there is some conviction that the tax will not be payable within three years.[10] As might be expected, the deferred income taxes that are reported are relatively immaterial in amount.

Business Environment

Form of Business.   The business entity in Italy that most closely approximates the U.S. corporation is the joint stock company, or the *Società per Azioni (S.p.A.)*. Italian law requires an *S.p.A.* to have minimum capital of L200 million ($111,670). An *S.p.A.* must create and maintain a legal reserve to which it allocates 5 percent of after-tax profits each year until the reserve equals 20 percent of paid-in capital. In addition, an *S.p.A.* must have more than one shareholder to be granted limited liability status under the law; owners of

---

[10]R. Khalaf, "Buyer Beware," *Forbes,* June 20, 1994, pp. 204–5.

100 percent of the stock of an *S.p.A.* are personally liable without limitation for all debts of the business. An *S.p.A.* may operate either under a single director or a board of directors, however. It is the preferred form of business for large enterprises.

The **Società a Responsibilità Limitada** *(S.r.l.)* is the other major limited liability entity; it is often used to form small businesses and closely held concerns. An *S.r.l.* must possess minimum capital of only L20 million (about $11,167), which is represented not by shares but by quotas or parts held by investors. Quotas may differ in amount but may not be less than L1,000 (about 56¢). Quota holders are liable only to the extent of their capital contributions.

Italy's first antitrust law was passed in 1990 and applies to both state-owned and private companies. In general, it seeks to outlaw agreements that restrict free competition and abuses of dominant position, and it subjects all mergers of a certain size to scrutiny for their effect on competitive forces. Historically, Italian industry has been dominated by public and private conglomerates that enjoy close relations with certain banks, newspapers, and insurance companies. Skeptics believe the new antitrust law will do little to alter this scenario. It is expected, however, that the law will offer consumers and small businesses real opportunities for redress against abuses of the large industrial units' dominant positions, as well as to society at large, in hindering the corporate tendency to seek easy gain via alliances that thwart competition.

A particularly unique feature of the Italian business landscape is the preponderance, on the one hand, of relatively small companies and, on the other, of large state-owned conglomerates. For example, Germany's 320 machine-tool companies average 200 workers per company whereas Italy's 450 companies average 70 workers.[11] Moreover, Italy is the world's fourth largest machine tools manufacturer but it has only a handful of companies ranked among Europe's 40 largest. Stated in a slightly more comprehensive manner, 39 percent of all Italian companies have less than 100 employees as compared to 21 percent in the United Kingdom.[12] Historically, Italian small businesses' only source of external financing has been short-term bank loans, with a real dearth of long-term loans and venture capital available.[13] At the other end of the spectrum, "of all Western economies, Italy still depends most heavily on state-owned entities that dominate whole [industrial] sectors."[14] These goliath-like conglomerates have not had to rely on an equities market for financing. Thus, given these two dominating features of the Italian business portfolio, there has been no real industrial demand for a broad, deep, sophisticated equity market and the business disclosures and governance that typically accompany such a market.

Audit and Reporting Requirements.   Every *S.p.A.* and every *S.r.l* with capital of more than L200 million must appoint a board of statutory auditors to monitor company management and ascertain that the company's books and financial statements conform to the requirements of the Italian civil code. These auditors must have some degree of independence: They may not be related to directors by blood or marriage and may not be employees of the corporation, but they may hold stock in it. At least one of the members must have certain business qualifications (not necessarily in auditing). In general, however, the role of the statutory auditor is not that of the trained independent auditor who undertakes the fairness attest function.

---

[11]"The Complications of Clustering," *The Economist,* January 2, 1999, pp. 53–54.

[12]A. Hill, "The Small Imbroglio," *Financial Times,* May 9, 1995, p. 14.

[13]See "Change in the Heartland," *The Economist,* April 2, 1994, pp. 63–64, and J. Simkins, "Shift towards Bigger Units," *Financial Times,* October 13, 1993, p. 28.

[14]J. Valente, "Two Paths, Two Problems," *The Wall Street Journal,* September 30, 1994, p. R8.

In addition to the largely formal oversight of statutory auditors, certain companies must submit their annual statements to an examination by an officially authorized auditing firm. (Independent audits were virtually unknown in Italy before 1975.) These companies include those listed on stock exchanges, those controlled or financed by the state, insurance companies, publishers with substantial income from periodicals, contractors bidding on large public construction projects, and several other types of enterprises. The agency that authorizes firms to perform independent audits is Italy's version of the SEC, the *CONSOB*. According to a law passed in 1981, Italian firms may retain an auditor for a maximum of nine years, after which it must hire a new one. (This law applies even to very large companies.) Accountants and managers alike have complained bitterly about the hardships this measure entails on auditors and their clients.

The nature of an independent auditor's attestation has evolved during the 20th century. Prior to the 1942 code, *S.p.A.s* were required to file financial statements that depicted

[w]ith straightwardness and truth the financial situation and the economic results of the company. The 1942 Civil Code [set forth the concept that] the balance sheet and profit and loss account should present with clearness and precision a company's financial position and results. [Then a 1974 law establishing the CONSOB also established] the fundamental innovation of the introduction of compulsory external audit for listed companies. [A 1975 presidential decree further noted that] independent auditors had to verify whether the company's financial statements complied with both legal rules and correct accounting principles.[15]

The dual focus created in 1975 was not always compatible, and audit reports often went to great lengths to try to clarify the auditor's conclusions as they pertained to a particular focus. This situation was somewhat alleviated with the adoption of the EU's Fourth Directive, which became effective for fiscal years ending December 1993. In its adoption of the Fourth Directive, Italy embraced the audit attestation objective of true and correct in contrast to the British notion of true and fair. Moreover, the clearness principle, a notion akin to the U.S. concern for full disclosure, was reiterated. As recently as July 1998, a new corporate law further clarified the auditors' role. In particular, external auditors have the exclusive responsibility of auditing the accounts, whereas the statutory auditor will monitor corporate management's conduct.[16]

For nonresident readers of Italian financial statements, it is difficult to ascertain the appropriate level of comfort afforded by a true and correct assertion. Does *correct* suggest legal compliance or perhaps the correct application of an accounting practice or standard? Is *correct* synonymous with *fair?* Even in Italy, "there is great concern as to how the 'true and correct representation' formula should be interpreted, and about the consequences of its introduction."[17] Perhaps as a result of that confusion, contemporary Italian audit opinions are not yet uniform (as they would be in the United States or Great Britain). Indeed, Exhibit 13–1 includes three different opinion statements, one each from three global accounting firms, all applicable to the same period of time.

Accounting Profession—Qualifications. Italy's accounting profession includes two tiers of qualifications: the *dottore commercialista* (doctor of commerce) and the *ragioniere collegiato* (accountant and commercial expert). Requirements for the former include completing a four-year course of study at a university and three years of apprenticeship in addition to passing a special examination administered by the government, after which the candidate is admitted to membership in the *Ordine de Dottori Commercialisti*. Requirements

---

[15]Zambon and Saccon, "Accounting Change in Italy," p. 247.
[16]"Corporate Law Reform," *Accountancy,* June 1998, p. 84.
[17]Zambon and Saccon, "Accounting Change in Italy," p. 251.

EXHIBIT 13–1
Excerpted Auditor Opinions in Italy

Panel A: Fiat
To the Stockholders of Fiat S.p.A.:
In our opinion, the consolidated financial statements as a whole have been properly prepared and give a true and fair view of the Group's financial position and the consolidated results of its operations in conformity with Italian law governing consolidated financial statements. Therefore, we issue this certificate to the consolidated financial statements of the Fiat Group for the year ended December 31, 1997.
Price Waterhouse S.p.A.
Turin, Italy May 27, 1998

Panel B: Benetton Group S.p.A.
In our opinion, based on our audit and the reports of other auditors, the consolidated financial statements referred to above present fairly, in all material respects, the consolidated financial position of BENETTON GROUP S.p.A. and subsidiaries as of December 31, 1996 and 1997, and the results of their operations and their cash flows for the three years ended December 31, 1997, in conformity with the accounting principles established or adopted by the Italian Law and the Italian Accounting Profession.
Deloitte & Touche S.p.A.
Treviso, Italy, April 30, 1998

Panel C: Montedison S.p.A.
To the Stockholders of Montedison S.p.A.
In our opinion, the consolidated financial statements taken as a whole have been prepared in a clear manner, giving a true and correct view of the Group's assets and liabilities, financial position and results for the year in accordance with the regulations governing consolidated financial statements. We therefore issue our certification on the consolidated financial statements of the Montedison Group as of December 31, 1997.
Deloitte & Touche
Milan, Italy (no date)

---

for the *ragioniere collegiato* include graduating from a special five-year secondary school (a kind of advanced high school for business), obtaining a "short" three-year university degree, passing a national examination, and gaining three years of experience in public practice under the supervision of a *dottore commercialista* or a *ragioniere collegiato*. The candidate is then admitted into the *Collegio dei Ragionieri e Periti Commerciali*.

The distinction in titles has little or no effect on professional activities; a *ragioniere collegiato* is permitted to perform the same tasks as a *dottore commercialista*. Italy is served by approximately 50,000 accounting professionals, 60 percent of whom are in practice and half of whom are *dottore commercialistas*.[18] A shortage of professionals has presented particular problems because of the large amount of complex legislation in recent years covering various aspects of financial reporting.

Independent audits (as opposed to the examination made by statutory auditors) may be undertaken only by firms approved by *CONSOB*. For an accounting firm to obtain such approval, a majority of its partners must be certified as *dottori* or *ragionieri* and have five years of experience in auditing.

Accounting Profession—Policy Formation.   The creation of accounting policy in Italy is a complex and multilayered process. Although Italian accounting standards have traditionally been created by government legislation, the process of policy formation is becoming more a partnership between the accounting profession and the government. It must be understood, though, that the government is still clearly the senior partner. To that end, the civil code and tax law prescribe the contents of financial statements and set broad principles for valuing assets and liabilities. *CONSOB*, as the primary regulator of capital

---

[18]Ibid.

markets, oversees the enforcement of existing financial reporting standards and imposes rules of its own when necessary. To date, the accounting profession's role has been as a consultant to legislators and as a promulgator of accounting and auditing procedures that clarify and/or supplement the civil code's guidelines.

The Civil Code prescribes the content and format of the required balance sheet and income statement in quite some detail. The Compart Group financial statements in Exhibit 13–2 follow the prescribed forms. The following should be noted:

> The balance sheet is organized according to the German-based "destination principle," which leads to an apparently inappropriate application of the Anglo-Saxon financial approach based on items' liquidity. Balance sheet memorandum accounts have to [also] be disclosed. Their role is to point out future risks and obligations. As for the income statement, the implemented format is of the progressive type, and is based on the cost classification by nature rather than by destination. This German-derived model starts with the "value of production" and shows some intermediate results but unfortunately not the operating income. An attempt to overcome the problematic relationship between commercial law and fiscal rules has been made by trying to separate the influence of taxation from accounting profit calculation [in that] . . . the final section of the income statement include adjustments of valuations and provisions resulting purely from the application of the tax legislation. In this way . . . there has taken place an institutionalization of the linkage between commercial and tax accounting. . . . Only additional charges caused by tax allowances being greater than commercial accounting ones may be entered in these adjustment lines. Where the difference is the other way, the difference cannot be included in these two lines, and therefore the reconciliation between the tax profit and the commercial profit is one-sided and partial.[19]

The detail presented in Exhibit 13–2 is, at one level, overwhelming and perhaps more than one needs to make an investment decision. At another level, however, various company constituencies are likely to find various parts of the detail useful. As a set of financial statements for public consumption, it is out of step with the international norm. For this reason, most Italian companies that publish financial statements such as those in Exhibit 13–2 also publish a more succinct, more generally recognizable balance sheet and income statement. Indeed, Exhibit 13–3 presents such statements as provided by Compart Group. Moreover, some Italian companies (e.g., Eni) do not publish statements such as those in Exhibit 13–2 for general public use, instead using statements similar to those in Exhibit 13–3. For most investor analytical purposes, users of the Compart annual report are likely to find information presented in Exhibit 13–3 sufficient.

The accounting body with the most influence on policy formation is the *Consiglio Nazionale dei Dottori Commercialisti* (CNDC), a national association roughly analogous to the American Institute of CPAs. The CNDC not only advises the government on accounting legislation, but also has begun to issue guidelines delineating "good accounting practices" and standards for performing audits. The strengths of the CNDC standards are their attentiveness to international developments and their provision of detailed guidance. However, it will be some time before the CNDC can catch up with the need for agreed-upon interpretations of the complex web of laws governing Italian financial reporting. In a major move to integrate more closely with emerging international capital markets, Italy passed a law in February 1998 allowing "enterprises listed on national or international capital markets to use internationally recognised accounting standards for consolidated financial statements, if they are consistent with accounting directives of the EU."[20] Thus, Italian companies may choose to adopt IASC standards for their local filings of consolidated financial statements.

---

[19]Ibid., pp. 252–56.
[20]"Europe Opens to IAS," *IASC Insight,* March 1998, p. 1.

EXHIBIT 13–2

COMPART GROUP
Financial Statements
Prepared in Civil Code Format

12/31/97 (in millions of ECU)	*Assets*	*12/31/97*		*12/31/96* (in billions of lire)
–	**A) Receivables from stockholders**	–		–
	B) Fixed assets			
	I– Intangibles:			
57	1) Start-up and expansion costs	110		147
–	2) Research, development and advertising expenses	–		18
2	3) Industrial patents and intellectual property rights	4		291
95	4) Permits, licenses, trademarks, and similar rights	185		208
209	5) Goodwill	405		426
1,259	–) Consolidation difference	2,444		2,480
2	6) Work in progress and advances	4		50
104	7) Other intangibles	202		180
1,728	Total	3,354		3,800
	II– Property, plant and equipment:			
1,638	1) Land and buildings	3,178		3,581
4,270	2) Plant and machinery	8,286		9,932
53	3) Manufacturing and distribution equipment	102		143
97	4) Other assets	188		146
288	5) Construction in progress and advances	559		1,357
6,346	Total	12,313		15,159
	III– Financial assets:			
	1) Equity investments in:			
551	a) unconsolidated subsidiaries	1,068		1,355
–	–) jointly controlled companies	–		–
122	b) affiliated companies	237		648
52	d) other companies	101		76
725	Total equity investments	1,406		2,079

		Amounts Due within One Year			
		12/31/97	*12/31/96*		
	2) Long-term loans to:				
78	a) unconsolidated subsidiaries	30	1	151	206
6	b) affiliated companies	–	3	13	15
35	d) other companies	19	20	68	180
119	Total long-term loans	49	24	232	401
3	3) Other securities			6	3
847	Total			1,644	2,483
8,921	**Total fixed assets (B)**			**17,311**	**21,442**
	C) Current assets				
	I– Inventories:				
739	1) Raw materials, auxiliaries, and supplies			1,435	1,318
154	2) Work in progress and semi-finished goods			298	361
1,550	3) Contract work in process			3,008	3,036
1,499	4) Finished goods and merchandise			2,909	2,839
45	5) Advances			87	40
3,987	Total inventories			7,737	7,594

EXHIBIT 13–2 (continued)

		Amounts Due after One Year			
		12/31/97	*12/31/96*		
	II– Accounts receivable:				
1,598	1) Trade accounts receivable	7	37	3,101	3,769
6	2) Accounts receivable from unconsolidated subsidiaries	–	2	12	7
–	–) Accounts receivable from jointly controlled companies	–	–	–	27
18	3) Accounts receivable from affiliates	–	–	35	45
1,467	5) Accounts receivable from outsiders	730	1,118	2,845	2,780
3,089	Total accounts receivable	737	1,157	5,993	6,628
	III– Financial assets not held as fixed assets:				
2	4) Other equity investments	Amounts Due after One Year		4	6
20	6) Other securities			40	32
	7) Long-term loans to:	*12/31/97*	*12/31/96*		
2	a) unconsolidated subsidiaries	–	–	4	30
1	b) affiliated companies	–	1	1	2
85	c) other companies	47	7	165	101
88	Total loans receivable	47	8	170	133
110	Total financial assets	47	8	214	171
	IV– Liquid assets:				
2,345	1) Bank and postal accounts			4,550	2,275
–	2) Checks in transit			–	44
73	3) Cash on hand			141	205
2,418	Total liquid assets			4,691	2,524
9,604	**Total current assets (C)**			**18,635**	**16,917**
87	**D) Accrued income and prepaid expenses**			**168**	**192**
18,612	**Total assets**			**36,114**	**38,551**

Liabilities and Stockholders' Equity

	A) Stockholders' equity		
	Group interest in capital and reserves:		
1,474	I– Capital stock	2,860	2,860
1,216	II– Additional paid-in capital	2,360	2,360
–	III– Reserve for inflation adjustments	–	–
–	IV– Statutory reserve	–	–
–	V– Reserve for treasury stock	–	–
–	VI– Reserves under the Bylaws	–	–
	VII– Other reserves:		
–	1) Reserve for reverse stock split	1	1
3	2) Reserve for surplus on cancellation of merger	5	5
8	3) Reserve for surplus on exchange upon merger	15	15
(406)	4) Consolidation reserve	(788)	(957)
(395)	Total other reserves	(767)	(936)
(1,128)	VIII– Retained earnings (Loss carryforward)	(2,188)	(2,145)
79	IX– Group interest in net income (loss)	154	96
1,246	Group interest in total stockholders' equity	2,419	2,235
	Minority interest in capital and reserves:		
4,864	–Minority interest in capital and reserves	9,438	9,061
868	–Minority interest in net income (loss)	1,685	668
5,732	Minority interest in total stockholders' equity	11,123	9,729
6,978	**Total stockholders' equity (A)**	**13,542**	**11,964**

EXHIBIT 13–2   (continued)

		Amounts Due after One Year			
		12/31/97	*12/31/96*		
	B) Reserves for risks and charges				
153	1) Reserve for pensions and similar obligations			297	339
277	2) Reserve for taxes			538	601
1,126	3) Other reserves			2,185	2,100
43	–) Consolidation reserve for future risks and charges			82	78
1,599	**Total reserves for risks and charges (B)**			**3,102**	**3,118**
222	**C) Reserve for employee severance indemnities**			**430**	**520**

		Amounts Due after One Year			
		12/31/97	*12/31/96*		
	D) Liabilities				
1,031	1) Bonds	1,942	1,465	2,001	2,165
4,256	3) Due to banks	4,326	5,844	8,258	11,411
130	4) Due to other lenders	159	157	252	270
1,625	5) Advances	2,703	3,146	3,152	3,380
1,732	6) Trade accounts payable	41	9	3,360	3,654
13	8) Accounts payable to unconsolidated subsidiaries	–	–	26	20
–	–) Accounts payable to jointly controlled companies	–	–	–	15
10	9) Accounts payable to affiliates	–	–	20	19
271	11) Taxes payable	3	2	526	574
71	12) Contributions to pension and social security institutions	–	–	137	118
533	13) Other liabilities	11	39	1,035	974
9,672	**Total liabilities (D)**	**9,185**	**10,662**	**18,767**	**22,600**
141	**E) Accrued expenses and deferred income**			**273**	**349**
18,612	**Total liabilities and stockholders' equity**			**36,114**	**38,551**

Memorandum Accounts

	1) Guarantees provided		
	a) Sureties provided on behalf of:		
23	–unconsolidated subsidiaries	45	7
1	–affiliated companies	2	38
1,558	–outsiders	3,022	3,121
1,582	Total sureties	3,069	3,166
	b) Other guarantees provided on behalf of:		
43	–unconsolidated subsidiaries	84	10
9	–affiliated companies	17	11
1,047	–outsiders	2,031	2,573
1,099	Total other guarantees	2,132	2,594
2,681	**Total guarantees provided**	**5,201**	**5,760**
	2) Collateral provided for		
	a) Borrowings and other obligations of outsiders on behalf of:		
29	–outsiders	57	–
29	Total	57	–
2,093	b) Liabilities listed on the balance sheet	4,062	5,631
4	c) Obligations of the company	7	29
2,126	**Total collateral provided**	**4,126**	**5,660**

Exhibit 13–2   (continued)

3) Commitments, risks and other memorandum accounts

a) Forward contracts and derivatives:

	1. Purchases and sales:			
5	1.1. Securities:	Sales	10	15
642	1.2. Currencies:	Between foreign currencies	1,246	15
22		Purchases against lire	43	69
357		Sales against lire	693	536
	2. Derivatives:			
	2.1 With exchange of principal:			
853	a) Currencies:	Between foreign currencies	1,656	2,675
47		Purchases against lire	91	1,360
591		Sales against lire	1,146	1,300
	2.2. Without exchange of principal:			
112	a) Currencies:	Purchases against lire	217	907
210		Sales against lire	408	22
2,377	b) Other instruments:	Purchases	4,613	2,474
1,626		Sales	3,154	2,204
6,842	Total		**13,277**	**11,577**

b) Transactions in the forward commodities markets:

597	–rights to receive commodities	1,159	769
661	–obligations to deliver commodities	1,282	988
1,258	Total	**2,441**	**1,757**

c) Unsecured counterguarantees provided by outsiders

166	to guarantee obligations of Group companies	322	392

d) Other memorandum accounts:

137	–commitments under leasing and similar agreements	266	409
302	–commitments to purchase fixed assets	585	422
2,900	–assets of Group companies held by outsiders	5,627	2,425
16	–assets of outsiders held by Group companies	31	469
72	–miscellaneous memorandum accounts	140	434
3,427	Total other memorandum accounts	**6,649**	**4,159**
11,693	**Total commitments, risks and other memorandum accounts**	**22,689**	**17,885**
16,500	**Total memorandum accounts**	**32,016**	**29,305**

Consolidated Statement of Income at December 31, 1997

1997 *(in millions of ECU)*		*1997*	*1996*
		(in billions of lire)	
	A) Production value		
12,639	1) Sales and service revenues	24,525	24,910
129	2) Changes in inventory of work in progress, semifinished goods and finished goods	250	121
(42)	3) Changes in contract work in process	(81)	174
33	4) Increase in company-produced additions to fixed assets	64	139
	5) Other revenues and income:		
87	a) operating grants	169	160
154	b) miscellaneous revenues and income	298	381
241	Total other revenues and income	467	541
13,000	**Total production value (A)**	**25,225**	**25,885**

EXHIBIT 13–2   (continued)

	B) Cost of production		
7,989	6) Raw materials, auxiliaries, supplies and merchandise	15,502	15,209
1,508	7) Outside services	2,926	3,383
128	8) Use of property not owned	249	296
	9) Personnel:		
940	a) wages and salaries	1,825	2,052
247	b) social security contributions	479	561
30	c) provision for employee severance indemnities	58	91
9	d) provision for pension and similar obligations	17	29
59	e) other personnel costs	114	113
1,285	Total personnel costs	2,493	2,846
	10) Depreciation, amortization and writedowns:		
180	a) amortization of intangibles	349	380
492	b) depreciation of property, plant and equipment	954	1,129
3	c) other writedowns of fixed assets	7	61
	d) writedowns of loans included in current assets		
21	and liquid assets	41	29
696	Total depreciation, amortization and writedowns	1,351	1,599
	11) Change in inventory of raw materials,		
(16)	auxiliaries, supplies, and merchandise	(31)	(2)
16	12) Provisions for risks	30	27
12	13) Other provisions	24	32
278	14) Miscellaneous operating costs	539	514
11,896	**Total cost of production (B)**	**23,083**	**23,904**
1,104	**Net production value (A-B)**	**2,142**	**1,981**
	C) Financial income and expense		
	15) Income from equity investments:		
–	a) dividends and other income from affiliated companies	–	32
2	b) dividends and other income from other companies	5	11
2	Total	5	43
	16) Other financial income from:		
	a) loans included in financial fixed assets:		
5	1) to unconsolidated subsidiaries	10	16
–	2) to affiliated companies	–	1
–	3) to outsiders	–	16
5	Total	10	33
	c) securities included in current assets		
1	other than equity investments	3	19
	d) other financial income from:		
2	1) unconsolidated subsidiaries	5	6
1	2) affiliated companies	1	1
340	3) outsiders	659	700
343	Total	665	707
349	Total	678	759
	17) Interest and other financial expense paid to:		
2	a) unconsolidated subsidiaries	4	5
–	b) affiliated companies	–	–
699	c) outsiders	1,357	1,713
701	Total	1,361	1,718
(350)	**Total financial income and expense (15+16−17) (C)**	**(678)**	**(916)**
	D) Value adjustments on financial assets		
	18) Upward adjustments of:		
12	a) unconsolidated equity investments	23	41
12	Total	23	41

Exhibit 13–2   (concluded)

	19) Writedowns of:		
191	a) unconsolidated equity investments	370	220
	b) financial assets		
11	other than equity investments	21	1
	c) securities, other than equity investments,		
–	included in current assets	–	1
1	d) loans receivable included in current assets	3	3
203	Total	394	225
(191)	**Total value adjustments (18-19) (D)**	**(371)**	**(184)**
	E) Extraordinary income and expense		
	20) Income:		
790	a) gains on disposals	1,532	550
235	b) other extraordinary income	457	1,136
1,025	Total	1,989	1,686
	21) Expense:		
20	a) losses on disposals	38	31
–	b) taxes attributable to prior fiscal years	1	4
400	c) other extraordinary expense	777	1,372
420	Total	816	1,407
605	**Total extraordinary items (20-21) (E)**	**1,173**	**279**
1,168	**Income before taxes (A−B+−C+−D+−E)**	**2,266**	**1,160**
220)	22) Income taxes	(427)	(396)
868	**Minority interest in net income (loss)**	**1,685**	**668**
80	**Group interest in net income (loss)**	**154**	**96**

Banking.   The 1990 Amato Law has been referred to as Italy's most important piece of financial legislation since the watershed Banking Law of 1936.[21] The law gives Italy's approximately 85 public sector banks the chance to privatize, listing up to 49 percent of their shares on the stock market. The intent of the law is to allow government-dominated banks to restructure to overcome their historical shortcomings of being too localized, too small, too numerous, and too inefficient to compete effectively with their larger international rivals. To encourage the restructuring, the law exempts banks from any tax on the capital gains associated with asset revaluations booked at the time of reorganization so that the total, real value of an institution's assets can be recorded. This provision has the effect of boosting a bank's capital base, providing room for subsequent loan growth and expansion. Recently, the Amato Law was viewed as having "failed miserably."[22]

It may be, however, that Italy's recent adoption of the EU's second banking directive will become the real catalyst for change in a banking industry that is long overdue for one. Italian banks are now allowed to be shareholders in Italian companies, make long-term loans, and provide universal banking services.[23] Such changes, along with a planned privatization of the banking system, consolidation of the industry, and growing public sentiment to stop the practice of *lottizzazione* (appointing bank managers as part of the political reward system rather than based on qualifications), bode well for converting the banking industry to a more competitive, professionally managed basis on which credit

---

[21]D. Lane, "Year of Profound Structural Change," *Financial Times,* November 19, 1990, p. II.
[22]"Half a Renaissance," *The Economist,* March 21, 1992, pp. 86–87. See also, "Italian Banking," *The Economist,* June 15, 1995, pp. 55–56.
[23]"Inching Forward," *The Economist,* June 5, 1993, pp. 90–91.

Exhibit 13–3

COMPART GROUP FINANCIAL STATEMENTS
Prepared for Easier International Comparisons
Reclassified Consolidated Balance Sheet

(in billions of lire)	12/31/97	12/31/96
A. Fixed assets		
Intangibles	3,354	3,800
Property, plant and equipment	12,313	15,159
Financial fixed assets	1,644	2,484
	17,311	**21,443**
B. Net working capital		
Inventories	7,737	7,594
Trade accounts receivable	3,130	3,841
Other assets	3,035	2,984
Trade accounts payable (−)	(6,521)	(6,755)
Reserves for risks and charges (−)	(3,102)	(3,118)
Other liabilities (−)	(1,971)	(2,327)
	2,308	**2,219**
C. Invested capital, net of operating liabilities (A+B)	**19,619**	**23,662**
D. Reserve for employee severance indemnities (−)	**(430)**	**(520)**
E. Net invested capital (C−D)	**19,189**	**23,142**
Covered by:		
F. Stockholders' equity before minority interest	**13,542**	**11,964**
G. Net borrowings (Liquid assets)		
Long-term debt	6,427	7,465
Long-term financial assets (–)	—	—
	6,427	**7,465**
Short-term borrowings	4,121	6,401
Liquid assets and short-term financial assets (–)	(4,901)	(2,688)
	(780)	**3,713**
	5,647	**11,178**
H. Total coverage sources (F+G)	**19,189**	**23,142**

Reclassified Consolidated Statement of Income

A. Net revenues	**24,911**	**25,625**
Changes in inventory of work in progress, semifinished goods and finished goods	250	121
Increase in company-produced additions to fixed assets	64	139
B. Production value	**25,225**	**25,885**
Raw materials and outside services (−)	(18,646)	(18,886)
Miscellaneous expense (−)	(580)	(543)
Provisions for risks and charges (−)	(54)	(59)
C. Value added	**5,945**	**6,397**
Labor costs (−)	(2,493)	(2,846)
D. Gross operating result	**3,452**	**3,551**
Depreciation, amortization and writedowns (−)	(1,310)	(1,570)
E. Net operating income	**2,142**	**1,981**
Net financial expense	(683)	(959)
Interest in the result of companies valued by the equity method and dividends from companies valued at cost	(237)	(69)
Other income (expense), net	(129)	(72)
F. Result before extraordinary items and taxes	**1,093**	**881**
Extraordinary income (expense)	1,173	279
G. Income before taxes and minority interest	**2,266**	**1,160**
Income taxes	(427)	(396)
H. Net income		
Minority interest in net income (loss)	**1,685**	**668**
Group interest in net income (loss)	**154**	**96**

risk might be assessed in regard to a company's cash-generating ability as opposed to the extent of its fixed-asset holdings.[24]

Capital Markets.   Of Italy's 10 stock exchanges, by far the most important is the ***Borsa Valori di Milano***—the Milan Bourse (the Bourse was privatized in early 1998). It accounts for about 90 percent of the total daily trading volume in shares and about 80 percent of the total trading volume in fixed-income securities throughout Italy. But yet, about "75 percent of dealings in Italy involved the 30 largest quoted companies."[25] As well as its regular market, the Bourse is seeking to join the London–Frankfurt stock exchange alliance and has plans for "a new market for small and medium-sized high-growth stocks participating in the EuroNM network linking similar markets in Paris, Amsterdam, Frankfurt, and Brussels."[26]

CONSOB is the regulatory agency overseeing the Italian stock exchanges, and it was created in 1974 to improve the efficiency and fairness of Italian capital markets. Since then, it has established a number of requirements for listing on Italian exchanges, including the following:

- Net shareholder equity must be at least L50 billion (about $27.9 million) for banks and insurance companies and at least L10 billion (about $5.6 million) for other companies.

- The applicant must present financial statements showing a profit for the last three years. The most recent set of statements must have been audited by an authorized firm.

- A minimum of 25 percent of the company's outstanding shares must be publicly owned (as opposed to government owned).

- Bond offerings must be at least L13 billion (about $7.3 million), of which at least 25 percent must be offered for sale to the public.[27]

Once listed, a company must furnish *CONSOB* with audited financial statements annually, directors' reports semiannually, and any other information the agency requests. Although fairly large by continental European standards, the Milan exchange is still far from becoming an international financial center. Only about 200 companies are currently listed on it, as compared to more than five or six times that many listings in New York, London, or Tokyo. Moreover, deposit requirements make trading in foreign equities on the Milan Bourse highly disadvantageous. Investors in foreign securities are required to deposit an amount equal to 15 percent of their purchase in a noninterest-bearing account in the Bank of Italy, to be held there until they sell the securities. Nonresidents are allowed to invest in Italian securities with few restrictions.

Although exchange restrictions, most of which are in the process of being lifted, must bear some responsibility for scaring investors away from the Italian stock ex-

---

[24]See "Unmasking Italian Banking," *The Economist,* February 12, 1994, pp. 77–78; H. Simonian, "Italian Shares Boom on Shaky Foundations," *Financial Times,* September 17, 1993, p. 17; J. Blitz, "Ill-prepared for a Host of New Hurdles," *Financial Times,* December 21, 1997, p. IV; and P. Betts, "Italy's Keen Interest in Financial Affairs," *Financial Times,* February 11, 1998, p. 20.

[25]P. Betts, "Stock Market Transparency in Italy," *Financial Times,* April 8, 1998, p. 3.

[26]P. Betts, "Italian Bourse Plans New Segment," *Financial Times,* June 26, 1998, p. 23; see also P. Betts, "Milan Set to Join Exchange Alliance," *Financial Times,* November 9, 1998, p. 2.

[27]*Doing Business in Italy* (New York, NY: Price Waterhouse, 1996).

changes, a much larger problem involves the provinciality and lack of openness that characterize Italian bourses. The confidence of international investors has been dampened by the lack of liquidity and of an effective regulatory infrastructure to protect outsiders, minority interest, and small investors (e.g., insider trading was legal until the early 1990s). In addition, potential investors are wary of the closed structure of Italian stock markets: Most companies listed on the Milan Bourse are controlled by a small circle of powerful business families. The five largest business groups in Italy, all controlled by families, account for 70 percent of the country's stock market capitalization. As a result of these problems, leading Italian equities are often traded more actively in London than in Milan.

In late 1990, stock market reform legislation was passed creating a new brand of financial institution, *Societá di Intermediazione Mobiliare* (SIM). The new SIM law calls for all business in equities to go through a stock exchange, thus ending widespread prior practices among banks of matching buy-and-sell orders in-house. Estimates at the time of the SIM law put the level of "off-floor" trading at twice that done in the exchanges. As might be surmised, such a requirement has generated a flurry of activity in the banking industry to develop or acquire an SIM or enter into a joint venture with one to retain that phase of their business. Such reform, along with a 1991 prohibition on insider trading, suggests a concerted attempt to position the Milan Bourse as a major equities market for global and Italian investors. This came at a time when historically "fewer than 10 percent of Italian families hold shares—the lowest level among the industrialized countries [and] only 4 percent of household savings were held in shares and 36 percent in [government bonds]."[28] These facts have not gone unnoticed in Italy and, the further development of its capital markets is a main goal of the government. Indeed, at the beginning of 1999, "thanks to privatizations and rock-bottom interest rates (and the fraying of old-boy relationships) Italian savers are shifting massively into equities."[29]

The next decade is likely to witness further changes in Italy's stock market. The *CONSOB* is pushing for accounting reform to bring greater transparency to corporate financial affairs. As one recent Italian broker noted, "Money flows towards transparency" and Italian firms are starting to catch on. Indeed, Mediobanca, an old-guard, large, powerful, publicly traded bank, appointed its first investor-relations officer in 1998 and was contemplating scheduling its first-ever presentation to financial analysts.[30] Perhaps even more noteworthy as a harbinger of how attitudes toward equity investors are likely to change is the 1998 appointment of a former assistant to General Electric's CEO Jack Welch as chairman of Fiat. The *Business Week* article announcing this monumental appointment begins, "Shareholder value. Transparency. Customers coming first."[31] For sure, such mantras may become as Italian as pasta and chianti.

---

[28]A. Hill, "Equities for the Family," *Financial Times,* July 7, 1994, p. 28.

[29]J. Rossant, K. Capell, and J. Ewing, "Raiders at the Gate," *Business Week,* March 8, 1999, pp. 51–52.

[30]See "Unmasking Italian Investor Relations," *The Economist,* August 8, 1998, p. 59, and B. Coleman, "Olivetti Case Spurs Italian Regulators to Press for Tougher Financial Rules," *The Wall Street Journal,* October 12, 1998, p. A19.

[31]J. Rossant, "Management, American-Style," *Business Week,* July 6, 1998, p. 50.

Selected Financial Reporting Practices

As particular Italian accounting conventions are discussed, remember that the general concepts undergirding its financial reporting are that (1) company taxable income, in principle, should be about the same as that reported for external purposes and (2) certain expenses are not tax deductible unless reported in the external financial statements.[32] Springing from these premises, at least in part, has been an historical tendency for financial reporting conservatism and secrecy.

As an overview, consider that interim financial statements are on a semiannual basis and earnings per share data are not required. A cash flow statement is not required but is sometimes voluntarily provided. Footnotes are often extensive and quite detailed and provide analysis of changes to certain accounts. Lastly, audit opinions may not be qualified (i.e., they must be without reservation or totally negative).

It is also worth noting that whatever the state of Italian accounting practices, the world's modern-day standard of double-entry accounting was founded and has been practiced in Italy since the 14th century. Luca Pacioli, an Italian monk, is credited with preparing the first treatise on double-entry accounting. Also indicative of Italy's long-standing accounting tradition is the fact that the first professional society of accountants was formed in Venice in the 16th century.[33] Italy's modern-day practices have evolved from such roots.

Valuation

The Italian civil code requires the use of the historical cost convention as the basis of valuation for all assets. Specific laws passed in 1975, 1982, 1990, and 1991, however, permit the revaluation of certain fixed assets, using government specified indexes, if a company can show that the current economic value of an asset exceeds its proposed valuation. The offsetting credit is to a revaluation reserve account in the shareholders' equity section of the balance sheet. Over time, a revaluation reserve account may become quite substantial, thus indicating sizable holding gains likely to be recognized by the company sometime in the future. (In 1997, ENI's revaluation reserve equaled 25 percent of the company's consolidated owners' equity.)

Consolidation

Beginning in 1994, the Italian civil code required consolidated financial statements following the adoption of the EU's Fourth and Seventh Directives. In addition, *CONSOB* requires companies listed on stock exchanges to prepare and publish consolidated statements. As a consequence, all "controlled" subsidiaries are consolidated, except those whose line of business differs substantially from the principal business of the group, where control is temporary, or on grounds of immateriality. In such cases, the unconsolidated company is accounted for under the equity method.[34]

A firm is considered to be "controlled" if another company directly or indirectly controls a majority of its voting power (whether through stock ownership or some other means) or if another company exercises significant influence over it by virtue of special ties. A firm is considered to be an "associate" if another company holds more than 5 percent of its capital if it is listed on a stock exchange or more than 10 percent of its capital

---

[32]Zambon and Saccon, "Accounting Change in Italy."

[33]G. Mann, "The Origins of Double-Entry," *Australian Accountant,* July 1994, pp. 17–21.

[34]Under the Italian equity method, changes in the value of the investment account are also reflected in an undistributable reserve account in the shareholders' equity section of the balance sheet, thereby bypassing the income statement (and hence current income taxes).

if it is not; investments in associate companies are often accounted for under the cost method for tax reasons, although the equity method is also permitted.

Investment Incentives

It is common for the Italian government to provide cash grants to companies to stimulate capital investment. These grants are usually carried in a special section of shareholders' equity without being included in income. Treatment may vary, however, according to the type of the grant and the accounting policy of a given company. For example, in the past Fiat has deferred such grants and credited them to income over the life of the related assets. Conversely, at other times, Fiat has credited them directly to an equity reserve account without including them in income.

Marketable Securities

Securities held as short-term investments are carried at cost or, in the case of listed securities, the lower of cost or market (on an individual security basis). Market value is determined by calculating the average daily market price of a security over the last three months of the financial year.

Inventories

Inventory must be carried at the lower of cost or market, calculated on an individual item basis. Common valuation methods include LIFO, FIFO, specific identification and average cost (although standard cost is also acceptable if it approximates cost under one of the other methods). A version of LIFO is popular because it permits high tax deductions; other methods are allowable for both book and tax purposes so long as they do not result in a lower inventory value than LIFO.

Leases

Because Italian tax law does not provide for the capitalization of leases, long-term leases are generally accounted for as operating leases by both parties, regardless of the substance of the lease agreement.

Goodwill

Goodwill may be recorded only if it arises from the acquisition of a business. It is defined as the difference between the consideration given and the agreed upon value of identifiable net assets and is amortized over its estimated useful life (but rarely in excess of 10 years). The charge-to-equity method is also permitted. Negative goodwill may be capitalized to the balance sheet and systematically amortized to income or written off against the depreciable assets acquired, as in the United States.

Long-Term Contracts

Accounting for long-term contracts is dictated by Italian tax law, which permits both the completed contract method and the percentage of completion method, which is more commonly used. If a loss is anticipated, it is fully accrued currently but is not tax deductible until realized. If the percentage of completion method is used, a provision for contractual risks equaling 2 to 4 percent of expected revenues is permitted under Italian tax law.

Segment Reporting

With the recent integration of the EU's Fourth Directive into the Italian civil code, Italian companies are now required to report results by geographical area or by line of business. Few of them did so voluntarily prior to the implementation of the Fourth Directive.

Shareholders' Equity

Shareholders' equity consists of capital reserves, legal reserves, revaluation reserves, retained earnings, and various other reserves. Capital reserves include share capital—namely, the par or nominal value of shares issued—and share premium—or the excess of share price over par (or nominal) value. The share premium reserve is distributable to shareholders when the legal reserve (see the next paragraph) equals 20 percent or more of share capital. Treasury stock is carried as an asset, usually under the heading other long-term investments.

The legal reserve is a reserve representing the withholding of 5 percent of annual earnings. Withholding is required until the legal reserve equals 20 percent of share capital. The legal reserve may not be distributed. Revaluation reserves are created when non-current assets are revalued above original historical cost, as permitted or required by legislative action and when long-term investments accounted for under the equity method are revalued. Revaluation reserves are distributable. If retained earnings reflects a deficit, it may be carried on the debit side of the balance sheet.

Analytical Considerations

As illustrated by Exhibit 13–4, generally accepted accounting practice in Italy in many instances parallels U.S. GAAP. Significant differences, however, are noteworthy in the following areas:

- *Valuation of property, plant, and equipment.* Unlike U.S. companies, Italian corporations are permitted—and sometimes required—by special legislative action to revalue certain fixed assets in excess of historical cost using government-specified coefficients developed from Italian inflation statistics. The corresponding revaluation surplus is carried as part of consolidated shareholders' equity, and the revalued assets are depreciated over their normal remaining useful life. Annually, a portion of the revaluation reserve is transferred to retained earnings to reflect (i.e., offset) the excess depreciation taken on the revalued assets.

- *Goodwill.* Goodwill may be capitalized to the balance sheet (as in the United States) and then amortized against earnings or may be written off in total at the time of acquisition against shareholders' equity.

- *Debt valuation.* Unlike U.S. GAAP, all debt instruments are valued at their face or settlement value; in the United States, present value is the dominant valuation approach.

- *Lease accounting.* Italian law does not recognize the capitalization of lease agreements; consequently, regardless of a contract's inherent substance, all leases are treated as operating leases.

- *Research and development costs.* Unlike U.S. GAAP, accepted Italian accounting practice permits the capitalization of recoverable R&D expenditures that relate to new products, projects, or technologies. When such costs are capitalized, it is customary to amortize them over five years.

- *Treasury stock.* Under Italian GAAP, treasury stock may be carried as an asset (usually under long-term investments); in the United States, treasury stock is accounted for as a contra owners' equity account.

- *Deferred income taxes.* Under Italian GAAP, deferred income taxes for temporary differences between book and tax income are rarely recorded (or are relatively immaterial because of the short three-year time horizon used in assessing timing differences); the flow-thru approach is most common, where the reported provision for income taxes is the actual taxes due and/or paid by a company.

EXHIBIT 13–4

Comparison of Italian and U.S. Accounting and Reporting Standards

Item	Italy	United States
Asset valuation	Historical cost with selected revaluation (e.g., property, plant, and equipment revaluations may be mandated by law)	Historical cost with selected revaluation (principally downward)
Inventory valuation	Specific identification, LIFO, FIFO (principally), and average cost	Principally LIFO (because of tax considerations); also FIFO and average cost methods
Inventory year-end	Lower of cost or market value (defined as replacement cost or net realizable value)	Lower of cost or replacement cost
Depreciation	Principally straight-line-method at rates permitted by tax law; "additional depreciation" during the first three years of an asset's life also frequently taken if permitted by tax law	Principally straight line with accelerated and production-based methods permitted
Goodwill	Principally capitalized and amortized over a 5- to 10-year period; immediate charge-to-equity method also permitted; negative goodwill written off immediately against the value of purchased assets or capitalized to the balance sheet and amortized to income	Capitalized to balance sheet with amortization (principally straight line) over a maximum of 40 years; negative goodwill not permitted (i.e., eliminated against long-term depreciable assets)
Research and development costs	Consistent with tax law, may be either expensed as incurred or capitalized and amortized over 5 years; must expense capitalized R&D judged to be nonrecoverable	Research costs expensed currently; development costs expensed currently except in certain industries (i.e., software, oil and gas)
Capitalized interest costs	Capitalization of interest during period of asset construction permitted (but required for tax purposes)	Capitalization required for self-constructed assets
Intercorporate investments:		
Marketable securities (current asset trading)	Lower of cost or market value on an individual investment basis	Mark to market (individual security basis) with unrealized gains and losses taken to income
Long-term investments: 0–20% ownership (available for sale)	Lower of cost or market value on an individual investment basis	Mark to market (individual security basis) with unrealized gains and losses reported on balance sheet (i.e., owners' equity)
20–50% ownership	Equity method	Equity method
51–100% ownership	Consolidated, unless a subsidiary's line of business differs substantially from the rest of the group (in which case, the equity method used); both pooling (merger) and purchase (acquisition) accounting permitted	Consolidated using pooling (until 2001) or purchase accounting
Debt valuation	All debt valued at face or settlement value	Long-term debt (except deferred income taxes) valued at present value; all other debt valued at face or settlement value
Leases	All leases treated as operating leases	Capital leases reflected in balance sheet; operating leases disclosed in footnotes
Deferred income taxes	Generally unnecessary because tax law usually subjects the reported accounting income to taxation (hence tax and book income are equivalent); when deferred taxes present, the liability method is used	Computed under liability method
Pension liabilities	Private pension plans rare but when present and unfunded, liability reported on balance sheet	Reflected on balance sheet
Discretionary reserves	Restricted to identifiable operational losses that are probable and can be reasonably estimated	Restricted to identifiable operational losses
Statement of cash flows	Permitted but not required	Required

The effects, in general, of these noted differences on the financial statements of Italian companies, as compared to their U.S. counterparts, can be summarized as follows:

Item	Financial Statement Impact
Revaluation of fixed assets	Total assets and shareholders' equity overstated with net earnings understated (due to excess depreciation on the revalued assets); hence, ROA and ROE relatively understated
Goodwill	Total assets and shareholders' equity understated (assuming the charge-to-equity approach) with net earnings overstated; hence, ROA and ROE relatively overstated
Lease accounting	Total assets and total debt understated by the present value of any capital leases; effect on net earnings not readily predictable
Capitalization of R&D	Total assets and current earnings overstated with future earnings relatively understated (due to the rear-end loading of R&D expenditures); ROS likely to be overstated with ROA and ROE not predictable
Treasury stock carried as asset	Total assets and shareholders' equity overstated; hence, ROA and ROE relatively understated
Deferred income taxes not reported	Net earnings and shareholders' equity overstated with total debt understated; hence, debt-to-equity ratio relatively overstated

To gain some sense of the relative financial effects attributable to these accounting differences on the reported earnings of one company, consider the case of ENI *S.p.A.*, a diversified oil and gas company. The company's 1997 audited financial statements revealed consolidated earnings of $2,893 million based on Italian GAAP. Under U.S. GAAP, ENI would have reported net income of $4,799 million, an increase of over 65 percent. In addition, the company disclosed the magnitude (in millions) of the various accounting differences between Italian and U.S. GAAP as depicted in Exhibit 13–5.

On the basis of these limited data, drawing the generalization that the net earnings of all Italian companies under Italian GAAP are consistently understated relative to their earnings under U.S. GAAP is inappropriate. In 1995, for example, these same adjustments would have *lowered* ENI's net earnings from $4,327 million under Italian GAAP to just $3,924 million under U.S. GAAP. Nonetheless, other evidence also exists to

---

EXHIBIT 13–5

ENI *S.p.A.*
Reconciliation of Italian GAAP versus U.S. GAAP Net Earnings

Balance as reported in the consolidated profit and loss account	2,893
Items increasing (decreasing) reported net profit (loss)	
Reduction in depreciation of fixed assets	313
Capitalized interest expense	93
Successful-efforts accounting	111
Change in provision for deferred taxes, including effect of the above adjustments	1,493
Other	(6)
Effect on minority interests of the above adjustments	(99)
Total net increase (decrease)	1,906
Balance in accordance with accounting principles generally accepted in the United States	4,799

suggest that the Italian GAAP–based earnings of Italian companies are consistently and systematically understated, on average, as compared to those of U.S. companies.[35] Consider, for example, the average price-earnings multiples for 1998:

| | Average P/E Ratio* |
	1998
Italy	29.1
United States	26.6

*Source: Morgan Stanley Capital International.

Assuming efficient world global markets, these data suggest a persistent biasing of reported earnings by Italian companies. Since security prices are thought to correctly reflect all available information about a company, Italian and U.S. firms with equivalent earnings potential should be equivalently priced, *ceteris paribus*. Consequently, the higher price-earnings multiples afforded Italian companies in general numerically result from the understatement of reported earnings characteristic of those firms. Thus, this institutionalized fiscal biasing must be considered by analysts when making interfirm comparisons involving Italian companies.

Summary

"Acceptance into the [EU's] single currency would mark Italy's coming of age as a modern nation."[36] This declaration by *The Economist* in 1997 indeed came to pass in January 1999—Italy qualified as, and was, one of the initial entrants into the European Monetary Union. Despite this remarkable accomplishment, Italy must resolve some seriously destabilizing conditions and hold steady for a number of years before one can proclaim her as having "come of age."[37] In particular the uncertainty created and momentum lost by frequently changing governments must be ameliorated by greater constancy of ruling coalitions. Second is the continued need to reform and streamline the banking system. Third, high tax rates facilitated the country's ability to qualify for EMU but they also encourage the existence of Italy's underground economy, the largest in Europe and perhaps as large as 25 percent of Italy's GDP. Last is the problematic nature of the economic discrepancies between the vibrant North versus the not-so-vibrant southern part of Italy. Perhaps the new government that assumed power in the fall of 1998 will have the answers. Then again, 56 prior postwar governments did not.

---

[35]M. Hagigi and A. Sponza, "Financial Statement Analysis of Italian Companies: Accounting Practices, Environmental Factors, and International Corporate Performance Comparisons," *International Journal of Accounting* 25, no. 4 (1990), pp. 234–51.

[36]"A Survey of Italy," *The Economist,* November 8, 1997, p. 1.

[37]See J. Blitz, "Italy's Sluggish Growth," *Financial Times,* July 22, 1998, p. 12; J. Blitz, "Promoted to Europe's Premier League," *Financial Times,* June 15, 1998, p. I; and "Light on the Shadows," *The Economist,* May 3, 1997, pp. 63–64.

Suggested Readings

Hagigi, M., and A. Sponza. "Financial Statement Analysis of Italian Companies: Accounting Practices, Environmental Factors, and International Corporate Performance Comparisons." *International Journal of Accounting* 25, no. 4 (1990), pp. 234–51.

"Italy—A Survey." *Financial Times,* June 15, 1998, pp. I–VI.

"Italy." *The Economist,* November 8, 1997, Survey 1–23.

Khalaf, R. "Buyer Beware." *Forbes,* June 20, 1994, pp. 204–5.

Nobes, C., and S. Zambon. "Piano, Piano: Italy Implements the Directives." *Accountancy,* July 1991, pp. 84–85.

Price Waterhouse. *Doing Business in Italy.* New York, NY: Price Waterhouse, 1996.

Valente, J. "Two Paths, Two Problems." *The Wall Street Journal,* September 30, 1994, p. R8.

Vigano, E. "Accounting and Business Economics Traditions in Italy." *European Accounting Review,* 7, no. 3 (1998), pp. 381–403.

Zambon, S., and C. Saccon. "Accounting Change in Italy." *European Accounting Review,* September 1993, pp. 245–84.

Exercises

13.1 Corporate Debt

In a February/March 1995 *OECD Observer* report (p. 47), "Italy: Corporate Governance," A. Goldstein and G. Nicoletti note that "for the vast majority of firms, debt-financing has mostly taken the form of short-term borrowing from a plethora of banks." Moreover, in a September 17, 1993, *Financial Times* article (p. 17), H. Simonian asserts that Italian banks have extended credit "too freely." In a related vein, P. Betts and J. Blitz quote an Italian banker in their February 23, 1999, *Financial Times* article (p. 15) as describing Italy's corporate financing as "capitalism without capital."

Required:

(a) Report on the nature and extent of debt disclosures and discussions contained in an Italian corporate annual report of your choosing.

(b) Compare and contrast what you find with the annual report from a U.S. company in the same industry.

13.2 Information Needs

In a July 7, 1994 *Financial Times* article (p. 28), "Equities for the Family," A. Hill asserts that "a more sophisticated personal and professional investor is emerging in Italy." Moreover, in a March 8, 1999, *Business Week* article (p. 52), J. Rossant, K. Capell, and J. Ewing report that "you are going to see increasing levels of shareholder activism in Italy."

Required:

Assume these statements are true and that the equity market will become a more significant source of corporate capital in Italy. Identify and discuss at least three ways that trend would be reflected in the information desired from companies.

13.3 Privatization

In early 1994, the Italian government announced the sale of 69 percent of its state-controlled electrical equipment company, Nuovo Pignone, to an investment group led by General Electric Co. for $420 million. After the sale, ownership of the company would be distributed as follows:

Ownership Interest	Ownership
25%	General Electric Co.
12	Ingersoll-Rand Co.
12	Dresser Industries, Inc.
20	A consortium of Italian banks
20	Ente Nazionale Idrocarburi (the Italian state-controlled energy conglomerate)
11	Italian private investors
100%	

The sale of a controlling interest in Nuovo Pignone was part of Italy's continuing privatization effort.

Required:

(a) Based on the ownership interest data, what restrictions appear evident for foreign investors involved in Italy's privatization program?

(b) Based on the available data, what value would you assign to GE's investment?

(c) How should GE, Dresser, and Ente Nazionale Idrocarburi account for their investments in Nuovo Pignone?

13.4 Statement of Cash Flows

Luxottica Group *S.p.A.* is an Italian-based corporation involved in the design, manufacture, distribution, and marketing of traditional and designer lines of frames for eyeglasses and sunglasses. The company's products are principally manufactured in Italy and are distributed worldwide by a variety of wholly owned foreign subsidiaries. The company's shares trade on the New York Stock Exchange via American depositary receipts under the symbol LUX.

The following are the company's balance sheets for the years ended December 31, 19x8 and 19x9, as they appeared in its 20-F filing with the SEC. The footnotes accompanying Luxottica's 20-F filing also revealed the following information for 19x9 (in millions of lire):

- Net income of 91,914.
- Depreciation and amortization of 24,695.
- Dividends declared and paid of 27,030.
- Currency translation effects of 21,748 (relating to the translation of foreign subsidiary financial statements into the Italian lire, the functional currency), which was recorded directly in retained earnings.

Required:

Using the available data, prepare a statement of cash flows for 19x9 for Luxottica and comment on the company's financial health vis-à-vis its cash flows.

LUXOTTICA GROUP *S.p.A.* **AND SUBSIDIARIES**
Consolidated Balance Sheets
December 31, 19x8 and 19x9

	(Millions of Lire)	
Assets	*19x8*	*19x9*
Current assets		
Cash	48,390	30,568
Marketable securities	16,741	77,373
Accounts receivable		
Less: Allowance for doubtful accounts, L3,776 and L4,565, respectively	135,732	168,928
Sales and income taxes receivable	12,507	5,150
Inventories	88,345	88,870
Prepaid expenses and other	7,167	19,895
Deferred income tax benefits	10,488	8,142
Total current assets	319,370	398,926
Property, plant, and equipment—net	122,335	139,449
Other assets		
Intangible assets—net	32,721	28,207
Investments	803	705
Security deposits and other	1,308	1,365
Sales and income taxes receivables	2,081	2,915
Total other assets	36,913	33,192
Total	478,618	571,567
Current liabilities		
Bank overdrafts	54,138	39,341
Current portion of long-term debt	2,400	10,890
Accounts payable	35,381	59,669
Accrued expenses and other	36,557	40,847
Accrual for customers' right of return	5,148	6,791
Income taxes payable	24,008	5,881
Total current liabilities	157,632	163,419
Long-term debt	20,450	14,181
Liability for termination indemnities	17,553	21,100
Deferred income taxes	20,698	22,970
Minority interests in consolidated subsidiaries	3,078	5,695
Shareholders' equity		
Capital stock; par value L1,000–45,050,000 ordinary shares authorized and issued, 44,584,500 shares outstanding	45,050	45,050
Surplus from monetary revaluations of assets	7,828	6,191
Retained earnings	223,788	310,420
Total	276,666	361,661
Less: Treasury shares at cost	17,459	17,459
Shareholders' equity	259,207	344,202
Total	478,618	571,567

13.5 Intangible Asset Amortization

Goodwill, an intangible asset, represents the excess purchase price paid in an acquisition of another company over the fair market value of identifiable assets acquired, less any liabilities assumed. Under Italian GAAP, purchased goodwill is recorded as an asset and amortized over a 5- to 10-year period. It is also permissible to immediately write off any goodwill incurred as a consequence of an acquisition against retained earnings.

Luxottica Group *S.p.A.* is one of the world's largest manufacturers and marketers of frames for eyeglasses and sunglasses. In recent years, the company had been active in the acquisition of competing companies. According to the company's December 31, 19x8 and 19x9 balance sheets, Luxottica had L32,721 million and L28,207 million, respectively, in intangible assets largely composed of goodwill (see following table and balance sheets in exercise 13–4). The company amortized this goodwill over a 10-year period.

The company's annual report revealed the following information about its intangible assets (amounts in millions of lire):

	December 31	
	19x8	*19x9*
Goodwill		
which arose in connection with the acquisition of the remaining 50% interest in Luxottica United Kingdom—net of amortization of L300 million and L450 million at December 31, 19x8 and 19x9, respectively.	1,197	1,047
Goodwill		
which arose in connection with the acquisition of Florence Line *S.r.l.*—net of accumulated amortization of L3,237 million and L4,316 million at December 31, 19x8 and 19x9, respectively.	7,554	6,475
Goodwill		
which arose in connection with the acquisition of Fidia S.p.A.—net of accumulated amortization of L4,253 million and L5,672 million at December 31, 19x8 and 19x9, respectively.	9,925	8,506
Goodwill		
which arose from the acquisition of the remaining 50% interest in Avant Garde Optics Inc. net of accumulated amortization of L22,736 million and L25,984 million at December 31, 19x8 and 19x9, respectively.	9,744	6,496
Other, principally trademarks		
net of accumulated amortization	4,301	5,683
Total	32,721	28,207

Required:

Using the income statement and balance sheet data from E.13.4 as well as the data in this table, restate Luxottica's 19x9 net income and balance sheet assuming the following:

(a) A 40-year amortization period for goodwill (as per U.S. GAAP).

(b) The direct write-off of goodwill against retained earnings.

13.6 Accounting for Shareholder Reserves

Luxottica Group *S.p.A.* produces more than 700 traditional eyeglass frame styles and over 500 designer frame styles. Since Luxottica's shares trade over the NYSE as ADRs (1 ADR is equivalent to 1 ordinary Luxottica share, par value of L1,000), it files with the Securities and Exchange Commission form 20-F to report its annual financial results and form 6-K to report its quarterly financial results.

The company's 20-F reported the following data (in millions of lire) as of December 31, 19x9:

Shareholders' Equity	19x9	19x8
Capital stock	45,050	45,050
Surplus from monetary revaluations of assets	6,191	7,828
Retained earnings	310,420	223,788
Total	361,661	276,666
Less: Treasury shares (at cost)	17,459	17,459
Total shareholders' equity	344,202	259,207

The company's SEC filing also disclosed the following footnote information:

- At the company's annual shareholders' meeting in April 19x9, cash dividends of L27,030 million were approved and were subsequently paid in July. Italian civil code requires that 5 percent of net income be retained as a legal reserve until this reserve is equal to one-fifth of the issued share capital. (Net income in 19x9 was L91,914 million.)

- Part of Luxottica's property, plant, and equipment (see exercise 13.4 for Luxottica's 19x9 balance sheet) was revalued in accordance with the provisions of Italian Laws No. 576 as of December 2, 1975, No. 72 as of March 19, 1985, and No. 413 as of December 30, 1991. The revaluation was undertaken to partially account for the change in the purchasing power of money (i.e., monetary revaluation).

On December 31, 19x7 (effective January 1, 19x8), the Italian government passed a law requiring the compulsory revaluation of industrial buildings. This revaluation resulted in a net write-up of the carrying value of assets and, accordingly, an increased charge for depreciation over a building's remaining useful life, such lives approximating 15 years. For financial reporting purposes, building costs and accumulated depreciation were increased by a like amount, resulting in no net write-up to either fixed assets or shareholders' equity.

Required:

   (a) Calculate the required value of Luxottica's legal reserve. Where would you expect this reserve to be disclosed? Do you think that the legal reserve constrained Luxottica's ability to declare dividends?

   (b) Use journal entries to explain how the account Surplus from Monetary Revaluations of Assets was created and why it declined from 19x8 to 19x9.

13.7 Analyzing Research and Development Costs

Montedison *S.p.A.* is a diversified food product and pharmaceutical company headquartered in Milan, Italy. Because of the company's involvement in chemicals and pharmaceuticals, it has had significant expenditures for research and development (see the following data).

	(Lire, in Billions) Year Ended		
	12/31/x9	*12/31/x8*	*12/31/x7*
Trademarks, licenses, and research	106	229	194
Deferred charges	485	164	159
Total	591	393	353
Annual amortization	166	170	106
Net income before tax	514	1,403	2,164
Shareholders' equity	5,363	5,312	2,120

According to the company's 19x9 annual report, the accounting policy with respect to intangible assets and deferred charges was as follows:

Licenses, trademarks and know-how are recorded at acquisition or internal production cost. These intangible assets are amortized on a straight-line basis over their expected useful lives. Amortization is provided over five years when no contract exists or there is no other way of determining useful life.

Industrial technology patents are amortized over their expected useful lives or the duration of the related licenses, if shorter.

Pure research costs, those relating to pharmaceutical and pharmacological research and the development of improvements to existing products or production processes are expensed as incurred.

The cost of research into new products or processes (excluding pharmaceuticals) and related development is deferred only if it relates to projects that are expected to be profitable. Such costs are amortized on a straight-line basis over five years.

Deferred industrial research costs are written off in the year the research proves unsuccessful.

When research is completed successfully, the residual costs are reclassified as industrial technology patents.

Required:

(a) Compare and contrast Montedison's accounting policy for research and development costs with (1) *IAS No. 9* and (2) *SFAS No. 2*.

(b) Restate Montedison's (1) net income before tax and (2) shareholders' equity (assume a tax rate of 36 percent) for 19x8 and 19x9 assuming that all deferred charges and research and development costs are expensed as incurred.

(c) Calculate the company's return on equity both before and after your restatement.

(d) Do you agree with Montedison's R&D policy? If so, why? If not, why not?

13.8 Accounting for Treasury Stock

At the end of 19x8, Montedison *S.p.A.* merged with and into Ferruzzi Agricola Finanziaria *S.p.A.*, its controlling shareholder. The resulting company was renamed Montedison *S.p.A.* Today it maintains operations in such diverse products as sugar, starch and derivatives, consumer products, industrial oils, animal feeds, chemicals, pharmaceuticals, and energy. Following the merger, certain shares in the new company were repurchased, and under the Italian civil code, treasury shares may be carried as an asset. According to the footnotes to the company's 19x9 annual report,

Long-Term Investment Securities

Long-term investment securities, amounting to Lire 1,202 billion, include shares of the parent company Ferruzzi Finanziaria S.p.A., acquired for Lire 200 billion, as well as treasury stock totaling Lire 267 billion. The treasury stock is not expected to be sold or canceled in the near future.

The company's balance sheet as of 31 December 19x9 also revealed the following capitalization:

	Lire, in Billions
Long-term debt	5,529
Shareholders' equity	
Share capital	2,917
Legal reserve	154
Additional paid-in capital	224
Retained earnings and other reserves	1,900
Net income	168
Total shareholders' equity	5,363
Total liabilities and shareholders' equity	27,704

Required:

(a) Restate Montedison's shareholders' equity section on a basis consistent with U.S. GAAP.

(b) Calculate Montedison's (1) long-term debt-to-shareholders' equity ratio and (2) shareholders' equity-to-total assets ratio, both before and after your restatement in part (a).

(c) List arguments (1) supporting the classification of treasury stock as an asset and (2) arguments against the treatment of treasury stock as an asset.

13.9 Analyzing Changes in Shareholders' Equity

Benetton Group S.p.A. is a well-known manufacturer of casual apparel which it markets under the brand name The United Colors of Benetton. The company was founded in 1965 by the Benetton family in Ponzano Veneto, Italy, and became a public company in 1978. In 1989, the company made its first public offering of American depositary receipts, each representing two ordinary shares (par value L 500), which trade on the NYSE.

Benetton's statement of changes in consolidated stockholders' equity for the years ended December 31, 19x7, 19x8, and 19x9, is presented as it appeared in the company's 19x9 20-F filing with the SEC. The company's footnotes to the 20-F report also revealed the following information about other reserves which were aggregated with retained earnings in the statement of changes in stockholders' equity:

Other Reserves Are as Follows (Lire, in Millions):

	31 December	
	19x8	*19x9*
Exchange fluctuation reserve	20,055	55,561
Risk reserve	14,210	7,099
Taxation reserve	—	7,580
Reserve for agents' termination indemnities	8,992	9,219
	43,257	79,459

The exchange fluctuation reserve reflects the net effect of adjusting foreign currency balances of payables and receivables of the Italian companies in the Group using year-end exchange rates.

The risk reserve prudently covers various business contingencies, including outstanding legal cases.

The taxation reserve prudently covers liabilities which may arise on the final settlement of outstanding tax disputes with the authorities.

BENETTON GROUP S.p.A.
Statement of Changes in Consolidated Stockholders' Equity
For the Years ended December 31, 19x7, 19x8, and 19x9
(in millions of lire)

	Capital Stock	Additional Paid-in Capital	Surplus from Monetary Revaluation of Assets	Other Reserves and Prior Years' Retained Earnings	New Income for the Year	Total
BALANCES AS OF DECEMBER 31, 19x6	81,777	186,661	19,118	165,776	133,271	586,603
Allocation of 19x6 net income to reserves	—	—	—	133,271	(133,271)	—
Dividends distributed, as approved at the stockholders' meeting of April 30, 19x7	—	—	—	(40,888)	—	(40,888)
Effect of monetary revaluation	—	—	27,104	(23,074)	—	4,030
Differences arising from the translation of foreign currency financial statements	—	—	—	2,004	—	2,004
Net income for the year	—	—	—	—	164,783	164,783
BALANCES AS OF DECEMBER 31, 19x7	81,777	186,661	46,222	237,089	164,783	716,532
Allocation of 19x7 net income to reserves	—	—	—	164,783	(164,783)	—
Dividends distributed, as approved at the stockholders' meeting of April 29, 19x8	—	—	—	(49,066)	—	(49,066)
Disposal of Prince Holdings Inc.: recovery of goodwill on acquisition previously charged against consolidation reserves	—	—	—	56,534	—	56,534
Differences arising from the translation of foreign currency financial statements	—	—	—	14,052	—	14,052
Net income for the year	—	—	—	—	184,709	184,709
BALANCES AS OF DECEMBER 31, 19x8	81,777	186,661	46,222	423,392	184,709	922,761
Allocation of 19x8 net income to reserves	—	—	—	184,709	(184,709)	—
Dividends distributed, as approved at the stockholders' meeting held on April 29, 19x9	—	—	—	(57,244)	—	(57,244)
Differences arising from the translation of foreign currency financial statements	—	—	—	(10,277)	—	(10,277)
Net income for the year	—	—	—	—	208,038	208,038
BALANCES AS OF DEC. 31, 19x9	81,777	186,661	46,222	540,580	208,038	1,063,278

Required:

Using journal entries, explain the changes in Benetton's stockholders' equity accounts from year-end 19x8 to year-end 19x9.

13.10 Reconciling U.S. and Italian Net Income

The ADRs of Benetton Group *S.p.A.* trade on the NYSE, and, consequently, the company files a Form 20-F (annual report) with the SEC. A key component of that report is the reconciliation of generally accepted accounting principles in Italy and the United States. Excerpts from that report include the following:

Differences which have an effect on net income and stockholders' equity:

- Revaluation of Fixed Assets and Trademarks
  In 19x7 and prior years, certain categories of property, plant and equipment and trademarks were revalued to amounts in excess of historical cost. This procedure, which was authorized by Italian law, was allowed under Italian accounting practice to give consideration to the effects of local inflation. Revaluations (totaling L46,222 million) were credited to stockholders' equity and revalued assets are depreciated over their remaining useful lives on a straight-line basis.

- Accounting for Goodwill
  In prior years, goodwill on investments acquired were charged or credited to stockholders' equity at the date of purchase. The adjustment in the accompanying reconciliation has been made to recognize the goodwill on acquisitions, originally amounting to L11,519 million. Goodwill is amortized over a 10 year period, corresponding to the estimated useful lives of the underlying assets acquired. The relevant decrease in 19x8 is due to the sale of the company's interest in Prince Holdings, Inc., and the consequent reversal of the related goodwill.

	Year Ended December 31 (Lire, Millions)		
	19x7	*19x8*	*19x9*
Net income, per Italian GAAP	164,783	184,709	208,038
Reduction in depreciation and amortization on revalued fixed assets and trademarks	2,067	2,575	3,134
Amortization of goodwill	(6,724)	(338)	(1,252)
Net income per U.S. GAAP	160,126	186,946	209,920
Stockholders' equity per Italian GAAP	716,532	922,761	1,063,278
Elimination of revaluations of fixed assets and trademarks	(19,494)	(16,919)	(13,785)
Reinstatement of goodwill previously written off	57,101	7,295	6,043
Stockholders' equity per U.S. GAAP	754,139	913,137	1,055,536

Required:

(a) Recreate the journal entries necessary to (1) revalue Benetton's fixed assets and trademarks and (2) write off purchased goodwill to stockholders' equity.

(b) Compare and contrast Benetton's return on equity under Italian GAAP with its return on equity under U S. GAAP. What generalizations can you draw about the profitability of Italian companies under Italian GAAP versus U.S. companies under U.S. GAAP?

13.11 Annual Report Analysis

An interesting and important challenge for students of international financial reporting is to study the published annual reports of various companies from different countries. Your instructor will provide you with a recent copy of an Italian corporate annual report. To facilitate your delving into this annual report, undertake the following endeavors.

Required:

(a) List the key differences between that annual report and what you would expect to see for a U.S. company in the same industry.

(b) Calculate the following ratios, taking care to note the assumptions you found necessary to make and where you found the appropriate pieces of data in the annual report.

$$(1) \text{ Current ratio} = \frac{\text{Total current assets}}{\text{Total current liabilities}}$$

$$(2) \text{ Quick ratio} = \frac{\text{Cash} + \text{Marketable securities} + \text{Accounts receivable}}{\text{Total current liabilities}}$$

$$(3) \begin{array}{l}\text{Operating cash flow to} \\ \text{current liabilities}\end{array} = \frac{\text{Operating cash flow}}{\text{Average total current liabilities}}$$

$$(4) \text{ Debt-to-equity ratio} = \frac{\text{Long-term debt}}{\text{Owners' equity}}$$

$$(5) \text{ Debt-to-total capitalization ratio} = \frac{\text{Long-term debt}}{\text{Long-term debt} + \text{Owners' equity}}$$

$$(6) \text{ Interest coverage ratio} = \frac{\text{Net income before interest and income taxes}}{\text{Interest expense}}$$

$$(7) \begin{array}{l}\text{Operating cash flow to interest} \\ \text{charges}\end{array} = \frac{\text{Operating cash flow}}{\text{Interest expense}}$$

$$(8) \begin{array}{l}\text{Operating cash flow to total} \\ \text{liabilities}\end{array} = \frac{\text{Operating cash flow}}{\text{Average total liabilities}}$$

$$(9) \text{ Receivables turnover ratio} = \frac{\text{Net sales}}{\text{Average accounts receivable}}$$

$$(10) \text{ Inventory turnover} = \frac{\text{Cost of goods sold}}{\text{Average inventory}}$$

$$(11) \text{ Asset turnover} = \frac{\text{Net sales}}{\text{Average total assets}}$$

$$(12) \text{ Average collection period ratio} = \frac{365 \text{ days}}{\text{Receivables turnover ratio}}$$

$$(13) \begin{array}{l}\text{Average number of days'} \\ \text{inventory on hand ratio}\end{array} = \frac{365 \text{ days}}{\text{Inventory turnover ratio}}$$

$$(14) \text{ Return on assets (ROA)} = \frac{\text{Net income}}{\text{Average total assets}}$$

$$OR = \text{ROS} \times \text{Asset turnover}$$

$$(15) \text{ Return on equity (ROE)} = \frac{\text{Net income}}{\text{Average total owners' equity}}$$

$$OR = \text{ROA} \times \text{Financial leverage}$$

(16) Return on sales (ROS) $= \dfrac{\text{Net income}}{\text{Net sales}}$

(17) Financial leverage $= \dfrac{\text{Average liabilities} + \text{Average owners' equity}}{\text{Average owners' equity}}$

(18) Basic earnings per share (EPS) $= \dfrac{\text{NI applicable to common shareholders}}{\text{Weighted average common shares}}$

(19) Cash dividend yield $= \dfrac{\text{Cash dividend per common share}}{\text{Market price per common share}}$

(20) Cash dividend payout $= \dfrac{\text{Total cash dividend to common shareholders}}{\text{Net income}}$

(c) What do you conclude about the availability of the appropriate data in the annual report for calculating these ratios?

(d) What does this financial analysis tell you about the Italian company?

(e) What analytical metrics did the company choose to report for itself? What do those choices say about the message the company is striving to tell and the audience it is addressing?

Appendix I
Comparative Accounting and Reporting Practices Around the World

Item	Australia
Asset valuation	Principally historical cost with selected revaluation (i.e., noncurrent assets at revalued amount; inventory and marketable securities at LCM)
Inventory valuation	Principally FIFO or average cost, but specific identification and standard cost methods permitted; LIFO, base stock, and other current cost methods not permitted
Inventory: year-end	Lower of cost or net realizable value
Depreciation	Principally straight-line and declining balance methods
Goodwill	Purchased goodwill capitalized as a noncurrent intangible asset and amortized to income over the expected period of benefit but not to exceed 20 years; negative goodwill not permitted (i.e., charged off against nonmonetary assets acquired until eliminated)
Research and development costs	Generally expensed as incurred; however, costs possibly deferred if recoverability is beyond a reasonable doubt; amortization of deferred costs match recoverability or receipt of related benefits
Capitalized interest costs	Generally permitted if interest costs clearly associated with bringing related asset to revenue-producing state
Intercorporate Investments:	
Marketable securities	Stated at lower of cost or net realizable value (on an individual basis); unrealized gains and losses taken into income
Long-term investments:	
0–20% ownership	Stated at cost, with revaluation permitted; revaluation amounts taken to revaluation reserve
20–50% ownership	Equity method
51–100% ownership	Consolidated, using purchase accounting; pooling of interests not permitted
Debt valuation	Long-term debt valued at present value; all other debt valued at face value
Leases	Finance leases capitalized to balance sheet; operating leases disclosed in footnotes
Deferred income taxes	Computed under liability method
Pension liabilities	Reflected on balance sheet; underfunding measured as projected benefit obligation less fair value of plan assets
Discretionary reserves	Permitted if authorized by board of directors
Statement of cash flows	Required

APPENDIX I *(continued)*
COMPARATIVE ACCOUNTING AND REPORTING
PRACTICES AROUND THE WORLD

Item	*Canada*
Asset valuation	Principally historical cost with selected revaluation (principally downward)
Inventory valuation	Principally average cost and FIFO, although specific cost and standard cost also permitted; LIFO not permitted for tax purposes, hence rarely used for reporting purposes
Inventory: year-end	Lower of cost or market with market approximated by replacement cost or net realizable value
Depreciation	Principally straight line, but unit-of-production and declining balance methods also permitted
Goodwill	Purchased goodwill is capitalized to balance sheet and amortized to income (straight-line basis) over expected life, but not to exceed 40 years; negative goodwill not permitted (i.e., eliminated against nonmonetary assets)
Research and development costs	Research costs expensed as incurred; development costs must be deferred and amortized if (a) product/process clearly defined, (b) technical feasibility established, (c) clear intent to produce and market the product, (d) the future market is clearly defined
Capitalized interest costs	Capitalization of interest on constructed assets permitted but not required
Intercorporate investments:	
Marketable securities	Lower of cost or market, applied individually or on a portfolio basis; unrealized gains and losses taken to earnings
Long-term investments:	
0–20% ownership	Principally at cost, adjusted for permanent value declines. Write-downs taken directly to earnings
20–50% ownership	Equity method
51–100% ownership	Consolidated, principally using purchase accounting; pooling of interest permitted if acquirer cannot be identified
Debt valuation	Long-term debt valued at present value; all other debt valued at face value
Leases	Finance leases capitalized to balance sheet; operating leases disclosed in footnotes
Deferred income taxes	Computed under deferral method
Pension liabilities	Reflected on balance sheet; both pension liability and asset disclosure required
Discretionary reserves	Generally not permitted (except for specific losses or liabilities)
Statement of cash flows	Permitted but not required (if statement of changes in financial position presented instead)

APPENDIX I *(continued)*
**COMPARATIVE ACCOUNTING AND REPORTING
PRACTICES AROUND THE WORLD**

Item	*China**
Asset valuation	Principally historical cost
Inventory valuation	Principally FIFO, LIFO, and weighted average; other methods (e.g., standard cost) also permitted
Inventory: year-end	Lower of cost or net realizable value
Depreciation	Principally straight line, production-based methods also permitted; accelerated methods less common but permitted
Goodwill	Treatment of purchased goodwill not currently addressed by Ministry of Finance's accounting regulations
Research and development costs	Treatment of research and development costs not currently addressed by Ministry of Finance's accounting regulations
Capitalized interest costs	Interest directly related to the acquisition or construction of an asset capitalized
Intercorporate investments:	
Marketable securities	Historical cost on individual security basis
Long-term investments:	
0–20% ownership	Historical cost on individual security basis
20–50% ownership	Principally historical cost
51–100% ownership	Consolidated, unless unconsolidated (i.e., equity method) accounting is approved by Ministry of Finance, usually on grounds of nonhomogeneity of operations
Debt valuation	All liabilities valued at face or settlement value
Leases	The treatment of leases not currently addressed by Ministry of Finance's accounting regulations
Deferred income taxes	Treatment not addressed by Ministry of Finance's accounting regulations
Pension liabilities	Not an issue in PRC because foreign investment enterprises do not maintain pensions for their employees; foreign investment enterprises do pay retirement insurance premiums according to national labor laws
Discretionary reserves	Generally not permitted (except for specific losses or liabilities)
Statement of cash flows	Not required, although statement of changes in financial position required on an annual basis

---

*The accounting principles listed here apply to foreign investment enterprises and need not apply to state or collective enterprises or to joint stock limited companies.

APPENDIX I *(continued)*
COMPARATIVE ACCOUNTING AND REPORTING PRACTICES AROUND THE WORLD

Item	*Denmark*
Asset valuation	Principally historical cost; revaluation permitted
Inventory valuation	Principally FIFO, specific identification, or standard cost; average cost also permitted; LIFO not recommended
Inventory: year-end	Lower of cost or net realizable value
Depreciation	Principally straight line and declining balance methods
Goodwill	Principally charged to equity at time of acquisition; capitalization and amortization (although not in excess of 5 years) also permitted
Research and development costs	Principally expensed as incurred; deferral permitted if clear relation exists between expenditure and future earnings; maximum amortization period of 5 years if capitalized
Capitalized interest costs	Permitted but not widely practiced
Intercorporate investments:	
Marketable securities	Lower of cost or net realizable value on an individual security basis; unrealized losses to income and unrealized gains to revaluation reserve (unless a prior unrealized loss is reversed)
Long-term investments:	
0–20% ownership	Mark to market, on individual security basis; write-ups taken to revaluation reserve unless a prior write-down taken to income reversed
20–50% ownership	Equity method
51–100% ownership	Principally consolidated; nonconsolidation permitted if disclosed; principally purchase accounting, although pooling of interests permitted
Debt valuation	All liabilities valued at face value
Leases	Generally, all leases treated as operating leases; companies increasingly adopting *IAS No. 17*
Deferred income taxes	Principally calculated under liability method; deferral method also permitted
Pension liabilities	Disclosed in balance sheet if underfunded
Discretionary reserves	Generally not permitted except for specific losses or liabilities
Statement of cash flows	Not required

APPENDIX I *(continued)*
COMPARATIVE ACCOUNTING AND REPORTING
PRACTICES AROUND THE WORLD

Item	*France*
Asset valuation	Principally historical cost, with revaluation of property, plant, equipment, and investments permitted
Inventory valuation	Principally FIFO and weighted-average cost; LIFO may be used in consolidated statements
Inventory: year-end	Lower of cost or replacement cost
Depreciation	Principally straight line and declining balance methods; excess depreciation to reduce a company's tax liability also permitted (accumulated excess depreciation classified under shareholders' equity)
Goodwill	Purchased goodwill (and negative goodwill) capitalized to balance sheet; amortization over a period of expected benefit, with no maximum period specified
Research and development costs	Generally expensed as incurred but may be deferred if feasibility of product is established and costs clearly identifiable; maximum amortization period of 5 years
Capitalized interest costs	May be capitalized but not required
Intercorporate investments:	
Marketable securities	Lower of cost or net realizable value on either an individual or portfolio basis; unrealized gains and losses to income statement
Long-term investments:	
0–20% ownership	Lower of cost or assumed (by management) value on an individual basis; revaluations taken to revaluation reserve in shareholders' equity
20–50% ownership	Equity method
51–100% ownership	Consolidated except when (1) operations of parent and subsidiary nonhomogeneous, (2) control temporary or impaired, (3) subsidiary immaterial to the group as a whole; pooling of interests not permitted, hence purchase accounting only
Debt valuation	All debt valued at face amount
Leases	For consolidated statements, finance leases generally capitalized to the balance sheet; in statutory statements, all leases accounted for as operating leases
Deferred income taxes	For consolidated statements, computed using either the deferral method or the liability method; not required in statutory financial statements
Pension liabilities	Reflected in balance sheet if unfunded
Discretionary reserves	Generally not permitted except for liabilities and losses reasonably estimated .
Statement of cash flows	Not required but recommended

APPENDIX I *(continued)*
COMPARATIVE ACCOUNTING AND REPORTING PRACTICES AROUND THE WORLD

Item	Hong Kong
Asset valuation	Principally historical cost with revaluation of noncurrent assets permitted
Inventory valuation	Principally FIFO and average cost
Inventory: year-end	Lower of cost or net realizable value
Depreciation	Principally straight line and declining balance methods; other methods permitted
Goodwill	Charge to equity and capitalization/amortization permitted; negative goodwill is credited to shareholder reserves
Research and development costs	Currently no prescribed accounting standard
Capitalized interest costs	Capitalization generally recommended for significant interest costs
Intercorporate investments:	
Marketable securities	Lower of cost or net realizable value on either individual or portfolio basis; unrealized gains and losses to income statement
Long-term investments:	
0–20% ownership	Principally cost with revaluation permitted; revaluation adjustments taken to shareholders' reserve
20–50% ownership	Equity method
51–100% ownership	Principally consolidated; many exceptions for excluding subsidiaries; principally purchase accounting; pooling of interests permitted
Debt valuation	All debt valued at face value except capitalized leases
Leases	Finance leases capitalized to the balance sheet; operating leases disclosed in footnotes
Deferred income taxes	Computed under the liability method
Pension liabilities	Currently no prescribed accounting standard
Discretionary reserves	Made at the discretion of management
Statement of cash flows	Required using either direct or indirect method

APPENDIX I *(continued)*
COMPARATIVE ACCOUNTING AND REPORTING
PRACTICES AROUND THE WORLD

Item	*India*
Asset valuation	Principally historical cost with selected revaluation (i.e., fixed assets) usually on basis of independent appraisal
Inventory valuation	Principally FIFO, average cost, or LIFO; specific identification and standard cost methods permitted
Inventory: year-end	Lower of cost or net realizable value
Depreciation	Principally straight line and declining balance methods; excess depreciation due to revaluation recovered from the revaluation reserve
Goodwill	Purchased goodwill capitalized and amortized over the expected period of benefit or charged against any available capital reserve account
Research and development costs	Charged to expense as incurred, except costs associated with products for which (1) costs clearly identified, (2) technical feasibility demonstrated, (3) management intent to produce and market, (4) costs likely to be recovered, and (5) resources exist to produce and market
Capitalized interest costs	Actual interest costs incurred on construction or installation of fixed assets capitalized
Intercorporate investments:	
Marketable securities	Lower of cost or net realizable value on an individual security basis
Long-term investments:	
0–20% ownership	Principally cost adjusted for any permanent declines
20–50% ownership	Equity method permitted but not required
51–100% ownership	Consolidation permitted but not required
Debt valuation	Principally valued at face value
Leases	Generally all leases accounted for as operating leases
Deferred income taxes	Generally the flow-thru approach used when no deferred taxes arise; liability method recommended
Pension liabilities	Disclosed on balance sheet if unfunded; rare since most currently funded for tax consideration
Discretionary reserves	Generally not permitted unless loss probable and reasonably estimable
Statement of cash flows	Permitted but not required

APPENDIX I *(continued)*
COMPARATIVE ACCOUNTING AND REPORTING
PRACTICES AROUND THE WORLD

Item	*New Zealand*
Asset valuation	Principally historical cost with selected revaluation of fixed assets either annually or at least every 3 years
Inventory valuation	Principally FIFO, weighted average, or specific identification; LIFO and base stock not permitted
Inventory: year-end	Lower-of-cost or net realizable value
Depreciation	Principally straight line method; others permitted
Goodwill	Purchased goodwill capitalized and amortized usually over a 10–20 year period; negative goodwill eliminated against nonmonetary assets
Research and development costs	Research expensed as incurred; development outlays capitalized if (1) costs of products clearly identifiable, (2) technical feasibility demonstrated, (3) management intends to manufacture and sell product, (4) future market exists, and (5) resources ensure project completion
Capitalized interest costs	Permitted but not generally practiced
Intercorporate investments:	
Marketable securities	Principally lower of cost or market
Long-term investments:	
0–20% ownership	Either cost (adjusted for any permanent impairment) or market value
20–50% ownership	Equity method
51–100% ownership	Principally consolidated; subsidiaries excluded if immaterial to group, if resulting consolidated data misleading, or if substantially nonhomogeneous; principally purchase accounting, although pooling of interests permitted if acquirer cannot be identified
Debt valuation	Generally valued at face value; present value permitted
Leases	Finance leases capitalized at the lower of the fair value of the asset or present value; operating leases disclosed in footnotes
Deferred income taxes	Calculated using liability method
Pension liabilities	Generally disclosed if unfunded but not required
Discretionary reserves	Generally not permitted except for reasonable future estimable costs
Statement of cash flows	Generally presented principally using direct method

APPENDIX I *(continued)*
COMPARATIVE ACCOUNTING AND REPORTING
PRACTICES AROUND THE WORLD

Item	*Spain*
Asset valuation	Principally historical cost; periodic revaluation (or "actualization") of fixed assets required by legislation using specified coefficients
Inventory valuation	Principally weighted average or specific identification; FIFO and LIFO also permitted
Inventory: year-end	Lower-of-cost-or-market value
Depreciation	Principally straight line method; declining balance also permitted
Goodwill	Purchased goodwill capitalized and amortized over 5–10 years; negative goodwill capitalized and amortized only to offset anticipated losses associated with acquired business
Research and development costs	Principally expensed as incurred but may be capitalized if (1) costs clearly identifiable and (2) recoverability relatively certain
Capitalized interest costs	Permitted for fixed assets purchased or constructed
Intercorporate investments:	
Marketable securities	Lower-of-cost-or-market value with unrealized losses taken to income
Long-term investments:	
0–20% ownership	Lower-of-cost-or-market value with unrealized losses taken to income
20–50% ownership	Equity method
51–100% ownership	Generally consolidated using purchase accounting except for subsidiaries (1) with pending sale, (2) immaterial value, (3) with nonhomogeneous principal business, or (4) with restricted control due to bankruptcy filing
Debt valuation	All liabilities valued at settlement value
Leases	Finance leases capitalized to balance sheet; operating leases disclosed in footnotes
Deferred income taxes	Calculated using liability method
Pension liabilities	Disclosed on balance sheet if underfunded
Discretionary reserves	Restricted to specific, probable and estimable losses
Statement of cash flows	Not presented, although statement of sources and uses of funds is frequently disclosed

APPENDIX I *(continued)*
COMPARATIVE ACCOUNTING AND REPORTING
PRACTICES AROUND THE WORLD

Item	*Switzerland*
Asset valuation	Principally historical cost; current or replacement cost of fixed assets also permitted
Inventory valuation	FIFO, specific identification, average cost, standard cost
Inventory: year-end	Lower-of-cost-or-market value (i.e., replacement cost or net realizable value)
Depreciation	Straight line or declining balance methods
Goodwill	Not separately disclosed; no required amortization
Research and development costs	Normally expensed as incurred, but capitalization permitted if recoverability highly certain
Capitalized interest costs	Permitted but not generally practiced
Intercorporate investments:	
Marketable securities	Cost or current market value applied either on individual or portfolio basis
Long-term investments:	
0–20% ownership	Cost or current market value applied either on individual or portfolio basis
20–50% ownership	Cost or equity method
51–100% ownership	Generally consolidated with few standards as to procedures
Debt valuation	All debt valued at face value
Leases	All leases treated as operating leases
Deferred income taxes	Generally unnecessary due to consistency between tax and publicly reported data
Pension liabilities	Disclosed in balance sheet if underfunded; disclosure rare due to conformity of tax and book statements
Discretionary reserves	Fully permitted
Statement of cash flows	Not required; usually not presented

APPENDIX II
OVERVIEW OF U.S. GAAP

U.S. GAAP is, without doubt, the most detailed and extensive set of financial reporting standards ever created. The purpose of this appendix is to serve as a brief summary of U.S. GAAP for those readers (1) trained in accounting outside of the United States and (2) who desire a broad-based review of U.S. GAAP. For those who may wish to use this appendix as a starting point for studying U.S. GAAP in greater depth, we begin with a brief description of its roots and development. We note references to the appropriate accounting standards at the beginning of each major section.

Sources of U.S. GAAP and Their Hierarchy

Modern U.S. GAAP has its origins with the Securities Act of 1933 and the Securities Exchange Act of 1934. The "'33 Act" requires delivery of a prospectus in public offerings of securities. The "'34 Act" requires updating (for the most part via annual and quarterly financial reports) of the information contained in the prospectus to satisfy the informational needs of secondary market participants. Both of these statutes require that financial statements be prepared in accordance with generally accepted accounting principles (GAAP). The Securities and Exchange Commission (SEC), which was created by the '34 Act, has the legal authority to establish GAAP.

The SEC delegated its authority to establish GAAP to the American Institute of Certified Public Accountants (AICPA), which initially formed the Committee on Accounting Procedure. The publications of this rather informal committee were referred to as Accounting Research Bulletins. The AICPA reorganized the standard-setting process as the Accounting Principles Board in 1959, which issued opinions and numerous interpretations of those opinions.

In 1973, the Accounting Principles Board was disbanded under political pressure, and the Financial Accounting Standards Board (FASB) was established apart from the AICPA to follow a process that gave all stakeholders in U.S. GAAP an opportunity to express their views and be duly considered. Although the AICPA designates the FASB to lead the process of establishing accounting standards, it retains significant participation through the Accounting Standards Executive Committee (AcSEC). To date, the FASB has issued 134 statements of financial accounting standards, 6 statements of financial accounting concepts, and numerous supplemental publications including interpretations, technical bulletins and "Q & A's" issued by the FASB staff, and consensus positions of the Emerging Issues Task Force (EITF).

U.S. auditing standards[1] specify a hierarchy of this vast accounting literature for cases in which the accounting guidance from two or more sources may conflict:

1. Accounting principles promulgated by a body designated by the AICPA. These include FASB Statements (SFAS) and FASB Interpretations (FIN), APB Opinions (APBO), and Accounting Research Bulletins (ARB).
2. Pronouncements of bodies composed of expert accountants that have exposed their pronouncements for public comment and have been cleared by one of the bodies in category 1. These currently include technical bulletins of the FASB staff (TB), AICPA Industry Audit and Accounting Guides (IAG), and the statements of position of AcSEC (SOP).

---

[1] AICPA, Statement of Auditing Standards No. 69, *The Meaning of Present Fairly in Conformity with Generally Accepted Accounting Principles in the Independent Auditor's Report,* 1992.

3. Pronouncements of bodies similar to those in category 2, but their pronouncements have not been exposed to public comment. The principal body currently in this category is the EITF of the FASB.

4. Practices or pronouncements that are widely recognized as being generally accepted because they represent prevalent practice in a particular industry, or the knowledgeable application to specific circumstances of pronouncements that are generally accepted. These currently include interpretations of the APB (AIN), "Q and A's" published by the FASB staff, and widely recognized industry practices.

It may be difficult to imagine, but often the accounting treatment of a transaction or event is not specified by a pronouncement covered by *any* of the sources in these four categories. In these cases, the reporting must justify a conclusion that the adopted treatment is generally accepted. This is usually accomplished by reference to "other literature," which principally includes FASB Concepts Statements (SFAC), AICPA Issues Papers, and statements of the IASC. The weight given to items within this uncategorized literature depends on the authority of the issuer.

Finally, the SEC has retained its option to reject, augment, and interpret GAAP. *Thus, SEC regulations also belong in category 1 for public companies filing their financial statements with the SEC.*[2] SEC Regulation S-X governs the form and content of financial statements, including certain supplementary disclosures. Staff Accounting Bulletins (SAB), Financial Reporting Releases (FRR) and Accounting, Auditing and Enforcement Releases (AAER) frequently interpret existing GAAP, and sometimes establish new GAAP for public companies.

Reporting Categories of Income (APB 30, APB 20, SFAS 16, SFAS 128)

Income Statement Format

The five major components of the income statement are:

- Income from continuing operations, including unusual items.
- Results from discontinued operations.
- Extraordinary items.
- Cumulative effects of changes in accounting principles.
- Earnings per share.

Under income from continuing operations, separate presentation is made of net sales revenue, cost of sales, operating expenses, other revenues and expenses, and income tax expense related to continuing operations. For public companies, SEC regulations set forth the major captions depending on the type of business entity; however, there is a fair amount of flexibility afforded to all reporting entities.

Extraordinary Items

Extraordinary items are transactions or events that are distinguished by (1) their unusual nature (i.e., abnormal and unrelated to typical activities) *and* (2) their infrequency of occurrence (i.e., cannot be reasonably expected to recur in the foreseeable future). Events that meet both of these criteria are rarely encountered in practice. However, gains and losses from the early retirement of debt are classified as extraordinary items. Extraordinary items are presented net of their tax effects.

---

[2]For nonpublic companies, SEC regulations would be classified as "other literature."

Discontinued Operations

The results of discontinued operations refers to the operations and/or disposal of a component of a firm whose activities represent a separate, major line of business. As with extraordinary items, the effects on income of discontinued operations are presented net of their tax effects.

Separate presentation is made for (1) earnings from the operating activities of discontinued operations to be sold (or were sold during the period) and (2) gains or losses on the disposal of discontinued operations.

Cumulative Effect of Accounting Changes

U.S. GAAP distinguishes between changes in an accounting estimate and changes in accounting principle. Changes in estimates are necessary when new information indicates that old estimates are no longer valid—for example, changes in the estimated lives of assets. Changes in estimates are recorded prospectively, that is, previous years are not restated to reflect the new estimate.

Changes in an accounting principle *usually* require that the cumulative effective on the income of earlier periods be presented in income in the period of the change. Again the

presentation is net of related income tax effects and clearly distinguished from income from continuing operations. Exceptions, such as restatement of prior periods, may occur when new accounting pronouncements mandate a change in accounting principles, and rules for transition to the new principle are specified by the pronouncement itself. Since GAAP contains few areas that provide a choice of accounting principles to follow, most changes in accounting principles result from the mandated adoption of a new accounting standard.

Earnings per Share

The current standard for presentation of earnings per share (EPS) information is the result of a joint project between the FASB and the IASC. Consequently, U.S. GAAP and IASC No. 33 are nearly identical. Most observers agree that U.S. standards prior to this project were needlessly complicated and out of step with the approach taken by most other countries.

"Basic" EPS is intended to measure performance over a reporting period and is calculated as:

$$\frac{\text{Net income available to common shareholders}}{\text{Weighted average number of common shares outstanding for the period}}$$

"Diluted" EPS is intended to measure performance over a reporting period while giving effect to all potentially dilutive securities. Dilution could occur upon the exercise of stock options, stock warrants or similar instruments, conversion of preferred stock or debt to common stock, or securities to be issued in the future based upon the occurrence of a specific event (i.e., "contingently issuable shares"). In calculating diluted EPS, the numerator of the above equation is adjusted for preferred claims

and any appropriate interest addbacks, and the denominator is increased by all common shares issuable from potentially dilutive securities.

For example, conversion of preferred stock to common stock will have both a numerator effect and a denominator effect on the calculation of dilutive EPS. The numerator of basic EPS is adjusted upward by the preferred dividends eliminated if the preferred stock were converted, and the denominator increases by the number of common shares issuable upon conversion of the preferred shares. If the effect of the conversion were to make dilutive EPS greater than basic EPS (i.e., the conversion is "antidilutive"), then the convertible preferred shares would be left out of the calculation of dilutive EPS.

In addition to a presentation of basic and diluted EPS, a reconciliation between the two must be included in the financial statement notes. Disclosures of securities not entering into the dilutive EPS calculation are also required. Companies with simple capital structures (i.e., with only common stock and nonconvertible preferred stock) need not present dilutive EPS and its related disclosures.

Revenue Recognition (SFAC 5, ARB 43, SOP 81-1, SOP 97-2)

SFAC No. 5, a source of GAAP below category 4, is the only source of general revenue recognition guidance:

> [Revenue recognition] involves considerations of two factors, (a) being realized or realizable and (b) being earned, with sometimes one and sometimes the other being the more important consideration.[3]

In most transactions, both of the above conditions are satisfied at the time goods are delivered or services are performed. There are, however, frequent situations in which special guidance is available in U.S. GAAP. It would be impossible to review the scores of more specific pronouncements,[4] but two areas will be discussed that are frequently encountered or applied by analogy to similar circumstances and are recognized to be susceptible to abuse: long-term construction contracts and software revenue recognition. Publications of the SEC's Division of Enforcement clearly indicate that questionable revenue recognition practices have long been an area of accounting abuse and fraud that is one of their greatest financial reporting concerns.

Long-Term Construction

Long-term contract accounting requires the use of the percentage-of-completion method if estimates of cost to complete a project and its stage of completion over time are reasonably estimable. Otherwise, the completed contract method is used. Under the percentage-of-completion method, the amount of revenue and cost recognized in a period is based on the proportion of total work performed during the accounting period. This may appear to violate the concept of realizability enunciated in SFAC No. 5, but two points are worth mentioning in support of percentage-of-completion:

- It results in a fairer presentation over time of the value created by a contractor if the criteria of reasonable estimation can be met.
- Most contracts or U.S. law give both parties to a construction contract enforceable rights. The contractor's activities may be seen as a sale or transfer of those rights as the contract progresses.

The completed contract method postpones revenue recognition and cost matching until the construction project is completed.

Software Sales

Under U.S. GAAP, software revenue is not recognized until all of the following conditions exist:

- All significant production, modification or customization has been completed.
- There is an arrangement between buyer and seller, usually in the form of a signed contract, purchase order, or on-line authorization.
- Delivery has occurred.

- The fees of the seller are fixed or determinable.
- Collectibility is probable.

Instructions for implementation of these criteria are set forth in SOP 97-2, where an attempt is also made to consider the many variations that can affect the elements of a sale, such as: conditions for customer acceptance, payment and pricing terms, warranties and future service commitments, options for returns, licensing arrangements and more.

---

[3]FASB, Statement of Financial Accounting Concepts No. 5, *Recognition and Measurement in Financial Statements of Business Enterprises,* ¶83, 1984.

[4]This condition may speak to the difficulty of describing the earnings process in general terms. But more likely, it indicates an expectation on the part of U.S. accounting standards setters that too many reporting companies will seek every opportunity to report revenues—even when doing so clearly violates the spirit and intent of general accounting rules and concepts governing revenue recognition.

Inventory (ARB 43)

Inventories of manufacturing and retail enterprises are reported at lower of cost or market. The allowable methods for measuring cost are LIFO, FIFO, weighted average cost, and specific identification. Inventory costs may be estimated using a standard cost system, and there is broad discretion over the types of costs to be included in inventory.

Market, or the utility of inventory to an enterprise, is taken to mean its replacement cost if an enterprise intends to replenish the stocks after they are sold. Because the replacement assumption is not always valid, market may not: (1) exceed net realizable value (the estimated selling price in the ordinary course of business, less costs of completion and disposal), nor (2) be less than net realizable value less a normal profit margin. The lower of cost or market rule is applied separately to each item of inventory, and once written down, subsequent recoveries may not be recognized until sale (through lower cost of goods sold).

Other pronouncements provide inventory measurement guidance in specific industry settings: long-term construction contracts, motion picture films, computer software, agricultural production.

Inventory disclosure standards are principally found in SEC regulations.[5] They include

- Major classes (finished, work-in-process, raw materials).
- Elements of cost, valuation, and cost flow methods.
- If LIFO is used, the excess of replacement or current value amounts over LIFO valuation.
- When LIFO liquidations occur, the amount of income realized from liquidation.

Investments (SFAS 115, SFAS 133, APB 16)

Passive Investments in Marketable Debt and Equity Securities

In addition to cost flow assumptions for inventories, management has broad discretion in determining accounting policies for marketable securities. The one constant, however, is that all passive investments in marketable *equity* securities are measured at their fair values on the balance sheet.

For securities classified by management as "trading," unrealized gains and losses are reported in income in the period they occur. For securities classified as "available for sale," gains or losses are not reported in income until they are either realized or a loss is determined to be caused by "other than temporary" declines in market value. Unrealized gains or losses that are not "other than temporary" bypass the income statement and are reported on the balance sheet in shareholders' equity as Accumulated Other Comprehensive Income.[6]

In addition to trading and available-for-sale categories, a third category, "held to maturity," is available for debt instruments. These securities are measured at cost and amortized to maturity value.

Investments in Derivative Securities

The accounting for investments in derivative securities and hedging activities are described in Chapter 6 of the text.

---

[5]U.S. Securities and Exchange Commission, *Regulation S-X,* Rule 5-02.

[6]See the discussion of hedge accounting in Chapter 6 for a description of Other Comprehensive Income.

Consolidation of Controlling Interests
Criteria for Consolidation[7]

A subsidiary must be consolidated with the results of its parent when the parent holds a majority voting interest in the shares of the subsidiary. Exceptions occur only if (1) majority voting control is likely to be temporary or (2) actual control does not rest with the parent. An example of the first exception is a subsidiary of an acquired company that will be sold soon as part of a plan to acquire the company.

Examples of the second exception are subsidiaries in bankruptcy (control may rest with a court of law, or with creditors) and foreign subsidiaries whose activities are highly controlled by a foreign government.

Translation of subsidiary financial statements denominated in a foreign currency is discussed in Chapter 6.

Pooling of Interests Accounting

Pooling of interests accounting for a business combination is applied when it is deemed that two companies are joined together in the absence of an acquisition transaction. Generally, a pooling is considered to have occurred when substantially all of the common stock of an autonomous entity is acquired. The common stock of the acquiring company is the only consideration given to the shareholders of the acquired entity, and no transactions are planned by the acquiring company to convert the common shares held by the former shareholders of the acquired company to cash.

Since under pooling of interests accounting no purchase is deemed to have occurred, the business combination is recorded without revaluation of the assets or liabilities of the acquired company and no goodwill is recognized. The consolidated financial statements will appear as if the two companies had been combined for all periods presented.

Purchase Accounting

Business combinations that do not meet the criteria for pooling of interests accounting are accounted for as purchases. Goodwill, the excess of the purchase price over the fair value of the acquired net assets, is amortized to expense over a period not to exceed 40 years. Measurement of minority interest is based on the book values of the subsidiary's assets and liabilities *before* the acquisition occurred, and is presented on the balance sheet between liabilities and consolidated shareholders' equity. Minority interest in the earnings of the consolidated entity is displayed as an operating expense.

Equity Method

The equity method is used to account for those investments that are neither passive nor controlling. SEC Regulation S-X requires footnote disclosure of summarized financial information of the assets, liabilities, and earnings for those equity investees (and unconsolidated subsidiaries) that individually or collectively account for a significant portion of a company's income or total assets.

Revaluation of Assets (SFAS 121)

Upward revaluations of assets are permitted only for those assets that are measured at their fair value. Noncurrent assets are to be revalued downward to fair value when the estimated undiscounted future cash flows stemming from the asset (or the smallest asset grouping for which cash flows can be measured) is less than its book value.

---

[7]At the time of this writing, the FASB has announced an intention to eliminate pooling of interests accounting, to revise criteria for consolidation, and revise accounting for goodwill. These projects are controversial, and the outcome of the board's future deliberations is highly uncertain.

Interest Capitalization (SFAS 34)

Interest cost must be capitalized when a company constructs property or equipment. The amount to be capitalized is the theoretical amount that could have been avoided if costs to construct the asset had not been incurred. Thus, it is not necessary for a project to be actually financed with interest-bearing debt in order for its cost basis to be increased by capitalized interest costs. The theoretical amount to be capitalized is based on the company's capital structure and incremental borrowing rate.

Deferred Costs (SOP 98-5, SOP 93-7, IAG—Casinos)

For the most part, cost deferrals are not allowed under U.S. GAAP, even for businesses that have not yet begun their principal operations or generated significant revenues ("development stage enterprises"). However, some exceptions do exist, primarily in the area of promotional costs. For example, direct-response advertising costs may be deferred and allocated to expense over the periods in which revenues are expected to be generated. Restaurant or casino preopening costs may be deferred until the period in which the opening occurs.

Pensions (SFAS 87)

Pension plans in the United States usually entail contributions by employers for the purpose of funding an employees' retirement. The contributions are usually made during the employees' working life to a "pension trust," which is a special-purpose entity set up to hold and invest contributed assets and make payments to employees over the period of their retirement. A "defined contribution" pension plan makes payments to employees based on past contributions to the trust and the investment income from the assets in the pension trust. A "defined benefit" plan obligates the employer to a fixed amount of payments to a retiree, without consideration of the return on the assets in the pension trust. The actual amount of the defined benefit obligation is usually determined at the retirement date as a function of years of service and average salary in the final years of employment. Thus, employers bear the investment risk under a defined benefit plan; conversely, employees bear the investment risk under a defined contribution plan.

The accounting for a defined contribution plan is straightforward. The employer recognizes an expense as required contributions to the pension trust accrue. Accounting for a defined benefit plan is the topic of the remainder of this section and entails measurement of two components of the plan: (1) the present value of the estimated future payments to be made to employees (i.e., "pension obligation), reduced by (2) the fair value of the assets in the pension trust (i.e., "pension plan assets").

With respect to measurement of the pension plan obligation, two measures are used, one for measurement of the net pension obligation on the balance sheet and one for measurement of pension expense:

1. *Accumulated Benefit Obligation.* This measure of the pension obligation is based on current salaries and years of service as of the balance sheet date. If the accumulated benefit obligation exceeds the fair value of plan assets—that is, the plan is "underfunded"—the net liability must be reported on the balance sheet.

2. *Projected Benefit Obligation.* This measure of the pension obligation is based on *expected future* salaries and years of service as of the balance sheet date. The amount of pension expense to be reported on the income statement each period is derived from this projected benefit obligation.

Note, most importantly, that periodic pension expense is not determined by changes in the net pension liability reported on the balance sheets as of the beginning and end of the period because two different measures of the pension obligation are used.[8] Thus, the income statement will not articulate with the balance sheets! The difference between the two measures of pension obligation is added or subtracted to Accumulated Other Comprehensive Income in the shareholders' equity section of the balance sheet.[9]

Because of the complex accounting for defined benefit pension plans, extensive disclosures of the elements of pension expense and pension liability are required. To aid in the ability to read and interpret these disclosures, the factors that influence periodic pension expense are summarized below:

- *Service cost*—The increase in the present value of the pension obligation attributable to employee service during the year.

- *Interest cost*—The increase in the present value of the pension obligation due to the passage of time. In other words, becoming one year closer to anticipated payment dates increases the present value of the payments.

- *Expected return on plan assets*—The anticipated increase in the value during the year of the pension plan's assets.

- *Actuarial gains or losses*—The effect of actual experience or changes in estimates, for example, unanticipated salary increases, changes in the estimate of return on pension plan assets, or returns on assets that were higher than expected.

- *Amortization of prior service cost*—The increase in the present value of estimated pension payments resulting from employees' receiving retroactive credit for enhancements of pension plan benefits. The total value of this retroactive credit is amortized to expense over the expected remaining years of employment of the employees receiving the credit.

- *Amortization of the transition obligation*—The amount of the pension liability as of the date of adoption of SFAS 87 is amortized to expense over the expected remaining years of employment at the time of the adoption.[10]

Post Retirement Benefits Other Than Pensions (SFAS 106)

In addition to pensions, some companies commit to paying additional benefits, principally health care costs, of retirees. The estimated amount of this obligation is accrued as employees provide service and reported as an expense in those periods.

While accruals of health care costs years before they are to be paid may be conceptually justified, some argue that the low reliability of the estimates results in questionable relevance, principally because of the inherent unpredictability of future health care costs. Nonetheless, expected benefits to be paid are reported on the balance sheet at their present value. Those companies that elect to prefund these benefits in a manner similar to pension funding may offset the liability by the fair value of the assets in the plan.

Leased Assets (SFAS 13)

The accounting for leases attempts to reflect the substance of a transaction rather than its legal form. Capital lease accounting is meant to capture those circumstances in which nearly all of the benefits and costs of ownership of an asset have been transferred to the lessee. An asset and corresponding liability are recognized at lease inception for the present value of minimum lease payments if the lease satisfies at least one of the following criteria for "capital lease" accounting:

- Ownership of the asset will be transferred to the lessee by the end of the lease term.

---

[8]There is no conceptual justification for this approach. It is widely acknowledged to be the result of a political compromise between the FASB and reporting companies, who wanted to avoid reporting potentially significant amounts of pension underfunding as measured by the projected benefit obligation.

[9]See the discussion of hedge accounting in Chapter 6 for a description of Other Comprehensive Income.

[10]FASB, Statement of Financial Accounting Standards No. 87, *Employers' Accounting for Pensions,* 1985, 77.

- The lessee holds an option to purchase the asset at a "bargain price."
- The term of the lease is greater than 75 percent of the estimated useful life of the asset.
- The present value of the minimum lease payments is greater than or equal to 90 percent of the fair value of the asset to be leased.

Under capital lease accounting, the booked leased asset is amortized to expense over the term of the lease. The lease payments on the lease obligation are allocated to interest expense and principal retirement over the term of the lease. When none of the conditions for capital lease accounting are met, then "operating lease" accounting is applied. There is no balance sheet recognition of an asset or liability at the inception of the lease, and therefore, there is no recognition of leased asset amortization or principal reduction on a lease liability. Each lease payment is recorded as an expense when incurred.

Income Taxes (SFAS 109)

The measurement of income tax expense can be one of the most significant differences in accounting systems around the world, since it is often the largest single component of expense on the income statement. Also, book-tax conformity varies widely in its impact on financial reporting throughout the world. The extensive discussion of income taxes in this appendix reflects these considerations as well as the complexity of recently enacted U.S. GAAP. To set the context, we begin with a basic discussion of the range of approaches available to standard setters for measuring periodic tax expense.

Measuring Tax Expense—the Alternative Approaches

Alternatives for measuring tax expense exist because some revenues and expenses that enter into the calculation of pretax income in published financial reports (hereinafter referred to as "pretax book income") for one period are reflected in taxable income—that is, on the tax return—in some other period. There are three basic approaches to financial reporting that deal with this problem, and their differences may be best illustrated via a simplistic example as the one contained in Exhibit A-1 for Impuesto Company. The example spans Impuesto Company's first four years of existence.

We assume that the only source of difference between Impuesto's pretax book and taxable income arises from applying straight-line depreciation for financial reporting and accelerated depreciation for tax purposes to noncurrent assets. Although total depreciation expense is equal over the four years of the example, depreciation for tax purposes is greater than (less than) book depreciation expense in the earlier (later) years of the example. Relatedly, the book value of the related noncurrent asset is consistently higher than the tax basis of the asset until the end of Year 4 when book value and tax basis are both zero.

EXHIBIT A-1

Impuesto Company

	Year 1	Year 2	Year 3	Year 4	Total
Data					
Statutory income tax rate	40%	40%	30%	30%	
Taxable income per tax return	70	110	90	130	400
Pretax book income	100	100	100	100	400
Preliminary Calculations					
Taxes due per the tax return	28	44	27	39	138
Difference between book value and tax basis					
of net assets at year-end	30	20	30	-	
Flow-Through Method					
Income Statement					
Tax expense	28	44	27	39	138
After-tax book income	72	56	73	61	262
Balance Sheet					
No effect					
Tax expense/pretax book income	28%	44%	27%	39%	35%
Deferral Method					
Income Statement					
Current tax expense	28	44	27	39	138
Deferred tax expense	12	(4)	4	(12)	-
Total tax expense	40	40	31	27	138
After-tax book income	60	60	69	73	262
Balance Sheet					
Deferred tax liability at end of period	12	8	12	-	
Tax expense/pre-tax book income	40%	40%	31%	27%	35%
Asset-Liability Method (U.S. GAAP)					
Income Statement					
Current tax expense	28	44	27	39	138
Deferred tax expense	12	(4)	1	(9)	-
Total tax expense	40	40	28	30	138
After-tax book income	60	60	72	70	262
Balance Sheet					
Deferred tax liability at end of period	12	8	9	-	
Tax expense/pre-tax book income	40%	40%	28%	30%	35%
"Current tax rate"	28%	44%	27%	39%	35%
Note: Basis Difference under Asset-Liability Method	30	20	30	-	

Flow-through Method

This method ignores differences between pretax book income and taxable income per the tax return, allowing taxes due per tax returns to "flow through" to tax expense per books. Critics of the flow-through approach point to its failure to match a proper amount of tax expense to the pretax book income for the period; since pretax book income is the same in the first two years, the matching principle requires that after-tax income should also be the same. As the historical cost-rooted accounting concept of matching is not well observed by the flow-through approach, it is not well received by accounting standard setters.

Deferral Method

This method matches tax expense with pretax book income. The time series of after-tax income trends can parallel the trend in pretax income by allocating the tax effects of temporary differences between book and taxable income on the basis of the difference between pretax book and taxable income. The effect of this method is to recognize $12 ([$100 − $70] × 40%) of "deferred tax expense" in addition to the $28 of taxes due for the first year.

The amount of deferred tax expense reverses itself when the sign of the temporary difference changes, *so long as the tax rate applied to the reversal of the temporary difference is the same rate used when the timing difference first originated.* Note, however, that the deferral method does not match tax expense to pretax income when the tax rate changes after the origination and before the reversal of a temporary difference. This is illustrated in Exhibit A-1 where after-tax book income in Year 4 is different from Year 3, even though the tax rate and pretax book income are the same for both years.

Asset-Liability Method (U.S. GAAP)

This method measures appropriate amounts of deferred tax assets and liabilities each period and determines tax expense through the changes in deferred tax assets and liabilities. A deferred tax liability of $12 in the first year results from the $30 difference in *book values* and *tax bases* of net assets (i.e., assets minus liabilities) that existed at the end of Year 1. Deferred tax expense for any year is the net change in deferred tax assets and liabilities from the beginning to the end of the year. Total tax expense is the sum of current and deferred tax expense components.

The major difference between the deferral and the asset-liability methods is seen in Year 3, when the enacted tax rate changes to 30 percent. The deferred tax liability is remeasured because of this change to reflect the expected amount payable under the new tax rate.

Measuring Tax Expense under U.S. GAAP

Deferred tax expense is measured under the asset-liability method as the net change in deferred tax assets and liabilities during the year, which means that identification of deferred tax assets and liabilities drives the measurement of deferred tax expense. Deferred tax assets and liabilities come from any of the following sources:

- "Taxable temporary differences" in book values and tax bases of assets and liabilities that give rise to deferred tax assets. If the book value of an asset is *greater* than its tax basis, a deferred tax liability is recognized in the amount of the enacted tax rate multiplied by the difference. The justification is as follows: If the income realized from the use of an asset is at least as much as its book value, then taxable income of at least the difference between the book and tax bases will be reported. When reported, the amount of taxes due is found by multiplying the taxable income by the tax rate. Similarly a deferred tax liability is recognized when the book value of a liability is *less* than its tax basis.

- "Deductible temporary differences" in book values and tax bases of assets and liabilities give rise to deferred tax assets, which may be reduced by a "valuation allowance." If the book value of an asset is *less* than its tax basis, a deferred tax asset is recognized in the amount of the enacted tax rate multiplied by the difference. The justification is as follows: If the income realized from the use of an asset is equal to its book value, then a tax deduction of at least the difference between the book and tax bases will be reported. When reported, the amount of taxes due is found by multiplying the taxable income by the tax rate. Similarly a deferred tax asset is recognized when the book value of a liability is *greater* than its tax basis.

- Other temporary differences that cannot be identified with a particular asset or liability, but nonetheless (1) result from events that have been recognized in the financial statements and (2) result in taxable or deductible amounts based on applicable tax law. Tax loss and tax credit carryforwards, for example, give rise to deferred tax assets, which may be reduced by a valuation allowance.

"Permanent differences" between pretax book and taxable income (for example, tax-free interest earned) do not give rise to deferred tax assets or liabilities.

Exhibit A-2 lists and briefly explains some of the most commonly encountered taxable and deductible differences in the United States.

EXHIBIT A-2

Common Sources of Taxable Differences

Source	*Description*	*Taxable or Deductible*
Property, plant and equipment	Straight-line depreciation for book and accelerated depreciation used for tax purposes	Taxable
	Change in book value as a result of a business combination, but no change for tax purposes.	Usually taxable
	Reduction in tax basis for investment tax credit	Taxable
Accounts receivable	Allowance not allowed for tax purposes, or a reserve for tax purposes is different than net book value	Usually taxable
Marketable securities	Securities marked to market for book purposes and maintained at cost for tax purposes	Taxable or deductible
Intercorporate investments	Cost method used for tax purposes and equity method used for book	Taxable or deductible
	Basis difference in assets resulting from consolidation	Taxable or deductible
Pension liability	Tax basis different from book value	Taxable or deductible
Liability for postretirement benefits	Not recognized for tax purposes	Deductible
Deferred income	Installment method used for tax purposes	Taxable
Debt	Differences in treatment of debt discount and issue costs	Taxable or deductible
Inventory	Valuation reserves for book purposes not allowed for tax purposes	Deductible

Income Tax Disclosures

Understanding income tax disclosures in the footnotes to financial statements is a challenging task requiring some knowledge of financial reporting and tax codes of various jurisdictions throughout the world. It is no wonder that no two companies, even in the same industry, can be expected to have identical income tax disclosure items. However, the payoff to analysts who are capable and willing to invest the time in reading these disclosures is that they are often a convenient way to grasp the economic effects of significant events, identify potentially aggressive financial reporting practices, and for significant refinements to tax components of earnings and cash flow forecasts.

Income tax disclosures rules for public companies are driven by SFAS 109 and SEC Regulation S-X. Required disclosures for most companies include:

- The components and amounts of deferred tax assets and liabilities.
- The components of pretax income as either domestic or foreign.
- The components of income tax expense for the period, including domestic and foreign sources.
- A reconciliation (using percentages or dollar amounts) between tax expense that would have been recognized at the federal statutory tax rate and the effective tax rate.
- A description of types of temporary differences for which a deferred tax liability has not been recognized (e.g., investments in foreign subsidiaries or foreign corporate joint ventures).

Contingencies (SFAS 5, SOP 96-1, SAB 92)

A contingency is defined as an existing uncertain condition that will be resolved when one or more future events occurs. Gain contingencies are never booked and loss contingencies are recorded when it is "probable" that an asset has been impaired or a liability has been incurred, *and* the range of losses can be reasonably estimated.

The amount of loss accrued is the amount most likely to occur. If a range of losses is judged to be equally likely, then the minimum of the range is reported as the loss. If a loss is less than probable of occurrence, but reasonably likely, then footnote disclosure only is required.

SEC regulations supplement contingency accounting and disclosures by requiring additional disclosures outside of the financial statements and footnotes pertaining to forward-looking information. Such information is contained in Management's Discussion & Analysis of Operations, Liquidity and Capital Resources (MD&A) when ". . . known trends, demands, commitments, events and uncertainties . . . [are reasonably expected to have] . . . a material impact on operations or liquidity."[11] Quantitative and qualitative disclosures of potential losses due to market risk (e.g., exchange rates, interest rates, commodity prices, equity prices) are also required.[12]

Unusual Items (APB 30, EITF 94-3)

An event or transaction that is distinctive because it is unusual *or* infrequently occurring (but not both) is reported as a separate component of income from continuing operations. While extraordinary items (discussed earlier in this appendix) are not frequently encountered in financial statements, unusual items are being reported with increasing frequency by U.S. companies, often to "restructure" operations or to exit an activity that does not qualify to be accounted for as a discontinued operation.

Unusual items may not be reported on the income statement net of taxes, and no subtotal should be made to set them apart from other components of income from continuing operations. However, supplemental disclosures in financial statement notes and MD&A invariably contain a high level of detail to comply with SEC regulations.

---

[11]SEC *Regulation S-K,* Item 303.
[12]SEC *Regulation S-K,* Item 305.

In addition to restructurings, examples of items reported as unusual are asset write-downs (i.e., "impairments"), accruals of litigation, and environmental remediation costs.

Shareholders' Equity

Categories of shareholders' equity exist primarily for legal or historical reasons. The specific categories include:

- Contributed capital—often referred to as paid-in capital. It includes amounts for both preferred and common stock.[13]
- Additional paid-in capital—includes contributed capital in excess of par or stated value of stock issued and the effects on equity of treasury stock transactions.
- Retained earnings—accumulated earnings of the corporation since inception, less dividends paid out of earnings (i.e., nonliquidating dividends). A portion of retained earnings may be reported as restricted, possibly as a result of sinking-fund provisions of bond indentures or legal requirements to protect creditors after treasury stock purchases.
- Accumulated Other Comprehensive Income—changes to shareholders' equity that do not result from transactions with shareholders or items recognized as income.
- Treasury stock—Reductions in shareholders' equity resulting from net repurchases of the company's own stock. When treasury stock is reissued at an amount different than its book value, the difference is debited or credited to additional paid-in capital.

---

[13]SEC *Regulation S-X,* Rule 5-02 requires that redeemable preferred stock (i.e., preferred stock that can be redeemed for cash at the option of the holder) lack sufficient characteristics of equity. It must be reported outside of shareholders' equity.

Glossary

accelerated depreciation   A cost allocation method in which depreciation deductions are largest in an asset's earlier years but decrease over time.

accounting   A language used by businesspeople to communicate the financial status of their enterprise to interested parties.

accounting exposure (risk)   The hazard of recognizing and reporting foreign exchange gains (losses) in the income statement for a given period.

accounting period   The time, usually a quarter or one year, to which accounting reports are related.

accounting policies   The specific accounting principles and practices adopted by a company to report its financial results.

Accounting Principles Board (APB)   An organization of the AICPA that established U.S. GAAP during the period 1957–1973; some of the APB's opinions remain in force today.

Accounting Standards Committee (ASC)   The principal accounting standards-setting organization in Great Britain (and the U.K.) until 1990; issued statements of standard accounting practice or SSAPs.

accounts receivable   An asset representing the future receipt of cash (or other assets), usually as a consequence of a sale of goods or services; see also *debtors*.

accounts receivable turnover ratio   A measure of the effectiveness of receivable management calculated as net credit sales for the period divided by the average balance in accounts receivable.

accrual concept (accrual basis of accounting)   An accounting measurement system that records the financial effects of transactions when a business transaction occurs without regard to the timing of the cash effects of the transaction.

active investment   An intercorporate investment by an investor company that allows the investor to exercise influence or control over the operations of the investee-company.

additional paid-in-capital   Amounts paid by shareholders in excess of the minimum amount required for the shares to be fully paid (e.g., par or stated value); also known as *paid-in capital in excess of par value* and *share premium reserve.*

Advance Corporation Tax (ACT)   A British tax paid by corporations based on the level of dividends expected to be distributed to shareholders.

affiliated company   A company in which an investor company holds an equity investment in excess of 20 percent of the voting capital stock.

aging of accounts receivables   A method of accounting for uncollectible trade receivables by which an estimate of the bad debts expense is determined by classifying the specific receivable balances into age categories and then applying probability estimates of noncollection.

Aktiebolag (AB)   A limited liability company in Sweden.

Aktiengesellschaft (AG)   A publicly held corporation in Germany.

American depositary receipt (ADR)   A security issued by a bank or other recognized trustee representing an actual shareholding in a foreign company; these beneficial ownership shares are issued to avoid problems relating to the collection of dividends denominated in a foreign currency and to facilitate rapid ownership transfer; also referred to as *stock depositary receipts.*

amortization   A cost allocation process that spreads the cost of an intangible asset over its expected useful life.

annual report   The report prepared by a company at year-end for its shareholders and other interested parties that frequently includes a letter to the shareholders from the chairperson of the board, management's discussion and analysis of financial performance, and a variety of financial highlights in addition to the basic financial statements; it also includes the auditor's report in which the independent auditors express an opinion as to the fairness of the financial data presented in the financial statements.

asset management The effective utilization of a company's revenue-producing assets; a measure of management's ability to effectively utilize a company's assets to produce income.

asset turnover The rate at which sales (or revenues) are generated from a given level of assets; a measure of a company's effectiveness in generating revenues from the assets at its disposal, calculated as net sales divided by average total assets.

assets Tangible and intangible resources of an enterprise that are expected to provide it future economic benefits.

associated company One that is not a legal subsidiary of another company (i.e., control is less than 50+ percent) but in which the other company exercises significant influence (i.e., presumably at least a 20 percent shareholding).

audit A process of investigating the adequacy of a company's system of internal controls, its consistent use of generally accepted accounting principles, and the presence of material errors or mistakes in its accounting data.

auditor's opinion A report to a company's shareholders and the board of directors issued by an independent auditor summarizing his or her findings with regard to the company's financial statements; the four types of opinions are clean or unqualified, qualified, adverse, and disclaimer.

authorized shares The total number of shares of capital stock authorized to be sold under a company's charter of incorporation.

average cost method An inventory cost-flow method that assigns the average cost of available finished goods to units sold and, thus, to cost of goods sold.

average number of days' inventory on hand ratio A measure of the effectiveness of inventory management, calculated as 365 days divided by the inventory turnover ratio; a measure of the appropriateness of current inventory levels given current sales volume.

average receivable collection period ratio A measure of the effectiveness of accounts receivable management, calculated by dividing the receivable turnover ratio into 365 days.

balance sheet (statement of financial position) An accounting statement describing, as of a specific date, the assets, liabilities, and shareholders' equity of an enterprise.

blocked funds risk The hazard that a government will restrict the flow of funds either into or out of a given locale.

book value (per share) The dollar amount of the net assets of a company on a per share of common (ordinary) share basis; calculated as total assets minus total liabilities divided by the number of outstanding shares of ordinary or common shares.

book value (of an asset) The original cost of an asset less any accumulated depreciation (depletion or amortization) taken to date; also known as *carrying value.*

Borsa Valori di Milano The Italian stock exchange in Milan, Italy.

business combination The purchase of one or more businesses that are merged together as one accounting entity but not necessarily into one legal entity.

capital expenditure An expenditure for the purchase of a noncurrent asset, usually property, plant, or equipment.

capital intensity ratio A measure of a company's operating leverage calculated as fixed assets divided by total assets.

capitalization The process of assigning value to a balance sheet account, such as a capitalized asset (e.g., a leased asset) or a capitalized liability (e.g., a lease liability).

capitalization (of a company) The composition of a company's long-term financing, specifically, shareholders' equity and long-term debt.

capital lease A noncancelable lease obligation accounted for as a liability on the balance sheet; a lease agreement in which the risks and rewards of asset ownership pass (either formally or informally) to the lessee.

cash dividend payout A measure of the cash return to common shareholders, calculated as the cash dividend per common share divided by the basic earnings per share.

cash dividend yield A measure of the cash return to common shareholders calculated as the cash dividend per common share divided by the average market price per common share.

cash equivalents Bank deposits usually in the form of short-term certificates of deposit and short-term investments in relatively risk-free securities (e.g., U.S. government securities).

cash flow adequacy ratio A cash flow ratio calculated as the cash flow from operations divided by the sum of capital expenditures, dividends paid, and long-term debt repayment; indicates the extent to which cash flows from operations are sufficient to cover asset replacement and capital carrying costs.

cash flow from operations (CFFO) A measure of the net cash flows from transactions involving sales of goods or services and the acquisition of inputs used to provide the goods or services sold; the excess of cash receipts over cash disbursements relating to the operations of a company for a given period; net income calculated on a cash basis.

CFFO to current liabilities ratio A measure of firm liquidity calculated as the cash flow from operations (CFFO) divided by average current liabilities; reflects the short-term debt coverage provided by current cash flows from operations.

CFFO to interest charges ratio A measure of solvency calculated as the cash flow from operations divided by interest charges; reflects the extent to which interest charges are covered by current cash flows from operations.

CFFO to total liabilities ratio A measure of solvency calculated as the cash flow from operations divided by average total liabilities; reflects the extent to which current cash flow from operations is sufficient to satisfy both long-term and short-term obligations.

chaebol Korean business conglomerates (similar to Japan's *keiretsu*), numbering approximately 30, which dominate that country's economy (e.g., Samsung, Hyundai, Lucky Gold-star, and Daewoo).

chartered accountant (CA) A certified public accountant in Great Britain (and elsewhere).

classified balance sheet A balance sheet that delineates the assets and liabilities as current and noncurrent.

Chusik Hoesa A Korean joint-stock company formed by seven or more investors with a minimum capitalization of W50 million.

collateral The value of various assets used as security for various debts, usually bank borrowings, that will be transferred to a creditor if the obligation is not fully paid.

collectivism The extent to which the societal ties between individuals are strongly coupled; the opposite of individualism.

Commercial Code of Japan Dates to 1899, provides general rules for the valuation of assets and liabilities, provision of reserves, and the accounting for legal and capital reserves.

Commissione Nazionale per le Societa e la Borsa (CON-SOB) The Italian equivalent of the U.S. Securities and Exchange Commission; regulates listing requirements and accounting disclosures for publicly held Italian companies.

commitment A type of contingent liability in which the value of the future obligation is known but that is not currently an obligation because various future events or conditions have not transpired or are currently satisfied.

common-size balance sheet A balance sheet in which all account balances are expressed as a percentage of total assets or total equities.

common-size financial statements Financial statements in which the dollar amounts are expressed as a percentage of some common statement item (e.g., a common-size income statement might express all items as a percentage of sales).

common-size income statement An income statement in which all revenue and expense items are expressed as a percentage of net sales.

common equity share of operating earnings (CSOE) A measure of the proportion of a company's operating earnings allocable to common shareholders.

common shareholders' capital structure leverage ratio (CSL) A measure of a company's financial leverage calculated as average total assets divided by average common equity.

common stock (shares) A form of capital stock (shares) that usually carries the right to vote on corporate issues; a senior equity security; see also ordinary shares.

common stock equivalents A subset of convertible securities, for example stock options and stock warrants, that enable the holder to become a common shareholder by exercising various rights.

Companies Act of 1985 Important British regulation governing the formation of corporations in that country.

compensating balances The percentage of a line of credit or of a loan that a bank requires a borrower to keep on deposit at the bank; the amount increases the effective interest rate of any amount borrowed.

consolidated financial statements Financial statements prepared to reflect the operations and financial condition of a parent company and its wholly or majority-owned subsidiaries.

consolidated reporting A reporting approach in which the financial statements of the parent and subsidiary companies are combined to form one set of financial statements.

contingent asset An asset that may arise in the future if certain events occur.

contingent liability A liability that may arise in the future if certain events occur.

contributed capital The sum of the capital stock accounts and the capital in excess of par (or stated) value accounts.

convenience statement A set of foreign financial statements translated into the language and the currency of another country.

convenience translation A set of foreign financial statements translated into the language (not currency) of another country.

countertrade A trade practice equivalent to barter or the exchange of goods and/or services for other goods and services (i.e., no currency is exchanged); typically occurs as a consequence of restrictive currency laws.

country risk analysis A process of identifying the various types of risks associated with investing or doing business in a given country.

cross-sectional analysis A process of analyzing financial data between or among firms in the same industry, or between a firm and industry averages, to identify comparative financial strengths and weaknesses.

currency risk See *foreign exchange risk.*

current asset Resources of an enterprise, such as cash, accounts receivable, inventory, or prepaid expenses, whose consumption or use is expected to occur within the current operating cycle.

current cost accounting A method of accounting in which financial data are expressed in terms of current rather than historical cost.

current liability An obligation of an enterprise whose settlement requires the use of current assets or the creation of other current liabilities, usually within one year.

current maturity of long-term debt The portion of a long-term obligation payable within the next operating cycle or one year.

current rate method A method of restating foreign financial statements in which assets and liabilities are restated using the current exchange rate at the balance sheet date, and revenues and expenses are translated at a weighted average rate for the period.

current ratio A measure of liquidity and short-term solvency calculated as current assets divided by current liabilities.

debt-to-equity ratio A measure of solvency calculated as long-term debt divided by total shareholders' equity.

debt-to-total capitalization ratio A measure of solvency, calculated as long-term debt divided by the sum of total shareholders' equity and long-term debt.

debtors An alternative designation for accounts and notes receivables, principally used in the financial statements of Great Britain and other Commonwealth companies.

declining balance method A method to depreciate the cost of a tangible asset in which the allocated cost is higher in the early periods of the asset's life (i.e., an accelerated method).

default risk The probability (or hazard) that a company will be unable to meet its short-term or long-term obligations.

defeasance A method of early retirement of debt in which risk-free securities are purchased and then placed in a trust account (i.e., sinking fund) to be used to retire the outstanding debt at its maturity.

deferral A postponement in the recognition of an expense (i.e., Prepaid Insurance) or a revenue (i.e., Unearned Rent) account.

deferred charge An asset that represents an expenditure whose related expense will not be recognized in the income statement until a future period; prepaid rent is an example.

deferred income taxes The portion of a company's income tax expense not currently payable; postponed because of differences in the accounting policies adopted for financial statement purposes versus those policies used for tax reporting purposes.

deficit An accumulated loss in the retained earnings or profit and loss reserve account; a debit balance in Retained Earnings.

depreciation A systematic allocation process that allocates the acquisition cost of a long-lived asset over the expected productive life of the asset.

devaluation A material downward adjustment of the exchange rate between two currencies.

direct financing type lease A capital lease in which the lessor receives income only from financing the "purchase" of the leased asset.

discretionary cash flows A measure of a company's cash flows from operations that are available to finance such discretionary corporate activities as the acquisition of another company, the early retirement of debt or equity, or some form of capital asset expansion.

dividend yield A measure of the level of cash actually distributed to common (ordinary) shareholders calculated as the cash dividend per common (ordinary) share divided by the market price per common (ordinary) share.

double-declining-balance depreciation A method of calculating depreciation by which a percentage equal to twice the straight-line percentage is multiplied by the declining book value to determine the depreciation expense for the period; salvage value ignored when calculating it.

Du Pont formula An overall indicator of corporate performance obtained by multiplying a company's asset turnover by its profit margin; equivalent to ROA or ROI.

earned surplus A term synonymous with *retained earnings* or *profit and loss reserve*.

earnings per share A standardized measure of performance calculated as net income after taxes, less preferred dividends, divided by the weighted-average number of common (ordinary) shares outstanding during an accounting period; also known as *basic EPS*.

economic exposure (risk) The risk of experiencing a real gain (loss) in purchasing power as a consequence of foreign exchange rate fluctuations.

efficient market hypothesis A theory to explain the functioning of capital markets in which share and bond prices always reflect all publicly available information, and any new information is quickly impounded in security prices.

equity in earnings of investee An income statement account representing an investor company's percentage ownership of an investee's (or subsidiary's) net earnings.

equity method A method to value intercorporate equity investments by adjusting the investor's cost basis for the percentage ownership in the investee's earnings (or losses) and for any dividends paid by the investee.

European currency unit (ECU) A currency intended to be used by all European Union members when conducting trade; also known as the euro.

European exchange rate mechanism (ERM) A system created by the EU to stabilize the rate of exchange of currency between EU member–nations.

European Union (EU) An organization of politically independent European nations (currently numbering 15), united to act as a single economic (i.e., trading) entity (or bloc); includes three cooperative alliances intended to improve the efficiency and competitive ability of its member-nations: the European Coal and Steel Community, the European Atomic Energy Commission, and the European Economic Community.

exchange Currency or legal tender used to facilitate trade between parties.

exchange rate The rate at which one unit of currency may be purchased by another unit of currency.

executory contracts A category of legal agreements requiring some type of future performance.

expense An expenditure whose revenue-producing value has been fully consumed and thus has no future revenue-producing value.

expropriation exposure (risk) The likelihood that a company's assets located in a foreign domain will be involuntarily appropriated by the local government, with or without compensation.

extraordinary item A loss or gain that, according to U.S. GAAP, is both unusual in nature and infrequent in occurrence.

face amount (maturity value) The value of a security as stated on the instrument itself; see also settlement value.

Financial Accounting Standards Board (FASB) An independent, private sector organization responsible for establishing U.S. generally accepted accounting principles.

Financial Reporting Council (FRC) An accounting standard-setting organization in the United Kingdom founded in 1990 that succeeded the Accounting Standards Committee; issues financial reporting standards.

financial reporting standard (FRS) An official accounting pronouncement issued by the Financial Reporting Council of the United Kingdom.

financial statement analysis The process of reviewing, analyzing, and interpreting the basic financial statements to assess a company's operating performance and/or financial health.

first-in, first-out (FIFO) An inventory cost-flow method that assigns the first cost value in finished goods inventory to the first unit sold and thus to cost of goods sold.

fiscal year Any continuous 12-month period, usually beginning after a natural business peak.

footnotes Written information by management designed to supplement the numerical data presented in a company's financial statement.

foreign currency option contract A contract providing the right to buy or sell a set quantity of foreign currency at a preset exchange rate within a specified future time frame; typically used to hedge foreign exchange risk exposure and often thought of as *currency insurance*.

foreign currency translation adjustment A shareholders' equity account measuring the change in value of a company's net assets held in a foreign country attributable to changes in the exchange rate of the foreign currency as compared to the U.S. dollar; arises under the current rate method.

foreign exchange Any currency other than the one in which a company prepares its basic financial statements.

foreign exchange exposure (risk) The risk associated with changes in exchange rates between the U.S. dollar and foreign currencies when a company maintains operations in a foreign country.

Form 8-K A special SEC filing required when a material event or transaction occurs between Form 10-Q filing dates. Events usually necessitating the filing of Form 8-K: a change in control or ownership of an enterprise, the acquisition or disposition of a significant amount of assets, a bankruptcy declaration, the resignation of an executive or director of an enterprise, or a change in the independent external auditor.

Form 10-K The annual financial report filing with the SEC required of all publicly held enterprises in the U.S.

Form 10-Q The quarterly financial report filing with the SEC required of all publicly held enterprises in the United States; filed only for the first three quarters of a fiscal year.

Form 20-F The annual financial report filing with the SEC required of all foreign companies whose debt or equity capital is available for purchase/sale on a U.S. exchange.

forward exchange contract A contract providing for the payment (receipt) of a foreign currency at a future date at a specified exchange rate; typically used to hedge foreign exchange risk exposure.

forward exchange rate An exchange rate between two currencies quoted for 30, 60, 90, or 180 days in the future; a rate quoted currently for the exchange of currency at some future specified date.

Fourth Directive A European Union agreement, adopted in 1978, to (1) eliminate legal and bureaucratic obstacles to economic activity between EU member-nations and (2) establish the basic reporting requirements and financial statement formats (i.e., comparability) for companies operating in EU member-nations.

front-end loading An accounting process by which revenues (expenses) are recognized for income statement purposes before they have been earned (incurred).

functional currency The currency of the primary business environment (i.e., country) of a company's operations.

generally accepted accounting principles (GAAP) Methods identified by authoritative bodies (i.e., APB, FASB, SEC) as being acceptable for use in the preparation of external accounting reports.

generally accepted auditing standards (GAAS) Auditing practices and procedures established in the U.S. by the AICPA (or other comparable professional organizations in other countries) and used by CPAs to evaluate a company's accounting system and financial results.

Gesellschaft mit beschränkter Haftung (GmbH) A privately held corporation in Germany.

goodwill An intangible asset representing the excess of the purchase price of acquired net assets over their fair market value.

gross profit (gross margin) A measure of a company's profit on sales calculated as net sales minus the cost of goods or services sold.

gross profit margin ratio A measure of profitability that assesses the percentage of each sales dollar that is recognized as gross profit (i.e., after deducting the cost of goods sold) and that is available to cover other operating expenses (e.g., selling, administrative, interest, and taxes).

harmonization The attempt by various organizations (e.g., the IASC. the EU, IOSCO) to establish a common set of international accounting and reporting standards.

hedge A process of buying or selling commodities, forward contracts, or options for the explicit purpose of reducing or eliminating foreign exchange risk.

hedged items Those accounts (assets, liabilities, revenues) or contracts for which an artificial or natural hedge exists.

hedging instrument A forward exchange contract or option contract acquired to hedge some type of exposure (e.g., currency risk, expropriation risk, political risk).

highest-in, first-out (HIFO) An inventory cost-flow method that assigns the highest cost value available in finished goods inventory to the first unit sold and thus cost of goods sold.

historical cost concept An accounting concept that stipulates that all economic transactions be recorded using the dollar value incurred at the time of the transaction.

holding company (parent company) A company that owns a majority of the voting capital shares of another company.

impairment A temporary or permanent reduction in asset value; usually necessitates a write-down in the asset's balance sheet value.

income A generic term used to indicate revenue from miscellaneous sources (e.g., interest income or rent income) or the excess of revenue over expenses for product sales or services.

income smoothing An accounting practice that implicitly or explicitly attempts to present a stable (but growing) measure of net income (e.g., straight-line depreciation).

income statement (profit and loss statement) An accounting statement describing the revenues earned and expenses incurred by an enterprise for a given period.

independent auditor A professionally trained individual whose responsibilities include the objective review of a company's financial statements prepared for external distribution.

individualism According to G. Hofstede, a cultural construct related to the extent to which the societal ties between individuals are loosely coupled; the opposite of collectivism.

inflation A phenomenon of generally rising prices.

initial public offering (IPO) The first or initial sale of voting stock to the general market by a previously privately held concern.

insolvent (bankrupt) A condition in which a company is unable to pay its current obligations as they come due.

intangible assets The resources of an enterprise, such as goodwill, trademarks, or trade names, that lack an identifiable physical presence.

intercompany profit The profit resulting when one related company sells to another related company; removed from the financial statements when consolidated financial statements are prepared.

intercorporate investments Investments in the shares and bonds of one company by another.

interest coverage ratio See *times-interest-earned ratio.*

interim financial statements Financial statements prepared on a monthly or quarterly basis, usually unaudited.

internal control The policies and procedures implemented by management to safeguard a company's assets and its accounting system against misapplication or misuse.

international accounting standards (IAS) The accounting and reporting standards adopted and promulgated by the IASC.

International Accounting Standards Committee (IASC) An organization established in 1973 by the leading professional accounting groups of the major industrial countries; goals: (1) to formulate, publish, and promote the worldwide acceptance and observance of international accounting standards and (2) to harmonize the accounting standards and procedures relating to the presentation of financial statements on a worldwide basis.

International Federation of Accountants (IFAC) An association of professional accounting organizations from more than 70 nations founded in 1977; largely concerned with developing international guidelines for the accounting profession in the areas of auditing, ethics, and education.

International Organization of Securities Commissions and Similar Organizations (IOSCO) An organization of securities regulatory agencies representing various member-countries, whose goal is to assist in the creation and regulation of orderly international capital markets.

International Stock Exchange (ISE) The largest securities exchange in the United Kingdom.

interperiod tax allocation The process of allocating the actual taxes paid by a company over the periods in which the taxes are recognized for accounting purposes.

inventory The aggregate cost of salable goods and merchandise available to meet customer sales; sometimes referred to as *stocks*.

inventory turnover A measure of the rate of inventory sales.

inventory turnover ratio A measure of the effectiveness of inventory management calculated as the cost of goods sold for a period divided by the average inventory held during that period.

investment ratio A cash flow ratio calculated as capital expenditures divided by the sum of depreciation and proceeds from the sale of assets; indicates the relative change in a company's investment in productive assets.

investment tax credit A reduction in a company's current income taxes payable earned through the purchase of various applicable assets.

investor company A company that holds an equity investment in another company (the investee company).

issued shares The authorized shares of capital stock sold to shareholders less any shares repurchased *and* retired.

Japanese Securities and Exchange Law of 1948 Based largely on the U.S. securities laws of 1933 and 1934; requires companies issuing securities to the public to file financial statements (zaimushohyo) audited by an independent auditor with the Ministry of Finance; also known as shokentorihikiho.

keiretsu An association of Japanese companies with interlocking shareholdings that provide economic support to one another; literally interpreted as "headless combines."

krona The basic unit of currency in Sweden.

last-in, first-out (LIFO) An inventory cost-flow method that assigns the last cost value in finished goods inventory to the first unit sold and thus to cost of goods sold.

lease An agreement to buy or rent an asset.

lessee An individual or company who leases an asset.

lessor The maker of a lease agreement; an individual or company that leases an asset *to* another individual or company.

leverage The extent to which a company's long-term capital structure includes debt financing; a measure of a company's dependency on debt; a company with large quantities of debt is said to be *highly leveraged;* sometimes referred to as *gearing.*

liabilities A company's obligations to repay monies loaned to it, to pay for goods or services received by it, or to fulfill commitments made by it.

life cycle The cycle that an enterprise normally follows throughout its existence: introduction, growth, maturity, decline; see *product life cycle.*

LIFO liquidation The sale of inventory units acquired or manufactured in a prior period at a lower cost; results when the level of LIFO inventory is reduced below its beginning-of-period level.

LIFO reserve An amount presented in the footnotes to the financial statements of companies employing the LIFO me-thod of inventory valuation; calculated as the current cost of ending inventory minus the LIFO cost of ending inventory.

limited company (Ltd) A limited liability but privately held company in the United Kingdom having no minimum capital requirement.

limited liability The concept that shareholders in a corporation are not held personally liable for its losses or debts.

line of credit An agreement with a bank (or other financial institution) by which an organization obtains authorization for short-term borrowings up to a specified amount.

liquid assets Current assets, such as cash, cash equivalents, or short-term investments, that either are in cash form or can be readily converted to cash.

liquidating dividend A cash dividend representing a return of invested capital and, hence, a liquidation of a previous investment.

liquidation The process of selling off the assets of a business, paying any outstanding debts, and distributing any remaining cash to the owners.

liquidity The short-term debt repayment ability of a company; a measure of a company's cash position relative to currently maturing obligations.

listed company A company whose shares or bonds have been accepted for trading on a recognized securities exchange (e.g., NYSE).

lire The basic unit of currency in Italy.

long-term liabilities (noncurrent liabilities) A company's obligations payable after more than one year.

long-term orientation According to G. Hofstede, a cultural societal inclination for the long-term and one that values persistence and thrift.

lower of cost or market A method to value inventories and marketable securities (both current and long term); the lower of an asset's cost basis or current market value used to value the asset accounts for balance sheet purposes.

market price The current fair value of an asset as established by an arm's-length transaction between a buyer and a seller.

marketable securities Short- or long-term investments in the stocks or bonds of other corporations.

matching principle A fundamental accounting concept stipulating that all expenses incurred to generate a given level of revenues should be matched with those revenues in the same accounting period in which the revenues are recognized on the financial statements.

merger A combination of one or more companies into a single corporate entity.

minority interest An account that reflects the percentage ownership in the net assets of a subsidiary held by investors other than the parent company.

monetary assets Resources of an enterprise, such as cash and marketable securities, whose principal characteristic is its monetary denomination.

multinational corporation (MNC) A for-profit organization with operations in two or more countries.

multinational enterprise (MNE) A for-profit or not-for-profit organization with operations in two or more countries (e.g., a multinational corporation).

multiple reporting Reporting by a company that requires the preparation of multiple sets of financial statements in the language and currency of another country.

natural hedge A hedging instrument that exists as a consequence of the normal course of business.

negative goodwill The excess of the net book value of an acquired company over the consideration paid for it.

net assets Total assets minus total liabilities; equivalent to shareholders' equity.

net current assets Current assets minus current liabilities; working capital.

net income (net earnings) The difference between the aggregate revenues and aggregate expenses of an enterprise for a given accounting period; referred to as *net loss* when aggregate expenses exceed aggregate revenues; sometimes referred to as *profit*.

net realizable value The amount of funds expected to be received upon the sale or liquidation of an asset.

net worth (of an enterprise) Total assets minus total liabilities; the value of owners' equity; also known as the *book value* of an enterprise.

noncurrent assets The long-lived resources of an enterprise, such as property, plant, and equipment, whose consumption or use is *not* expected to be completed within the current operating cycle.

noncurrent asset turnover ratio A measure of the effectiveness of noncurrent asset management; calculated as net sales for the period divided by the average balance of noncurrent assets.

noncurrent liability An obligation of an enterprise whose settlement is not expected within one year.

nondiversifiable risk Unique, nonsystematic risk associated with an investment that cannot be effectively hedged (e.g., through portfolio diversification).

nonmonetary assets Resources of an enterprise, such as inventory or equipment, whose principal characteristic is other than its monetary denomination or value.

off–balance sheet debt Economic obligations that are not reported on the face of the balance sheet (e.g., operating leases).

operating cycle The average length of time between the investment in inventory and the subsequent collection of cash from the sale of that inventory.

operating funds index A cash flow ratio calculated as net income divided by cash flow from operations that indicates the portion of operating cash flow provided by net income.

operating lease A lease agreement in which the risks and rewards of asset ownership are retained by the lessor.

operating leverage The extent to which a company operates with a high proportion of fixed costs.

operational risk The probability that unforeseen or unexpected events will occur and consequently reduce or impair the revenue, earnings, and cash flow streams of a company.

option contract Usually used for hedging purposes to grant one party to it the right to choose whether (and sometimes when) a currency exchange will actually take place.

Organization for Economic Cooperation and Development (OECD) Formed in 1960, an association of representatives from various countries whose purpose is to promote economic cooperation among nations.

outstanding shares The number of authorized shares of capital stock sold to shareholders that are currently in the possession of shareholders; the number of issued shares less the shares held in treasury.

owners' equity (shareholders' equity) The dollar value of the owners' (or shareholders') investment in an enterprise; may take two forms—the purchase of shares of stock or the retention of earnings in the enterprise for future use.

paid-in capital in excess of par value (contributed capital in excess of par value) An owners' equity account reflecting the proceeds from the sale of capital stock in excess of the par value (or stated value) of the capital stock; sometimes referred to as *capital surplus reserve* or *premium*.

par value A legal value assigned to a share of capital stock that must be considered in recording the proceeds received from the sale of the stock; see also *stated value*.

passive investment An intercorporate investment in which the investor cannot (or does not) attempt to influence the operations of the investee company.

payback period The time required to recover the cash outlay for an asset or other investment.

permanent difference A difference in reported income or expenses between a company's tax return and its financial statements that will never reverse (i.e., the difference is permanent).

permanent earnings (cash flows) The recurring earnings (cash flows) of a company; earnings (cash flows) expected to recur in future periods.

pledging Using assets as collateral for a bank loan.

political exposure (risk) The degree of stability (or lack thereof) among political groups and the established government in a given country.

pooling of interests A consolidation method that combines the financial results of a parent company and its subsidiary on the basis of existing book values.

power distance According to G. Hofstede, a cultural concept pertaining to the extent members of an institution or a society expect and accept that power is distributed unequally.

preferred stock A (usually) nonvoting form of capital stock whose claims to the dividends and assets of a company precede those of common shareholders; also known as *preference shares*.

premium An amount paid in excess of the face value of a security or debt instrument.

present value The value today of a future stream of cash flows calculated by discounting the cash flows at a given rate of interest.

price-earnings (P-E) ratio A market-based measure of the investment potential of a security calculated as the market price per share divided by the earnings per share; also known as *P-E multiple.*

price-level-adjusted financial statements Financial statements in which the account balances have been restated to reflect changes in price levels due to inflation.

prior period adjustment An accounting adjustment that does not affect the current period's earnings but instead is reflected as an adjustment to beginning retained earnings (or profit and loss reserve).

private placement The sale, or "placement," of a significant number of stocks or bonds to a limited group of buyers (i.e., the securities are not offered for sale to the general marketplace).

privatization The sale of all or part of a previously state-controlled entity to the general public.

product life cycle The cycle of introduction, growth, maturity, and decline that all products and their companies are assumed to pass through in a natural evolutionary fashion.

productivity index A cash flow ratio calculated as the cash flow from operations divided by the capital investment; indicates the relative cash productivity of a company's capital investments.

profit The excess of revenues over expenses.

profit and loss reserve The amount of retained earnings of a company; see *retained earnings.*

profit margin The excess (or insufficiency) of operating revenues over operating expenses; a measure of a company's ability to generate profits from a given level of revenues; calculated as net income after tax divided by net sales; also known as the *return on sales.*

profitability The relative success of a company's operations; a measure of the extent to which accomplishment exceeded effort.

pro forma financial statement A forecasted or projected financial statement for a future accounting period.

proportionate consolidation A method of consolidating the financial results of a parent company and its subsidiary in which only the proportion of net assets owned by the parent are consolidated; as a consequence there is no need for a minority interest account.

proprietary company A label used in some countries to describe a privately held (or nonpublic) company.

prospectus A document describing the nature of a business and its recent financial history, usually prepared in conjunction with an offer to sell capital stock or bonds by a company.

proxy A legal document granting another person or company the right to vote for a shareholder on matters involving a shareholder vote.

prudence The criterion used under German GAAP to establish the appropriateness and necessity of recognizing a loss contingency.

public company One whose voting shares are listed for trading on a recognized securities exchange or are otherwise available for purchase (sale) by public investors.

public limited company (Plc) A limited liability publicly held company in the United Kingdom; must have share capital of at least £50,000.

purchase accounting A consolidation method in which the financial results of a parent company and its subsidiary are combined using the fair market value of the subsidiary's net worth.

qualified opinion Issued by an independent auditor indicating that the financial statements of a company are fairly presented on a consistent basis and use generally accepted accounting principles but for which some concern or exception has been noted.

quick assets Highly liquid, short-term assets such as cash, cash equivalents, short-term investments, and receivables.

quick ratio (acid test ratio) A measure of liquidity and short-term solvency calculated as quick assets divided by current liabilities.

ratio A financial indicator (e.g., the current ratio) formed by comparing two account balances (e.g., current assets and current liabilities).

ratio analysis The process of analyzing and interpreting the ratios formed from two or more financial statement numbers.

realized loss (gain) The amount recognized in the financial statements usually due to the sale of an asset.

rear-end loading An accounting process by which expenses (revenues) are deferred for income statement purposes despite being incurred (earned).

receivable turnover A measure of the rate of collections on sales.

receivable turnover ratio A measure of the rate of collections on sales, calculated as net sales divided by the average receivable balance; the rate at which a company's receivables are converted to cash.

reconciliation report A statement or report reconciling the financial statements of a foreign entity to the accepted or prevailing accounting practice of another country.

registrar An independent agent, normally a bank or a trust company, that maintains a record of the number of a company's shares of capital stock that have been issued and to whom.

reorganization A process of changing the ownership structure of a company, usually as a direct result of a deficit in retained earnings.

replacement cost The cost to reproduce or repurchase a given asset (e.g., a unit of inventory).

reporting currency The currency used to measure and report a company's net assets (i.e., the "local" currency).

reserve An owners' equity account including the profit and loss reserve (i.e., retained earnings), revaluation reserve, capital reserve, or share premium reserve (i.e., paid-in capital in excess of par value), and legal reserves (those mandated by a given country's laws of incorporation).

retained earnings Earnings of an enterprise that have been retained in the enterprise (i.e., have not been paid out as dividends) for future corporate use; see *profit and loss reserve.*

retained earnings—appropriated The amount of total retained earnings that has been allocated for specific corporate objectives, such as the redemption of debt or capital stock.

retained earnings—restricted The amount of total retained earnings that is legally restricted from being paid out as dividends to shareholders usually because of a borrowing agreement with a bank or other financial institution.

return on common equity (ROCE) ratio A measure of profitability calculated as the net income available to common shareholders divided by average total common equity for the period.

return on owners' equity (ROE) ratio A measure of profitability; a measure of the relative effectiveness of a company in utilizing the assets provided by the owners to generate net income; calculated as net income after tax divided by average shareholders' equity.

return on sales ratio (net profit margin ratio) A measure of profitability calculated as the percentage of each sales dollar earned as net income (i.e., net income after tax divided by net sales).

return on total assets (ROA) A measure of profitability that assesses the relative effectiveness of a company in using available resources to generate net income; also called *return on investment* (ROI); calculated as net income after tax divided by average total assets.

revaluation A material upward adjustment of the exchange rate between two currencies; an upward adjustment in asset value, usually undertaken to reflect the economic effects of inflation.

revenues The inflow of assets, the reduction in liabilities, or both, from transactions involving an enterprise's principal business activity (e.g., sales of products or services); also referred to as *turnover* or *total trading transactions.*

sales-type lease A capital lease that generates two income streams: (1) from the "sale" of the asset and (2) from financing the "purchase" of the asset.

salvage value (residual value) The amount expected to be recovered when an asset is retired, removed from active use, and sold.

self-sustaining foreign operation A foreign entity financially and operationally independent of its parent company.

sensitivity analysis A process by which the effect of a change in a given assumption is assessed (i.e., as in a pro forma analysis).

Seventh Directive A European Union agreement adopted in 1983 governing the preparation of consolidated financial statements for companies operating in EU member-nations.

short-term orientation A societal inclination that values personal stability, protecting "face," and respect for tradition.

Società a Responsabilità Limitada (S.r.l.) A closely held, limited liability entity in Italy.

Società per Azioni (S.p.A.) A publicly held (joint stock) company in Italy.

solvency The long-term debt repayment ability of a company; a measure of a company's long-term liquidity.

specific identification An inventory cost-flow method that assigns the actual cost of producing a specific unit to that unit; the only inventory method that matches exactly the cost flow and physical flow.

spot rate The prevailing exchange rate between two currencies on a given date.

stated value The recorded accounting value of capital stock; see also *par value.*

statement of cash flows An accounting statement describing the sources and uses of cash flows for an enterprise for a given period.

statement of changes in financial position An accounting statement describing the inflows and outflows of a company's funds or working capital.

statement of fund flows An accounting statement describing a company's inflows and outflows of funds over a given period; *funds* defined with reference to a company's cash, liquid assets, or working capital.

statement of owners' equity (statement of shareholders' equity) An accounting statement describing the principal transactions affecting the owners' (or shareholders') interests in an enterprise for a given period.

statement of retained earnings An accounting statement describing the beginning and ending balances in retained earnings and the major changes to the retained earnings account (e.g., dividends and net income).

Statement of Standard Accounting Practice (SSAPs) Official accounting pronouncements issued by the Accounting Standards Committee of the United Kingdom.

stock depositary receipt (SDR) A beneficial ownership share in a foreign entity held by a trustee (e.g., a bank or brokerage firm) on behalf of the investor; see *American depositary receipt.*

stockholders' equity The owners' equity of a corporation; comprises paid-in capital and retained earnings, as well as any reserve accounts; also known as *shareholders' equity.*

straight-line method A method to depreciate the cost of a tangible asset or to amortize the cost of an intangible asset in which the allocated cost is constant over the life of the asset.

strategic business units (SBUs) Autonomous business segments of a company that could be managed and run as viable isolated entities.

subsidiary A company in which an investor company (the parent) holds an equity investment in excess of 50 percent of the voting shares of the investee company.

sum-of-the-years'-digits method A method to depreciate the cost of a tangible asset in which the allocated cost is higher in the early periods of the asset's life (i.e., an accelerated method).

take-or-pay contract An executory contract by which one party agrees to pay for certain inventory (or other products) regardless of whether the inventory is physically received or not.

tangible asset Resources of an enterprise, such as property, plant, and equipment, that possess physical characteristics or have a physical presence.

temporal method A method of translating foreign financial statements in which cash, receivables, and payables are translated at the exchange rate in effect at the balance sheet date; other assets and liabilities translated at historical rates;

revenues and expenses translated at the weighted-average rate for the period.

times-interest-earned (interest coverage) ratio A measure of solvency and leverage calculated as net income before income taxes plus interest charges divided by interest charges; a measure of the extent to which current interest payments are covered by current earnings.

time value of money The concept that money can always be invested at a bank to earn interest for the period it is on deposit.

total asset turnover ratio A measure of asset management effectiveness reflecting the rate at which sales are generated from a company's investment in assets; calculated as net sales divided by average total assets.

total debt-to-total assets ratio A measure of solvency or long-term liquidity calculated as total debt divided by total assets.

transaction exposure (risk) A source of foreign exchange risk resulting from exchange rate fluctuations between the date on which a contract is signed or goods delivered and the date of payment.

transitory earnings (cash flows) The nonrecurring earnings (cash flows) of a company; earnings (cash flows) that are not expected to reoccur in future periods.

translation exposure (risk) A source of foreign exchange risk resulting from the restatement of foreign financial statements denominated in a foreign currency into U.S. dollar equivalents; also known as *accounting exposure.*

treasury stock Outstanding capital stock that has been repurchased but not retired and usually held to be reissued at some future date.

trend analysis The analysis of ratios or account balances over one or more accounting periods to identify the direction or trend of a company's financial health.

true and fair view The current standard of precision required of all audited financial data in the EU; analogous to the "fairly presented" standard used in the United States.

turnover A measure of the rate of sales of goods or services; in the United Kingdom, a measure of net sales or net revenues.

uncertainty avoidance According to G. Hofstede, a cultural construct related to the extent to which the members of a society feel threatened by uncertain or unknown situations; the opposite of uncertainty acceptance.

unleveraged ROA (UROA) A refinement of the return on assets (ROA) ratio obtained by restating net income to include interest charges on an after-tax basis (i.e., net income plus interest expense net of tax benefits).

unrealized loss (gain) A loss (gain) recognized in the financial statements but not associated with an asset sale; usually involves a revaluation of an asset value.

useful life   The estimated productive life of a noncurrent asset.

value-added statement   A financial statement prepared by some foreign companies reflecting a measure of the wealth created by the operations of the company and the distribution of that wealth among its major constituents (e.g., employees, investors, and the government).

value-added tax   A tax levied at each stage in the production and distribution chain on the basis of the value that is added to a product as it passes through a given stage.

weighted-average cost method   An inventory cost-flow method that assigns the average cost of available finished goods, weighted by the number of units available at each price, to a unit sold and thus cost of goods sold, and to ending inventory.

Wirtschaftsprüfer (WP)   A certified public accountant in Germany.

won   The basic unit of currency in Korea.

working capital   A measure of liquidity or short-term solvency calculated as total current assets minus total current liabilities.

working capital maintenance agreement   An executory contract by which one entity guarantees to maintain the level of working capital of a second entity; usually arises as a consequence of a borrowing agreement by the second entity for which the first party becomes a guarantor.

world standards report   A set of financial statements prepared according to IASC accounting standards.

zaibatsu   Japanese industrial conglomerates that existed prior to World War II but were disbanded and have been subsequently replaced by *keiretsu.*

Index